LEARNING AND INSTRUCTION
Theory into Practice

FIFTH EDITION

Margaret E. Gredler
University of South Carolina

PEARSON
Merrill
Prentice Hall

Upper Saddle River, New Jersey
Columbus, Ohio

Library of Congress Cataloging in Publication Data

Gredler, Margaret E.
    Learning and instruction : theory into practice / Margaret E. Gredler.—5th ed.
      p. cm.
    Includes bibliographical references and indexes.
    ISBN 0-13-111980-X
      1. Learning. 2. Cognition in children. 3. Teaching.   I. Title

LB1060.G73 2005
370.15′ 23—dc22   2004040024

Vice President and Executive Publisher: Jeffery W. Johnston
Publisher: Kevin M. Davis
Editorial Assistant: Amanda King
Production Editor: Mary Harlan
Production Coordinator: Rena Cutchin, nSight, Inc.
Design Coordinator: Diane C. Lorenzo
Cover Design: Bryan Huber
Cover Image: Corbis
Production Manager: Laura Messerly
Director of Marketing: Ann Castel Davis
Marketing Manager: Autumn Purdy
Marketing Coordinator: Tyra Poole

This book was set in TimesTen by Laserwords. It was printed and bound by R. R. Donnelley & Sons, Inc. The cover was printed by Coral Graphic Services, Inc.

Pearson Education Ltd.
Pearson Education Singapore Pte. Ltd.
Pearson Education Canada, Ltd.
Pearson Education–Japan

Pearson Education Australia Pty. Limited
Pearson Education North Asia Ltd.
Pearson Educación de Mexico, S.A. de C.V.
Pearson Education Malaysia Pte. Ltd.

10 9 8 7 6 5 4 3 2 1
ISBN: 0-13-111980-X

In memory of my beloved daughter,
Margaret Lynn,
and for her sister,
Elizabeth Lee

EDUCATOR LEARNING CENTER: AN INVALUABLE ONLINE RESOURCE

Merrill Education and the Association for Supervision and Curriculum Development (ASCD) invite you to take advantage of a new online resource, one that provides access to the top research and proven strategies associated with ASCD and Merrill—the Educator Learning Center. At **www.EducatorLearningCenter.com** you will find resources that will enhance your students' understanding of course topics and of current educational issues, in addition to being invaluable for further research.

How the Educator Learning Center will Help Your Students Become Better Teachers

With the combined resources of Merrill Education and ASCD, you and your students will find a wealth of tools and materials to better prepare them for the classroom.

Research
- More than 600 articles from the ASCD journal Educational Leadership discuss everyday issues faced by practicing teachers.
- A direct link on the site to Research Navigator™ gives students access to many of the leading education journals, as well as extensive content detailing the research process.
- Excerpts from Merrill Education texts give your students insights on important topics of instructional methods, diverse populations, assessment, classroom management, technology, and refining classroom practice.

Classroom Practice
- Hundreds of lesson plans and teaching strategies are categorized by content area and age range.
- Case studies and classroom video footage provide virtual field experience for student reflection.
- Computer simulations and other electronic tools keep your students abreast of today's classrooms and current technologies.

Look into the Value of Educator Learning Center Yourself

A four-month subscription to Educator Learning Center is $25 but is FREE when used in conjunction with this text. To obtain free passcodes for your students, simply contact your local Merrill/Prentice Hall sales representative, and your representative will give you a special ISBN to give your bookstore when ordering your textbooks. To preview the value of this website to you and your students, please go to **www.EducatorLearningCenter.com** and click on "Demo."

Preface

In the new millennium, both new and continuing developments pose challenges to the design and implementation of events that support learning. Among them are the pervasive influence of television, the questions raised by research on the human brain, and the increasing importance of schooling in advanced technological societies. New in this edition are discussions of the current research on the human brain and the cognitive models and theories of academic motivation, an expanded review of the philosophy known as constructivism, and further clarification of the key concepts in Vygotsky's cultural-historical theory.

I would like to thank the following individuals for reviewing the last edition and suggesting improvements for this one: Frank N. Dempster, University of Nevada; Stuart R. Ellins, California State University; and Robert L. Hohn, University of Kansas.

Margaret E. Gredler

Brief Contents

Contents

variety of skills, strategies for functioning in the world, and attitudes and values. It begins in infancy, with the baby's learning to recognize its mother, and continues into adulthood, with the acquisition of knowledge in various subject areas, competencies essential to a chosen profession or career as well as social interaction patterns.

Learning also can contribute to a rich and diverse lifestyle for the individual. Sewing, basic home repair, waterskiing, playing Scrabble, and mountain climbing are only a few of the leisure-time activities acquired through learning. In our society, we are not surprised to find engineers who are gourmet cooks and college professors who grow prize-winning roses.

The capacity for continued learning is particularly important for the individual in today's information age. New developments in technology are increasing both the store of knowledge and the ways that information and knowledge are transmitted. Continued learning is important both for changing job markets and for taking advantage of new opportunities to access information.

Second, for society, the developments produced by individuals that evolve from their learning contribute to new discoveries and inventions by subsequent generations. For example, telescopes, computers, and electronic guidance systems set the stage for unmanned space probes to the outer edges of our solar system, and cell analysis has led to explorations of gene replacement therapy to address debilitating diseases. In other words, the inherited experience described by Vygotsky (1924/1979) is essential for human progress.

Third, learning is essential for societies to preserve the values, language, and developments of the particular culture. Suppose that each new generation would only be able to learn those things that are half as difficult as the things currently learned (Thorndike, 1931). For example, instead of members of the present generation learning calculus, they would learn only algebra. Then the next generation would learn only arithmetic, and so on. The result is obvious. Most of human civilization's accomplishments would be unusable in one generation, and civilization itself would soon disappear from the face of the earth (Thorndike, 1931).

Fourth, the study of learning is important because both the individual and society have a vested interest in the successful management of learning. Individuals who become skilled at self-directed learning are able to acquire expert knowledge in their chosen fields, to change careers, and to endow their lives with creativity and variety.

Society, on the other hand, cannot risk leaving the acquisition of learning to chance. Some system is needed to teach the cultural heritage to the young and to train them to take on productive adult roles. In early societies, the collective wisdom and folklore often were acquired by each member, usually by word of mouth. In technological societies, the available knowledge and information is so vast that no one can begin to learn all of it. Instead, formal educational systems address both broad areas of knowledge and areas of particular expertise that individuals select for further study. This process requires several years and often includes the learning of particular prerequisite knowledge, such as chemistry for pharmacists and music theory for symphony conductors.

In addition, changing conditions pose new challenges for the successful planning and management of learning. An example is the increasing dependence on technology. Benefits include the accessibility of information and communication via the Internet and developments such as online instruction. Problems include the need for learners to develop skills to address information authenticity, the potential for lack of meaningful interaction, and social isolation.

Further, the nature of worldwide problems such as global warming and the related flooding, depletion of the ozone layer and the related widespread growth of skin cancer, have led to discussions about the need to focus on teaching children to think about others and about society (Sternberg, 2001, p. 271). Implications for the management of learning, therefore, include "helping all students learn to use their minds well" (Jackson & Davis, 2000, p. 11). The challenge is to address both the skills of thinking critically (e.g., supporting reasons with evidence, evaluating reasons, and examining and evaluating opposing reasons) and the value of engaging in such hard work (Kuhn & Udell, 2001).

Finally, learners construct their own meanings for themselves and from the contexts in which they live. That is, individuals select information from interpersonal and other interactive events occurring in the family, school, peer, community, and work environments. Individuals then relate the selected information to their prior knowledge, analyze it, and construct a representation in memory. In this view of learning, the knowledge in the mind is coextensive with the relationships that compose one's interpersonal and societal environments. From this perspective, each new generation constructs a new society for itself (Meacham, 1993, p. 259). The key question then becomes, Can adults in democratic societies, for example, be confident that the next generation will construct society so as to reproduce the society's traditions, values, commitments, and hopes? (p. 264). For example, how will farm children in the Midwest, growing up in an environment of worry, hopelessness, fear, and alienation as large numbers of independent family farms collapse, construct society? Or others of the one in four children under the age of 6 whose families are below the poverty line? According to Meacham (1993), these and similar questions have serious implications for any discussion of learning.

Discussed in the remainder of this chapter are the sources of knowledge about learning, the role of research and theory in knowledge development, and the functions of learning theory. The chapter concludes with an overview of the organization of the text.

WHAT ARE THE SOURCES OF KNOWLEDGE ABOUT LEARNING?

Each generation seeks an explanation of the contemporary reality to which it belongs. Early societies sought to explain the mysteries of the four seasons, thunder, lightning, and other natural forces in their lives. Contemporary cultures, in contrast, are seeking to understand the causes and effects of global viruses, the effects of and countermeasures to widespread pollution, and the ramifications of cloning.

The search for understanding by any generation is restricted by the methods available at the time. Early societies lacked the methods to systematically analyze events. Instead, they developed different beliefs to explain the world. First were folklore and myths, which gradually gave way to logically reasoned explanations referred to as philosophies. In the 20th century, empirical research and formal theories have replaced these early types of beliefs as sources of knowledge.

Folklore, Traditional Wisdom, and Myths

Folklore consists of customs, tales, or sayings that typically are preserved orally among people. Traditional wisdom, (a subset of folklore) consists of proverbs and maxims that often are derived from experience. An example is, "Spare the rod and spoil the child." However, one problem with this information is that it may be interpreted in a variety of ways. Therefore, such sayings are inadequate as guidelines for educational practice.

Some individuals, however, contend that good teaching practice constitutes a "traditional wisdom" that can inform others about learning and instruction. According to this view, more can be learned from good teachers than from either research or psychology. Of course, much can be learned from skilled teachers (Hilgard, 1964). However, ignoring the possibility of improving instruction through well-designed research is like "returning medical practice to the prescientific physician because we still value the bedside manner" (Hilgard, 1964, p. 404).

Several cultures explained events in the natural world by creating myths about powerful gods and goddesses who were responsible also for particular events in both the natural world and human affairs. The early Greeks, for example, believed that ocean storms were caused by Poseidon, the sea god, and lightning bolts were Zeus's arrows unleashed in punishment. In human affairs, the goddess Aphrodite was believed to influence love relationships, and wisdom was the gift of Athena. Such a system led to activities to placate the gods and goddesses, so that events would go well. However, these myths did not advance society's knowledge about the actual workings of the physical or social environment.

The Original Role of Philosophy

The early myths were replaced gradually by logically consistent belief systems known as philosophies. Unlike folklore and myths, which tend to be loosely organized, philosophies are structured belief systems based on reasoned judgment and logic. The purpose of a philosophy is to provide a coherent set of values that describes the relationship between the human race and the universe.

A philosophy first describes the nature of reality and then defines the nature of truth and beauty consistent with the stated assumptions about reality.

Some philosophers also developed views about the human role in society, the function of the mind, and the nature of knowledge. The questions addressed are, What is knowledge? What is the origin of knowledge? and What does it mean "to know"? The answers, of course, are required to be logically consistent with the philosopher's view of reality.

One of early views on learning was developed by the Greek philosopher Plato (417–327 B.C.). His philosophy (idealism) describes mind or spirit as basic to everything that exists. Reality, therefore, consists of the pure ideas of the mind. Thus, human knowledge is derived from the ideas and concepts that are present in the mind at birth in the form of shadowy images. Learning, then, is the process of developing these innate or inborn ideas into a knowledge system. In Plato's view, the mind was developed through the study of the pure forms of mathematics, such as the circle and the square, and the classics.

Aristotle, Plato's pupil, developed a contrasting view of learning. According to Aristotle, reality exists in the physical world, not in the mind's conception of it. Universal laws are not innate ideas. Instead, they are the relationships observed in nature. The source of knowledge, therefore, is the physical environment, and learning occurs through contact with the environment. In Aristotle's system, the individual initially acquires knowledge by forming images of sensory experiences and by making associations among the images.

From 400 B.C. to the 19th century, philosophy served as the primary source of information about the human mind. Although experimentation on the physical world began in the 16th century, research methods were not applied to the study of mental activity for another 300 years. First, the mind, like the soul, was viewed as the gift of God. To conduct research on the mind would call into question that gift. Second, the primary function of the mind was to become attuned to the universe, the ultimate reality. Therefore, descriptions of reality developed by philosophers were sufficient for this task.

Two problems arise, however, when philosophy is used to develop knowledge about real-world events. First, the information is likely to be limited because only general questions are addressed, such as the nature of learning. For example, learning, according to Plato, is the development of the innate or inborn ideas in the mind. Methods for identifying these innate ideas, however, are not described.

Second, a philosophy develops information about major concepts (e.g., virtue, truth, knowledge, learning) using logic and reasoning. The resulting definitions, however, are only required to be logically consistent. They are not explicit hypotheses about the processes that are components of learning.

Current Influences of Philosophical Beliefs

Early philosophical beliefs about knowledge and learning have influenced theoretical developments and educational practice in various ways. First, some general concepts developed by early philosophers in their efforts to describe the nature of knowledge have appeared in contemporary theories. For example, Aristotle's recommended practice, in which public orators were taught to form vivid, active images of ideas to be remembered, is a device currently used to recall foreign language words and their meanings. Similarly, the association of ideas described by early philosophers reappears later in behaviorism. However, instead of the association of ideas, the behaviorists describe learning as the association of responses to particular objects or events known as stimuli.

Second, philosophical beliefs about the origins of knowledge have influenced educational practice. The belief in the innate nature of knowledge led to the development of and reliance on only intelligence tests for major educational decisions about students in the early 20th century.

In addition, different views on the origins of knowledge contributed to the nature/nurture controversy. For several years, the debate revolved around whether intelligence is an inborn trait (Plato) or is developed through experience with the environment (Aristotle). John Dewey, a well-known American philosopher, psychologist, and educator, noted that this focus on origins of knowledge had led to 30-year cycles of different emphases in educational practice. That is, American education has swung in a wide arc from the view that education is development from within to education as formation from without (Dewey, 1939, p. 5). One problem with a reliance on philosophical beliefs about the origins of knowledge, according to Dewey (1929), is that the focus is like looking in a rearview mirror. Instead, the factors that convey value on one's thoughts or ideas are the results of outcomes they produce (Dewey, 1929).

Philosophical concepts also have influenced aspects of the cognitive-development theories developed by Jean Piaget and Lev S. Vygotsky. For Piaget, answering the philosophical questions, What is the nature of knowledge? and What is the relationship between the knower and reality? are essential to establish a framework for theory development and research. Knowledge, according to Piaget, is not a static objective reality. Instead, knowledge is synonymous with human intelligence as it constructs the structures it needs to adapt to the environment (Piaget, in Bringuier, 1980, p. 3). Also, the learner and the world cannot be separated in the individual's construction of cognitive structures because the relationship cannot be specified in advance and it is always changing. The infant, for example, learns about the world by putting objects into its mouth and other similar actions whereas researchers develop information about the world through detailed experiments.

Vygotsky, in contrast, drew on the beliefs about dialectical change described by the German philosopher G. W. F. Hegel. That is, a movement or event (thesis) is countered by an opposing force (antithesis). The resolution, which is a qualitatively new phenomenon, combines elements of both and is referred to as a synthesis. According to Vygotsky (1930/1966), cognitive development is "a complex dialectical process characterized by disproportion in the development of some (cognitive) functions, metamorphoses or qualitative transformations of some forms into others, ... and a complex process of surmounting difficulties and of adaptation" (p. 36). Specifically, primitive or natural cognitive functions were transformed into higher cognitive functions referred to as categorical perception, logical memory, conceptual thinking (verbal and mathematical), and voluntary (self-organized) attention.

In summary, a philosophy provides a coherent set of values about the nature of reality, truth, beauty, and knowledge. Philosophies do not develop testable hypotheses about causes and effects in real-world settings. However, some of the concepts and ideas developed by philosophers have influenced the thinking of contemporary learning theorists.

3. Research Methods

In the mid-16th century, Galileo introduced experimentation with objects as a new method of developing knowledge about the physical world. An often repeated anecdote about Galileo is that he dropped objects of the same material (such as lead balls), but of different weights from the top of the Leaning Tower of Pisa. According to the anecdote, the balls fell at the same speed. That is, they did not fall at speeds proportional to their weight, as Aristotle and his followers maintained (Sharratt, 1994, p. 47).

Conducting experiments greatly expanded knowledge about the physical environment. Mystical beliefs and untested maxims gradually were replaced by reliable laws and principles. The science of chemistry supplanted the practice of alchemy, and the methods of astrology were replaced by the science of astronomy.

Rationale for Psychological Research

For almost 300 years, research methods were confined to the natural sciences. One reason was that to conduct research on the mind would call into question the gift of God. Second, philosophy was an adequate knowledge base for the mind's task of becoming attuned to an ultimate reality.

Two events in the 19th century set the stage for scientific investigations of mental functions. One was the publication of Charles Darwin's *Origin of Species* in 1859. Instead of viewing biological species as static preestablished groups, Darwin postulated that species survive, perish, or develop variations as a result of their ability to adapt biologically to changing conditions. Darwin's theory defined a new reality, one characterized by change and not a static order. An important result was a new perspective of the mind. That is, if the human mind is part of the evolutionary process, then defining the static relationship between the human mind and the mind of God is no longer a major issue.

The second key event that set the stage for psychological research of mental functions was Hermann von Helmholtz's introduction of the concept of scientific empiricism. Von Helmholtz, a medical doctor, scientist, and philosopher, maintained that because ideas are products of human experience, they are subject to human observation and analysis. The term scientific empiricism refers to the accumulation of facts through carefully designed experiments. He demonstrated the usefulness of experimentation on ideas by his invention of the ophthalmoscope for observing the operations of the eye.

From research on the senses, which are living tissue, to research on the mind was only one short step. That step was taken by Wilhelm Wundt. In addition to publishing a text that summarized the research on sensory functions,

Wundt established the first psychological research laboratory in 1879 at the University of Leipzig. The first studies included research on reaction time, sensation, auditory perception, and attention. Individuals from around the world, including the United States, came to study and conduct research in Wundt's laboratory.

However, the shift in ideas from the mind as the gift of the Creator to that of the brain as the key to mental activity was gradual rather than immediate. Books on psychology at the end of the 19th century continued to assert that psychology could not be an exact science because humans could never predict the interventions of the Creator to produce particular mental events in an individual's life (Reed, 1997). Nevertheless, Wundt's text on physiological psychology and his laboratory dominated Western thought. These developments initiated psychology as an experimental discipline and formally marked its separation from the discipline of philosophy. By 1895, 24 laboratories were in existence in the United States as well as 3 journals and several textbooks, including *Principles of Psychology* (1890) by William James, the father of American psychology.

Experimentation gradually became the primary mechanism for developing knowledge about psychological processes. Researchers tested propositions in the form of hypotheses by collecting quantitative data on specified variables, such as the relationship of curriculum to achievement. An example is the study conducted by Edward L. Thorndike in the 1920s. He investigated the popular "mental discipline" concept derived from Plato's philosophy. According to this view, the study of certain difficult subjects, such as Greek, Latin, or geometry, functioned as kinds of mental exercises that would enable students to think clearly and deeply (Cox, 1997, p. 42), i.e., discipline the mind. Thorndike compared the postcourse achievement of high school students enrolled in classical and vocational curricula and found no significant differences. He concluded that learning a particular subject, such as Greek, would not benefit intellectual performance in other areas.

Although Wundt's work on sensations captured the attention of Western scholars, he also advocated a "second psychology" that should address higher psychological functions, such as deliberate remembering, reasoning, and language (Cole, 1996). This second psychology was based on the concept proposed by two other German scholars that collective mentality exerts a powerful influence on individuals (see Jahoda, 1993, for a discussion). Referring to the second psychology as *Völkerpsychologie* (roughly translated, *folk psychology*), Wundt maintained that this area required historical and anthropological methods rather than experimentation. The purpose was to study reasoning and language, which are created by a community of individuals. He used the term *Kultur* (*culture*) to designate art, science, and sophistication, the products of advanced civilizations (Jahoda, 1993). Wundt's early writings on Völkerpsychologie were not translated into English, and the work (which later grew to 10 volumes) fell into oblivion (Jahoda, 1993). However, the identification of culture as the primary agent in the individual's development of higher psychological functions re-emerged in the theory of Vygotsky in the early 20th century.

Other Methods

In recent years, anthropological and other methods that (1) are nonmanipulative and (2) yield data in the form of words (rather than numbers) have emerged in education. Observational methods for use in classrooms and other settings include narrative and field research (ethnographic) methods that record speech, descriptions of events, and interpretations (Turner & Meyer, 2000, p. 75). Other methods from anthropology and sociology are structured interviews with predesignated questions, unstructured interviews, and discourse analysis (the analysis of verbal interactions). Referred to as qualitative methods (in contrast to quantitative), these methods result in detailed information about particular events and descriptions.

Implementation of such methods can fulfill any of three research roles in the educational setting. One is the development of inferences about a particular setting that can then be tested empirically in other settings. Second is that of clarifying the ways that established variables or constructs function in different situations. For example, quantitative studies have identified the relationship (correlation) of students' skills in self-regulating their learning to achievement. Observations of classroom events have indicated the particular teacher actions and verbalizations that influence the development of students' self-regulation in the classroom (Meyer & Turner, 2002; Perry, Van deKamp, Mercer, & Nordby, 2002). In other words, the use of qualitative methods can enrich the understanding of important cognitive and motivational constructs.

A third role is to serve as a major component in an approach referred to as design-based research (The Design-Based Research Collective, 2003). Implemented in mathematics and science, the focus of design-based research is (1) to analyze learning environments through continuous cycles of design, enactment, analysis, and redesign, and (2) to account for the ways the design of the learning environment functions in actual settings. The commitment is to use "theory-driven design to generate complex interventions that can be improved through empirical study and that contribute to more basic understanding of the underlying theory" (p. 7). Documentation, for example, may include extensive video recordings of student and teacher activity supplemented with textual material, interviews, and questionnaires (Shavelson, Phillips, Towne, & Feuer, 2003, p. 6). Retrospective analysis systematically examines the extensive longitudinal data and produces a situated narrative account of learning and the ways it can be supported and organized (p. 27).

Pitfalls

By the early 20th century, empirical research had become a primary mechanism for generating information about psychological processes. However, the difficulty with the use of empirical research as the *sole* source of knowledge is that data collection does not necessarily advance knowledge about important phenomena. Vygotsky (1993) decried the pedagogical anarchy that resulted from efforts to use "uncoordinated compendia of empirical data and techniques."

Furthermore, Suppes (1974) referred to the educational research of the 1920s as "the golden age of empiricism." This period was characterized by

CHAPTER QUESTIONS

1. Self-directed learning is important to the individual because it contributes to a varied and creative lifestyle. What are some reasons for the importance of self-directed learning to society?
2. One of the activities undertaken in the data collection efforts of the 1920s was determining the cost of teaching certain topics, such as Latin verbs. What is the problem with this particular piece of research, according to Suppes?
3. A maxim sometimes provided to novice teachers is "Don't smile until Christmas."

Why is such a directive of little help in the classroom?
4. The view that one should study great books to improve one's mind is consistent with which philosophy?
5. What is the major difference between the methods used by philosophy and the new psychology?
6. A collaborative learning group in seventh grade, using print resources and the Internet, develops a travel brochure on South America. Included are major historical sites. According to Vygotsky, what type of experience is this?

REFERENCES

Bandura, A. (1971). *Social learning theory*. Upper Saddle River, NJ: Prentice Hall.

Bringuier, J. C. (1980). *Conversations with Jean Piaget* (B. M. Gulati, Trans.) Chicago: University of Chicago Press.

Bronfenbrenner, U. (1993). The ecology of cognitive development: Research models and fugitive findings. In R. H. Wozniak and K. W. Fischer (Eds.), *Development in context: Acting and thinking in specific environ-ments* (pp. 3–44). Hillsdale, NJ: Erlbaum.

Brophy, J. (1981). Teacher praise: A functional analysis. *Review of Educational Research, 51*, 5–32.

Cole, M. (1996). *Cultural psychology*, Cambridge, MA: Belknap Press of Harvard University Press.

Cox, B. D. (1997). The rediscovery of the active learner in adaptive contexts: A developmental-historical analysis of the transfer of training. *Educational Psychologist, 32*(1), 41–55.

Cronbach, L. J. (1975). Beyond the two disciplines of scientific inquiry. *American Psychologist, 30*, 116–127.

Dewey, J. (1929/1988). The quest for certainty. In J. A. Boydston (Ed.), *John Dewey: The later works, 1925–1953, Vol. 14*. Carbondale, IL: Southern Illinois University Press.

Dewey, J. (1939/1988). Experience and education. In J. A. Boydston (Ed.), *John Dewey: The later works, 1925–1953, Vol. 14*. Carbondale, IL: Southern Illinois University Press.

Gagné, R. M. (1972). Domains of learning. *Interchange, 3*(1), 1–8.

Gagné, R. M. (1977). *The conditions of learning* (3rd ed.). New York: Holt, Rinehart, & Winston.

Gagné, R. M. (1984). Learning outcomes and their effects: Useful categories of human performance. *American Psychologist, 37*(4), 377–385.

Gagné, R. M. (1985). *The conditions of learning* (4th ed.). New York: Holt, Rinehart, & Winston.

Goldberg, E. (2001). *The executive brain: Frontal lobes and the civilized mind*. New York: Oxford University Press.

Hilgard, E. R. (1964). A perspective on the relationship between learning theory and educational practices. In E. R. Hilgard (Ed.), *Theories of learning and instruction: The sixty-third yearbook of the National Society for the Study of Education, Part I* (pp. 402–415). Chicago: University of Chicago Press.

Hull, C. L. (1935). Conflicting psychologies of learning: A way out. *Psychological Review, 42*, 491–516.

Jackson, A., & Davis, G. (2000). *Turning points 2000: Educating adolescents in the 21st century*. New York: Teachers' College Press.

Jahoda, G. (1993). *Crossroads between culture and mind*. Cambridge, MA: Harvard University Press.

James, W. (1890). *Principles of psychology*. New York: Henry Holt.

Joyce, B., & Weil, M. (1996). *Models of teaching*. Boston: Allyn & Bacon.

Kuhn, D., & Udell, W. (2001). The path to wisdom. *Educational Psychologist, 36*(4), 261–264.

Meacham, J. A. (1993). Where is the social environment? A commentary on Reed. In R. H. Wozniak and K. W. Fischer (Eds.), *Development in context: Acting and thinking in specific environments* (pp. 255–267). Hillsdale, NJ: Erlbaum.

Meyer, D. K., & Turner, J. C. (2002). Using instructional discourse analysis to study the scaffolding of student self-regulation. *Educational Psychologist, 37*, 17–25.

Perry, N. E., Van de Kamp, K. L., Mercer, L. K., & Nordby, C. J. (2002). Investigating teacher-student interactions that foster self-regulated learning. *Educational Psychologist, 37*, 5–15.

Piaget, J. (1963). *The origins of intelligence in children*. New York: Norton.

Pintrich, P., & Schunk, D. (2002). *Motivation in education: Theory, research and applications* (2nd ed.). Upper Saddle River, NJ: Merrill/Prentice Hall.

Reed, E. S. (1997). *From soul to mind: The emergence of psychology from Eramus Darwin to William James*. New Haven, CT: Yale University Press.

Sfard, A. (1998). On two metaphors for learning and the dangers of choosing just one. *Educational Researcher, 27(2)*, 4–13.

Sharratt, M. (1994). *Galileo: Decisive innovator*. Cambridge, MA: Blackwell.

Shavelson, R. J., Phillips, D. C., Towne, L., & Feuer, M. J. (2003). On the science of education design studies. *Educational Researcher, 32*(1), 25–28.

Skinner, B. F. (1968). *The technology of teaching*. New York: Appleton-Century-Crofts.

Sternberg, R. (2001). How wise is it to teach for wisdom? A reply to five critiques. *Educational Psychologist, 36*(4), 269–272.

Suppes, P. (1974). The place of theory in educational research. *Educational Researcher, 3*(6), 3–10.

The Design-Based Research Collective (2003). Design-based research: An emerging paradigm for educational inquiry. *Educational Researcher, 32*(1), 5–8.

Thorndike, E. L. (1931). *Human learning*. New York: Century.

Turner, J. C., & Meyer, D. K. (2000). Studying and understanding the instructional contexts of classrooms: Using our past to forge our future. *Educational Psychologist, 35*, 69–85.

van der Veer, R., & Valsiner, J. (1991). *Understanding Vygotsky: A quest for synthesis*. Cambridge, MA: Blackwell.

Vygotsky, L. S. (1966). Development of the higher mental functions. In A. N. Leont'ev, A. R. Luria, & A. Smirnol (Eds.), *Psychological research in the U.S.S.R., Vol. I* (pp. 11–45). (Original work published 1931.)

Vygotsky, L. S. (1979). Consciousness as a problem in the psychology of behavior. *Soviet Psychology, 176*(4), 3–35. (Original work published 1924.)

Vygotsky, L. S. (1993). *The collected works of L. S. Vygotsky: Vol. 2. The fundamentals of defectology (abnormal psychology and learning disabilities)* (J. E. Knox and C. B. Stevens, Trans.). New York: Plenum.

CHAPTER 2
Early Behaviorist Theories

At any one time, a science is simply what its researches yield, and the researches are nothing more than those problems for which effective methods have been found and for which the times are ready. Each step in scientific progress depends on the previous one, and the process is not much hurried by wishing. (Boring, 1950)

Wilhelm Wundt's laboratory for research on the senses initiated the separation of psychology as a discipline from philosophy. One year later, in 1875, Harvard University introduced the first graduate course in psychology. By 1900, the 24 laboratories, three journals, and the new American Psychological Association indicated the rapid growth of American psychology.

Major questions for the emerging discipline were What should be the focus of study? and What should be the scope of psychology? Several perspectives proposed answers and competed to be the major voice of the new discipline. Psychologists also aspired to develop a precise science, like physics and chemistry. However, early directions suggested for psychology lacked precise research methods. Into that breach came behaviorism, championed by its founder, John B. Watson. From the 1920s to the 1950s, behaviorism was the dominant movement in psychology and with it, the study of learning became a major focus.

CLASSICAL CONDITIONING AND CONNECTIONISM

The research method that initiated behaviorism was reflex or classical conditioning. Discovered by two Russian physiologists in independent experiments and adapted by John Watson, classical conditioning seemed to be the precise methodology sought by psychologists. The other approach implemented in the early 20th century was Edward Thorndike's connectionism.

A Rationale for Behaviorism

In addition to the disagreements within psychology, changes in American society and the discipline of philosophy also contributed to setting the stage for the study of behavior (Leahey, 1992). Specifically, industrializing cities were replacing rural communities and the urban migrants needed to learn new skills. Also, pragmatism, the emerging American philosophy, identified concrete consequences (outcomes) as the test for validating ideas (p. 312). Truth, in other words, is "what works."

In this context, John Watson advocated the study of behavior rather than mental processes or states. His goal was the final separation of psychology from philosophy and physiology, and the establishment of psychology as a science. Toward that end, he proposed a common subject of study—behavior—that could unite all psychologists (Todd & Morris, 1992, p. 1447).

In the 1913 article "Psychology as the Behaviorist Views It," Watson made a case for the study of behavior. He noted that in some 50-odd years, psychology had failed to establish itself as a natural science. The focus on consciousness and mental processes had led psychology into a dead end where the topics were "threadbare from much handling" (Watson, 1913, p. 174). Furthermore, when human consciousness is the reference point for research, the behaviorist is forced to ignore all data that do not relate to human mental processes. Other sciences, such as physics and chemistry, he noted, do not restrict their definitions of the subject matter to the extent that information must be discarded.

The starting point for psychology, therefore, should be the fact that all organisms adjust to the environment through responses (Watson, 1913). Because certain responses follow certain stimuli, psychologists should be able to predict the response from the stimulus, and vice versa. When this goal is achieved, according to Watson, psychology will then become an objective, experimental science. In addition, the discipline also would provide useful knowledge for the educator, physician, business leader, and others.

After the appeal to study behavior, Watson discovered the motor-reflex research of V. M. Bekheterev, a Russian physiologist (not the research of Pavlov, as is often believed [Boakes, 1934; Coleman, 1988]). Bekheterev's work was important because he had successfully manipulated simple behavioral reactions in the laboratory. On reading the research, Watson was convinced that behavioral control in the real world was within reach. His prediction was wrong, but his views were a major force in the use of precise methods of research and measurement by psychologists (Kratochwill & Bijou, 1987).

Basic Assumptions

The term *behaviorism* refers to several theories that share three basic assumptions about learning. They are:

1. Observable behavior, rather than internal mental events or verbal reconstructions of events, should be the focus of study.

2. Behavior should be studied in terms of its simplest elements, i.e., specific stimuli and specific responses. Examples of behavioral reactions investigated by different researchers include reflexes, observable emotional reactions, and motor and verbal responses.

3. The process of learning is behavioral change. That is, a particular response becomes associated with the occurrence of a particular stimulus. In other words, the response occurs in the presence of a particular stimulus.

Reflex or Classical Conditioning

The motor reflex experiments conducted by Bekheterev "trained" reactions such as finger retraction to respond to a variety of sights and sounds associated with an electric shock stimulus (Murphy, 1949). The best-known experiments, however, were conducted in the research laboratories of Ivan Pavlov.

The story handed down through the years about Pavlov's research features the lonely scientist who, quite by accident, discovered that an involuntary reaction, salivation, could be trained to respond to sounds unrelated to food. However, far from being a lonely scientist, Pavlov directed several physiological laboratories, which produced more than 530 research papers from 1897 to 1936. As director, Pavlov assigned research topics to co-workers and students and monitored their work, but he rarely experimented himself (Todes, 1997; Windholz, 1997).

Pavlov and the Bolsheviks

The years of the Bolshevik revolution (1917–1921) were particularly difficult for Pavlov, his family, and his laboratory. Pavlov's home was searched several times, he scavenged for firewood, and fed his family from a garden he tended at the Institute of Experimental Medicine. The Nobel Prize money he had received in 1904 for the work on digestive processes was confiscated and work in his laboratories almost ceased for lack of electricity, kerosene, and candles (Todes, 1995, p. 384).

In June 1920, at the age of 70, Pavlov wrote to the government for permission to emigrate. Considering the emigration of an internationally known scientist impermissible, the government accorded Pavlov special status. He received improved living quarters, liberal food rations for himself and his co-workers, and extensive laboratory support (Todes, 1995).

Of interest is that throughout the 1920s, Pavlov attacked state policies in public, including the ouster of various scientists from academic positions. Because of his special status, Pavlov was not silenced. Although his public criticisms tempered somewhat in the 1930s, Pavlov did not relinquish his basic criticisms of governmental actions (Todes, 1995, p. 46).

The Research in Pavlov's Laboratory

The accepted belief about the salivary reaction was that (1) food texture did not influence the reaction, and (2) contact between food and the animal's sensory receptors is essential to produce salivation. However, an early laboratory finding by a student indicated greater salivation for dry foods placed in a dog's mouth than for moist foods. Another student testing this finding serendipitously discovered that "teasing" dogs from a distance with dry and moist foods produced the same greater and lesser amounts of salivation (Windholz, 1997, p. 942). Pavlov initially named the reaction to sight of the food as a conditional reflex.

Subsequent research by V. N. Boldyrev found that the salivary reflex also may be conditioned (trained to respond) to stimuli (objects or events) from virtually any sensory modality (sight, sound, touch) (Windholz, 1997). An often-described experiment is that of sounding a tuning fork moments before the placement of meat powder on the animal's tongue. After several such pairings, the tuning fork alone elicited the salivation reaction.

The research in Pavlov's laboratory was important for two reasons. First, it demonstrated that the salivation reaction is a reflex. That is, it is a spontaneous reaction that occurs automatically to a particular stimulus. Second, to alter the "natural" relationship between a stimulus and a reaction was viewed as a major breakthrough in the study of behavior. To manipulate even a simple reaction held out the promise that the causes of complex behaviors also might be discovered. Thus, the research demonstrated the potential of laboratory studies to discover new knowledge.

The Classical Conditioning Paradigm

The process by which new events or stimuli acquire the power to trigger responses became known as reflex or **classical conditioning**. In the classical conditioning methodology, the naturally occurring stimulus and the reflex response are unconditioned. That is, they occur together without training and are referred to as the **unconditioned stimulus (UCS)** and **unconditioned response (UCR)**. The UCS is said to *elicit* the UCR; for example, a foreign object in the eye elicits an eye blink.

After training, the new stimulus that elicits the reflex response is referred to as the **conditioned stimulus (CS)**. The reflex, formerly unconditioned, became known as a **conditioned** (instead of conditional) **response (CR)** after training (see Table 2.1).

TABLE 2.1
Examples of Classical Conditioning

Preexperimental ("Natural") Relationship		Experimental Trials		Postexperimental (Conditioned) Relationship	
Unconditioned (Eliciting) Stimulus (UCS)	Associated Reflex Response (UCR)	Paired Stimuli	Reflex Responses	Conditioned Stimulus (CS)	Conditioned Reflex (CR)
Meat powder	Salivation	Meat powder Tuning fork	Salivation	Tuning fork	Salivation
Air puff	Eye blink	Air puff Bright light	Eye blink	Bright light	Eye blink
Electric shock	Finger retraction	Electric shock Buzzer	Finger retraction	Buzzer	Finger retraction

The development of classical conditioning introduced a number of variables and new relationships that could be researched and precisely measured in the laboratory setting. Included are the amount or strength of the response (referred to as amplitude), the length of time between the stimulus and the response (latency), and the tendency of similar stimuli to elicit the reflex (stimulus generalization). For example, studies indicated that a reflex conditioned to a sound pitch of 256 also is conditioned to sound pitches of 255 and 257 (Murphy, 1949).

Three other relationships introduced in classical conditioning include **resistance to extinction, inhibition**, and **higher-order conditioning**. Resistance to extinction is the tendency of a response to persist for a time after the supporting conditions are withdrawn. Inhibition refers to the reduction in a response caused by the introduction of extraneous stimuli.

In contrast, higher-order conditioning produces a second conditioned stimulus (CS2) by pairing it with the initial conditioned stimulus (CS1) instead of with the unconditioned stimulus (US). For example, Pavlov (1927) conditioned the salivary reaction to a black square (CS2) by pairing it with the sound of a metronome (CS1) that previously had been paired with food (US). However, one difficulty with higher-order conditioning is that the relationships appear to be short-lived.

Current Applications.   In addition to the discovery of new variables that have become part of the foundation of behavioral psychology, Pavlovian research had three other enduring effects. One is the research on animal survival mechanisms in the natural environment in which an animal learns to respond to cues that precede biologically important events (Hollis, 1997). An example is the particular locations or sites that signal the likely presence of a predator.

Second, Pavlovian research in the 1920s identified animal neuroses and methods to counter maladaptive reactions. Animal neurosis develops when powerful conditioned environmental stimuli (such as repeated mild electric shock) overwhelm an animal's typical reactions and elicit anxiety or neurotic reactions (such as howling and rapid pacing). However, pairing an aversive stimulus, such as mild electric shock, with the presentation of food precipitated salivation instead of the animal's defensive behaviors. Termed counterconditioning, this finding, along with the Pavlovian research on animal neuroses, became the foundation for clinical behavior therapy for these problems in humans (Wolpe & Plaud, 1997).

Third is the research into drug reactions identified as the causes that signal different human responses. Pavlov found that conditioned responses (CRs) associated with drug injections also were elicited by cues that precede the injection. Contemporary research by Siegel (1991) and others indicates that reliable cues associated with the ingestion or injection of several drugs (including opiates, alcohol, and caffeine) elicit a set of CRs that counter the physiological and biological reaction to the particular drug. The result is drug tolerance, the decreasing effect of a drug over several administrations (Hollis, 1997, p. 960).

John Watson's Behaviorism

One of Watson's contributions to psychology was his organization of the findings of current research into a new perspective and persuading other psychologists of the importance of his views. Behaviorism, as Watson (1916a) viewed it, should apply the techniques used in conditioning animal behavior to human beings. He therefore redefined mental concepts as behavioral responses. Thinking, for example, was identified as subvocal speech (Watson, 1924).

An original contribution of Watson's work was his extension of the role of classical conditioning beyond reflexes and motor reactions to emotional responses (Rilling, 2000b). Watson, in his theory of emotion (Watson & Morgan, 1917), agreed with Freud that the adult's emotional life began in infancy. However, he disagreed with Freud's psychoanalytic methods. Instead, the psychologist should rely on direct behavioral observations conducted in the laboratory (Rilling, 2000b, p. 308). Furthermore, the theory also specified rage and fear as instinctive emotional responses of infants, in addition to the response of love (Watson, 1928; Watson & Morgan, 1917). For example, the fear response was observed in the natural environment after a loud noise or loss of support for the infant. The fear response begins with the jumping or starting of the body and an interruption in breathing.

Particularly important in terms of emotional development is that Watson accepted Freud's concept of transference. For example, Watson and Morgan (1917) suggested that, in the laboratory, fear responses may be transferred from one object to another through classical conditioning (Rilling, 2000b, p. 308). Later, Watson (1928) maintained that an adult's complex emotional life is the result of the conditioning of the three basic responses to a variety of situations.

The Conditioning Experiment with Albert.   The purpose of Watson's well-known experiment with an 11-month-old child named Albert was to test his theory of emotion (Rilling, 2000b, p. 309). The experiment extended prior research, which addressed motor and salivary reflexes, to a third category, emotional reactions (Watson, 1916b). In the experiment, unethical by today's standards, Watson and his graduate assistant, Rosalie Rayner, conditioned Albert's fear reaction to several soft furry objects (Watson & Rayner, 1920).

Albert was tested first to confirm that live animals and objects (such as a human mask and cotton) did not elicit his fear response. Then, for several trials, a white rat was presented to Albert and a laboratory assistant behind Albert struck a steel bar with a hammer. On the first pairing of the white rat and the loud noise, the infant jumped violently; on the second trial (pairing), he began to cry. On the eighth trial, the white rat alone elicited crying and crawling away (Watson & Rayner, 1920).

Five days later, the fear reaction also appeared in response to a white rabbit. Non-furry objects, such as the child's blocks, did not elicit the fear response, but mild fear reactions occurred in response to a dog and a sealskin fur coat. The child's emotional response had transferred to furry animals and objects, and it persisted for longer than a month.

Albert's conditioned emotional response of crying on the presentation of a rabbit, which had not been paired with the loud sound, demonstrated Freud's concept of transference (Rilling, 2000b). Contemporary behavioral psychology later would label the crying reaction to the rabbit (in addition to the conditioned stimulus of the white rat) as stimulus generalization.

In recent years, questions have been raised about the experiment because the requirements for classical conditioning were not strictly followed. The loud noise was not paired with the presentation of the rat; instead, the noise occurred as Albert reached out his hand to touch the animal. However, the experiment demonstrated that emotions could be studied by controlled research methods, and it promoted research on conditioning (Kratochwill & Bijou, 1987).

A related topic, the elimination or "unconditioning" of children's fear reactions, was pioneered by Mary Cover Jones. She found that efforts to talk the child out of the fear or relying on extinction to eliminate the fear were ineffective (Jones, 1924). Instead, a planned program was required. The two successful strategies were (1) the child's observation of other children's acceptance of the feared object, and (2) the gradual presentation of the feared object during a favorite activity, such as eating.

Watson's Predictions.   In the "behaviorist manifesto," Watson (1913) foresaw practical goals for behaviorism (Logue, 1994, p. 112). He predicted that educators, physicians, jurists, and business executives could utilize behavioral data as soon as it was experimentally available (Watson, 1913, p. 168).

Some years later, Watson (1924) made the following claims for conditioning, although he stated he was going beyond his facts:

> Give me a dozen healthy infants, well formed, and my own specified world to bring them up in, and I'll guarantee to take any one at random and train him to become any type of specialist I might select—doctor, lawyer, artist, merchant-chief—regardless of his talents, penchants, tendencies, abilities, vocations, and race of his ancestors. (p. 82)

In addition to extending classical conditioning to emotional responses, Watson organized the findings of current research into a new perspective and persuaded other psychologists of the importance of his views. He also increased the status of learning as a topic in psychology (Rilling, 2000a, p. 277).

One result of Watson's work was that the simplicity of the method for conditioning responses and the novelty of the procedure led to a multitude of applications and experiments. In the 1920s almost every psychologist seemed to be a behaviorist, and none appeared to agree with any other (Boring, 1950). The term behaviorism became attached to several developments, including a particular research method, objective data in general, and a materialistic view of psychology.

Watson also believed that behaviorism would place psychology in the ranks of the "true" sciences, along with zoology, physiology, physical chemistry, and others. These same views on the potential of behaviorism were to be reiterated in the 1950s by B. F. Skinner.

In fact, conditioned reactions were not shown to add up to complex voluntary behavior. However, it was *believed* that they would, very likely because the resulting conception of psychology responded to the general scientism of the times (Baars, 1986, p. 53).

Conditioned Emotional Reactions

Through paired association, positive and negative reactions may be conditioned to a variety of objects and events. For example, a whiff of the paste used to fasten labels to bottles brought back painful memories of a miserable childhood for the well-known author Charles Dickens (Ackerman, 1990). The bankruptcy of Dickens's father had driven him to abandon the young Charles to a workhouse where such bottles were made.

In addition, current research indicates that parental reactions paired with a novel stimulus facilitates the conditioning of the child's approach or avoidance reaction to the stimulus. For example, parental disgust reactions when confronted with spiders facilitated children's acquisition of spider fear (deJong, Andrea, and Muris, 1997). In another study, Gerull and Roper (2002) found that mothers' positive (happy/encouraging) or negative (fearful/disgusted) reactions to novel stimuli (rubber snake or rubber spider) significantly influenced the approach and avoidance reactions of their toddlers.

Emotional reactions may, in certain situations, be conditioned in a single pairing of stimuli. An example is an automobile driver who narrowly misses a fatal accident with a large truck on a particular S-shaped curve. He experiences a rapid pulse, sweating palms, and increased blood pressure. A few days later, on approaching the same S-shaped curve, he experiences the same physiological reaction.

However, "pure" examples of classical conditioning to aversive stimuli are difficult to find in the natural setting. Typically, individuals are not "trapped" by emotion-producing stimuli. They may engage instead in escape behaviors that may, in some situations, produce satisfying outcomes. For example, Albert's fear responses of crying and whining (conditioned response) to the furry object (conditioned stimulus) were followed by crawling away (escape behavior). In the natural setting, the baby's mother would likely pick him up and comfort him, perhaps even rock him a few minutes. Thus, a selected response, the escape behavior of crawling away, is followed by receiving the mother's attention and comfort.

A positive example of classical conditioning is the nostalgic reaction (response) to a song (conditioned stimulus) that was a hit during a former love affair. The song has acquired the power to elicit some of the same feelings originally associated with the person in the former relationship. Such emotional reasons often occur without the awareness of the individual; thus, their origin may be difficult to identify.

Classical Conditioning in the Classroom

An essential step in developing the appreciation of literature, art, science, and other subjects is that of associating students' early experiences with positive reactions (Estes, 1989). However, the problem is that negative emotional reactions may become attached to the same situations and lead to the passive escape behaviors of apathy and "tuning out."

One strategy is to make use of already-established relationships that elicit positive reactions. For example, sustained reading is an important activity in learning to appreciate literature. Carpeting one corner of the room and furnishing it with large sofa cushions to create an area for sustained reading may, over time, elicit positive reactions to the free-time reading included in the daily schedule.

Such strategies are particularly important in situations in which a particular setting or activity is expected to elicit a negative reaction. For example, for some children, unfamiliar situations generate anxiety reactions. Introducing a difficult activity, such as a mathematics activity, on the first day of school may lead to the association of an anxiety reaction to mathematics (see Figure 2.1a). Positive strategies observed in some elementary school classes included greeting the children warmly as they arrived and starting the day with drawing or coloring activities (Emmer, Evertson, & Anderson, 1980) (see Figure 2.1b). In addition, no difficult activities were introduced the first week while the children were becoming accustomed to classroom routines. Instead, the potential for anxiety was reduced by repeatedly pairing the unfamiliar setting with relaxing activities.

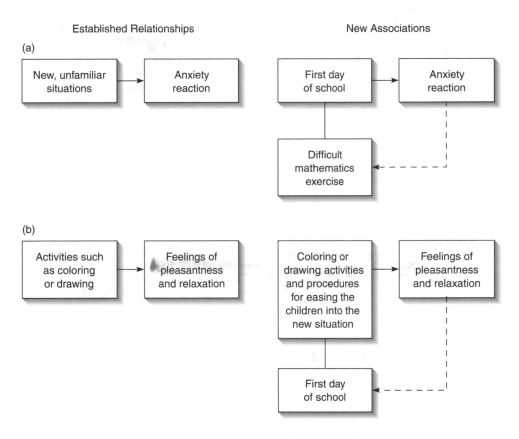

FIGURE 2.1
Applying classical conditioning in the classroom

Summary

Reflex conditioning began with the motor-reflex experiments of Bekheterev and the research on salivation in Pavlov's laboratory. Early studies on dogs found that dry foods elicited greater salivation than moist foods and that "teasing" the animals from a distance with food also elicited the salivary reflex. Subsequent research indicated that the salivary reaction could be trained to respond to a variety of sights and sounds. The importance of this research is that it demonstrated salivation is a reflex and the "natural" relationship between a stimulus and the associated reflex could be altered. These manipulations held out the promise that reflex conditioning might lead to the causes of complex behaviors.

The paradigm by which a reflex is trained to respond to a new stimulus involves the repeated pairing of the new stimulus with the stimulus that naturally elicits the reflex. In addition, Pavlovian research indicated that particular objects or events can precipitate reactions in several areas of psychological functioning. Among them are animal responses to cues associated with danger, the associations that become the basis for counterconditioning, and the drug reactions referred to as drug tolerance and enigmatic overdose.

John Watson applied the concepts of classical conditioning to emotional reactions. Maintaining that newborns possess only three emotional responses, Watson believed that an adult's complex emotional life resulted from the conditioning of these responses to various situations. His now-famous experiment with baby Albert reportedly conditioned the fear reaction to several soft furry objects. Of interest is that another researcher, Mary Cover Jones, demonstrated the unconditioning of children's fear reactions through the gradual presentation of the feared object during a favorite activity.

Although Watson's prediction about the role of classical conditioning was not realized, positive and negative emotional reactions may be conditioned to a variety of objects and events. In the classroom, for example, the teacher can utilize already-established relationships to elicit positive reactions.

Edward Thorndike's Connectionism

Although typically referred to as a behaviorist theory, Edward Thorndike's connectionism differs from classical conditioning in two major ways. First, Thorndike was interested in mental processes, and his first experiments were designed to provide information about the nature of the thought processes of animals. Second, instead of reflex or involuntary reactions, Thorndike researched voluntary or self-directed behaviors.

The publication of Thorndike's doctoral thesis in 1898 was a breakthrough in the study of behavior in North America (Galef, 1998). Prior to his research, the literature in comparative psychology was a morass of questionable anecdotes and engaging tales (p. 1128). Thorndike (1911) noted that "dogs get lost hundreds of times and no one ever notices it or sends an account of it to a scientific magazine. But let one find his way from Brooklyn to Yonkers and the fact immediately becomes a circulating anecdote" (p. 24).

Instead of depending on chance observations of intriguing bits of behavior and attempting to describe the animal's likely mental processes, Thorndike insisted on experimentation under controlled conditions. In the experiments, animals were confined in cages or food was placed in a latched box. The task for the hungry animal was to open the box or cage and get to the food. Thorndike referred to his experiments as **instrumental conditioning** to reflect the differences from classical conditioning. The theory also is known as **connectionism** because connections were established between particular stimuli and voluntary behaviors.

Experimental Procedure

Thorndike experimented with baby chicks, dogs, fish, cats, and monkeys. (While he was a student at Harvard, his landlady forbade him to continue hatching chicks in his room. William James offered the basement of his home for Thorndike's research, to the dismay of Mrs. James and the excitement of the children.) The typical experimental procedure required each animal to escape from a confined space to reach food. A puzzle box was used that required the tripping of a latch or some other mechanism to effect escape (Figure 2.2).

When confined, the animal often engaged in a variety of behaviors, including scratching, biting, clawing, and rubbing against the sides of the box. Sooner or later the animal tripped the latch and escaped to the food. Repeated confinements were characterized by a decrease in the behaviors unrelated to escape and, of course, a shorter escape time. The most dramatic change was observed with monkeys. In one experiment, a box containing a banana was placed inside

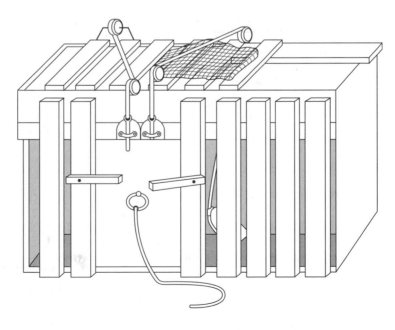

FIGURE 2.2
Puzzle cage used in some of Thorndike's experiments

the cage. The monkey took 36 minutes to pull out the nail that held the wire fastener closed. On the second trial, the monkey successfully released the fastener in only 2 minutes 20 seconds (Thorndike, 1911).

The experimental data from a series of trials were recorded as a learning curve illustrating the faster escape times. Thorndike concluded from this data that the escape response gradually became associated with the stimulus situation in trial-and-error learning. For this reason, his theory is referred to as an *association* theory.

The Laws of Learning

During the series of trials in the experiment, the correct response was gradually "stamped in" or strengthened. Incorrect responses were weakened or "stamped out." In other words, problem solving involves establishing associations or connections between the stimulus (the problem) and appropriate responses.

Thorndike originally identified three major laws of learning to explain this process. They are the law of effect, the law of exercise, and the law of readiness. The *law of effect* states that a satisfying state of affairs following the response strengthens the connection between the stimulus and the behavior, whereas an annoying state weakens the connection. Thorndike later revised the law so that punishment was not equal to reward in its influence on learning.

The *law of exercise* describes the conditions implied in the adage "Practice makes perfect." Repetition of the experience, in other words, increases the probability of a correct response. However, repetition of a task, such as drawing lines blindfolded, does not enhance learning in the absence of a satisfying state of affairs (Thorndike, 1913b, p. 20).

The *law of readiness* describes the conditions that govern the states referred to as "satisfying" or "annoying" (Thorndike, 1913a). Briefly summarized, the execution of an action in response to a strong impulse is satisfying, whereas the blocking of that action or forcing it under other conditions is annoying.

Thorndike's views were not immediately accepted. Galef (1998) noted that one early review maintained he has studied "starved, panic-stricken cats and dogs that had temporarily lost their normal wits, so that their intelligence was grossly underestimated" (Mills, 1899 in Galef, 1998, p. 1130). However, Thorndike's work became better known, and laboratories to study comparative psychology were established.

Applications to School Learning

In the laboratory, Thorndike researched the relationship between physical stimuli and physical actions, and his interpretations of learning were based on these behavioral studies. However, his theory also includes references to mental events. It thus occupied a middle ground between the concerns of some early views of psychology and the "pure" behaviorism of other researchers.

Thorndike described human mental life as composed of both mental states and movements with connections between each type (Thorndike, 1905, p. 12). In his view, connections between ideas accounted for the major portion of "knowledge" in its popular sense (Thorndike, 1913b, p. 19). The process of learning, in other words, is simply that of connecting: "The mind is man's connection system" (Thorndike,

(The Brain)

1913b, p. 122). This connection system includes both specific examples, such as $9 \times 5 = 45$, and connections to multiple configurations. An example is the concept that $1 \times 1 = 1/2 \times 2 = 1/3 \times 3$ (Cox, 1997). Other examples include events and dates, such as Columbus and 1492 and persons and characteristics, such as John and blue eyes.

Thorndike's rules for teaching arithmetic, for example, identify the requirements for establishing connections between stimuli and responses. Examples are (1) do not form a bond that will have to be broken, and (2) form bonds in the way they are later required to act (Thorndike, 1922, p. 101). He also described five minor laws that are the first effort to account for the complexity of human learning. These subsidiary laws and their applications to school learning are summarized in Table 2.2. These laws were believed to interact with the laws of effect and exercise to account for human learning.

Connectionism, with its emphasis on establishing bonds between stimuli and responses, was particularly relevant for school learning in the early 20th century. At that time, the emphasis was on the learning of information and specific procedures.

The application of connectionism to school subjects is an example of Thorndike's focus throughout his career—that of developing an educational psychology based on empirical data (Beatty, 1998). A series of studies on **transfer of learning** conducted by Thorndike and Woodworth (1901) found that

TABLE 2.2
Application of Thorndike's Minor Laws to Education

Law	Description	Example
1. Multiple response or varied reaction	A variety of responses often occurs initially to a stimulus	Pronunciation of foreign language Skill in tennis Coherence in English composition
2. Attitudes, dispositions, or states	Condition of the learner that influences the learning; includes stable attitudes and temporary factors of the situation	Individual competing to throw a ball the longest distance or throw a player out in a baseball game Instructions for the problem 7 6 – to add or to subtract
3. Partial or piecemeal activity of a situation	The tendency to respond to particular elements or features of a stimulus situation (also referred to as analytic learning)	Responses to the qualities of shape, color, number, use, intent, and others Responses to relations of space, time, causation, and others
4. Assimilation of response by analogy	The tendency of situation B to arouse in part the same response as situation A	The foreigner pronouncing English
5. Associative shifting	Successively altering the stimulus until the response is bound by a new stimulus	*abcde* is altered to *abcdef* to *abcdefg* and so on

Note: From *Educational Psychology: Vol. II. The Psychology of Learning* (pp. 19–31) by E. L. Thorndike, 1913. New York: Teachers' College Press.

training in particular tasks facilitated the later learning only of similar tasks, not dissimilar ones. Some behaviorists interpreted the findings to be the result of identical stimulus elements between the training and transfer tasks. However, Thorndike and Woodworth (1901) viewed the commonality to be that of similar mental actions or habits related to stimuli (Cox, 1997, p. 42).

An aspect of Thorndike's investigations into transfer of learning was his study of the effects of difficult subjects on students' thinking (the mental discipline study). He noted that the main reason that certain school subjects, such as trigonometry and physics, superficially seemed to produce good thinkers was that good thinkers tended to enroll in those courses. Furthermore, students became better thinkers because of the "inherent tendency of the good to gain more than the poor from any study" (Thorndike, 1924, p. 98). In succeeding years, Thorndike's research was named as a major influence in turning curriculum designers away from the mental discipline concept and toward the practice of designing curriculum for more useful purposes (Cushman & Fox, 1938; Gates, 1938).

In addition to founding the *Journal of Educational Psychology* and developing tests of mathematics and handwriting, Thorndike produced more than 500 publications in his career, including 50 books (Dewsbury, 1998). His son later noted that his father was a workaholic primarily because he enjoyed analyzing data more than anything else (R. L. Thorndike, 1991).

Summary.   Seeking to determine the nature of mental life in animals, Thorndike confined animals in cages with food nearby. Observing the faster escapes in repeated confinements, he concluded that the correct response is "stamped in" through association with eating the food, a satisfying state (the law of effect). Describing human mental life as the connections between ideas, Thorndike described five minor laws that further address human learning.

Thorndike's school-related research illustrates his goal of developing an educational psychology based on empirical data. His research on the transfer of learning found that training on particular tasks facilitated only the learning of similar tasks. Other studies demonstrated that the learning of difficult subjects, such as Greek, Latin, or geometry, does not function as a type of mental exercise that enhances thinking skills.

THE RETREAT TO THE LABORATORY (1930–1950)

Thorndike cautioned his fellow psychologists that the proper laboratory for research was the classroom and the appropriate experimental subject was the student (Shulman, 1970). For the most part, however, the theorists from 1930 to 1950 ignored Thorndike's advice. Research was conducted instead on animals and human beings in artificially contrived situations: Rats ran mazes, rats escaped from boxes, and humans were given puzzles to solve.

The goal of the research also shifted in this period. In this "era of grand theories," the goal was to integrate all known facts around the principal theme of describing, predicting, and controlling learning (DiVesta, 1987, p. 207). In other words, the purpose of research was to develop the one comprehensive theory that would explain all learning.

The Refinement of Behaviorism

The dominant movement in the 1930s and 1940s continued to be behaviorism. However, it was by no means a unitary theory, nor was it the only approach to behavioral analysis. Some psychologists, influenced by Sigmund Freud's psychoanalytic theory, were searching for deeper meanings in behavior beyond observed relationships between events and responses. Included were Robert Woodworth's "dynamic psychology" and William McDougall's "hormic psychology." McDougall described "drives" as behavioral activators. For example, the "thirst drive" activates the go-to-water mechanism (Boring, 1963, p. 723). In contrast, McDougall developed an extensive list of instincts that he identified as goal directed (flight, fear, reproduction, and so on).

Three theories emerged from the 1930s and 1940s, referred to as "neobehaviorist" to distinguish them from the work of Watson and Thorndike. These theories are Clark Hull's behavior system, Edwin Guthrie's contiguity theory, and B. F. Skinner's operant conditioning. The views of Hull and Guthrie are referred to as *S–R theories* because they define learning as an associative link between a particular stimulus and a particular response. They differ, however, in the identification of the specific factors believed to be of primary importance in establishing the S–R association. Hull's theory emphasized processes within the organism, specifically, intervening variables. Guthrie, however, maintained that the temporal relationship between the stimulus and the response was the critical factor in learning. In contrast, Skinner began with Edward Thorndike's law of effect. He redefined "reward" as reinforcement and described behavioral change as a function of response consequences.

Two S–R Theories

Hull's behavioral system and Guthrie's contiguity theory are in sharp contrast to each other. Hull's theory is rigorous, abstract, and complex; Guthrie's theory is informal and loosely organized. Practical advice for parents and teachers also is included in Guthrie's work.

Clark Hull's Behavior System

Hull's theory is a rigorous example of his recommendations for theory development, the hypothetico-deductive method. That is, testable propositions are derived from explicitly stated assumptions. Then controlled experimentation either verifies or fails to support the propositions.

Influenced by the concept of evolution, Hull (1943) maintained that behavior functions to ensure the organism's survival. Therefore, the central concepts in his theory revolve around biological needs and need satisfaction, which is essential for survival. Needs were conceptualized by Hull (1943, 1952) as "drives," such as hunger, thirst, sleep, relief from pain, and others. Stimuli, referred to as *drive stimuli*, are associated with primary drives and therefore "motivate" behavior.

For example, stimuli associated with pain, such as the sounds of a dentist's drill, can also arouse fear, and the fear motivates behavior.

Reinforcement also was incorporated into the theory; however, reinforcement is a biological condition. Satisfaction of the biological need, referred to as **drive reduction**, strengthens the link between the drive stimulus and the response. For example, giving an animal a sip of water after turning right in a maze reduces the drive stimulus of a dry mouth. The water, therefore, strengthens the link between the dry mouth and turning right in the maze.

The final version of Hull's theory combined 17 assumptions into 133 propositions on theorems (Hull, 1952). Also included in the system are concepts such as incentive, generalized habit strength, the power of a stimulus to elicit a particular response, and others. However, the testable propositions in the theory often were not verified. Further, Hill (1990) noted that, depending on which assumption is used, the theory yields conflicting predictions. More important for educators, the theory did not generalize beyond the laboratory. Although dominant into the 1940s, Hull's system was eclipsed in the 1950s by Skinner's operant conditioning (discussed in chapter 6).

Edwin Guthrie's Contiguity Theory

A refreshing contrast to the other theories of this period, contiguity theory relied on one major learning principle. Known as the **law of contiguity**, it states that a combination of stimuli accompanied by a movement will tend to be followed by the same movement on its recurrence (Guthrie, 1952, p. 23). Also, movements can bridge the distance between the initial stimulus and the response. For example, the ringing of the telephone leads to standing up, followed by walking to the telephone, then lifting the receiver (Guthrie, 1935, p. 34).

Reinforcement, however, is not an essential factor in learning. Instead, learning occurs because the last movement that is made changes the stimulus situation and no other response can occur. For example, in solving a puzzle, the last action changes the stimulus (i.e., completes the puzzle). Similarly, in the earlier example, lifting the telephone receiver terminates the ringing. Therefore, in the same situation again, the same response will be repeated. Reinforcement simply protects the new learning from unlearning by preventing the acquisition of new responses (Guthrie, 1942, 1952).

Breaking Habits. A habit is defined in the theory as a response that is associated with several different stimuli (Guthrie, 1952). The greater the number of associations, the stronger the habit because the response is "cued" on many different occasions. Smoking is an example of a strong habit because so many different cues trigger lighting up a cigarette. Included are finishing a meal, taking a coffee break, sitting down to watch television, and so on.

Breaking habits requires breaking the associations between the cues (eliciting stimuli and the response). To break a habit, one must practice another response in the presence of the cues that elicit the undesirable response. The three methods suggested by Guthrie (1938, p. 62) are equivalent because they all involve presenting the cues that typically elicit a particular undesirable response while preventing the performance of the response (see Table 2.3).

TABLE 2.3
Summary of Three Methods for Breaking Habits

Method	Characteristic	Example
Threshold method	1. Introduce the eliciting stimulus at weak strength	*Breaking a horse to the saddle*: Begin with a light blanket, then heavier blankets, and finally, a light saddle
	2. Gradually increase the stimulus strength, always keeping it below the response "threshold" (i.e., strength that will elicit the response)	
Fatigue method	"Exhaust" the response in the presence of the eliciting stimulus	*Breaking a horse*: Throw the saddle on the horse and ride him until he quits kicking, bucking, and trying to throw the rider; the saddle and rider become the stimulus for walking and trotting calmly
Incompatible response method	Pair the eliciting stimulus (S^1) for the inappropriate behavior with a stimulus (S^2) that elicits appropriate responses; the appropriate behavior associated with S^2 becomes linked to S^1	Overcome fear and avoidance by pairing the frightening object, such as a large toy tiger, with a stimulus that elicits warm feelings, such as mother

Guthrie (1938) suggested that the threshold method is appropriate for introducing new foods to a young child. Parents should begin with small tastes that are not enough to cause rejection and gradually build toward a teaspoonful.

The fatigue method involves executing the response in the presence of the stimuli until it is no longer fun. However, practical applications of this method for parents and teachers are difficult to identify. For example, the student who is caught writing notes in class should not be punished by having to write sentences on the blackboard for an hour after school. As discussed later in the chapter on operant conditioning, such practices evoke resentment and other undesirable emotional reactions.

The incompatible response method, however, does have practical applications. It is appropriate for overcoming the fear of a particular object. The method used by Mary Cover Jones earlier in this chapter for unconditioning children's fears by introducing the feared object during a favorite activity is an example.

Uses of Punishment.   To be effective, punishment must (1) be delivered appropriately in the presence of a stimulus that elicits inappropriate behavior, and (2) cause the subject to do something different. An example is the girl who came home repeatedly from school each day and threw her hat and coat on the floor. The girl's mother made her put her hat and coat back on, go back outside, come in again, and hang up her wraps. After a few occasions, the response of hanging up the coat and hat became associated with the stimulus of entering the house (Guthrie, 1935).

Suggestions for Educators. Associating stimuli and responses appropriately is the core of Guthrie's advice to teachers. The student must be led to perform what is to be learned. Students, in other words, learn only what the stimuli in lectures or books cause them to do (Guthrie, 1942, p. 55). Therefore, if students use notes or textbooks simply to memorize quantities of information, books will be the stimuli that cue rote learning.

In managing the classroom, the teacher is cautioned not to give a directive that is permitted to be disobeyed. A request for silence, if followed by a disturbance, will become the cue for disruptive behavior.

SUMMARY

At the beginning of the 20th century, the newly formed discipline of psychology was searching for a direction and major focus. Unlike other proposed courses of action, behaviorism, advocated by John Watson, was represented by the newly discovered reflex or classical conditioning. Watson's directive to discover the mechanisms that explain why certain responses follow certain stimuli soon became the dominant perspective. Demonstrations of the new linkages established between stimuli and reflex reactions by classical conditioning led to application of the paradigm to emotional reactions and application to animal neuroses and counterconditioning. Classical conditioning, however, was unable to explain the mechanisms that account for complex, self-initiated behaviors.

The advent of Thorndike's connectionism initiated the study of voluntary behaviors and set the stage for Skinner's operant conditioning. According to Thorndike, positive consequences in the form of a satisfying state of affairs establish connections between stimuli and appropriate responses. Thorndike also demonstrated the applicability of research methods to school learning through his studies of transfer of training and the mental discipline concept.

Contrary to Thorndike's advice, the neobehaviorist theories retreated to the laboratory. Hull's behavior system, which incorporated biological needs, drives, and need satisfaction, did not generalize beyond the laboratory. Guthrie's perspective analyzed the movements in acts. However, he provided little direction for establishing appropriate connections, suggesting instead methods for breaking already-established habits.

APPLICATIONS TO EDUCATION

The behaviorist and neobehaviorist theories of the early 20th century differed in their research goals and methods. As a result, their suggestions for education address different aspects of behavior. Classical conditioning, which relies on stimulus pairing to link reactions to new stimuli, identifies the importance of avoiding the association of anxiety and other negative feelings to the school setting. Implementing activities that elicit positive feelings during the first few days of kindergarten or elementary school is suggested.

In contrast, Thorndike emphasized the importance of establishing connections between ideas and the avoidance of introducing opportunities to establish inaccurate bonds or connections. Guthrie's contiguity theory also focused on the link between the stimulus and the response. Of importance in the classroom is that (1) students learn what they do, and (2) teachers ensure that stimuli do not cue wrong responses. For example, the teacher should ensure that directives such as to begin seatwork or to line up for lunch are not followed by disruptive behavior. The problem is that these directives can become the cues for disruptions in the future. If punishment is to be used for inappropriate responses, then it must "undo" the association between a stimulus and the inappropriate behavior. In other words, if students are disruptive following a directive to line up by rows for lunch, they should be sent back to their seats to respond appropriately to the teacher's statement.

CHAPTER QUESTIONS

1. What are the implications for the classroom inherent in the major differences between Thorndike's connectionism and classical conditioning?
2. At summer camp, a spider is thrust in a child's face at the same time that some girls scream and shout, "Boo!" The next night, the girls scare her just as she turns down the sheet and finds a spider. Diagram these events and predict the outcome of these experiences.
3. Identify a school activity that may tend to elicit negative reactions. What prior relationship may be the basis for this reaction?
4. Apply Guthrie's "incompatible response method" to address the problem in question 2.
5. A student who relies on coffee to wake up in the morning finds, over time, that he requires a stronger brew to be alert. How does classical conditioning explain the problem?
6. In the 1980s, some advocates of teaching computer programming skills maintained that such learning would promote the broad skills of rigorous thinking (Cox, 1997). These beliefs reflect what concept that was refuted in the early 20th century?

REFERENCES

Ackerman, D. (1990). *A natural history of the senses*. New York: Random House.

Baars, B. J. (1986). *The cognitive revolution in psychology*. New York: Guilford.

Boakes, R. (1934). *From Darwin to behaviorism*. New York: Cambridge University Press.

Beatty, B. (1998). From laws of learning to a science of values. *Celebrating E. L. Thorndike: American Psychologist, 53*(1), 1145–1152.

Boring, E. G. (1950). *A history of experimental psychology* (2nd ed.). New York: Appleton-Century-Crofts.

Boring, E. G. (1963). *History, psychology, and science: Selected papers*. New York: Wiley.

Coleman, S. R. (1988). Assessing Pavlov's impact on the American conditioning enterprise. *Pavlovian Journal of Biological Science, 23*, 102–106.

Cox, B. D. (1997). The rediscovery of the active learner in adaptive contexts: A developmental–historical analysis of transfer to training. *Educational Psychologist, 32*(1), 41–55.

Cushman, C. L., & Fox, G. (1938). Research and the public school curriculum. In G. Whipple (Ed.), *The scientific movement in education. The thirty-seventh yearbook of the National Society for the Study of Education, Part II* (pp. 67–78). Chicago: University of Chicago Press.

deJong, P. J., Andrea, H., & Muris, P. (1997). Spider phobia in children. Disgust and fear before and after treatment. *Behaviour Research and Therapy, 35*, 559–562.

Dewsbury, D. A. (1998). Celebrating E. L. Thorndike a century after animal intelligence. *Celebrating E. L. Thorndike: American Psychologist, 53*(1), 1121–1124.

DiVesta, F. J. (1987). The cognitive movement and education. In J. A. Glover & R. R. Ronning (Eds.), *Historical foundations of educational psychology* (pp. 203–233). New York: Plenum.

Emmer, E., Evertson, C., & Anderson, L. (1980). Effective classroom management at the beginning of the school year. *The Elementary School Journal, 80*(5), 219–231.

Estes, W. (1989). Learning theory. In A. Lesgold & R. Glaser (Eds.), *Handbook of research on teaching* (pp. 1–49). Hillsdale, NJ: Erlbaum.

Galef, B. G. (1998). Edward Thorndike: Revolutionary psychologist, ambiguous biologist. *Celebrating E. L. Thorndike: American Psychologist, 53*(1), 1128–1134.

Gates, A. (1938). Contributions of research on the general methods of education. In G. Whipple (Ed.), *The scientific movement in education. The thirty-seventh yearbook of the National Society for the Study of Education, Part II* (pp. 79–80). Chicago: University of Chicago Press.

Gerull, F. C., & Rapee, R. M. (2002). Mother knows best: Effects of maternal modelling on the acquisition of fear and avoidance behaviour in toddlers. *Behaviour Research and Therapy, 40*, 279–287.

Guthrie, E. R. (1935). *The psychology of learning.* New York: Harper.

Guthrie, E. R. (1938). *The psychology of human conflict.* New York: Harper.

Guthrie, E. R. (1942). Conditioning: A theory of learning in terms of stimulus, response, and association. In N. B. Henry (Ed.), *The psychology of learning: The forty-first yearbook of the National Society for the Study of Education, Part II* (pp. 17–60). Chicago: University of Chicago Press.

Guthrie, E. R. (1952). *The psychology of learning.* New York: Harper & Row.

Hill, W. F. (1990). *Learning: A survey of psychological interpretations* (5th ed.). New York: Harper & Row.

Hollis, K. L. (1997). Contemporary research on Pavlovian conditioning. *American Psychologist, 52*(9), 956–965.

Hull, C. L. (1943). *The principles of behavior.* New York: Appleton-Century-Crofts.

Hull, C. L. (1952). *A behavior system.* New Haven, CT: Yale University Press.

Jones, M. C. (1924). Elimination of children's fears. *Journal of Experimental Psychology, 7*, 382–390.

Kratochwill, T. R., & Bijou, S. W. (1987). The impact of behaviorism on educational psychology. In J. A. Glover & R. R. Ronning (Eds.), *Historical foundations of educational psychology* (pp. 131–157). New York: Plenum.

Leahey, T. H. (1992). The mythical revolutions of American psychology. *American psychologist, 47* (2), 308–318.

Logue, A. W. (1994). Watson's behaviorist manifest: Past positive and current negative consequences. In J. T. Todd & E. K. Morris (Eds.), *Modern perspectives on John B. Watson and classical behaviorism* (pp. 109–123). Westport, CT: Greenwood Press.

Mills, W. (1899). The nature of animal intelligence and the method of investigating it. *Psychologi-cal Review, 6*, 262–274.

Murphy, G. (1949). *Historical introduction to modern psychology.* New York: Harcourt, Brace, & World.

Pavlov, I. P. (1927). *Conditioned reflexes: An investigation of the physiological activity of the cerebral cortex* (G. V. Anrep, trans.). New York: Dover.

Rilling, M. (2000a). How the challenge of explaining learning influenced the origins and development of John B. Watson's behaviorism. *American Journal of Psychology, 113*(2), 275–301.

Rilling, M. (2000b). John Watson's paradoxical struggle to explain Freud. *American Psychologist, 55*(3), 301–312.

Shulman, L. (1970). Reconstruction of educational research. *Review of Educational Research, 40*, 371–396.

Siegel, S. (1991). Feedforward processes in drug tolerance. In R. G. Lister & H. J. Weingartner (Eds.), *Perspectives in cognitive neuroscience* (pp. 405–416). New York: Oxford University Press.

Thorndike, E. L. (1905). *The elements of psychology*. New York: A. G. Seiler.

Thorndike, E. L. (1911). *Animal intelligence*. New York: Macmillan.

Thorndike, E. L. (1913a). *Educational psychology: Vol. I. The original nature of man*. New York: Teachers' College Press.

Thorndike, E. L. (1913b). *Educational psychology: Vol. II. The psychology of learning*. New York: Teacher's College Press.

Thorndike, E. L. (1922). *The psychology of arithmetic*. New York: Croswell-Collier and Macmillan.

Thorndike, E. L. (1924). Mental discipline in high school studies. *Journal of Educational Psychology, 15*, 1–22, 83–98.

Thorndike, E. L., & Woodworth, R. S. (1901). The influence of improvement in one mental function upon the efficiency of other functions I, II, & III. *Psychological Review, 8*, 247–261, 384–395, 553–564.

Thorndike, R. L. (1991). Edward L. Thorndike: A professional and personal appreciation. In G. A. Kimble, M. Wertheimer, & C. White (Eds.), *Portraits of pioneers in psychology, Vol. 1* (pp. 139–151). Washington, DC: American Psychological Association.

Todd, J. T., & Morris, E. K. (1992). Case histories in the power of misrepresentation. *American Psychologist, 47*(1), 1441–1453.

Todes, D. P. (1995). Pavlov and the Bolsheviks. *History and Philosophy of the Life Sciences, 17*, 379–418.

Todes, D. P. (1997). From the machine to the ghost within: Pavlov's transition from digestive physiology to conditioned reflexes. *Commemorating Pavlov's Work: American Psychologist, 52*(9), 947–955.

Watson, J. B. (1913). Psychology as the behaviorist views it. *Psychological Bulletin, 20*, 158–177.

Watson, J. B. (1916a). The place of the conditioned reflex in psychology. *Psychological Review, 23*, 89–108.

Watson, J. B. (1916b). Behavior and the concept of mental disease. *Journal of Philosophy, Psychology, and Scientific Methods, 13*, 589–597.

Watson, J. B. (1924). Behaviorism. New York: Norton.

Watson, J. B. (1928). Chapter I. What the nursery has to say about instincts; Chapter II. Experimental studies on the growth of emotions. In C. Murchison (Ed.), *Psychologies of 1925* (pp. 1–37). Worcester, MA: Clark University Press.

Watson, J. B., & Morgan, J. J. B. (1917). Emotional reactions and psychological experimentation. *American Journal of Psychology, 28*, 163–174.

Watson, J. B., & Rayner, R. (1920). Conditioned emotional reactions. *Journal of Experimental Psychology, 3*, 1–14. (Reprinted in *American Psychologist* [2000], *555*, 313–317.)

Windholz, G. (1997). Ivan P. Pavlov: An overview of his life and psychological work. *Commemorating Pavlov's Work: American Psychologist, 52*(9), 941–946.

Wolpe, J., & Plaud, J. J. (1997). Pavlov's contributions to behavior therapy. *Commemorating Pavlov's Work: American Psychologist, 52*(9), 966–972.

CHAPTER 3
Gestalt Psychology: The Cognitive Perspective

A general theory in psychology is something like a political platform, in that its policies are stated as of larger scope, and in a form to encourage enthusiastic adherents, and often equally committed opponents. (Hilgard, 1987, p. 416)

The dominant perspective in the first half of the 20th century was behaviorism. In the early years, under Watson's influence, it had acquired some of the characteristics of a political platform. However, the rise of behaviorism was not completely unchallenged. The opposing view was that of Gestalt psychology, which, ironically, had originated as a reaction against the study of sensations in psychology. When transported to this country, Gestalt psychology became the reaction to the behaviorist perspective. The primary reasons for the attention of American psychologists to Gestalt psychology were dissatisfaction with the strictures of behaviorism and the limited intellectual appeal of Thorndike's connectionism (Hilgard, 1996).

MAJOR CONCEPTS

The original focus of Gestalt research was the experience of perception. Max Wertheimer, the founder of Gestalt psychology, initiated the movement with an innovative experiment that illustrated the differences between visual perceptions and physical phenomena. Together with Kurt Koffka and Wolfgang Köhler, Wertheimer proceeded to develop the laws of perception and to apply these concepts to learning and thinking.

The theory was introduced in the United States in 1922, 10 years after its inception. In the 1930s, the three leaders left Germany to continue their writing and teaching in the United States. In general, Gestalt theory was viewed by American psychologists as interesting but by no means the final solution to major issues. However, the theory established the experimental study of perception and social psychology, neglected topics in the heyday of behaviorism (Baars, 1986, p. 71). In addition, the theory raised new questions about problem solving and thinking.

Origins of the Gestalt Perspective

The foundation for Gestalt psychology was established in an 1890 paper by a German named Christian von Ehrenfels. He maintained that qualities appear in perception in addition to the separate sensory elements that are components of the experience. For example, when the same melody is played in different keys, the tone sensation (sensory elements) change but the melody is recognized as the same. The term applied to this process was *Gestaltqualitat*, which may be translated roughly as "the quality conferred by a pattern" (Murphy, 1949, p. 226).

Research conducted by the Gestalt psychologists into visual perception demonstrated that (1) global features are detected as a whole, rather than as simple elements, and (2) the process is constructive in that individuals often transform incomplete visual input into a more explicit perceptual image (Lehar, 2003, p. 51). Legend indicates that Max Wertheimer got the idea for his research on perception while traveling from Vienna to Germany for a vacation (Watson, 1963). Leaving the train at Frankfurt to follow up a sudden hunch, he bought a toy stroboscope. The device presents pictures at such a rapid rate that it creates the illusion of motion, and was popular before the invention of motion pictures.

At the time Wertheimer began his research, the silent films shown in nickelodeons also were making use of apparent motion (the perception of motion from the rapid presentation of stable images) (Steinman, Pizlo, & Pizlo, 2000). However, Wertheimer's (1912) research revealed subtle differences in perception associated with minor differences in the presentation of a simple geometric figure, such as a line, first at position *a* and then at position *b* at different time intervals (60 to 200 ms). Logically, the subject should see two brief illuminations. However, depending on the time interval, the subjects saw different illuminations. Included were *a* followed by *b* (successive images) and *a* and *b* appearing simultaneously.

Wertheimer's (1912) novel discovery was that of "pure" motion, designated as the *phi phenomenon*. That is, with different time intervals, subjects saw the vertical line *a* "falling" to the right to point *b*, or the two lines (*a* and *b*) moving toward each other (Sekular, 1996, p. 1247). However, the lines are stationary; thus, the movement is "pure" or "objectless motion" (Steinman et al. 2000, p. 2260). Specifically, *phi* "signifies what is present other than the perception of *a* and *b*" (Wertheimer, 1912, p. 186 in Sekular, 1996, p. 1252).

The discovery was important because it demonstrated the relationships between stimulus configurations and "experienced wholes." In other words, the relationships between stimulus configurations and perceptions were not haphazard. Instead, they could be studied and categorized.

Basic Assumptions

Four basic assumptions support the Gestalt perspective (see Table 3.1). First, unlike the behaviorists, Gestalt theorists maintained that "molar" behavior

TABLE 3.1
Basic Assumptions of Gestalt Theory

Assumption	Example
1. Molar behavior, rather than molecular behavior (muscle contractions or gland secretions), should be studied.	1. A college student's performance that occurs in a classroom in which a lecturer holds forth (Koffka, 1935, p. 27).
2. Organisms respond to "segregated sensory wholes" or *Gestalten* (Köhler, 1929, p. 174) rather than to specific stimuli as isolated and independent events.	2. A geometrical arrangement of 11 dots is perceived as a cross.
3. The geographical environment, which is the way things are, differs from the behavioral environment, which is the way things appear to be. The behavioral environment is the individual's subjective reality.	3. Koffka (1935, p. 29) described the incident of a man on horseback who rode across a windswept plain in a snowstorm to arrive safely at an inn. When asked where he came from, the man pointed in the direction away from the inn. Amazed, the landlord asked the man if he knew he had ridden across a lake. The story goes that the man dropped dead from the shock that he had ridden miles across thin ice.
4. The organization of the sensory environment is a dynamic interaction of forces within a structure that influence an individual's perception.	4. The three patterns below are projections of the same wire-edged cube, but are perceived differently because of the relationships of the lines to each other.

a   b   c

should be studied, rather than "molecular" behavior. Chemical processes illustrate these concepts. Suppose, for example, that HNO_3 is produced in one part of a factory out of its elements and that the product is used in another part of the factory to dissolve silver (Köhler, 1929, p. 180). Do we say that the silver reacts to nitrogen, hydrogen, and oxygen? Of course not, because the effect on the silver depends on the chemical organization of the product. The effect on the silver cannot be understood either as a reaction to the individual elements or to their sum.

Examples of the related assumption (organisms respond to organizations of stimuli or "segregated sensory whole") include the names of groupings of stars in the sky. These names, such as the hunter Orion, reflect the particular images suggested by the star clusters. Similarly, cloud formations often are perceived as faces, mountains, and other familiar objects.

The third assumption, the differences between the geographical and the behavioral environments, provides the foundation for studying individuals' perceptions. As illustrated in the examples in Table 3.1, the individual responds to his or her perception of the environment, not to the geographical environment.

Finally, the organization of stimuli in the environment is itself a process and this process influences an individual's perception. Koffka (1935, p. 159) noted that when pattern a in the example in Table 3.1 is presented without the others, it is seen as a plane figure, either as a hexagon with diagonals or as a type of cross or starlike pattern. In pattern a, the plane figure is both symmetrical and simple; therefore, it is dominant.

In contrast, pattern c appears as a three-dimensional cube. Here, the plane figure is very irregular and difficult to see. Pattern b, on the other hand, is seen as either two- or three-dimensional. It may be seen as a plane figure in which the

pattern [bowtie figure] is lying on top of a hexagon or it may be seen as a cube. The

reason is that the two- and three-dimensional forces are more balanced in pattern b than in the others. Figure 3.1 illustrates another example in which the forces within the perceptual field are balanced. In this figure, the viewer typically sees either a black Maltese (German iron) cross or a white propeller (Hartmann, 1942, p. 176).

The description of the behavioral environment and the dynamic organization of the sensory equipment illustrate Gestalt efforts to apply the concept of field theory in physics to psychology. Briefly, a field is a dynamic interrelated system in which every component influences all the other components. In the psychological theory, the behavioral environment is a field and small groups of stimuli (such as the examples in Table 3.1) are each a small field.

FIGURE 3.1
Geometrical figure with
balanced forces in the
perceptual field

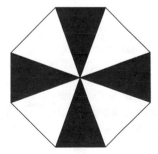

In summary, Gestalt theory emphasized wholeness and organization. For example, individuals respond to complete geometric figures rather than the separate lines. Also, because individuals may perceive a situation in particular ways, the behavioral environment (the perceived field) rather than the geographical environment should be studied. Therefore, psychological research should identify the dynamic interaction of elements in a field that influence the individual's perception.

The Laws of Perceptual Organization

The primary task for psychology, according to the Gestalt theorists, was to answer the question, How does the individual psychologically perceive the geographical environment? First, Gestalt psychology defined the process of perception as that of organizing the observed stimuli. That is, the observer conveys meaning on the stimulus array.

Second, the arrangement of elements in the total stimulus is a major factor in perception (Koffka, 1935). For example, 11 dots distributed in the shape of a parallelogram would be perceived as a four-sided figure. The next step was to determine the characteristics of the stimulus display that influence perception. These influences are described in a basic law, the law of Prägnanz, and four related primary laws.

The Law of Prägnanz.   The term **Prägnanz** refers to essence. The law of Prägnanz, introduced by Wertheimer, states that "a psychological organization will only be as 'good' as prevailing conditions allow." In this definition, the term *good* is undefined. It embraces such properties as "regularity, symmetry, similarity, and others" (Koffka, 1935, p. 110).

In other words, in any particular group of stimuli, the organization that prevails is the one that is the most comprehensive and the most stable and one that is also free of the casual and the arbitrary (Murphy, 1949). An example is a particular type of puzzle picture popular several years ago. The picture, a line drawing, typically portrayed a landscape, and hidden in various parts of the drawing were faces and sometimes objects. However, the structure that prevailed was that of the overall scene, and often much searching was required to find the "hidden" objects.

Related Laws.   A principle closely related to the law of Prägnanz is the law of membership character. Specifically, each element manifests particular qualities depending on its place in the total structure of context. For example, a patch of color in a landscape depends for its value on the context in which the artist places it (Murphy, 1949, p. 288). Similarly, "faces" are so difficult to find in a line drawing of a forest because the lines that make up the faces take on the character of roots, leaves, and other aspects of the forest context that surround them. In other words, important aspects of the components of a structure are defined by their relationship to the system as a whole.

Another example of membership character is the presentation of a red cross in a gray field. After viewing the cross for 20 seconds, the subject perceives a green border around the cross. Then the subject is asked to predict the color if a notch is cut in one of the arms of the cross. The logical answer is green, like the border. The Gestaltists, however, predict accurately that the color will be red. The cross is an organized whole that forces the elements within it to take on those attributes that support the total structure (Murphy, 1949, p. 288).

This example also illustrates the dynamic nature of the organization of the sensory environment. That is, the sensory field includes forces that exert particular effects on the individual stimuli. The definite outline of the arms of the cross have a higher degree of Prägnanz than the outline of the notch (Murphy, 1949). Therefore, the organization of the cross prevails and the notch "disappears."

Four primary characteristics of the visual field that influence perception were also identified by Wertheimer (1938). They are *proximity, similarity, open direction*, and *simplicity*. Specifically, the nearness of elements to each other (proximity), shared features such as color (similarity), the tendency of elements to complete a pattern (open direction), and the contributions of stimulus elements to a total simple structure (simplicity) are factors that govern the perception of groups from separate elements (Figure 3.2).

The laws of perceptual organization operate in conjunction with the general law of Prägnanz. That is, psychological events tend to be meaningful and complete, and the four characteristics influence the completeness.

Since Wertheimer's (1938) work on the laws of perception, research has continued to explore the characteristics of the visual field that influence perception. For example, Tse (1998, 1999) describes the contour of penetration (COP). It is a smooth curve in an image that leads to the perception of (a) a complete perceptual entity for less-than-complete visual input, and (b) the illusion that the image is three-dimensional. For example, the illusion in Figure 3.3 is that of a sphere intersected by spikes.

The "Insight" Experience

Perhaps the best-known contribution of Gestalt theory to the study of learning is the so-called "insight" experience. Introduced by Wolfgang Köhler in his experiments with anthropoid apes, the concept also was researched in experiments with humans. It continues to be studied by contemporary cognitive psychologists.

The Initial Experiment.   Assigned by the Prussian Academy to the Canary Islands in World War I, Köhler conducted several innovative experiments in learning. The basic experimental situation included two components: food placed out of the animal's reach and a type of mechanism placed nearby. If properly utilized, the mechanism would help the animal obtain the food. In the simplest experiment, food was hung from the roof near a scaffold. In other experiments food was placed outside the cage with a stick or dead branch nearby. In one complex situation, reaching the food required the fitting together of two separate sticks.

1. **Proximity:** The lines tend to be perceived as three columns or three sets of two lines.

2. **Similarity:** Although the letters are equidistant from each other, they tend to be perceived as columns.

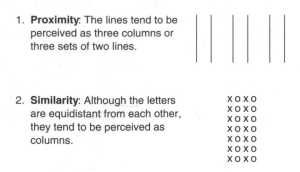

3. **Open direction:** The figure tends to be perceived as a circle although it is not a closed figure.

4. **Simplicity** (total structure): In figure (*c*) the total structure (*a*) is perceived, rather than the hexagonal figure (*b*) that is embedded in it.

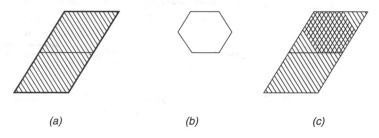

(a)   (b)   (c)

FIGURE 3.2
Examples of four primary laws of perceptual organization

Köhler (1928, 1929) noted that when the animal perceived the stick, branch, or other mechanism as a tool, the problem was solved. This phenomenon is referred to in Gestalt psychology as *insight*. Köhler therefore maintained that the learning formula of "stimulus-response" should be replaced. Instead, he recommended that the learning formula should be a "constellation of stimuli-organization-reaction to the results of the organization" (Köhler, 1929, p. 108). In other words, insightful behavior does not occur by following predetermined courses of action. Instead, it "presupposes the processes of organization and reorganization" (Koffka, 1935, p. 628).

Of importance is that the term *insight* refers to one type of behavior that cannot be reduced to another type (Koffka, 1935, p. 628). However, it is not an

FIGURE 3.3
The illusion of a sphere intersected by spikes.
Note: From "Illusory Volumes from Confirmation," by
P.U. Tse, 1998, *Perception*, 27(8), p. 984. Copyright
1998 by Pion Ltd. Reprinted with permission.

explanation; it is simply the name of a particular type of reorganization of the perceptual field. In addition, insight does not necessarily occur in a single step. Sometimes two or more steps are required, in which each is a case of partial insight (Koffka, 1935).

The Pendulum Problem.   In an experiment with human subjects, Norman R. F. Maier investigated the processes related to the discovery of a creative solution in the well-known pendulum problem. Sixty-one subjects, one at a time, were placed in a room in which two cords that reached the floor were hung from the ceiling. One hung near a wall and the other was near the center of the room. The task was to tie the ends of the two cords together. However, if one cord were held in either hand, the subject could not reach the other one (Maier, 1931, p. 182). The room also contained many other objects including poles, ringstands, clamps, pliers, extension cords, tables, and chairs.

Using the objects, four solutions to the problem were possible and all but one were obvious. Maier studied the difficult solution because it required originality and was least likely to be linked to prior experience. The three obvious solutions were (1) anchoring one cord with a heavy object near the other, (2) lengthening one cord with an extension cord so as to reach the other, (3) holding one cord and pulling the other in with a pole. The difficult solution was to tie a weight to the cord in the center of the room and set it in motion, thus making it a pendulum. The other cord would then brought near the center and the swinging cord would catch it as it approached the midpoint between the two cords (Maier, 1931, p. 183).

In the experiment, when subjects found one solution, they were directed to find another. If the subject did not discover solution 4 or was ready to give up after working conscientiously for 10 minutes, the experimenter walked to the window, passing the cord in the middle of the room and gently setting it in motion (hint 1). If, after a few minutes, solution 4 still was not found, the experimenter gave the subject the pliers and said, "With the aid of this and no other object, there is another way to solve the problem" (Maier, 1931, p. 183).

Of the 61 college students in the study, 24 solved the problem without the hints, and 14 failed to solve it at all, even with assistance. Of the 23 subjects who solved the problem with assistance, 19 found the solution after one hint. Of interest, however, is that 16 students reported having the idea "all at once." In contrast, for 7 subjects, the idea of swinging the cord and that of attaching a weight occurred separately. They threw things at the cord, said they wished the wind would blow harder, or mentioned the need for a magnetic force to draw in the cord (Maier, 1931, p. 186). A little later the utilization of the weight occurred to the subject and the individual tied the pliers to the end of the cord. Maier concluded that insight may be either an "all or nothing" experience or a partial experience.

Subsequent Analysis of Insight. One of the difficulties in conducting research on insight is the lack of a clear definition (Schooler, Fallshore, & Fiore, 1995). The two characteristics acknowledged by most cognitive researchers are that insight (1) represents seeing clearly into the heart or essence of a situation (the essential structural relationship [Wertheimer, 1945/1959]); and (2) involves, at least partially, an automatic nonconscious process that does not include step-by-step reasoning (Gick & Lockhart, 1995).

A current model of insight focuses on problem restructuring (Ohlsson, 1992). The individual initially fails to solve a problem despite possession of the prerequisite knowledge. This impasse results from an incorrect interpretation of the problem, which means that relevant operators for executing a solution will not be activated. Restructuring the problem is the essential factor that can lead to insight.

According to Ohlsson, the three possible mechanisms for achieving restructuring are (1) re-encoding, (2) elaboration, and (3) constraint relaxation. Re-encoding refers to the correction of an improper interpretation of problem elements. For example, in Maier's (1931) pendulum problem, the pliers must be re-encoded as a weight in order to use them to set one cord in motion. Elaboration involves the addition of either unnoticed information in the problem or the retrieval of information from long-term memory.

Constraint relaxation refers to the removal of unnecessary constraints imposed by the problem solver on his actions (e.g., MacGregor, Ormerod, & Chronicle, 2001; Ormerod, MacGregor, & Chronicle, 2002; Smith & Blankenship, 1991). An example is the eight-coin problem in which the task is to move only two coins so that each coin exactly touches three others (Ormerod et al. 2002, p. 792). The unnecessary constraint typically imposed by the problem solver is that coins may only be moved in two dimensions (left, right, up, or down). However, as illustrated in Figure 3.4, the necessary insight involves the removal of this assumption so that each of the two coins may be stacked on top of the other coins.

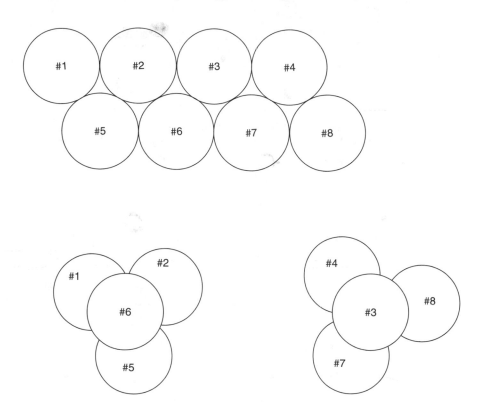

FIGURE 3.4
Solution to the eight-coin problem
Note: From "Dynamics and Constraint in Insight Problem Solving," by T.C. Ormerod et al., 2002,
Journal of Experimental Psychology: Learning, Memory, and Cognition 28, p. 793. Copyright
2002 by the American Psychological Association. Adapted by permission.

One study implemented a training program for problem restructuring that
included strategy instructions, and pairs of problems with their respective answers, for which participants wrote a method for solving both problems in each
pair. Feedback and discussion followed. The average solution rate for transfer
problems was 60.77% (Ansburg & Dominowksi, 2000, p. 47).

Some researchers identify the suddenness of a solution as a criterion, i.e.,
the "Aha! Experience." References to anecdotes about the experiences of famous mathematicians and scientists appear to support this view. An example is
the discovery of a particular type of mathematical function by Henri Poincare as
he was boarding a bus. Another is Alexander Fleming's discovery of penicillin
following his accidental notice that bacteria flourishing in the laboratory dish did
not grow near mold (Seifert, Meyer, Davidson, Patalano, & Yaniv, 1995, p. 93).

Some creative insights in various disciplines may indeed occur in this manner. However, research on introspective reports and interviews of creative individuals indicates that four phases often are involved. They are (1) hard work
and research (mental preparation), (2) a period of idle time (incubation), (3) the

moment of insight (illumination), and (4) work, including elaboration, to develop the idea (verification) (Csikszentmihalyi & Sawyer, 1995; Hadamard, 1949; Wallas, 1926). For example, by Poincare's own account, his mathematical discovery involved several weeks of work with seemingly no progress, a brief seaside vacation in which an idea came to him, further work followed by an impasse, a second insight, and work to develop a finished product (Gruber, 1981, 1995).

Although insight is unpredictable, the long-term and short-term conditions most likely to lead to insight may be identified (Simonton, 1995). Long-term preparation includes (1) an early home environment that provides extensive cultural and intellectual stimulation, including an appetite for reading, (2) development by the individual of a huge reservoir of discipline-relevant information interconnected into a complex network of meanings and unusual associations, (3) study with more than one mentor, and (4) keeping abreast of developments beyond the boundaries of a particular specialty area. Such a background makes possible the linkage of disparate ideas that become breakthroughs in a discipline.

In everyday life, preparation involves phases one and two of the four-stage process mentioned previously. That is, a favorable climate for insight involves preliminary work, including exploring possibilities and recognizing dead ends, followed by a period of incubation in which the individual focuses on other activities (Simonton, 1995).

Summary

In the first half of the 20th century, Gestalt psychology served as the foil to behaviorism. Maintaining that molar rather than molecular behavior should be studied, the Gestalt psychologists focused on perception in learning. Specifically, organisms respond to sensory wholes rather than specific stimuli, and the organization of the sensory environment influences the organism's perception. In addition to the laws of perceptual organization that indicate the factors influencing visual perception, Gestalt psychology introduced the concept of insight. In the early studies, animal and human subjects were presented problems that required a novel solution. Perceptual reorganization of the situation led to a solution.

Currently, insight is described as seeing clearly into the heart of a situation or problem through a nonconscious process. Suddenness of a solution sometimes is mentioned as a characteristic. However, research indicates the importance of preparatory work on a problem and an incubation period, followed by elaboration and other activities, to develop the idea.

OTHER GESTALT DEVELOPMENTS

Although concerned primarily with perceptual processes, the Gestalt psychologists also applied their concepts to other areas of interest in psychology. By the mid-1930s, Gestalt psychology had redefined the major issues in psychology in terms of a theory of form or structure (Murphy, 1949, p. 293). Not surprisingly, their work focused on the role of perception in learning and thinking. Major developments were the distinctions between arbitrary and meaningful learning, additional studies of problem solving, Edward Tolman's purposive behaviorism, and Kurt Lewin's theory of motivation.

Arbitrary and Meaningful Learning

In applying the concepts of structure and wholeness to the analysis of learning, Wertheimer differentiated between arbitrary or "senseless" learning and meaningful learning (Katona, 1967). This distinction was made in two ways. First, some simple connections are arbitrary or senseless. An example is the fact that John's telephone number is 782-9031. It is a senseless connection because the telephone number cannot be derived from the name or character of John.

Some simple connections, however, are meaningful. An example is $(a + b)^2 = a^2 + 2ab + b^2$. If one side of this equation is presented, the other may be derived from it. In other words, they are connected in a nonarbitrary, meaningful way.

The major focus for Wertheimer, however, was not the nature of particular connections. Instead, he was concerned primarily with the distinction between senseless and meaningful learning methods in the classroom. In other words, meaningful structures should not be learned in a senseless or rote manner.

Wertheimer (1945) reported a classroom visit in which students learned to determine the area of a parallelogram by dropping two perpendicular lines to the baseline. However, when faced with another form of the parallelogram, the students were at a loss as to an appropriate course of action. Their reaction was, "We haven't had that yet."

In working with another group of children, Wertheimer first showed them how to calculate the areas of rectangles. He then presented them a parallelogram and asked if they could make use of their knowledge of rectangles to determine the area. After some false starts, some children cut off the "triangle" at one end of the parallelogram and placed it on the other end, thereby forming a rectangle (see solution a, Figure 3.5). They then proceeded to solve for the area of the rectangle that they had just constructed. Others, however, perceived the rectangle formation in a different way. They cut the parallelogram in half, inverted one of the halves, and placed the diagonal ends together to form a rectangle (see solution b, Figure 3.5). Solving the problem depended on the children's reorganization of the field and their reaction to the reorganization.

Wertheimer did not recommend specific teaching methods based on Gestalt theory. However, the implication from this example is that providing information that assists students to reorganize their view of the problem should be an integral component in teaching problem solving.

The relevance of Wertheimer's concern for meaningful learning is apparent in a discussion of the "Mathnet" segments of the public television program *Square One TV*. In the program, a problem-solving duo fashioned after the *Dragnet* detective series duo (with calculators in their holsters) act as sleuths to solve problems (Blau, 1990). Important in the program format is that the "detectives" use various ways of solving problems, such as drawing a picture of the situation or recalling the way a similar problem was solved.

FIGURE 3.5
Children's solutions to the parallelogram
problem

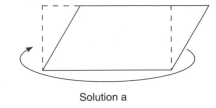

Solution a

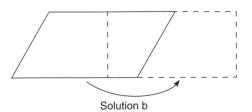

Solution b

Results of pre- and posttesting of viewers and a control group indicated differences in problem-solving skills. Viewers improved an average of 46% in the number and variety of techniques they used to solve problems and by an average of 56% in the sophistication and completeness of their answers. Also of interest is the rationale for developing the program. The developers had noted a tendency among 8- to 12-year-olds, when given a problem, either to see the solution instantly or to say, "We haven't had that yet."

Research on Problem Solving

Of continuing interest to the Gestalt theorists was a further analysis of factors that influenced perception in problem solving. Concepts identified by the researchers that are relevant to today's classrooms are **transfer of training**, **problem approach** and **functional fixedness**, and **problem set**.

Transfer of Training

The effects of different ways of demonstrating problem solutions on problem-solving skills were investigated by George Katona. He conducted a series of experiments on matchstick problems in which the task was to change the number of squares formed by the matchsticks by moving a minimal number of matches. A typical example is to move three matchsticks to make five squares, illustrated in Figure 3.6.

One experiment involved teaching two groups of students different approaches to the problems. In one group, the instructor illustrated the solutions to four variations of the same task that were all solved in the same way. In contrast, the method used with the second group was referred to by Katona (1940) as "guided discovery." The instructor illustrated six transitions in the matchstick configuration by moving only a few matches. For example, removing only three matchsticks created a "hole" in the center of the configuration. This method provided hints to solving other problems by illustrating that major changes

Problem: Solution:

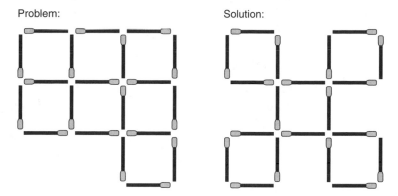

Move three matchsticks to make five squares

FIGURE 3.6
Matchstick problem
Note: From *Organizing and Memorizing* (p. 79), by G. Katona, 1940, New
York: Columbia University Press. Reprinted by permission.

could be made by moving only a few matchsticks. That is, the important structural principle in these problems is that a matchstick may serve as a side in two squares simultaneously. Results comparing the two groups of subjects indicated that the quantity and quality of the solutions to new problems were greater in the guided discovery group.

Problem Approach and Functional Fixedness

Karl Duncker (1926) noted that most theories seek to explain problem solving in terms of a "third factor." That is, they name some extraneous factor such as past experience or imitation to account for the connection between a problem situation and the solution.

Duncker analyzed the protocols of subjects as they attempted to solve several unique problems. His analysis indicated that the first step taken by successful problem solvers is that of a "comprehended conflict." The next step, sometimes taken after some false steps and perhaps hints from the experimenter, is a clear identification of the basic difficulty. The final step is that of a problem solution that addresses the basic difficulty. Such solutions, in his view, are examples of productive thinking and they are therefore referred to as *solutions with functional value.*

One example, referred to as the "X-ray problem," is illustrated in Table 3.2. The key to solving the problem is to note that the rays are too "thick," i.e., too concentrated (felt difficulty). The solution as illustrated in Table 3.2 is to provide "thin" rays from various angles that converge on the tumor.

As indicated in Table 3.2, a key factor in a successful solution is getting to the heart of the problem, i.e., identifying the basic difficulty. Productive thinking, in other words, is distinguished by an inventory of the problem situation,

TABLE 3.2
Problem Solutions with Functional Value

Problem	Comprehended Conflict	Difficulty	Solution with Functional Value
Ape wants the food outside the cage.	Ape cannot reach the food.	Ape's arm is too short.	Make use of something that extends the animal's reach.
Man needs X-ray treatment for tumor inside his body.	X-ray cannot cure man because surrounding tissue would be damaged.	Bundle of X-rays is too concentrated, too united (or too "thick").	Scatter out X-rays, send weak (thin, momentary) rays from various angles.

Note: Summarized from "A Qualitative (Experimental and Theoretical) Study of Productive Thinking (Solving of Comprehensible Problems)" by K. Duncker, 1926, *Pedagogical Seminary, 33,* 642–708.

and the recognition of a definite lack (Aufgabe) that is supplied by the thinking process (Duncker, 1926, p. 702).

Students who are unable to perceive the elements of the situation in a new way are said to suffer from **functional fixedness** (Duncker, 1945). Examples include the inability of some apes to see that a stick can be used as a tool and the subjects in Maier's pendulum experiment who failed to "see" a new use for the pliers.

Problem Set

Functional fixedness is one perceptual difficulty in problem solving. A related concept is **problem set** or **Einstellung**, identified by Abraham Luchins (1942). Briefly, problem set refers to rigidity in problem solving because the individual perceives that a series of problems are to be solved in the same way. In the well-known water jar problems, subjects receive three jars of different capacities and are asked to measure a particular amount of water. The solution to each problem requires pouring certain amounts of water from one jar to another (Table 3.3).

In the experiment, problems 2 through 6 are the set-inducing or "E" problems. Problems 7 through 11 are the test problems because they can be solved by the simple A – C method. However, for problems 7, 8, 10, and 11, the more cumbersome strategy used in problems 1 through 6 will also yield a correct solution. Problem 9 is referred to as the extinction problem because the strategy B – A – 2C will not produce 25 units. The subject who fails problem 9 is regarded as demonstrating rigid behavior because he or she adheres to a repeated strategy although it is completely inadequate (Luchins & Luchins, 1959, p. 111).

Luchins demonstrated that, in the series of problems, the strategy used for problems 1 through 6 was applied also by the subjects to problems 7 through 11. Of 1,039 subjects, 83% used the B – A – 2C in problems 7 and 8, and 64% failed problem 9 (Luchins & Luchins, 1959, p. 110).

TABLE 3.3
Series of Water Jar Problems on Problem Set

	Problem	Solution
1. Task: Given:	Measure 20 units of water Jug A = 29 units; B = 3 units	Fill Jar A and pour off into B three times: 29 − (3 × 3) = 20 A − 3B
2. Task: Given:	Measure 100 units Jug A = 21 units, B = 127, C = 3	Fill Jar B, pour into A, and then fill C twice from jar A B − A − 2C or 127 − 21 − 6 = 100
3. Task: Given:	Measure 99 units A = 14 units, B = 163, C = 25	Same as above: B − A − 2C
4. Task: Given:	Measure 5 units A = 18, B = 43, C = 10	B − A − 2C
5. Task: Given:	Measure 21 units A = 9, B = 42, C = 6	B − A − 2C
6. Task: Given:	Measure 31 units A = 20, B = 59, C = 4	B − A − 2C
7. Task: Given:	Measure 20 units A = 23, B = 49, C = 3	A − C*
8. Task: Given:	Measure 18 units A = 15, B = 39, C = 3	A + C*
9. Task: Given:	Measure 25 units A = 28, B = 76, C = 3	A − C only
10. Task: Given:	Measure 22 units A = 18, B = 48, C = 4	A + C*
11. Task: Given:	Measure 6 units A = 14, B = 36, C = 8	A − C*

*Solvable also by B − A − 2C

Note: Summarized from *Rigidity of Behavior: A Variational Approach to the Effects of Einstellung* by A. S. Luchins and E. H. Luchins, 1959, Eugene, OR: University of Oregon Books.

In contrast, of 970 subjects who received only problems 7 through 11, less than 1% used B − A − 2C in 7 and 8, and only 5% failed problem 9. This phenomenon was named *Einstellung* to denote a certain kind of set that immediately predisposes one to a particular conscious act (Luchins & Luchins, 1959).

In one variation of the basic experiment, the solutions of elementary school children to the first six problems were collected prior to the distribution of problems 7 through 11. The children also were told not to use the same method on these problems.

Although the children heeded the warning, most of them failed problems 7 and 8 and others again used the earlier strategy on problems 10 and 11. Some of the children explained that the old method "kept 'popping up' in their minds and they could not help using it" (Luchins & Luchins, 1959, p. 134).

Efforts to answer the question, What is learned? during the problem-solving activity revealed a variety of answers. Some subjects learned to generalize a rule, others learned to begin with the middle jar, and others learned to begin with the largest jar. Thus, problem rigidity appears to be not one factor, but many.

Summary

Gestalt psychologists also applied their views of structure and perception to issues in school learning. Wertheimer differentiated arbitrary (senseless) and meaningful learning in which the student learned the relevant structure of a situation or problem. Assisting students to reorganize their view of a problem can facilitate meaningful learning. Katona's experiments demonstrated the role of guided discovery in facilitating an understanding of structural principles in visual problems and transfer to new situations.

Other issues in problem solving are clearly identifying the problem goal to develop a solution with functional value, and avoiding the impasses referred to as functional fixedness and problem set. Functional fixedness refers to the inability to see elements of the problem in a new way, and problem set refers to rigidity in problem-solving procedures.

Edward Tolman's Purposive Behaviorism

Tolman (1932) referred to his theory as a "subvariety of Gestalt psychology" (p. 230), and he, too, studied molar behavior. Examples included "a rat running a maze, a cat getting out of a puzzle box, a man driving home to dinner, and a pupil marking a test sheet" (Tolman, 1932, p. 8). Although the theory focused on goal-directed behavior, Tolman defined the term as behavior that is maintained by the environment. An example is the behavior of a rat moving through a maze that ends when the animal gets to the food. Although the animal appears to be seeking a goal, the behavior is governed by the stimuli of the turns in the maze and the food.

The Process of Learning

Instead of specific S–R connections, the subject learns the critical events that lead to some goal, referred to as a "sign-Gestalt-expectation." For example, Pavlov's dogs learned that "waiting-in-the-presence-of-sound" leads to food. According to Tolman, learning occurs because the subjects bring certain expectancies to the learning situation, referred to as hypotheses. The expectations that are confirmed are the ones that survive. Confirmation, in other words, is similar to reinforcement in other theories.

Latent Learning

The term **latent learning** refers to knowledge that is acquired, but which is not necessarily enacted. In other words, learning and performance are not interchangeable. Albert Bandura later incorporated this distinction into his theory of learning.

Tolman and his associates designed several ingenious experiments that challenged the concepts in S–R theory. In one experiment, three different groups of rats ran a maze on 10 successive days. One group received food at the end of each run and another group received no food. The third group, however, received no food for the first 10 days, but were fed from the goalbox on the 11th day. For the remaining 6 days of the experiment, the error rate of this group fell dramatically and was not significantly different from that of the group rewarded daily with food (Tolman & Honzik, 1930).

Tolman (1932) maintained that this experiment demonstrated that the subjects in the third group "learned" from being fed from the goalbox on the 11th day. That is, running the maze (performance) and receiving the food reward for correct maze-running was not essential for learning. In other words, learning and performance are not synonymous.

Some behaviorists, however, suggested that reinforcement was present for the subjects that did not receive the food. Specifically, removal of the subject from the goalbox at the end of the run may act as a reinforcer for reaching the goalbox. This suggestion may also explain the slight improvement of the first group, which never received food for a successful run.

Cognitive Learning

Tolman (1932) maintained that subjects learn "cognitive maps" of the environment. Behaviorists, in contrast, maintain that responses are learned. To address these different views, one study compared the performance of two groups of rats, labeled the "response learners" and the "place learners." The food reward for the response learners was located in different places on different days; however, they always had to turn in only one direction (right or left) to find the food. This group was the response learners. In contrast, the food reward for the place learners was always in the same place. However, they were started through the maze at different points; therefore, to find the reward they had to take different routes (Figure 3.7). The performance of the place learners was superior, supporting the hypothesis that learners acquire cognitive maps of the environment (Tolman, Ritchie, & Kalish, 1946).

Tolman defended the use of rats to demonstrate cognitive learning. Rats "do not go on binges the night before one has planned an experiment; they do not kill each other off in wars; . . . they avoid politics, economics, and papers on psychology. They are marvelous, pure, and delightful" (Tolman, 1949, p. 166).

Applications to Social Psychology

In the early 1930s, Gestalt psychologists began to apply the concept to the formation of social groups and motivation and personality. Koffka (1935) maintained that the principles of field organization in perception also apply to the formation of groups. Maier (1970) investigated the dynamics of problem solving in the work setting, including supervisors and employees.

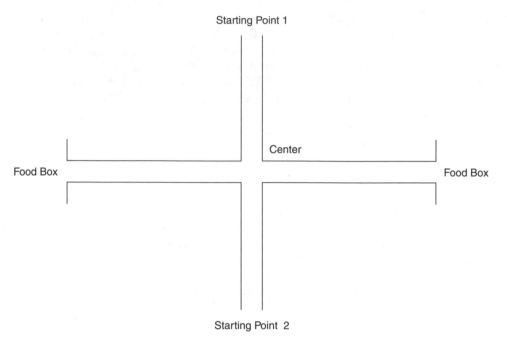

FIGURE 3.7
Maze with different starting points used in Tolman's latent learning experiments

Another theorist associated with the Gestaltists was Kurt Lewin. His work on motivation led to the focus now referred to as group dynamics. Analysis begins with the situation referred to as the individual's life space, and proceeds to identify the interacting psychological forces that influence behavior. The basic concept in his theory is that "to understand or predict the psychological behavior (B) one has to determine for every kind of psychological event (actions, emotions, expressions, etc.) the momentary whole situation, that is, the momentary structure and state of the person (P) and the state of the psychological environment (E). B = f(P, E)" (Lewin, 1933, p. 598). In other words, behavior is a function of the person and the psychological environment. Albert Bandura later used this formula in his analysis of learning in the social setting.

Lewin (1942) also distinguished between learning information and motivational learning. Saying that "the spastic child has to learn to relax" is quite different from "learning French vocabulary," which also has little in common with "learning to like broccoli." Therefore, we should not expect identical laws to hold for these different processes (Lewin, 1936, p. 220). Lewin also coined the term *cognitive structure* to differentiate knowledge learning from motivational learning. The term was then used by Tolman and later was adopted by cognitive psychology.

SUMMARY

In the first half of the 20th century, Gestalt psychology served as the cognitive response to behaviorism, the dominant movement. The major focus of Gestalt writings and research was the dynamic nature of perception. Emphasizing the importance of sensory wholes in perception as the meaningful alternative to the discrete elements of behaviorism, the Gestalt psychologists first developed several laws that govern the dynamic nature of visual perception.

Creative problem situations in which the subject must develop a novel solution illustrated the importance of reorganizing one's perceptions in order to "see" the solution. Referred to as insight, the concept, from the Gestalt perspective, represented understanding the essence or key structural relationships in a situation. Currently, the term also refers to new discoveries in a subject discipline.

Other contributions of Gestalt psychology include the role of guided discovery in meaningful learning, types of problem impasses, and the work of Tolman and Lewin.

APPLICATIONS TO EDUCATION

Issues raised for education by the Gestalt perspective were meaning, understanding, and insight, which are distinctly human characteristics (Wertheimer, 1991). Computer programs, in contrast, can model human problem solving only after the relevant information about the problem has been extracted and fed into the program. In other words, the computer can address a problem once it has been understood (Wertheimer, 1991). The organizing, the thinking, and the understanding are, instead, in the mind of the programmer (p. 203). Therefore, education should address these issues, rather than the steps undertaken after understanding and reorganization have occurred. In other words, situations or problems include some elements that are structurally central and others that are peripheral. Of major importance in learning to solve problems is to grasp the structurally central elements and differentiate them from the peripheral or unimportant features (Wertheimer, 1945).

The difficulty in applying the Gestalt perspective in the classroom is the lack of a set of clearly defined principles of learning. Instead, Gestalt researchers developed general suggestions for problem-solving instruction. First, embed the problem or learning task in concrete, actual situations (Wertheimer, 1945). Finding the area of a rectangle, for example, may be embedded in the situation in which two farmers wish to exchange two plots of land (p. 272). In other words, the teacher should provide reasonable problem situations that the student attempts to address. Then cooperative help should be provided as needed.

Second, the assistance provided during problem solving should not be that of copying or repeating procedures. Instead, the teacher should provide guided discovery in the form of cues or hints to help learners reorganize their view of the problem and overcome inadequate or inaccurate views of the problem (referred to as functional fixedness). The goal is for students to discover a solution with functional value; that is, a solution that addresses the basic difficulty posed by the problem. The test of the occurrence of real learning is to determine if the individual can solve a related problem or task (the principle referred to as transfer) (Cox, 1997; Wertheimer, 1945). If the student has only memorized some steps, he or she will not be able to recognize the similarities of the two situations and will be unable to solve the situation.

Third, instruction should not present students with sets of trite problems that can be solved by learning a series of rote steps. This approach leads to the difficulty referred to as problem set.

Of interest is that two Gestalt concepts, problem set and insight, continue to be discussed by contemporary cognitive psychologists. Problem set (referred to as stereotypy) occurs with poor students who may have the appropriate skills but stick to one strategy, even when it is not successful (Kaplan & Davidson, 1988). However, an incubation period sometimes permits the unproductive associations to weaken. Further, when students reach an impasse on problems that require creative solutions, researchers suggest that taking a break accompanied by hints and self-reflection can lead to insight (Seifert, Meyer, Davidson, Patalano, & Yariv, 1995).

A COMPARISON OF BEHAVIORISM AND GESTALT THEORY

Early behaviorism and Gestalt theory differed from philosophical views of learning in the identification of textable principles, reliance on observation for verification, and application of the principles to real-world situations. Thorndike applied his habit-formation theory to the analysis of school subjects, Watson conditioned Albert's fear reaction, and the Gestalt theorists investigated problem solving.

Among the contributions of this period were the applications of classical conditioning to emotional reactions, the key to effective punishments, the role of guided discovery in problem solving, and the importance of organization in perception. However, in the mid-1930s, both behaviorism and Gestalt theory became overextended. Each perspective attempted to develop the one comprehensive theory that would explain all learning. (See Table 3.4.)

As early as the 1940s, the conflict between the S–R and Gestalt positions was criticized for nonproductivity. Two practices contributed to this problem (McConnell, 1942). First, the terms used by each perspective magnified the differences between them. For example, the terms "insight" and "connection" represent extreme descriptions of the learning process. Also, task difficulty may be a factor in the learning process ultimately described by the theorist. If the task is so difficult that the learner cannot establish relationships with the situation, the subject must resort to trial and error. In contrast, less difficult tasks, in which past experience may play a role, may be reacted to quickly and accurately. Therefore, the flashes of insight described by the Gestalt psychologists may, in some cases, be included under transfer through identical elements (McConnell, 1942, p. 26).

Second, different descriptions of learning arose, in part, from differences in the experimental context. Tasks can be classified according to the amount of

TABLE 3.4
A Comparison of Behaviorism and Gestalt Theory

Major Characteristics	Behaviorism	Gestalt Theory
Basic assumption(s)	Learning is the formation of associations between elements.	Individuals react to unitary, meaningful wholes; therefore, learning is the organization and reorganization of a sensory field. The whole possesses emergent properties that differ from that of the elements. *Tolman:* Learning is essentially the acquisition of cognitive maps that direct behavior.
Typical experiment(s)	(a) *Trial and error:* Rats run mazes; animals escape from cages. (b) *Emotional or reflex responses:* Stimulus pairing.	(a) *Reorganization:* Subjects are placed in situations that require restructuring for solution. (b) Animals run mazes from different starting points and under different reward conditions.
Learning formula	(a) Stimulus-response-reward (b) Emotional responses: Stimulus 1⌉ ⊢ Response Stimulus 2⌋	Constellation of stimuli-organization-reaction

discovery required to make a correct response. Rote learning, for example, is reflected in the simple conditioning experiments whereas complicated unstructured situations require the learner's reorganization of past experience and discovery of the appropriate behavior pattern (McConnell, 1942).

Of importance is that Thorndike's theory was not a strictly behaviorist perspective. In his view, connections between ideas accounted for a major portion of knowledge.

As the decade of the 1950s approached, interest in the development of all-encompassing theory declined. Hilgard (1964), in his review of the end of this period of theory development, noted that the "great debate" among comprehensive theories was now over.

CHAPTER QUESTIONS

1. Katona (1940) differentiated between arbitrary or "senseless" connections and meaningful connections. Describe an example of each.
2. Students in mathematics sometimes complain that they cannot solve word problems that have been rearranged or restated in some way. According to Wertheimer, what is the source of the student's difficulty?
3. Katona (1940) found that illustrating different ways that the matches may be rearranged ("guided discovery") was successful in assisting students in solving certain matchstick problems. According to

Gestalt theory, why should this type of assistance be helpful?

4. The following problem on the National Assessment of Educational Progress (NAEP) is mishandled frequently. One hundred thirty children are waiting to go on a field trip. How many buses are needed if each bus holds 50 students? Students often produce a fractional answer, not recognizing the absurdity. Silver (1986) maintained this error results in part from the division word problems in the curriculum that require partitioning a number into groups of a particular size. What is the Gestalt explanation for this phenomenon?

5. How do the insight problems used by the Gestalt psychologists differ from insight in a subject domain?

REFERENCES

Ansburg, P. I., & Dominowski, R. L. (2000). Promoting insightful problem solving. *The Journal of Creative Behavior, 34*(1), 30–60.

Baars, B. J. (1986). *The cognitive revolution in psychology.* New York: Guilford.

Blau, E. (1990, March 26). Making math come alive on television. *New York Times,* p. C18.

Cox, B. D. (1997). The rediscovery of the active learner in adaptive contexts: A developmental-historical analysis of transfer of training. *Educational Psychologist, 32*(1), 41–55.

Csikszentmihalyi, M., & Sawyer, K. (1995). Creative insight: The social dimension of a solitary moment. In R. J. Sternberg & J. E. Davidson (Eds.), *The nature of insight* (pp. 329–363). Cambridge, MA: MIT Press.

Duncker, K. (1926). A qualitative (experimental and theoretical) study of productive thinking (solving of comprehensible problems). *Pedagogical Seminary, 33,* 642–708.

Duncker, K. (1945). On problem solving. *Psychological Monographs, 58* (Whole No. 270).

Gick, M. L., & Lockhart, R. S. (1995). Cognitive and affective components of insight. In R. J. Sternberg and J. E. Davidson (Eds.), *The nature of insight* (pp. 197–228). Cambridge, MA: MIT Press.

Gruber, H. E. (1981). On the relation between the "Aha! experiences" and the construction of ideas. *History of Science, 19,* 41–59.

Gruber, H. E. (1995). Insight and affect in the history of science. In R. G. Sternberg and J. E. Davidson (Eds.), *The nature of insight* (pp. 397–432). Cambridge, MA: MIT Press.

Hadamard, J. (1949). *The psychology of invention in the mathematical field.* Princeton, NJ: Princeton University Press.

Hartmann, G. W. (1942). The field theory of learning and its consequences. In N. B. Henry (Ed.), *The 41st yearbook of the National Society for Study of Learning, Part II. The Psychology of Learning* (pp. 165–214). Chicago: University of Chicago Press.

Hilgard, E. R. (1964). Postscript: Twenty years of learning theory in relation to education. In E. R. Hilgard (Ed.), *Theories of learning and instruction. The sixty-third yearbook of the National Society for the Study of Education* (pp. 416–481). Chicago: University of Chicago Press.

Hilgard, E. R. (1987). Perspectives on educational psychology. In J. A. Glover & R. R. Ronning (Eds.), *Historical foundations of educational psychology* (pp. 425–429). New York: Plenum.

Hilgard, E. R. (1996). History of educational psychology. In D. C. Berliner & R. C. Calfee (Eds.), *Handbook of educational psychology* (pp. 990–1004). New York: Macmillan Library References.

Kaplan, C. A., & Davidson, J. E. (1988). *Hatching a theory of incubation effects.* (Tech. Rep. No. C.I.P. 472). Pittsburgh: Carnegie Mellon University, Department of Psychology.

Katona, G. (1940). *Organizing and memorizing.* New York: Columbia University Press.

Katona, G. (1967). *Organizing and memorizing: Studies in the psychology of learning and teaching.* New York: Hafner.

Koffka, K. (1935). *Principles of Gestalt psychology.* New York: Harcourt Brace.

Köhler, W. (1928). Chapter VII. Intelligence in apes; Chapter VIII. An aspect of Gestalt psychology. In C. Murchison (Ed.), *Psychologies of 1925* (pp. 145–195). Worcester, MA: Clark University Press.

Köhler, W. (1929). *Gestalt psychology.* New York: Horace Liveright.

Lehar, S. (2003). *The world in your hand: A Gestalt view of conscious experience.* Mahwah, NJ: Erlbaum.

Lewin, K. (1933). Environmental influences. In C. Murchison (Ed.), *A handbook of child psychology* (2nd ed., pp. 590–625). Worcester, MA: Clark University Press.

Lewin, K. (1936). *Principles of topological psychology.* New York: McGraw-Hill.

Lewin, K. (1942). Field theory of learning. In N. B. Henry (Ed.), *The psychology of learning: The forty-first yearbook of the National Society for the Study of Education, Part II* (pp. 215–242). Chicago: University of Chicago Press.

Luchins, A. S. (1942). Mechanization in problem solving: The effect of Einstellung. *Psychological Monographs, 54* (Whole No. 248).

Luchins, A. S., & Luchins, E. H. (1959). *Rigidity of behavior: A variational approach to the effects of Einstellung.* Eugene, OR: University of Oregon Books.

MacGregor, J. N., Ormerod, T. C., & Chronicle, E. P. (2001). Information processing and insight: A process model of performance on the nine-dot and related problems. *Journal of Experimental Psychology: Learning, Memory, and Cognition, 27,* 176–201.

Maier, N. R. F. (1931). Reasoning in humans II. *Journal of Comparative Psychology, 12,* 181–194.

Maier, N. R. F. (1970). *Problem solving and creativity in individuals and groups.* Belmont, CA: Brooks/Cole.

McConnell, T. R. (1942). Reconciliation of learning theories. In N. B. Henry (Ed.), *The psychology of learning. The forty-first yearbook of the National Society for the Study of Education* (pp. 371–401). Chicago: University of Chicago Press.

Murphy, G. (1949). *Historical introduction to modern psychology.* New York: Harcourt, Brace, and World.

Ohlsson, S. (1992). Information-processing explanations of insight and related phenomena. In M. T. Keane & K. J. Gilhooly (Eds.), *Advances in the psychology of thinking, Vol. 1* (pp. 1–203). London: Harrester.

Ormerod, T. C., MacGregor, T. N., & Chronicle, E. P. (2002). Dynamics and constraints in insight problem solving. *Journal of Experimental Psychology: Learning, Memory, and Cognition, 28*(4), 791–799.

Schooler, J. W., Fallshore, M., & Fiore, S. (1995). Epilogue: Putting insight into perspective. In R. J. Sternberg & J. E. Davidson (Eds.), *The nature of insight* (pp. 559–587). Cambridge, MA: MIT Press.

Sekular, R. (1996). Motion perception: A modern view of Wertheimer's 1912 monograph. *Perception, 25,* 1243–1258.

Seifert, C. M., Meyer, D. E., Davidson, N., Patalano, A. L., & Yariv, I. (1995). Demystification of cognitive insight: Opportunistic assimilation and the prepared-mind perspective. In R. J. Sternberg & J. E. Davidson (Eds.), *The nature of insight.* Cambridge, MA: MIT Press.

Silver, R. (1986). Using conceptual and procedural knowledge: A focus on relationships. In J. Hierbert (Ed.), *Conceptual and procedural knowledge: The case of mathematics* (pp. 181–198). Hillsdale, NJ: Erlbaum.

Simonton, D. K. (1995). Foresight in insight? A Darwinian answer. In R. J. Sternberg & J. E. Davidson (Eds.), *The nature of insight* (pp. 466–494). Cambridge, MA: MIT Press.

Smith, S. M., & Blankenship, S. E. (1991). Incubation and the persistence of fixation in problem solving. *American Journal of Psychology, 104,* 61–87.

Steinman, R. M., Pizlo, Z., & Pizlo, F. J. (2000). Phi is not beta, and why Wertheimer's discovery launched the Gestalt revolution. *Vision Research, 40,* 2257–2264.

Tolman, E. C. (1932). *Purposive behavior in animals and men.* New York: Appleton-Century-Crofts.

Tolman, E. C. (1949). There is more than one kind of learning. *Psychological Review, 56,* 144–155.

Tolman, E. C., & Honzik, C. H. (1930). Introduction and removal of reward, and maze performance in rats. *University of California Publications in Psychology, 4*, 257–276.

Tolman, E. C., Ritchie, B. F., & Kalish, D. (1946). Studies in spatial learning, II. *Journal of Experimental Psychology, 36*, 221–229.

Tse, P. U. (1998). Illusory volumes from conformation. *Perception, 27*(8), 977–994.

Tse, P. U. (1999). Volume completion. *Cognitive Psychology, 39*, 37–68.

Wallas, G. (1926). *The art of thought.* New York: Harcourt Brace & Jovanovich.

Watson, R. I. (1963). *The great psychologists* (4th ed.). Philadelphia: Lippincott.

Wertheimer, M. (1912). Experimentelle studien über das Schen von Bewegung. *Zeitschrift für Psychologie, 61*, 161–265.

Wertheimer, M. (1938). Laws of organization in perceptual forms. In W. Ellis (Ed.), *A source book of Gestalt psychology* (pp. 71–88). New York: Harcourt Brace.

Wertheimer, M. (1959). *Productive thinking.* New York: Harper. (Original work published in 1949.)

Wertheimer, M. (1991). Max Wertheimer: Modern cognitive psychology and the Gestalt problem. In G. A. Kimble, M. Wertheimer, & C. White (Eds.), *Portraits of pioneers of psychology* (pp. 189–207). Hillsdale, NJ: Erlbaum.

PART II
Major Trends

The early behaviorist and Gestalt proponents each sought to build the one comprehensive theory that would explain all learning. However, by the 1940s, these efforts were reaching a dead end. Also, the need to design effective training for the military in World War II established new priorities. Then, from the late 1950s to the 1990s, changes in society and the schools introduced new roles for learning and new issues for theory and research. Chapter 4 briefly describes four trends that emerged from the 1950s to the mid-1980s. Chapter 5 discusses the 1990s interest in brain imaging techniques and the field of cognitive neuroscience.

CHAPTER 4
Influences on Theory and Research

Theories are nets to catch what we call "the world"; to rationalize, to explain, and to master it. We endeavor to make the mesh ever finer and finer. (Popper, 1968, p. 59)

Social changes in the second half of the 20th century influenced theory and research in several ways. Among them were the fear of losing the cold war to the U.S.S.R. in the 1950s, the advent of the computer and the high-speed processing of information in the 1960s, and the recognition of the role of personal and social factors in learning in the early 1980s.

In addition, various philosophical and pedagogical beliefs, generally referred to as constructivism, emerged in the late 1980s. These beliefs either reconceptualized the nature of the academic disciplines or the nature of the classroom interactions, and they entered discussions of educational policy in the 1990s.

THE EXPANSION OF THEORY

The years from 1950 to the present may be described in terms of three trends. The first, from 1950 to approximately 1975, is the shift from laboratory research to instructionally relevant research. The second, from the mid-1970s to approximately 1990, is the rise of cognitive psychology. Overlapping with this focus, from the mid-1980s to the present, is the rise of social, cultural, and personal factors in learning.

The Shift from the Laboratory to the Classroom (1950–1975)

Two major trends in this period are (1) the emergence of instructional psychology and (2) the influence of B. F. Skinner's behaviorism.

The Emergence of Instructional Psychology
The military training problems of World War II included complex tasks that challenged existing concepts of learning developed in the laboratory. Examples

include training for aircraft gunners, radio operators, and troubleshooters (Gagné, 1962). Specifically, the recommended learning principles of reinforcement, distribution of practice, and response familiarity did not lead to successful instruction (Gagné, 1962). Instead, efforts to design effective instruction indicated that topic sequencing and providing instruction on competent tasks enhanced learning (Gagné, 1962). These concepts were later developed by Robert Gagné into hierarchies of skills, the basis for his theory of conditions of learning (see chapter 7).

Although initiated by military training needs, instructional research did not become a priority until the late 1950s. The precipitating event was the successful launch of the space capsule *Sputnik* by the Soviet Union in 1957. This technological feat by a Cold War opponent was viewed by the American public as a failure of the country's educational system. The intensity of the international power struggle had magnified the role of education as the guardian of a free society's scholarship and technological achievements.

The launch of *Sputnik* sparked a massively funded curriculum reform in the United States. The learning of isolated facts was to be replaced by a focus on developing thinking and discovery learning. Mathematics, science, and foreign languages—subjects identified as essential to national security—were targeted first for development.

The new emphasis on curriculum development attracted subject matter experts, psychologists, social scientists, and educators. Research on classroom learning, formerly regarded as less prestigious than "pure" laboratory research, became legitimate.

Faced with the problem of curriculum redesign for thinking skills and perhaps influenced by the precision of space technology, researchers expressed the need for an instructional technology. Such a technology would translate learning theory into educational practice (see Bruner, 1964; Hilgard, 1980). Jerome Bruner (1960) called for an instructional theory that would describe principles for the design of effective classroom instruction. In Bruner's view (1964), a theory of learning is descriptive, whereas a theory of instruction is prescriptive.

The impact of the curriculum redesign effort was less than originally expected. However, the new focus on instructional research led to the identification of a new area in psychology. Introduced in 1969 as instructional psychology (see Gagné & Rohwer, 1969), this focus incorporated the interests of educators, curriculum design teams, psychologists, sociologists, and others.

Although instructional theory did not remain a priority, learning theorists began to address the needs of the classroom. Four theoretical perspectives applicable to the classroom gained prominence in this period. The most well known is B. F. Skinner's operant conditioning (see chapter 6). The others are Robert Gagné's conditions of learning (chapter 7), Jean Piaget's cognitive-development theory (see chapter 10), and Jerome Bruner's cognitive approach to curriculum development.

Jerome Bruner's Cognitive-Development Perspective
Director of the Harvard Center for Cognitive Studies in the 1960s, Jerome Bruner (1964) recommended the cognitive-development approach to curriculum

design. Like John Dewey, Bruner described the knowledgeable person as one who is a problem solver; that is, one who interacts with the environment in testing hypotheses and developing generalizations. The goal of education, therefore, should be intellectual development. Furthermore, the curriculum should foster the development of problem-solving skills through the processes of inquiry and discovery.

Degree of cognitive development is described by Bruner in three levels or stages. The first stage, *enactive*, is the representation of knowledge in actions. An example is that of a child operating a balance beam by adjusting his or her position, although the child may be unable to describe the procedure. The second stage, *iconic*, is that of the visual summarization of images. The child at this stage can represent the balance beam in a drawing or diagram. The third and most advanced stage is that of *symbolic representation*. It is the use of words and other symbols to describe experience. The learner at this stage can explain the operation of the balance beam, using the concepts of fulcrum, length of the beam, and weights to be balanced.

The subject matter, therefore, should be represented in terms of the child's way of viewing the world—enactive, iconic, or symbolic. The curriculum should be designed so that the mastery of skills leads to the mastery of still more powerful ones (Bruner, 1966, p. 35). Therefore, the fundamental structure of the subject matter, referred to as organizing concepts, should be identified and used as the basis for curriculum development. Such a practice, according to Bruner (1964, p. 33), permits the teaching of any subject effectively in an intellectually honest form to any learner at any stage of development. Referred to as a spiral curriculum, this organization is represented in the social studies curriculum developed by Bruner, "Man: A Course of Study."

Bruner (1961) also advocated learning by discovery, which he defined as "obtaining knowledge for oneself by the use of one's own mind" (p. 22). Further, new information often is not required for discovery. That is, it requires only a rearrangement or transformation so that the student develops new insights. Benefits that accrue from learning by discovery, according to Bruner (1961), are (1) an increase in the student's capabilities in asking strategic questions, detecting patterns and regularities, and persistence, (2) relying on reinforcement in the form of successful completion of tasks, (3) learning the heuristics (rules of thumb) of discovery, and (4) efficient use of memory.

Finally, in psychology Bruner (1990) maintained that culture should become a central concept. An individual's participation in culture and the realization of one's mental capabilities through culture make the development of a human psychology on the basis of the individual alone impossible (p. 12). Of particular importance is the crucial feature of culture that Bruner (1990) refers to as "folk psychology." Briefly, a folk psychology consists of the culturally shaped notions through which people organize their views of themselves, others, and the world in which they live (p. 137). Therefore, one cannot understand the individual without understanding his or her culture.

The Influence of Skinner's Behaviorism

Unlike other psychologists, B. F. Skinner is known outside the profession of psychology. He is the only post–World War II psychologist to be featured on the cover of *Time* magazine, and a survey of American college students in 1975 indicated he was the best-known American scientist (Gilgen, 1982, p. 97).

Skinner first attracted public attention with his 1945 article in *Ladies' Home Journal* on his invention, the baby tender, also known as the air crib (Rutherford, 2003, p. 2). Designed for Skinner's second daughter, the baby tender was an enclosed, humidity- and temperature-controlled space with a Plexiglas front, in which the baby could sleep unencumbered by sheets and blankets.

He also subsequently wrote three books for the educated public. *Walden Two* described life in a utopian society, *Beyond Freedom and Dignity* applied his behavioral management techniques to social engineering, and *Beyond Behaviorism* both responded to his critics and related his concepts to daily life. In *Walden Two*, Skinner argued that advances in the physical and biological sciences alone cannot provide solutions to such problems as environmental pollution, the hazards of ghetto living, the population explosion, and nuclear war. Instead, societies must rely on advances in the understanding of human behavior (Dinsmore, 1992, p. 1456).

The two major developments that are educational and/or clinical applications of Skinner's operant conditioning are programmed instruction and behavioral management.

Programmed Instruction.   At about the same time that the curriculum reform was getting underway, Skinner developed the teaching machine for classroom use. The purpose was to make instruction more effective and learning more successful (Rutherford, 2003, p. 7).

The instruction consisted of self-paced "stand-alone" materials that did not require teacher intervention. The subject matter was sequenced from simple to complex and students interacted with the materials by responding to a series of incomplete statements. The lesson on morphemes at the end of chapter 6 is an example.

The teaching machine and the accompanying materials, programmed instruction, became a component of a widespread educational technology movement. However, the programmed instruction movement lasted less than 10 years, from approximately 1957 to 1965. Although the hope was to improve education, at least three factors contributed to the demise of programmed instruction. One was the concern, voiced in the popular press, about technology contributing to the dehumanization of education (Rutherford, 2003, p. 9). Second, as teaching machines became popular, individuals who did not understand the basic design principles produced dull programs that were ineffective. Third was the clumsiness of the teaching machine, which was eclipsed by high-speed computers.

Behavioral Management.   The term *behavior modification* first appeared in *Psychological Abstracts* in 1967 (Gilgen, 1982). It refers primarily to behavioral management based on operant conditioning principles, specifically the manipulation of reinforcers to appropriate behaviors.

During the 1960s and 1970s, programs for behavioral change were implemented in a variety of clinical, institutional, and educational settings. Included were schools, businesses, hospitals, clinics, prisons, and governmental settings. The programs have been referred to as *applied behavioral analysis, behavioral modification*, and *contingency management*. Some programs used tokens to reinforce appropriate behaviors that later were exchanged for privileges and thus are known as *token economies*.

Publications in cognition currently dominate the major journals in psychology. However, behavior analysis continues to thrive, even in the absence of its mentor, B. F. Skinner (Pierce, 1996), and behavioral methods continue to be widely used by researchers and clinicians to describe and study human behavior (Robins, Gosling & Craik, 1999, p. 4).

The Rise of Cognitive Psychology (1975–1990)

During the height of behaviorism in psychology, research focused on the analysis of observable responses and their related environmental conditions. Interest in mental events had not disappeared, but remained on the periphery of psychology. Of interest is that the key causes and supports for the revival of cognitive psychology came from outside the discipline (Leahey, 1992, p. 314). One was the communications research initiated in World War II, which led to the conclusion that the learner is a complex information-processing system. Training problems related to the sophisticated equipment included the perception, judgment, and decision-making processes of the human operators. The term *information*, already a foundation concept in the fundamental sciences, became a legitimate topic for psychology.

A second major influence was the development of high-speed computers. Machines that followed a set of instructions (whether they involved logic, arithmetic, or natural language) placed internal processes in the realm of tangible events. Research on such processes thereby became legitimate. Newell and Simon (1961), for example, applied computer operations to the development of a model of human problem solving. Also, computer capabilities in symbol manipulation, transformation, and storage of information provided an analogy for the information-processing model of human memory. Proposed in 1958 by Donald Broadbent, this model of memory includes (1) sensory registers, (2) short-term memory, and (3) long-term memory.

A third influence was the work of Noam Chomsky (1957) in psycholinguistics, which contributed to the legitimization of "rule-following" explanations of language processing (Greenwood, 1999). Not until the late 1960s did psychology get its own influential statement of cognitive science in Ulric Neisser's (1967) *Cognitive Psychology* (Leahey, 1992, p. 314). Although Jerome Bruner and others emphasized perception and cognition, the information-processing model became the dominant view of mental processes. Bruner (1990) noted that the focus in cognitive psychology was not constructing and making sense of their world and themselves. That is, the focus became "information" instead of "meaning" and the processing of information instead of the construction of meaning.

Some discussions have described this period as that of the cognitive revolution. Leahey (1992), however, maintained that the advent of cognitive psychology did not meet the requirements for a revolution. Specifically, the requirements are (1) anomalies or problems that the dominant world view cannot explain provoke a crisis, (2) an emerging world view proposes new solutions to the problems, and (3) the emerging world view passes critical review and converts others to its ideas. First, behaviorism was not a unified world view. Some theorists maintained that only behavior should be studied (e.g., Skinner) and others proposed intervening variables that mediated the process between stimulus and response (e.g., Hull).

Second, the anomalies faced by behaviorism, such as the discovery of biological limits on conditioning, did not lead to the abandonment of the principles of behaviorism (Greenwood, 1999, p. 2). Third, this and other anomalies of behaviorism were not the primary stimulus for the emergence of cognitive theory. Instead, new developments in fields other than psychology introduced new possibilities and questions to be addressed. Cognitive psychology, in other words, bypassed behaviorism and focused on cognitive states and processes as legitimate objects of theoretical focus and explanation (p. 13). In other words, the story of psychology is a narrative of research traditions, not revolutions (Leahey, 1992, p. 316).

The Rise of Social, Cultural, and Personal Factors in Learning (1980–present)

Early studies of learning presented a stimulus or task to the learner, often in a laboratory setting. Extrapolations from these studies were then made to classrooms and other settings. Other perspectives, however, began to focus on different aspects of the natural setting. Three such perspectives that gained prominence in the late 20th century are Lev Vygotsky's cultural-historical theory, Albert Bandura's social-cognitive theory, and other theories of motivation (see Table 4.1).

The theory developed by Lev S. Vygotsky in the early 20th century has been reintroduced in the United States in recent years. Referred to as cultural-historical, the theory addresses the concerns voiced by Bruner. The theory describes two broad cultural factors that determine the nature of learning. One is the ways that signs and symbols developed by a particular culture influence the thinking of its members. The other describes the role of social interaction with knowledgeable members of the culture in the individual's development.

Vygotsky's theory addressed the role of cultural signs and symbols in the individual's cognitive development. Bandura's (1977) theory, however, began with his analysis of the importance of models in the learning of both prosocial and reprehensible behaviors. That is, in the naturalistic setting, observation of models and the effects of their actions leads to the learning of new behaviors by the observers. Bandura's (1986) later work explored the role of self-efficacy in learning. Specifically, perceived self-efficacy is the learner's belief that he or she can be successful in a particular endeavor.

TABLE 4.1
Some Major Events from 1950 to 2000

1950

	1956	Broadbent's model of human memory		
	1957	Soviet Union launches *Sputnik*		
			1958	Newell and Simon's artificial intelligence

1960

1960–1969	Curriculum redesign		1960	Bruner calls for a theory of instruction
1960–1963	Piagetian concepts introduced to American education		1961	Skinner describes importance of teaching machines
	1965	Gagné's conditions of learning		
	1967	Publication of Neisser's *Cognitive Psychology*		
	1968	Publication of Skinner's *Technology of Teaching*		

1970

1970–1975	Various models of human memory proposed		1970	Piaget summarizes major concepts for psychologists
			1971	Bandura's social learning theory introduced
			1972	Weiner introduces attribution theory
	1977	Gagné expands his theory to include information processing		

1980

Dominance of research on cognitive processes

	1984	Application of Vygotsky's concepts in reciprocal teaching		
	1985	Cognitive psychology emphasizes strategy instruction and metacognition	1985	Social, cultural, and personal factors in learning acquire prominence

1990

1990–1994	Various constructivist curricula are implemented
	1995	Interest in neuroscience emerges

2000

Motivational theories address classroom learning

The learner's self-efficacy is one factor that influences the individual's motivation to address challenging or difficult tasks. Other factors addressed by motivational theories include the individual's expectancy for success, the value of the task to the individual, and his or her goal orientation and perceived causes of success and failure. These theories are discussed in chapter 13.

Summary

Three trends have guided theory development and research in the second half of the 20th century. The first, instructional psychology, emerged in response to the need to design training for complex tasks in World War II, and continued as a part of the post-*Sputnik* curriculum redesign. Developments during this period include Gagné's conditions of learning, Piaget's cognitive-development theory, Bruner's curriculum development model, applications of operant conditioning to classroom instruction, and the management of behavior.

Dissatisfaction with behaviorist tenets contributed to the second trend, the rise of cognitive psychology, in the late 1970s. The original goal was to bring "mind" back into the human sciences. However, influenced by communications research and the development of high-speed computers, the focus on the movement shifted to information processing. In the 1980s, research began to address related issues. Included are novice and expert knowledge and metacognition.

Emerging in the early 1980s, the third trend introduced social, cultural, and personal factors into the study of learning. Three theories that address some of these issues are Vygotsky's cultural-historical theory, Bandura's social-cognitive theory, and cognitive/affective theories of motivation.

CONSTRUCTIVIST BELIEFS

The term *constructivism* currently appears in philosophical, sociological, and educational discussions. However, these disciplines, and the various schools of thought within them, define the term in diverse and changing ways (Bredo, 2000, p. 128). In addition, constructivism is used on many levels to address such issues as the formation of scientific knowledge, the development of children's knowledge, and the relationship between knowledge and reality (p. 128). Also, educational discussions frequently suggest classroom strategies based on a particular conception of constructivism.

Currently, constructivism may refer to either of two broad areas. One is the nature of the disciplines or bodies of human knowledge built up in human history (epistemology). That is, what is the nature of physics, calculus, or American history? The other area consists of beliefs about educational practices (educational constructivism) (Phillips, 2000a, p. 6). Furthermore, both moderate and extreme views are found in each of these areas and there may be no linkage between a particular philosophical orientation and beliefs about the nature of educational practices. For example, Thomas Kuhn held a constructivist view of science, but advocated an anti-constructivist pedagogy (Matthews, 2000, p. 163). In other words, one may accept a particular constructivist view of the nature of knowledge and favor any of several classroom practices. Similarly, advocates of constructivist classroom practices may justify them in a variety of ways and some may not be philosophically constructivist (Phillips, 2000b, p. 18).

Discussed in this section are constructivist beliefs about the nature of knowledge, beliefs about educational practices, and concerns expressed by some scholars about aspects of constructivism.

The Nature of Disciplines of Knowledge

Constructivist views of the nature of knowledge are social-constructivist perspectives. That is, depending on the particular emphasis, they either greatly reduce or set aside the role of external reality in shaping beliefs. Instead, they emphasize the importance of social processes in the production of knowledge (Phillips, 1997, p. 85). Also, much of the discussion has focused on the disciplines of science and mathematics, particularly the former (Phillips, 2000a, p. 30). That is, social constructivists address the extent to which physics, for example, is a human construction and whether it may, in some way, reflect an external world.

The rough subgroupings of social constructivism identified by Latour (1992) illustrate the varying conceptions of the nature of science. The conservative view maintains that science is free of society, but social factors still "leak in" and influence its development. In contrast, the progressivists state that social relations "partially" construct knowledge, but nature "leaks in" at the end (Latour, 1992, p. 276, cited in Phillips, 2000a, p. 10). However, the subgroup that has generated the most controversy and that has major implications for both the nature of science and science education is radical social constructivism (Phillips, 1997a, 2000a, Slezak, 2000).

The Radical Social-Constructivist Perspective

Unlike the other social-constructivist views, the radical perspective maintains that knowledge is entirely constructed out of social relations. As indicated in Table 4.2, objects in the natural world are not part of an external pre-existing reality. Instead, objects are constructed by humans in the course of their inquiries. In other words, atoms, molecules, and quarks are human constructions. They are social artifacts that are products of social forces, interests, and other historical characteristics of the local context (Woolgar, 1988; Bloor, 1976).

One version of radical social constructivism, known also as radical social constructionism, maintains that language represents a culture's accumulation of knowledge (Gergen, 1995, p. 23). Also, meaning in language is achieved through social interdependence in a particular community (Gergen, 1995, p. 24). That is, entities such as molecules are constructed through words that "take on their meaning only within the context of ongoing relationships" (Gergen, 1994, p. 49). In other words, "scientific enclaves" form a "conversational world" by choosing "certain configurations to count as 'objects,' 'processes,' or 'events,' and by generating consensus about the occasions to which the descriptive language is to apply" (p. 50).

TABLE 4.2
Premises of the Radical Social-Constructivist View of Science

1. Objects in the natural world are not real or objective, and do not have an independent pre-existence. Instead, they are constituted by our inquiries (Woolgar, 1988, p. 94).
2. Therefore, the ideas of scientific theories do not explain or describe the real world. Instead, they are "rhetorical accomplishments" of a particular discourse community (Woolgar, 1988, p. 26). That is, "knowledge is a matter of conversation and social practice, rather than an attempt to mirror nature" (Rorty, 1979, p. 171; see also Gergen, 1994).
3. Scientific theories reflect the social milieu in which they emerge. They are the product of social forces, interests, and other historically contingent aspects of the local context (Woolgar, 1988, p. 95; see also Bloor, 1976).

Criticisms.   Scholars have identified some major problems with radical social constructivism. First, social constructivist views go beyond typical sociological studies that address the effects of peripheral social phenomena (such as institutional politics) that surround the production of science (Slezak, 2000, p. 96). Instead, social constructivist views attempt to explain the cognitive contents of theories (Phillips, 1997, p. 93; Slezak, 2000 p. 96). However, one implication of maintaining that a social milieu is the causative agent of the contents of a particular theory leads to the illogical inference that Sir Isaac Newton may have articulated an inverse cube law of gravitation if society had been different (Slezak, 2000, p. 98).

Second, radical social constructivism does not rely on reasoning or scientific/physical evidence as criteria for the development and verification of theory (Phillips, 1997, p. 93; Matthews, 2000; Slezak, 2000). For example, if balls rolling down inclined planes did not act in ways observed by Galileo and subsequent countless physicists, the contents of physics would have been different, regardless of the social milieu (Phillips, 1997, p. 95).

Four criticisms of radical social constructivism address implications for science education. First, if knowledge is a product of social conventions, then ideas reflect conformity to social consensus (see Table 4.3). Therefore, individual creativity or genius, such as Albert Einstein's theory of the interrelationships among light, matter, energy, and time, cannot be explained in this framework.

Second, addressing independent critical thinking, viewed by many as important in the survival of society, is no longer needed. Third, there is no basis for evaluating the falsity or implausibility of a theory or of discounting theories that subvert the scientific process. Finally, reliance on consensus as a criterion for the acceptance of ideas allows ideology or group self-interest to identify educational policy.

Summary.   Constructivist views of the nature of knowledge either greatly reduce or set aside the role of external reality in the production of knowledge. Some views consider that the development of scientific knowledge is a mix of social factors and the influence of nature. So, much of the discussion has focused on the disciplines of science and mathematics.

TABLE 4.3
Implications of Radical Social Constructivism for Science Education

1. If knowledge involves only consensus on arbitrary conventions, then education need only ensure that ideas conform prevailing interests (Slezak, 2000, p. 91).
2. Because knowledge involves only consensus, efforts to develop students' capabilities for logical and critical thinking are not needed (Slezak, 2000, p. 93).
3. Because logic, evidence, and other accepted criteria for theories are not relevant to the status of a theory, some theories cannot be judged as false or implausible (Slezak, 2000, p. 93). Therefore, there are no grounds for teaching that Hitler's view of a superior race was a perversion of scientific truth (Slezak, 2000, p. 94).
4. The barrier between evidence and theory leaves space for ideology, group self-interest, or simply "feel-goodness" to identify educational policy (Matthews, 2000, p. 169).

The radical social-constructivist view maintains that knowledge is entirely a product of social processes. Objects are social artifacts, and the rhetorical accomplishments of a particular discourse community and scientific theories simply reflect the social milieu in which they emerge. One radical social-constructivist perspective places the emphasis for knowledge construction on language. The task of describing the world, in other words, is a linguistic rather than a cognitive process.

Scholars have identified some major problems with radical social constructivism. One is the illogical conclusion that, had society been different, a particular scientist would have developed a different theory. Second, logical reasoning and scientific/physical evidence are not criteria for acceptance of a theory. In science education, if knowledge is a product of social conventions, then education need only ensure that ideas conform to prevailing interests. Also, developing students' critical thinking skills is not needed; there is no basis for judging theories as false or implausible; and educational policy may be identified through group self-interest.

Educational Constructivism

Three factors primarily contributed to the emergence of constructivism in education. One was dissatisfaction with information-processing theory. Criticisms include (1) the "overselling" of the computer as a metaphor for learning, which excludes the everyday capabilities of individuals, everyday problems, and the role of context (Bredo, 1994), and (2) the transmission model of learning (Marshall, 1996). That is, some constructivists maintain that information-processing theory views learners as passive receptacles that receive preformed knowledge (O'Connor, 1998).

The other two factors contributing to interest in constructivism are (1) concerns that students are acquiring isolated, decontextualized skills and are unable to apply them in real-world situations, and (2) an interest in Vygotsky's cultural-historical theory. A basic premise of his theory is that the cultural context, particularly the signs and symbols, shape a child's view of reality. Furthermore, these symbols also can serve as psychological tools that are important in developing higher cognitive functions, such as self-organized attention and conceptual thinking (verbal and mathematical).

Currently, like constructivist views that address the nature of disciplines, educational constructivism is not a unified perspective. It consists of different theoretical views and varied classroom perspectives in different subject areas. However, the shared belief of these perspectives is that learners are active constructors of their own knowledge.

Three major varieties of educational constructivism may be identified. They are personal or individual, social, and aphilosophical.

Personal or Individual Constructivism

Like radical social constructivism, personal or individual constructivism considers all knowledge to be a human construction. That is, reality is not accessible to rational human knowledge (von Glaserfeld, 1995). Instead, reality consists of "the network of things and relationships that we rely on in our living" (p. 7).

Also, unlike radical social constructivism, the individual creates knowledge and constructs concepts. Thus, an individually constructed viewpoint cannot be judged as less "correct" than another. However, individual perspectives can be judged partly according to their correspondence to consensually accepted norms (e.g., the Earth revolves around the sun; the Earth is not flat). Personal constructivism also is referred to as a type of radical constructivism (von Glaserfeld, 1991, 1995), and the chief proponent is Ernst von Glaserfeld.

Personal constructivism originated with Jean Piaget's cognitive-development theory. A key difference, however, between Piaget's perspective and von Glaserfeld's view is that Piagetian theory maintains the existence of an external reality. Further, the focus of Piagetian theory is the changes in the thinking of young children, school-age children, and adolescents as they accommodate their strategies of understanding the world to that reality. A second key difference between the two perspectives is that Piaget focused on the development of reasoning and logical thinking whereas personal constructivism focuses on classroom tasks.

However, two Piagetian principles also advocated by the current view of personal constructivism are (1) learning is an internal process that occurs in the mind of the individual, and (2) essential learning processes are the cognitive conflict and reflection that occur when one's thinking is challenged (see chapter 10 for details). The teacher's role, as in Piagetian theory, is to develop an adequate model of each student's way of viewing an idea, devise situations that challenge the child's way of thinking, and help students examine the coherence in their current mode of thinking (Confrey, 1985). The students' reorganizations, however, refer to the specific information associated with particular topics, such as photosynthesis.

Also important is that the emphasis in learning is not on the correspondence with external reality. Instead, the focus is "the construction by the learner of schemes that are coherent and useful to them" (Driver, 1995, p. 387). The goal is to shift the focus from correctly replicating the teacher's words and actions to the successful organization by the student of his or her own experiences (von Glaserfeld, 1987, 1995).

In addition, learners must be granted access to the models and concepts of "conventional science" (Driver, 1995, p. 395). That is, the teacher must introduce the conventions of science that students cannot discover from experience. This goal can be accomplished through carefully developed questions that "shape students' reasoning toward the accepted science view" (p. 397).

Social Constructivism

Social-constructivist beliefs differ from personal or individual constructivism in three major ways: (1) the definition of knowledge, (2) the definition of learning, and (3) the locus of learning (see Table 4.4). That is, social constructivists view the classroom as a community charged with the task of developing knowledge. Furthermore, they view knowledge as inseparable from the activities that produced it (Bredo, 1994; Dewey & Bentley, 1949). Therefore, knowledge is transactional; learning is socially constructed and is distributed among the co-participants. The role of the learner in such situations is to participate

TABLE 4.4
Shared Beliefs of Social-Constructivist Philosophy

Definition of knowledge	A product of the particular classroom or participant setting to which the learner belongs; the endpoint or product of a particular line of inquiry that is inseparable from the occasions and activities that produced it (Bredo, 1994; Dewey & Bentley, 1949).
Definition of learning	Socially shared cognition that is a process of becoming a member of a sustained community of practice (Lave, 1991); social interaction that constructs and reconstructs contexts, knowledge, and meanings (Marshall 1996).
Locus of learning	Not confined to the individual's mind (Marshall, 1996); occurs in a community of participants and is distributed among the co-participants (Bredo, 1994).

in a system of practices that are themselves evolving (Cobb & Bowers, 1999). Mathematics, for example, is not viewed as objective knowledge. Instead, it is an active construction by individuals that is shared with others (Wood, Cobb, & Yackel, 1995, p. 405). Therefore, classroom learning over several months can be analyzed in terms of a sequence of evolving mathematical practices in a community of learners. For example, first-grade children early in the fall may be using counters in various ways to determine the number of days remaining in the week and, in the spring, discussing different ways to address three-digit problems (Cobb & Bowers, 1999).

Subvarieties within social constructivism vary on the precise relationship of the individual to the community, the exact nature of the learning goals, and the role of language. For example, the most fully articulated social-constructivist view, referred to as emergent, was developed "to account for students' mathematical development as it occurs in the social context of the classroom" (Cobb & Yackel, 1996, p. 176). Described by Paul Cobb (1994), the emergent perspective is a coordination of personal and social-constructivist theories. This view, therefore, permits analyses of learning from both the social (group) and the individual perspective in situations in which neither is primary. For example, social norms (rules of discourse) jointly negotiated by a teacher and her second-grade pupils included explaining and justifying one's solutions, attempting to make sense of the explanations of others, and questioning proposed alternatives (Cobb & Bowers, 1999). Analyses from the individual perspective addressed the child's mathematical beliefs and beliefs about one's role and that of others in the general nature of school mathematical activity (p. 177).

This perspective is based on the view that neither cognitive nor social processes should be considered secondary in efforts to understand mathematics learning and teaching in classrooms (Wood et al., 1995, p. 401). That is, accounts of cognitive activity cannot be derived from analyses of social processes. Also, mathematics learning and teaching is more than a cognitive process that is influenced by social processes. In other words, mathematics should be viewed as "both cognitive activity constrained by social and cultural processes and a sociocultural phenomenon that is constituted by a community of actively cognizing individuals" (p. 402).

A very different view, described by Bredo (1994) as neo-Marxist, is the apprenticeship perspective of Jean Lave (1991; Lave & Wenger, 1991). Citing the current alienated condition in capitalism, which lacks opportunities for individuals to develop deep knowledgeable skill and identities of mastery, Lave (1991) called for research on situated social practice or situated learning. Examples include Mayan midwives and West African tailors. Essential characteristics of such situations are the seamless immersion of the learner into a community of practice with gradual movement from peripheral tasks to full participation. Further, learning proceeds with no didactic structuring (Lave, 1991).

Situated social practice also maintains that no strict knowledge boundary exists between the intra- and extracranial aspects of human cognition (Lave, 1991, p. 68). Instead, knowing is *located in relations among practitioners*, their practice, and the social organization and political economy of communities of practice in a world in which social practices themselves are in the process of reproduction, transformation, and change (Lave & Wenger, 1991, p. 122). Although typical of informal and craft apprenticeship, the pedagogy can involve specially designed social activities that can permit novices to gain mastery of simplified domains of knowledge and activity (Ernst, 1995, p. 471). In this way, this approach can be applied to formal educational systems.

In the classroom, social constructivists consider their approach as an alternative to learning by discovery (Wood et al., 1995, p. 404). One difference is that the constructivist teacher of mathematics creates situations that may be personally meaningful to students at different conceptual levels (p. 407). Children, in pairs or small groups, develop their own ways of solving the problems. Requirements in the classroom also include (1) children's explanations and justifications of their approach to the problem, (2) their listening to and trying to make sense of the explanations of others, and (3) verbalizing agreement, disagreement, or a failure to understand the explanations of others (p. 411). In this way, the children participate in and contribute to a communal mathematical practice. That is, they construct for themselves such concepts as even numbers as those numbers that can be divided into two equal whole-number groups with no remainder (Ball & Bass, 2000, p. 217).

A few educators (e.g., Packer & Goioechea, 2000) maintain that socially situated views of learning should not be labeled as constructivist. The reason is that socially situated perspectives focus on the characteristics of social participation, relationships, and the setting of the activity. More important, they do not emphasize the ways that knowledge is constructed on qualitatively different, and more progressively adequate, levels (p. 227). Therefore, according to this description, they should be viewed as sociocultural approaches instead of social constructivist.

Aphilosophical Constructivism

Constructivist approaches to educational practice that make no assumptions about the nature of knowledge may be categorized as aphilosophical. At least three subgroups are in this category. One consists of those educators who "simply use the label 'constructivist' to refer to anything which is pupil-centered, engaging, questioning, and progressive" (Matthews, 1997, p. 8).

The two other subgroups interpret constructivism as representing the ways that students make meaning when reading and writing. Perhaps best known is the "holistic" approach to literacy known as whole language (Au, Mason, and Scheu, 1995; Poplin & Stone, 1992). Teachers should become facilitators of learning by creating authentic contexts that stimulate students to meet their own learning needs. In other words, the belief is that all forms of language, including written language, are most easily learned in the context of use. Therefore, literacy development requires immersion in authentic literacy events—activities that use language in functional ways and that have personal meaning for the student.

The third classroom-focused constructivist approach describes readers and writers as "building, shaping, and elaborating meanings when they understand or produce texts" (Spivey, 1995, p. 313). For example, a particular text has different meanings for readers with different perspectives and purposes. In reading, the constructive process involves choosing relevant content suggested by the text, organizing it, and linking it to the reader's prior knowledge (Spivey, 1987). When composing a text, the writer considers the potential meaning that readers may build from the textual clues. That is, the writing is influenced by the writer's anticipation of the reader's knowledge and what the reader needs to know. In other words, composing is a constructivist process that focuses on the meanings to be generated from the final text.

Concerns

Currently, some educators have voiced concerns about the social-constructivist classroom in which students construct knowledge through participation in a group. One is the exclusion of direct classroom instruction. Howe & Berv (2000) note that collaborative learning seems inappropriate for tasks such as learning the sounds of "A." Matthews (1997) doubts that children will be able to develop knowledge of complex conceptual schemes built by human minds over hundreds of years unless knowledge can be imparted to students (p. 12). Furthermore, he doubts that learners can construct for themselves such concepts as potential energy, mutation, linear inertia, or valence without the teacher illustrating and explaining them, and showing their relationships to other concepts (p. 13).

A second concern is the difficulties faced by low-ability learners and those from other cultures. Specifically, the participation structure can create barriers for them because they lack the knowledge and skills to participate (Cobb & Bowers, 1999; Delpit, 1988). Similarly, a reliance on authentic tasks that involve implicit rather than explicit instruction can also tax the cognitive skills of students at risk for learning difficulties (Foorman, Francis, Fletcher, Schatschneider, & Mehta, 1998).

Third is the burden on the classroom teacher who faces challenges both within and outside the classroom. Windschitl (2002) identified four broad areas of dilemmas. They are conceptual (grasping the underpinnings of constructivism); pedagogical (honoring students' efforts to think for themselves while remaining true to accepted disciplinary ideas); cultural (taking advantage of individual students' knowledge and experiences while managing the transformation of beliefs and practices according to constructivist norms); and political (facing issues of accountability and negotiating to teach for understanding) (p. 133).

Within the classroom, the teacher must (1) balance the competing demands of discovery and efficient understanding, and (2) exercise sensitive clinical judgments moment-by-moment to know when to intervene and when to allow interactions to continue (Palinscar, 1998; Perkins, 1999). Some observers note that, in some cases, teachers do not ask challenging questions (Howe & Berv, 2000, p. 38), and do not challenge incoherence and inconsistencies (MacKinnon & Scarff-Seatter, 1997). In other words, the social-constructivist classroom requires teacher skills in establishing a discourse community with intellectual standards and a commitment to joint construction of meaning (Green & Gredler, 2002). Observations indicate opportunities for learning and success differ as a function of teacher skills in establishing social norms and intellectual standards (Cobb & Bowers, 1999; Palinscar, 1998).

Summary.   Three factors primarily contributed to the emergence of constructivism in education. They are dissatisfaction with the information-processing model, concerns that students were acquiring isolated, decontextualized skills they are unable to apply in the real world, and an interest in Vygotsky's cultural-historical theory. Currently, three major types of educational constructivism may be identified.

Personal or individual constructivism considers all knowledge to be a human construction, that the individual creates knowledge and constructs concepts, and that viewpoints can only be partially judged according to their correspondence with consensually accepted norms. In the classroom, personal constructivism does advocate two Piagetian principles. They are that learning is an internal process, and cognitive conflict and reflection result from challenges to one's thinking. The teacher's role is to develop an adequate model of each student's way of viewing an idea, and to devise situations that lead students to question and reflect on their ideas. The goal is the successful reorganization by the student of his or her own experiences. Some educators, however, also note that the student must also be granted access to the concepts of conventional science.

In contrast, social constructivists believe that knowledge is transactional. That is, learning is socially constructed and is distributed among the co-participants. Classroom learning over several months can be described in terms of the evolving mathematical practices in a community of learners. One social-constructivist view, however, analyzes learning from both the social and the individual perspectives. Group activities include negotiating the rules of discourse and participating in an exchange of views, accompanied by questions and explanations. Analyses from the individual perspective address the child's mathematical beliefs and one's role in the classroom activity.

Another social-constructivist perspective is that of apprenticeship. That is, knowing is located in relationships among practitioners. Although typical of craft apprenticeships, proponents maintain that specially designed social activities can permit novices to develop mastery of simplified domains of knowledge. A few educators, however, maintain that socially situated views of learning should not be labeled as constructivist. One reason is that they do not emphasize the ways that knowledge is constructed on qualitatively different and more adequate levels.

The third approach, which may be designated as aphilosophical, makes no assumptions about the nature of knowledge. Rather, some educators refer to classroom practices that are pupil-centered and progressive. Others, such as the holistic approach to literacy and the view that writers build and elaborate meanings, focus on the ways that readers and writers develop meaning. Therefore, literacy development requires immersion in activities that use language in functional ways and that have personal meaning for students.

Some educators have expressed concerns about constructivism in the classroom. Included are (1) that collaborative learning seems inappropriate for some learning, (2) the difficulties faced by low-ability learners and those from other cultures, and (3) the burdens on the classroom teachers.

CHAPTER QUESTIONS

1. What is Bruner's rationale for the centrality of culture in psychology?
2. What is Leahey's argument that the so-called cognitive revolution was not a revolution?
3. In what ways does personal constructivism agree with Piaget?
4. In education, how does aphilosophical constructivism differ from social-constructivist beliefs?

REFERENCES

Au, K., Mason, J., & Scheu, J. (1995). *Literacy instruction for today*. New York: Harper Collins.

Ball, D. L., & Bass, H. (2000). Making believe: The collective construction of public mathematical knowledge in the elementary school classroom. In D. C. Phillips (Ed.), *Constructivism in education. Ninety-ninth yearbook of the Society for the Study of Education* (pp. 193–224). Chicago: University of Chicago Press.

Bandura, A. (1977). *Social learning theory*. Upper Saddle River, NJ: Prentice Hall.

Bandura, A. (1986). *Social foundations of thought and action: A social cognitive theory*. Upper Saddle River, NJ: Prentice Hall.

Bredo, E. (1994). Reconstructing educational psychology: Situated cognition and Deweyian pragmatism. *Educational Psychologist, 29*(1), 23–25.

Bredo, E. (2000). Reconsidering social constructivism. In D. C. Phillips (Ed.), *Constructivism in*

education. Ninety-ninth yearbook of the Society for the Study of Education* (pp. 127–157). Chicago: University of Chicago Press.

Bloor, D. (1976). *Knowledge and social imagery*. London: Routledge Kegan Paul.

Broadbent, D. E. (1958). *Perception and communication*. London: Pergamon.

Bruner, J. S. (1960). *The process of education*. Cambridge, MA: Harvard University Press.

Bruner, J. S. (1961). The act of discovery. *Harvard Educational Review, 31*, 21–32.

Bruner, J. S. (1964). Some theorems on instruction illustrated with references to mathematics. In E. R. Hilgard (Ed.), *Theories of learning and instruction. The sixty-third yearbook of the National Society for the Study of Education, Part I* (pp. 306–355). Chicago: University of Chicago Press.

Bruner, J. S. (1966). *Toward a theory of instruction*. Cambridge, MA: Harvard University Press.

Bruner, J. S. (1990). *Acts of meaning*. Cambridge, MA: Harvard University Press.

Chomsky, N. (1957). *Syntactic structures*. Berlin: Mouton de Gruyter.

Cobb, P. (1994). Where is the mind? Constructivist and sociocultural perspective on mathematics development. *Educational Researcher, 23*, 13–20.

Cobb, P., & Bowers, J. (1999). Cognitive and situated learning perspectives in theory and practice. *Educational Researcher, 28*(2), 4–15.

Cobb, P., & Yackel, E. (1996). Constructivist, emergent, and sociocultural perspectives in the context of developmental research. *Educational Psychologist, 31*(3/4), 175–190.

Confrey, J. (1985). Toward a framework for constructivist instruction. In L. Streefland (Ed.), *Proceedings of the Ninth International Conference for the Psychology of Mathematics Education, Vol. 1* (pp. 477–478, 483).

Delpit, L. (1988). The silenced dialogue: Power and pedagogy in educating other people's children. *Harvard Educational Review, 58*, 280–298.

Dewey, J., & Bentley, A. (1949). *Knowing and the known*. Boston: Beach Press.

Dinsmore, J. A. (1992). Setting the record straight: the social views of B. F. Skinner. *American Psychologist, 47*(1), 1454–1463.

Driver, R. (1995). Constructivist approaches to science teaching. In L. P. Steffe & J. Gale (Eds.), *Constructivism in education* (pp. 385–400). Hillsdale, NJ: Erlbaum.

Ernst, P. (1995). The one and the many. In L. P. Steffe & J. Gale (Eds.), *Constructivism in education* (pp. 459–486). Hillsdale, NJ: Erlbaum.

Foorman, B., Francis, D., Fletcher, J., Schatschneider, C., & Mehta, P. (1998). The role of instruction in learning to read: Preventing reading failure in at-risk children. *Journal of Educational Psychology, 90*, 37–55.

Gagné, R. M. (1962). The acquisition of knowledge. *Psychological Review, 69*, 355–365.

Gagné, R. M., & Rohwer, W. (1969). Instructional psychology. *Annual Review of Psychology, 20*, 381–418.

Gergen, K. J. (1994). *Realities and relationships: Soundings in social construction*. Cambridge, MA: Harvard University Press.

Gergen, K. (1995). Social construction and the educational process. In L. P. Steffe & J. Gale (Eds.), *Constructivism in education* (pp. 17–39). Hillsdale, NJ: Erlbaum.

Gilgen, A. R. (1982). *American psychology since World War II*. Westport, CT: Greenwood.

Green, S. K., & Gredler, M. E. (2002). A review and analysis of constructivism for school-based practice. *School Psychology Review, 31*(1), 53–70.

Greenwood, J. D. (1999). Understanding the "cognitive revolution" in psychology. *Journal of the History of the Behavioral Sciences, 35*(1), 1–22.

Hilgard, E. R. (1980). The trilogy of mind: Cognition, affection, and conation. *Journal of the History of the Behavioral Sciences, 16*, 107–117.

Howe, K. R., & Berv, J. (2000). Constructing constructivism, epistemological and pedagogical. In D. C. Phillips (Ed.), *Constructivism in education. Ninety-ninth yearbook of the National Society for the Study of Education* (pp. 19–40). Chicago: University of Chicago Press.

Latour, B. (1992). One more time after the social turn. In E. McMullin (Ed.), *The social dimensions of science*. Notre Dame, IN: University of Notre Dame Press.

Lave, J. (1991). Situated learning in communities of practice. In L. Resnick, J. Levine, & S. Teasley (Eds.), *Perspectives on socially shared cognition* (pp. 63–82). Washington, DC: American Psychological Association.

Lave, J., & Wenger, E. (1991). *Situated learning: Legitimate peripheral participation*. New York: Cambridge University Press.

Leahey, T. H. (1992). The mythical revolutions of American psychology. *American Psychologist, 47*(2), 308–318.

MacKinnon, A., & Scarff-Seatter, C (1997). Constructivism: Connections and confusions in teacher education. In V. Richardson (Ed.), *Constructivist teacher education* (pp. 38–56). Washington, DC: Falmer Press.

Marshall, H. (1996). Clarifying and implementing contemporary psychological processes. *Educational Psychologist, 31*(1), 29–34.

Matthews, M. R. (1997). A bibliography for philosophy and constructivism in science education. *Science and Education 6*(1–2), 197–200.

Matthews, M. R. (2000). Appraising constructivism in science and mathematics education. In D. C. Phillips (Ed.), *Constructivism in education*.

Ninety-ninth yearbook of the National Society of the Study for Education (pp. 161–192). Chicago: University of Chicago Press.

Neisser, J. (1967). *Cognitive psychology*. New York: Appleton-Century-Crofts.

Newell, A., & Simon, H. (1961). *Human problem solving*. Santa Monica, CA: Rand.

O'Connor, M. G. (1998). Can we trace the "efficacy of social constructivism"? In P. D. Pearson & A. Iran-Nejad (Eds.), *Review of Research in Education, 23* (pp. 25–71). Washington, DC: American Educational Research Association.

Packer, M. J., & Goioechea, J. (2000). Sociocultural and constructivist theories of learning: Ontology, not just epistemology. *Educational Psychologist, 35*(4), 227–241.

Palinscar, A. (1998). Social constructivist perspectives on teaching and learning. *Annual Review of Psychology, 49*, 345–375.

Perkins, D. N. (1991). What constructivism demands of the learner. *Educational Technology, 31*, 19–21.

Perkins, D. (1999). The many facets of constructivism. *Educational Leadership 57*(3), 6–16.

Phillips, D. C. (1997). Coming to grips with radical social constructivism. *Science and Education 6*(1–2), 85–104.

Phillips, D. C. (2000a). An opinionated account of the constructivist landscape. In D.C. Phillips (Ed.), *Constructivism in education. Ninety-ninth yearbook of the National Society of the Study of Education* (pp. 1–16). Chicago: University of Chicago Press.

Phillips, D. C. (2000b). Constructivism as an epistemology and philosophy of education. In D. C. Phillips (Ed.), *Constructivism in education. Ninety-ninth yearbook for the Study of Education* (pp. 17–18). Chicago: University of Chicago Press.

Pierce, W. D. (1996). Behavior analysis is alive and well. *Contemporary Psychology, 41*, 461.

Poplin, M. M., & Stone, S. (1992). Paradigm shifts in instructional strategies: From reductionisn to holistic constructivism. In W. Stainback & S. Stainback (Eds.), *Controversial issues confronting special education* (pp. 153–180). Boston: Allyn & Bacon.

Popper, K. (1968). *The logic of discovery*. New York: Harper & Row.

Robins, R. W., Gosling, S. D., & Craik, K. H. (1999). An empirical analysis of trends in psychology. *American Psychologist, 54*(2), 117–128.

Rorty, R. (1979). *Philosophy and the mirror of nature*. Princeton: Princeton University Press.

Rutherford, A. (2003). B. F. Skinner's technology of behavior in American life: From consumer culture to counterculture. *Journal of the History of the Behavioral Sciences, 39*(1), 1–23.

Slezak, P. (2000). A critique of radical social constructivism. In D. C. Phillips (Ed.), *Constructivism in education. Ninety-ninth yearbook of the National Society for the Study of Education* (pp. 91–126). Chicago: University of Chicago Press.

Spivey, N. N. (1987). Construing constructivism: Reading research in the United States. *Poetics, 16*, 169–192.

Spivey, N. N. (1995). Written discourse: A constructivist perspective. In L. P. Steffe & J. Gale (Eds.), *Constructivism in education* (pp. 313–366). Hillsdale, NJ: Erlbaum.

von Glaserfeld, E. (1987). Learning as a constructivist activity. In C. Janvier (Ed.), *Problems of representation in the teaching and learning of mathematics* (pp. 3–17). Hillsdale, NJ: Erlbaum.

von Glaserfeld, E. (1991). *Radical constructivism in mathematics education*. Dordrecht, The Netherlands: Kluwer.

von Glaserfeld, E. (1995). A constructivist approach to teaching. In L. P. Steffe & J. Gale (Eds.), *Constructivism in education* (pp. 3–15). Hillsdale, NJ: Erlbaum.

Windschitl, M. (2002). Framing constructivism in practice as the negotiation of dilemmas: An analysis of the conceptual, pedagogical, cultural, and political challenges facing teaching. *Review of Educational Research, 72*(2), 131–175.

Wood, T., Cobb, P., & Yackel, E. (1995). Reflections on learning and teaching mathematics in elementary school. In L. P. Steffe & J. Gale (Eds.), *Constructivism in education* (pp. 401–422). Hillsdale, NJ: Erlbaum.

Woolgar, S. (1988). *Knowledge and reflexivity*. Newbury Park, CA: Sage.

CHAPTER 5
The Human Brain

The human brain is the most complex natural system in the known universe; its complexity rivals and probably exceeds the complexity of the most intricate social and economic structures. It is science's new frontier. (Goldberg, 2001, p. 23)

Several events have contributed to an unprecedented interest in the human brain. One was the designation of the 1990s as the decade of the brain by a congressional resolution. Second were extrapolations from the neurobiological research of the 1970s and 1980s to educational policy in the 1990s. Third is the increasing application of brain neuroimaging technologies to the study of cognitive tasks. Accompanying this development are questions about the possibilities of obtaining answers about the brain similar to the breakthroughs in genetics resulting from the discovery of the structure of DNA (Damasio, 1994, p. 260).

The problem is that the equivalent for the mind-producing brain involves detailing the activities of several billion neurons in their micro- and macro-levels of organization, as well as the host of local and global influences on their performance. Moreover, the performance of each neuron occurs in tens of milliseconds. In other words, the mind/brain puzzle (the construction of a mind from the activity of the brain) does not have a single answer, but many answers (Damasio, 1994). Required in this effort are various techniques that address the many levels of structure and function in the human brain. Through the use of neuroimaging techniques, new findings are accumulating rapidly. However, the potential problem is that the flood of new facts may overwhelm the ability to think clearly (Damasio, 1994, p. 258).

A further complication is the increased interest in the brain, fueled by media reports and commentaries (see Thompson & Nelson, 2001) and discussions among scientists and others. This interest has led to speculations about the ways research findings can improve or enrich educational practice (Organisation for Economic Co-operation and Development, 2002, p. 69). One result is that some who promulgate brain-based research to teachers fail to communicate the relative paucity of the research from which they draw their claims. Others advocate brain-based teaching strategies that are not based on research (p. 69). Moreover, expectations of the utility of brain research have contributed to the rapid growth of myths.

Therefore, one purpose of this chapter is to provide an overview of the organization and development of the human brain. A second purpose is to discuss the cognitive and educational issues related to brain research.

ORGANIZATION AND DEVELOPMENT

Discussed first is an overview of the basic units of the brain, the microscopic structure. Then this section discusses various areas of the brain, the macroscopic structure.

Overview of the Microscopic Structure

Both structural and chemical components constitute the microscopic organization of the brain. The building blocks are the neurons, which are the basic unit of communication, and glial cells, which provide structural support for the neurons. Glial cells also produce the fluid that cushions the brain and spinal cord against the bumps and jarrings of daily life. The cerebral cortex of the human brain contains between 10 and 20 billion (approximately 10^{10}) neurons and five to 10 times as many glial cells (Blinkov & Gleser, 1968).

The three components of the neuron are (1) the cell body, (2) an axon (the "tail" of the neuron), and (3) dendrites or branches. The neurons are connected in circuits such that each serves as both a receiver and a transmitter.

The axons and dendrites are the communication "wires" between neurons. Each axon transmits signals to a dendrite of the associated neuron across a microscopic gap known as the synapse. However, the architecture formed by the axons, synapses, and dendrites is not a set of neatly constructed circuits. Instead, they resemble a "jungle" where the various extensions of thousands of different neurons are entangled (Changeux, 1985, p. 54). Many neurons communicate within relatively local circuits in particular areas of the brain (Damasio, 1994, p. 30); however, others project across regions of the brain. The length of the axon cables that form neuron circuits in the brain is approximately several hundred thousand miles (Damasio, 1994, p. 259).

When a neuron becomes active, an electric current is transmitted down the axon to the synapse. This action of the neuron is referred to as "firing" (Damasio, 1994, p. 29). The time frame for firing is minute, approximately tens of milliseconds, and the brain produces millions of firing patterns over a large variety of circuits (p. 259).

Typically, when the electrical current arrives at the synapse, it is transported across that minute gap by a chemical messenger known as a neurotransmitter. This process requires less than 10 millionths of a second. The effect of the neurotransmitter on the receiving neuron may be to increase the likelihood that the receiving neuron will be activated (excitatory) or decrease the likelihood of activation (inhibitory). The functioning of neurons suggests the image of a "gigantic assembly of billions of interlacing neuronal spiders' webs, in which billions of electrical impulses flash by, relayed from time to time by a rich array of chemical signals" (Changeux, 1985, p. 126).

Scientists have identified more than 50 transmitters (Fischbach, 1992), although information about their effects is incomplete. One of the main neurotransmitters found in the brain is serotonin, which includes approximately 14 types and contributes to almost all aspects of cognition and behavior (Damasio, 1994, p. 76).

One of the difficulties in understanding the complex role of neurotransmitters on perception, cognition, memory, and emotion is that the same neurotransmitter can have different effects depending, in part, on the area or region of the brain in which the chemical is acting and the nature of the receptors of the receiving neurons. For example, the degeneration of neurons that produce dopamine leads to Parkinson's disease. However, an excess of dopamine in another part of the brain contributes to the hallucinations that occur with schizophrenia (Hockenbury & Hockenbury, 1997).

During prenatal development, factors such as physical injury, malnutrition of the mother, and harmful substances ingested by the mother can cause structural and functional problems. An example is heavy consumption of alcohol. Another is Accutane, the medication for severe acne. Researchers have documented severe mental, physical, and behavioral disorders in children whose mothers accidentally conceived while taking the medication (Rafshoon, 2003).

Following birth, unlike other species, the human brain undergoes a lengthy period of development (Changeux, 1985, p. 242). For example, development of the cortical area of the brain (the site of executive functions such as goal setting and evaluation) extends approximately four times longer in humans than in other primates (Johnson, 1997, p. 59). Also, by age 20, the average weight of the human brain has increased to approximately 1350 grams from the birth weight of 350 grams (Blinkov & Gleser, 1968).

The term "growth," when used in reference to the brain, refers to the lengthening and branching of nerve fibers that connect the cell bodies to their targets (Changeux, 1985, p. 212). In many parts of the brain, in the early months and years of life, neurons exhibit "exuberant" growth. That is, they extend axons to other neurons in addition to the target neuron (Nowakowski & Hayes, 2002, p. 74). This growth is accompanied by a dramatic increase in the number of dendrites and synapses. For example, synapses in the visual and auditory cortices attain a maximum density that is 150 percent of adult levels between 4 and 12 months (Huttenlocher, de Courten, Garey, & Van der Loos, 1982; Huttenlocher, 1990, 1994a, b; Johnson, 1997).

The bursts in synaptic development are followed by a period of loss and reduction in the number of synapses to adult levels (Changeux, 1985, pp. 216–219, 227–229). The timing of this loss, however, varies across cortical regions of the brain. Synapse elimination in the visual cortex, the area of the brain that processes visual input, begins at about 1 year and is completed by approximately age 10 (Huttenlocher, 1994a, p. 143). Synapse elimination is somewhat slower in the frontal cortex, the area of the brain that integrates and interprets information. The process appears to occur between age 7 and adolescence (p. 143). Data from other species that also indicate bursts in synaptic development followed by elimination of synapses suggest that this is a universal phenomenon.

In addition to these structural developments, some chemical neurotransmitters that assist neurons in communicating with each other also undergo a developmental rise and fall (Johnson, 1997, p. 37). Among them are glutamate and serotonin (Benes, 1994).

Researchers suggest that the overproduction of synapses fulfills an important function. First, it reduces the genetic load that would be required to reprogram the huge number of synapses required to deal with the complexities of life (Chugani, Phelps, & Mazziotta, 2002, p. 112). That is, the number of genes is insufficient to determine the precise structure and location of the billions of neurons and their synapses (Damasio, 1994, p. 108). Second, a brain determined entirely by genes would be "rigid." The number of possible operations would be limited, and the organization of the brain would not be open to the social and cultural environment (Changeux, 1985, p. 278).

Furthermore, early theories that maintained the brain is "hard wired" at birth are not supported by research. Many studies on rats through the years have indicated that training and experience led to changes in the brain (e. g., Krech, Rosenzweig, & Bennett, 1960; Holloway, 1966; Greenough & Volkmar, 1973; Turner & Greenough, 1985). More recently, neuroimaging studies of identical twins, who have the same genes, indicated striking differences in cortical areas (Johnson, 1997, p. 38).

The current view is that of structural plasticity, in which development of the brain emerges from the complex and variable interactions between genes and the environment (Johnson, 1997; Oyama, 1985). Particularly important is that structural plasticity is not restricted to the early years of life. Studies with both rats and humans indicate that stimulating environments can lead to cerebral changes throughout the lifespan (e.g., Bennett, Diamond, Krech, & Rosenzweig, 1964; Black, Isaacs, Anderson, Alcantara, & Greenough, 1990; Greenough, 2002; Nelson & Bloom, 1997; Riego, 1971). For example, autopsy studies of university graduates and high school dropouts indicated 40 percent more synaptic connections in the university graduates (Jacobs, Schall, and Scheibel, 1993). However, university graduates who had not led mentally stimulating lives had fewer dendritic connections.

Research also suggests that cognitive challenges throughout life may provide some protection against the debilitating effects of Alzheimer's disease. Autopsies indicated that more educated individuals, although their brain cells were damaged, did not experience the devastating symptoms of Alzheimer's disease (Albert et al., 1995; Katzman, 1993; Snowdon et al., 1996; Stern, Gurland, & Tatemichi, 1994).

In summary, the basic building blocks of the microscopic structure of the brain are neurons and the supporting glial cells. The basic communication sequence is the transmission of an electric current down the axon of a neuron across the synapse to a dendrite of the targeted neuron. In the chemical synapse, signals are transported by neurotransmitters, and the effect on the receiving neuron may be inhibitory or excitatory. After birth, in the absence of trauma, disease, or disuse, the brain continues to develop throughout the lifespan. In the early years of life, some areas of the brain undergo a dramatic increase in the number of dendrites and synapses. These bursts are followed by a period of synaptic loss and reduction to adult levels. Although early theories maintained that the brain is "hard wired" at birth, research indicates that the complex and variable interactions between genes and environment are responsible for brain development. Furthermore, structural plasticity throughout life is indicated by the differences in brain anatomy between those who engage in mentally stimulating activities and those who do not.

The Macroscopic Organization

At the macroscopic level of the organization of the brain, neurons are grouped into cohesive structures, either nuclei or cortical regions, and each consists of millions of neurons (Goldberg, 2001, p. 29). Further, the nuclei and cortical regions interconnect to form systems and systems of systems as they execute the functions of the brain (Damasio, 1994, p. 28). Two useful ways to categorize the structures in the brain are subcortical and cortical.

The Subcortical Structures

The category "subcortical" reflects the location of particular structures in the brain of particular structures, which is below the cortex. Some researchers, who describe the development of the brain in terms of evolution, state that the subcortical structures developed millions of years before the cortex and managed the complex behaviors of several organisms (e.g., Changeux, 1985; Goldberg, 2001; Johnson, 1997). Four of the subcortical structures are the thalamus, hypothalamus, amygdala, and cerebellum. Each is divided into two twin halves, left and right. Thus they are part of the left and right hemispheres of the brain. With the exception of the cerebellum, which is attached to the back of the brain stem, the subcortical structures are buried deep in the brain.

Briefly, the thalamus is a collection of many nuclei that serves as a routing station to send information to other parts of the brain and also integrates some types of sensory information. In contrast, the hypothalamus monitors the organism's internal states (e.g., food intake, body temperature). The amygdala, a small almond-shaped structure, regulates the organism's interactions with the external world that are critical to survival. Specifically, it provides rapid, precognitive, affective assessment of a situation in the context of survival value (Goldberg, 2001, p. 13).

Finally, the cerebellum is responsible for muscle coordination, fine motor movements, and equilibrium. However, research also indicates it contributes to complex planning (e.g., Grafman et al., 1992).

(?. motor)

The Cortex

Like the subcortical structures, the areas in the cortex also have two halves, referred to as the right and left hemispheres. From an evolutionary perspective, the cortex emerged late in the development of species (Changeaux, 1985; Goldberg, 2001; Johnson, 1997). Initially, this development included the hippocampus (the "seahorse") that fulfills a critical role in memory, and the cingulate cortex, which seems to be implicated in emotions (Goldberg, 2001, p. 31).

Then the neocortex, which resembles a blanket with many folds and creases, appeared. In mammals, it is a thin sheet, approximately 3 to 4 millimeters, and it covers the subcortical structures in the brain. Between the subcortical structures and the neocortex is the corpus callosum. It is a large "C" shaped bundle of fibers that links the left and right hemispheres of the cortex.

The neocortex is more highly developed in primates, particularly humans. For example, the cortex of a cat is approximately 100 square centimeters, whereas the human neocortex is approximately 2400 square centimeters (Johnson, 1997, p. 28). This large area accounts for its creased appearance, because it is too large to fit within the available space in the skull. If the human brain were in the form of a cube, the surface of the neocortex would be 700 square centimeters (Changeux, 1985, p. 45). Thus, to fit into the skull, the surface is creased and two-thirds of the neocortex is hidden deep in the fissures (p. 45).

The neocortex consists of four major lobes; each is involved in processing a different type of information. An area of the occipital lobes (which are at the back of the head) receives input from the eyes, whereas the auditory cortex (a portion of the temporal cortex which is just above the ears) receives auditory information (see Figure 5.1). The remainder of the occipital and temporal cortices are engaged in processing information and serving as a communication link between the prefrontal cortex and the physical receptors for visual and auditory data. The parietal lobe (above the occipital and temporal lobes and at the rear) processes tactile sensations. (The wide strip at the front of the parietal cortex, which goes from ear to ear, is the somatosensory cortex. It receives information about sensations.)

The frontal cortex (behind the forehead) includes the primary motor cortex (the wide strip at the back), which controls voluntary movements, and also the prefrontal lobes. The importance of the prefrontal lobes is that they are required for goal setting, planning, evaluating alternatives, and emotional expression and control.

In summary, four of the subcortical structures of the brain are the thalamus, hypothalamus, amygdala, and the cerebellum. They are involved in monitoring and maintaining important functions of the organism essential to survival. In contrast, the cortical structures, for the most part, are engaged in processing and integrating different types of information, or in solving problems.

COGNITIVE AND EDUCATIONAL ISSUES

Among the cognitive and educational issues related to the brain are approaches to linking brain structures and functions, misinterpretations of some brain research, and the role of cognitive neuroscience.

Linking Brain Structures and Functions

Through the years, researchers have proposed different relationships between the structures of the brain and the functions it executes. An early concept was that of brain centers, each of which was responsible for a particular function. This view was followed by the perspective of areas of specialization in the brain. The most recent perspective is that of brain systems.

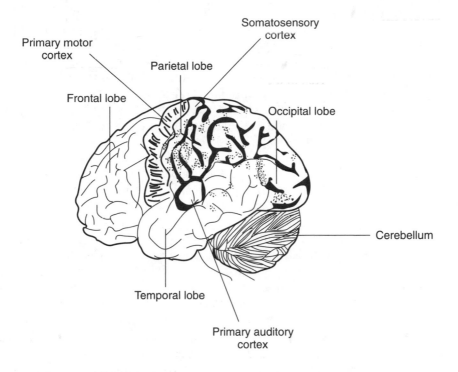

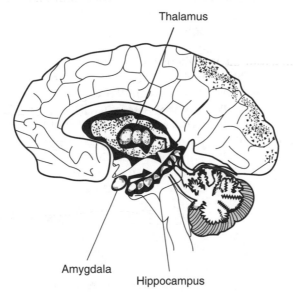

FIGURE 5.1
Key structures of the brain

Brain Centers

(Oldest)

In the early 1700s, Franz Joseph Gall introduced the perspective that the brain consisted of many organs, each of which had a particular psychological function. Named phrenology by a younger colleague, this view also stated that brain organs could be identified by particular bumps in the skull.

Although wrong on several points, Gall's perspective was unusual for that time in that he raised the issue of specialization within the human brain (Damasio, 1994). This belief also led to the idea of "brain centers," each responsible for separate functions such as speech and hearing.

Two subsequent discoveries reinforced belief in the concept of brain centers. First, in the late 19th century, Pierre Paul Broca, a French neuroanatomist, found that autopsies of his patients who had difficulty speaking, but who understood written and spoken language, indicated brain damage in the lower left frontal lobe. Problems range from the capability to produce only a single syllable (Changeux, 1985, p. 19) to reliance on nouns and the infinitive form of verbs (p. 120).

A few years later, Karl Wernicke, a German neurologist, found that damage to a particular area of the left temporal lobe resulted in the inability to understand spoken or written communication. Also, patients spoke in nonsense syllables and were unable to construct meaningful sentences (Changeux, 1985, p. 121). These brain areas were named, respectively, Broca's area and Wernicke's area.

Problems with the concept of these areas as brain centers are (1) other areas of the brain also are involved in speech production and comprehension and (2) the brain injury also may influence other areas (Goldberg, 2001, p. 53). In the absence of corroborating data from other sources, inferences about the functioning of a normal brain based on data from injured brains is somewhat spurious (p. 53).

Areas of Specialization (Ⓛ vs. Ⓡ brain)

(older)

Since the identification of Broca's area and Wernicke's area in the left hemisphere, other research has indicated that language is more intimately concerned with the left hemisphere than the right. In the early literature, the right hemisphere often was referred to as "the silent hemisphere" or "the minor hemisphere" (Goldberg, 2001, p. 43).

Subsequent studies began to pursue the role of each of the hemispheres in the functioning of the brain. However, media reports of some isolated studies oversimplified and overgeneralized the results (Coren, 1993). For example, a talk by a psychologist reported that university students recognized melodies heard only through the left ear, not those heard only through the right ear. Inaccurate media interpretations said that the right side of the brain controls musical ability, musicians are right-brained, and the study explained the large number of left-handed musicians.

Other inferences about differences in hemispheric activity also are unsupported by research. Included are that individuals who are analytic are left-brained and creativity is linked to the right brain. These beliefs about hemispheric dominance were identified as "neuromythologies" in the forums on cognitive neuroscience sponsored by the Organisation for Economic Co-Operation and Development (2002, pp. 69–77).

What about the fMRI, the PET evidence?

Moreover, the close relationship between language and the left hemisphere requires further exploration (Goldberg, 2001, p. 41). First, describing the functioning of one hemisphere as executed through language and the functioning of the other hemisphere as related to spatial processing is counterintuitive. Other organs of the body with two halves, such as the kidneys and the lungs, do not divide the organ's functions.

Second, biochemical and structural differences between the hemispheres have been cited as evidence for the assignment of different functions to different hemispheres. However, these same hemispheric differences also are found in orangutans, gorillas, and chimpanzees, although they do not possess language (Goldberg, 2001, p. 42).

A potential explanation of the stronger association between the left hemisphere and language offered by Goldberg (2001) is that it is a special case of another phenomenon. Specifically, hemispheric differences may be related to cognitive novelty and cognitive routines (p. 43). That is, the relationship between the hemispheres may be dynamic, in which novel tasks are addressed by the right hemisphere and control shifts to the left hemisphere as tasks become routinized (p. 46). Three of the studies that are consistent with this view indicated that (1) musically naive individuals process music primarily with the right hemisphere whereas trained musicians process music primarily with the left hemisphere (Berer & Chiarello, 1974); (2) PET imaging revealed that, for a variety of tasks, changes in blood flow in the brain indicated right hemisphere activation when the task was novel, with decreased activation on the second presentation (Martin, Wiggs, & Weisberg, 1997); and (3) obscure faces are processed primarily by the right hemisphere, and familiar faces with the left (Marzi & Berlucci, 1977). In other words, the novelty-routinization concept may describe hemispheric involvement in cognitive tasks (Goldberg, 2001).

The Concept of Brain Systems

(current)

The current view is that interconnected units of the brain each contribute to "systems" that are themselves responsible for relatively separable functions (Damasio, 1994, p. 15). In other words, no single locales in the brain are responsible for vision, language, social behavior, or other complex capabilities. The interconnectedness is indicated by the six layers of neurons in the neocortex, some of which communicate with different locations in the brain. The neurons in layers one through three form horizontal connections that link different cortical areas. Layers four through six are responsible for communication with subcortical regions. Layer four is the termination point of axons from subcortical areas, and layers five and six send their axons to subcortical areas.

An example of the systems functioning of the brain is the processing of sensory data. Studies of brain tissue using electron microscopes indicate that the axons of the sense organs (eyes, ears, etc.) terminate in subcortical areas of the brain, primarily the nuclei of the thalamus. Then neurons in the thalamus relay the data to layer four of the appropriate cortical structure (e.g., occipital, parietal, temporal) for further interpretation. Neurons in layers five and six of the particular cortical structure send information back to the appropriate subcortical structure. In addition to sensory information, information on motor activity also is received in the cortex from a particular nucleus in the thalamus, and the cortex also sends information to that subcortical area (Changeaux, 1985, p. 54).

The neuroscience analysis of Pavlovian fear conditioning also indicates different pathways for different types of stimuli. When the conditioned stimulus is auditory, the pathways of the input come from both the auditory thalamus and the auditory cortex to the lateral nucleus of the lateral amygdala (LA) and then to the central amygdala, which controls the expression of fear responses (LeDoux, 2000, p. 163). However, contextual fear conditioning, in which fear responses are executed in the chamber in which the tone and shock were paired, follows a different pathway that involves the hippocampus and the amygdala (p. 163). In other words, an integrated cerebral function cannot be assigned to a single center or a single neurotransmitter. Instead, it "belongs to a system of 'transit stations,' where different states of electrical and chemical activity are integrated" (Changeux, 1985, p. 204).

In summary, Gall introduced the perspective that the brain consists of many organs, each of which is responsible for a particular function. The concept of brain centers was strengthened with the discovery of Broca's area, which plays a critical role in speech production, and Wernicke's area, which is important in the comprehension of spoken and written symbols. However, other brain areas also are involved in these tasks. Included are the structures that process the input to which the individual responds, and the prefrontal cortex, which participates in executive planning and monitoring. The current view is that of brain systems, in which various cortical and subcortical areas participate in the execution of integrated brain functions.

Misapplications of Some Brain Research

Calls for linking educational policy to brain research in the 1990s primarily referred to some animal studies conducted in the 1970s and 1980s (Bruer, 1998a, 1998b). Referring to the neuroscientific research, the rationale of policymakers for providing enriched environments to children prior to the age of three was (1) this age is the critical period in brain development, (2) the most crucial learning opportunities occur before the age of five, and (3) enriched environments can influence brain development in uniquely beneficial ways (see Begley, 1996; Newman, 1997; Shore, 1997). Some recommendations for enriched environments for infants and young children included listening to Mozart and looking at colored mobiles.

Providing such experiences to infants and toddlers may be important for a variety of reasons, such as socialization. However, the impetus to focus educational efforts on the toddler and preschool years is not supported by the neurobiological data (Bruer, 1997, 1998a, 1998b, 1999; Schoenfeld, 1999). Three types of animal studies, although unrelated, were erroneously applied to early childhood development.

One type reflects the so-called "sensitive period" or "critical period" concept (Bateson, 1979), which is the brief opening of a window in which experience can influence development in major ways. Most of the research data, however, is from studies in which kittens were reared in darkened environments devoid of visual movement (Cynader & Chernenko, 1976), or one eye was sutured shut for the first three months of life (see Bruer, 1997 for a discussion). Visually deprived cats had fewer synapses per visual cortex than non-deprived cats (Cragg, 1975). Subsequent research, however, has indicated a period following sensory deprivation in which training and therapy led to near-normal functioning (Daw, 1995).

(2) Second is the research that documents the postnatal burst of synaptic growth followed by a period of synaptic loss and pruning. The popular belief (referred to as a "neuromyth") (Organisation for Economic Co-operation and Development, 2002) is that "enriched" learning experiences at an appropriate time can prevent synaptic loss, thereby promoting greater intelligence or greater learning potential (p. 73). However, as stated earlier, the rapid growth of synapses followed by loss seems to be a universal and natural development.

A related perspective is that of "phrenoblysis" or growth spurts of the *entire* brain during particular developmental periods (see Greenough, Black, & Wallace, 1987 for a discussion of this view). Although a proponent of this perspective recommended educational changes to correspond to "whole brain spurts," research has discredited the analysis (Marsh, 1985).

(3) The third line of research compared rats raised either (1) in environmentally complex environments, (2) in pairs with food and water, or (3) in isolation with food and water (Greenough, Hwang, & Gorman, 1985; Greenough & Volkmar, 1973; Turner & Greenough, 1985). The complex environments were large cages with various objects for exploration and play, and housed about a dozen animals. Findings indicated a greater number of visual synaptic connections in the rats raised in the complex environment (Greenough et al., 1987, p. 197). However, the research does not support the introduction of early educational interventions for children. Instead it concurs with the studies of Romanian orphans that indicated the ill effects of severely limited environments (see O'Connor, Bredencamp, & Rutter, 1999).

Furthermore, the term "complex" does not translate into "enriched," which typically refers to activities selected according to one's value system (Bruer, 1997). Examples include *Sesame Street* but not other programs, and Mozart rather than Hootie and the Blowfish. Neuroscience, in other words, does not provide support for such choices (Bruer, 1997, 1998a).

In summary, some policymakers maintain that birth to ages three or five is *the* critical period in brain development, and particular experiences must occur during that period or learning opportunities will be lost. However, the studies on visual deprivation of kittens, the documentation of early synaptic growth followed by loss, and the comparison of rats raised in complex and deprived environments do not support this belief.

The Role of Cognitive Neuroscience

The aim of cognitive neuroscience, a relatively new discipline, is to determine the links between neural activity in the brain and cognitive behaviors (Kosslyn & Shin, 1992). A major impetus to the emergence of the discipline was the development of neuroimaging methods that can monitor brain activity during cognitive or behavioral tasks (Sarter, Berntson, & Cacioppo, 1996). This development is analogous to the importance of the invention of the telescope which made possible detailed investigations of the heavens (Goldberg, 2001). Neuroimaging methods can provide information about particular regions of the brain involved in specific cognitive processes (Gur & Gur, 1991). For example, portions of the cerebellum may be important in problem solving (Kim, Uqurbik & Strick, 1994), and areas of the prefrontal cortex are activated in 8- to 10-year-olds during spatial memory tasks (Truwit et al., 1996).

Although neuroimaging methods are a landmark development, there is some controversy about their efficacy. Also, some studies use cognitive tasks that are fairly simple. Examples include reading words or sentences, naming objects, identifying words as concrete or abstract, and simple addition. Discussed in this section are current research methods and the potential of research on the human brain for conceptualizations of human learning.

Current Research Methods

Early methods of researching the brain included case studies of individuals with brain damage from illness or injury, and the practice of surgically altering animals' brains to observe the effects on behavior. One limitation of studies of brain-damaged individuals is that, as stated earlier, damage in one area of the brain also may disturb functioning in another area that otherwise would function normally. A limitation of animal studies is that the findings may not be applicable to the human brain.

More recent methods differ from prior research in that they produce "maps" of brain activity based on changes in electrical activity, cerebral metabolism, or blood flow in the brain. Summarized in Table 5.1, they are electroencephalography (EEG), positron emission tomography (PET), and functional magnetic resonance imaging (fMRI). The availability of MR scanners has led to an exponential increase in the number of articles that have implemented brain imaging; they "present data as visually appealing multicolored 'brain images'" (Fitzpatrick & Rothman, 2002, p. 806). The color-coded areas are those areas in which statistically significant differences in signal intensity between a task state and a reference or control state were found.

As indicated in Table 5.1, EEG can measure electrical activity associated with a stimulus presentation or action (ERP) (Johnson, 1997, p. 13). However, the electrical signal recorded at any particular electrode may not accurately reflect the area of the brain that produced it. Instead, it reflects both local activity and distant activity that may have proceeded through neural networks to that electrode.

PET scans and fMRI methods, although referred to as neuroimaging methods, do not measure neural activity directly (Gabrieli, 1998). Instead, they are based on the assumption that incremental changes in regional cerebral metabolism or blood oxygenation are related to brain activity. However, yet to be defined is the nature of the link between changes in the blood and neural activity (Fitzpatrick & Rothman, 2002, p. 807).

As indicated in Table 5.1, the data obtained in PET studies typically is derived from paired image subtraction (Raichle, 1994). The difference image

TABLE 5.1
A Comparison of Neuroimaging Methods

Method	Characteristics	Advantages	Disadvantages *(Sources of Error)*
Electroencepha-lography (EEG)	Electrodes on the scalp record electrical activity; records brain wave activity; can measure electrical activity time-locked to a stimulus presentation (ERP)	Non-invasive	1. Some uncertainty about the exact location of brain activity 2. Individual differences in skull thickness and cell densities associated with processing variables may confound interpretations of the data (Byrnes, 2001, p. 21)
Positron emission tomography (PET)	A radioactive isotope, such as glucose or oxygen, is injected into the bloodstream; amount in the brain is measured in a control and a task state and images are subtracted from each other. Data are converted to a standard brain space; data are averaged across subjects	*(?)*	1. Indirect measure of brain activity *(brain metabolism)* 2. High cost of equipment 3. Requires radioactive isotope 4. Differences in individual brains raise questions about averaging and data conversion to a standard space 5. Diffusely organized circuits may yield weak signals that cannot be discerned *(Blood flow)*
Functional magnetic resonance imaging (fMRI)	Subject is placed in a magnetic tube; a magnetic field is passed over the brain. The most popular signal, blood oxygen level dependent (BOLD) imaging, measures changes in intensity of the nuclear MR signal related changes in metabolism	1. Non-invasive 2. Does not involve radiation 3. Equipment is less costly and more widely available than MR scanners 4. Produces a sharper image than PET scanners	1. Indirect measure of neural activity *(Blood flow)* 2. Cognitive tasks are completed while subject is in a noisy tube 3, 4, & 5. Same as PET scans

presumably represents the brain areas involved in the mental activity uniquely associated with the task (Sarter et al., 1996, p. 16).

One concern about the methodology is the conversion of the coordinates that indicate particular brain activation areas in the difference images to the coordinates of a standard brain space. The standard is a stereotaxic brain atlas developed by the French neuroradiologist Talairach and his colleagues (Raichle, 1997, p. 20; Talairach & Tournoux, 1988). This practice, along with averaging the data across subjects, contributes to the impression that performance is more localized than indicated by brain lesion studies (Byrnes, 2001, p. 21). Marcus Raichle's (1997) response to the concerns is that general organizing principles emerge that transcend individual differences (p. 24). For example, PET studies indicate that metabolic activity in the frontal cortex lags behind all the other areas in the cortex and continues to develop at least until the early teens (Nelson, 2002, p. 163).

Further, characteristics of statistical software packages used to analyze the data can influence the information that is reported. Specifically, the software identifies statistically significant differences (i.e., between control and task states). Depending on the design of the study, for example, the same signal obtained in fMRI studies may be statistically significant in one individual but not another (Fitzpatrick & Rothman, 2002, p. 807). In addition, some statistical packages are biased to support localization of brain functions, because the packages delete the areas common to both tasks (p. 812). For example, the brain activity maps in an article about a bilingual subject speaking two languages indicated different and discrete areas of activation, which was interpreted as supporting the view that different areas of the brain were involved in each language. However, careful examination of the data indicated that the differences between speaking the two languages reflected only a small shift in the same mental processes involved in producing one language, rather than a separate area for the second language.

Efforts to determine the involvement of particular areas of the brain in cognitive tasks also are complicated by the diffuse organization of some of the neural circuits; their activation produces a weak signal that is undetected (Sarter et al., 1996, p. 16). Finally, two key questions have yet to be addressed by neuroimaging methods. One is, In the efforts to localize brain activity, what exactly is localized? (Sarter et al., 1996, p. 15). That is, cognitive functions often involve multiple processes, including sensory-perceptual analysis, learning, and memory processing. Each of these processes may involve different neural activities in different areas of the brain (p. 15). Therefore, cognitive models of mental activities may not precisely correspond to complex brain systems and neural activities that support these functions. This lack of correspondence can complicate further the efforts to understand brain–behavior relationships (p. 15).

Answering this question also is complicated by the various tasks used in different studies. That is, the labels for the tasks often are so broad that generalizations across studies cannot be made. An example is "semantic decisionmaking" (Gernsbacher & Kaschak, 2003, p. 108).

The second question yet to be addressed by the research is, How does the processing identified in different areas of the brain occur and what does it mean?

That is, the research does not address the role of the microscopic structure of the brain in the various cognitive tasks.

The Potential of Brain Research.   Fitzpatrick and Rothman (2002) note that the excitement generated by fMRI methods has contributed to many researchers overlooking what can and cannot be said in response to the question, What can the fMRI signal tell us about neural and mental processes? (p. 806). Despite this problem, some well-designed studies provide a glimpse into the potential of brain research for four areas of cognitive development and learning.

Two areas are the principles of cognitive development and learning disabilities. An example is information developed in cognitive neuroscience that appears to shed further light on Jean Piaget's description of preoperational thinking. Briefly, children at that level of thinking are unsuccessful on so-called "conservation" problems. When water is poured from a tall, thin container into a short, wide container, the child may focus only on the height of the first container and state that it holds more water. Or she may focus on the wide container, maintaining that it contains more water. The preoperational child is unable to hold the two different perceptions (the water level in the two containers) in mind at the same time, relate them to each other, and inhibit a response based on initial perception.

Research on patients with damage in the dorsolateral prefrontal cortex (DL–PFC) indicated they made the same kinds of errors on problems similar to the Piagetian tasks (cf. Price, Daffner, Stowe, & Mesulam, 1990). Further, other research suggested that one maturational change in the DL–PFC that makes possible cognitive advances in solving such problems is increasing levels of the neurotransmitter dopamine in that area (cf. Luciana, Depue, Arbisi, & Leon, 1992; Simon, Scatton, & LeMoal, 1980).

In addition, an extended research program on children treated for Phenylketonuria (PKU) found that they also have difficulties with Piagetian-type tasks that require holding two rules in mind while resisting acting on the basis of perception (Diamond, 2002). Briefly, PKU is a genetic metabolic disorder that, untreated, leads to extensive brain damage and mental retardation. However, when treated early and continuously with diet, PKU children test in the normal range on IQ measures. Nevertheless, they have the specific cognitive deficit associated with preoperational thinking. In addition, the research indicates that these children have reduced levels of dopamine in the DL–PFC (p. 478). In other words, the studies indicate the role of the DL–PFC in Piagetian-type tasks, the importance of dopamine, and the particular cognitive deficit in PKU-treated children.

A third area of cognition and learning to which cognitive neuroscience may contribute is that of principles of information processing. For example, models have identified two levels of processing, automatic and controlled or deliberate. That is, some actions have been practiced so extensively that they require no conscious control. Others, however, require deliberate processing.

Raichle (1994), using neuroimaging, assessed the neural differences in deliberate and automatic processing. He first required the subjects to generate verbs for 40 nouns presented one at a time for 1.5 seconds (deliberate processing). Then, after 15 minutes of practice (nine practice blocks), subjects repeated the task a 10th time while a second image of their brain activity was taken. Of interest is that the two images indicated that the production of verbal responses, whether automatic or non-automatic, represents two different distributed neural processes with several widely separated areas of brain activity (p. 342). Furthermore, the prefrontal cortex is a major participant in the subjects' initial selection of a verb for each noun. However, it is not involved in the practiced execution of the task. This finding is congruent with other research that indicates that patients with frontal lobe damage cannot complete tasks that involve some free choice by the subject. In other words, the frontal lobes are critical in tasks in which the subject must decide on the interpretation of the situation (Goldberg, 2001, p. 80).

Another concept informed by research is episodic memory, which involves the recall of events in one's past life. These tasks also involve (1) going back in time, (2) an awareness of subjective time in which events occurred (autonoetic awareness), and (3) a sense of self (Tulving, 2002, p. 2). Studies that support the view that episodic memory differs from semantic (declarative) memory include clinical studies of brain-damaged patients with intact semantic memory and impaired episodic memory (summarized in Kapur, 1999 and Wheeler & McMillan, 2001), and an analysis of PET data pooled from several studies that suggested different retrieval sites for semantic memory and episodic memory (Lepage, Ghaffar, Nyberg, & Tulving, 2000).

A fourth area to which cognitive neuroscience may apply is the role of life-long learning in maintaining cognitive proficiency. Recall the research findings reported earlier in the chapter about the importance of cognitive challenges throughout life in providing some protection against the effects of Alzheimer's disease. Perhaps the most dramatic example is that of the School Sisters of Notre Dame in Mankato, Minnesota (Goldberg, 2001, p. 208). In addition to longevity was the absence of Alzheimer's disease. This phenomenon was attributed to their lifelong habit of engaging in cognitively challenging activities such as puzzles, card games, debates of current policy issues, and other similar activities. One nun, Sister Mary, demonstrated excellent performance on cognitive tasks prior to her death at age 101. However, the autopsy on her brain indicated the multiple tangles in the neural fibers and the plaques of Alzheimer's disease (p. 208). One inference is that developing the lifelong habit of taxing one's mind provided a protective effect such that, despite some debilitating changes in the brain, sufficient neural connections remained to execute cognitive activity.

SUMMARY

The development of neuroimaging methods that can monitor brain activity during cognitive or behavioral tasks is a major factor in the emergence of the field referred to as cognitive neuroscience. Early methods of researching brain activity included case studies of brain-damaged patients and surgical alterations of the brains of animals.

The new methods can produce maps of brain activity based on changes in electrical activity (electroencephalography, or EEG), brain metabolism (positron emission tomography, or PET), or blood oxygenation (functional magnetic resonance imaging, or fMRI). Disadvantages include the accuracy of the electrical activity recorded (EEG), the links between changes in the blood and neural activity, the image subtraction methodology conversion of the data to a standard brain image, possible shortcomings of statistical packages that analyze the data, and the failure to detect relevant brain circuitry that may emit only a weak signal (PET and fMRI). Also, cognitive functions often involve multiple processes, and cognitive models may not correspond precisely to complex brain systems and neural activities. In other words, the issue of the precise processes that are localized is not answered. Furthermore, the methods can identify areas of the brain involved in different tasks, but not how the various neural activities occur.

Despite these shortcomings, well-designed studies can contribute to information in four areas of cognitive development and learning. They are principles of cognitive development, learning disabilities, principles of information processing, and lifelong learning.

CHAPTER QUESTIONS

1. Why are the new brain imaging technologies unlikely to obtain detailed information about the brain in the near future?
2. What does the term "growth" mean in relation to the brain?
3. What information supports the "structural plasticity" view of the brain as opposed to a genetic "hard-wired" view?
4. What is the major difference between the subcortical and cortical structures of the brain?
5. How does the research on synaptic development refute the "early critical period" concept?

REFERENCES

Albert, M. S., Jones, K., Savage, C. R., Berkman, L., Seeman, T., Blazer, D., & Rowe, J. W. (1995). Predictors of cognitive change in older persons: MacArthur studies of successful aging. *Psychology of Aging, 10*(4), 578–589.

Bateson, P. P. G. (1979). How do sensitive periods arise and what are they for? *Animal Behavior, 27*, 470–486.

Begley, S. (1996). Your child's brain. *Newsweek, 127*(8), 55–62.

Benes, F. M. (1994). Development of the cortico-limbic system. In G. Dawson & K. W. Fischer (Eds.), *Human behavior and the developing brain* (pp. 176–206). New York: Guilford Press.

Berer, T. G., & Chiarello, R. J. (1974). Cerebral dominance in musicians and nonmusicians. *Science, 185* (150), 537–539.

Bennett, E. L., Diamond, M. C., Krech, D., & Rosenzweig, M. R. (1964). Chemical and anatomical plasticity of brain. *Science, 164*, 610–619.

Black, J. E., Isaacs, K. R., Anderson, B. J., Alcantara, A. A., & Greenough, W. T. (1990). Learning causes synaptogenesis, whereas motor activity causes angiogenesis in cerebellar cortex of adult rats. *Proceedings of the National Academy of Science* (USA), *87*, 5568–5572.

Blinkov, S. M., & Gleser, I. I. (1968). *The human brain in figures and tables: A quantitative handbook*. New York: Plenum Press.

Bruer, J. T. (1997). Education and the brain: A bridge too far. *Educational Researcher, 26*(8), 4–16.

Bruer, J. T. (1998a). Brain science, brain function. *Educational Leadership, 56*(3), 14–18.

Bruer, J. T. (1998b). The brain and child development: Time for some critical thinking. *Public Health Reports, 113*, 389–397.

Bruer, J. T. (1999). *The myth of the first three years: A new understanding of early brain development*. New York: The Free Press.

Byrnes, J. P. (2001). *Minds, brains, and learning*. New York: Guilford.

Changeux, J. P. (1985). *Neuronal man*. New York: Pantheon.

Chugani, H. T., Phelps, M. E., & Mazziotta, J. C. (2002). Positron emission tomography study of human brain functional development. In M. H. Johnson, Y. Munakata, & R. O. Gilmore (Eds.), *Brain development and cognition* (pp. 101–128). Malden, MA: Blackwell.

Coren, S. (1993). *The left-hander syndrome: The causes and consequences of left-handedness*. New York: Vintage Books.

Cragg, B. G. (1975). The development of synapses in kitten visual cortex during visual deprivation. *Experimental Neurology, 46*, 445–451.

Cynader, M. & Chernenko, G. (1976). Abolition of direction selectivity in the visual cortex of the cat. *Science, 193*, 504–505.

Damasio, A. R. (1994). *Descartes' error: Emotion, reason, and the human brain*. New York: Putnam.

Daw, N. (1995). *Visual development*. New York: Plenum Press.

Diamond, A. (2002). A model system for studying the role of dopamine in prefrontal cortex during early development in humans. In M. H. Johnson, Y. Munakata, & R. O. Gilmore (Eds.), *Brain development and cognition: A reader* (pp. 441–493). Malden, MA: Blackwell.

Fischbach, G. D. (1992, September). Mind and brain. *Scientific American, 267*, 24–32.

Fitzpatrick, S. M., & Rothman, D. L. (2002). Meeting report: Choosing the right MR tools for the job. *Journal of Cognitive Neuroscience, 14*(5), 806–815.

Gabrieli, J. D. (1998). Cognitive neuroscience of memory. In J. T. Spence, J. M. Darley, & D. J. Foss (Eds.), *Annual Review of Psychology, 49* (pp. 87–115).

Gernsbacher, M. A., & Kashak, M. P. (2003). Neuroimaging studies of language production and comprehension. *Annual Review of Psychology, 54*, 91–114.

Goldberg, E. (2001). *The executive brain: Frontal lobes and the civilized mind*. New York: Oxford University Press.

Grafman, G. J., Litvan, I., Massaquoi, S., Stewart, M., Sirigu, A., Hallett, M. (1992). Cognitive planning deficit in patients with cerebrellar atrophy. *Neurology 42*(8), 1493–1496.

Greenough, W. T. (2002). Brain adaptation to experience: An update. In M. H. Johnson, Y. Munakata, & R. O. Gilmore (Eds.), *Brain development and cognition: A reader* (2nd ed.) (pp. 213–216). Malden, MA: Blackwell.

Greenough, W. T., & Volkmar, F. R. (1973). Pattern of dendritic branching in occipital cortex of rats reared in complex environments. *Experimental Neurology, 40*, 491–504.

Greenough, W. T., Black, J. E., & Wallace, C. S. (1987). Experience and brain development. *Child Development, 58*, 539–559.

Greenough, W. T., Hwang, H. M., & Gorman, C. (1985). Evidence for active synapse formation, or altered postsynaptic metabolism, in visual cortex of rats reared in complex environments. *Proceedings of the National Academy of Sciences* (USA), *82*, 4549–4552.

Gur, R. C., & Gur, E. R. (1991). The impact on neuroimaging on human neuropsychology. In R. G. Lister & H. J. Weingartener (Eds.), *Perspectives on cognitive neuroscience* (pp. 417–436). Oxford: Oxford University Press.

Hockenbury, D. H., & Hockenbury, S. E. (1997). *Psychology*. New York: Worth Publishers.

Holloway, R. L. (1966). Dendritic branching: Some preliminary results of training and complexity in rat visual cortex. *Brain Research, 2*, 393–396.

Huttenlocher, P. R. (1990). Morphometric study of human cerebral cortex development. *Neuro-psychologia, 28*, 517–527.

Huttenlocher, P. R. (1994a). Synaptogenesis in human cerebral cortex. In G. Dawson & K. W. Fischer (Eds.), *Human behavior and the developing brain* (pp. 137–152). New York: Guilford.

Huttenlocher, P. R. (1994b). Synaptogenesis, synapse elimination, and neural plasticity in human cerebral cortex. In C. A. Nelson (Ed.), *Threats to optimal development: The Minnesota Symposia on Child Psychology, Vol. 27* (pp. 35–54). Hillsdale, NJ: Erlbaum.

Huttenlocher, P. R., de Courten, C., Garey, L. G., & Van der Loos, H. (1982). Synaptogenesis in human visual cortex—evidence for synapse elimination during normal development. *Neuroscience Letter, 33*, 247–252.

Jacobs, B., Schall, M., & Scheibel, A. R. (1993). A quantitative dendritic analysis of Wernicke's area in humans. II. Gender, hemispheric, and environmental factors. *Journal of Comparative Neurology, 327*, 97–106.

Johnson, M. H. (1997). *Developmental cognitive neuroscience*. Cambridge, MA: Blackwell.

Kapur, N. (1999). Syndromes of retrograde amnesia: A conceptual and empirical analysis. *Psychological Bulletin, 125*, 800–825.

Katzman, R. (1993). Education and the prevalence of dementia and Alzheimer's disease. *Neurology, 43*, 13–18.

Kim, S. G., Ugurbik, K., & Strick, P. L. (1994). Activation of a cerebellar output nucleus during cognitive processing. *Science, 265*, 949–951.

Kosslyn, S. M., & Shin, L. M. (1992). The status of cognitive neuroscience. *Current Opinion in Neurobiology, 2*, 146–149.

Krech, D., Rosenzweig, M. R., & Bennett, E. L. (1960). Effects of environmental complexity and training on brain chemistry. *Journal of Comparative Physiological Psychology, 53*, 509–519.

Lepage, M., Ghaffar, O., Nyberg, L. & Tulving, E. (2000). Prefrontal cortex and episodic memory retrieval mode. *Proceedings of the National Academy of Sciences* (USA), *97*, 506–511.

LeDoux, J. E. (2000). Emotion circuits in the brain. *Annual Review of Neuroscience, 23*, 155–184.

Luciana, M., Depue, R. A., Arbisi, P., & Leon, A. (1992). Facilitation of working memory in humans by a D2 dopamine receptor agonist. *Journal of Cognitive Neuroscience, 4*, 58–68.

Marsh, R. W. (1985). Phrenoblysis: Real or chimera? *Child Development, 56*, 1059–1061.

Martin, A., Wiggs, C. L., & Weisberg, J. (1997). Modulation of human medial temporal lobe activity by form, meaning, and experience. *Hippocampus, 7*(6), 587–593.

Marzi, C. A., & Berlucci, G. (1977). Right visual field superiority for accuracy of recognition of famous faces in normals. *Neuropsychologia, 15*(6), 751–756.

Nelson, C. A. (2002). The ontogeny of human memory: A cognitive neuroscience perspective. In M. H. Johnson, Y. Manakata, & R. O. Gilmore (Eds.), *Brain development and cognition: A reader* (pp. 151–178). Malden, MA: Blackwell.

Newman, F. (1997). Brain research has implications for education: Is first grade too late? *State Educational Leader, 15*, 1–2.

Nowakowski, R. S., & Hayes, N. L. (2002). General principals of CNS development. In M. H. Johnson, Y. Munakata, & R. O. Gilmore (Eds.), *Brain development and cognition* (pp. 57–82). Malden, MA: Blackwell.

O'Connor, T. G., Bredenkamp, D., & Rutter, M. (1999). Attachment disturbances and disorders in children exposed to early severe deprivation. *Infant Mental Health Journal, 20*(1), 10–20.

Organisation for Economic Co-operation and Development (2002). *Understanding the brain*. Paris: Author.

Oyama, S. (1985). *The ontogeny of information*. Cambridge: Cambridge University Press.

Price, B. H., Daffner, K. R., Stowe, R. M., & Mesulam, M. M. (1990). The compartmental learning disabilities of early frontal lobe damage. *Brain, 113*, 1383–1393.

Raichle, M. E. (1994). Images of the mind: Studies with modern imaging techniques. *Annual Review of Psychology, 45*, 333–356.

Raichle, M. E. (1997). Brain imaging. In M. S. Gazzaniga (Ed.), *Conversations in the cognitive neurosciences* (pp. 15–33). Cambridge, MA: Massachusetts Institute of Technology.

Rafshoon, E. (2003, April 27). What price beauty? *Boston Globe Magazine*, 15–17, 19–23.

Riego, W. H. (1971). Environmental influences on brain and behavior of old rats. *Developmental Psychobiology, 4*, 157–167.

Sarter, M., Berntson, G. G., & Cacioppo, J. T. (1996). Brain imaging and cognitive neuroscience. *American Psychologist, 51*(1), 13–21.

Schoenfeld, A. H. (1999). Looking toward the 21st century: Challenges of educational theory and practice. *Educational Researcher, 28*(7), 4–14.

Shore, R. (1997). *Rethinking the brain: New insights into early development*. New York: Families and Work Institute.

Simon, H., Scatton, B., & LeMoal, M. (1980). Dopaminergic A10 neurons are involved in cognitive functions. *Nature, 286*, 150–151.

Snowdon, D. A., Kemper, S. J., Mortimer, J. A., Greiner, L. H., Weksten, D. R., & Markesbery, W. R. (1996). Linguistic ability in early life and cognitive function and Alzheimer's disease in late life: findings from the Nun Study [see comments]. *Journal of the American Medical Association, 275*(7), 528–532.

Stern, X., Gurland, B., & Tatemichi, T. K. (1994, April 6). Influence of education and occupation on the incidence of Alzheimer's disease. *Journal of the American Medical Association, 271*(13), 1004–1007.

Talairach, J., & Tournoux, P. (1988). *Co-planar stereotaxic atlas of the human brain*. New York: Thieme Medical.

Thompson, R. A., & Nelson, C. A. (2001). Developmental science and the media: Early brain development. *American Psychologist, 56*(1), 5–15.

Truwit, C. L., Le, T. H., Lim, J. C., Hu, X., Carver, L., Thomas, K. M., Monk, C., & Nelson, C. A. (1996, June). *Functional MR imaging of working memory task activation in children: Preliminary findings*. Paper presented to the American Society of Neuroradiology, Seattle, WA.

Tulving, E. (2002). Episodic memory: From mind to brain. *Annual Review of Psychology, 53*, 1–25.

Turner, A. M., & Greenough, W. T. (1985). Differential rearing effects on rat visual cortex synapses, I. Synaptic and neural density and synapses per neuron. *Brain Research, 329*, 195–203.

Wheeler, M. A., & McMillan, C. T. (2001). Focal retrograde amnesia and the episodic-semantic distinction. *Cognitive and Affective Behavioral Neuroscience, 1*, 22–37.

PART III
Learning-Process Theories

Three theories address the particular events and conditions necessary for the learning of information and/or skills. Continuing the behaviorist tradition, B. F. Skinner's operant conditioning describes the environmental events and conditions responsible for complex patterns of voluntary behavior. Examples are pigeons learning to bowl and children learning to read. Skinner's analyses include the various types of consequences that influence behavioral change, the emotional by-products of aversive consequences, and a mechanism for individualizing classroom instruction.

Robert Gagné, in contrast, began with an analysis of the various tasks found in the range of human learning. He identified five major types of capabilities, each reflected in a particular performance. His theory details the cognitive processes and learner states essential for each type of task, as well as the essential steps for instruction.

The cognitive perspective began with a model for the ways that the learner receives, processes, and later recalls information. At present, cognitive theory and research also address problem-solving and learner strategies for the management of learning.

CHAPTER 6
B. F. Skinner's Operant Conditioning

A baby shakes a rattle, a child runs with a pinwheel, a scientist operates a cyclotron—and all are reinforced by the results. (Skinner, 1968b, p. 153)

The principles of B. F. Skinner initiated a new direction in the 1930s for a behaviorism that was dominated by Pavlov's model. Skinner disagreed with the S–R position that "cues" or "drive stimuli" trigger all behavior like some "inexorable force" (Skinner, 1966b). Instead, his research indicated that the important event in changing behavior, whether that of a baby or a scientist, is the outcome produced by the action (Skinner, 1953). The baby's accidental movement of a rattle produces a new sound, and soon the baby is shaking the toy for several minutes at a time. Similarly, a scientist discovers an efficient way to stain slides for cell analysis. He then begins to spend evenings and weekends in the laboratory perfecting the technique. The increased frequency of the baby's and scientist's actions is influenced by the outcome produced by each behavior.

Skinner's analysis led to more than 50 years of research on what seems, at first glance, to be a very simple principle. Consider, however, the situation in which a well-meaning teacher delays helping a student so that he can show what he can do (Skinner, 1968b). When the student shows discouragement, the teacher quickly comes to his aid. For the anxious or insecure student, giving up on a difficult problem has "produced" adult attention and assistance. The reaction of the careless teacher has strengthened an undesirable behavior, which is likely to be repeated.

Skinner's work began with an analysis of the differences between reflexes and other behaviors (Skinner, 1935), and his principles of operant conditioning soon followed (Skinner, 1938, 1953). He later turned his attention to the school setting with the development of the teaching machine (Skinner, 1961) and a technology of classroom teaching (Skinner, 1968a, 1968b, 1973). His later comments on education include recommendations for microcomputer instruction (Skinner, in Green, 1984; Skinner, 1989b).

In the 1980s, Skinner continued to apply his concepts to various aspects of the human condition. His work encompassed an analysis of the similarities and differences in natural selection and operant conditioning (Skinner, 1981, 1987), an analysis of aging (Skinner & Vaughan, 1983), a description of cultures and their development (Skinner, 1981, 1987, 1989b), and a further analysis of rule-governed behavior (Skinner, 1987). His work has been described as including (1) a philosophy of science, (2) a theory of behavior, and (3) a system for applying the principles in the natural setting (Kratochwill & Bijou, 1987, p. 138).

PRINCIPLES OF LEARNING

Skinner agreed with the position taken earlier by John Watson (1913). That is, psychology can become a science only through the study of behavior.

Basic Assumptions

Like Clark Hull, B. F. Skinner established rigorous procedures for the study of behavior. Unlike Hull, however, he did not believe in the use of theory as a research framework. Instead, the cornerstone of operant conditioning is Skinner's beliefs about the nature of a behavioral science and the characteristics of learned behavior.

The Nature of a Behavioral Science

The goal of any science, according to Skinner (1953), is to discover the lawful relationships among natural events in the environment. Therefore, a science of behavior must discover the lawful or "functional" relationships among physical conditions or environmental events and behavior. The challenge is to determine which changes in independent variables (conditions or events) lead to changes in the dependent variable, behavior. For example, what are the conditions or events responsible for one student's attending to academic tasks and another's avoidance of homework? To refer to the one student as "motivated" and the other as "unmotivated" does not, in Skinner's view, answer the question.

The development of a science of behavior is difficult because behavior is both complex and varied (Skinner, 1953). In addition, it is a temporal, fluid, and changing process. The task for the scientist is to discover its order and uniformity (Skinner, 1953).

Of importance is that neither theories nor discussions of inner states should be used as a basis for behavioral research (Skinner, 1950, 1966b). Theories create an artificial world of order and lawfulness by explaining one statement in terms of another. The result is that the yet undiscovered lawful relationships are obscured. Moreover, theories may stifle the scientist's sense of curiosity, thereby ending the search for clarification (Skinner, 1950).

Problems with Internal States.   At least three problems result from describing behavior as "caused" by some mental state or set of feelings. First, such explanations simply raise another issue—that of explaining the states themselves (Skinner, 1963a). For example, if anxiety is proposed as an explanation for poor test-taking skills, then what causes the anxiety?

Second, the emphasis on states treats behavior as merely an indicator or "symptom" of an inner mental or physiological activity (Skinner, 1966b, p. 213). Behavior becomes a "second-class variable" when it is viewed as merely an indicator of a process (e.g., learning or maturation), a state (such as alertness), or a drive, emotion, or available psychic energy.

Third, attention is diverted from research that may identify both the sources of problems and the solutions. For example, the state referred to as "consumer lack of confidence" in the economy is described as a "problem" in the restoration of economic growth. However, people plan to buy less when their money does not go very far, and the decreased buying is described as lack of confidence. Thus governmental actions to "restore confidence" are, in reality, actions taken to restore consumer buying—that is, to change behavior.

A similar situation is the depression that one experiences when moving to a new city. The problem is that the old set of behaviors is now useless (Skinner, 1987, p. 155). The old stores, restaurants, theaters, and friends are no longer present, and a new set of behaviors must be acquired. When this is done, the depression is relieved.

In the classroom, a student who demonstrates poor reading skills also will perform poorly in his academic subjects. The student may be labeled as lacking in self-esteem, or as having a poor self-concept, which refers to his lack of initiative in school. However, the problem is not that of the student's internal state, but is, instead, a lack of reading skills (Belfiore & Hornyak, 1998, p. 186).

Experimental Analysis.   To study behavior, the researcher must manipulate observable events in a controlled setting. This procedure is referred to as the experimental analysis of behavior (Skinner, 1953, 1968b).

To control environmental conditions, Skinner designed an experimental space that was free of distractions. A soundproof darkened box was used that included one or more response devices, such as levers, keys, or discs. Mechanisms to provide reinforcers (e.g., food and water) were also included. Sometimes other stimuli were used, such as lights, loudspeakers, or mechanisms for the delivery of mild shock. The chamber was automated so that reinforcers were delivered immediately after an appropriate response, and automated devices recorded the frequency of responses.

In addition, the behavior of individual subjects rather than of groups was recorded. In Skinner's view, group averages do not provide a clear picture of behavior. For example, the average 68.33 provides little information about the three scores from which it was obtained: 55, 60, and 90.

The first subjects in Skinner's experiments were rats; later he used pigeons. The information collected on these subjects also reveals information about the interactions between all organisms and the environment. "The schedule of reinforcement which makes the pigeon a pathological gambler is to be found at the racetrack and the roulette table, where it has a comparable effect" (Skinner,

1969, p. 84). Thus the research on these processes in the laboratory is considered to be applicable to human behavior.

A Definition of Learning

In Skinner's view, learning is behavioral change. As the subject learns, responses increase, and when unlearning occurs, the rate of responding falls (Skinner, 1950). Learning, therefore, is formally defined as a change in the likelihood or probability of a response.

Because the likelihood of responding is difficult to measure, the rate, or frequency, of responding is measured instead. Although not precisely the same as the probability of future performance, it is an initial step in the analysis of behavioral change (Skinner, 1963b). Also, response rate may be applied to a variety of behaviors, from the behavior of pigeons in the laboratory to student responses in the classroom.

In summary, six assumptions form the foundation of operant conditioning:

1. Learning is behavioral change.
2. Behavioral change (learning) is functionally related to changes in environmental events or conditions.
3. The lawful relationships between behavior and the environment can be determined only if behavioral properties and experimental conditions are defined in physical terms and observed under carefully controlled conditions.
4. Data from the experimental study of behavior are the only acceptable sources of information about the causes of behavior.
5. The behavior of the individual organism is the appropriate data source.
6. The dynamics of an organism's interaction with the environment is the same for all species. 7

Summary

Like John Watson, Skinner believed that psychology could become a science only through the study of behavior. The goal of any science is to discover the lawful relationships among natural events in the environment. Therefore, a science of behavior must discover the lawful relationships among environmental events and behavior.

Of importance in developing a science of behavior is that both theories and discussions of inner states should be excluded. Theories create an artificial world of orderliness, and the use of inner states as explanations simply raises other issues to be explained. In addition, behavior is treated merely as a symptom of some inner state, and it becomes a second-class variable. Third, a reliance on inner states diverts attention from research that may identify both problems and solutions.

To study behavior, the researcher must manipulate both behavior and observable events in a controlled setting. Behavioral properties and experimental conditions are defined in physical terms, and the behavior of the individual organism can assist the researcher in identifying the processes of behavioral change, that is, learning.

The Components of Learning

Development of the principles of operant conditioning began with the analysis of Pavlov's classical conditioning. According to Skinner (1938), Pavlov's model is restricted to those responses that are already associated with a particular stimulus, such as the leg jerk that follows a hammer tap to the knee. Such responses are involuntary reactions referred to as reflexes. Skinner described these reflexes as **elicited responses** or respondent behavior. Because the method of conditioning these responses requires stimulus substitution, Skinner designated Pavlov's model as *Type S conditioning*.

Analysis of complex behaviors, such as painting a picture or singing a song, indicated that they are not elicited by particular stimuli (events or conditions) (Skinner, 1935). These behaviors were named **emitted responses**. In addition, emitted responses act on the environment to produce different kinds of consequences that affect the organism and thereby alter future behavior. Singing a song, for example, may "operate" on the environment to produce consequences such as praise, applause, or money. These behaviors were therefore named **operants** (Skinner, 1935).

The key to understanding operant behaviors, in Skinner's view (1953, 1963b), was Edward Thorndike's law of effect. Specifically, an animal's escape behavior resulted in food, and under similar confinement conditions, the escape response was repeated. The importance of Thorndike's research was that it included the effects of the subject's action among the causes of behavioral change. Therefore, concepts such as purpose, intention, and expectancy were not needed to explain future behavior (Skinner, 1963b, p. 503).

Although Thorndike used some terms that lead to misunderstandings, the law of effect identified the three essential components in behavioral change (Skinner, 1953). They are (1) the occasion on which the response occurs, (2) the subject's response, and (3) the reinforcing consequences. These three components of learning are described as the discriminative stimulus (S^D), the response (R), and the reinforcing stimulus ($S^{reinf.}$). The sequence of learning events is (S^D)–(R)–($S^{reinf.}$).

The Discriminative Stimulus

Any stimulus that is consistently present when a response is reinforced is a **discriminative stimulus**. For example, after repeated reinforcement for tripping the latch of a cage, a confined animal responds only to the fastener and ignores other parts of the cage. The latch is referred to as the discriminative stimulus. Through association with the reinforced response, the discriminative stimulus serves as a cue for behavior.

The process by which the stimulus becomes a behavioral cue was demonstrated in an experiment in which a pigeon's behavior of pecking a red key was reinforced several times (Skinner, 1953). When the color was changed to green in mid-stroke, the pigeon's head stopped and its beak did not strike the key. The process is typically referred to as discrimination; however, the organism is simply responding more often to settings with certain properties (Skinner, 1989a, p. 128).

Behavioral change can, of course, be explained without reference to the preceding stimulus (Skinner, 1953). An example is neck stretching in the pigeon, which typically occurs without an S^D. Like other behaviors, neck stretching will increase in rate as a result of continued reinforcement. However, if neck stretching is reinforced only when a signal light is on, then eventually the behavior will occur only in the presence of the light (Skinner, 1953, p. 107).

The Role of Discriminative Stimuli.   The probability that a response will be repeated is maximized by the presence of a discriminative stimulus. Examples that exercise control over behavior in everyday life include red and green traffic lights, stop signs, and other signals (Skinner, 1953). Also included are countless verbal commands, such as "Take out your pencils" and "Please pass the salt." However, signals, verbal commands, and other discriminative stimuli do not automatically trigger (elicit) operant behaviors. Rather, they acquire behavioral control as a result of prior reinforcements for particular responses in their presence.

Discriminative stimuli for human behavior are not restricted to environmental events. In many situations, individuals construct discriminative stimuli to which they can respond. People construct such stimuli when they make resolutions, announce expectations or intentions, and develop plans (Skinner, 1963b, p. 513). However, to be most effective in controlling behavior, these self-generated stimuli must be visible in some durable form, such as drafting a written plan or posting the resolution on a bulletin board (Skinner, 1963b).

Two or more different stimuli that share a common feature may also acquire control over a particular response. A pigeon's pecking response to both a lighted bar and a lighted disc and a child's verbal identification of $\wp$, *P,* and p are examples. This process is referred to by Skinner as **induction** (commonly known as **stimulus generalization**).

Summary

The key to understanding complex behaviors is to understand the events and processes responsible for emitted responses. These responses, unlike Pavlov's elicited responses, are not automatically associated with a particular stimulus. The key, in Skinner's view, was Thorndike's law of effect. That is, emitted responses act on the environment to produce different kinds of consequences that affect the organism and thereby alter future behavior. The three essential components of learning that Skinner derived from Thorndike's paradigm are the discriminative stimulus (S^D), the response (R), and the reinforcing stimulus ($S^{reinf.}$).

The discriminative stimulus is any stimulus that is consistently present when a response is reinforced. Through repeated association with the reinforced response, the discriminative stimulus becomes a behavioral cue for the response. Examples of discriminative stimuli that exercise control over behavior include "Take out your pencils" and "Please pass the salt." Discriminative stimuli often are environmental events and the verbal statements of others. However, individuals also construct discriminative stimuli for themselves, such as lists and written plans.

Essential Principles of Reinforcement

The essential principles of reinforcement include the dynamics of reinforcement and factors that influence the role of behavioral consequences.

The Dynamics of Reinforcement.

Thorndike's experiments illustrated that certain consequences influence behavioral change. However, Thorndike emphasized the terms *rewarding, satisfying,* and *trial-and-error learning,* and these terms do not describe behavioral properties. Furthermore, reward implies remuneration for services performed (Skinner, 1989b, p. 92) or compensation that offsets a loss or sacrifice of some kind (Skinner, 1963b, p. 505).

Skinner substituted the terms **reinforcing consequence** and **reinforcement** for reward. **Reinforcement** is defined as any behavioral consequence that strengthens behavior (i.e., increases the frequency of responding). The particular response that occurs immediately prior to the reinforcement has passed into history. However, the organism is changed by the particular consequence and later responds as a changed organism (Skinner, 1989b, p. 64).

The two key processes in operant conditioning are *variation* (of behavior) and *selection by consequence.* In other words, different behaviors are executed, only some of which are strengthened by the outcomes. For example, the rat's behaviors of sniffing the corners of the cage and looking at the ceiling do not produce a food pellet. Because important outcomes do not follow these behaviors, they decrease in frequency.

Also important is that not every behavioral consequence is a reinforcer. If the rat has been fed recently, producing a food pellet will not lead to an increase in lever pressing. To determine whether a particular event is reinforcing, a direct test is needed (Skinner, 1953, p. 73). The frequency of a selected response is first observed, and then a particular event is made contingent on that response. The rate of responding with the added consequence is observed. If the response frequency increases, the selected event is reinforcing in the given condition.

To be effective in altering behavior in a particular way, reinforcement also must be immediately contingent on the execution of an appropriate response. In the laboratory, lever pressing produces a food pellet instantaneously. Similarly, when a baby moves an arm so as to shake the rattle vigorously, he or she is reinforced at once by the sound.

Sometimes behaviors are reinforced accidentally. Such contingencies lead to the development of superstitious behavior (Skinner, 1953, p. 85). That is, random behavior that is reinforced accidentally will increase in frequency and very likely receive accidental reinforcement again.

Superstitious behavior in the laboratory was demonstrated by providing food to a pigeon every 15 seconds. Behaviors that were strengthened were those actions that were occurring when the food was delivered. Examples include strutting, wing flapping, bowing and scraping, and others (Skinner, 1948).

Random behaviors also are reinforced in the natural setting. For example, a man waiting for a bus may look in the direction that the bus is to appear, then pace up and down and look at his watch several times. None of these actions makes the bus arrive, yet all are reinforced by the appearance of the vehicle (Skinner, 1989a). When the man waits for a bus again (or a train), he is likely to pace up and down and to check his watch repeatedly.

Reinforcement increases the rate of responding; however, elimination of the reinforcing consequence decreases the rate. This decreased rate in the absence of a reinforcing outcome is known as **extinction** (Skinner, 1938, 1963b). If reinforcement is withdrawn completely, behavior will gradually cease. Thus, an important function of reinforcement in everyday life is to prevent the extinction of behavior.

Factors That Influence the Role of Behavioral Consequences.   At least three factors influence the extent to which particular events may function as reinforcers. They are (1) the individual's past reinforcement history, (2) the skills repertoire of the individual, and (3) the particular characteristics inherited by the individual.

As already indicated, food is not likely to strengthen the behavior of a rat that has eaten recently. However, food *is* a powerful reinforcer if the rat has been deprived of food. Similarly, consider the child who has been deprived of parental love and affection for a period of time. Almost any form of attention from the parent, even if abusive, is likely to be reinforcing.

The importance of the individual's behavioral repertoire is that as skills become more complex, new reinforcement contingencies begin to operate (Skinner, 1987, p. 59). For example, when a researcher, writer, or student learns to operate a microcomputer, another set of reinforcement contingencies comes into play. Examples include success in operating the equipment, solving problems, and editing text quickly.

Both the individual's past reinforcement history and particular skills repertoire are products of a person's daily life. However, inherited characteristics, such as differences in mental ability, also influence the types of consequences that are likely to be reinforcing.

In addition, the current generation has inherited susceptibilities to at least four kinds of reinforcement from early humans. They are susceptibilities to reinforcement from overeating, the tastes of sugar and salt, sexual contact, and the outcomes of aggressive behavior.

Early humans lived in a difficult and dangerous environment, and certain behaviors were powerfully reinforced by survival. Included were eating as much as possible at one time whenever food was found and eating the few foods that were sweet, which often were especially nutritious (Skinner, 1987, p. 174). Western civilization, however, has an abundant food supply, and many individuals today often face health problems from overeating as well as from consuming excessive amounts of salt and sugar.

In addition, sexual contact that led to procreation and aggressive behavior against predators also led to survival of the strong breeders and fighters. Problems currently faced by their descendants include overpopulation and a susceptibility to reinforcement by the outcomes of aggression.

Summary

A reinforcing event is any behavioral consequence that strengthens behavior. That is, it increases the frequency of responding. The two key processes involving reinforcement that result in complex behaviors are variation of behavior and selection by consequence. Many behaviors are executed, but only some are strengthened. That is, they are selected by the consequences of reinforcement.

For a behavioral consequence to be effective, it must increase the rate of responding under particular environmental conditions. Also, it must be immediately contingent on the execution of the appropriate response. If reinforcement for a particular response is withdrawn, extinction or cessation of the behavior will occur.

Three factors that influence the extent to which stimuli may function as reinforcers are the individual's past reinforcement history, the skills repertoire of the individual, and the particular characteristics inherited by the individual. Inherited characteristics include mental ability and susceptibilities to certain reinforcers, such as food and the taste of sugar and salt.

Categories of Reinforcement

Three broad classifications of reinforcement are primary or secondary reinforcers, generalized reinforcers, and positive or negative reinforcement.

Primary and Secondary (Conditioned) Reinforcers.   As societies grow more complex, a greater variety of events can function as reinforcers (Skinner, 1989a). Included are getting a key to the executive washroom, winning an Olympic medal, and finding information on the Internet.

How do such events become reinforcers? The process begins with a small group of stimuli known as **primary reinforcers** (Skinner, 1953, 1963b). Under appropriate conditions, primary reinforcers are the stimuli that can increase the frequency of behavior without training. They also are essential to the survival of the species. Primary reinforcers include food, drink, shelter, and sexual contact.

Other events that strengthen behavior are **conditioned** or **secondary reinforcers**. They acquire reinforcing power by association with events that already reinforce behavior. A typical example in the laboratory is the sound of the food mechanism that occurs just prior to the delivery of food. Through repeated association with food (the primary reinforcer), the click of the mechanism acquires reinforcing power. In the everyday world, smiles and being rocked or cuddled often accompany the feeding of the young infant. In this way, receiving affection and the approval of others become secondary reinforcers.

Events also may acquire reinforcing power by association with other well-established secondary reinforcers. For example, the different trophies and medals awarded for winning various kinds of contests are reinforcing through association with the secondary reinforcers of social approval and recognition.

Conditioned reinforcers play an important role in the development of complex human behaviors. First, if behavior were strengthened only by primary reinforcers, the human behavioral repertoire would be limited to those actions that produce food, drink, sleep, shelter, and sexual contact.

Second, conditioned reinforcers bridge the gap between early stages of complex behavior and some future consequence. For example, "people are said to write articles or books for money or acclaim. Those may be rewards, but they do not occur soon enough to be reinforcers. At one's desk the reinforcers are the appearances of sentences that make sense, clear up puzzles, answer questions, make points" (Skinner, 1986, p. 109). These conditioned reinforcers, rather than ultimate publication or acclaim, maintain the day-by-day behavior of writing.

Generalized Reinforcers.   Some secondary reinforcers are restricted to a particular setting because they are linked to only one primary reinforcer. The click of the food magazine, for example, functions only in the laboratory. Others, however, are found in a variety of situations; they are **generalized reinforcers**. Examples include the reinforcements that are provided by other individuals, such as attention, approval, and affection (Skinner, 1953). Smiles, commendations, and the agreement of peers are all expressions of approval that function as reinforcers in numerous social situations.

Money also has been referred to as a generalized reinforcer because it has been associated with the primary reinforcers of food, drink, and shelter. However, Skinner (1987, p. 18) noted that money becomes reinforcing only when exchanged for strongly reinforcing goods or services. More important, money strengthens specific work behaviors only when it is paid on commission or for piecework. In contrast, money paid for a specified amount of time worked (such as per hour or per week) does not strengthen particular behaviors (Skinner, 1987, p. 19). Instead, the real function of money is to establish a standard of living that the worker, under certain circumstances, may lose (Skinner, 1987).

One powerful generalized reinforcer that often is overlooked is the reinforcement provided by successful manipulation of the physical environment. Our tendency to participate in activities that depend on skill, such as crafts, artistic creations, and skill sports such as bowling and tennis, may be a function of this generalized reinforcer (Skinner, 1953, p. 79). Similarly, in playing video games, "No one really cares whether PacMan gobbles up all those little spots on the screen. Indeed, as soon as the screen is cleared, the player covers it again with more little spots to be gobbled up. What is reinforcing is successful play" (Skinner, 1984, p. 24).

Positive and Negative Reinforcement.   The categories of primary and secondary reinforcement refer to the ways that events acquire reinforcing power. However, reinforcers also may be categorized in terms of the nature of the reinforcing consequence. In the examples already discussed, certain behaviors are followed by the appearance of a new object or event. Lever pressing produces a food pellet, correctly identifying the primary colors produces approval, and so on. These situations, in which a new stimulus is added to the situation, are defined as positive reinforcement (Skinner, 1953, 1989b).

In contrast, some behaviors result in the removal of or escape from a situation. For example, a rat is exposed to mild shock through an electrified floor grid. Backing into or touching the wall terminates the shock. The response—touching the wall—increases in frequency (is strengthened) because it removes the electric shock. Any behavior that provides escape from a situation typically increases. However, this form of reinforcement is referred to as **negative reinforcement** (Skinner, 1953, 1989b). Specifically, "a negative reinforcer is properly defined as 'a stimulus the *reduction* or *removal* of which strengthens behavior'" (Skinner, 1989b, p. 127). Further, "behavior which is followed by the withdrawal of an aversive stimulus is called escape" (Skinner, 1953, p. 171). An everyday example is the loud buzz in some cars when the ignition is turned on. The intent is that the driver's behavior of fastening the seat belt will increase because it removes the irritating buzz.

Negative reinforcement is also known as escape conditioning because it strengthens escape behaviors. Consider, for example, a boy who has not made friends and is not doing well in school. One day he says that his stomach hurts, and he is allowed to leave class. A few days later he avoids school by saying he has a stomachache. The next Monday morning, he insists he does not feel well enough to attend classes. This set of events, which has strengthened an escape behavior, is one of negative reinforcement. The learning sequence is (1) the school (discriminative stimulus), (2) feigning illness to avoid school (escape response), and (3) avoiding school (reinforcement). Initially, the school (discriminative stimulus) was followed by the boy feigning illness (response) and leaving class (termination of the aversive stimulus—reinforcement). The avoidance of school, on the subsequent days, is not quite the same because the avoided condition (being in school) does not directly affect the boy (Skinner, 1953, pp. 176–177). However, by feigning illness in the morning while he is getting dressed or at the breakfast table, the boy avoids a particular situation that served as a negative reinforcer.

The similarities and differences between positive and negative reinforcement are illustrated by the examples in Table 6.1. Notice that the consequence in positive reinforcement is the addition of a new stimulus. In contrast, the consequence in negative reinforcement is the removal of or escape from the discriminative stimulus.

TABLE 6.1
Examples of Positive and Negative Reinforcement

Discriminative Stimulus	Response	Consequence	Type of Consequence	Type of Reinforcement*
Coffee machine	Subject puts change in machine and pushes button.	Subject receives a cup of coffee.	Subject's behavior "produces" a new stimulus.	Positive
Parent nags teenager to clean up room.	Subject straightens up his room every day for two weeks.	Nagging stops	Subject's behavior has been followed by the withdrawal of the discriminative stimulus.	Negative

*The assumption here is that the response increases in frequency; therefore, the described consequence is functioning as reinforcement.

In the analysis of behavior, the terms *pleasant* and *unpleasant* should not be used as a basis for differentiating positive and negative reinforcers (Skinner, 1953). Such a classification can lead to errors in behavioral analysis. For example, praise, typically considered to be pleasant or satisfying, often is treated as a positive reinforcer. Consider, however, the situation of a teenage male in the classroom who is seeking status in the eyes of his peers. Teacher praise is an aversive stimulus that the student seeks to escape. Teacher attention and praise for such a student is a discriminative stimulus for any of a variety of behaviors from apathy to minor classroom disruptions.

Emotional By-Products. The use of negative reinforcement to regulate behavior introduces undesirable emotional by-products that accompany the subject's escape or avoidance behavior (Skinner, 1953, 1989b). Included are the emotions referred to as "anxiety" and "fear." The set of reactions called anxiety, for example, includes conditioned reflexes of the intestinal muscles, such as gastric changes, a sudden loss of blood from the face, and possibly, increased blood pressure.

Because these emotional reactions accompany the escape response, they become conditioned to situational characteristics that accompany the aversive stimulus. A horse that has been whipped by a rider, for example, will roll its eyes, become restive, and possibly rear up at the sight of a riding crop. On a more subtle level, the child who has been scolded for not completing his or her chores may become agitated when the parent comes home.

Interactive Examples. In many situations, both positive reinforcement and mild negative reinforcers function to strengthen the same behaviors. For example, the scientist's long hours of work in the laboratory may be reinforced positively by the conditioned reinforcers of manipulating the experimental situation and, intermittently, by identifying new facts. In addition, perhaps social "small talk" with other people is mildly aversive. If the scientist leaves a party to go to work in the laboratory, escaping from the party is functioning as a negative reinforcer.

In interactions between two or more people, a careful analysis is required to determine discriminative stimuli, responses, and reinforcers. For example, a child may begin to cry whenever the parents entertain guests. The parents may turn their attention momentarily to the disruptive child so that they can continue to enjoy the visit. In that situation, the child's interruption is the **aversive stimulus** for the parent's attention (Figure 6.1). Their attention terminates the interruption (withdrawal of the aversive stimulus). Terminating the child's interruption serves as a negative reinforcer for the parents. However, the attention of the adults, particularly if prolonged, serves as positive reinforcement for the child's crying and whining.

Summary

Three broad classifications of reinforcement may be identified. One is that of primary and secondary (conditioned) reinforcers. Primary reinforcers are those that, under appropriate conditions, can increase the frequency of behavior

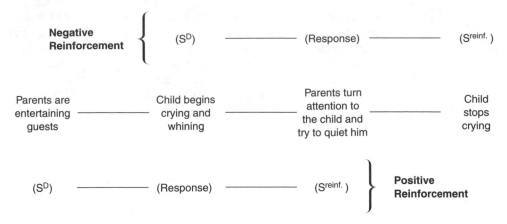

FIGURE 6.1
Behavioral analysis of parent-child interaction

without training. They are food, shelter, drink, and sexual contact. Secondary or conditioned reinforcers acquire reinforcing power through association with events that already function as reinforcers. Examples are smiles and expressions of social approval that often are associated with the baby's first feedings.

The second category, generalized reinforcers, refers to reinforcers that function in a variety of settings. Examples are attention, approval, and affection. One powerful generalized reinforcer that often is overlooked is the successful manipulation of the physical environment. Participation in sports, skill activities, and hobbies may be a function of this generalized reinforcer.

The third category, positive or negative reinforcement, refers to the nature of the reinforcing consequence. In positive reinforcement, the response produces a new stimulus, for example, a lever press produces a food pellet. In contrast, negative reinforcement refers to the withdrawal or reduction of the discriminative stimulus. Fastening one's seat belt to terminate the annoying buzzing sound is an example. Another term for negative reinforcement is escape conditioning because behaviors that represent escape from aversive stimuli are reinforced. One problem associated with negative reinforcement is that undesirable emotional responses accompany the subject's escape or avoidance behavior. Included are the emotions referred to as anxiety and fear.

In many situations, both positive and mild negative reinforcement function to strengthen behavior. Also, both positive and negative reinforcement may be operating in interactions between individuals. A careful analysis is needed to determine the discriminative stimuli, responses, and reinforcers.

Punishment
The term *punishment*, like many commonly used words, is associated with a variety of meanings. Typically, punishment is viewed as imposing unwanted consequences on the individual to stop a particular behavior.

Behavior may be punished in either of two different ways. One form of punishment is the removal of a positive reinforcer (Skinner, 1953, 1968b). Withdrawing the privilege of watching television is an example. The other form of punishment is the addition of a negative reinforcer to a situation. Examples include being sent to one's room and writing 50 times "I will not talk in class."

Because both punishment and negative reinforcement involve aversive stimuli, they often are confused. However, two major differences may be identified. One is the relationship of the individual to the aversive stimulus. In negative reinforcement, the individual successfully escapes from or avoids the aversive situation. In contrast, in punishment, the individual is placed in an aversive situation. Second, the effects on behavior differ. Negative reinforcement (successful escape or avoidance of an aversive situation) strengthens a particular behavior. In contrast, punishment only temporarily suppresses behavior. For example, a child punished for scribbling on the furniture may decorate a bedroom wall a few days later.

Also, in terms of effect, punishment is not the opposite of reinforcement (Skinner, 1953). At least four undesirable effects of punishment may occur. First, as already mentioned, punishment only temporarily suppresses behavior; it is not a permanent solution. Second, punishment also produces undesirable emotional reactions, such as frustration, anger, and guilt. Third, actions other than the unwanted behavior also may be punished. Red marks on a term paper and a low grade for misspelled words punish the errors. Also punished, however, are the student's time and effort in writing the paper.

The major shortcoming associated with punishment, however, is that it does not generate positive behaviors (Skinner, 1953, 1968b). Interest in schoolwork does not result from the punishment of indifference (Skinner, 1968b, p. 149). Similarly, students do not learn correct speech by being punished for bad grammar.

If punishment should not be used, then what are some alternatives? First, avoid the conditions that make punishment necessary. For example, punishing students for shouting out in class can be avoided by eliminating events that ask for call-out behavior, such as "Who has their homework done?" Also, lessons with purpose that move briskly with clear signals to students leave few opportunities for misbehavior. Interruptions and confusion resulting from missing props, unclear directions, false starts, and backtracking do not occur.

Second, reinforce a behavior that is incompatible with the undesirable behavior. For example, we suppress competitive behavior when we reinforce cooperation (Skinner, 1968b). In other words, punishing a student for being out of his or her seat may be unnecessary if the student has tasks to complete that earn reinforcement (in-seat behavior).

In summary, both negative reinforcement and punishment involve aversive stimuli. However, negative reinforcement strengthens an escape behavior, whereas punishment temporarily suppresses behavior. The shortcomings of punishment are the negative emotional reactions, the punishment of behaviors associated with the punished behavior, the inability to generate positive behaviors, and the fact that the punished behavior is only temporarily suppressed.

Cultural Practices and Operant Conditioning

Skinner (1981) maintained that the essential processes in conditioning individual behavior also operate at two other levels. One, already discussed, is the biological evolution of the species. The other is the development of cultures.

Specifically, a culture or a set of social practices is defined as the contingencies that are maintained by a group (Skinner, 1989b, p. 52). An example is the American practice of joining family members or friends on Thanksgiving. Celebrating this holiday is positively reinforced by good food and social reinforcers such as affection, companionship, and the approval of others. It is also negatively reinforced through escape from work.

The reinforcement contingencies in cultural practices shape the behavior of each member of the group. Also, social practices are transmitted when members shape the behavior of new or younger members. Young parents, for example, reinforce the participation of their children when they continue the same rituals as their parents.

Cultures, and governments in particular, also often control their members through the use of aversive stimuli, either as negative reinforcers or as punishments for undesirable behavior. Citizens obey laws primarily to escape from or to avoid fines and imprisonment (Skinner, 1989b, p. 53).

Some cultural practices, however, erode the contingencies available through operant conditioning (Skinner, 1987). For example, families no longer must grow their own food or weave the material for their clothing. Although some aversive consequences are avoided by paying someone else for goods and services, opportunities for reinforcement, such as pride in the finished product, are also lost.

In addition, the degree of job specialization in contemporary society has reduced the opportunities for reinforcement. Although society gains from a division of work (more products are available), the assembly line worker who completes one part of the circuitry in a television set does not directly experience reinforcement from the final product.

Another problem in Western civilization is the abundance of things described as "interesting, beautiful, delicious, entertaining, and exciting" (Skinner, 1987, p. 231). Included are beautiful pictures, beautiful music, and exciting entertainments. However, the only behaviors reinforced by such easy access to beautiful and exciting things are the behaviors of looking and listening. However, this is only a very small sample of human behavior (compared with the vast range of behaviors that might receive reinforcement) (Skinner, 1987, p. 24). In other words, easy access to pleasing reinforcers creates a situation in which "the reinforcers are not contingent upon the kinds of behavior that sustain the individual or promote the survival of (either) the culture or the species" (Skinner, 1987, p. 24).

The Nature of Complex Learning

The law of effect specifies the temporal relationship between a response and a consequence (Skinner, 1953, 1963b). However, it does not explain the acquisition of complex behaviors such as pigeons playing ping-pong, or table tennis, and humans working with computers. Instead, the development of new and complex patterns or "topographies" of behavior results from complex and subtle contingencies of reinforcement. For example, a child learns to pull itself up, to stand, to walk, and to move about through the reinforcement of slightly exceptional instances of behavior (Skinner, 1953). Later, this same process is responsible for the individual's learning to sing, to dance, and to play games, as well as all the other behaviors found in the normal adult repertoire (Skinner, 1953, p. 93).

Shaping Behavior

The acquisition of complex behaviors is the result of the process referred to as shaping (Skinner, 1954, 1963b, 1989b). This process involves a carefully designed program of discriminative stimuli and reinforcements for subtle changes in responses. An example is that of teaching a pigeon to bowl (Skinner, 1958). The desired terminal behavior is that of swiping a wooden ball with a sideways movement of the beak so that the ball is sent down a miniature alley toward a set of toy pins.

The shaping process begins by providing reinforcement for responses that indicate approaches to the ball. Reinforcement is then withheld until the pigeon's beak makes contact with the ball. After initial reinforcements for contact, reinforcement is withheld again until further refinement in the behavior occurs (i.e., the pigeon sideswipes the ball). The procedure of first reinforcing responses that only remotely resemble the desired response and then reinforcing only refinements in the response is referred to as *reinforcing successive approximations* (Skinner, 1953, 1968b, 1989b) or differential reinforcement. Shaping is effective because it is sensitive to the continuous nature of a complex act, and it illustrates the utility of constructing complex behavior by a continual process of **differential reinforcement** (Skinner, 1953).

The importance of shaping is that it can generate complex behaviors that have an almost zero probability of occurring naturally in the final form (Skinner, 1963a). A complex behavior is shaped by a series of changing contingencies referred to as a **program** (Skinner, 1963b, p. 506). Each stage of the program evokes a response that also prepares the organism to take the next step in the behavioral sequence.

Shaping differs from the modification of behavior that occurs with puzzle boxes, mazes, and memory drums. In those situations, the organism is thrown into a problem situation and must discover the successful behaviors through trial and error. However, performance of the appropriate response has been left to chance, and random, incorrect responses also occur.

Contingencies of Reinforcement

Behavior that acts on the immediate physical environment, in general, is reinforced consistently (Skinner, 1953, p. 99). Standing and walking are examples. However, a large part of behavior generates only intermittent reinforcement, such as writing.

In the laboratory, intermittent reinforcement may be delivered precisely according to different schedules or combinations of schedules (see Ferster & Skinner, 1957). The schedule may be controlled by either (1) a system outside the organism or (2) the behavior itself (Skinner, 1953, p. 100). The former may be determined by the clock and is referred to as **interval reinforcement**. The latter, which is determined by the number of responses emitted by the organism, is known as **ratio reinforcement** (Table 6.2).

When fixed schedules are used, ratio or interval, the timing of reinforcement is certain. Typically, responding slows down immediately after reinforcement and then gradually increases in rate. The slowdown in response rate can be avoided through the use of a variable schedule. The delivery of reinforcement is uncertain, and the rate of responding is more nearly constant.

Intermittent reinforcement for a particular response can sustain behavior for long periods of time. One particularly effective schedule is the **variable-ratio** schedule. Reinforcement is frequent at first, but then it is gradually reduced. For example, a television program may become less reinforcing as jokes or story lines become less interesting. Someone who has followed the program from the beginning, however, may continue to watch the program for a long time (Skinner, 1966a, p. 164).

The Concept of Negative Utility

The variable-ratio schedule is useful because it maintains behavior against extinction when reinforcement is infrequent (Skinner, 1989b, p. 77). The behavior of dedicated artists and scientists, for example, is sustained by occasional, unpredictable reinforcements.

In some situations, however, the variable-ratio schedule can lead to the long-term detriment of the subject. For instance, pigeons reinforced on a variable-ratio schedule for pecking a disc at a high rate will peck until their beaks become inflamed. Similarly, the compulsive gambler is reinforced periodically for betting at the roulette table or playing the slot machine. Every winning play,

TABLE 6.2

Comparison of Ratio and Interval Schedules of Reinforcement

Ratio Reinforcement	Interval Reinforcement
Reinforcement delivery is based on number of responses emitted.	Reinforcement delivery is based on elapsed time. *Examples:* Reading books, going to the theatre, watching television (Skinner, 1966a)
Fixed: A constant number of responses generates reinforcement (e.g., every fifth response) *Examples:* Selling on commission; pay for piecework in industry	*Fixed:* Reinforcement for a correct response at a constant time interval (e.g., every 15 seconds)
Variable: Reinforcement delivered after a varying number of correct responses (e.g., every fifth, eighth, third, etc.) *Examples:* Payoffs from slot machines, roulette, horse races, and other games of chance	*Variable:* Reinforcement delivered for an appropriate response at varying time intervals (e.g., every 10 seconds, 4 seconds, 7 seconds, etc.)

of course, is reinforcing, but they do not occur often and eventually the gambler exhausts his or her resources. This situation, in which a stretched variable-ratio schedule leads to the long-term detriment of the subject, is one of **negative utility** (Skinner, 1987, p. 24).

Gambling sustained by a variable-ratio schedule to the point of negative utility is one form of addiction. Another form of addiction occurs when substances are used that initially are positively reinforcing but that subsequently are taken to escape from physical states known as "withdrawal symptoms" (Skinner, 1989b, p. 76). The long-term condition is one of negative utility; greater and greater amounts of the substance are required to provide escape from the physical symptoms, while the general physical and emotional states of the individual steadily deteriorate.

Rule-Governed Behavior

The process known as shaping exposes the subject to changing contingencies of reinforcement for the performance of progressively more accurate behaviors. This method is referred to as **contingency-governed behavior** (Skinner, 1969).

For the human learner, however, not all behaviors are acquired through direct exposure to response consequences. "Few people drive a car at a moderate speed and keep their seat belts fastened because they have actually avoided or escaped from serious accidents by doing so" (Skinner, 1953, p. 168). Instead, people often do what others tell them to do; that is, they follow advice (Skinner, 1987, p. 21). Typically, the advice is in the form of verbal suggestions or instructions, such as, "If you wish to avoid the grid-lock near Sumner Tunnel on the way to Logan Airport, take McGrath Highway" (Vaughan, 1987, p. 260). The instructions are verbal stimuli that alter the listener's behavioral repertoire. Such behavior is known as *rule-governed* (Skinner, 1987).

In addition to informal advice, rule-governed behavior may be acquired through formal rules, such as maxims, proverbs, and the rules of grammar and spelling. Also included are the legal, ethical, and religious practices of a society that are compiled into laws and other codified procedures. These rules and laws are important to a culture in two ways. First, they help the individual benefit from the experience of others. Second, they also help the group to command and censure consistently (Skinner, 1989b).

Why do individuals follow advice or rules? The primary reason is that following advice in the past has produced particular consequences. For example, we follow the directions for assembling a piece of equipment if similar behavior has produced the outcome of properly assembled equipment (Skinner, 1987, p. 180). Also, when parents provide positive reinforcers for following directions and rules, children will do as they are told because positive reinforcers have followed (Skinner, 1989b, p. 80).

Rule-governed and contingency-governed behavior differ in two ways. One is that behavior is more effectively executed in the contingency-governed condition. When learning to drive a car, for example, the procedures executed by the learner in response to instructions are awkward and halting. Skilled behaviors are acquired in the contingency-governed condition when the novice driver experiences the consequences of his or her actions.

The second difference is that only the immediate response consequences alter the probability of future occurrence of the response. In the rule-governed condition, however, the probability of a response remains undetermined (Skinner, 1953, p. 147). "For example, having learned that 'procrastination is the thief of time,' we are probably no less likely to put off unpleasant tasks" (Skinner, 1989b, p. 41).

A particular problem in efforts to change behavior is advice based on probable adverse consequences, such as warnings about cigarette smoking. One does not stop smoking as a result of the statistical probabilities of dying from a heart attack or lung cancer. In other words, statistical predictions are ineffective in establishing rule-governed behavior.

Summary

The acquisition of a complex set of behaviors results from the process known as shaping. This process consists of a series of discriminative stimuli with reinforcement for subtle changes in responses. Shaping illustrates the development of complex behavior through differential reinforcement. It also generates behaviors that have an almost zero probability of occurring naturally in the final form. In the laboratory, reinforcement may be delivered according to different schedules. If determined by the clock, the schedule is referred to as interval reinforcement. However, if based on the number of responses emitted by the organism, the schedule type is ratio reinforcement. The timing for each schedule also may be fixed or varied.

One advantage of variable-ratio reinforcement is that it maintains behavior against extinction when reinforcement is infrequent. The behavior of dedicated artists and scientists is an example. However, when a variable-ratio schedule leads to long-term detriment of the organism, the process is referred to as negative utility. An addiction to gambling is an example.

When the execution of particular behaviors receives reinforcement, the learned responses are referred to as contingency-governed behavior. However, not all behaviors are acquired through direct exposure to response consequences. Instead, individuals often follow advice, instructions, or directions that constitute the discriminative stimulus. The instructions alter the listener's behavioral repertoire. This behavioral change occurs because individuals have been reinforced in the past for compliance with verbal directives. Such behavior, referred to as rule-governed, differs from contingency-governed behavior in two ways. One is that behavior is more effectively executed in the contingency-governed condition. The other is that the probability of a response in the rule-governed condition remains undetermined.

PRINCIPLES OF INSTRUCTION

Skinner became interested in education when his children entered school, and he began in the 1950s to apply operant conditioning to the classroom. He devised techniques for developing step-by-step instruction, mechanical devices for instruction referred to as teaching machines, and a technology of class-room teaching. He also wrote essays on the problems in education.

Basic Assumptions

Assumptions about the nature of learning and the nature of science estab-lished the parameters within which the principles of operant conditioning were developed in the laboratory. Similarly, B. F. Skinner's beliefs about the nature of schooling and classroom learning established the parameters for his technology of teaching.

The Nature of Education

The educational system is extremely important because the welfare of any cul-ture depends on it. A culture is no stronger than its capacity to transmit its skills, beliefs, and practices to the next generation, and this responsibility be-longs to education (Skinner, 1953).

Contemporary education, however, faces three major problems in fulfill-ing this mission. One is that it takes place in an artificial setting. That is, schools prepare students for a world that lies in the future (Skinner, 1989b, p. 87). Educators have tried to bring real life into the classroom, for example, by teaching botany with a few plants (Skinner, 1989b, p. 88). The problem is that so little of the world actually can be made available to the student during 12 years of schooling. Because the school has access to so few of the natural rein-forcers found in the world, educators face the task of designing reinforcement contingencies to bridge the gap between initial learning and later real-world contingencies.

Second, the public school was established to provide the services of a pri-vate tutor to more than one student at a time (Skinner, 1989b, p. 85). However, by the time classes reach 25 or 30, personal attention is intermittent and brief, at best. "The larger the class or the school, the worse the problems faced by the teacher" (Skinner, 1989b, p. 86).

The third problem is an outgrowth of the other two. Because students are placed in groups to read and hear about events rather than experience them, the individual student seldom does anything that is immediately or visibly suc-cessful (Skinner, 1987, p. 91).

Faced with these three problems, the school has resorted to the use of aver-sive control. The result is that students complete their work primarily to avoid the consequences of not doing so (Skinner, 1968b, 1989b). Moreover, the educa-tional system again is facing criticism much like the reaction to Russia's launch-ing of *Sputnik*. Skinner (1987) noted that a report of the National Commission on Excellence in Education described American schools as comparing poorly with those in other nations in several fields. Among the current suggested solu-tions were extending the school day, lengthening the school year, raising schol-arship standards, and increasing teacher salaries.

These proposed solutions are like those recommended in the curriculum reform of the 1960s following Russia's launching of *Sputnik*. That is, a basic omission in all the suggestions is that they contain no indication that teaching should be improved (Skinner, 1987, p. 114). However, in Skinner's view, no institution can realize progress and improvement until it analyzes the basic processes for which it is responsible.

Learning in the Classroom Setting

The specific characteristics of the educational setting differ from those of the laboratory. The dynamics of behavioral change, nevertheless, are the same (Skinner, 1968b, 1987). In the laboratory, internal states such as "hunger" were redefined as observable conditions or events. In the classroom, the state referred to as "readiness" is defined as the set of skills already in the student's behavioral repertoire.

When a teacher is responsible for 20 to 30 students at one time, several problems for instruction arise. Included are (1) the infrequency of positive reinforcement, (2) the excessive lengths of time between behavior and reinforcement, and (3) the lack of programs that lead the child through a series of approximations to the final behavior (Skinner, 1954).

To correct these problems, programs of carefully selected stimuli and reinforcements are needed. In basic arithmetic alone, approximately 50,000 reinforcements for each student would be needed to ensure that the skills are acquired (Skinner, 1968b). Because the teacher cannot provide the needed reinforcements, machines such as computers and other current technology are necessary in the classroom. Appropriate applications of these aids would then free the teacher to spend more time listening and talking with individual students (Skinner, 1987).

In summary, three assumptions support Skinner's approach to a technology of teaching. First, the experimental analysis of behavior also applies to the classroom. Second, behavioral repertoires in the classroom may be shaped in the same manner as other behaviors. Third, technology is needed to provide the large number of reinforcements for behavioral responses.

The Components of Instruction

Skinner (1989a) emphasized that teaching is more than telling. Teaching occurs when a response is evoked for the first time and is then reinforced. Thus, the design of effective instruction requires careful attention to two important issues: the selection of the discriminative stimuli and the use of reinforcement.

Selecting the Stimulus

In classroom instruction, the selection of stimuli includes two major concerns. One is that stimulus discrimination and stimulus generalization are important prerequisites for the learning of more complex verbal behaviors. In discrimination, for example, the student must learn to respond verbally "p" to the *p*, but not to *r, d, b*, and so on. Then the response must be reinforced in the presence of different forms of the stimulus, such as *P*.

In the social environment of the classroom, a variety of verbal stimuli, such as "Look at this picture" and "Take out your pencils" may serve as discriminative stimuli to direct student attention. However, good classroom management can also make use of nonverbal stimuli and thus reduce the need for oral directions. In one classroom, for example, the teacher used colored name tags for the children. A particular color indicated the work or study group to which the child was to report that day. This technique permitted the teacher to rotate group membership easily and without confusion. In addition, any child who needed help with seatwork set up a little red tent provided in each work folder. The tent served as a discriminative stimulus for the teacher's behavior and eliminated hand and arm waving (Becker, 1973).

The other important consideration is the transfer of stimulus control. For example, when pictures are associated with words to assist the student in saying the correct word, the picture is the stimulus that controls the student's response. A picture of a flag, for example, induces the student to respond "flag" to the four-letter word. Inducing a response through prompting is not learning, however (Skinner, 1968b). The picture must be gradually withdrawn so that the word alone has control over the student's response. In other words, the transfer of stimulus control refers to the gradual withdrawal of contrived cues or hints that signal the correct response so that stimuli within the learner or other events are followed by appropriate responses.

The failure to provide for the transfer of stimulus control is one of the major errors found in microcomputer instruction (Vargas, 1986). For example, a program that consistently highlights words that students are to type teaches them to copy whatever is highlighted rather than to think about the content on the screen.

Providing Reinforcement

To be effective, reinforcement must be immediately contingent on the emission of the correct response. The two types of reinforcers available in the classroom are natural reinforcers and contrived reinforcers. Also important is phasing out contrived reinforcers, the timing of reinforcement, and the problems with aversive control.

Natural Reinforcers.   The events available in the setting that provide nonaversive feedback are referred to as natural reinforcers (Skinner, 1954). Examples include playing with mechanical toys, painting, and cutting with scissors. Others include finding the right word to describe something, resolving a temporary confusion, and having the opportunity to advance to the next stage of an activity (Skinner, 1958, p. 380). Further, a child learning to read is reinforced when the material "makes sense."

The research conducted by David Premack (1959) indicated that children's preferred activities will reinforce their participation in their less-preferred activities. For the child who prefers playing with mechanical toys to painting, time with the toys may be used to reinforce participation in art activities.

In two studies, high-priority academic activities were used to strengthen other academic behaviors. Gallant, Sargeant, and Van Houten (1980) made access to a highly preferred subject area, a science lab activity, contingent on accurately completing assignments in reading and mathematics. Moreno and Hovell (1980) used access to a language laboratory to reinforce a Spanish-speaking teenager for answering questions in English. However, care should be exercised in the use of academic activities so that students are not denied access to important methods of instruction.

Contrived Reinforcers.   In many situations, the use of natural reinforcers alone is insufficient to change behavior. For example, people should consume lesser amounts of certain kinds of goods because the by-products of those goods irreversibly foul the environment (Skinner, 1989b, p. 118). However, such a consequence is too remote to have an immediate effect on behavior. Contrived contingencies are needed to alter behaviors of overconsumption.

In education, contrived reinforcers also are often needed to bridge the gap between the early stages of learning and the setting in which natural reinforcers can function. Teaching reading and writing are examples in which the behavior is too much a product of an advanced culture to rely on natural reinforcers such as reading for information or for pleasure.

In some of the learning centers in the United States, students listen to instructions on cassette recorders and respond on work sheets. A magic-ink effect immediately indicates whether their behavior is correct or incorrect. Although no natural contingency exists between correct responses to a word or a passage and the appearance of a reaction, children nevertheless learn to read quickly (Skinner, 1987, p. 176). Contrived reinforcers also include verbal comments, gold stars, early dismissal, and free time.

Phasing out Contrived Reinforcers.   Im portant in planning the use of contrived reinforcers is (1) gradually stretching the ratio between responses and reinforcers, and (2) pairing the contrived reinforcer with other reinforcers that can gradually be replaced with natural reinforcers. Reinforcing oneself, for example, with a special treat for diligently working on a manuscript for an hour a day, particularly when paired every few days with the verbal reinforcers of noting the number of pages completed, can sustain early writing efforts while the individual is developing writing fluency and competency.

Also important is to withdraw or fade the special treat as the appearance of paragraphs that make sense, answer questions, or clarify important points begin to strengthen behavior (natural reinforcers).

Furthermore, a teacher initially may implement concrete reinforcers, such as tokens, for socially appropriate behaviors in the classroom. The tokens later may be exchanged for a prescribed number of minutes of free time. Of importance is to pair the tokens with verbal comments in the form of positive feedback to recognition. Also, the teacher should teach the students to commend themselves for appropriate behavior, and gradually phase out the tokens.

The key to using contrived reinforcers effectively is (1) to restrict their use to early stages of developing complex behavior, (2) plan the use of discriminative stimuli to include transfer to internal or non-arbitrary stimuli, (3) plan for the emergence of natural reinforcers, and (4) gradually fade (phase out) the contrived reinforcers as the behavior develops and natural reinforcers are functioning. Step three can be aided by a respected teacher, for example, who reads several paragraphs when the student completes them and verbally confirms good points made or improvement in fluency or expression.

The Timing of Reinforcement.   Particularly important in the effectiveness of reinforcement is timing the delivery of reinforcing stimuli. "A fatal principle is 'letting well enough alone'—giving no attention to a student so long as he behaves well and turning to him only when he begins to cause trouble" (Skinner, 1968b, p. 180). Because the attention of the teacher often is reinforcing in the classroom, the careless teacher will unintentionally reinforce the attention-getter and the show-off. Furthermore, at-risk students in a class who are not receiving attention for their academic behaviors will engage in nonacademic behaviors because nonacademic behaviors are producing reinforcement (Belfiore & Hornyak, 1998, p. 187).

Another example is that of dismissing the class early. If the class is dismissed when the students are loud or disruptive, the early dismissal reinforces inappropriate behavior. The teacher must time the dismissal to occur when the class is quiet and busy.

The mistiming of reinforcement also occurs with brightly colored and attractive learning materials. Bright colors, animated sequences, and other innovations have a temporary effect—they induce the student to look at the materials (Skinner, 1968b, p. 105). Computers also have used such techniques to attract the attention of students (Vargas, 1986).

The problem is that the student is not taught to look and listen. In effective instruction, the student should attend to the situation because previous encounters were reinforcing. Similarly, an attractive school building reinforces the behavior of coming in view of it, and a colorful classroom reinforces only the behavior of entering it (Skinner, 1968, p. 105). Although attending is important, good instruction reinforces the student *after* he or she has read the page, listened to the explanation, solved the problem, and so on.

Equally important in planning reinforcement is to avoid the overuse of reinforcers. For example, research data indicate that excessive praise for right answers to teacher questions is both intrusive and counterproductive (Brophy, 1981).

Problems with Aversive Control.   Classroom control often includes both the use of aversive stimuli and the withdrawal of positive reinforcement. Governments use punishment to suppress the behavior of troublesome individuals. Punishing students for such things as "not studying," however, is different (Skinner, 1989b, p. 88). First, the aim of education is to strengthen behavior, not suppress it. Second, the use of aversive stimuli as negative reinforcers and punishments leads to unwanted by-products. Specifically, this practice generates unwanted emotional reactions and escape behaviors. Escape behaviors include forgetting, inattention, truancy, and vandalism, as well as subtle forms of behavior, such as looking at the teacher while not paying attention (Skinner, 1968b, p. 97). The emotional side effects include reactions typically described as apathy, anxiety, anger, and resentment, all of which inhibit learning.

The third problem associated with the use of aversive control is that punishment does not generate positive behaviors. "We do not strengthen good pronunciation by punishing bad, or skillful movements by punishing awkward" (Skinner, 1968b, p. 149).

Reprimands can be used effectively, if they are in the form of "gentle admonitions" for small units of behavior (Skinner, 1968b, p. 101). Slight reprimands to the child who is learning to tie a shoelace for holding the lace wrong or moving it in the wrong direction, for example, are acceptable. They provide the opportunity for the learner to select the correct response from a small number of possibilities.

Summary

Effective instruction requires the careful selection of discriminative stimuli and reinforcement for changes in responding. An important classroom consideration in the selection of stimuli is that stimulus discrimination and stimulus generalization are important prerequisites for learning complex verbal behaviors. Another important issue is the transfer of stimulus control. Cues and other events that signal the appropriate response must be gradually withdrawn so that stimuli within the learner or other events are followed by appropriate responses. In other words, prompting responses does not ensure learning. In the classroom, discriminative stimuli range from teacher directions and signals to color-coded materials and printed text.

The teacher must rely often on contrived reinforcers because natural reinforcers are either unavailable or are remote consequences for expert performance. Success in the form of confirmation of a correct answer is an example. Important in implementing reinforcement is the judicious use of contrived reinforcers, avoidance of the overuse of reinforcement, and ensuring that reinforcement is contingent on appropriate behavior. Aversive control should be avoided if possible because it is accompanied by negative emotional reactions and escape behaviors. Moreover, punishment does not generate appropriate behavior.

Designing Instruction for Complex Skills

The development of complex skills should not be left to chance. One of the problems with Thorndike's experiment is that the animal was placed in the cage and left to "discover" the correct method of escape (Skinner, 1953). Similar situations occur in the school setting with the practice of "assign and test" or asking students to write a term paper without teaching them the subordinate skills. Skinner refers to these situations as placing the learner in a set of **terminal contingencies**. The situation is one in which the learner is left, through trial and error, to discover the complex skill or series of skills required for success.

Shaping Human Behavior

Developing complex skills in the classroom involves the key ingredients identified in teaching pigeons to play ping-pong and to bowl. The key ingredients are (1) inducing a response, (2) reinforcing subtle improvements or refinements in the behavior, (3) providing for the transfer of stimulus control by gradually withdrawing the prompts or cues, and (4) scheduling reinforcements so that the ratio of reinforcements to responses gradually increases and natural reinforcers can maintain the behavior.

Consider learning to pronounce new words in a foreign language. For instance, the teacher typically holds up an object or picture, pronounces the words or phrases, and the student is induced to repeat the words. Reinforcement is provided initially for sounds that only remotely resemble correct pronunciation. Then reinforcement is withheld briefly until the pronunciation improves slightly. The teacher continues to prompt the pronunciation of difficult syllables or sounds and to provide reinforcement for improved pronunciation. The prompts then are gradually withdrawn. Instruction is complete when the student can identify the new objects or pictures correctly without assistance.

In the classroom, the first step in shaping behavior is to clearly specify the behavior that is to be learned (Skinner, 1989b, p. 122). For example, one mathematics teacher wanted the students to learn to follow a course of logical reasoning. This expectation is too vague to be of assistance in planning instruction. However, examples of specific expectations (subskills) include identifying the "givens" in a word problem, determining what the problem is asking, and so on.

The second step is to identify the entry skills of the learners (Skinner, 1987). This step is important because any missing skills should be included in the instruction. The third step is to program the subject matter in carefully graded steps and teach first things first (Skinner, 1987). One temptation is to move too quickly to the final product (i.e., the terminal contingency). However, a well-designed program takes small steps and guarantees a great deal of successful action (Skinner, 1987, p. 125).

The purpose of the step-by-step instruction is to provide a series of reinforcements, contrived if necessary, for increasingly refined or complex behavior. However, the reinforcements are programmed so that eventually natural reinforcers in the environment come into play and/or the activity itself becomes reinforcing for the learner. In learning to read, for example, a magic-ink effect may indicate initial success, whereas later the student is reinforced when a sentence makes sense, answers a question, or solves a problem. The activity of reading becomes reinforcing when the individual reaches the stage of reading for pleasure.

Shaping often has been viewed as limited to highly specific skills, such as discriminating sounds, words, or colors. However, Glaser (1990) identifies elements of shaping in representative instructional programs for developing self-regulatory skills. All of the programs incorporate features to ensure student success and to minimize student errors. In addition, Brown (1994) noted that operant conditioning developed fading and scaffolding. Scaffolding refers to the supports provided to the student in the early stages of learning. Currently, for example, the program referred to as reciprocal teaching uses successive approximations and the gradual fading of support. The goal is for students to learn to monitor their own reading comprehension. First, the teacher structures the situation so that students implement only what they are able to do. Supporting cues from the teacher, close monitoring, and frequent feedback improve students' skills. As the students become more proficient, the teacher relinquishes control of parts of the comprehension monitoring process, that is, withdraws the supporting cues. (The process is referred to as "vanishing" in programmed learning.) After a few weeks, the students are monitoring their reading comprehension without assistance and are being reinforced by their success in extracting meaning from printed text.

The techniques of teaching new routines and procedures at the beginning of the school year that effective classroom managers use in elementary school classrooms also incorporate elements of shaping. Such teachers spend considerable time in the early weeks of school teaching the routines for use of storage areas, the pencil sharpener, and the bathroom, step by step with encouragement for each step (Doyle, 1986; Emmer, Evertson, & Anderson, 1980). Effective classroom managers consistently use cues to signal appropriate behavior, carefully monitor the classroom, provide reinforcement for appropriate behaviors, and redirect student behavior when small errors occur.

In addition, the methods for developing appropriate behaviors have been expanded to the secondary school classroom (Emmer et al., 1984) the management of adolescent behavior (Gottfredson, Gottfredson, & Hybl, 1993), and the development of positive school-wide discipline systems (Horner & Suqai, in press; Suqai & Horner, 2002). Of importance in such implementations is to develop clear expectations for student behavior and to remove the environmental events that reinforce inappropriate behavior.

Teaching Machines and Computers

Teaching machines were designed to provide sequenced instruction and the reinforcing power of immediate consequences (Skinner, 1989b). The importance of a mechanical device is that it gives reinforcement only for correct responses. When programmed instruction is implemented in a book format, students may look ahead, skip frames, or lose their places. The first teaching machine was developed in 1954, and Skinner (1989b) described it as a mechanical anticipation of the computer.

The early mechanical teaching machines provided contingent reinforcement for right answers in the form of (1) confirmation for correct answers, (2) the opportunity to move forward to new material, and (3) the opportunity to operate the equipment. The machine functioned as a patient tutor with no reprimands for errors, and a student moved forward at his or her own pace.

Current versions of the teaching machine include desktop models that are equipped with earphones and voice feedback. Some 400 Skinnerian learning centers around the country were established to provide remedial work in reading and mathematics. They use an advanced version of the original teaching machine (Skinner, in Green, 1984).

Skinner (1989b) considered the computer as the ideal teaching machine. He noted, however, that it tends to be used to provide drill or to teach in the same way as teachers in large classes. In contrast, computers can bring aspects of "real life" into the classroom. In industry, for example, meltdowns in nuclear power plants can be simulated on computers.

Another advantage of computers is that they expand the range of potential reinforcers and can be programmed to provide appropriate feedback for a variety of responses. Included in the potential reinforcers are opportunities (1) to change the screen display, (2) to play simple games, and (3) to develop one's own games. One group of games to teach math skills embeds the games in fantasy themes (e.g., a scavenger hunt theme in San Francisco) and allows the children to choose the problem type, game piece, and level of game. The games use the contrived reinforcers of verbal praise and an item needed in the scavenger hunt for helping a game character solve a problem (Azar, 1998).

Skinner cautioned, however, that computer programs that try to "jazz up" the material with fancy graphics often are doing the students a disservice. When programs seek to attract students' attention through animation or color graphics, they may actually be distracting the student from learning (Skinner, in Green, 1984). According to Skinner, there is no substitute for discovering that one can learn and for experiencing increasing levels of success.

Summary

Shaping behavior in the classroom first requires the clear specification of the behaviors to be learned. Second, entry skills of the learner must be identified. Then the subject matter should be programmed carefully in graded steps so that the instruction guarantees a great deal of successful action. Programs that initially provide instructional support, gradually fade or withdraw the support, and use successive approximations are using operant conditioning techniques. Effective classroom managers also use the methods to teach appropriate classroom behavior.

Mechanical devices known as teaching machines were developed by Skinner to teach programmed subject matter. Computers are improvements over teaching machines because they can bring aspects of real life into the classroom and also expand the range of potential reinforcers that may be used. However, computer programs should not be overloaded with animation or fancy graphics to attract student attention because they may distract the student from learning.

Operant Analysis of the Intrinsic and Extrinsic Motivation Discussion.

In the early 1970s, two experiments explored the effect of giving a reward to nursery school children for engaging in an activity that they had previously engaged in spontaneously (Lepper & Greene, 1973, 1974). Children who had drawn pictures with magic markers during free-choice time were each brought to the experimental room individually and asked if he or she would like to draw some pictures for an important person who was to visit the school. In the 6-minute experimental condition, some children also were told they would receive a Good Player certificate. In the other situations (also 6 minutes in duration), children simply received the certificate or were simply thanked.

Post-session observations indicated that the average percentage of free-choice time spent by children who were told of the expected reward was significantly less than that of the other two groups.

The researchers concluded that offering and providing the certificate "undermined" the children's interest in the activity, and schools should avoid the use of extrinsic rewards such as gold stars or special privileges (Lepper & Greene, 1973, p. 136). In subsequent years, some discussions in the literature (1) equated the term "extrinsic motivation" with the use of contrived reinforcers, and (2) urged school personnel to focus on intrinsic motivation because "extrinsic" rewards can undermine intrinsic interest or motivation (Deci & Ryan, 1990). These suggestions are a component of the belief in an internal wellspring for action in which psychological needs can precipitate learning.

First, from the operant conditioning perspective, the offer of the certificate and acceptance of that condition by the children for the drawing activity constituted a pre-experimental contract between the assistant and the child. Second, in the absence of baseline data on the free time spent coloring, conclusions about whether post-experimental drawing time increased or decreased cannot be made. Third, the example was a one-shot implementation of particular outcomes, whereas behavioral change typically involves more than one discriminative stimulus–response–outcome sequence. Moreover, subsequent analyses of studies of extrinsic rewards suggest that negative effects are produced when the rewards connote failure or are not directly linked to behavior (Cameron & Pierce, 1994a, 1994b).

Fourth, a persistent behavior that is executed in the absence of observable reinforcers is under the control of internal discriminative stimuli and/or natural reinforcers. Finally, teachers do not implement concrete reinforcers for activities in which students already have demonstrated interest.

EDUCATIONAL APPLICATIONS

Like Watson's behaviorism in the 1920s, Skinner's methodology has enjoyed wide popularity. Its rapid popularization, however, has led to a variety of misapplications of the principles. Many of the behavioral management programs that emerged in the 1950s were a combination of operant conditioning and other methods (Kazdin, 1989). (See Belfiore & Hornyak [1998] for a discussion of self-monitoring programs that combine operant and other principles.) For example, many programs use time-out and response cost procedures. *Time-out* is a brief period of removal of the individual from a setting that provides reinforcement. *Response cost* is the loss of a reinforcer for misbehavior and requires paying a penalty. Because both techniques involve loss of reinforcers, they are a form of punishment (Becker, 1973; Kazdin, 1989). According to Skinner, punishment is to be avoided.

In addition, many of the individualized materials for verbal behaviors copied the stimulus–response–feedback format of programmed instruction but not the substance. Textbook materials subdivided into sentences with blanks do not shape verbal behaviors. The disillusionment of educators with these poorly developed programs and the clumsiness of the original teaching machines contributed to the rapid decline of the programmed instruction movement. Also, the token-economy programs developed for behavioral management in the classroom often focused on trivial behaviors, contributing to the view that the methodology has only limited applications.

A commercial program developed in the 1960s to teach reading, DISTAR, continues to be successful with at-risk children. Now known as SRA Reading Mastery, the program is a highly structured, scripted program in which children are taught according to skill level (Foorman et al., 1998).

Classroom Issues

B. F. Skinner's approach to learning is in terms of the factors responsible for behavioral change. Therefore, the issues of importance to education are discussed either as behaviors or as stimuli that lead to behavioral change.

Learner Characteristics

In the Skinnerian framework, learner characteristics are particular behaviors that students bring to the learning situation, and they may influence the acquisition of new behaviors.

Individual Differences.   According to Skinner (1953), individual differences in student behaviors result from (1) the organism's genetic endowment and (2) a particular history of reinforcement. The behavior of mentally retarded individuals, for example, is primarily the product of a defective genetic endowment. However, planned programs can develop new skills (Skinner, 1968b).

In Skinner's view (1968b), defective reinforcement contingencies in the individual's experience result in the failure to acquire a variety of skilled behaviors. An example is rhythm (Skinner, 1958). Some individuals, such as skilled typists and musicians, are under the influence of reinforcers that generate subtle timing. However, the development of this and other skills that influence career choices, artistic interests, and participation in sports is typically unplanned. Yet, important skills that presently contribute to such individual differences can be taught. A simple machine can teach a child first to tap in unison and then to echo more and more subtle rhythmic patterns that constitute a sense of rhythm.

Mechanical devices that present instruction (Skinner, 1968b) can both provide the necessary individual reinforcement and correct the problems caused by multitrack systems and ungraded classes. In these situations, large groups of students move forward at the same speed and are required to meet the same criteria, usually those of the mediocre or average student. However, no teacher can teach 30 to 40 students at one time and allow each one to progress at an optimal speed (Skinner, 1987, p. 124). In contrast, new technologies such as microcomputers can accommodate different entry skills and also may present self-paced instruction.

Readiness for Learning.   In the operant conditioning framework, "readiness" is the behavioral repertoire that the student brings to the learning situation.

Deficiencies in particular entry skills may be corrected through the use of carefully designed programs.

The concept of readiness interpreted as age or maturational level is unacceptable in the Skinnerian concept of designing instruction. Chronological age is of little help in determining the presence or absence of important skills (Skinner, 1953, p. 156). Also, developmental studies may indicate the amount usually learned by a child of a given age; however, such studies do not indicate the extent of a child's intellectual development under an appropriate schedule of events (Homme, deBaca, Cottingham, & Homme, 1968). For example, once a child can discriminatively respond to objects, planned contingency management can advance the child's reading levels in a systematic way independent of age.

Motivation.   Behaviors that illustrate interest, enthusiasm, appreciation, or dedication are included in descriptions of motivation. The diligent and eager student, the individual who enjoys "reading good books," and the scientist who works long hours in the laboratory are all said to be motivated (Skinner, 1968b).

Such sustained activity in the absence of observable reinforcement is the result of a particular history of reinforcement. It is not the result of natural contingencies. No child really learns to plant seeds because he or she is reinforced by the resulting harvest, nor do we learn to read because we enjoy interesting books (Skinner, 1968b, p. 154). Such long-range natural contingencies are insufficient to develop and maintain "dedicated" behavior. Instead, dedication is the result of exposure to a gradually increasing variable-ratio schedule of reinforcements. The individual first receives an immediate payoff for engaging in the activity (Skinner, 1968b). Then the reinforcements are gradually extended (referred to as stretching the ratio) until the activity itself acquires secondary reinforcing power. Ironically, the same reinforcement schedule produces both the compulsive gambler and the dedicated scientist (i.e., a variable-ratio schedule). However, only the scientist is considered by society to be "dedicated" (Skinner, 1963b).

Cognitive Processes and Instruction

Internal or mental events are included in the operant conditioning paradigm only to the extent that they can be translated into identified behaviors. Therefore, transfer of learning is excluded from Skinner's formulations, but learning "how-to-learn" skills and problem solving, defined behaviorally, are included.

Transfer of Learning.   Thorndike and Woodworth's (1901) experiments explained students' performance on learning tasks as caused in part by the degree of similarity between those tasks and prior learning tasks. Therefore, training in particular skills, such as playing the piano, is said to improve performance in playing other instruments. According to Skinner (1953), however, transfer merely appears to strengthen behavior without reinforcing it directly. Many responses, in fact, possess common elements, such as the use of the same musculature. Skill in manipulating tools and instruments, for example, may be a part of a number of different responses. "Transfer," then, is simply the reinforcement of "common elements wherever they occur" (Skinner, 1953, p. 94).

Learning "How-to-Learn" Skills.   According to Skinner (1953, 1968b), the process commonly referred to as "thinking" often means behaving in a particular way with regard to certain stimuli. When a child responds to certain stimulus properties, the child's response has come under the control of those stimuli. An example is a child's identification of a closed, three-sided plane figure as a triangle. The child's identification is under the control of the figure. Little is gained in such situations by describing the learning as that of "forming an abstraction."

Certain activities typically identified with thinking, however, should be analyzed and taught (Skinner, 1968b). Such behaviors are called precurrent responses because they either change the environment or change the learner so that an effective response becomes possible. Thus, precurrent responses are defined as "behavior which affects behavior" (Skinner, 1966b, p. 216). Precurrent responses are covert; that is, they are private events that are not observable.

Also, they are the self-management behaviors that increase the probability of an effective response to a stimulus. Included are (1) reviewing the characteristics of a particular problem or calculating a mathematical answer by speaking silently to oneself and (2) visualizing a problem or situation in the "mind's eye" (i.e., covert seeing) (Skinner, 1968b).

Other self-management behaviors that are precurrent responses are (1) attending to stimuli, (2) underlining important ideas in textual material, (3) using mnemonic devices or other cues to remember important ideas, and (4) rearranging the elements in a problem situation so that a solution is more likely.

Teaching Problem Solving.   In the true "problem situation," the subject has no response immediately available that will reduce the deprivation or remove the aversive stimulus (Skinner, 1953, p. 246). If the room is too warm, for example, a problem exists if we cannot open the window (Skinner, 1968b). The problem is solved when we change the situation so that either the available response can occur or the deprivation or aversive stimulation is reduced in some other way. We find either some way to get the window open or some other means to cool the room (Skinner, 1968b).

Formally defined, problem solving is "any behavior which, through the manipulation of variables, makes the appearance of a solution more probable" (Skinner, 1953, p. 247). The "difficulty" of a problem depends on the availability of a response in the subject's repertoire that solves the problem. If no response is immediately available, the problem is difficult. To maximize the likelihood of a response (solution), the individual must change the situation so that he or she can respond appropriately. Steps that may be taken include (1) reviewing the problem carefully and clarifying the problem, (2) rearranging or regrouping the components of the problem, and (3) searching for similarities between the problem and others that have been solved. In anagrams, for example, the player maximizes the chances of forming a word from the set of letters by regrouping the letters in logical sequences (i.e., vowels separated by consonants).

Individuals learn to solve problems effectively by manipulating stimuli and receiving reinforcement for the behavior. Reinforcement for the effective manipulation of the problem situation will reduce the occurrence of haphazard or trial-and-error responses to problems.

The Social Context for Learning

Reinforcers that require the mediation of another person are referred to as *social reinforcers*. This group includes the positive reinforcers of attention, approval, and affection (typically, positive reinforcers) and the negative reinforcers of disapproval, insult, contempt, and ridicule (typically, negative reinforcers).

Social reinforcers, both positive and negative, have been used in group settings for the modification and maintenance of behavior. However, the relationships between stimuli, responses, and reinforcers in a social setting are both dynamic and reciprocal. For example, two children alone in a room with few toys provide an ideal situation for the shaping of selfish behavior (Skinner, 1958).

Behavior in the classroom is also a product of ongoing and complex contingencies that include teacher and students reinforcing each other both positively and negatively (Skinner, 1968a, p. 252). If a student is not punished by his or her peers for answering the teacher's questions and is reinforced by the teacher, he or she will answer as often as possible. If the teacher calls only on students whose hands are raised, the student will raise his or her hand. Similarly, teachers who are reinforced by right answers will call on students whose hands are raised. However, teachers who are reinforced by wrong answers are exercising aversive control, and they typically call on students who do not raise their hands (Skinner, 1968a).

Therefore, designing a classroom environment to modify behavior must take into account the reciprocal reinforcement characteristics of a social setting. Brigham (1978, p. 266) describes one study in which special education children were taught to reinforce the positive comments of other children and teachers. As their behavior changed, so did the environment, and they became skillful at manipulating the environment. Furthermore, the children's behaviors changed the teacher's environment as well because the children became the source of social reinforcement for their teachers.

Relationships to Other Perspectives

Unlike cognitive approaches to learning, operant conditioning addresses behavior rather than knowledge or internal states. That is, evidence of learning is behavioral change. Moreover, student actions such as contributing verbally to classroom discourse (constructivism), manipulating objects (Piagetian theory), or observing the reinforcement received by others (Bandura's social-cognitive theory) are not indicators of learning unless they are new behaviors.

The application of operant conditioning to the priorities of other theoretical perspectives lies in the implementation of reinforcement to develop complex behaviors. Examples include reinforcing children's explanations of their problem-solving steps and listening respectively to the strategies of others (radical constructivism and cognitive theory), developing persistence in academic tasks (Weiner's attribution theory) and monitoring one's own learning (cognitive theory). Further, reciprocal teaching makes use of reinforcing successive approximations and the gradual fading of cues for student responses.

Operant conditioning would not support presenting open-ended problems or tasks to groups of children in the absence of prior teaching of required behaviors. This practice is conducive to trial-and-error learning, does not ensure the acquisition of essential behaviors, and can precipitate the learning of incorrect responses. Further, not all children in the group situation may receive reinforcement for appropriate responses.

Developing a Classroom Strategy

The classroom teacher can make use of Skinner's technology in two ways. One is the appropriate use of reinforcement in classroom interactions, and the other is the development of individualized instructional materials.

Developing a Positive Classroom Climate (appropriate use of ®)

An important application of Skinner's technology is that of developing a positive classroom climate. This goal differs from that of implementing an extensive behavior modification program. Skinner (1973) noted that an obvious approach, such as a token economy, may indeed be necessary in a totally disruptive classroom. However, a teacher can make the transition from punishment to positive reinforcement with one simple change—merely by responding to student successes rather than to student failures (Skinner, 1973, p. 15). Instead of pointing out what students are doing wrong, point out what they are doing right. The result, in Skinner's view, will be an improved classroom atmosphere and more efficient instruction.

Applying the technology developed by Skinner in the classroom can make use of the following steps:

Step 1: Analyze the current classroom environment.

    1.1 What are the positive student behaviors currently receiving reinforcement in the classroom? What are the undesirable behaviors that are receiving reinforcement? For example, withholding help so that the child has an opportunity to demonstrate his or her knowledge and then providing help when the child shows discouragement may be reinforcing behavior that indicates discouragement (Skinner, 1968b, p. 252).

    1.2 For which behaviors is punishment currently dispensed in the classroom? (Recall Skinner's definition of punishment: removal of a positive reinforcer or introduction of an aversive stimulus from which the individual seeks escape.)

    1.3 What is the frequency of punishment? Have the punished behaviors been suppressed but other, related behaviors appeared?

Step 2: Develop a list of potential positive reinforcers.

    2.1 What are the students' preferred activities? (Students can rank their preferences on a list; young children can identify pictures.)

    2.2 Which of the punished behaviors identified in step 1.2 may be used as reinforcers? For example, if talking with peers currently is punished, consider incorporating it occasionally as a reinforcer for less-preferred activities, such as completing seatwork assignments quietly.

    2.3 Which activities that you have observed in the natural setting may serve as positive reinforcers for other behaviors? One reading teacher, for example, expressed difficulty in keeping children on task because they constantly interrupted to discuss the progress of their favorite TV shows that aired the previous evening. Discussing the TV programs for 10 to 15 minutes is a potential reinforcer in that setting.

Step 3: Select the behavioral sequences to be initially implemented in the classroom. Include discriminative stimuli and reinforcers.

    3.1 Which of the punished behaviors identified in step 1.2 may be restructured in the form of positive behaviors? For example, use positive reinforcement for promptness instead of punishment for tardiness. Becker (1973) suggested that instead of punishment for fighting, a student may earn 1 minute of recess for no fighting.

    3.2 Which of the positive student behaviors from the list in step 1.1 are occurring infrequently? Examples may include demonstrating independence in learning by getting and putting away needed materials on time, attending to relevant characteristics of stimuli during instruction, and so on.

    3.3 What are the initial discriminative stimuli to be used? To which stimuli is the transfer of behavioral control to be made? For example, the verbal statement "Time to begin" may be replaced by a signal, such as a bell, and then by the students' observations of the clock time.

Step 4: Implement the behavioral sequences, maintaining anecdotal records and making changes when necessary.

    4.1 Are the rules for classroom behavior clear and consistent?

    4.2 Is the method for earning reinforcement clear, and is reinforcement provided for improved behavior?

    4.3 Does every child have the opportunity to earn reinforcement for behavioral change? If reinforcement is provided only for one or two behaviors that must meet a high standard, some children have no means of earning reinforcement in the classroom and are likely to seek attention in disruptive ways (Resnick, 1971).

    4.4 Following initial behavioral change, are reinforcements provided after longer intervals (stretching the ratio), and are other reinforcers also implemented?

Programming Instruction

Programs to develop verbal behaviors should be designed to lead the student from a state of no knowledge to proficiency in one or more skills. The following steps are recommended in the development of a Skinnerian or constructed-response program:

Step 1: Identify the terminal skill to be acquired and analyze the subject matter to be learned.

    1.1 What is the nature of the terminal behavior? Is it a discrimination skill, such as learning color names, or is it the application of a rule, such as carrying in addition?

    1.2 What terms or definitions must be learned to acquire the skill?

    1.3 What types of examples should the student respond to during learning (e.g., color bands, simple and complex addition problems)?

Step 2: Develop the initial sequence of frames and response confirmations.

    2.1 What information should be placed in the first frame to induce a response (referred to as a *copying frame*)?

    2.2 What is a logical sequence of responses (behaviors) that can be expected of the student?

    2.3 What sequence of discriminative stimuli that progress from simple to complex can provide for the transfer of stimulus control?

Step 3: Review the sequence of frames, reordering if necessary.

    3.1 Does the sequence progress from simple to complex?

    3.2 Are the prompts gradually vanished in the sequence?

    3.3 Does the student respond to meaningful rather than trivial content?

Step 4: Implement the instruction with a few students and revise if necessary.

    4.1 Do any students experience difficulty with any of the frames? Such frames may need to be rewritten.

    4.2 Do the students race through any of the frames, getting the right answer by only reading part of the frame? The frame may be superfluous or it may be asking for trivial information.

    4.3 Does the program lead to mastery performance on the criterion posttest?

Classroom Example

The frames on the following pages were developed to teach the concept "morpheme" to advanced high school students or college freshmen. The terminal skills are that (1) the student can define *morpheme* and (2) the student can identify examples of free morphemes and bound morphemes.

Discussion of Classroom Example

Skinner originally developed programmed instruction for mechanical devices known as teaching machines. However, Skinner (in Green, 1984) recommended that microcomputers be utilized to present the instruction. A partial program for teaching the student to discriminate morphemes is illustrated in Figure 6.2. The style of programming is referred to as *constructed response* because the student writes or constructs the answer. After a brief introduction to the lesson on morphemes (including lesson objectives), the next screen and the computer feedback is programmed as follows:

> **One aspect of linguistics is the analysis of words into the smallest units that carry meaning. The study of such word parts is an area of study in l_____.**

Computer feedback for correct answer: The correct answer is linguistics. Good. Continue with the program. When you enter the correct answer, the program will display it on the screen. For a wrong answer, you will be asked to try again.

Computer feedback for wrong answer: Sorry your answer is not correct. Try the question again.

The first frame is referred to as a copying frame because essentially it involves the student's copying or repeating basic information in the stimulus. Each frame includes one item of information to which the student responds. The cues, or prompts, for the correct answers are gradually withdrawn so that stimuli within the learner or other textual stimuli are generating appropriate responses (see frame 15).

Care should be taken in the design of programmed instruction to lead the students from no knowledge to skill proficiency. Notice the examples in the unit on morphemes shown in Figure 6.2. Frames 2 and 3 present the definition, later followed by the definition of bound and free morphemes.

The advantage of several short units of programmed instruction on specific skills is twofold. Remediation is provided that is targeted to specific deficiencies. Often students are unable to participate in ongoing instruction because they lack a particular skill. Continuation of the deficiency, however, only compounds the problem. In this example, students will be unable to analyze complex word meanings unless they first are able to differentiate commonly used morphemes.

The second advantage is that such materials can assist the teacher in individualizing instruction. Students who enter a grade lacking some essential skills or students who experience difficulty with the initial instruction for a topic may be given the material while the teacher works with other students on other problems.

1. One aspect of linguistics is the analysis of words into the smallest units that carry meaning. The study of such word parts is an area of study in l_____. (linguistics)

2. The smallest word parts that carry meaning are *morphemes.* In the word "unhappy," the part "un-" means "not." Therefore, "un-" is a m_____. (morpheme)

3. Some words are composed of only one morpheme or unit of meaning. An example is *cat.* In this case, the morpheme making up the word is ___. (cat)

4. Sometimes morphemes may be added to existing words, for example, the letter "s." When added to some words, "s" means "more than one." In such a situation, the "s" is a _____. (morpheme)

5. Of course, some letters do not carry any meaning in words, such as the "s" in "slide." In this case, "s" is ___ a morpheme. (not)

6. Some words are composed of two or more morphemes. An example is "biology," which includes "bio-" (life) and "-logy" (study of). Biology, therefore, is composed of _____ _____. (two morphemes)

7. The word "morpheme" itself may be analyzed as follows: "Morph-" = unit or form and "-eme" = "small." The complete word is composed of ____ _____. (two morphemes)

8. Prefixes and suffixes are word parts that frequently function as units of meaning. An example is "pre-" (before or prior) as in "preview." In this example, the prefix is also a _____. (morpheme)

9. In the earlier example, "un-" in "unhappy" was identified as a morpheme. This prefix is a morpheme because it is a u___ __ _____. (unit of meaning)

10. Language includes two kinds of morphemes, one of which is "free morphemes." They are the smallest unit of meaning that can stand alone. For example, in the word "cats," the word part "cat" is a ____ _____. (free morpheme)

11. Some words are composed only of free morphemes. The word "cowboy" is composed of two free morphemes. They are ___ and ___. (cow, boy)

12. The other type of morpheme is a "bound morpheme." It is a unit of meaning that cannot stand alone. For example, the morpheme "s" in the word "cats" is a _____ _____. (bound morpheme)

13. The letter "s" in the word "cats" is a bound morpheme because it is a unit of meaning that can/cannot stand alone. (cannot)

14. Some words may be composed of only bound morphemes. An example is the word "biology," composed of "bio-" and "-logy." This word includes two _____. (bound morphemes)

15. Still other words, like "cats," may be composed of both bound and free morphemes. Another example is the word "unhappy," which includes _____ free morpheme(s) and _____ bound morpheme(s). (one, one)

16. The study of morphemes can be a means for building vocabulary. We have learned, for example, that "-logy" means "study of." Further, "psycho-" is a morpheme that means mind or mental life. Therefore, "psychology" means "study of the mind or mental life," based on the two _____ _____. (bound morphemes)

Figure 6.2
Introductory frames on morphemes
Source: Terry L. Norton, Winthrop College

Review of the Theory

B. F. Skinner's principles of operant conditioning continued the tradition established by John Watson. That is, for psychology to become a science, the study of behavior must become the focus of psychological research. Unlike the other S–R theorists, Skinner avoided the contradiction posed by Pavlov's classical conditioning model and Thorndike's instrumental conditioning. He proposed a paradigm that includes both types of responses and analyzed the conditions responsible for emitted responses or operant behavior (Table 6.3).

Skinner's analyses yielded a parsimonious system that was applied to the dynamics of behavioral change in both the laboratory and the classroom. Learning, represented by increased response rate, was described as a function of the three-component sequence $(S^D)–(R)–(S^{reinf})$. Skinner described the typical practice of placing experimental animals in puzzle boxes and mazes as that of placing the subject in a "terminal contingency"; that is, the animal must either sink or swim in the search for escape or food. Instead, the appropriate procedure is to shape the animal's behavior through carefully established stimulus-response-reinforcement sequences. Approximations to appropriate responses are reinforced

TABLE 6.3
Summary of Skinner's Technology

Basic Elements	Definition
Assumptions	Behavioral change is a function of environmental conditions and events.
Learning	A change in behavior represented by increased response frequency
Learning outcomes	New responses (behaviors)
Components of learning	$(S^D)–(R)–(S^{reinf.})$
Designing instruction for complex learning	Design sequences of stimuli–responses–reinforcements to develop sets of complex responses.
Major issues in designing instruction	Transfer of stimulus control, timing of reinforcement, avoidance of punishment
Analysis of the Technology	
Disadvantages	1. Technology for complex situations is incomplete; successful analysis depends on the skill of the technologist. 2. Response frequency is difficult to apply to complex behaviors as a measure of probability.
Contributions to classroom practice	1. Analysis of states such as "readiness" and "motivation" 2. Analysis of aversive classroom practices and interactive classroom situations 3. Individualized learning materials: teaching machines, microcomputers

on intermittent schedules until the behavioral repertoire is acquired, such as pigeons playing ping-pong.

In the classroom, Skinner cited the practice of "assign-and-test" as one example of placing the human learner in a terminal contingency. Instead, Skinner recommended the practice of reinforcing the component behaviors, such as attending to stimuli and executing appropriate study behaviors. Punishment should be avoided because it produces unwanted emotional side effects and does not generate the desired positive behaviors.

Included in Skinner's analyses are the role of conditioned and natural reinforcers, positive and negative reinforcers, and generalized reinforcers. Also included is the development of programmed learning for verbal behaviors. Individual differences in entry skills and rates of learning may be accommodated by such materials.

Disadvantages

Two major problems in the application of Skinner's recommendations may be identified. One is that the technology for the experimental analysis of complex human behaviors is incomplete. Some students respond well in highly structured situations in which objectives and the steps to be taken are clearly specified. Others, however, are reinforced by the opportunity to explore on their own and to relate ideas without external directives. The procedures for identifying these and other differences in the variety of potential reinforcements is yet to be developed.

Second, in the classroom, response frequency as a measure of learning may be applied to simple behaviors, such as naming colors or adding two-digit numbers. Complex behaviors, however, such as diagnosing an illness or calculating one's taxes, are not conducive to response frequency as a measure of learning.

Contributions to Classroom Practice

Three major contributions to educational practice are illustrated in Table 6.3. First, the search for conditions and behaviors that represent states such as "unmotivated" is an important step in the identification of an appropriate course of action. Second, observations of contemporary classrooms reveal many inconsistent and noncontingent uses of reinforcement that contribute to classroom discipline problems. An analysis of these interactive situations in terms of discriminative stimuli, responses, and reinforcements is an important step in correcting the problems. Third, programmed learning materials, if properly designed, can provide for individual differences in the classroom.

CHAPTER QUESTIONS

1. Skinner (1989b) stated that governments make use of aversive situations both as punishment and as negative reinforcers. His examples are having to pay a fine for parking in a "no parking" zone and the directive "Pay your taxes and avoid a fine." Identify the type of consequence in each example.

2. Which reinforcement concept is most likely to explain a person's involvement with the Sunday crossword puzzle?

3. Good and Power (1976) have identified five types of students in the classroom. Three are briefly described on the following page. Name some potential reinforcers that may be effective for each type.

_____ a. *successful*—does not require structure or praise from the teacher

_____ b. *social*—is more person-oriented than task-oriented

_____ c. *dependent*—seeks teacher structure and teacher support

4. For the dependent student, which behaviors should the teacher seek to reinforce? What problems should be avoided in the use of reinforcement with this type of student?

5. One of the concerns about Internet use is that of individuals spending hours and days in computer chat rooms to the exclusion of eating and sleeping regularly and no engagement in face-to-face interactions. Which concept in operant conditioning describes this phenomenon?

REFERENCES

Azar, B. (1998). Research-based games enhance children's learning. *APA Monitor, 29*(8), 18, 20.

Becker, W. D. (1973). Application of behavior principles in typical classrooms. In C. E. Thoresen (Ed.), *Behavior modification in education: The seventy-second yearbook of the National Society for the Study of Education, Part I* (pp. 77–106). Chicago: University of Chicago Press.

Belfiore, P. J., & Hornyak, R. S. (1998). Operant theory and application to self-monitoring in adolescents. In D. Schunk & B. J. Zimmerman (Eds.), *Self-regulated learning: From teaching to self-reflective practice* (pp. 184–202). New York: The Guilford Press.

Brigham, T. A. (1978). Self-control: Part II. In A. C. Catania & T. A. Brigham (Eds.), *Handbook of applied behavioral analysis* (pp. 259–274). New York: Irvington.

Brophy, J. (1981). Teacher praise: A functional analysis. *Review of Educational Research, 51,* 5–32.

Brown, A. L. (1994). The advancement of learning. *Educational Researcher, 23*(4), 4–11.

Cameron, J., & Pierce, W. D. (1994a). Reinforcement, reward, and intrinsic motivation: A meta-analysis. *Review of Educational Research, 64,* 363–423.

Cameron, J., & Pierce, W. D. (1994b). Reinforcement, reward, and intrinsic motivation: The myth continues. *The Behavior Analyst, 24,* 1–44.

Deci, E. L., & Ryan, R. M. (1990). A motivational approach to self: Integration in personality. In D. Diensthier (Ed.), *Nebraska Symposium on Motivation* (pp. 237–288). Lincoln, NE: University of Nebraska Press.

Doyle, W. (1986). Classroom organization and management. In M. C. Wittrock (Ed.), *Handbook of research on teaching* (3rd ed., pp. 392–431). Upper Saddle River, NJ: Merrill/Prentice Hall.

Emmer, E., Evertson, C., & Anderson, L. (1980). Effective classroom management at the beginning of the school year. *The Elementary School Journal, 80*(5), 219–231.

Emmer, E. T., Evertson, C. M., Sanford, J. P., Clements, B. S., Worsham, M. E. (1984). *Classroom management for secondary teachers.* Englewood Cliffs, NJ: Prentice Hall.

Ferster, C. B., & Skinner, B. F. (1957). *Schedules of reinforcement.* New York: Appleton-Century-Crofts.

Foorman, B. R., Francis, D. J., Fletcher, J. M., Schatschneider, C., & Mehta, P. (1998). The role of instruction in learning to read: Preventing reading failure in at-risk children. *Journal of Educational Psychology, 90*(1), 37–55.

Gallant, J., Sargeant, M., & Van Houten, R. (1980). Teacher-determined and self-determined access to science activities as a reinforcer for task completion in other curriculum areas. *Education and Treatment of Children, 3*(2), 101–111.

Glaser, R. (1990). The reemergence of learning theory within instructional research. *American Psychologist, 45*(1), 29–39.

Good, T., & Power, C. (1976). Designing successful classroom environments for different types of students. *Journal of Curriculum Studies, 8,* 1–16.

Gottfredson, D. C., Gottfredson, G. D., & Hybl, L. G. (1993). Managing adolescent behavior: A multiyear, multischool study. *American Educational Research Journal, 30*(1), 179–215.

Homme, L. E., deBaca, R., Cottingham, L., & Homme, A. (1968). What behavioral engineering is. *The Psychological Record, 18,* 424–434.

Horner, R. H., & Suqai, G. (2004). School-wide positive behavior support: An alternative approach to discipline in schools. In L. Bambara & L. Korn (Eds.), *Positive behavior support.* New York: Guilford.

Kazdin, A. (1989). *Behavior modification in applied settings* (4th ed.). Pacific Grove, CA: Brooks/Cole.

Kratochwill, T., & Bijou, S. (1987). The impact of behaviorism on educational psychology. In J. Glover & R. Ronning (Eds.), *Historical foundations of educational psychology* (pp. 131–157). New York: Plenum.

Lepper, M. R., & Greene, D. (1973). Undermining children's intrinsic interest with extrinsic reward: A test of the "overjustification" hypothesis. *Journal of Personality and Social Psychology, 28*(1), 129–137.

Lepper, M. R., & Greene, D. (1974). Effects of extrinsic rewards on children's subsequent intrinsic interest. *Child Development, 45*(4), 1141–1145.

Moreno, R., & Hovell, M. (1980). Teaching survival English skills and assessment of collateral behavior. *Behavior Modification, 6*(3), 375–388.

Premack, D. (1959). Toward empirical behavior laws. I. Positive reinforcement. *Psychological Review, 66*(4), 219–233.

Resnick, L. (1971). Applying applied reinforcement. In R. Glaser (Ed.), *The nature of reinforcement* (pp. 326–333). New York: Academic Press.

Skinner, B. F. (1935). Two types of conditioned reflex and a pseudotype. *Journal of General Psychology, 12,* 66–77.

Skinner, B. F. (1938). *The behavior of organisms.* New York: Appleton-Century-Crofts.

Skinner, B. F. (1948). "Superstition" in the pigeon. *Journal of Experimental Psychology, 38,* 168–172.

Skinner, B. F. (1950). Are theories of learning necessary? *Psychological Review, 57,* 193–216.

Skinner, B. F. (1953). *Science and human behavior.* New York: Macmillan.

Skinner, B. F. (1954). The science of learning and the art of teaching. *Harvard Educational Review, 24*(2), 86–97.

Skinner, B. F. (1958). Reinforcement today. *American Psychologist, 13,* 94–99.

Skinner, B. F. (1961). Why we need teaching machines. *Harvard Educational Review, 31*(4), 377–398.

Skinner, B. F. (1963a). Behaviorism at fifty. *Science, 140,* 951–958.

Skinner, B. F. (1963b). Operant behavior. *American Psychologist, 18,* 503–515.

Skinner, B. F. (1966a). Contingencies of reinforcement in the design of a culture. *Behavioral Science, 11,* 159–166.

Skinner, B. F. (1966b). What is the experimental analysis of behavior? *Journal of the Experimental Analysis of Behavior, 9*(3), 213–218.

Skinner, B. F. (1968a). Teaching science in high school—What is wrong? *Science, 159,* 704–710.

Skinner, B. F. (1968b). *The technology of teaching.* New York: Appleton-Century-Crofts.

Skinner, B. F. (1969). *Contingencies of reinforcement.* New York: Appleton-Century-Crofts.

Skinner, B. F. (1973). The free and happy student. *Phi Delta Kappan, 55,* 13–16.

Skinner, B. F. (1981). Selection by consequence. *Science, 213,* 501–504.

Skinner, B. F. (1984, February). In J. O. Green, Skinner's technology of teaching. *Classroom Computer Learning,* pp. 23–29.

Skinner, B. F. (1986). Programmed instruction revisited. *Phi Delta Kappan,* 103–110.

Skinner, B. F. (1987). *Upon further reflection.* Upper Saddle River, NJ: Merrill/Prentice Hall.

Skinner, B. F. (1989a). The origins of cognitive thought. *American Psychologist, 44*(1), 13–18.

Skinner, B. F. (1989b). *Recent issues in the analysis of behavior.* Upper Saddle River, NJ: Merrill/Prentice Hall.

Skinner, B. F., & Vaughan, M. (1983). *Enjoy old age.* New York: Norton.

Suqai, G., & Horner, R. H. (2002). The evolution of discipline practices: School-wide positive behavior supports. *Child and Family Behavior Therapy, 24,* 23–50.

Thorndike, E. L., & Woodworth, R. S. (1901). The influence of improvement in one mental function upon the efficiency of other functions: I, II, and III. *Psychological Review, 8,* 247–261, 384–395, 553–564.

Vargas, J. S. (1986). Instructional design flaws in computer-assisted instruction. *Phi Delta Kappan, 64,* 738–744.

Vaughan, M. (1987). Rule-governed behavior and higher mental processes. In S. Modgil & C. Modgil (Eds.), *B. F. Skinner: Consensus and controversy* (pp. 257–264). New York: Falmer.

Watson, J. B. (1913). Psychology as the behaviorist sees it. *Psychological Bulletin, 20,* 158–177.

CHAPTER 7
Robert Gagné's Conditions of Learning

Human skills, appreciations, and reasonings in all their great variety, as well as human hopes, aspirations, attitudes, and values, are generally recognized to depend for their development largely on the events called learning. (Gagné, 1985, p. 1)

Robert Gagné's conditions of learning shifted the focus in theory development from the laboratory to the classroom. Beginning with the training needs of the armed forces in World War II, he addressed the question, What are the conditions essential to developing expertise in real-world tasks?

Assigned to the Aviation Psychology Program, Gagné worked to develop realistic analyses of a broad class of human skills, including those of radar operators, pilots, and bombardiers. Later tasks, which were part of the weapons system planning of the air force, included analyzing man-machine systems and forecasting training requirements for weapons systems yet to be built (Gagné, 1987b, 1989).

Three principles of instruction identified by Gagné in the analysis of training tasks were (1) providing instruction on the set of component tasks that build toward the final task, (2) ensuring that each component task is mastered, and (3) sequencing the component tasks to ensure optimal transfer to the final task (Gagné, 1962a, 1962b).

Convinced that the analysis procedures that were successful for the armed forces also were applicable to school learning, Gagné began to analyze problem solving in mathematics. Incidental observations of students indicated that the lack of success experienced by some students was the result of apparent gaps in their knowledge of procedures, such as simplifying fractions (Gagné, 1987b, p. 398). Identification of subcomponents of the final task led to the concept of a **learning hierarchy**, or a progression of prerequisite skills (Gagné, 1968a, 1968b). Various research technologies applied in the verification of learning hierarchies (see Airasian & Bart, 1975; White, 1974), indicate that properly identified prerequisite skills contribute to the learning of more complex capabilities.

Continued research in classrooms and other educational settings on the question, What kinds of things are learned in school? led to several developments. Included are the identification of five distinct domains or varieties of learned capabilities, the internal states and information-processing steps required for learning in each domain, and the supporting requirements for instruction. Included in the guidelines for designing instruction are media selection guidelines.

Gagné's concepts of analyzing tasks into component tasks and identifying needed prerequisite skills became the core design components of instructional programs in a variety of areas (see, e.g., Griffin, Case & Siegler, 1994; Jonassen, Tessmer, & Hannum, 1999). In addition, Gagné's principles of systems design are found in a framework that combines instructional design with research (see Bannon-Ritland, 2003).

PRINCIPLES OF LEARNING

The key to the development of a comprehensive learning theory, according to Gagné (1974a, 1977a), is to identify the factors that account for the complex nature of human learning. This view contrasts with earlier approaches that typically began with an explanation of the learning process based on laboratory research and then attempted to fit the conclusions to human learning. Instead, the principles developed by Gagné are derived from the analysis of the variety of performances and skills executed by human beings.

Basic Assumptions

The basic assumptions of Gagné's theory address the unique characteristics of human learning and the diversity of learning.

The Nature of Human Learning

Several elements are included in Gagné's conception of learning. Key factors are the relationship of learning to development, and the cumulative nature of learning.

A major task for psychologists interested in learning is that of separating the changes that result from learning from those that result from maturation or growth. According to the growth-readiness model (often referred to as the Gesellian model), certain growth patterns must occur before learning can be beneficial. This model maintains that body growth is closely related to mental growth. One suggestion, for example, is that the acquisition of permanent teeth is an indicator of the appropriate developmental age to begin reading instruction (see Gredler, 1992, for a review).

In contrast, the model described by Gagné assigns a primary role to learning. According to Gagné (1968a), learning is an important causal factor in the individual's development. Within the broad parameters established by growth, "behavioral development results from the cumulative effects of learning" (Gagné, 1968a, p. 178).

Two characteristics of learning account for its importance in development. One is that human learning is not simply acquiring isolated bits of information. Instead, much of human learning generalizes to a variety of situations. Addition, for example, applies to situations such as computing wages and deductions, constructing a family budget, calculating taxes, and many others.

The other important contribution of learning to development is that complex skills that are learned build on prior learning. In other words, human learning is *cumulative*. Again, addition serves as an example. The skill of adding numbers contributes to the learning of long division. The child does not need to learn to add all over again when learning to divide. Instead, addition merely is incorporated into the new skill.

In summary, intellectual development "may be conceived as the building of increasingly complex and interesting structures of learned capabilities" (Gagné, 1968a, p. 190). These learned capabilities contribute to the learning of more complex skills, and they also generalize to other situations. The result is that an ever-increasing intellectual competence is generated.

The Diversity of Learning

According to Gagné, prior theories presented limited views of the nature of human learning. For the most part, the ideas presented by the early theories are tied to specific situations, such as dogs salivating at the sight of food or people recalling words or syllables that have been paired with other words (Gagné, 1984, p. 388).

One group of theories includes those derived from laboratory studies of learning; examples are the theories of Pavlov, Thorndike, Hull, and Skinner. However, these models do not account for the human capacity to learn complex skills and abilities, according to Gagné (1977a). Some of them do describe the subcomponents of human learning, but these subskills are not the major objectives of learning. Examples are signal learning (Pavlov's model), S–R associations, and chainlike skills. Signal learning involves feelings of well-being generated by a favorite stuffed toy or a favorite melody. Chainlike skills include buttoning, fastening, printing, and writing, and verbal sequences, such as the "Pledge of Allegiance."

Although the S–R model has been used to characterize human learning, Gagné (1977a) observes that "pure" examples of S–R learning are difficult to find. Such learnings rapidly are incorporated into longer sequences. Letters of the alphabet, for example, soon become a part of decoding words.

Like the S–R model, the "insight" experience identified by Gestalt psychologists also attempted to explain the "true" nature of learning. However, although Gestalt theorists maintained that learning occurs when a subject "sees" a new relationship, the process of insight is not a spontaneous occurrence (Gagné, 1977a). Instead, it is influenced by transfer from prior learnings to new situations. In the school setting, children may display insight when they are led to understand relationships. An example is the relationship between weight and the pull of gravity (Gagné, 1977a, p. 14). The major problem with the Gestalt explanation, however, is that it, too, does not explain all learning. For example, learning to speak a foreign language and learning to read are not the result of insight.

This analysis indicates that learning is not a single process (Gagné, 1970, 1972). Neither the learning of word associations nor the problem solving described by the Gestalt theorists can be reduced one to the other. The learning of associations cannot be explained by insight, nor can problem-solving behavior be explained by the pairing of stimulus elements (Gagné, 1977a). Therefore, no one set of characteristics can be applied to all learning.

Efforts to force-fit all learning into a single description are one error in the development of learning principles. Equally erroneous is the view that psychology should develop principles of specific subject-matter learning, such as principles of mathematics learning, science learning, and computer-repair learning (Gagné, 1984). Important general principles are overlooked unless one searches for the similarities in learning outcomes between reading and mathematics, for example, or between the procedures of office management and those of aircraft maintenance (Gagné, 1984, p. 333).

In addition, an adequate conception of human learning must not be restricted to the learning found only in the laboratory or the school. Instead, an adequate perspective should apply also to, for example, masons, carpenters, astronauts, politicians, housewives, and word-processing operators (Gagné, 1984, p. 378). Thus, the task is to identify principles of learning that generalize to the various situations and circumstances in which learning occurs.

A Definition of Learning

The human capacity for learning makes possible an almost infinite variety of behavioral patterns (Gagné, 1977a). Given this diversity, no one set of characteristics can account for such varied activities as learning to define a word, to write an essay, or to lace a shoe (Gagné, 1972, p. 2). Therefore, the task for learning theory is to identify a set of principles that accommodates both the complexity and the variety of human learning.

If human learning is indeed a complex, multifaceted process, how is it to be defined? First, learning is the mechanism by which an individual becomes a competently functioning member of society (Gagné, 1977a). The importance of learning is that it is responsible for all the skills, knowledge, attitudes, and values that are acquired by human beings. Learning, therefore, results in a variety of different kinds of behaviors, referred to by Gagné (1972, 1977a) as **capabilities**. They are the outcomes of learning.

Second, these capabilities are acquired by human beings from (1) the stimulation from the environment and (2) the cognitive processing undertaken by the learner. In other words, the learner is not passive. Formally defined, learning is the set of cognitive processes that transforms the stimulation from the environment into the several phases of information processing necessary for acquiring a new capability (Gagné & Briggs, 1979, p. 43).

Summary

The key to the development of a comprehensive learning theory, according to Gagné, is to account for the complex nature of human learning. First, unlike the growth-readiness model, in which maturation governs learning, Gagné maintains that learning is an important causal factor in development. Second, human learning is cumulative. That is, the learning of certain skills contributes to the learning of more complex skills. The result is an ever-increasing intellectual competence.

Third, human learning is both complex and diverse. That is, human learning cannot be reduced to either S–R associations or the insight experiences described by the Gestalt theorists. Instead, an adequate description of human learning must apply to, for example, masons, carpenters, astronauts, politicians, housewives, and word-processing operators. That is, the principles must generalize to the various situations and circumstances in which learning occurs. Learning, in other words, results in a variety of different behaviors, referred to as capabilities. Learning is the set of cognitive processes that transforms the stimulation from the environment into capabilities.

The Components of Learning

The essential components in a theory of learning, according to Gagné, must account for the diversity of human capabilities. In addition, theory must describe the processes by which the capabilities are acquired.

The Learning Framework

A major focus in Gagné's principles is the identification of categories or varieties of learning that reflect the range and complexity of human experience. According to Gagné (1984, p. 2), any set of categories that purports to describe human learning should meet at least four major criteria:

1. Each category should represent a formal and unique class of human performance that occurs through learning.
2. Each category should apply to a widely diverse set of human activities and be independent of intelligence, age, race, socioeconomic status, classroom, grade level, and so on.
3. Each category should require different instructional treatments, prerequisites, and processing requirements by the learner.
4. Factors identified as affecting the learning of each category should generalize to tasks *within* the category but not across categories (with the exception of reinforcement).

The five varieties of learning identified by Gagné meet the foregoing criteria. They are verbal information, intellectual skills, motor skills, attitudes, and cognitive strategies (Gagné, 1972, 1977a, 1985). Like the S–R associations and the insight experience, none of these categories may be reduced to the other. However, unlike associations and insight, they represent the range of human learning.

The five varieties represent the outcomes of learning. That is, they reflect the distinct types of skills or capabilities that individuals acquire as a result of learning. In addition, Gagné (1977a, 1985) has identified the internal states required in the learner to acquire the new skills. These states are referred to as the **internal conditions of learning**.

However, the conditions for acquiring new skills or capabilities are not all within the individual. Also important are the particular kinds of interactions between the learner and the external environment. Therefore, the third component in learning includes the types of environmental stimuli that are required to support the internal learning processes. These environmental supports are referred to as the **external conditions of learning**. (Gagné, 1974b, 1977a, 1985). They also are referred to as the events of instruction, and they are designed to support learning (Gagné 1977a, 1977b, 1985) (Figure 7.1). They are described further in the Principles of Instruction section. Discussed here are the five varieties of learning outcomes and the essential internal conditions for each category.

The Varieties of Learning

In the 1960s, attempts to identify instructional objectives led to an awareness that different classes of behaviors are acquired through learning. Efforts began with the identification of behavioral categories that consistently would indicate particular requirements for instruction (Gagné, 1965a, 1965b). However, accounting for the diversity of human learning in a systematic and comprehensive way is a difficult task. Some approaches attempted to reconcile laboratory learning descriptions and the behaviors taught in the classroom (Melton, 1964). For school subjects, Gagné (1972) noted that categories such as "cognitive learning," "rote learning," "discovery learning," and "concrete versus symbolic learning" often were used. The difficulty, however, is that these learning categories do not generalize to different settings. Examples may be classified as rote learning in one context and as conceptual in another (Gagné, 1972).

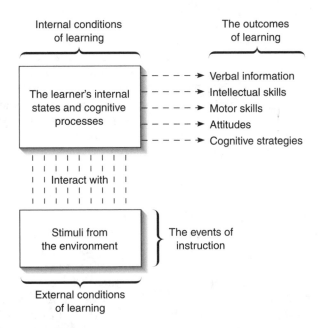

FIGURE 7.1
Essential components of learning and instruction

The five **varieties of learning** are summarized in Table 7.1. They are referred to as capabilities because they make possible the prediction of many instances of performance by the learner (Gagné & Briggs, 1979, p. 51). An individual who has acquired an intellectual skill, for example, can interact with the environment using symbols. Composing sentences, adding two-digit numbers, and identifying colors are all intellectual skills. In contrast, the student who has learned verbal information can restate or paraphrase definitions and major points in bodies of knowledge. Examples include stating the formula for salt and defining *fulcrum*. However, the capability of stating information does not in itself imply that the individual can apply the information in new ways. In other words, the capability of defining *fulcrum* does not imply that one can identify different examples of fulcrums or use them in any way.

Verbal Information.   The capability represented by this category is that of acquiring (1) labels and facts, (2) meaningfully connected selections of prose or poetry, and (3) organized bodies of knowledge. *Declarative knowledge* is another term that also may be used, implying the capability to "declare" or "state" something (Gagné, 1984, 1985). In learning labels, for example, a consistent verbal response or "name" is applied to an object or an object class, such as "rose" or "tiger."

When a fact has been learned, the response is an oral or written statement of the relationships between two or more objects or events. "Columbus discovered America in 1492" and "Rectangles have four sides" are examples. Recalling selections such as the salute to the flag or Hamlet's soliloquy are longer verbatim reinstatements of particular words and phrases than the recall of a fact.

TABLE 7.1
Overview of the Five Varieties of Learning

Category of Learning	Capability	Performance	Example
Verbal information	Retrieval of stored information (facts, labels, discourse)	Stating or communicating the information in some way	Paraphrasing a definition of patriotism
Intellectual skills	Mental operations that permit individuals to respond to conceptualizations of the environment	Interacting with the environment using symbols	Discriminating between red and blue; calculating the area of a triangle
Cognitive strategies	Executive control processes that govern the learner's thinking and learning	Efficiently managing one's remembering, thinking, and learning	Developing a set of note cards for writing a term paper
Motor skills	Capability and "executive plan" for performing a sequence of physical movements	Demonstrating a physical sequence or action	Tying a shoelace; demonstrating the butterfly stroke
Attitudes	Predisposition for positive or negative actions toward persons, objects, and events	Choosing personal actions toward or away from objects, events, or people	Electing to visit art museums; avoiding rock concerts

Larger bodies of knowledge also are learned as information. Examples include the biblical story of creation and the contents of a local ordinance on littering. The performance is slightly different from other forms of verbal information. Typically, the performance is that of paraphrasing or reporting a summary of learned information.

In summary, the nature of the learning outcome for verbal information may be defined as (1) the reinstatement in speech or writing of a word or series of words in the order presented or (2) the reconstruction of the organized presentation of a verbal passage, including the main and subordinate ideas (Gagné, 1984). Internal conditions for learning verbal information include a preexisting set of organized knowledge (referred to as a "cognitive structure" by David Ausubel) and strategies for processing (encoding) the new information.

Intellectual Skills.   The essential characteristic of intellectual skills is that they involve interacting with the environment using symbols. Instead of simply stating or paraphrasing information, the learner is making decisions about a variety of events. The range of capabilities that are intellectual skills includes everyday skills such as analyzing the evening news as well as applying the rules that govern speaking, writing, and reading. In mathematics, such skills are using the rules for computation, interpreting word problems, and verifying problem solutions (Gagné, 1984). Intellectual skills may be described as "the basic and, at the same time, the most pervasive structures of formal education" (Gagné & Briggs, 1974, p. 24).

Intellectual skills also are found in a host of occupations, such as a technician in a nuclear power plant or a computer programmer. In other words, intellectual skills are the capabilities that make human beings competently functioning members of society.

Unlike factual information, however, intellectual skills cannot be learned by simply hearing them or looking them up (Gagné, 1977a, p. 11). The major difference between information and intellectual skills is the difference between knowing *that* and knowing *how* (Gagné, 1974b, p. 55). The student learns how to add integers, how to make the verbs and subjects of sentences agree, and countless other skills (Gagné, 1974b). Each skill is that of interacting with the environment using a variety of symbols. Such symbols include numbers, letters, words, and pictorial diagrams.

Unlike the other four varieties of learning, intellectual skills include four discrete skills. From simple to complex, they are discrimination learning, the learning of concrete and defined concepts, rule learning, and higher-order rule learning (problem solving). These skills are discussed in the Learning Hierarchies section and are summarized in Table 7.3. Internal conditions of learning for any of the intellectual skills include (1) recalling prerequisite skills, (2) interacting in a variety of ways with the new learning, and (3) applying the new skills to a range and variety of different situations and contexts.

Motor Skills.   To a certain extent, all performances are "motor" (i.e., stating something, pushing a button, or pointing at something) (Gagné, 1984). Identifying a category that represents new learning, however, refers to activities such as fly casting, lariat twirling, using a typewriter, or others that have not been previously executed. Included are simple skills learned early in life, such as fastening clothing and executing communicable speech sounds (Gagné, 1977a). In the early years of schooling, important motor skills include printing and writing letters and symbols, skipping rope, and balancing on a beam. Later, motor skills include learning the separate skills involved in playing tennis, basketball, and other sports.

The common characteristic of all these skills is the requirement to develop smoothness of action, precision, and timing (Gagné, 1977a, 1985). Novice and expert performances differ in these qualities.

Three major phases may be identified in the learning of motor skills. First is the learning of the sequence of the movements in the skill, referred to as the executive routine (Gagné, 1984). Then practice enables all the parts of the skill to be fitted together. Finally, continued practice results in improved timing and smoothness of performance. Practice continued over long periods of time eventually leads to automatization of the skill. In other words, the skill can be executed in the presence of potentially interfering activities, such as the roar of the crowd at an athletic event.

The feature of motor skills that sets this category apart from the others is that such skills improve through practice. Repetition of the basic movements with feedback from the environment is essential for learning. It leads to the identification of the kinesthetic cues that signal the differences between inaccurate and error-free performance (Gagné, 1977a, p. 19).

Attitudes.   Capabilities that influence an individual's choice about the kinds of actions to take are attitudes. In other words, they are inferred internal states that appear to modulate behavior (Gagné, 1984). In general, attitudes are considered to include three different aspects. One is a cognitive aspect, that is, an idea or a proposition. The second is an affective aspect, the feelings that accompany the idea. The third is a behavioral aspect that pertains to the readiness or predisposition for action (Gagné, 1985, p. 222).

An important characteristic, however, is that attitudes do not determine specific acts. Rather, they only make classes of individual actions more or less likely to be engaged in (Gagné, 1977a, p. 231). For example, the student develops attitudes toward reading books or constructing art objects (Gagné & Briggs, 1979, p. 86).

In contemporary society, various institutions and individuals attempt to establish and modify attitudes. The most pervasive medium in this effort is television. Both commercials and other aspects of television, such as soap operas, influence attitudes toward the various problems of everyday life (Gagné, 1984).

In contrast to the other categories of learning, the specific conditions for learning attitudes are yet to be identified. One clear requirement, however, is that being told what to do does not facilitate learning (Gagné, 1984). Reading a printed message, such as "Avoid harmful drugs," is not expected to have any effect on a learner's attitude (Gagné, 1974a).

Efforts to establish attitudes directly, such as through emotional appeal or persuasive logic, also have been found to be ineffective. However, one essential component appears to be Bandura's (1977) concept of the human model of behavior (Gagné, 1984, 1986). When the model is perceived as admirable, powerful, and credible, learning is most effective (Gagné, 1986). Imitation of the model's actions is most likely to occur when the model receives reinforcement for his or her choices of action.

Important considerations for future research on technology include the precise effects of modeling via television (Gagné, 1986). Examples are the relation of the model to different viewers, the importance of the context in which the model appears, and the nature of the messages that are being sent to viewers (Gagné, 1986, p. 4).

Cognitive Strategies.   Prior to the extensive development in information-processing theories and cognitive theory, Gagné (1972) identified another category of skills essential for learning. Referred to as cognitive strategies, this category includes the capabilities that control the management of learning, remembering, and thinking. Other terms for these skills include *strategic knowledge* (Greeno, 1978) and *executive control processes.* Cognitive strategies also are similar to Skinner's (1968) self-management behaviors and Rothkopf's (1970) mathemagenic behaviors (Gagné, 1977a, 1985). Currently, cognitive theory uses the term *metacognition* to refer to these strategies. Metacognition, however, also includes one's knowledge about learning tasks and one's learning capabilities. Gagné's cognitive strategies, in contrast, describes skills.

Unlike verbal information and intellectual skills, which are directly content related, the object of cognitive strategies is the learner's own thought processes. Cognitive strategies influence the learner's attending to stimuli, the ways that learners encode information for memory storage, and the size of the "chunks" of information that are stored. They also influence the learner's search and retrieval strategies and the organization of the learner's responses. In addition, they enable the learner to choose the relevant verbal information and intellectual skills to apply during learning and thinking (Gagné, 1984).

Three levels of cognitive strategies may be identified. One is that of task-specific strategies. An example is telling children to remember a set of pictures by putting them into categories (Gagné, 1984). In some situations, such as troubleshooting equipment, specific strategies are particularly important. One is to weigh the difficulties and potential benefits of tests prior to their use (Gagné in Twitchell, 1991).

The second level includes general strategies that are applicable to a variety of tasks. An example is the general problem-approach strategy described by Greeno (1978). The strategy includes constructive search, limiting the problem space, and dividing a problem into parts.

A third level of cognitive strategy is that of a "strategy to select strategies" or an executive strategy (Gagné, 1980a). Success in problem solving, for example, has been found to be related to the learner's ability to shift strategies and even to consider each strategy in rapid succession to reach a solution. Current research has yet to determine whether learners can readily or quickly acquire strategies that enable them to review, select, and reject their available cognitive strategies and to persist in the search for the best strategy for a given stage of problem solving (Gagné, 1980a, p. 89). General observation indicates that a period of time, a variety of situations, and reflective thought are essential in the development of an efficient executive strategy.

Research indicates that the disadvantaged students in chapter 1 programs, in particular, are most likely to need extensive strategy training (Brophy, 1988). Low-achieving students tend to rely primarily on rote memorization and other inefficient strategies. They also fail to organize their learning and tend to skip over material they do not understand (p. 262).

Summary

The framework of learning described by Gagné consists of (1) the five varieties of learning, (2) the cognitive processing phases, referred to as internal conditions, and (3) the environmental supports for learning, referred to as external conditions of learning. The five varieties of learning are verbal information, intellectual skills, motor skills, attitudes, and cognitive strategies. Each category represents a unique class of performance that is learned, is independent of individual characteristics, generalizes across situations, and requires different instructional treatments.

Verbal information refers to the acquisition of labels, facts, meaningfully connected selections of text, and organized passages. Intellectual skills, in contrast, involve interacting with the environment using symbols. Motor skills consist of both simple skills, such as fastening clothing, and complex skills, such as those involved in playing tennis, basketball, and other sports. Attitudes, in contrast, are the states that influence an individual's choices about the kinds of actions to take in a situation. The fifth category, cognitive strategies, consists of the capabilities that control the management of learning, remembering, and thinking.

Internal Conditions of Learning

The five varieties of human capability are one component of Gagné's framework of learning. The other key component consists of the internal prerequisites for each type of learning and the set of internal learning processes. These cognitive processes are executed in somewhat different ways for each of the five varieties of learning.

Internal learning conditions are composed of (1) the learner's internal states that are required for the particular capability to be acquired and (2) the set of cognitive processes involved in learning. Internal states consist of the prerequisite skills and attitudes that influence the new learning.

Internal Prerequisites. The two types of internal states required for learning are *essential* and *supportive prerequisites* (Gagné & Briggs, 1979; Gagné, Briggs, & Wager, 1988). Supportive prerequisites are the capabilities that facilitate learning, regardless of the type of outcome. An attitude of confidence in learning is an example. Verbal information, for example, requires a context of meaningful information for the new associations to be learned.

In contrast, essential prerequisites are particular skills that become an integral part of the new learning (Gagné & Briggs, 1979, p. 106). In other words, essential prerequisites are "folded into" the more complex skill when it is learned. An example is learning to discriminate between three-cornered geometric figures and those with four or more corners. This discrimination skill later becomes a part of the skill of classifying and labeling triangles. In contrast, learning a motor skill requires knowledge of the steps in the sequence and, if a complex skill, the related part-skills.

The essential prerequisites for a capability to be learned are obtained by analyzing the skill into the subskills that must be learned first (Gagné et al., 1988). For example, the task of "supplying the definite article" for writing a noun in German requires the skills of identifying gender and identifying number (singular or plural). They are component skills that become a part of the final task.

The Nine Phases of Learning.   Developments in cognitive psychology indicate that the learner's cognitive processes interact with the environment in several ways during learning. Included in these processes are the individual's perception of stimuli in the environment, the transformation of stimuli into codes to be remembered, and the later recall of stored information. Also important are the concepts "long-term memory" and "working memory." The memory system in which all our memories and learning are stored is **long-term memory**. In contrast, **working memory** is responsible for processing stimuli from the environment. It also is referred to as **short-term memory** because it has a limited capacity for holding information.

Gagné (1977a, 1985) has applied the cognitive processing concepts to his analysis of learning. He has identified nine stages of processing that are essential to learning and that must be executed in sequential order. The nine stages are referred to as **phases of learning** (Gagné, 1985). In this text, for the purposes of understanding the functions of the learning phases, the nine phases are categorized into three stages: (1) preparation for learning, (2) acquisition and performance, and (3) transfer of learning. The importance of these stages is that they are enacted in different ways for the different varieties of learning (see Table 7.2).

Implementing the Phases of Learning

Preparation for learning sets the stage for the learning task, and these steps typically require only a few minutes. Acquisition and performance, however, are the "core events" that are responsible for the learning of the new capability. Depending on the complexity of the skill to be learned, these phases may require from one to several sessions. Finally, transfer of learning provides for retrieval of the new skill from long-term memory and generalizability of the skill to new contexts. Transfer of learning may take place a few days after acquisition of the new skill.

Preparation for Learning.   The initial phases of learning are attending, expectancy, and retrieval of relevant information and/or skills from long-term memory. These activities set the stage for learning. The learner first "takes in," or apprehends, the relevant stimulus, and an expectancy for learning is established.

TABLE 7.2
Summary of the Nine Phases of Learning

Description	Phase	Function
Preparation for learning	1. Attending	Alerts the learner to the stimulus
	2. Expectancy	Orients the learner to the learning goal
	3. Retrieval (of relevant information and/or skills) to working memory	Provides recall of prerequisite capabilities
Acquisition and performance	4. Selective perception of stimulus features	Permits temporary storage of important stimulus features in working memory
	5. Semantic encoding	Transfers stimulus features and related information to long-term memory
	6. Retrieval and responding	Returns stored information to the individual's response generator and activates response
	7. Reinforcement	Confirms learner's expectancy about learning goal
Transfer of learning	8. Cueing retrieval	Provides additional cues for later recall of the capability
	9. Generalizability	Enhances transfer of learning to new situations

The stimulus may be the spoken or printed word, a still or moving picture, an object, or a human model. (Selection of stimuli to support learning is discussed later in the Selecting Instructional Events section.)

The importance of the learner's expectancy is that it represents the specific motivation of the learner to attain the learning goal (either set by others or self-selected) (Gagné, 1985, p. 78). Expectancy orients the learner toward goal accomplishment; thus, it enables the learner to select appropriate output at each subsequent stage of processing information. For example, if the learner has the expectancy of learning ways to find the resistances of electric circuits, certain characteristics of the circuit relevant to that goal will be processed and others will be ignored (Gagné, 1985, p. 78).

Expectancy is followed by the retrieval from long-term memory of previously learned capabilities essential to the new learning. In learning the concept "triangle," for example, the child first must recall that three-sided figures differ from other geometric shapes (discrimination learning).

Acquisition and Performance.   The four phases known as selective perception, semantic encoding, retrieval and responding, and reinforcement are here referred to as the core phases of learning. The first phase, *selective perception,* requires only a few seconds. In this phase, the learner transforms physical stimuli into recognizable features and permits the brief retention of those features in working memory so that encoding may occur.

The next phase, encoding, is the process whereby the stimulus features are given a conceptual or meaningful framework and then stored in long-term memory. This process is the central and critical stage in learning (Gagné, 1977a, p. 66). Without it, learning has not occurred.

The stored code may be a concept, proposition, or some other meaningful organization (see Gagné & White, 1978). In learning the concept "triangle," for example, the child encodes typical examples of triangles. For motor skills, however, the learner encodes a visual image of the skill and the executive routine required to enact the component performances.

The core events of learning conclude with performance and confirmation of the new learning. The learner *retrieves* the newly stored code from long-term memory and executes a *response*. If the child is learning the concept "triangle," he or she identifies examples of triangles that include various sizes, colors, and materials. For a motor skill, the student demonstrates the physical performance.

Feedback about the achievement of the learning goal is the next step. The feedback may be provided by the environment, or it may result from the learner's observation of his or her performance (Gagné, 1977a). The importance of the feedback, according to Gagné (1985, p. 79), is derived from Estes's (1972) concept of *reinforcement*. That is, feedback is reinforcing to the learner when it confirms that the goal has been attained or is close to being accomplished. In other words, feedback acquires reinforcing power by confirming the learner's expectancy.

Transfer of Learning.   Providing for transfer of learning is important for two reasons. One is that the new learning should not be limited to one or two examples or situations. Instead, the learner should be able to generalize the capability to several new situations. This generalizability is known as *lateral transfer* (Gagné, 1985). For example, the learner should be able to pick out the triangles in a geometric painting, as well as those drawn on a sheet of paper.

Second, the importance of applying the new learning in several contexts also provides the learner with additional cues that later can be used in searching long-term memory for the new capability.

Acquiring additional cues for retrieval and generalizability may not immediately follow the other phases of learning. Short delays of a day or two may intervene between the initial learning and opportunities for transfer (Gagné, 1974b).

In summary, the cognitive processes required for learning include nine phases that translate physical stimuli from the environment into new capabilities. The set of nine learning phases is executed in different ways for each of the five varieties of learning.

Summary

The internal conditions of learning consist of the learner's internal states required to learn particular capabilities and the set of cognitive processes involved in learning. The two types of internal states are essential and supportive prerequisites. Supportive prerequisites facilitate learning, whereas essential prerequisites are particular skills that become integral parts of the new learning.

The cognitive processes in learning consist of nine phases of information processing that may be categorized into three general stages. They are preparation for learning, acquisition and performance, and transfer of learning. Each of these stages is important in learning new capabilities.

The Nature of Complex Learning

Gagné's analysis of learning includes two organizations of capabilities that represent complex learning. The two organizations are *procedures* and *learning hierarchies*.

Procedures

A set of different actions that must be executed in a sequential or steplike fashion is referred to as a procedure (Gagné, 1985, p. 262). Examples of procedures include writing a check, balancing a checkbook, parking a car, and changing a tire.

Procedures are organizations of skills that include both motor and intellectual skills. The motor skills in parallel parking, for example, include positioning the vehicle appropriately, backing at low speed in a certain direction, and turning the wheels straight from the turn (Gagné, 1977a, 1985). The intellectual skills include identifying the correct angle of approach, identifying alignment with the other car, and so forth. Learning the procedure involves learning to perform the discrete motor skills as well as learning the essential concepts and rules.

Some procedures, such as parking a car or changing a tire, require learning the step-by-step actions that constitute the total sequence. Others, however, require decisions about alternative steps at certain points in the procedure. This type is sometimes referred to as a **conditional procedure**. In such a procedure, the outcome of one step provides clues to the choice to be made in the next step (Gagné, 1977a, p. 271). When balancing a checkbook, for example, an individual first must determine if the checks are in numerical order. If not, the next step is to arrange the checks in sequence by date of issue.

Learning Hierarchies

Procedures are organizations of both motor and intellectual skills. Learning hierarchies, in contrast, are organized sets of intellectual skills only. The concept of cumulative learning is represented in the set of skills referred to as a **learning hierarchy**. Briefly summarized, a learning hierarchy is a set of subordinate skills or capabilities such that each skill is essential to the learning of the next higher skill. Figure 7.2 illustrates the subordinate skills for learning to subtract whole numbers. Subtracting when a single borrowing is required—skill VII, for example—is prerequisite to skills VIII, IX, and X, which involve several or successive borrowings across columns. In other words, in a valid hierarchy, a connection exists between two skills if the higher element cannot be learned without first learning the lower element (Gagné, 1977a, 1985).

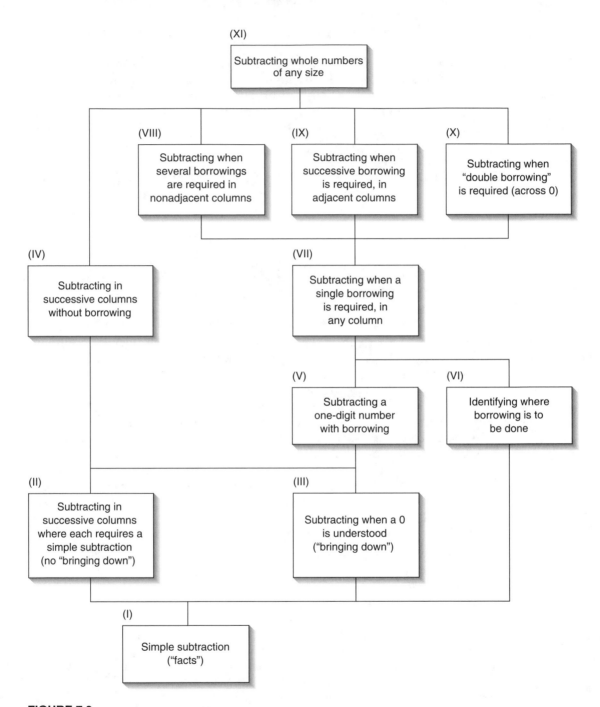

FIGURE 7.2

A learning hierarchy for subtracting whole numbers

Note: From *Principles of Instructional Design, 2nd edition,* by R. M. Gagné, © 1979. Reprinted with permission of Wadsworth, a division of Thomson Learning: www.thomsonrights.com. Fax: (800) 730-2215.

Of importance in understanding learning hierarchies is that they are *psychological organizations of skills.* In other words, a learning hierarchy is neither a logical ordering of information nor a description of the ways in which verbalized knowledge is acquired (Gagné, 1968b). Within intellectual skills, four kinds of discrete psychological capabilities have been identified. They are **discrimination learning, concept learning** (both concrete and defined concepts), **rule learning**, and **higher-order rule learning** (problem solving). Each of these skills is an essential prerequisite to the next higher-order skill. They are summarized in Table 7.3.

At least two major implications for curriculum may be derived from learning hierarchies. One is that curricula may be designed to reflect "process" as opposed to content. In the development of "Science—A Process Approach," emphasis was on the skills involved in classifying, measuring, and predicting rather than that of verbalizing the accomplishments of science (Gagné, 1968b).

The second implication is that careful attention to prerequisite skills may reduce greatly the need for remedial education. When remedial education is necessary, the case often is that some basic skill or set of skills has not been learned. When remedial students attempt problems using basic math operations, they typically make use of rules they have developed themselves—the wrong rules. Similarly, one of the major differences between good and poor readers is the lack of essential prerequisite skills (Gagné, 1982).

In summary, the two organizations of capabilities that represent complex learning are procedures and learning hierarchies. Procedures are sets of actions that must be executed sequentially, and they consist of both motor skills and intellectual skills. Learning hierarchies, in contrast, are organized sets of intellectual skills in which each skill is an essential prerequisite to the next higher skill. The intellectual skills are discrimination learning, concept learning, rule learning, and higher-order rule learning or problem solving.

TABLE 7.3

Summary of Intellectual Skills from Simple to Complex

Type of Skill	Description
Discrimination learning	Child responds differentially to characteristics that distinguish objects, such as shape, size, color
Concept learning/ Concrete concepts	Child identifies object or event as a member of a concept class, learned through direct encounters with concrete example, such as triangles
Defined concepts	Cannot be learned through concrete examples; acquired by learning a classifying rule, such as "liberty," "patriotism"
Rule learning	Student can respond to a class of situations with a class of performances that represents a relationship; for example, student responds to 5 + 2, 6 + 1, and 9 + 4 by adding each set of integers
Higher-order rule learning (problem solving)	Student combines subordinate rules in order to solve a problem; most effective learning strategy is guided discovery

PRINCIPLES OF INSTRUCTION

Robert Gagné framed his analysis of the conditions that affect human learning from the perspective of the question, "What factors really can make a difference in instruction?" (Gagné, 1985, p. xiii). This view derives from the realization that children's experiences play a major role in their development. This heavy dependence of learning on environmental circumstances implies a great responsibility for society because the situations in which learners are placed have great effects on them (Gagné, 1985, p. 1). These situations may encourage the development of great artists and scientists, or they may inhibit the development of the human intellect (Gagné, 1977a, p. iv).

As a result of the perspective from which the theory was developed, the transition from the principles of learning to the principles of instruction requires no translation. The five varieties of learning as outlined in Table 7.3 are capabilities that are the outcomes of school learning. Similarly, the essential internal states for each of the five varieties are important prerequisites for school learning. Finally, each of the nine phases of learning is supported by a particular type of event during classroom instruction.

Basic Assumptions

The importance of instruction is a major consideration in Gagné's discussions of learning. His assumptions about classroom learning therefore include the nature of instruction and the process referred to as instructional design.

A Definition of Instruction

Learning can occur whether or not instruction is present (Gagné, 1987a, p. 400). However, each of the learning processes may be influenced in some way by events external to the learner. When these events are deliberately planned to support learning, they are referred to as *instructional events*. An important characteristic of instruction is that these external events occur in the context of the learner's internal control processes. Therefore, the external events do not *produce* learning; instead, they can only support the learner's internal processing (Gagné, 1974a).

A second characteristic of instruction is that it does not have a single unitary purpose. Instead, instruction has several functions that correspond to the different information-processing phases of learning. That is, an external event appropriate for one phase may be inappropriate or irrelevant for another phase (Gagné, 1974a). An instructional event to arouse attention, for example, is different from one to provide transfer of learning.

Third, decisions about instruction must be made in the context of the skill or skills to be learned. Instruction for information, for example, is not the same as instruction for motor skills. Therefore, the question Is this example of instruction good? cannot be answered. Instead, the relevant question is, Is this instruction good for learning (information, intellectual skills, motor skills, attitudes, cognitive strategies)? (Gagné, 1974a).

The Nature of Instructional Design

The focus in Gagné's principles is on instruction rather than simply teaching. The intent is to address all the events that may directly influence an individual's learning (Gagné & Briggs, 1979). In addition to teaching, instruction may be delivered by print materials, pictures, television, computers, and other media. The design and development of instruction in such detail is an essential element of the larger enterprise known as **instructional systems design** (Gagné, 1987a, p. 400).

Five assumptions support Gagné's recommendations for designing instruction (Gagné & Briggs, 1979). First, instruction should be planned to facilitate the learning of an individual student. Although students often are grouped for instruction, learning takes place within the individual. Therefore, the needs of the learner are placed in the planning sequence prior to grouping.

Second, both immediate and long-range phases are included in the design of instruction. The teacher or instructional designer plans daily lessons, but the lessons occur within the larger segments of units and courses, which also must be planned. Third, instructional planning should not be haphazard or provide merely a nurturing environment. Such a course of action can lead to the development of individuals who are not competent. In other words, to influence human development as much as possible, instruction should be designed systematically (Gagné & Briggs, 1979, p. 5).

Fourth, instruction should be designed using the systems approach. The systems approach to planning is defined as the organized, sequential selection of components that makes use of information, data, and theoretical principles as input at each planning stage (Gagné et al., 1988, p. 15). At each step in the development process, the prospective outcomes are checked against the goals originally established by those who will implement the final product. In the last step, the product is tested in real-world situations both during development and at the completion of the development process.

In designing curriculum and instruction, the application of the systems approach should begin with the analysis of needs, continue with the development of goal statements, and then proceed step by step to develop the instruction. Empirical evidence is then obtained about the effectiveness of the instruction in order to revise the materials. Tryout and revision continue until the standards established for the instruction are met.

Finally, instructional design should be developed from knowledge about how human beings learn (Gagné & Briggs, 1979, p. 5). These five assumptions are consistent with Gagné's definition of instruction. Specifically, instruction has several functions that correspond to the different information-processing phases of learning. Equally important, decisions about instruction should be made in terms of the skills to be learned.

The Components of Instruction

The various kinds of capabilities and the ways of analyzing the different learning requirements are combined by Gagné (1985) in a theory of instruction. The cornerstone of the theory is the designation of the five varieties of learning. They serve as a frame of reference to identify the capability or capabilities to be learned for a particular lesson. Instructional outcomes in the form of performance objectives are developed first. Then instruction is planned using the set of nine instructional events that support the nine phases of learning.

Designing Performance Objectives

All five varieties of learning reflect important outcomes for school learning. Motor skills are found in physical education and dance and also are subcomponents of other school subjects. Examples include the physical skills in printing and writing. In contrast, cognitive strategies and attitudes include hoped-for outcomes. Specifically, they are developing the learner's management strategies and fostering positive, self-confident attitudes toward learning.

The content of the curriculum is for the most part represented by the learning of information and the acquisition of intellectual skills, regardless of the subject area. Performance objectives for these two varieties of learning are found in all courses in the curriculum.

The function of performance objectives for instruction is that they are unambiguous statements of the capabilities to be learned. Terms such as *understand, comprehend,* and *appreciate* should be replaced with more precise terms that clearly communicate the skill or attitude to be acquired. An example of a performance objective is "The student demonstrates, by solving verbally stated examples, the addition of positive and negative numbers" (rule learning) (Gagné et al., 1988, p. 124).

Because each of the five learning varieties represents a different class of performances, the verbs used also will differ. For example, *states* or *defines* are appropriate verbs for information objectives. However, they are not appropriate for intellectual skills that require learner decision making and interaction with the subject matter. Instead, depending on the level of intellectual skill, verbs such as *selects, classifies, demonstrates,* or *solves* are needed. (See Table 7.4 for a listing of sample verbs.)

TABLE 7.4
Suggested Verbs for the Varieties of Learning

Capability	Verbs
Information	States, defines, paraphrases
Motor skill	Executes, performs, enacts, pronounces
Attitude	Chooses to . . ., freely elects to . . ., selects (a preferred activity)
Cognitive strategy	Originates (a strategy)
Intellectual skills	
Discriminate	Selects (same and different)
Concept	Identifies (examples), classifies (into categories)
Rule	Demonstrates, predicts, derives
Higher-order rule	Generates (a problem solution), solves

Stating capabilities to be learned as performance objectives fulfills two important functions in the school setting: (1) the needs of instruction are identified, and (2) the method of testing is determined. That is, different capabilities are both taught for and tested in different ways. Specifically, verbal information may be tested by asking the student to define or state the particular item of information. The testing of intellectual skills, however, requires that the student (1) interact with the stimulus situations using symbols and (2) respond to a new set of situations that is not the same as that used in instruction.

Selecting Instructional Events

As a guideline for planning instruction, nine instructional events have been identified. Their function is to support the learner's cognitive processes during learning. For example, saying "Today we are going to learn to figure earned run averages of baseball players" (stating the objective) assists the student to establish the purpose and key elements of the events that are to follow (expectancy for learning). Similarly, providing hints or cues can facilitate the encoding and storage of the new learning in long-term memory. Table 7.5 lists the instructional events for each of the nine learning phases.

Preparation for Learning.   Gaining attention, informing the learner of the objective, and stimulating the recall of prior learning are three instructional events that set the stage for new learning. Gaining the learner's attention may be accomplished by asking a provoking question, depicting an unusual event, or appealing to a child's particular interests. For example, a lesson on the Earth's atmosphere may begin with a question, such as "Did you know that one of the things we breathe every day is sulfuric acid?" (Gagné & Driscoll,

TABLE 7.5
Relationships Between Learning Phases and Instructional Events

Description	Learning Phase	Instructional Event
Preparation for learning	1. Attending	Gain learner's attention through unusual event, question, or change of stimulus
	2. Expectancy	Inform the learner of the objective
	3. Retrieval (of relevant information and/or skills) to working memory	Stimulate recall of prior learning
Acquisition and performance	4. Selective perception of stimulus features	Present distinctive stimulus features
	5. Semantic encoding	Provide learning guidance
	6. Retrieval and responding	Elicit performance
	7. Reinforcement	Provide informative feedback
Transfer of learning	8. Cueing retrieval	Assess performance
	9. Generalizing	

1988, p. 73). The teacher may say, "Today we are going to learn why leaves change colors and fall from the trees" or "Let's find out why the liquid changes colors when certain drops are added." The answer to the initial question or the response to the unusual event provides closure and informs the learner of the new objective (event 2).

The importance of informing students of the objective should not be underestimated, particularly for elementary school children. Research reported by Peterson (1988) indicated that most of them are unable to determine the skills and concepts to be learned from their academic tasks. Typically, they report that the goal, particularly for seatwork, is to get the task finished (p. 323).

Next, to prepare the student for a new level of learning, the instruction should stimulate the recall of important prerequisites (event 3). Relevant information, concepts, and rules, such as how plants make food, may be needed. Recall is stimulated through the use of questions such as Do you remember ...? or What did we do yesterday that might help us answer this question?

Materials and objects also may stimulate recall. In a unit on linear measurement, children were given sticks of different lengths. Then they were asked to think about using the sticks to measure the height of a box (Gagné & Briggs, 1979, p. 167). Recall of the skill of counting numbers was initiated as each of the children used a particular length of stick to determine height.

Acquisition and Performance. The core phases of learning are selective perception, semantic encoding, retrieval and responding, and reinforcement. Each of these four phases also is supported by a particular instructional event. Specifically, the four events are presenting distinctive stimulus features, providing learning guidance, eliciting performance, and providing feedback.

The stimulus characteristics, or situations with which the learner is to interact during instruction, are presented first. Next, specific situations accompanied by hints or prompts as needed are presented to the learner. This activity is that of providing learning guidance. The communications to the learner should stimulate a particular direction of thought and therefore prevent the learning from getting off the track (Gagné & Briggs, 1974, p. 129).

Providing learning guidance is a critical event in instruction (Gagné, 1980b). First, it helps the learner transform the new capability into a code for later recall. Second, it "makes the difference between learning that is facile and learning that is hard; and also between learning that is relatively effective and learning that is ineffective" (Gagné, 1980b, p. 61).

To determine the effectiveness of encoding, the learner's performance of the new skill is elicited. Feedback is then provided that indicates either necessary corrections or provides reinforcement by confirming that the objective has been achieved.

The core events, in particular, should be flexibly implemented for different kinds of learning. For example, instruction for the concept "circle" may include a variety of circles of different colors or sizes (presenting the stimulus). Examples made of string or rope also may be used (Gagné & Briggs, 1974, p. 129). In addition, the children might be asked to join hands and form a circle.

Then the children may be presented with a variety of pictures and other examples that include different geometric figures. They may be asked to look carefully at each picture in the set and to decide which ones represent circles. Hints or prompts concerning the characteristics of circles may be provided by the teacher as each picture is introduced and included in the set (providing learning guidance).

After identification with teacher assistance of several circles, the children may be asked to point to examples in a new set of geometric figures or pictures (eliciting performance). Incorrect identifications are followed by reminders about the characteristics of circles and comparisons with the examples already identified (providing informative feedback).

In contrast, if the objective is that the students are to discover a rule, the core instructional events are executed somewhat differently. For example, the task may be to discover the rule of prime numbers. The rule is that these numbers are divisible only by one set of factors (the number itself and the number 1).

The student first may be asked to recall that any number can be expressed as the product of various factors (e.g., $4 = 2 \times 2; 4 \times 1$). Then the student may be presented with a succession of numbers from 1 to 15 and asked to write out all the various factors for the set of numbers (presenting distinctive stimulus features). The learner is asked next if the factors for any of the numbers vary in any way (learning guidance). However, this suggestion may not be sufficient for the student to discover that certain numbers are divisible only by themselves and 1. The student then may be asked the differences between the numbers 3, 5, 7, and 4, 8, 10 (Gagné & Briggs, 1974, p. 129). Learning guidance in the form of questions and prompts continues in this way until the learner discovers the prime numbers.

Retrieval and Transfer. The concluding segment of instruction provides for assessment of the new learning followed by cues for retrieval and transfer. For assessment, new situations or examples should be presented to students to be certain that learning is not restricted to only a few examples.

Then instruction should conclude with stimuli specifically designed to enhance retention and transfer. This phase may take the form of spaced reviews after a reasonable delay of a day or more following the initial learning (Gagné, 1974b). For example, if the student has learned to define *legislative* with regard to the U.S. Congress, the spaced reviews may include the meaning of *legislative* with regard to state and city lawmaking bodies (Gagné, 1974b, p. 116).

In summary, teachers and instructional designers select verbal statements, questions, objects, diagrams, and other stimuli to stimulate the learner's internal processing. These stimuli are selected to meet the requirements of the nine instructional events.

Applicability to the Learning Varieties. Each of the nine instructional events supports a particular phase in the learning process. However, these events are executed in somewhat different ways for each of the five varieties of learning. Table 7.6 illustrates the unique external conditions (requirements for instructional events) for the five learning varieties.

TABLE 7.6
Unique External Conditions of Learning for the Five Varieties

	Preparation for Learning	Core Instructional Events	Transfer of Learning
Verbal information	Relate new content to learner's framework of information.	Provide meaningful context of information for encoding. Provide elaborations, imagery, or other encoding cues. For bodies of knowledge, present information so that it can be learned in chunks.	Give cues for effective retrieval and generalization.
Intellectual skills	Stimulate recall of prerequisite skills.	Provide varied concrete examples and rules. Provide opportunities for interacting with examples in different ways. Assess in new situations.	Use a variety of contexts and novel situations to promote transfer.
Cognitive strategies	Elicit recall of necessary intellectual skills.	If task-specific, describe the strategy; if general, demonstrate the strategy. Provide opportunities for strategy practice with support and feedback.	Provide unfamiliar problems for strategy use.
Motor skills	Show performance of skill to be learned. Stimulate recall of part-skills, if appropriate.	Establish executive subroutine and provide for mental rehearsal. Arrange several repetitions of skill with corrective feedback.	Supply opportunities for performing skill in new physical setting.
Attitudes	Learner is *not* directly informed of the objective. Establish that learner respects the model.	Provide respected model(s) who enact positive behavior and reinforce the model. When learner enacts the behavior, provide reinforcement.	Provide opportunities for learner to continue to enact behavior, and provide reinforcement.

As indicated, specific requirements for instructional events vary for preparation for learning, the core events, and learning transfer. For example, in introducing instruction for attitudes, the teacher does not inform students of the objective but must first establish respect for the model who is to execute the desired behavior. In contrast, introducing instruction for intellectual skills requires stimulating the recall of the prerequisite discriminations, concepts, or rules that are subcomponents of the new skills to be learned.

Also important is that the instructional events should not be treated as an ironclad sequence. Learning a complex concept, for example, may require cycling through the core events two or three times, given the number of criteria essential for identifying concept examples. The instructional plan presented later in this chapter is an example.

Although the instructional events were developed for teacher and other media-directed instruction, Flynn (1992) observed them in a fourth-grade cooperative learning environment. The teacher set the stage (preparation for learning), and the core events of instruction occurred in peer interactions in small groups. Flynn (1992) suggested that these events contribute to the effectiveness of the co-operative learning model over large-group instruction because the group interactions provide enhanced opportunities for their occurrence.

In summary, instructional events are selected for performance objectives based in large measure on the variety of learning represented by the objective. However, events are included as needed for the types of students and complexity of the information, skill, strategy, or attitude to be learned.

The Role of Media in Instruction

The term *media* typically conjures up images of computer-assisted instruction, instructional television, videocassette and CD/DVD recordings, and similar mechanized delivery systems. However, instructional media also include the teacher's voice, printed text, and real objects—in short, any physical means that communicates an instructional message (Gagné & Briggs, 1979; Reiser & Gagné, 1983).

The typical approach to media selection is to choose a media form and then plan the instruction. However, this approach is deficient in two ways. First, research on media utilization indicates that no one medium is universally superior to all others for every type of learning outcome for all learners (Gagné et al., 1988, p. 204). Therefore, to choose arbitrarily a computer, television, or some other medium for a lesson is to ignore factors such as learner characteristics and task variables that can influence the effectiveness of a particular delivery system. Computer-assisted instruction, for example, can provide the interactive tutoring capability for the core events in intellectual skills for some learners. For example, it can provide the practice in basic skills that is essential for children in grades K–3 (Gagné in Twitchell, 1991). Further, interactive videodiscs can provide instruction on intellectual skills and cognitive strategies. Harvard Law School, for example, has developed interactive videodiscs in which students learn direct and cross-examination skills in a tenant-landlord case, applications of search and seizure law, and so on (Miller, 1990). Television or film, however, does not include this capability but can provide the meaningful context required for verbal information.

Second, the arbitrary selection of media can result in the omission of essential instructional events. A film or audiotape, for instance, may provide content but exclude instructional events such as providing learning guidance or pauses for student responding and feedback (Gagné et al., 1988, p. 199). Also, with a few notable exceptions, many of the computer materials developed for the public school classroom are inadequate examples of instruction. For example, the majority of computer exercises labeled "simulations" are either competitive games or drill-and-practice exercises accompanied by animated graphics (Gredler, 1986). Like other models of media selection, the model developed by Reiser and Gagné (1983) first provides for the identification of a range of appropriate choices and then narrows the choices to one or two.

Criteria to be considered first are the nature of the learning outcome and the characteristics of the learners. For example, computer instruction, interactive television, and interactive videodisc instruction are three possible choices for an intellectual skill. Then important learner characteristics, such as age and extent of reading comprehension, are considered. Interactive television may be selected for nonreaders, for example.

The next step is to review the choices for the capability of providing the required instructional events. The final selection is based on practical factors, such as cost, size of the group to be accommodated at one time, and ease of implementation.

The media selection model is useful for expanding one's thinking about the various types of media for instruction. It is particularly useful when the same unit of instruction will be replicated several times with similar groups of students.

Summary

Application of the nine instructional events to the five varieties of learning leads to differences in instruction for the different learning outcomes. Elaboration, imagery, and methods for encoding chunks of information are sufficient core events for verbal information. However, they are not appropriate for intellectual skills. Instead, students must interact with situations and examples in a variety of ways. Attitude change, in contrast, depends on respected models and reinforcement for positive behaviors.

Also important in the use of instructional events to plan instruction is that they are not an ironclad sequence. Once the instructional events are identified, media may be selected. In other words, one does not first select media, such as television or the computer, and then design instruction. Instead, media are selected to fit the requirements of particular instructional events.

Designing Instruction for Complex Skills

Defining each capability to be learned in the form of a performance objective and selecting the appropriate instructional events are important steps in the design of instruction. Also important, however, is providing for the cumulative nature of human learning. Thus, Gagné (1977a) describes the methods by which instruction is to be developed for organizations of complex skills. As described earlier, the two types of capabilities organized from simple to complex are procedures and learning hierarchies. Instructional planning for these two different organizations of skills occurs in somewhat different ways.

Instructional Design for Procedures

The first step in developing instruction for complex skills is to determine the set of skills to be taught. For a procedure, each separate step is identified first. For example, for the procedure of changing a tire, the identified sequential skills include removing the wheel cover, placing a block under the other wheel, using the jack to raise the wheel, and so on (Gagné, 1977a, p. 360).

The motor skills in the sequence are then analyzed into part-skills that also may need to be taught. An example is the skill of backing up a car, which is an essential step in parallel parking. Stopping the car at the right point so that it is neither too close nor too far away from the curb is a part-skill in backing up a car.

For some procedures, choices between alternative steps may be required. For example, one step in reconciling a bank statement with check records is to determine if the checks are numbered. If the answer is yes, the checks are arranged in numerical order. If the answer is no, the checks are arranged by date of issue (Gagné, 1977a, p. 262). Both alternatives must be included in the instruction.

After the skills and part-skills are identified, the type of capability of each skill is identified. Performance objectives then are written for the skills and part-skills, and instruction is planned for the set of objectives.

Instructional Design for Learning Hierarchies

The task of deriving a learning hierarchy is not necessarily an easy one (Gagné & Briggs, 1974, p. 112). Correct identification of subordinate skills requires the identification of component mental operations, not the identification of items of information (p. 113).

Essential prerequisites for the intellectual skills are determined by the method referred to as **learning task analysis** (Gagné & Briggs, 1979). This method, essentially a questioning approach, is first applied to the most complex skill to be taught; it asks, What simpler skill is essential to the learning of the present skill? The key to the identification of the immediate prerequisite is the word *essential.* Many simpler skills may be identified that are not integral components of the skill to be learned. The prerequisite skill is the one that must be recalled by the student if the learning is to proceed rapidly and without difficulties.

An example is the skill "subtracting a one-digit number with borrowing" in Figure 7.2. An immediate prerequisite skill is "subtracting when a zero is understood (bringing down)." Learning to subtract zero from a one-digit number is essential to learning to subtract one-digit numbers that do not require borrowing.

The importance of learning task analysis is illustrated by the objective "converting Fahrenheit to Celsius temperature readings" (Gagné & Briggs, 1974, p. 113). One might be tempted to identify a prerequisite as "knowing that $C = \frac{5}{9}(F - 32)$." This statement, however, is an item of information. In contrast, the prerequisite skills include "finding numerical values of an unknown variable by solving equations" and "substituting numerical values of variables in equations to yield a single numerical value for a variable" (p. 113).

Each skill identified by the questioning procedure also is subjected to the same question to determine the next simpler set of prerequisites. This analysis by questioning is repeated until a logical endpoint is reached for the particular group of learners. The logical endpoint is the set of prerequisite skills that the students already have learned. These skills are identified as the entry capabilities for the unit or course of instruction.

Each skill to be taught then is categorized as to type of capability and is written in the form of a performance objective. The relevant verbal information and attitudes also are identified and written as performance objectives. Instruction is developed for each objective, using the instructional events described earlier.

EDUCATIONAL APPLICATIONS

Programs in several areas have implemented the concepts of component sub-tasks and prerequisite skills. For example, Reading Recovery, a program for the poorest readers, has found that understanding basic concepts about print is essential to success in reading instruction. Among the basic concepts are identifying the front of the book, indicating that print (not pictures) carries the message, identifying the purpose of the spaces between words, and so on (Clay, 1999). In arithmetic, Griffin, Case, & Siegler (1994) found that a signifi-cant number of low-income inner-city children lack central essential prerequi-sites for beginning formal arithmetic. They also use maladaptive strategies, such as counting up from either addend in a simple addition problem. The es-sential capabilities, which most middle-income children acquire prior to school, include counting reliably, quantifying sets, matching sets of numbers, and correctly identifying the larger and smaller numbers in a pair (p. 37).

Classroom Issues

Gagné's approach to the analysis of learning is from the perspective of the needs of instruction. As a result, his work addresses several issues of impor-tance in the classroom.

Learner Characteristics

Individual differences, readiness, and motivation are issues for both the sys-tems approach to designing instruction and the classroom teacher. Gagné (1974b, 1980a) and Gagné and Briggs (1979) discuss these issues with regard to both instructional design and the delivery of instruction.

Individual Differences. The effectiveness of instruction is influenced by sev-eral kinds of individual differences among students. Included are differences in cognitive strategies and rate of learning. Particularly important, however, are differences in student entry capabilities (Gagné, 1974b) (see the Readiness sec-tion). Entry capabilities are "the raw materials with which instruction must work" (Gagné, 1974b, p. 125). They may be assessed at several beginning points within the curriculum, such as the beginning of a school year or the start of a new course or unit.

Methods of compensating for individual differences in the delivery of in-struction include small-group instruction, the tutorial mode, independent learn-ing (Gagné, 1974b), and individualized instructional systems (Gagné & Briggs, 1979). The advantage of individualized systems is that they are delivery systems for adjusting instruction to the individual student in a group of 25 or more (Gagné & Briggs, 1979, p. 261).

Readiness. For Gagné (1968a, 1977a), developmental readiness is viewed as the individual's relevant capabilities. Readiness is not a matter of maturation in which certain growth changes must take place before learning can occur (referred to as the growth-readiness model; Gagné, 1968a). Nor is readiness a matter of the gradual internalization of logical forms of thought as Piaget (1970) suggested. Both of these models, Gagné notes, have assigned a secondary role to the influence of learning in human development. However, because learning is cumulative, readiness for new learning refers to the availability of essential prerequisite capabilities. As discussed earlier, readiness includes the lower skills in the hierarchy of intellectual skills and the essential rules, concepts, and part-skills in procedures.

Motivation.   Designing effective instruction includes the identification of student motives and the channeling of those motives into productive activities that accomplish educational goals (Gagné, 1977a, p. 287).

Although often treated as a single characteristic, motivation includes both general and specific types. General motivational states include David McClelland's achievement motivation (1965) and R. W. White's competence motivation (1950) (Gagné, 1977a). More specific types include incentive motivation and task motivation, both of which may be developed through the careful use of reinforcement contingencies. That is, reinforcement for the activities of working with other children, relating to school tasks, and for mastery and accuracy can establish incentive motivation (Gagné, 1977a).

Cognitive Processes and Instruction
Gagné's analysis of learning is conducted from the perspective of the factors that make a difference in instruction. Therefore, the issues of transfer of learning, the students' self-management skills, and the teaching of problem solving are integral components of the conditions of learning.

Transfer of Learning.   The concept of learning transfer is the heart of Gagné's model of cumulative learning. First, Gagné describes essential prerequisites for each of the five varieties of learning. Second, the essential prerequisites within intellectual skills provide for transfer in two ways. They contribute to the learning of the next higher-order skill, and they also generalize to other situations. Examples include the skills of adding, subtracting, multiplying, and dividing whole numbers and fractions.

The sequence of nine instructional events also includes attention to transfer of learning. At the conclusion of learning, cues are provided for retrieval of the capability, and new situations are introduced to which the student applies the skill.

Learning "How-to-Learn" Skills.   These skills are the cognitive strategies identified by Gagné (1972, 1977a). They are the ways that the individual manages his or her learning, remembering, and thinking. Gagné notes that improving students' how-to-learn skills so that each student is "working up to potential" is one of the challenging problems for education (Gagné, 1977a, p. 36).

Teaching Problem Solving.   According to Gagné (1977a, p. 34), the process of problem solving is one in which the learner discovers how to combine some previously learned rules to generate a solution to a problem that is new to the learner. Teaching problem solving requires that (1) the necessary rules are already acquired by the learner, and (2) a problem situation is presented to the learner that he or she has not encountered before (Gagné & Briggs, 1979, p. 71). The learner, in generating the solution, engages in "discovery learning" in that he or she must select from memory the appropriate rules and combine them.

Problem solving, although it includes discovery learning, differs from the solving of novel problems suggested for cognitive strategies. In cognitive strategies, the learner is *originating* a solution that may require the selection of information from a variety of sources and the combining of information in novel ways. In the problem solving included in intellectual skills, the learner is *generating* a solution that requires the recombination of previously learned related rules. The result is a higher-order rule.

The Social Context for Learning

The methods recommended by Gagné (1977a) and Gagné and Briggs (1979) focus on the design of instructional systems rather than on the development of models of teaching. A major difference between the two is that models of teaching place the teacher or other individual in the role of conducting and/or managing instruction for some identified group of learners. Instructional systems, in contrast, often include sets of materials and activities for which the pacing and management of instruction may reside in the learner. As a result, the context for learning with regard to instructional design is discussed in terms of the effects on the management of instruction (Gagné & Briggs, 1979). That is, the differences in the implementation of instructional events among the tutoring situation, small-group instruction, and large-group instruction are described. Gagné and Briggs also discuss the implications of different entry capabilities of students for each of these contexts.

Relationships to Other Perspectives

Unlike prior theorists, Gagné began his analysis with the various skills and capabilities that humans enact in diverse situations. Noting that some theories had identified at least part of the complex picture of human learning, his conditions of learning incorporate the Gestalt concept of partial insights and guided discovery in the description of intellectual skills, and the modeling plus reinforcement component from Bandura's theory in the description of attitudes.

Gagné's conditions of learning also is a bridge between the behavioral focus of operant conditioning and the cognitive approaches to learning. That is, learners acquire responses, and environmental events (the events of instruction) are essential to learning (behavioral principles). However, the responses reflect different kinds of internal capabilities and require different internal states (mental events). Further, the variety of learning referred to as cognitive strategies is also reflected in the information-processing concept referred to as metacognition.

Like operant conditioning, in the classroom, the sequence of instruction in the conditions of learning is teacher-directed and managed, and moves toward a predetermined outcome for learners. It differs from social constructivism in which the community of learners, with input from the teacher, largely determines the direction and depth of learning. It also differs from the cognitive perspectives, which, although discussing internal processing activities of the learner and instructional supports, often do not specify the learning outcome.

Developing a Classroom Strategy

According to the systems approach, the design of a classroom lesson is one component of a total process that includes both curriculum and instruction. Therefore, ideally, developing particular lessons is preceded by design at the curriculum and course levels.

The Systems Design Model

Systems models for instructional design are characterized by three major features. First, instruction is designed for specified goals and objectives. Second, the development of instruction utilizes media and other instructional technologies. Third, pilot tryouts, materials revision, and field testing of the materials are an integral part of the design process. In other words, systems models specify objectives, design the instruction, and try out the materials with students, revising the instruction until the desired achievement is produced. The design, tryout, and revision process is the major characteristic of systems models; the development is a "closed loop" process.

The systems model described by Gagné and Briggs (1979) includes all the stages in the design of curriculum and instruction (Figure 7.3). It begins with needs assessment and the development of goal statements. The model also entails the development of end-of-course objectives, specific performance objectives, instructional events, selection of media, and field testing of the final product.

One important feature of the model is that it places lesson development within the total context of curriculum design. In so doing, it extends the concept of cumulative learning beyond instruction to the curriculum level. The relationship between learning at the instructional and course levels is illustrated by the following set of objectives:

1. *Course objective.* The student can critically analyze events and situations in a country's judicial, governmental, economic, and political systems, consistent with that country's identified priorities.
2. *Unit objective.* The student can demonstrate the relationships between political and economic systems.
3. *Specific subskill.* The student can classify systems as "political" or "economic."

In the design model, the term *formative evaluation* (step 11) refers to materials tryout with small groups of students. The purpose is to identify areas in the instruction that are not working effectively and to revise them. After these

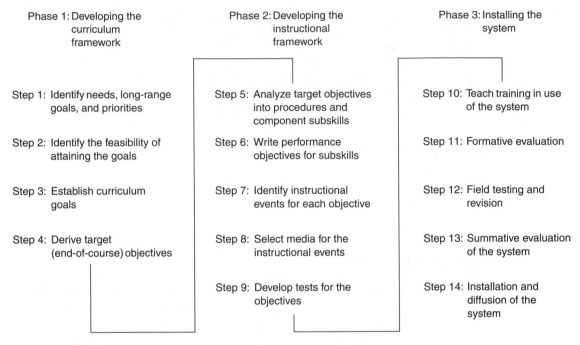

FIGURE 7.3
Summary of the phases in the Gagné-Briggs systems design model

changes are made, field testing is undertaken with a large group. Minor changes in the materials may be required after the field test. Finally, summative evaluation (step 13) assesses the materials with a typical population. This evaluation certifies the objectives that are met by the instruction and identifies the population for which the materials are effective.

Designing the Lesson.   The complete systems model is designed for curriculum development that includes both courses and units of instruction. However, the principles are applicable to the design of individual lessons.

Step 1: Write or select performance objectives.
> **1.1** What is/are the culminating skill(s) to be learned at the end of the lesson?
> **1.2** What are the related subordinate skills? If learning to use a rule is the end-of-lesson skill, what are the supporting concepts? If a cognitive strategy is to be learned, what are the related intellectual skills?
> **1.3** Determine which of the supporting skills are entry skills to the lesson and which are to be taught as part of the lesson.
> **1.4** Select appropriate verbs for the skills to be taught and write in the form of performance objectives.

Step 2: Select instructional events for each of the performance objectives.

    2.1 Identify the variety of learning for each objective. If intellectual skills, identify as to discrimination skill, concept learning, rule learning, or higher-order rule learning.

    2.2 Identify entry skills and particular characteristics of the group to be taught (e.g., average or poor reading ability).

    2.3 Given 2.1 and 2.2, select instructional events to meet the unique learning conditions for each objective (see Table 7.6).

Step 3: Select media for instructional events.

    3.1 Identify several choices that meet the requirements for the particular learning outcome.

    3.2 Eliminate media inappropriate for the age and/or reading level of the learners.

    3.3 Make final media choices for instructional events based on cost, size of the group, and ease of implementation.

Step 4: Develop tests for the objectives.

    4.1 Write four to eight items per objective that reflect the performance stated in the objective. For example, for "identifying the main idea," select several short paragraphs with a set of possible choices for each.

    4.2 Assemble the items for each objective into a test and check for length and item difficulty.

Classroom Example

The lesson in Table 7.7 is an example of instruction designed for the objective of identifying the main idea. The lesson builds on a concept learned previously, that of topic. The lesson illustrates the use of the nine instructional events in specific classroom activities.

Note that in step 4, present distinctive stimulus features, the teacher presents core information that illustrates the defining rule of the concept of main idea. This information is applied first by the teacher and then by the students in the identification of concept examples.

The use of the game in step 5 provides a chance for the children to try out their new skills prior to assessment of their performance. The game thus provides a source of feedback other than the teacher.

During the lesson, instructional events 5, 6, and 7 are repeated to give the children experience with two types of statements often confused with the main idea. The two types are general statements that do not describe the topic and specific details. Each type is contrasted separately with examples of the main idea so that the children may clearly understand the differences.

Retention and transfer is provided a few days after the initial instruction using a discussion of the children's favorite television programs. The children receive additional cues for later recall at this time.

TABLE 7.7
Classroom Example

Capability to be learned: The students can identify statements that represent the main idea for short selections (fourth and fifth graders).

Instructional Event	Medium for Instruction	Classroom Activity
1. Gain attention	Teacher communication	Teacher asks students to name their favorite TV show or story.
2. Inform learner of the objective	Teacher communication	Teacher asks the children if they know how to tell someone what the show (story) is about without retelling the story. Teacher explains that they are going to learn how to find the main idea of story so they can tell a friend what the story is about.
3. Stimulate recall of prior learning	Teacher communication	Learners asked to recall the term *topic* (who or what a story is about).
4. Present distinctive stimulus features	Transparency and teacher communication	*Transparency:* TOPIC + SOMETHING SPECIAL ABOUT THE TOPIC = MAIN IDEA Example: Three Little Pigs Main idea: The three pigs (topic) built houses, and the wolf blew down all except the brick house. Teacher explains why the statement is the main idea.
5. Provide learning guidance	Transparencies and group discussion	*Transparencies:* Brief situations plus set of three statements about each. In each set, one choice is the main idea; others are specific details. Teacher and student discuss options and reasons for correct choices. Students are divided into groups and play the game "Natural Topics" (Bell & Weikert, 1985, pp. 78–83). Students take turns drawing game cards, each of which has three statements, and select the main idea. Tokens are moved on a game board—one space for easy answers, two for more difficult choices.
	Academic game	

6. Elicit performance	Print material	Children are given brief situations, each with several choices from which they select the main idea.
		Example: Movie *E.T.*
		Choices: The main idea is
		  A. E.T. rode on the handlebars of Elliott's bicycle.
		  B. E.T. was left on Earth and wanted to go home, although he had friends on Earth.
		  C. E.T. hid in a closet full of toys in Elliott's house and was hard to tell apart from the toys.

7. Provide feedback | Group discussion and teacher communication | Class discusses the answers.

Instructional events 5, 6, and 7 are then repeated, with the difference that the other statements about the story are not details; they are general statements. However, they do not describe "something special" about the topic.

Example: A short selection describes edible grasses and includes wheat, rice, hay, and their uses as food.

Choices: The story is about
A. how to eat grass.
B. how grass grows.
C. the uses of grass.

Instructional events, 5, 6, and 7 are then repeated, using a wide selection of statements that may represent the main idea.

Example: A short selection describes tree rings (topic), how they are formed, and what they tell us about a tree's growth.

Choices: The story as a whole is about
A. tree rings that are close together.
B. how rain makes trees grow.
C. how tree rings tell about trees.

8. Assess performance | Print material | Children are given several short reading selections with choices for main ideas (general and specific), and they select the sentence that tells what the whole story is about.

9. Provide retention and transfer | Group discussion | Children talk about the stories and the TV shows mentioned in instructional event 1. The teacher introduces several choices for the main idea of each, and the children as a group make a decision about the main idea during a class discussion.

This lesson illustrates an important characteristic of effective instruction. Too often, too much information is presented to the learner too quickly. Confusion and mislearning often result. In this lesson, one new feature of the concept is presented at a time, with practice by the learner at each stage.

The lesson also demonstrates the major requirements for intellectual skills. Specifically, they are the integration with prior information and the learner's interaction with symbols.

Review of the Theory

Prior learning theorists developed explanations of the learning process in the laboratory and extended the findings to the human situation. Robert Gagné, in contrast, began with the complexity and variety that characterizes human learning and developed a system to account for that variety.

Gagné's analysis yielded five categories or varieties of learning that are distinguished by different performances and different requirements for learning. The five varieties are verbal information, intellectual skills, cognitive strategies, attitudes, and motor skills. In addition, intellectual skills include four discrete skills that form a hierarchy from discrimination learning to higher-order rule learning (problem solving). Unlike other designations, such as "rote learning" or "conceptual learning," the five varieties cut across school subjects, ages of learners, and grade levels.

Each learning variety requires a different set of internal and external conditions for acquisition of the particular capability. Internal conditions include (1) the necessary prerequisite skills and (2) the nine phases of cognitive processing required for learning. External conditions are the events of instruction that support the learner's cognitive processes.

A major goal of Gagné's theory is the planning of effective classroom instruction. The skills to be learned are written in the form of performance objectives, and the variety of learning is identified. Task analysis is then used to identify prerequisite skills, and instructional events are selected for each objective to be taught.

Disadvantages

The theory was developed to account for the range of psychological processes observed in prior research on learning and to specify precisely the sequence of instructional events for the identified processes. Thus the theory is easier for a curriculum design team to implement than for the classroom teacher to use (Table 7.8).

Contributions to Classroom Practice

The best-known contribution of the theory is that it operationalizes the concept of cumulative learning and provides a mechanism for designing instruction from simple to complex. The concepts of cumulative learning, task analysis, and the identification of component skills have become accepted curriculum components.

TABLE 7.8
Summary of Gagné's Conditions of Learning

Basic Elements	Definition
Assumptions	Within the parameters established by growth, development is the result of the cumulative effects of learning.
	Learning is characterized by more than a single process, and these processes cannot be reduced or collapsed into one.
Learning	The phases of information processing supported by stimulation from the environment executed for the different kinds of learning
Learning outcome	An internal capability manifested in a particular performance for each of the kinds of learning
Components of learning	*Five varieties of learning:* verbal information, intellectual skills, cognitive strategies, attitudes, and motor skills
	Internal conditions of learning: prerequisite skills and the nine phases of information processing
	External conditions of learning: the events of instruction
Designing instruction for complex skills	Provides instructional events for the sequences of skills in procedures and learning hierarchies
Major issues in designing instruction	Identification of capabilities to be learned; task analysis of objectives; selection of appropriate instructional events
Analysis of the Theory	
Disadvantage	Difficult for the classroom teacher to implement without special training
Contributions to classroom practice	Provides a mechanism for designing instruction from simple to complex; identifies the psychological processes in cumulative human learning
	Accounts for the diversity of human learning
	Links instructional events to specific phases in information processing

CHAPTER QUESTIONS

1. A classroom teacher is developing a unit on solving for the areas of plane geometric figures. She presents two formulas, $A = lw$ and $A = w \times \frac{1}{2} l$. She then uses the formulas to solve for the area of two rectangles and two triangles. The students are given several problems to complete for homework. According to Gagné's theory, what are some of the things that the teacher has done wrong?

2. Classify the following objectives as to the variety of learning. If the objective is an intellectual skill, identify the type.

_____ a. The learner can classify paintings as examples of cubism, impressionism, or realism.

_____ b. The computer analyst can debug computer programs for errors in program commands.

_____ c. The suburbanite voluntarily takes recyclable garbage to a community reclamation site.

_____ d. The student can develop a set of logical arguments to support U.S. trade restrictions to other civilized countries.

3. Identify at least two prerequisites for skills (b) and (d).
4. Discussions continue as to whether Head Start and other preschool programs are successful in reducing subsequent school failure. From Gagné's perspective, what key question should be asked in this debate?

REFERENCES

Airasian, P. W., & Bart, W. M. (1975). Validating a priori instructional hierarchies. *Journal of Educational Measurement, 12,* 163–173.

Bandura, A. (1977). *Social learning theory.* Upper Saddle River, NJ: Prentice Hall.

Bannon-Ritland, B. (2003). The role of design in research: The integrative learning design framework. *Educational Researcher, 32*(1), 21–31.

Bell, I. W., & Weikert, J. E. (1985). *Basic media skills through games* (Vol. 1, 2nd ed.). Littleton, CO: Libraries Unlimited.

Brophy, J. (1988). Research linking teacher behavior to student achievement: Potential implications for instruction of Chapter One students. *Educational Psychologist, 23*(3), 235–276.

Clay, M. M. (1999). *An observation survey of early literacy achievement.* Portsmouth, NH: Heinemann.

Estes, W. K. (1972). Reinforcement in human behavior. *American Scientist, 60,* 723–729.

Flynn, J. L. (1992). Cooperative learning and Gagné's events of instruction. *Educational Technology, 32*(10), 53–60.

Gagné, R. M. (1962a). The acquisition of knowledge. *Psychological Review, 69*(4), 355–365.

Gagné, R. M. (1962b). Military training and principles of learning. *American Psychologist, 17,* 83–91.

Gagné, R. M. (1965a). The analysis of objectives. In R. Glaser (Ed.), *Teaching machines and programmed learning: II. Data and directions* (pp. 21–65). Washington, DC: National Education Association.

Gagné, R. M. (1965b). *The conditions of learning.* New York: Holt, Rinehart & Winston.

Gagné, R. M. (1968a). Contributions of learning to human development. *Psychological Review, 75*(3), 177–191.

Gagné, R. M. (1968b). Learning hierarchies. *Educational Psychologist, 6,* 1–9.

Gagné, R. M. (1970). Some new views of learning and instruction. *Phi Delta Kappan, 51,* 486–472.

Gagné, R. M. (1972). Domains of learning. *Interchange, 3*(1), 1–8.

Gagné, R. M. (1974a). *Expectations for school learning.* Bloomington, IN: Phi Delta Kappa.

Gagné, R. M. (1974b). *Essentials of learning for instruction.* Hinsdale, IL: Dryden.

Gagné, R. M. (1977a). *The conditions of learning* (3rd ed.). New York: Holt, Rinehart & Winston.

Gagné, R. M. (1977b). Instructional programs. In M. H. Marx & M. E. Bunch (Eds.), *Fundamentals and applications of learning.* New York: Macmillan.

Gagné, R. M. (1980a). Learnable aspects of problem solving. *Educational Psychologist, 15*(2), 84–92.

Gagné, R. M. (1980b). Preparing the learner for new learning. *Theory into Practice, 19*(1), 6–9.

Gagné, R. M. (1982). Learning from the top down and the bottom up. *Florida Educational Research Journal, 24,* 1–10.

Gagné, R. M. (1984). Learning outcomes and their effects: Useful categories of human performance. *American Psychologist, 37*(4), 377–385.

Gagné, R. M. (1985). *The conditions of learning* (4th ed.). New York: Holt, Rinehart & Winston.

Gagné, R. M. (1986). Instructional technology: The research field. *Journal of Instructional Development, 8*(3), 7–14.

Gagné, R. M. (Ed.). (1987a). *Instructional technology: Foundations.* Hillsdale, NJ: Erlbaum.

Gagné, R. M. (1987b). Peaks and valleys of educational psychology. In J. A. Glover &

R. R. Ronning (Eds.), *Historical foundations of educational psychology* (pp. 395–402). New York: Plenum.

Gagné, R. M. (1989). *Studies of learning: Fifty years of research*. Tallahassee, FL: Learning Systems Institute.

Gagné, R. M., & Briggs, L. J. (1974). *Principles of instructional design*. New York: Holt, Rinehart & Winston.

Gagné, R. M., & Briggs, L. J. (1979). *Principles of instructional design* (2nd ed.). New York: Holt, Rinehart & Winston.

Gagné, R. M., Briggs, L. J., & Wager, W. W. (1988). *Principles of instructional design* (3rd ed.). New York: Holt, Rinehart & Winston.

Gagné, R. M., & Driscoll, M. P. (1988). *Essentials of learning for instruction*. Upper Saddle River, NJ: Prentice Hall.

Gagné, R. M., & White, R. T. (1978). Memory structures and learning outcomes. *Review of Educational Research, 48*(2), 187–222.

Gredler, G. R. (1992). *School readiness: Assessment and educational issues*. Brandon, VT: Clinical Psychology Publishing Company.

Gredler, M. B. (1986). A taxonomy of microcomputer simulations. *Educational Technology, 26*(3), 36–40.

Greeno, J. (1978). Nature of problem-solving abilities. In W. Estes (Ed.), *Handbook of learning and cognitive processes* (pp. 239–270). Hillsdale, NJ: Erlbaum.

Griffin, S. A., Case, R., & Siegler, R. S. (1994). Right-start: Providing the central conceptual prerequisites for first formal learning of arithmetic to students at risk for school failure. In K. McGilly (Ed.), *Classroom lessons: Integrating cognitive theory and classroom practice* (pp. 25–49). Cambridge, MA: MIT Press.

Jonassen, D. H., Tessmer, M., & Hannum, W. H. (1999). *Task analysis methods for instructional design*. Mahwah, NJ: Erlbaum.

McClelland, D. C. (1965). Toward a theory of motive acquisition. *American Psychologist, 20*, 321–323.

Melton, A. W. (Ed.). (1964). *Categories of human learning*. New York: Academic.

Miller, E. J. (1990). In videodisc veritas: Interactive video at Harvard Law School. *T.H.E. Journal*, March, 78–80.

Peterson, P. (1988). Selecting students and services for compensatory education: Lessons from aptitude-treatment interaction research. *Educational Psychologist, 23*(4), 313–352.

Piaget, J. (1970). Piaget's theory. In P. H. Mussen (Ed.), *Carmichael's manual of psychology* (pp. 703–722). New York: Wiley.

Reiser, R. A., & Gagné, R. M. (1983). *Selecting media for instruction*. Englewood Cliffs, NJ: Educational Technology.

Rothkopf, E. Z. (1970). The concept of mathemagenic activities. *Review of Educational Research, 40*, 325–336.

Skinner, B. F. (1968). *The technology of teaching*. New York: Appleton-Century-Crofts.

Twitchell, D. (Ed.) (1991). Robert M. Gagné and M. David Merrill in conversation. *Educational Technology, 31*(1), 34–40.

White, R. T. (1974). A model for validation of learning hierarchies. *Journal of Research in Science Teaching, 11*, 1–3.

White, R. W. (1950). Motivation reconsidered. The concept of competence. *Psychological Review, 66*, 297–333.

CHAPTER 8
Cognitive Perspectives:
I. The Processing of Information

The brain is not a passive consumer of information. . . . The stored memories and information-processing strategies of our cognitive system interact with the sensory information received from the environment, selectively attend to this information, relate it to memory, and actively construct meaning for it. (Wittrock, 1990, p. 348)

Development of the digital computer illustrated the ways a complex machine uses a set of instructions to engage in complex tasks, such as playing chess. This development led to the view of the mind as a set of processes for operating on symbols. Early research, based on computer-related models of memory structures, addressed the sequence of mental operations and the products (information) in the performance of a cognitive task (Anderson, 1990).

Criticisms of the computer-related models, which did not adequately address the human capabilities involved in constructing meaning, led to new research directions. The view of learners as active constructors of knowledge who can understand and control the learning process has led to a gradual shift toward studying learning in educational settings (Brown & Campione, 1994, p. 231). Current research includes the ways that individuals develop meaning from text and other information sources, and the ways that learners organize knowledge.

Theorists and researchers also address the development of metacognition and problem solving. These capabilities are the complex skills addressed by the cognitive perspective and they are discussed in chapter 9.

PRINCIPLES OF LEARNING

Information-processing theory, which addresses the basic steps in the ways individuals obtain, code, and remember information, is the central theory of the cognitive perspective. However, unlike Skinner's operant conditioning and Gagné's conditions of learning, information processing does include some variations. Nevertheless, researchers who adopt this perspective share the broad assumption that individuals transform much of the information impinging on the senses from the environment into memory codes that are stored for later use. From this foundation, researchers developed particular assumptions about the nature of human memory and the ways that knowledge is represented in memory. Essential components of learning are the organization of information to be learned, the learners' prior knowledge, and the processes involved in perceiving, comprehending, and storing information.

Basic Assumptions

Two key assumptions support information-processing research. They are (1) the memory system is an active, organized processor of information, and (2) prior knowledge plays an important role in learning. Related to these basic assumptions are beliefs about (1) the nature of the human memory system, (2) the ways that specific knowledge items are represented in long-term memory, and (3) the organization of bodies of knowledge in long-term memory.

The Nature of Human Memory

The early conception of human memory was that it served simply as a repository or passive collector of information over long periods of time. In the 1960s, however, researchers began to view human memory as a complex system that processes and organizes all our knowledge. It is not a passive repository; instead, it is a system that is both organized and active. That is, human memory actively selects the sensory data that are to be processed, transforms the data into meaningful information, and stores much of that information for later use. Four different perspectives on the nature of human memory portrayed in Table 8.1 are (1) the memory system concept, (2) the state concept, (3) levels of processing, (4) the connectionist perspectives, and (5) the multi-stage model. The dominant perspective, however, is the multistage concept.

Types of memory.   The memory system concept, the state concept, and levels of processing conceptualize human memory in terms of states or levels. The importance of episodic memory identified by Tulving (1985) is the uniqueness of the remembered information, which is personal or autobiographical. Each item in episodic memory, such as the hurricane one survived last year or the movie seen last week, is identified by a personal "tag." Typically these memories are recalled through association with a time or place. In education, the learning of particularly difficult concepts has the potential to be mediated by particularly memorable classroom episodes (Martin, 1993).

The state concept, the identification of information as active or inactive, accounts for such activities as memorizing a poem, repeating a telephone number, and carrying on a conversation with a friend while driving. The levels of processing concept, in contrast, addresses three basic processes in identifying words or phrases, but does not address more complex processes.

short - term — active
long - term - inactive

TABLE 8.1
Conceptions of Human Memory

Concept	Description	Limitations
1. ✳ The multi-stage model	1. Assumes that information is processed in stages linked to memory systems 2. Structures are the sensory register, short-term storage, working memory, and executive control processes 3. Structures are not locations in the brain	1. Lack of research confirmation of the capacity of the structures 2. Does not incorporate the wide variations in brain functioning that can occur (Edelman, 1987) 3. Mindful procedures are brain products, not processes (Iran-Nejad, Marsh, & Clements, 1992)
2. The memory system concept	1. Systems are episodic (personal or autobiographical information); semantic (general knowledge); procedural (steps that help in responding adaptively to the environment) (Tulving, 1985)	Differences in processing in semantic and procedural memories are not clear
3. The state concept	Conceptualizes memory in terms of the state of information (active or inactive)	Does not address processing steps in acquiring information
4. Levels of processing	1. A memory is a by-product of perceptual analysis in a series of sequential, hierarchial levels 2. Levels are sensory analysis, pattern recognition, and semantic association (Craik & Lockhart, 1972; Craik, 1979)	Depth of processing cannot be measured independently of the amount of information that is remembered (Neath, 1998)
✳ 5. Connectionist networks, also known as neural networks or parallel distributed processing (PDP)	1. Consist of nodes or elements and links or connection weights in a network structure 2. Described as a Frisbee/rubber band (elements/connection weights) network (Bereiter, 1991) 3. Oscillations of the rubber bands represent input signals traversing a portion of the network 4. The extent of tightness in the rubber bands (connection weights) represents learning	1. The need for a physical agent to alter the connection weights disqualifies these models as explanations of autonomous learning by the brain (Bereiter, 1991) 2. In computer simulations, the initial connection weights must be mechanically set by the designer (Iran-Nejad et al., 1992) 3. There is no guarantee that the network structure of the models represents the brain's network (Iran-Nejad et al., 1992)

The multi-stage model.   Broadbent's (1958) description of a multi-stage memory influenced the current general model derived from a computer metaphor. The sequential memory stages, managed by an executive control, are illustrated in Figure 8.1. As illustrated, an array of physical signals impinges on the sensory registers, primarily visual and auditory. Many signals are not processed, some are retained only briefly in the sensory registers (0.5–2.0 seconds), and some are selected for further processing. Information selected for further processing enters short-term or working memory, where much of it is encoded into some meaningful form and transferred to long-term memory for permanent storage. Some information, such as a little-used telephone number that is looked up, is retained only until the call is completed. Although the stages do not reflect brain structure, the processes associated with the stages (discussed in this chapter) are useful in addressing issues in learning.

Connectionist networks.   These networks differ from Thorndike's connectionism, which consists of stimulus–response pairs. The concept of networks in which nodes (thoughts) fire impulses through the connections to other nodes was first proposed by William James (1890; Neath, 1998). James was intrigued by the "restless flight" of one idea before another and conceptualized a network to account for the rapid generation of different thoughts.

In the current models, knowledge is stored in connection weights (links) that also modulate the transfer of activity from one unit to the next (Schneider & Graham, 1992).

Developers of connectionist models (e.g., McClelland & Rumelhart, 1986) note that many activities, such as interpreting language, require the processing of information from several sources at once. Further, only the connectionist

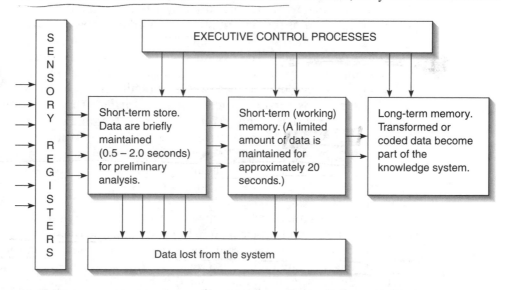

FIGURE 8.1
Generalized conceptualization of the human memory as a structural system

models account for such events. That is, multiple processing occurs simultaneously because information is stored in the strengths between the connections instead of in the form of static patterns. The models maintain that, in reading, for example, letter and word recognition and recognition of constraints are occurring and interacting simultaneously. Referred to as *parallel distributed processing,* this activity, according to the models, accounts for the instant recognition of THE CAT as "the cat."

Bereiter (1991) noted that some models referred to as "symbolic connectionist" models use elements (Frisbees) that represent concepts of propositions (Holyoak, 1991; Thagard, 1989). Although these models sidestep the issue of how the symbolic representations are acquired, the models function as people often do. That is, they illustrate the gradual change from vagueness (or imprecise impressions) to clarity that is found in much of human thought (Bereiter, 1991, p. 13).

The Representation of Knowledge

The mechanisms with which the human memory system functions are a major issue in the information-processing perspective. Another equally important issue is the nature of the symbolic form in which information is stored in memory. Early views described the representation of specific items of information in memory. Later perspectives address the organization of larger bodies of knowledge.

Representation of Specific Items.   The record of information that is stored is not a literal copy of the stimulus input because the physical signals received by the senses are not perfect representations of the world. Therefore, to be remembered, the physical signals must be transformed in some way.

Two major views on the form of stored information have been proposed. One is the dual-code model proposed by Paivio (1971, 1983, 1986). The other perspective maintains that information is stored in verbal form only.

The Dual-Code Model.   The essential characteristic of the **dual-code model** is that information may be stored in long-term memory in nonverbal as well as verbal form. The model describes two functionally independent, although interconnected, systems for the processing and storing of information. Abstract objects and events that do not refer to concrete, tangible objects or events are stored in verbal form. Examples are "success," "soul," "truth," and "ability." In contrast, nonverbal representations include environmental sounds, actions, visceral sensations, and other nonlinguistic objects and events. Examples include the sound of church bells, drawing lines, or pressing keys, and a clenched jaw or racing heart (Clark & Paivio, 1991).

Some events and objects, such as "house," that have both concrete and abstract characteristics may be coded in both systems. The overall likelihood of the activation of verbal or nonverbal representations depends upon the combined effects of the presented stimulus (verbal or objects/pictures), instructions, and other contextual stimuli and individual differences in abilities to process visually or verbally (Paivio, 1986, p. 69).

The importance of nonverbal encoding is reflected in the greater recall of concrete over abstract text and items in list memory tasks (Paivio, 1983; Clark &

Paivio, 1991). The explanation of the dual-code model for imagery effects is the additive effects of imagery and verbal codes. Moreover, when separate elements are integrated into a compound image, a partial cue can later reactivate the total representation (Clark & Paivio, 1991).

Critics of visual imagery maintain that information storage in picture form would exceed the storage capacity of the brain and also would require a "perceiver" in the brain to "read" the pictures (Pylyshyn, 1973). However, the visual encoding theorists maintain that the stored codes are not pictures but rather are analog representations or analog memories. Instead, Pylyshyn (2002) maintains that imagistic reasoning utilizes the same mechanisms and the same forms of representation as general reasoning, and only the content differs (p. 158). For example, if told to imagine a baseball thrown into the air, we can easily imagine the curved trajectory of the ball because we recall having seen a ball follow such a path (p. 159). Also, the difficulty in imagining a cube observed from all sides at the same time may be the result of no knowledge of the appearance of this event (p. 159).

Verbal Representations.   The theorists who advocate verbal representations in long-term memory do not question the importance of imagery in the processing of information for later recall. However, they maintain that the ultimate representation of information is in verbal form and that images are reconstructed from verbal codes.

Two types of knowledge are represented in verbal form. One, declarative knowledge, is stored in the form of verbal networks. The other, procedural knowledge, is stored in the form of condition–action pairs.

Declarative Knowledge.   Influenced by Noam Chomsky's work in linguistics, the early models described stored information as base strings (Tom is tall) plus related comparative information. An early network model developed by Quillian (1968; Collins & Quillian, 1969) used nodes to portray concepts and superordinate concepts. Properties of each concept, such as "has four legs," "has fur," and "is a predator," were attached to the concept by links or pointers. Deficiencies in Quillian's model in accounting for retrieval times as well as other problems led to the development of other network models.

The common dimensions of currently accepted structural networks are "nodes" and "links." The nodes represent central conceptual components joined (linked) to various relationships that may include features, properties, functions, other concepts, and facts (DiVesta, 1987, p. 212). The critical feature of these representations is that knowledge is composed of ideas linked by relations.

The network organization proposed by John R. Anderson (1983; 1990) is composed of propositions. Formally defined, a proposition is "the smallest unit of knowledge that can stand as a separate assertion; that is, the smallest unit about which it makes sense to make the judgment true or false" (Anderson, 1990, p. 123). Examples include "Mary is my sister" and "The Cadillac is beautiful." In other words, propositions are "atomic units of meaning" (Anderson, 1990, p. 143). Other proposed models of human memory describe a fixed architecture (as does Anderson) whereas others differ on the processing components (unitary or multicomponent) (see Miyake & Shah, 1999).

Procedural Knowledge.   Briefly, *procedural knowledge* is knowing how to execute a particular task or activity, such as parallel parking a car. Procedural knowledge may range from simple tasks, such as unlocking a door, to complex activities, such as using word processing software on a computer. According to the theorists, procedural knowledge is encoded in the form of condition–action pairs that are if–then statements (Anderson, 1993; Newell & Simon, 1972). For example, *if* a plural subject, *then* the present tense of the verb "to be" takes the form of "are."

Organizations of Knowledge (Memory)

The dual-code concept, verbal representations, and condition–action pairs describe hypothesized representations of specific information in long-term memory. Researchers, particularly those investigating school learning, often are interested in the ways that individuals acquire and make use of bodies of information or knowledge. Among the terms used in the research literature are prior knowledge, domain knowledge, schema, content-specific knowledge, and topic knowledge. Reviews of the uses of the terminology in the literature indicated that explicit definitions of terms typically are missing (Alexander, 1992; Alexander, Schallert, & Hare, 1991). However, analyses of implicit uses by Alexander et al. (1991) clarified the relationships among some of the various terms. The analysis first identifies two broad categories of knowledge, tacit and explicit. Then the components of explicit knowledge, referred to as conceptual and metacognitive, are described.

Tacit and Explicit Knowledge.   A large part of an individual's knowledge is tacit (Alexander, 1992; Alexander et al., 1991). Specifically, tacit knowledge is implicit and typically operates below the level of conscious awareness. Sociocultural knowledge, such as the appropriate ways to treat one's elders, is an example.

Another form of tacit knowledge is scripts. First described by Schank and Abelson (1977), scripts contain the general information found in familiar, frequently experienced events. For example, included in a "going to the movies" script are going to the theater, buying the ticket, buying refreshments, finding a seat, seeing the movie, leaving the theater, and going home. In the school setting, the first few weeks of the fall term in elementary school address the socialization of the children according to the scripts for the major events in the school day.

Research indicates that babies, by 7 months of age, show recall of caretaking scripts, such as teeth brushing and bath and peek-a-boo games (Ashmead & Perlmutter, 1980). Further, individuals tend to name the same major events when asked to state the important events in an episode such as going to a restaurant (Anderson, 1990). However, once learned, scripts tend to operate below the individual's level of conscious awareness, that is, as tacit knowledge.

Explicit knowledge, in contrast, is easily available to consciousness and is the object of thought (Prawat, 1989). One broad type of explicit knowledge is referred to as conceptual (see the following section).

The other broad type of explicit knowledge is referred to as *metacognitive*. ①
Included in metacognitive knowledge are knowledge of specific and general
strategies for learning new information; knowledge of plans, goals, and specific
tasks; and knowledge of oneself as a learner (Alexander et al., 1991). An example
is the knowledge that encountering words or sentences one does not understand
in a text passage is a signal to initiate a "fix-it" strategy to aid comprehension
(Dole, Duffy, Roehler, & Pearson, 1991). Metacognitive knowledge contributes
to the ways that the executive control processes illustrated in Figure 8.1 function.

② *Conceptual Knowledge.*   Conceptual knowledge includes subject-related
knowledge and knowledge about the communication of information, and both
are essential to learning. The two types of conceptual knowledge described by
Alexander et al. (1991) are content knowledge and discourse knowledge (see
Table 8.2). Content knowledge consists of information about the individual's
physical, mental, and social world (Alexander et al., 1991). Discourse or linguistic
knowledge consists of knowledge of text, syntax, and rhetoric of language. This
category is important because discourse knowledge interacts with content
knowledge. For example, the learner's knowledge of signal words, such as "on the
other hand," "nevertheless," and "exceptions are," alerts the learner to important
points that qualify or run counter to the concepts previously discussed.

TABLE 8.2
Two Broad Categories of Explicit Conceptual Knowledge

Content knowledge[*]—information about some aspect of one's physical, social, or mental world (corresponds roughly to the abstract structure referred to in the literature as content schemata)	*Discourse knowledge*[*]—information about language and its use (linguistic knowledge) (corresponds roughly to the abstract structure referred to in the literature as textual schemata)
May be informal or formal	May be informal or formal
May be organized and integrated at either of the following two levels:	Formal organization consists of the following types:
Domain knowledge—organized knowledge (1) about a defined area (such as baseball or computer programming) or (2) related to a discipline (such as biology)	*Text-structure knowledge*—understanding of the forms or frames of expository texts; the story schema or grammar activated by the learner during reading; and learner construction of hierarchies within the text
Discipline knowledge—extensive academic knowledge that is organized around the fundamental principles defining a particular field that is a discipline (such as biology or chemistry)	*Syntactic knowledge*—knowledge of the conventions of language; linguistic connections and ties *Rhetorical knowledge*—sense of audience style, or tone or register of language that can be used

Note: Summarized from "Domain Knowledge: Evolving Themes and Emerging Concerns," by P. A.
Alexander, 1992, *Educational Psychologist, 27*(11), 33–51 and Alexander et al., 1991.

[*]This category and the subtypes consist of declarative and procedural knowledge.

(progression?)

("Physical Theory")

Domain Knowledge and Discipline Knowledge.   As concepts become central to a defined area or a discipline, they contribute to the construction of formal organizations of content. The two major types are domain knowledge and discipline knowledge. Domain knowledge is less extensive and less comprehensive than discipline knowledge for one of two reasons. First, it may involve an area of study that is not a discipline, for example, baseball or computer programming. Second, the individual may be developing knowledge in a discipline, but that knowledge is limited. Examples are the extent of knowledge of first-semester students in biology or chemistry.

Discipline knowledge, in contrast, consists of extensive academic knowledge in a particular field designated as a discipline. Specifically, a discipline is an extensive field of study that is defined by sets of rules or generalizations, and has a history of knowledge construction. Examples are physics, biology, and chemistry. A senior who is majoring in biology and a third-year medical student, for example, are acquiring discipline knowledge.

(like the gossip game)

p

Schemas.   The term **schema** was first defined by Frederick Bartlett (1932) as an "active organization of past reactions" that is assumed always to be operating in an individual's response (p. 201). In a now-classic experiment to illustrate the influence of schemas, Bartlett (1932) gave the first subject a folk story from an unfamiliar culture to read. The individual then reproduced the events and gave this accounting to the second subject. The second subject read the first subject's version, laid it aside, reproduced the events, and handed that account to the third subject, and so on. By the time the story reached the tenth subject, it was no longer a folk story about mythical visitors ("The War of the Ghosts"). Instead, it had become a fishing trip. Unfamiliar information was dropped in the repeated stories, a few details were retained, and each story became more like the reader's expectations.

A recent definition of schema describes it as an "organized structure that reflects an individual's knowledge, experience, and expectations about some aspect of the world" (Neath, 1998, p. 328). Further, schemas represent knowledge at any of a variety of levels, from a schema of an office to a schema of social structure.

Three functions identified for schemas are (1) to provide a framework into which new data must fit in order to be comprehended, (2) to serve as a guide for goal-directed activities and to undertake searches of the environment, and (3) to fill in gaps in information received from the environment (Alba & Hasher, 1983; Neisser, 1967). An experiment on the influence of schemas on visual perception and memory used a room designed as a graduate student's office (Brewer & Treyens, 1981). However, items were included that did not fit in that setting, such as a skull, a toy top, and a picnic basket. Each subject on arrival was asked by the graduate assistant to wait in his office while he checked on the prior subject. After 35 seconds, the subject was escorted to a conference room and asked to write his or her recollections of the room. Of interest is that 88 objects were recalled by one or more subjects, of which 19 were objects not found in the room. Among the nonpresent items named by the subjects were books, a filing cabinet, coffee cup (a coffee pot was in the room), pens, and a lamp. These objects were highly relevant to the schema "office"; thus, the researchers concluded that schema knowledge became integrated with actual information about the room (p. 228). In other words, although schemas can aid in recall, as indicated by the prior study, they also can introduce errors (Neath, 1998).

The term schema is not included in the essential types of knowledge identified by Alexander et al. (1991) because the term has been interpreted in different ways over the years and has no fixed definition (Alba & Hasher, 1983; Hampson & Morris, 1996). For example, two of the problems are (1) knowing how much information to include in a schema and (2) deciding how much information should be designated as optional (Hampson & Morris, 1996). For example, the schema of a room would include walls, floor, and a ceiling. Then the question arises, should minimum dimensions be included (to differentiate "room" from "closet")? Further, should the schema of a room include windows as an option?

The most common criticism of the concept of schema is that it is too vague to be of use. That is, it explains everything, but predicts nothing (Neath, 1998, p. 331). Also the functions of schemas are met by the types of conceptual and tacit knowledge discussed earlier in this chapter.

Summary

Current models of human memory and concepts on the representation of knowledge are based on two key assumptions. They are (1) human memory is actively involved in the construction of knowledge and (2) the learner's prior knowledge plays an important role in learning. Four different views of the nature of human memory are the multistage concept, the state concept, levels of processing, and the connectionist perspectives.

The multistage model of memory identifies three structures involved in the processing of information and their associated processes. The structures are the sensory registers, short-term or working memory, and long-term memory. The associated processes are perception, encoding and the construction of meaning, and the storage and later recall of reconstructed information. The state concept, in contrast, specifies that working memory is simply an active state of information whereas long-term memory is inactive information. Tulving (1985) further described long-term memory as composed of three distinct memory systems. They are episodic, semantic, and procedural. Personal events experienced by the individual are stored in episodic memory, and general knowledge is found in semantic memory. Procedural memory enables the individual to respond adaptively to the environment. Similar to the state concept of memory is the levels of processing perspective. Specifically, a memory results from perceptual analysis that occurs in a series of sequential, hierarchical levels.

Connectionist models, in contrast, approximate the neural networks found in the brain. Memory consists of interacting connection nets composed of elements or units and links known as connection weights. Learning involves modifying the connection weights among certain units to produce output patterns.

Theorists also have proposed different forms of knowledge representation in long-term memory. (The exception is the connectionist models, which exclude the processing of symbols.) The dual-code model maintains that abstract objects and events are stored in verbal form. Environmental sounds, actions, and sensations are stored in nonverbal form. Some events and objects that have both abstract and concrete characteristics may be coded both verbally and nonverbally.

The verbal perspective, in contrast, identifies two major types of knowledge representation: declarative and procedural. Declarative knowledge is stored in the form of propositional networks, and procedural knowledge is stored in the form of if–then statements or condition–action pairs.

Larger bodies of knowledge also have been organized as to type. Tacit knowledge refers to knowledge that is implicit. Social knowledge about everyday events is an example. Included in tacit knowledge are scripts that consist of general information about the activities in frequently experienced events.

In contrast to tacit knowledge, explicit knowledge is easily available to consciousness and is the object of thought. Explicit knowledge consists of both conceptual and metacognitive knowledge. Conceptual knowledge includes both specific content and larger organizations at either the domain or discipline level. Knowledge of text structure and syntax (discourse knowledge) also is included in conceptual knowledge. Finally, metacognitive knowledge comprises the information that is essential in acquiring conceptual knowledge. Included are knowledge of oneself as a learner, task knowledge, knowledge of plans and goals, and strategy knowledge.

Another organization, schema, refers to organized knowledge, experience, and expectations about some aspect of the world. Although useful for educators, the vagueness of the concept limits its use in research.

The Components of Learning

The multistage concept of information processing identified particular processes that occur at each stage in the model. These processes are perception (short-term store), encoding (working memory), storage (long-term memory), and retrieval (long-term and working memory). Similar to computer processing, these human processes refer to activities in relation to specific items of information. Human cognition, however, often involves broader tasks, such as developing expertise in knowledge domains and disciplines. Moreover, cognitive processes do not occur in a vacuum. Instead, the information that is learned is strongly influenced by the learning framework. Included are the learner's prior knowledge and the nature of the information to be learned. In other words, learning is a product of the interactions between the learning framework and the individual's activities during learning.

The Learning Framework

The framework for learning consists of both internal and external factors. The internal factors are the types of knowledge in the individual's cognitive framework (tacit, conceptual, and metacognitive knowledge). The external factors consist of the nature and organization of the knowledge to be learned.

The Role of Learner Knowledge.   The extent and variety of knowledge that the individual brings to the learning situation influences all aspects of processing.

First, the learner's tacit and content knowledge base serves as the framework for identifying incoming information. This knowledge functions at the level of perception as the individual recognizes familiar objects, symbols, faces, and events. For example, a child may recognize a tall, leaf-bearing plant as a tree, whereas an adult perceives it as a willow, a poplar, and so on.

Second, both tacit and content knowledge are major determinants of the inferences that individuals make about new information. For example, if your friend tells you she has a big dog named Brutus, you infer that the animal has four legs and hair, barks, and is likely to be protective of his home territory (Adams, 1989). Prior knowledge also serves as the framework to minimize the potential confusion among similar types of information. For example, in reading about John Dean in *All the President's Men,* one does not confuse him with King John, Pope John, or a former classmate John (Adams, 1989).

More important, research indicates that individuals' prior knowledge predicts both rate of learning and retention scores for factual learning, general topics, and word meanings (Bors & McLeod, 1996). In other words, extent of prior knowledge has serious implications for learning.

Third, an extensive knowledge base can enhance the capacity of short-term memory by making it possible to chunk new information into large units (see the section on encoding). Fourth, prior knowledge also influences the speed of processing. For example, an art historian reading a detailed description of a particular type of Chinese porcelain can rapidly process the technical terms in the discussion because they were previously learned by the expert.

Organization of Information to Be Learned.   Two formal organizations of information to be learned are teacher presentations, including lectures, and text passages. Research on the nature of texts indicates that the ambiguity or complexity of the text influences the extent and nature of the learning. For example, expert readers briefly experience the same difficulties in constructing meaning as novice readers when faced with obscure or ambiguous text (Alexander et al., 1991).

An analysis by Garner (1992) indicated that many textbooks are difficult to read, include information that is irrelevant to the topic, seldom focus learner attention on important information, and contain long digressions (p. 53). This situation is particularly a problem for younger or less-skilled students with inadequate text-structure knowledge (a component of discourse knowledge). They are likely to acquire trivial details instead of important generalizations (p. 54). The inclusion of highly interesting details tangential to important concepts may interfere with the recall of key generalizations (Garner, 1992). However, early studies on the so-called seductive detail effect are flawed (Goetz & Sadoski, 1995). More recent studies with college students report that pictures as seductive details interfered with text recall (Harp & Mayer, 1998), but the effect was not found for all print text (Schraw, 1998). However, further research is needed with younger students.

In summary, the learner's tacit and content knowledge interact with text and other sources of information to influence learning. When the match between learner knowledge and complexity of text is poor or when learner knowledge is inaccurate or incomplete, faulty learning is likely to occur.

Perception

Both the internal and external organizations of knowledge are important components of learning. Equally important are the processing steps undertaken by the learner. Perception, the first step in comprehending information, is the process whereby information impinging on the senses is selected and recognized. Information from the environment is first detected in the form of physical energy by the sensory system (vision, hearing, touch, smell, and taste). Receptor cells in the senses transform the physical energy into neural signals that are then sent to the sensory register in the central nervous system.

However, we do not have a use for much of the environmental stimuli impinging on the senses. Thus, the sensory register serves as a brief temporary store so that some of the information may be selected for further processing. The brief availability of visual images is referred to as *iconic memory*, and the brief auditory store is known as *echoic memory*.

Information that is not attended to in the sensory registers is lost. The remaining information is rapidly compared with one's knowledge and assigned a preliminary meaning. This process, referred to as pattern recognition, is responsible for the identification of thousands of specific sensations and images, from the scent of a rose to the faces of one's friends.

Two important factors in the determination of the information that is perceived are learner attention and the learner's knowledge. **Attention** plays a key role because the individual must selectively address particular events, objects, symbols, and other stimuli if they are to be learned. Attention, however, is not an unlimited resource. Instead, it is similar to energy, fuel, or other resources that must be allocated among competing alternatives (see Grabe, 1986). As indicated earlier, for example, when vivid details in text distract learner attention, important generalizations in the material may not be attended to. Thus, learner attention may be described as a "front-line manager" that is instrumental in determining the information that will be available for encoding (Kulhavey, Schwartz, & Peterson, 1986).

One solution to the problem of the limited capacity of attention is to practice some essential tasks until they become *automatic*. Then they can be executed with little or no conscious attention. For example, the child's task of learning the shapes and names of letters requires concentration and effort. At this stage the task is described as dependent on *deliberate* or *controlled processing*. However, after extended practice and use, letter identification becomes an automatic perceptual task. Later, for good readers, word identification also becomes largely automatic, freeing attention for the tasks of comprehending meaning and developing relations among major concepts in the material.

In addition to attention, the individual's knowledge plays an important role in perception. Someone who has lived in the city all of his life, for example, may identify a large plant with a central trunk as a tree. In contrast, another individual who has lived in the country and majored in forestry in college may indicate that she has seen a hybrid American elm grafted onto a Chinese elm stock (Bruning, Schraw, & Ronning, 1995). Similarly, comparisons of the recall of chess pieces on a board viewed for 20 seconds indicated large differences between chess masters and novices (Chase & Simon, 1973). The chess masters perceived the arrangements as configurations while the beginners perceived them in terms of individual pieces.

Encoding and Constructing Meaning

In the information-processing model, **encoding** is the process whereby information is prepared so that it will be remembered. That is, perceived information is acted on in some way so that it is retained in long-term memory in an inactive state and can be retrieved later.

The process of encoding occurs in the state referred to as short-term or working memory. The capacity of working memory originally was described as "seven plus or minus two" (Miller, 1956). However, this analysis refers only to the number of items or "chunks" that can be held in short-term memory at any one time unless action is taken by the learner to retain the information. Also, a chunk varies in the amount of information it contains. For example, the letters *bkj* may be three chunks, but the three letters in *cow* are only one chunk for a fluent reader (DiVesta, 1987, p. 210).

Maintaining information in working memory is similar to the circus act of spinning plates on a reed (Anderson, 1990, p. 153). The performer must get each plate spinning in turn and then get back to the first one before it slows down and falls off. If we try to keep too many items in working memory, the first item, like the spinning plate, will fall off.

Types of Encoding Strategies.

Information can be retained in short-term memory and also remembered for later recall through various encoding strategies. These strategies are important because the accessibility of an item at a later time depends on two things: (1) the ways the item is encoded, and (2) the more ways of encoding, the greater the chances of later retrieval (Hampson & Morris, 1996).

The two major types of encoding strategies are maintenance, or **primary rehearsal,** and **elaborative rehearsal.** Reciting information over and over—such as names, dates, and definitions—is maintenance rehearsal. The problem, however, is that the effects usually are only temporary (McKeown & Curtis, 1987). In other words, studying for an examination by reciting information over and over may, on a recognition or verbatim recall test, facilitate performance. However, maintenance rehearsal does not relate the information to the student's knowledge, and the information is quickly forgotten.

In contrast, elaborative rehearsal transforms the information in some way. The information may be (1) modified so that it relates to the learner's prior knowledge, (2) replaced by another symbol (referred to as stimulus substitution by Tulving & Madigan, 1970), or (3) supplemented by additional information to aid in recall. Elaborative rehearsal makes use of associations and images and relates new information to the learner's existing knowledge. These additional connections to material already learned and additional cues to aid in recall lead to the construction of elaborated structures in memory. One perspective about the effectiveness of elaboration is that alternate routes are developed for later retrieval of the information (Anderson, 1990, p. 182). In other words, such elaborations increase the redundancy of the information that is stored in memory.

Different methods of elaborative encoding are appropriate for different kinds of information. Content knowledge that is specific and factual, such as dates of events, the spelling of words, or state capitals, requires linking the information to images or other cues that convey meaning. In contrast, concepts, principles, and ideas are related to each other in different ways. Elaborations should make use of the meaningful relationships among concepts and principles and establish connections to the student's prior knowledge.

Encoding Specific Items.   Depending on the nature of the encoding process, specific items and facts may be forgotten, stored as isolated fragments, or integrated into a larger framework. One method that enhances the encoding of specific items so that they may be remembered is additional assessment. Research on the learning of word lists indicates that a test prior to the final test increases the number of words recalled. Tests, in other words, are not merely neutral events that provide evidence of the person's knowledge (Dempster, 1996). Instead, they require individuals to retrieve information from long-term memory and interact with it again (Roediger & Guynn, 1996).

The best-known methods of encoding specific items are referred to as *mnemonics.* A mnemonic technique is "any mental strategy that facilitates the learning of material by using other, initially extraneous material as an aid" (Turnure & Lane, 1987, p. 331). Thus, mnemonic devices are one type of elaboration (Turnure & Lane, 1987). Mnemonic methods include both images and verbal cues. An example of imagery is associating the term roseola, a common viral disease of children, with the image of a spray of red rosebuds. An example of a verbal mnemonic is the acronym ROY G BIV for the seven primary colors (red, orange, yellow, green, blue, indigo, and violet).

Some advocates of imagery maintain that bizarre and vivid images are more effective than mundane images in enhancing recall (e.g., Bower, 1970). However, a review of 44 studies of normal versus bizarre images indicated that most bizarre images are effective only under certain conditions and in tests administered after only short delays (Epstein & McDaniel, 1987). Moreover, the use of bizarre images is counter to the traditional view that new information should fit into one's scheme of reality in some way (Bellezza, 1996, p. 365).

Some mnemonic methods serve as organizing frameworks for the information to be learned. A well-known organizing system that includes imagery is the **method of loci**. The method supposedly originated with the Greek poet Simonides, and it was used by the early Greek and Roman orators to remember the main points in their lengthy speeches. To use the method of loci, one should select a familiar setting, such as the rooms in a house or the pathway of a customary walk. Then, using mental images, each of the items to be remembered is associated with a particular location.

A variation of the method of loci appropriate for collections of important facts is to visualize a course of study or an area of content as a filing cabinet.

Each drawer is mentally labeled by major topics, periods of time, or some similar designation. Each folder in a drawer may represent a subtopic, a major event, a person, or some other important designation. During learning, the student visualizes the label on a particular drawer, the opening of the drawer, and the insertion of particular information in the relevant folder. For example, for a course in human development, a student may visualize the drawer labeled *early childhood* and mentally place information about children's types of play experiences in a folder labeled *play*.

To be effective as mental cues for the retrieval of information, mnemonic devices should meet three criteria. They are (1) constructibility, (2) associability, and (3) discriminability (Bellezza, 1996). Constructibility refers to the reliability *(reconstruct?)* that the cue can be generated from memory at the time of recall as well as at the time of learning. For example, the method of loci will not be effective if one or more of the locations cannot be generated at a later time.

The second criterion, associability, means that the mnemonic must be linked easily to the new information to be learned (p. 353). Typically, visual images are more readily associated with new information than abstract words.

Third, discriminability refers to the requirement that mnemonic devices must be dissimilar and easily identified as different. If they cannot be easily differentiated from each other, then more than one item of new information will become attached to basically the same cue. The result is confusion or forgetting (p. 354).

Encoding Concepts, Principles, and Ideas.   Two methods address the encoding of content knowledge that consists of concepts, principles, and ideas. They are (1) additional spaced presentations or reviews of the material, and (2) Wittrock's (1990, 1992) generative learning model.

Research indicates that presentations spaced over a period of time are almost twice as effective as two massed presentations separated by only a few hours (see Dempster, 1996, for a review). This phenomenon, referred to as "spacing effect," has been found for verbal learning tasks, addition facts, science concepts, and the processing of text materials (Dempster, 1996).

Spaced readings or reviews provide the learner with an opportunity to retrieve the information from long-term memory and to encode additional facts or details on the second reading. In contrast, the generative model, developed by Wittrock (1990, 1992), maintains that comprehension and understanding are the result of generating two types of relations. They are relations among concepts and between the student's prior experiences or knowledge base and the new information. Teaching for comprehension, according to the generative model, involves leading students to construct these two types of relations (Wittrock, 1992, p. 532). The importance of establishing relationships within the new information is supported in a study by Benton, Glover, & Bruning (1983). They found that students who answered one to three inferential questions after reading paragraphs recalled a greater number of idea units than students who read declarative versions of the question. Further, Spires and Donley (1998) found that ninth-grade students taught a prior knowledge activation strategy had higher comprehension scores than students taught a strategy for identifying the main idea.

Retrieval

The term *retrieval* refers to accessing information that has been stored in long-term memory. Although computer models may imply that retrieval is rapid and effortless, it is often reconstructive and effortful. For example, if asked to recall when a particular chair in one's living room was purchased, the owner searches her memory and recalls that it was when she lived in apartment X in town Y. This information assists in recalling that she saw it in a sale at store W (Conway, 1996).

Until the 1970s, the failure to produce information when needed was viewed as either an encoding problem or the result of the deterioration of the memory of the event (Roediger & Guynn, 1996). Tulving (1974), however, introduced the possibility that encoding and memory storage may be successful, but failure to recall an item of information occurs as a result of retrieval failure. In other words, recall of an event is a product of both (1) the encoding process and (2) the retrieval cue, which is the information in the individual's cognitive environment at the time of retrieval (p. 74). According to Tulving (1974), remembering is similar to other familiar psychological events. For example, a star in the sky can be seen if its light reaches our eyes *and* if no light is reflected from the sky around it. Similarly, we recall an event if encoding developed a memory trace *and* if something reminds us of the event (Tulving, 1974, p. 74). According to this view, information may be available in long-term memory, but may be inaccessible through lack of a retrieval cue.

The stimulus for retrieval may be an external cue, an internal cue, or a combination. In the prior example, the purchase date of the chair, the friend's question is an external cue that leads to the recall of the town and apartment lived in (internal cue), which then leads to the recall of the sale at store W.

Subsequent testing also suggests that learners develop internal cues. Experiments on the recall of categorized words, states, and other information indicate that subjects demonstrate a different pattern of recall when tested a second time. That is, they may forget some items, but recall others that were not remembered on the first test. Roediger and Guynn (1996) suggested that individuals use cues they generate themselves to guide retrieval.

Although individuals can generate mental cues that aid in recall, the encoding process is a critical step in the retrieval process. The rationale for using mnemonics for information that may be low in imagery or meaningfulness, for example, is to establish an internal mental cue that may be easily accessed at a later time.

Summary

The essential components of learning are the learning framework and the processes of perception, encoding, and retrieving the learned information from long-term memory when needed. The learning framework consists of (1) the learner's prior knowledge, both tacit and conceptual (content and discourse knowledge), and (2) the nature and organization of the information to be learned. The learner's knowledge serves as the framework for identifying incoming information and also influences the inferences made by the learner about new information. Extensive knowledge also can enhance the capacity of short-term memory to encode information in large chunks as well as the speed of processing.

Two formal organizations of material to be learned are teacher presentations and text passages. However, many textbooks are difficult to read and often include irrelevant information. Some texts use irrelevant vivid details, which can distract student attention from important information.

Perception, the first step in comprehending information, selects and recognizes information impinging on the senses. Two factors that influence perception are the learner's knowledge and learner attention. Learner attention functions as a front-line manager that determines which information will be selected for further processing while the learner's knowledge assists in the identification of incoming information.

Encoding is the process that prepares selected information for storage in long-term memory and later recall. Reciting information over and over (maintenance rehearsal) is only effective for recall within a short time period. Instead, elaborative rehearsal, which transforms information in some way and establishes links with previously learned knowledge, is an effective encoding approach. Two effective methods of elaboration for specific items of information are additional testing and mnemonics. Also important is to select a mnemonic device that can serve as a retrieval cue. Encoding concepts, principles, and ideas, in contrast, requires the construction of meaningful links between the new concepts or ideas and between the new material and the learner's prior knowledge.

PRINCIPLES OF INSTRUCTION

Information processing is a particular perspective within the larger domain of cognitive perspectives. Currently, instructional guidelines have been derived from classroom research in this area.

Basic Assumptions

The basic assumptions that underlie the information-processing view describe the nature of the human memory system and the representation of knowledge in memory. Classroom applications are derived from the assumption that human memory is an active system that selects, organizes, and encodes for storage the new information or skills to be learned. Another important goal is to develop in the learner a rich store of knowledge and effective strategies for understanding and comprehending information. In particular subject domains, such as mathematics, physics, and computer programming, the goal of instruction is to facilitate the learner's construction of new domains of knowledge that differ from the student's prior experiences.

The Components of Instruction

Major components in instruction are (1) structuring the framework for learning, (2) facilitating learner perception and encoding of information, and (3) teaching students strategies for constructing meaning.

The Learning Framework

The learning framework, in the information-processing view, consists of learner knowledge and the organization of the information to be learned. The role of instruction is (1) to contribute to the ways that learner knowledge interacts with new learning and (2) to structure the information to be learned in meaningful ways.

Enhancing the Learner's Prior Knowledge.   Both discourse knowledge, particularly text-structure knowledge, and the student's domain knowledge are important in the student's comprehension of teacher presentations and text materials.

Knowledge of Text Structure.   Garner (1990) suggested that students' lack of text knowledge hampers their ability to invoke and apply useful comprehension strategies, such as summarizing. Specifically, knowledge of text structure, particularly organization, is important in assisting readers to differentiate important from unimportant information (Dole et al., 1991; Garner, 1990). Lack of understanding of text structure is illustrated in two studies in which 20% of the seventh graders were unable to logically sequence seven randomly organized sentences into a coherent paragraph. Further, one-third of the third and fifth graders were unable to identify the topic sentence in the set of randomly ordered sentences (Garner et al., 1986).

Instruction on text structure can enhance students' comprehension of reading materials (Mayer, 1984). In addition to the organization of text, instruction on the recognition and understanding of signal words also is important. Signal words are noncontent words that emphasize the conceptual structure of the material. Examples include preview sentences, paragraph headings, and connectives such as "the problem is. . . ." Also included are "pointer words," such as *unfortunately* and *more important*.

Domain Knowledge.   Across all ages and ability levels, readers use their knowledge base as a filter to interpret and construct meaning from text passages (Dole et al., 1991). When learner knowledge is incomplete, naïve or misleading, interpretations will be incomplete or faulty (p. 24). Further, when the material to be learned is in conflict with or contradicts the learner's knowledge base, learner knowledge typically prevails (see Dochy, Segers, & Buehl, 1999, for a discussion). Inaccurate knowledge can be a major problem because the relationship between the learner's domain knowledge and text material becomes increasingly important as the student moves through the educational system (Alexander, Kulikowich, & Jetton, 1994). One reason is that texts become more important as information sources in the middle and high school grades. Thus, texts become a primary mechanism for increasing the student's domain knowledge. Paradoxically, however, the student's subject matter knowledge is an important factor in interpreting texts, which become lengthier and more complex in middle and high school (Alexander et al., 1991).

The relationship between the learner's domain knowledge and text comprehension is described by Stanovich (1986) as *Matthew effects*. The term is derived from the biblical passage in Matthew XXV:29, which states that those who have shall have abundance, but those who have not shall lose the little they have. Applied to school learning, those with more subject-matter knowledge are better able to process information from text and, therefore, acquire more domain-related information as they move from grade to grade. In contrast, students with weak domain knowledge become less able to address the more demanding texts and, thus, fall further and further behind (Alexander et al., 1994, p. 215).

One classroom strategy to address this problem is the use of classroom discussions following reading assignments. The purpose is to clarify difficult or unfamiliar concepts. For example, statements in one elementary school passage were "Plains Indians lived mainly in tepees; some California tribes lived in simple earth-covered shelters," and so forth. For children who did not know or who were unable to activate knowledge about the relationship of house style to lifestyle, climate, and availability of raw materials, the information is simply a list of arbitrary statements (Bransford, Vye, Adams, & Perfetto, 1989, p. 216). Classroom discussions in which students explore possible reasons for differences described in general statements provide experience in elaborating text and altering their prior knowledge about the topic.

Organizing the Information to Be Learned. As indicated earlier in the chapter, textbooks often are not well organized and are difficult to read. In a few studies, text material was restructured to illustrate key concepts within and between domains. The restructured material enhanced both learning and interest in the subject matter (Alexander et al., 1994). However, given that textbooks, for the most part, are unlikely to be restructured, teachers are faced with the responsibility of providing a meaningful organization for the text material. One suggested strategy is the use of **advance organizers**. As discussed in the following section, advance organizers serve as umbrellas into which the student can fit more detailed information as he or she reads. Advance organizers can assist in countering the seductive detail effect in which the reader misses the main point through focusing on vivid details.

Another possible strategy is the development of materials using nonlinear or hypercard computer materials. In such an arrangement, the learner can access portions of the information as he or she chooses. However, many of the initial hypercard texts that have been researched to date are quite lengthy (Alexander et al., 1991). Such texts can pose a problem for readers with poor processing strategies.

One hypercard development used as supplementary material in coordinated English and history high school courses addressed a key difficulty in designing an appropriate conceptual structure in the humanities and social sciences. That is, items of information often are multiply linked to different topics and the meaning of an abstract concept depends, in part, on the ways it relates to other concepts (Spoehr, 1994). The modules (hypercard stacks) were organized into three "conceptual neighborhoods" (themes): (1) historical periods, (2) literary movements/individual authors, and (3) themes in American culture (e.g., popular music, war and revolution). Initial entry generates a choice of one of three "neighborhoods." A choice typically provides the learner with a finer-grain subdivision of options. Of importance is that, when the learner selects an option, the program first displays an overview screen that diagrammatically illustrates the major relationships between the conceptual themes and the types of information on the topic.

Also, as the learner, in exploring the topic, "descends" into more detailed levels of information, the program also provides suboverviews of relationships at those levels (p. 895). In addition to assisting the learner to develop a conceptual organization of information, the overviews are intended to avoid the problems of learners wandering through the material in inefficient and disorganized ways, missing sections of relevant information, or getting lost. In other words, the information within the three major themes is organized hierarchically and laterally (Spoehr, 1994).

Facilitating Learner Attention

Of major importance in planning instruction is that the learner does not respond to instruction as presented. Instead, the learner responds to the instruction that he or she actively apprehends (Shulman, 1986). Thus, an important aspect of instruction is to first structure the environment so that student attention is focused on important tasks (Bruning et al., 1995) and then to informally assess learner perceptions. One approach is to introduce preteaching activities that activate students' relevant knowledge. For example, prior to a lesson on heat conduction and the relationship of an object's density to its heat conduction, students generate examples of objects that conduct heat. One girl named the handle of the metal frying pan on a hot stove burner, another the outside-facing wall of a room on a cold day, and so on. A carefully controlled experiment in which several different materials of the same size were placed in a flame led to a discussion as to why some of the materials became warm quickly while others seemed to remain cool (Bruning et al., 1995).

Advance Organizers.   The concept of advance organizers, introduced by Ausubel (1968), refers to highly inclusive concepts that would serve as "ideational scaffolding." Presented prior to instruction, the purpose is to serve as an "umbrella" into which more detailed information is incorporated as learning progresses. The material must be carefully selected to serve as a link between the student's present store of information and the new learning. According to Ausubel (1968), advance organizers provide a conceptual framework and also facilitate encoding. More recently, theorists have suggested that advance organizers are effective because they activate the learner's prior knowledge.

The two types of organizers identified by Ausubel (1968) are expository (used with unfamiliar material) and comparative (used to facilitate the integration of new ideas in relatively familiar material with similar, previously learned concepts).

Although some of the early research indicated no effects, Corkill (1992) noted that a variety of materials, such as prereading activities, paragraph headings, study objectives, and outlines, were mislabeled as advance organizers. Subsequent research indicated that written organizers should be concrete and contain an example that illustrates the analogous relationship between ideas in the advance organizer and ideas in the new material (Corkill, 1992, p. 63). Also important is that the advance organizer must be at the appropriate reading level for the student and assist the student in accessing relevant knowledge. Thus, different students may require different advance organizers, depending on their prior knowledge and reading levels.

Teaching Selective Attention Strategies.   The second major task for teachers in facilitating learner attention is to teach students to be strategic processors of information. The initial key step is focusing attention on important ideas, facts, concepts, and generalizations to be learned. However, researchers note that, particularly when reading text materials, the attention of both children and adults often is not strategic, conscious, or selective (Garner, 1992, p. 58). That is, when individuals process meaningful materials, they often do so superficially (Pressley et al., 1992).

Teachers can provide instruction on focusing attention, using questions first to direct students' attention to important material and then observing their use of these questions on their own. Appropriate questions to begin with are, Where should we look first for important information? (first or second sentence in the paragraph) and What other information do we need to include? (Garner, 1992).

Facilitating the Encoding of Specific Items (use of mnemonics)
Laboratory research on the encoding of word lists indicates that a test prior to the final assessment enhances recall. In the classroom, this practice can apply to spelling and vocabulary in the elementary grades. A practice test administered on Wednesday, for example, can indicate learning problems prior to the weekly graded test on Friday.

The method referred to as mnemonics is appropriate for arbitrary associations in different subject areas that must be learned. Sentences and acronyms, for example, are organizational mnemonics that assist in learning the information, and they also serve as retrieval cues for later recall. They are most effective for items that must be recalled in a certain order (Snowman, 1986). For example, a useful mnemonic for music students is the sentence, "Every good boy does fine." The initial letters of the words *(e, g, b, d, f)* are the notes printed on the lines of the treble clef. Similarly, the word *face* represents the notes printed in the spaces *(f, a, c, e)*.

Acronyms, rhymes, and sentences are most effective for items that must be recalled in a certain order (Snowman, 1986). An example useful for anatomy students is the rhyme, "On old Olympia's towering top, a Finn, Visigoth, and German vault, skip, and hop" (Solso, 1988, p. 227). The initial letter of each word of the first line represents the cranial nerves (olfactory, optic, oculomotor, trochlear, trigeminal, and so on).

Both visual and verbal learner-generated cues can enhance encoding. A flexible mnemonic technique, originally developed for foreign-language learning, is the keyword method. The method divides vocabulary learning into two major steps. The first step is for the learner to select an English word that sounds like some part of the foreign language word. This step is the acoustical link (Atkinson, 1975, p. 821). The second step is to form a mental image of the keyword interacting with the English equivalent of the foreign language word, referred to as an imagery link. For example, the Spanish word for *duck* sounds like "pot-o" (acoustical link). An interactive image is that of a duck hiding under an overturned flower pot. Another example (Jones & Hall, 1982) is the use of the keyword *wave* for the Spanish word *huevo* (wave-o), which means "egg." The visual image is that of a giant egg riding the crest of a wave.

Although designed for foreign language learning, the keyword method is applicable also to other learning tasks. It has been used in learning medical definitions, linking explorers with discoveries (Jones & Hall, 1982), enhancing memory for facts (Levin, 1986), and increasing learning from text (McCormick & Levin, 1984). Mnemonic imagery is also useful for learning information about totally unfamiliar concepts, such as information about unknown countries (Pressley, Johnson, Symons, McGoldrick, & Kurita, 1989, p. 12).

Several studies indicate that both mentally retarded and learning disabled students can learn imagery-based strategies to enhance learning and recall in several areas (see Mastropieri & Fulk, 1990, and Turnure & Lane, 1987). In some studies, regular classroom teachers implemented the methods over time and reported increased recall on both immediate and delayed posttests. However, Turnure and Lane (1987) caution that educators must not succumb to the illusion that installing an array of monolithic information-processing mnemonics can rescue students from all their learning, memory, and thinking problems (p. 330). To be effective, mnemonic techniques must be explained, demonstrated, and applied in many, many situations in which they are to be used. However, this method and other elaborative techniques can serve as mental cues to recall items that are low in imagery or meaningfulness (Bellezza, 1996).

In addition to enhancing the recall of specific items, mnemonic methods also may be useful in conveying both meaning and structure when terms are hierarchically organized. Levin and Levin (1990) developed a mnemonic system for plant classification terms in which (1) the particular terms were recoded into acoustically or orthographically similar concrete proxies (keywords), and (2) links between the terms were represented as pictorial semantic relationships. For example, angiosperm became an angel who is holding a pet leash attached to a monkey (for monocotylan) and the monkey is shooting an arrow (for arales) at a frying pan (for pandanales) (p. 302). The subordinate relationships were illustrated in the picture by placing the images in sequence from the top to the bottom of the picture beginning with the angel at the top. Results indicated that the system, when compared to a taxonomy chart, significantly increased recall on both immediate and delayed tests (2 months later) for college students. Also important is that the mnemonic group was more fluent in accurately placing the plant terms within the taxonomy.

Strategies Instruction

Teaching processes and strategies for learning concepts, principles, and ideas is important for two reasons. One is that students tend to overestimate their comprehension of text. Bradshaw (2000) found no relationship between the self-ratings of elementary school children on their text comprehension and their performance on specific comprehension questions. The other reason for strategic instruction is that many students fail to use effective strategies. Specifically, strategies are operations over and above the processes that are involved in a task (Pressley, Borkowski, & Schneider, 1987). Important issues in strategy instruction are the types of strategies for constructing meaning and the steps in strategy instruction. " *Constructively - Responsive Reading* "

Types of Strategies for Constructing Meaning.   Two specific strategies shown to be effective for constructing meaning from both text and orally presented material are summarizing and self-questioning. The purpose of these strategies is to assist students to construct a model of meaning from their prior knowledge from cues noted in the material and from the instructional context (Dole et al., 1991).

Summarizing.   The purpose of summarization is to capture the gist of instruction while, at the same time, reducing the material. Effective summarization requires that the learner sift through large organizations of information, distinguish important from unimportant ideas, and then synthesize the key ideas into a new coherent organization that represents the original (Dole et al., 1991). Brown and Day (1983) identified several rules for developing useful summaries. They are (1) delete unnecessary material, (2) eliminate redundancy, (3) substitute a superordinate term for groups of terms and/or lists of events, and (4) invent a topic sentence if none appears in the text.

Summarization often is recommended as a strategy for enhancing the meaning of reading passages. In addition, King (1992) found that the strategies enhanced the comprehension of orally presented material. She taught students a summarization strategy following notetaking during lectures. The strategy involved (1) turning the topic into a sentence that reflected the main idea and (2) successively linking subtopics (or the main idea) and related ideas together.

The effectiveness of summarization, however, depends on the student's ability to differentiate important from unimportant information (Dole et al., 1991). In reading, for example, research indicates that good readers use their general knowledge and domain knowledge as well as their knowledge of text structure to help them determine importance (Dole et al., 1991). Garner (1990) differentiates strategically inefficient from strategically efficient summarizers on the basis of this capability. That is, inefficient summarizers copy ideas verbatim from text and do not paraphrase or combine ideas. In contrast, efficient summarizers select only the most important text, use rules for condensing text, and produce coherent summaries (p. 263).

Self-Questioning.   Teacher-generated questions are a traditional practice in the teaching of reading. Current research, however, indicates that teaching students to generate their own questions stimulates their inferences and explanations about the material and, therefore, their understanding (Dole et al., 1991; King, 1991, 1992; Pressley et al., 1992).

The product generated in self-questioning is a set of questions and answers about the instruction. When the questions require inferences by the learner, that is, when they are high-level questions, they can assist the learner to organize the new material and to integrate the information with existing knowledge. In addition, self-questioning also is a metacognitive strategy because it is a way for learners to check their level of comprehension and understanding (King, 1992).

Asking high-level questions is particularly important in facilitating understanding. Pressley et al. (1992) note that questions that affect only selective attention or maintenance rehearsal do not require transformation of the material. The result is small, if any, learning gains.

One role of self-questioning is useful in relation to facts. Referred to as elaborative interrogation, the method involves asking "why" questions about factual statements in text passages. For example, for statements on Canadian provinces, Canadian university students asked questions such as, "Why would it make sense that the first radio stations were in Alberta?" (Pressley et al., 1992). For the students, the researchers hypothesized that the "why" questions activated the students' prior knowledge related to the new facts (p. 98).

One approach to generating thought-provoking questions is to teach specific stems (King, 1990, 1991, 1992). This strategy is appropriate for high school and college students. Examples are How would you use _____ to _____ ? What is a new example of _____ ? Explain why _____ . How does _____ affect _____ ? What do you think would happen if _____ ? (King, 1992, p. 114). Formulating such questions forces students to identify main ideas and the ways the ideas relate to each other and to the students' prior knowledge and experience. These two levels of elaborations are the essential components in Wittrock's (1990) model.

A strategy recommended by King (1994) is referred to as guided cooperative questioning. In small groups or pairs, students ask each other specific thought-provoking questions on the material presented in teacher-led presentations and lessons. Students were taught two types of specific stems: lesson-based questions and experience-based questions. Examples of lesson-based questions include What does _____ mean? Why is _____ important? How are _____ and _____ similar? What are strengths and weaknesses of _____ ? (p. 341). Examples of experience-based questions are What would happen if _____ ? How could _____ be used to _____ ? How does _____ tie in with _____ that we learned before? (p. 341). Combining the two types of questions for a science lesson was more effective than either lesson-based questions or learner construction of cognitive maps of science concepts.

A third approach to self-questioning addresses the identification of story themes by elementary school students (Williams et al., 2002). Children first are taught four organizing questions that assist them to identify important plot components that provide information for developing a theme. They are "Who is the main character? What is the main character's problem? What did the main character do about the problem? And then what happened?" (p. 236). The teacher should introduce these questions by both asking and answering them, providing a model for the students. After the students have demonstrated proficiency with these questions, four organizing items can lead to theme identification. They are "Was what happened good or bad? Why was it good or bad? The main character learned that he/she could _____ . We should _____ " (p. 237).

A fourth approach that raised the reading scores of poor comprehenders combined instruction on looking for clue words in passages with answering "who," "where," "why," and "when" questions (McGee & Johnson, 2003). Children between the ages of 6 and 9 identified as poor comprehenders participated in groups of five in two sessions per week (20 to 30 minutes each) for three weeks. For the children, looking for clue words was a novel activity; they had not deconstructed text in that way before (p. 56).

Recommendations for Strategy Instruction.   A frequent criticism of strategy instruction is that students do not continue using the strategies without specific directions to do so (Pressley & El-Dinary, 1992, p. 86). However, implementing particular steps along with strategy instruction does promote transfer to other similar tasks. A first step in strategy instruction is to determine the particular activities undertaken by students and the underlying rationales for their actions. To the extent that students are skimming a passage merely to get through it suggests an avoidance of school tasks and/or a sense that such tasks have no inherent meaning for life in the world outside of school.

Next, demonstrate the benefits of strategy use in both school assignments and other activities. For example, demonstrate the role of strategies in reading to construct a model of meaning from one's prior knowledge and cues noted in the text and the situational context (Dole et al., 1991). Another activity is for students to compare their performance before and after using the particular strategy (Pressley & El-Dinary, 1992).

Other essential steps in strategy instruction are (1) to describe and then model the strategy and (2) to provide teacher-guided practice accompanied by praise and corrective feedback. Practice should begin with simple materials and progress to grade-level tasks (Pressley et al., 1989, p. 25). Also important is to teach students when and where to use particular strategies. This information is an important component of the student's metacognitive knowledge (see chapter 9).

Strategy instruction is not a "quick fix." Strategies such as paraphrasing, summarizing, and self-questioning require time and practice to develop. Therefore, only one strategy should be taught at a time, and it should be learned well prior to the introduction of another strategy.

In summary, successful strategy instruction should not be viewed as remediation. Instead, the goal is to develop sophisticated comprehension skills in all students (Pressley et al., 1989).

Summary

Major components in instruction from the information-processing perspective are enhancing prior learner knowledge, organizing the material to be learned, facilitating learner attention, encoding and the construction of meaning, and teaching students strategies to enhance their understanding of text and oral presentations.

Both discourse knowledge and the student's domain knowledge are important in the comprehension of text materials and teacher presentation. Teachers can assist students in developing text-structure knowledge by teaching them to recognize signals such as preview sentences, paragraph headings, and signal words. For students with poor background knowledge or for texts that are poorly written, small group and class discussions can develop some of the missing links.

Of major importance in planning instruction is the realization that the student responds only to the instruction that he or she actively apprehends. Therefore, instruction should focus learner attention on important tasks and informally assess learner perceptions. One approach is to implement preteaching activities that activate prior knowledge and/or link prior knowledge to key concepts. Another approach is to use advance organizers. They are highly inclusive concepts that serve as a link between the student's present store of information and the new learning. Their purpose is to serve as a conceptual framework and also to facilitate encoding. Another instructional strategy is to teach students ways to find important information in text and other materials.

Methods for encoding specific items of information such as vocabulary words, dates, and facts include prior testing and various mnemonic techniques. Examples are rhymes, acronyms, sayings, and learner-generated cues, such as the keyword method. Designed for foreign language learning, the student first selects an English word that sounds like some part of the foreign word. Then the student forms a mental image of the keyword interacting with the English equivalent. Imagery-based strategies can also aid mentally retarded students and learning-disabled students with learning and recall.

Two strategies for the construction of meaning for complex information are summarizing and self-questioning. One summarization strategy involves turning the topic into a sentence that reflects the main idea and successively linking subtopics and related ideas together.

Self-questioning can be useful both for facts and other types of information. When used for facts, the method involves asking "why" questions about factual statements in text passages. The purpose is to activate students' prior knowledge related to the new facts. Self-questioning to generate the meanings in a passage should involve application questions in which the learner generates new examples, explains how the key concepts are used, and identifies relationships between major ideas. Use of such strategies also depends on the student's metacognitive strategies, which are discussed in chapter 9.

EDUCATIONAL APPLICATIONS

Information-processing theories began as a research effort to understand the cognitive operations undertaken by humans. Investigations of the ways that students process information in various subject areas are increasing (Lampert, 1990; Rohrer & Thomas, 1989; Schoenfeld, 1985). In addition, methods for developing students' understanding and use of strategies to facilitate processing also are being developed (see King, 1992, 1994; Pressley et al., 1992).

Classroom Issues

Classroom issues addressed by information-processing theory are those that are directly related to cognitive processes.

Learner Characteristics

The student characteristics that are important in the management of classroom learning are individual differences, readiness for learning, and motivation. Of these three, the concept of individual differences is addressed directly in relation to problem solving, which is discussed in chapter 9.

Cognitive Processes and Instruction

The focus in information-processing theories is the variety of processes whereby individuals perceive, encode, remember, recall, and apply information or knowledge. The issues of transfer of learning and learning "how-to-learn" skills are also addressed.

Transfer of Learning. Typically, transfer of learning refers to skills or knowledge learned in one context or situation that later are applied in new contexts. Mnemonic techniques and other mechanisms to assist encoding are generalizable to a variety of settings, as are text comprehension strategies and others.

However, transfer will not occur unless the appropriate prior knowledge is activated. This failure to activate relevant knowledge that has been learned is referred to as *inert knowledge* (Bransford et al., 1989; Whitehead, 1929). The problem of inert knowledge (i.e., lack of transfer) may be the result of (1) memorizing rather than learning the significance of new information, (2) acquiring concepts in a limited context, or (3) being unable to access acquired knowledge efficiently with minimal effort (Bransford et al., 1989, p. 214). Important in facilitating the transfer of strategies for specific tasks, such as comprehending text, are the student's skills in managing and directing his or her own learning.

Learning "How-to-Learn" Skills. The term *metacognition* refers to the capabilities required to direct one's learning, remembering, and thinking, discussed in chapter 9.

Teaching Problem Solving. This topic is discussed in chapter 9.

The Social Context for Learning

Information-processing theories focus on the cognitive mechanisms involved in the comprehension and retention of sensory data from the environment, as well as the application of learned information to solving problems. Although much of this learning occurs in a social environment, the theories have yet to address the influence of that environment on cognitive processing.

Relationships to Other Perspectives

Like Gestalt psychology, information-processing theory also assesses perception. However, the Gestalt psychologists discussed perception only in problem-solving situations that require a reorganization of visual stimuli. In contrast, information-processing theory treats perception as one of the major steps in acquiring and remembering information.

Information-processing theory also discusses strategies for constructing meaning that operate within a context of predetermined knowledge to be learned. Constructivists, however, maintain that such constraints prevent the "true" construction of knowledge, which, instead, must begin with the learner and does not build toward a performed outcome.

The comprehension of knowledge in a subject-matter area or domain is the focus of information processing. Unlike Gagné's conditions of learning, the theory does not address the different types of cognitive operations that may be developed in relation to knowledge.

Developing a Classroom Strategy

The importance of designing instruction for information processing is that logical meaning of the knowledge is transformed into psychological meaning. Logical meaning is the relationship of the symbols, concepts, and rules of the subject area. Psychological meaning is the relationship of the symbols, concepts, and rules to the student's cognitive structure (Ausubel, 1968). Developing psychological meaning in the comprehension of knowledge and in solving problems depends on student interaction with the subject matter.

Comprehension

Step 1: Develop cues to guide the reception of the new learning.

    1.1 What informal questions will access the learner's existing cognitive structure?

    1.2 Does the lesson include broadly written objectives or a statement of purpose that can direct the learner's attention?

    1.3 How will the new knowledge or skills enhance or build on the learner's existing knowledge?

Step 2: Select or develop conceptual supports that facilitate the encoding of information.

    2.1 What information should be included in advance organizers so that they bridge the student's knowledge and the new learning?

    2.2 What concepts, episodes, and images already acquired by the student may be used to illustrate the new terms, definitions, or concepts?

    2.3 Are there adjunct questions in the text or major points in the text that can be used as a basis for secondary rehearsal by the students?

    2.4 What are the logical points in the instruction for students to engage in secondary rehearsal (i.e., visual and/or verbal elaboration)? What are some examples of associative images and verbal codes that can be provided to students?

Step 3: Develop cues that aid in the retrieval of learned information.

    3.1 What are some comparisons with related concepts, terms, or ideas that may be made? For example, if the concept is *morpheme,* it may be contrasted with *phoneme* and compared with the term *word.*

    3.2 What inference questions may be used to conclude the lesson?

Comprehension Strategies

Step 1: Teach attention-focusing strategies.

    1.1 Use questions first to direct students' attention to important material.

    1.2 Provide opportunities for students to apply the questions.

Step 2: Teach summarization and self-questioning strategies.

    2.1 Demonstrate turning topic sentences into a statement of the main idea.

    2.2 Demonstrate linking the main idea to subtopics.

    2.3 Provide opportunities for student application, feedback, and further opportunities for application.

    2.4 Demonstrate the use of generic question stems to generate information from text.

    2.5 Provide opportunities for student application, feedback, and further opportunities for application.

Classroom Example

The following strategy is a component of the story grammar strategy developed to assist students with learning and/or writing problems to write better stories. The strategy is a component in a program developed by Graham and Harris (1994) to teach writing and self-regulation skills to students with learning problems. The purpose is to provide students with an explicit, context-based strategy.

> *Initial conference:* The purpose of instruction is explained. Teacher and students then discuss the common parts of a story and the goal for learning the story grammar strategy.

> *Pre-skill development:* Teacher and students discuss the common story parts (characters, place, time, setting) and story episodes (precipitating event, characters' goals, action to achieve goals, resolution, and characters' reactions).

> *Story grammar strategy:* The following steps to help the students write stories are taught by the teacher:

1. Think of a story you would like to share with others.
2. Let your mind be free.
3. Write down the reminders of the story parts (W-W-W; What = 2; How = 2).

> *W* — Who is the main character? Who else is in the story?
> *W* — When does the story take place?
> *W* — Where does the story take place?
> *What* does the main character do or want to do and what do the other characters do?
> *What* happens with other characters?

How does the story end?

How do the main character and the other characters feel? (Graham & Harris, 1994, p. 219)

4. Make notes of your ideas for the story parts.
5. Write the story. Use some parts, add, expand, or revise as you go (summarized from Graham & Harris, 1994).

Review of the Theory

The communications research of World War II and computer simulations of human intellectual capabilities introduced a new paradigm to the study of mental operations. This paradigm is reflected in the information-processing descriptions of mental operations. According to this paradigm, the human memory is an active organized system that selects the information to be processed and then transforms that information into meaningful codes for later use (see Table 8.3).

TABLE 8.3
Summary of Information-Processing Theory

Basic Elements	Definition
Assumptions	Human memory is a complex and active organizer of information; the memory system transforms information for storage (and later retrieval) in long-term memory.
Learning	The processes by which information from the environment is transformed into cognitive structures
Learning outcome	Some form of cognitive structure; the prevalent view is that of semantic networks.
Components of learning	The processes of perception, encoding, and storage in long-term memory
Designing instruction for complex skills	See chapter 9
Major issues in designing instruction	Relating new learning to existing knowledge; teaching students to monitor comprehension; and structuring learning to facilitate processing
ANALYSIS OF THE THEORY	
Disadvantages	Information-processing theory lacks a coordinated theoretical foundation; various perspectives are somewhat disjointed.
	Computer model of cognitive processes may or may not be valid.
Contribution to classroom practice	Identification of the importance of designing instruction for the cognitive processes in learning

The core of the theory comprises the processes by which individuals perceive, encode, and then store information in long-term memory for later use. The theorists agree that codes are stored internally in some type of cognitive structure. The prevalent view is that this structure takes the form of semantic networks, in which verbal elements are linked to each other. Large bodies of knowledge are categorized as tacit and explicit. Included in explicit knowledge are domain and discipline knowledge (content knowledge), discourse knowledge, and metacognitive knowledge.

Key components in learning include (1) the learning framework, which consists of the learner's knowledge and the organization of the information to be learned, and (2) the learner's cognitive processes, learning strategies, and metacognitive decisions. Applications to education include specific recommendations for enhancing the learner's prior knowledge, the use of advance organizers, and the use of learner-generated cues for encoding and constructing meaning. Included are the use of images, combinations of images and words, and students' summarization and self-questioning strategies.

Disadvantages

Information-processing theory is a collection of various approaches to the study of cognitive functions. Thus, the theory lacks an overarching framework for integrating the various research studies.

Contributions to Classroom Practice

Information-processing theory has described in detail the processes that the Gestalt theorists were attempting to identify. For classroom learning, the processes identified in encoding and constructing meaning indicate the importance of structuring lessons to support these processes and to teach strategies to enhance comprehension. Table 8.2 summarizes information-processing theory.

CHAPTER QUESTIONS

1. A student is faced with the task of learning the following information stated in a biology textbook: Arteries are thick, elastic, and carry blood rich in oxygen from the heart. Veins are thinner, less elastic, and carry blood rich in carbon dioxide from the body to the heart.

   _____a. What are some visual imagery and/or mnemonic elaborations that the student may generate to facilitate learning this information?

   _____b. What information can the teacher provide about the significance or relevance of these facts that may assist the student in remembering the information?

2. Why are the sentences in _Set A_ below easier to remember than the sentences in _Set B_?

   _____ _Set A_: Benjamin Franklin flew the kite. George Washington hid the ax. Santa Claus walked on the roof. Noah built a boat.

   _____ _Set B_: Jim flew the kite. John hid the ax. Ted walked on the roof. Malcolm built a boat (Bransford et al., 1989, p. 204).

REFERENCES

Adams, M. J. (1989). Thinking skills curricula. *Educational Psychologist, 24*(1), 25–77.

Alba, J. W., & Hasher, L. (1983). Is memory schematic? *Psychological Bulletin, 93,* 203–231.

Alexander, P. A. (1992). Domain knowledge: Evolving themes and emerging concerns. *Educational Psychologist, 27*(1), 33–51.

Alexander, P. A., Kulikowich, J. M., & Jetton, J. (1994). The role of subject-matter knowledge and interest in the processing of linear and nonlinear texts. *Review of Educational Research, 64*(2), 201–252.

Alexander, P. A., Schallert, D. A., & Hare, V. C. (1991). Coming to terms: How researchers in learning and literacy talk about knowledge. *Review of Educational Research, 61*(3), 315–343.

Anderson, J. R. (1983). *The architecture of cognition.* Cambridge, MA: Harvard University Press.

Anderson, J. R. (1990). *Cognitive psychology and its implications* (3rd ed.). New York: Freeman.

Anderson, J. R. (1993). Problem solving and learning. *American Psychologist, 48*(1), 35–44.

Ashmead, D. H., & Perlmutter, M. (1980). Infant memory in everyday life. In M. Perlmutter (Ed.), *New directions for child development: Children's memory* (Vol. 10, pp. 1–16). San Francisco: Jossey-Bass.

Atkinson, R. C. (1975). Mnemotechnics in second-language learning. *American Psychologist, 30,* 821–825.

Ausubel, D. P. (1968). *Educational psychology: A cognitive view.* New York: Holt, Rinehart & Winston.

Bartlett, F. C. (1932). *Remembering.* New York: Cambridge University Press.

Bellezza, F. S. (1996). Mnemonic methods to enhance storage and retrieval. In E. L. Bjork & R. A. Bjork (Eds.), *Memory: Handbook of perception and cognition* (2nd ed.) (pp. 345–380). San Diego, CA: Academic Press.

Benton, S. L., Glover, J. A., & Bruning, R. H. (1983). The effect of number of decisions on prose recall. *Journal of Educational Psychology, 75,* 382–390.

Bereiter, C. (1991). Implication of connectionism for thinking about rules. *Educational Researcher, 20*(3), 10–16.

Bors, D. A., & McLeod, C. M. (1996). Individual differences in memory. In E. L. Bjork & R. A. Bjork (Eds.), *Memory: Handbook of perception and cognition* (2nd ed.) (pp. 411–441). San Diego, CA: Academic Press.

Bower, G. H. (1970). Imagery as a relational organizer in associative learning. *Journal of Verbal Learning and Verbal Behavior, 9,* 529–533.

Bradshaw, B.K. (2000). Do students effectively monitor their comprehension? *Reading Horizons, 41*(3), 143–154.

Bransford, J. D., Vye, N., Adams, L. T., & Perfetto, G. (1989). Learning skills and the acquisition of strategies. In A. Lesgold & R. Glaser (Eds.), *Foundations for a psychology of education* (pp. 199–249). Hillsdale, NJ: Erlbaum.

Brewer, W. F., & Treyens, J. T. (1981). Role of schemata in memory for places. *Cognitive Psychology, 13,* 207–230.

Broadbent, D. E. (1958). *Perception and communication.* London: Pergamon.

Brown, A. L., & Campione, J. C. (1994). Guided discovery in a community of learners. In K. McGilly (Ed.), *Classroom lessons: Integrating cognitive theory and classroom practice* (pp. 229–274). Cambridge, MA: MIT Press.

Brown, A. L., & Day, D. (1983). Macrorules for summarizing texts: The development of expertise. *Journal of Verbal Learning and Verbal Behavior, 22,* 1–14.

Bruning, R. H., Schraw, G. S., & Ronning, R. R. (1995). *Cognitive psychology and instructions.* Upper Saddle River, NJ: Merrill/Prentice Hall.

Chase, W. G., & Simon, H. A. (1973). The mind's eye in chess. In W. G. Chase & H. A. Simon (Eds.), *Visual information-processing* (pp. 215–281). New York: Academic.

Clark, J. M., & Paivio, A. (1991). Dual coding theory and education. *Educational Psychology Review, 3*(3), 149–210.

Collins, A. M., & Quillian, M. R. (1969). Retrieval time from semantic memory. *Journal of Verbal Learning and Verbal Behavior, 8,* 240–247.

Conway, M. A. (1996). Autobiographical memory. In E. L. Bjork and R. A. Bjork (Eds.), *Memory: Handbook of perception and cognition* (2nd ed.) (pp. 165–194). San Diego, CA: Academic Press.

Corkill, A. J. (1992). Advance organizers: Facilitators of recall. *Educational Psychology Review, 4*(1), 33–68.

Craik, F. I. M. (1979). Levels of processing: Overview and closing comments. In L. S. Cermak & F. I. M. Clark (Eds.), *Levels of processing human memory.* Hillsdale, NJ: Erlbaum.

Craik, F. I. M., & Lockhart, R. S. (1972). Levels of processing: A framework for memory research. *Journal of Verbal Learning and Verbal Behavior, 11,* 671–684.

Dempster, F. N. (1996). Distributing and managing the conditions of encoding and practice. In E. L. Bjork & R. A. Bjork (Eds.), *Memory: Handbook of perception and cognition* (2nd ed.) (pp. 317–344). San Diego, CA: Academic Press.

DiVesta, F. J. (1987). The cognitive movement and education. In J. Glover & R. Ronnings (Eds.), *Historical foundations of educational psychology* (pp. 203–233). New York: Plenum.

Dochy, F., Segers, M., & Buehl, M. (1999). The relation between assessment practices and outcomes of studies: The case of research on prior knowledge. *Review of Educational Research, 69*(2), 145–186.

Dole, J. A., Duffy, G., Roehler, L. R., & Pearson, P. D. (1991). Moving from the old to the new: Research on reading comprehension instruction. *Review of Educational Research, 61*(2), 239–264.

Edelman, G. M. (1987). *Neural Darwinism: The theory of neuronal group selection.* New York: Basic Books.

Epstein, G. O., & McDaniel, M. A. (1987). Distinctiveness and the mnemonic benefits of bizarre images. In M. A. McDaniel & M. Pressley (Eds.), *Imagery and related mnemonic processes: Theories, individual differences, and applications.* New York: Springer-Verlag.

Garner, R. (1990). Children's use of strategies in reading. In D. Bjorklund (Ed.), *Children's strategies: Contemporary views of cognitive development* (pp. 245–268). Hillsdale, NJ: Erlbaum.

Garner, R. (1992). Learning from school texts. *Educational Psychologist, 27*(1), 53–64.

Garner, R., Alexander, P., Slater, W., Hare, V. C., Smith, T., & Rcis, R. (1986). Children's knowledge of structural properties of expository text. *Journal of Educational Psychology, 78,* 411–416.

Goetz, E. T., & Sadoski, M. (1995). The perils of seduction: Distracting details or incomprehensible abstractions? *Reading Research Quarterly, 30,* 500–511.

Grabe, M. (1986). Attentional processes in education. In G. Phye & T. Andre (Eds.), *Cognitive classroom learning* (pp. 49–82). Orlando, FL: Academic.

Graham, S., & Harris, K. R. (1994). The role and development of self-regulation in the writing process. In D. Schunk & B. J. Zimmerman (Eds.), *Self-regulation of learning and performance.* Hillsdale, NJ: Erlbaum.

Hampson, P. J., & Morris, P. E. (1996). *Understanding cognition.* Cambridge, MA: Blackwell.

Harp, S. F., & Mayer, R. E. (1998). How seductive details do their damage: A theory of cognitive interest in science learning. *Journal of Educational Psychology, 90*(3), 414–434.

Holyoak, M. (1991). Symbolic connectionism: A paradigm for third-generation theory of expertise. In K. A. Ericsson & J. Smith (Eds.), *Toward a general theory of expertise.* New York: Cambridge University Press.

Iran-Nejad, A., Marsh, G. E., & Clements, A. C. (1992). The figure and the ground of constructive brain functioning: Beyond explicit memory processes. *Educational Psychologist, 7*(4), 473–492.

James, W. (1890). *The principles of psychology.* New York: Henry Holt.

Jones, B. F., & Hall, J. W. (1982). School applications of the mnemonic keyword method as a study strategy for eighth graders. *Journal of Educational Psychology, 74,* 230–237.

King, A. (1990). Reciprocal peer-questioning: A strategy for teaching students how to learn from lectures. *The Clearing House, 64,* 131–135.

King, A. (1991). Effects of training in strategic questioning on children's problem-solving performance. *Journal of Educational Psychology, 83,* 307–317.

King, A. (1992). Comparison of self-questioning, summarizing, and notetaking review as strategies for learning from lectures. *American Educational Research Journal, 29*(2), 311–323.

King, A. (1994). Guiding knowledge construction in the classroom: Effects of teaching children how to question and how to explain. *American Educational Research Journal, 31*(2), 338–368.

Kulhavey, R. W., Schwartz, N. H., & Peterson, S. (1986). Working memory: The encoding process. In G. Phye & T. Andre (Eds.), *Cognitive classroom learning* (pp. 115–140). Orlando, FL: Academic.

Lampert, M. (1990). When the problem is not the question and the solution is not the answer: Mathematical knowing and teaching. *American Educational Research Journal, 27*(1), 29–63.

Levin, J. R. (1986). Educational applications of mnemonic pictures: Possibilities beyond your wildest imagination. In A. A. Sheikh (Ed.), *Imagery in the educational process* (pp. 202–265). Farmingdale, NY: Baywood.

Levin, M. E., & Levin, J. R. (1990). Scientific mnemonics: Methods for maximizing more than memory. *American Educational Research Journal, 27*(2), 301–321.

Martin, J. (1993). Episodic memory: A neglected phenomenon in the psychology of education. *Educational Psychologist, 28*(2), 169–183.

Mastropieri, M. A., & Fulk, B. J. M. (1990). Enhancing academic performance with mnemonic instruction. In T. E. Scruggs & B. Y. L. Wong (Eds.), *Intervention research in learning disabilities* (pp. 102–112). New York: Springer-Verlag.

Mayer, R. E. (1984). Aids to text comprehension. *Educational Psychologist, 19,* 30–42.

McClelland, J. L., & Rumelhart, D. E. (1986). A distributed model of human learning and memory. In J. L. McClelland & D. E. Rumelhart (Eds.), *Parallel distributed processing: Explanations in the microstructure of cognition, Vol. 2: Psychological and biological models.* Cambridge, MA: MIT Press.

McCormick, C. B., & Levin, J. (1984). A comparison of three different prose-learning variations of the mnemonic keyword. *American Educational Research Journal, 21,* 379–398.

McGee, A., & Johnson, H. (2003). The effect of inference training on skilled and less skilled comprehenders. *Educational Psychology, 23*(1), 51–59.

McKeown, M. G., & Curtis, M. E. (1987). *The nature of vocabulary acquisition.* Hillsdale, NJ: Erlbaum.

Miller, G. A. (1956). The magic number seven, plus-or-minus two: Some limits on our capacity for processing information. *Psychological Review, 63,* 81–97.

Miyake, A., & Shah, P. (Eds.). (1999). *Models of working memory.* New York: Cambridge University Press.

Neath, I. (1998). *Human memory.* Pacific Grove, CA: Brooks-Cole.

Newell, A., & Simon, H. A. (1972). *Human problem solving.* Upper Saddle River, NJ: Prentice Hall.

Niesser, U. (1967). *Cognitive psychology:* Appleton-Century-Crofts.

Paivio, A. (1971). *Imagery and verbal processes.* New York: Holt, Rinehart & Winston.

Paivio, A. (1983). The empirical case for dual coding. In J. C. Yuille (Ed.), *Imagery, memory, and cognition* (pp. 307–332). Hillsdale, NJ: Erlbaum.

Paivio, A. (1986). *Mental representations: A dual coding approach.* New York: Oxford University Press.

Prawat, R. S. (1989). Promoting access to knowledge, strategy, and disposition to students: A research synthesis. *Review of Educational Research, 59,* 1–41.

Pressley, M., & El-Dinary, P. B. (1992). Memory strategy instruction. In D. J. Hermann, H. Weingartner, A. Searleman, & C. McEvoy (Eds.), *Memory improvement: Explications for memory theory* (pp. 79–100). New York: Springer-Verlag.

Pressley, M., Borkowski, J., & Schneider, W. (1987). Cognitive strategies: Good strategy users coordinate metacognition and knowledge. *Annals of Child Development, 4,* 89–129.

Pressley, M., Johnson, C. J., Symons, S., McGoldrick, J. A., & Kurita, J. A. (1989). Strategies that improve children's memory and comprehension of text. *The Elementary School Journal, 90*(11), 3–32.

Pressley, M., Wood, E., Woloshyn, V., Martin, V., King, A., & Menke, D. (1992). Encouraging mindful use of prior knowledge: Attempting to construct explanatory answers facilitates learning. *Educational Psychologist, 27*(1), 91–109.

Pylyshyn, Z. (1973). What the mind's eye tells the mind's brain: A critique of mental imagery. *Psychological Bulletin, 80,* 1–24.

Pylyshyn, Z. (2002). Mental imagery: In search of a theory. *Behavioral and Brain Sciences, 25,* 157–238.

Quillian, M. R. (1968). Semantic memory. In M. Minsky (Ed.), *Semantic information processing* (pp. 216–270). Cambridge, MA: MIT Press.

Roediger, H. L., III, & Guynn, M. J. (1996). Retrieval processes. In E. L. Bjork & R. A. Bjork (Eds.), *Memory: Handbook of perception and cognition* (2nd ed.) (pp. 197–236). San Diego, CA: Academic Press.

Rohrer, W. D., & Thomas, J. W. (1989). Domain-specific knowledge, metacognition and the promise of instructional reform. In C. B. McCormick, G. E. Miller, & M. Pressley (Eds.), *Cognitive strategy research* (pp. 104–132). New York: Springer-Verlag.

Schank, R. E., & Abelson, R. (1977). *Scripts, plans, goals, and understanding.* Hillsdale, NJ: Erlbaum.

Schneider, W., & Graham, D. J. (1992). Introduction to connectionist modeling in education. *Educational Psychologist, 27*(4), 513–530.

Schoenfeld, A. H. (1985). Metacognition and epistemological issues in mathematical understanding. In E. A. Silver (Ed.), *Teaching and learning mathematical problem solving: Multiple research perspectives* (pp. 361–379). Hillsdale, NJ: Erlbaum.

Schraw, G. (1998). Processing and recall differences among seductive details. *Journal of Educational Psychology, 90*(1), 3–12.

Shulman, L. (1986). Paradigms and research programs in the study of teaching: A contemporary perspective. In M. C. Wittrock (Ed.), *Handbook of research on teaching* (pp. 1–36). New York: Macmillan.

Snowman, J. (1986). Learning tactics and strategies. In G. F. Phye & T. Andre (Eds.), *Cognitive classroom learning: Understanding,* *thinking, and problem solving* (pp. 243–275). Orlando, FL: Academic.

Solso, R. L. (1988). *Cognitive psychology* (2nd ed.). New York: Allyn & Bacon.

Spires, H. A., & Donley, J. (1998). Prior knowledge activation: Inducing engagement with informational tests. *Journal of Educational Psychology, 90*(2), 249–260.

Spoehr, K. T. (1994). Enhancing the acquisition of conceptual structures through Hypermedia. In K. McGilly (Ed.), *Classroom lessons: Integrating cognitive theory and classroom practice* (pp. 75–101). Cambridge, MA: MIT Press.

Stanovich, K. E. (1986). Matthew effects in reading: Some consequences of individual differences in the acquisition of literacy. *Reading Research Quarterly, 21,* 360–406.

Thagard, R. (1989). Explanatory coherence. *Behavioral and Brain Sciences, 12*(3), 435–502.

Tulving, E. (1974). Cue-dependent forgetting. *American Scientist, 62,* 74–82.

Tulving, E. (1985). How many memory systems are there? *American Psychologist, 40,* 385–398.

Tulving, E., & Madigan, S. A. (1970). Memory and verbal learning. *Annual Review of Psychology, 21,* 437–484.

Turnure, J. E., & Lane, J. F. (1987). Special education applications of mnemonics. In M. A. McDaniel & M. Pressley (Eds.), *Imagery and related mnemonic processes* (pp. 329–357). New York: Springer-Verlag.

Whitehead, A. N. (1929). *The aims of education.* New York: Macmillan.

Williams, J. P., Lauer, K. D., deCani, J. S., Hall, K. M., Lord, K. M., Gugga, S. S., Bak, S., & Jacobs, P. R. (2002). Teaching elementary school students to identify themes. *Journal of Educational Psychology, 94* (2), 235–248.

Wittrock, M. C. (1990). Generating processes of comprehension. *Educational Psychologist, 24*(4), 345–376.

Wittrock, M. C. (1992). Generative learning processes of the brain. *Educational Psychologist, 27*(4), 531–541.

CHAPTER 9
Cognitive Perspectives: II. Metacognition and Problem Solving

The reconceptualization of thinking and learning that is emerging suggests that becoming a good thinker in any domain may be as much a matter of acquiring the habits and dispositions of interpretation and sense-making as of acquiring any particular set of skills. (Resnick, 1988, p. 58)

In the preschool years, most situations that require learning or remembering are part of the child's daily experiences, and the reasons for learning are fairly obvious (Howe, 1988). Young children learn to feed and dress themselves, and they acquire a lexicon of terms for the people and objects in their daily environment.

In contrast, in the school setting, the reasons for learning are less obvious. As the child progresses through school, learning tasks become more complex and abstract. Some middle school textbooks in mathematics, for example, introduce the concepts of probability and statistics. In addition, students are responsible for tasks such as learning from text and applying their learning to solve problems in various knowledge domains.

The need for self-directed learning does not end with formal schooling. Rapid increases in knowledge in several disciplines, the explosion of technology into daily affairs, and technological advances are changing the workplace and placing new demands on individuals. Managing one's learning and learning to solve new problems are important capabilities in a variety of settings.

THE NATURE OF COMPLEX LEARNING

The basic learning processes studied by cognitive theorists are perception, encoding, and storage and retrieval. Also researched are comprehension-related strategies that can facilitate these processes (e.g., focusing attention, elaboration, and summarizing text).

Initially, the complex processes addressed by cognitive researchers were those involved in solving problems that were not related to school subjects.

Examples include Katona's matchstick problems and so-called "move" problems. An example of a move problem is the Tower of Hanoi where the goal is to transfer a stack of different-size discs from one peg to another without placing a larger disc on top of a smaller one. The rationale for studying these problems was that simple domains permitted a focus on the development of strategies, and this work could then be expanded into semantic-rich domains (Schoenfeld, 1992).

Since the early years, research on complex cognitive processes has expanded in two ways. One is the extension of research on problem solving to issues in subject-matter disciplines. Also included are the differences between novices and experts in areas such as physics and historical document analysis.

The second body of research addresses the knowledge of higher-order processes involved in the selection and management of specific activities in learning and thinking. An example is knowing that the skimming strategy used to read the newspaper is inadequate for obtaining information from a difficult text.

The concept of a particular knowledge base that addresses the organization and management of learning is relatively new. In the early 1970s, learning to use comprehension strategies, such as self-questioning and summarizing text, was viewed as moving from non-use to the spontaneous production of the effective strategy (Harnishfeger & Bjorklund, 1990). Spontaneous strategy production was attributed to increasing planning capabilities and acquisition of the component skills in the particular strategy (p. 9).

In the later 1970s and 1980s, an alternative view of strategy use emerged. This view introduced the concept of higher-order processes that control the use of specific strategies. An early development was the concept of metamemory (Flavell, 1971). Specifically, metamemory referred to one's verbalizable knowledge about memory storage and the person, task, and strategy variables that influence the performance of memory (Flavell & Wellman, 1977). In the late 1970s, research interests expanded to include knowledge about one's cognitive functioning in general (in addition to memory) (Harnishfeger & Bjorklund, 1990). The term **metacognition** was applied to this broad focus.

Metacognition

Important issues are the basic definitions of metacognition and differences between younger and older learners and between experts and novices in the use of metacognitive strategies.

Components

The terms *metacognition* and *metacognitive knowledge* have been defined in somewhat different ways by different researchers. In general, metacognition involves thinking about thinking. Some perspectives emphasize the individual's knowledge about cognition and strategy use. Others emphasize both the knowledge and regulation of cognition (Brown, 1987; Son & Schwartz, 2003).

Knowledge of Cognition.   Key components of metacognition are (1) knowledge about and awareness of one's own thinking and (2) knowledge of when and where to use acquired strategies (Pressley & McCormick, 1995, p. 2). Knowledge about one's thinking includes information about one's own capacities and limitations and awareness of difficulties as they arise during learning so that remedial action may be taken.

Knowledge of when and where to use acquired strategies includes knowledge about the task and situations for which particular goal-specific strategies are appropriate. For example, students are sometimes unaware that a difficult text for which they have little background knowledge should be read differently than a text on familiar topics. The students lack important metacognitive knowledge about reading. In other words, metacognitive knowledge is important because simply learning particular goal-specific strategies, such as summarizing, underlining, and note taking, is insufficient to be a good strategy user (Pressley, Borkowski, & Schneider, 1987).

Alexander, Schallert, and Hare (1991) also consider knowledge of plans and goals to be a component of metacognition. For example, young children sometimes believe that the purpose of reading is to pronounce all the words without mistakes. They also believe that good reading involves verbatim recall of the text. These children lack sufficient metacognitive knowledge about the purposes of reading.

Regulation of Cognition.   One issue in the regulation of cognition is the difference between metacognitive and cognitive strategies. The major difference is that they fulfill different goals. Cognitive strategies are applied to content or information whereas metacognitive strategies are applied to one's thinking. For example, a reader who is familiar with the Louisiana Purchase reads the chapter and takes notes on the major points. These activities are cognitive strategies that are undertaken to facilitate comprehension and learning. The goal is to improve the student's knowledge (Flavell, 1979).

Later, the reader is concerned about being prepared for an upcoming test. She then quizzes herself to evaluate her level of preparedness using the end-of-chapter questions and her own self-generated questions. As indicated in chapter 8, this strategy both assists the learner in constructing meaning and is a metacognitive strategy for checking one's level of learning (evaluation). An example of metacognitive evaluation methods in mathematics is the way in which students can judge the reasonableness of their answers (Van Haneghan & Baker, 1989).

Researchers have proposed somewhat different models of metacognition for different tasks. One model includes the three components of planning, evaluation, and monitoring (Jacobs & Paris, 1987). Planning consists of setting goals, activating relevant resources (including budgeting time), and selecting appropriate strategies. Evaluation involves determining one's level of understanding.

Monitoring, the third component, involves checking one's progress and selecting appropriate repair strategies when originally selected strategies are not working. Developing meaning from text while reading, which involves evaluation and monitoring, is referred to as *comprehension monitoring*. The term refers to one's awareness of the quality and degree of comprehension and knowing what to do and how to do it when one discovers comprehension failures (Dole, Duffy, Roehler, & Pcarson, 1991). For example, readers may proceed through a relatively easy reading assignment with rapid construction of meaning until a confusion or other comprehension problem occurs and is detected. Garner (1990, p. 251) describes this situation as cognitive failure (information processing is impaired) but a metacognitive success (the reader notices the problem and addresses it).

Research indicates that active monitoring and control of comprehension during reading increases the likelihood of one's understanding of text and one's knowledge that he or she understands (Hacker, 1998). When readers fail to monitor and control comprehension, "triggering events" that can alert them to comprehension failure (such as realizing they do not know the meaning of one or more of the words) simply do not occur. The result is that the reader erroneously believes he or she has comprehended the text.

A model of the metacognitive activities in studying describes four stages in which these activities occur (see Table 9.1). They are defining the task, goal setting and planning, enacting study tactics and strategies, and adapting studying (Winne & Hadwin, 1998). If the study task is very familiar, stage one may be skipped.

TABLE 9.1
A Model of the Metacognitive Activities in Studying[1]

Stage	Description	Example
Defining the task	Generate a perception of the nature of the studying task, available resources, and constraints.	Complete an assigned reading on volcanoes from *National Geographic*; language is complex for middle school students, but student has $1\frac{1}{2}$ hours to complete assignment.
Goal setting and planning	Select or generate goals and a plan for addressing the study task.	Read the article for deep processing to prepare for unit test; personal note taking and self-questioning are needed.
Enacting study tactics and strategies	Implement the activities selected in stage two, and fine-tune, if necessary.	Difficult vocabulary encountered during reading leads to pauses to look up term definitions and rereading.
Adapting studying	(1) Make large-scale adjustments to the task, goals, plans, and engagement.	Major difficulties in understanding the article lead to searching for basic information about volcanoes on the Internet.
	or	or
	(2) Alter one's conditions for future studying (knowledge, skills, beliefs, dispositions, and motivational factors).	Lower one's standard of proficiency for difficult material to shallow processing.

[1]Stages and definitions are summarized from Winne & Hadwin (1998).

Each stage generates a product that is evaluated (a metacognitive activity) and updates the conditions of work in the next stage. The student's perception of the learning task, for example, is the basis for setting goals in stage two.

Important in the model are the student's personal standards, which influence the actions at each stage. For example, students with an orientation to "just get by" may, in stage two, select simplistic tasks, such as paraphrasing headings and noting boldface terms in the text.

In stage three, the internal feedback generated by monitoring the enactment of study strategies may lead to adjustments. However, if the student perceives no tactics are available to achieve the goals, the task may be abandoned. Stage four, a broad metacognitive activity, does not refer to fine-tuning ongoing strategies. Instead, one of two adaptive decisions is made. One is to make large-scale adjustments to the student's understandings of the task, goals, plans, and strategies. The second is to make relatively permanent changes in future study conditions. An example is lowering one's personal standards for success (Winne & Hadwin, 1998, p. 285).

As indicated by these examples, metacognitive strategies are considered to be conscious and intentional. They involve an awareness of one's thinking processes and decisions about the actions to be taken if progress is unsatisfactory. In some cases, however, metacognitive processes can be highly automatized. For example, some studying tasks may be so familiar that defining the task (stage one in the model) is bypassed (Winne & Hadwin, 1998). Further, expert readers process text fluidly and rapidly without conscious attention allocated to their level of comprehension until a contradiction or other difficulty occurs. They then take steps to resolve the difficulty.

Relationship of Metacognition to Other Internal States

At least three internal learner states interact with or influence the implementation of the individual's metacognitive skills. They are the learner's knowledge about a topic or domain, achievement goal orientation, and beliefs about oneself as a learner (referred to as personal agency formulations [Zimmerman, 1995]).

The Learner's Topic or Domain Knowledge.   The cognitive resources available for processing and evaluation are limited. Therefore, detailed knowledge about a topic or in a domain allows an individual to process information about the domain efficiently and with little effort (Bjorklund, Muir-Broaddus, & Schneider, 1990, p. 95). In other words, metacognitive strategies play minor roles in comprehension and recall when an individual is well-informed on a topic. For example, a biology professor rarely has to monitor comprehension when reading about the effects of acid rain on the environment (Garner, 1990). However, when reading about Renaissance art, a domain in which he has little knowledge, he must use metacognitive strategies to generate knowledge from the text.

Metacognitive strategies can enhance learning when domain knowledge is weak. In one study, novices in knowledge about soccer with greater metacognitive knowledge of study tactics recalled more than novices with less metacognitive knowledge (Winne & Hadwin, 1998).

2.   *Achievement Goal Orientation.*   An achievement goal orientation refers to different conceptions of success with accompanying reasons for engaging in academic tasks. Three types of goal orientation are mastery, performance, and failure-avoidance (see chapter 13 for a discussion). Students with a mastery goal orientation, for example, seek to demonstrate their ability through developing new skills (Ames, 1992). These students, given the opportunity, also develop effective and sophisticated metacognitive skills.

In contrast, a performance goal orientation involves a focus on score attainment or counting the tasks to be completed (Ames, 1992; Elliott & Dweck, 1988). In one study, individuals who studied glossary terms more each week had lower final examination scores than students who prepared for frequent quizzes (Tuckman, 1996). The lower scores were attributed to a performance goal of adding terms to their glossary rather than a goal of expanding one's knowledge.

A third orientation, referred to as failure avoidance, involves a preoccupation with one's image in the class (Midgley, Kaplan, Middleton, & Maeke, 1998). Student attention is focused on avoiding such actions as responding in class and volunteering for difficult subtasks in small group work. In terms of learning, this orientation fosters nonproductive strategies.

3.   *Personal Agency Formulations.*   Metacognitive models of the management and control of learning emphasize knowledge states and reasoning about tasks, goals, resources, and learning progress. Factors that influence decision making include personal agency formulations—beliefs and judgment about one's competence that often are formed intuitively and are applied in particular contexts (Zimmerman, 1995). An example is believing that one "is terrible" at solving mathematical word problems. As a result, the individual is not motivated to attempt a solution or to monitor one's efforts (Hacker, 1998, p. 10). Such views, referred to as *self-efficacy*, are defined as beliefs in one's capabilities to organize and execute the actions necessary to manage and be successful in particular situations (Bandura, 1995, p. 2). Included are tasks in the academic sphere (Zimmerman, 1995). Individuals with high self-efficacy engage in challenging tasks, persist, even when confronted with difficulties, and flexibly alter their strategies when initial steps or strategies are ineffective.

Models of effective learners that incorporate the motivational construct of self-efficacy, along with goal setting and monitoring and evaluating learning, are referred to as models of self-regulated learning (see chapter 12; Schunk & Zimmerman, 1998). These perspectives address issues such as effort, persistence, and task choice. Whereas metacognitive models focus on the particular metacognitive skills enacted by individuals during learning, the self-regulated learning models focus on the relationship of self-efficacy to goal setting and other metacognitive activities.

In summary, the enactment of metacognitive capabilities is influenced at three types of internal learner states. They are the topic or domain knowledge of the individual, the individual's achievement goal orientation, and one's personal beliefs about his or her capabilities to be successful in particular situations.

Differences in Metacognitive Capabilities

Differences in metacognitive capabilities, in general, are found in two types of comparisons. They are (1) the differences between younger and older children and (2) the differences between experts and novices.

The differences between younger and older children, on occasion, have been referred to as developmental differences. However, in large measure, they are the result of an increasing knowledge as the child has more experience with formal schooling.

Differences Between Younger and Older Children.   Several differences in metacognition between younger and older students have been identified. Among them are the extent of awareness of the purposes of instruction and different task demands, monitoring one's comprehension and understanding, detection of mathematical errors, and awareness of strategy flexibility.

Awareness of Instructional Purposes and Task Demands.   School curricula and classroom lessons often reflect multiple purposes. For example, the general purpose of a mathematics exercise may be for students to learn to apply a particular procedure. In addition, the teacher expects the students' papers to be neat and handed in at the end of the class period. Young children typically are aware of the peripheral lesson requirements, but they often are unaware of the broader purposes of instruction. Thus, they may report that the goal of instruction is to finish seatwork on time. Or, as mentioned earlier, they may believe that the goal of reading is to pronounce all the words correctly (Alexander et al., 1991).

Lack of awareness of task performance is not universal, however. Fang and Cox (1999) found that some preschool children, when asked to dictate their favorite experience so that other children may read it, monitored and self-corrected their ongoing oral speech. Comments included, "What do I want to do here?" and "I wanna change that word."

Recognition of the need to remember as a purpose for working through instructional materials is a capability that develops slowly throughout childhood. One study asked young children what they would do to remember information (Jacobs & Paris, 1987). Options such as "to think hard and try to remember" and "to ask yourself questions about the ideas" were provided. Many of the children, however, selected the option that stated they would skip the parts they did not understand.

A second difference between younger and older children is that younger children often are unaware of task demands. They are likely to believe, for example, that reading a story for fun and reading for science or social studies do not differ. In other words, children often have only a rough idea about the factors that influence task difficulty (Bruning, Schraw, & Ronning, 1995). Karmiloff-Smith (1979) documented differences in children ages 4 to 9 who were to construct a railroad track in the form of a complete loop. The 4- and 5-year-olds picked up pieces at random and arranged them in that order. The 8- and 9-year-olds, however, first sorted the pieces into straight and curved and then chose systematically from each stack to complete the loop.

b) *Monitoring One's Comprehension and Understanding.*   Research indicates that children show little indication of monitoring their comprehension to determine whether it is successful (Kuhn, 1999, p. 21). Further, although improvement accompanies development, mastery often is not attained even by adulthood.

Evidence indicates that younger and older children differ in their ability to accurately monitor their comprehension (e.g., Garner, 1987, 1990; Jacobs & Paris, 1987). One measure of comprehension monitoring used in research studies is the error detection task. Subjects read or listen to a text that contains inconsistencies with either the text or world knowledge. Vosniadou, Pearson, and Rogers (1988) found that first graders were able to detect inconsistencies in texts that were read to them when the topic was a familiar one. However, they were unable to recognize anomalies in unfamiliar material they listened to, even if the contradiction appeared later in the text. In contrast, third and fifth graders were able to detect inconsistencies in texts on unfamiliar topics.

Other studies report similar differences in error detection, but note that both younger and older children read the contradictory statements more slowly than other lines in the story (for a discussion, see Garner, 1990). One explanation for the observed discrepancies between reading times and reported contradictions is that younger children have only a momentary awareness of comprehension difficulties, which they dismiss as unimportant (Garner, 1990).

c) *Detecting Mathematical Errors and Other Problems.*   Related to the concept of error detection in text is the detection of mathematical errors. One application is the use of strategies to check one's work at the completion of a problem. The other is the detection of logical inconsistencies in word problems.

A study by Van Haneghan (1986) found that first-, third-, and fifth-grade children differed in their strategies for checking their answers to grade-appropriate open-sentence problems. First graders typically used memorized addition and subtraction facts or counted on their fingers or with objects. In contrast, the older children checked their work against a computational standard, such as adding the column up in the opposite direction. Of interest is that most of the children who originally arrived at wrong answers were not led to change their answers on the basis of the checking.

In another study, children were presented with several problems that required dealing with "more than" and "less than" relations among quantities (Van Haneghan & Baker, 1989). The tasks included the problem text, an algorithmic form of the problem, and another child's answer. Problems ranged from correctly solved, to computational or operational error, to unanswerable, but "solved" anyway. (An example of an unsolvable problem is stating that Matt has 22 cents and Ken has 69 cents and asking how many more cents Matt has than Ken.) Results indicated that the fifth graders found more of the errors than the third graders. Of the various problem errors, calculational errors were most likely to be found, and unanswerable problems were least likely to be identified (p. 229).

One reason for the lack of identification of the unsolvable problems is that children develop a "word problem" schema in which word problems are divorced from real-world problems. Also, children often develop limited expectations for the structure of word problems. One group of third- and fifth-grade children, for example, stated that a legitimate problem was unsolvable because it differed from typical problems (Van Haneghan, 1986). The misjudged problem stated that Sam had 28 cookies and he had 13 more than John. The problem asked how many cookies John had. The two reasons given by the children as to the unsolvability of the problem were (1) the problem does not tell you how many John has, and (2) the problem says first that Sam has 28 cookies and then he has 13, and this does not make sense (p. 225).

A somewhat different problem detection skill is essential in writing. Specifically, revising one's writing depends on detecting sentences or passages that do not communicate clearly. However, students often fail to revise their writing because they assume the text is clear and understandable (Graham & Harris, 1994). Beal (1989) found that third-grade children revised more ambiguous messages than younger children. The performance differences were largely the result of the level of skill in finding the problem in the passage.

Awareness of Strategy Flexibility.   A fourth characteristic of children is that they often lack the knowledge about when and where to make use of different strategies. This component of metacognition is described by Paris, Lipson, and Wilson (1983) as *conditional knowledge.* The lack of conditional knowledge is indicated by children's inability to transfer learned strategies to new situations.

The development of conditional knowledge is related, in part, to children's reliance on primitive strategies that they have developed. These strategies, such as copying selected text sentences verbatim (used as a summarization strategy), hinder their development of more appropriate strategies. Moreover, these primitive strategies hinder their awareness of strategy flexibility.

Although the lack of conditional knowledge is most noticeable in young children, it is found in other age groups as well. For example, beginning graduate students may focus on memorizing content from textbooks instead of integrating information and ideas (Garner, 1990).

The Development of Cognitive Maturity.   Coming to cognitive maturity in complex societies is not an easy task, and it involves several factors. First, it depends on developing knowledge about the internal mental world. Basic information about this world includes the fact that people possess minds, mental processes are distinct from feelings and emotions, and a person can understand and react to his or her mental states (Wellman, 1985). Young children, however, have little knowledge of beliefs, certainties, illusions, mistakes, or deceptions (Garner, 1990). Thus, they are not skilled in identifying inconsistencies in text passages or monitoring their thinking. Older children, in contrast, have a more sophisticated theory of mind and also are able to treat language itself as an object of thinking. Thus, older children can use this knowledge to direct and manage their thinking.

Second, developing cognitive maturity also involves mastering tasks that may not be of interest to the child. Kindergarten children can differentiate classroom activities into work and play and can state that "work" activities are more important to the teacher than play activities (Garner, 1990). However, they may expend less cognitive effort on tasks that represent work. The often-cited example is the student who can cite earned run averages, runs batted in, and other baseball statistics of major players, past and present. The student, however, has difficulty in history and other fact-loaded subjects.

Expert-Novice Differences.   Several differences have been identified between experts and novices in metacognitive skills. For example, in contrast to novices, experts in diagnosing X-rays tested and revised their diagnoses until they accounted for all the characteristics of a particular situation (Lesgold et al., 1988).

In reading, the metacognitive skills of experts and novices differ in four major ways. First, experts are aware of the general goals of reading and studying and of the specific objectives of a particular task (Rohrer & Thomas, 1989). As a result, they allocate their time and effort differently to different tasks and typically expend greater time and effort on more difficult tasks. Also, in the rapid pace of the classroom, which often has an emphasis on task completion, experts weigh the costs of using different strategies against the benefits of the goals to be achieved (Garner, 1990).

In contrast, novices tend not to read for meaning. They do not adjust their reading behavior to different kinds of content or reading situations. Further, they do not slow down for difficult passages (Rohrer & Thomas, 1989).

Second, experts are aware of and use "fix-it" strategies when problems occur (Dole et al., 1991). In this way, difficulties are addressed before they become major problems. Third, experts are more likely to use available resources, such as the strategy of looking back at prior text when a difficulty occurs and the pause-and-reflect strategy.

Finally, the strategy use of experts is more flexible than that of novices in at least two important ways. They are more likely to use different strategies in different circumstances, and they also adapt question-asking strategies to different kinds of texts and task demands (p. 248). Novices, in contrast, tend to apply a single strategy across contexts. Moreover, although they may use strategies, such as context clues, when directed to do so, they do not apply them spontaneously (Rohrer & Thomas, 1989).

In one study, social science professors were asked to read aloud a text in their area of expertise that was important to them (Wyatt et al., 1993). The readers applied strategies that assisted them in abstracting important information from the articles. These strategies included anticipating and predicting information, testing predictions as they read, searching for information related to their reading purpose, looking backward and forward in the text to find particular information, and developing summary interpretations of the articles.

Pressley and Afflerbach (1995) developed a comprehensive catalog of the processes reported in verbal protocols of reading. They found 15 common processes, which included overviewing before reading, searching for and paying more attention to important information, and relating important points in the text to each other to understand the text as a whole. The authors concluded that skilled reading is constructively responsive reading. That is, the reader exploits text clues, reflects on the text after reading, and monitors his or her reading extensively (Pressley & Afflerbach, 1995; Pressley, 1995).

Summary

In the 1970s, the spontaneous production of effective strategies was thought to result from increases in planning skills and the learning of subskills in a strategy. The revised view of the 1980s is that higher-order processes control the use of cognitive strategies. Referred to as metacognition, this knowledge base includes two broad components. They are the knowledge of and regulation of cognition. Knowledge of cognition includes knowledge about tasks, strategies, instructional plans, and goals. Regulation of cognition involves setting goals, activating relevant resources, selecting appropriate strategies, evaluating one's understanding, checking one's progress, and redirecting effort, if necessary. Although conscious and internal, metacognitive processes can become highly automatized. Also, the greater the learner's knowledge base, the less need for metacognitive strategies.

Individual differences that can influence and interact with the execution of metacognitive strategies include the learner's topic or domain knowledge, achievement goal orientation, and beliefs about personal agency. Individuals with a mastery goal orientation seek to develop new skills and typically develop effective and complex metacognitive strategies. A performance goal orientation, in contrast, typically leads to simplistic or surface strategies whereas failure avoidance generates nonproductive monitoring and evaluation activities. Beliefs about personal agency—specifically, self-efficacy—influence goal setting and learner persistence and flexibility during learning.

Several developmental differences in metacognition between younger and older children have been identified. They are awareness of instructional purposes and changing task demands, the capability of monitoring one's comprehension and mathematical errors, and awareness of strategy flexibility. These differences result, in part, from increasing cognitive maturity in which children begin to recognize and react to their mental processes. Further, experts in metacognitive thinking allocate their time and effort differently for different tasks, use "fix-it" strategies when problems occur, and are more flexible in strategy use than novices.

Problem Solving

Problem solving, in general, involves dealing with new and unfamiliar tasks when the relevant solution methods (even if partly mastered) are not known (Schoenfeld, 1992, p. 354). Initially, research on problem solving focused on the strategies used by problem solvers to research the correct solution (see the section on prior research). However, various interpretations of the definition and the role of problem solving in the school curriculum have led to a reexamination of problem solving in the 1990s. That is, the focus is the learner's interpretation, structuring, and adaptation of knowledge (both content and strategic) to new situations (Resnick, 1989). Important topics are the different types of problems, the major subprocesses in problem solving, and the differences between expert and novice problem solvers.

Types of Problems

Formally defined, a problem consists of three components: givens, a goal, and allowable operators. The givens include the elements, the relations among

them, and conditions or constraints that constitute the initial form of the problem (Anderson, 1985; Davidson & Sternberg, 1998). The goal is the desired
outcome or solution and the allowable operators are the steps or procedures
that will transform the givens into the goal (Mayer & Wittrock, 1996).

In addition, the problem situation also may include obstacles (Davidson &
Sternberg, 1998). They are the characteristics of either the problem and/or the
student that make it difficult for the student to transform the initial form of the
problem into the desired outcome. The situations referred to as functional fixedness and problem set by the Gestalt researchers are examples.

Two types of problems mentioned in the literature are well-defined and ill-
defined. In well-defined problems, the givens, desired goal, and allowable operators are explicit. Computation problems, such as $2.69 \times .078 = \_\_\_\_$, are
examples. Well-defined problems are the type that Edward Thorndike addressed in his research on the applications of connectionism to school learning.

In ill-defined problems, the givens, desired goal, and allowable operators
(procedures) are not immediately clear to the problem solver (Mayer & Wittrock, 1996). The problems investigated by the Gestalt researchers are examples.
An example in the school setting is "Write a computer program that can serve
as a teacher's grade book" (p. 48). Although most educational materials address
well-defined problems, most problems in the real world are ill-defined.

Problems also may be categorized as routine and nonroutine (Mayer, 1992;
Mayer & Wittrock, 1996). Routine problems are those that the individual has
solved in the past and for which he or she instantly recognizes a solution. Nonroutine problems, in contrast, are those that the individual has not solved previously and for which he or she cannot generate a preexisting solution (Mayer,
1992, p. 4). These designations are analogous to the processes identified by the
Gestalt researchers as reproductive and productive thinking (Katona, 1940;
Wertheimer, 1945/1959). Reproductive thinking is the application of procedures
used to solve similar problems whereas productive thinking is the construction
of a novel solution.

These categories, however, actually identify the endpoints of a continuum.
Between these two extremes lie problems for which the individual does not
have a ready solution but which also do not require a novel solution. Instead,
they require the application of prior strategies in new ways or the restructuring
of prior strategies for different goals. Examples include the problems devised by
first-grade children who are learning to solve various types of simple word problems in mathematics. Among them are finding out how much older a book they
are reading is than they are and how old the book is this year (Fennema, Franke,
Carpenter, & Carey, 1993).

Prior Cognitive Research
Prior developments in the 1970s include the General Problem Solver (GPS),
discussions of heuristics, and artificial intelligence research.

The GPS.   Developed from tasks such as the Tower of Hanoi problems, the
GPS identifies three main steps in problem solving. First, represent the problem,

the givens, and the legal operators. Second, establish goals and subgoals and begin solving for the subgoals. Three, use means–ends analysis to assess progress; redefine subgoals, if necessary (Newell & Simon, 1972). Means–ends analysis involves assessing the differences between a present state and a desired state, searching for an appropriate operator to reduce the differences, and evaluating the results (Simon, 1980).

GPS is particularly appropriate for well-defined problems for which subgoals can be clearly defined and which are solved in sequential steps. Many problems, however, do not fit this category. Another difficulty is that most problems require domain-specific information to solve them. However, individuals cannot derive domain-specific strategies from general problem-solving approaches.

Heuristics.   A focus on well-defined problems led to discussions of heuristics, which typically refer to a rule of thumb for reducing uncertainty about a problem. In addition to means-ends analysis, examples are working backward from the goal state, hill climbing, and dividing the problem into subproblems. Hill climbing involves taking any step that moves the problem solver closer to the goal. One difficulty with such strategies is that they may or may not result in a solution. For example, the rule of thumb "Always take the smaller number from the larger number" in subtraction will result in errors some of the time (e.g., $3 - 7 = -4$, not +4).

In addition to the prior examples, Polya (1973) also included general heuristic strategies used to match conceptual and procedural knowledge to a particular problem. Examples are searching one's memory for similar problems for special cases and analogies.

In a pair of studies, Gick and Holyoak (1980, 1983) used the medical problem developed by Duncker (1945) discussed in chapter 3. Subjects were asked to solve the problem immediately after reading a brief analogous episode of a general dispersing his forces to invade a town. However, the results indicated that the presence of an analogous situation is insufficient for subjects to solve the target problem. Spontaneous transfer occurred in the majority of subjects (62%) only when they were given two priming stories, asked to write a summary of them, and then were given an explicit statement of the solution principle.

Like the GPS, one difficulty with heuristics is that most problems require domain-specific information in order to solve them. Another is that heuristics do not address the key thinking processes required by the problem.

Artificial Intelligence Research.   This research involves programming computers with humanlike rules inferred from think-aloud protocols of human subjects. A dramatic example of the artificial intelligence research is PARRY, a program that simulated a paranoid patient so well that psychiatrists communicating by computer terminal were unable to determine whether the "patient" was real or a computer program (Bereiter, 1991). The rules incorporated into PARRY included rules for reacting emotionally to the psychiatrist's language in addition to rules for interpreting the psychiatrist's words.

Despite the success of PARRY and other programs, some concerns about this approach to analyzing problem solving have emerged (Bereiter, 1991). One major concern is that the easiest tasks to simulate on the computer are those that are most difficult for humans, that is, extended chains of reasoning (p. 11). Conversely, the tasks that humans complete easily are extremely difficult to program with rule-based systems. Examples are associative memory retrieval and pattern recognition (Bereiter, 1991, p. 11). A second major concern is that human problem solving is not as neat and orderly as portrayed in the computer programs.

Subprocesses in Problem Solving

Research on problem solving in the 1970s primarily addressed move problems that require the physical movement and recombination of objects to fulfill a specific goal. In recent years, the shift in research focus to learner construction, interpretation, and adaptation of knowledge to new situations places primary importance on the thinking strategies of students. Further, expertise requires knowledge of principles in a domain rather than general heuristic strategies (Chi, Glaser, & Farr, 1991). Important in these activities are the metacognitive skills of planning and monitoring and evaluating one's decisions.

Table 9.2 illustrates the four major subprocesses of problem solving, all of which require metacognition. The major subprocesses are described as representing the problem, planning strategies, overcoming obstacles, and executing plans (Mayer & Wittrock, 1996; Davidson & Sternberg, 1998). Further, in addition to planning, the metacognitive skills of monitoring and evaluating one's decisions also are important.

TABLE 9.2
Subprocesses in Problem Solving and the Role of Metacognitive Skills

Subprocesses	Role of metacognitive skills
1. Representing the problem (identifying the most relevant features and creating a mental map of the components.)	1a. Assist in accessing relevant information from long-term memory that can contribute to the identification of key problem components.
	b. Assist in creating a "mental map" of the givens, the relations among them, the goal, and the constraints (Davidson & Sternberg, 1998).
	c. Assist in selective recoding, selective combination, and selective comparison, when necessary (Davidson & Sternberg, 1998).
2. Planning	2a. Review and select plans and strategies, perhaps engaging in structured exploration (Schoenfeld, 1992).
	b. Initiate 1a above, when necessary.
3. Overcoming obstacles	3a. Assist in searching LTM for new information.
	b. Initiate 1c above.
4. Executing plans (and overcoming obstacles)	4a. Monitor progress and modify plans when necessary.
	b. Return to 3, if necessary.

1, ***Representing the Problem.***   This phase, often overlooked by students, is essential to successful problem solving for both well-defined and open-ended situations. Important in identifying the key features of the problems and creating a mental map of the relationships of the related information in the learner's long-term memory. Included are informal and intuitive knowledge about the domain (tacit knowledge in the Alexander, Schallert, & Hare model), content knowledge, and metacognitive knowledge about problem approaches and strategies for similar problems.

Some problem solvers, however, possess inaccurate metacognitive knowledge about problems. For example, some schoolchildren thought that they need not read an entire math problem because the critical information was always in the last sentence (Briars & Larkin, 1994).

After identifying the key relevant information in the problem, creating a mental map of the relationships is important. This process assists the individual to organize the conditions, decide on appropriate steps, and keep track of his or her progress (Davidson & Sternberg, 1998).

Difficulties in constructing a mental map of the problem may require the processes of selective recoding, selective combination, and selective comparison. Selective recoding involves seeing elements that previously were unnoticed and selective combination involves putting the problem elements together in a new way. The result is a new mental representation of the problem and the goal. Selective comparison is the discovery of a nonobvious relationship between problem elements and already-acquired information (Davidson & Sternberg, 1998, p. 53).

These processes reflect the components of problem solving identified earlier by the Gestalt researchers. Specifically, they include "the restructuring of the given material" (Köhler, 1969, p. 146), mentally redefining and clarifying the problem, such as redefining the goal (Duncker, 1945), or reformulating the functions of the givens (Maier, 1930).

2. ***Planning.***   Effective problem solvers review strategies and tactics prior to implementing them (the structured exploration identified by Schoenfeld [1992]). The importance of this phase is that it helps the problem solver anticipate the consequences of particular approaches and helps to avoid costly mistakes (Holyoak, 1995). Unsuccessful identification of a viable strategy may require the review and possible reorganization of the learner's mental map of the problem (1 in Table 9.2).

The importance of representing the problem and planning is indicated in the differences in the problem-solving behavior of a faculty member and a group of students faced with a difficult two-part problem. The faculty member spent more than half his allotted time in analyzing and structured exploring before beginning to implement a solution (Schoenfeld, 1992). Students, however, began to work immediately on the problem. Also, although they had more of the facts and procedures readily accessible to them than the faculty member, few solved the problem. The faculty member generated a number of potential wild-goose chases, but he abandoned paths that did not bear fruit and solved the problem (p. 356). (See the following section on the differences between expert and novice problem solvers.)

3 *Overcoming Obstacles.*   One major obstacle that can occur during planning is the state referred to as stereotypy (Davidson & Sternberg, 1998), which consists of the problem set and functional fixedness identified by the Gestalt researchers. The other is the inability to generate any plans or procedures, which occurs most often in insight problems. One strategy is to search long-term memory for models, analogies, and metaphors that may provide a new perspective on the problem. Another is to take a break from the problem to allow one's thoughts to incubate (Davidson & Sternberg, 1998).

4 *Executing Plans.*   Students often fail to correctly solve problems because they do not monitor their execution of the selected strategy. Monitoring is important to keep track of the steps already executed and the actions yet to be completed. It also can prevent misapplication of routine steps in a strategy. For example, Vye et al. (1997) found that, in solving a complex multistage problem, use of inappropriate data and calculation errors accounted for 13% and 2% of the errors, respectively, of sixth-grade students. Further, Declos and Harrington (1991) found that requiring middle-school students to monitor their strategies in solving computer-based problems reduced errors and decreased problem-solving time.

Summary

The formal components of a problem are the givens, the goal, and the allowable operators or procedures that transform the given information. The situation also may include obstacles that impede progress in solving the problem.

Two categorizations of problems are well-defined (information is explicit) and ill-defined (information is implicit). From the learner's perspective, problems also may be described as routine (has an instantly recognizable solution) and nonroutine (involves developing a novel solution). However, between these two designations are problems that require the restructuring of prior strategies to fit a new goal.

Cognitive research in the 1970s primarily included development of the General Problem Solver (GPS), discussions of heuristics, and artificial intelligence research. A limitation of GPS and heuristics is that they do not provide for domain-specific knowledge. Currently, research is beginning to focus on the subprocesses of problem solving and the related metacognitive skills. Identified subprocesses are representing the problem, which includes identifying key elements and creating a mental map, planning, overcoming obstacles, and executing the plans. Overcoming obstacles often requires taking account of previously unnoticed elements, combining them in new ways, and discovering new relationships between problem elements and learner knowledge. In addition to metacognitive knowledge about problems and strategies, the skills of planning, monitoring, and evaluation are essential in successful problem solving.

Expert and Novice Problem Solvers

Efforts to simulate human capabilities in computer programs in the 1960s have led to increased interest in expertise as a subject for investigation (Glaser & Chi, 1988, p. xv). Research in the ensuing period has identified several key characteristics of expert performance that are generalizable across knowledge domains

(Glaser & Chi, 1988). First, expertise is developed over a lengthy period of time in a particular domain. Research indicates that around 5 years or approximately 10,000 hours are required (Hayes, 1988). Second, experts and novices differ both in the nature of their knowledge and their problem-solving strategies.

1. ***Knowledge Differences.***   The knowledge differences between novices and experts are substantial. They are found both in the amount of knowledge and the organization and accessibility of that knowledge. Specifically, the knowledge structures of novices are organized around the main phenomena in a domain, such as the behavior of objects on inclined planes in physics. In contrast, the knowledge structures of experts represent the phenomena in a domain in relation to higher-order principles, such as Newton's laws of force (Chi, Glaser, & Rees, 1982).

The organization of the expert's domain or discipline knowledge has implications for problem solving. Experts in the sciences use a different "problem schema" than novices to encode and represent problems (Glaser & Chi, 1988). That is, with experience, experts have encoded procedures for solving relevant problems and the conditions under which they are applied, along with representations of higher-order principles. Over time, problem and solution become entwined in the problem schema so that the activation of problem–solution strategies becomes more automatic. Thus, for the expert, strategies become one component of the knowledge base.

Knowledge differences also contribute to the more efficient use of short-term and long-term memory by experts. They are more efficient at searching a solution space because their recall is chunked (Bruning, Schraw, & Ronning, 1995). For example, in pattern recognition tasks using a chessboard, the knowledge base of the master chess player greatly simplifies recall. Both experts and novices were shown mid-game positions for a few seconds and were asked to replicate the configurations. Chess masters were able to construct 80% to 90% of the board positions of pieces after a few seconds' exposure. However, beginners were able to place only a few pieces. The chess expert has stored some 50,000 configurations in long-term memory, and new information is encoded in the form of these configurations. The beginner, however, depends on rote memory for the location of individual pieces (Chase & Simon, 1973).

As indicated in chapter 8, the extent of the individual's knowledge base also influences his or her capability to process verbal information in large chunks. For example, the expression $(a + b)^2$ may be one chunk for a mathematics teacher and several chunks for the beginning student in algebra. Also, experts in physics recall the equations linked with a particular physics principle in a single configuration or "bundle" (Bruning et al., 1995, p. 352). Thus, although the short-term memory capacity of experts is no larger than that of other individuals, their chunking of information makes efficient use of short-term memory.

2. ***Strategy Differences.***   As discussed earlier in the chapter, experts and novices differ in their metacognitive skills. In the area of problem solving, the metacognitive skills of experts and novices differ in three ways. They are (1) problem representation, (2) problem approach, and (3) self-monitoring skills (Glaser & Chi, 1988).

a) ***Problem Representation.*** For difficult or ambiguous problems, experts in mathematics and in the sciences often spend time in constructing representations of the problem (Rohrer & Thomas, 1989; Schoenfeld, 1992). The differences between the faculty member and students working on a difficult two-part problem is an example. Further, Voss (1989, p. 274) notes that when Michael Faraday was attempting to solve the problem of electromagnetic induction, he spent considerable time in developing a representation of the problem and subsequently proposed two possible solutions. Deductions then were made from these solutions and tested in the laboratory.

Similar processes were observed in a study of expert radiologists diagnosing difficult X-ray films (Lesgold et al., 1988). Experts viewed each film, constructed a tentative mental representation of the problem, and then proceeded to test this schema. If disconfirmed, the schema was set aside and the film was examined for clues to another representation of the problem. Medical residents, in contrast, were more likely to go with their initial perspective of the problem. They also tended to force-fit film features that should have signaled abnormality into their schemata for normal anatomy.

Experts also represent problems at deep structural levels in terms of basic principles in the domains, such as conservation of energy. Novices, in contrast, represent problems in terms of surface or superficial characteristics or objects stated in the problem. Examples include rotating discs on inclined planes.

b) ***Problem Approach.*** For easy or moderately difficult problems, experts in mathematics and in the sciences apply their well-developed problem schema. They also work forward from information given in the problem. The expert has solved many such problems in the past, and similar problems and their solutions are recalled with little effort.

Novices, on the other hand, typically use "working backward" strategies and, sometimes, trial and error. As already indicated, because they lack sophisticated problem schema, they must begin with the unknown in the problem. In science, for example, novices often begin with an equation that contains the unknown and work backward in hopes of finding the variable they need (Anzai, 1991). See Table 9.3 for a comparison of novice and expert problem solvers.

Expertise in mathematics and science typically involves bringing the appropriate problem schema to the task of solving well-structured problems. In contrast, expertise in the humanities depends more on constructing a context-specific schema tailored to specific events (Spoehr, 1994; Wineburg, 1991). That is, expertise requires searching for patterns of knowledge in the construction of explanations at abstract levels (Spoehr, 1994, p. 79). In one study, trained historians working with a group of fragmented and contradictory historical documents (1) looked first to the source of the document as a framework for reviewing the text, (2) carefully validated and rejected various details by checking and crosschecking the documents (corroboration), and (3) constructed sequences and locales of events as a means to verify witness accounts (Wineburg, 1991). Novices, in contrast, tended to not notice discrepancies and rarely looked back at previous documents. They also struggled with interpreting accounts, in part through failure to identify the writer or to construct sequences of events.

TABLE 9.3
A Comparison of Novice and Expert Problem Solvers in Mathematics and Science

Novices	Experts
1. Knowledge structures are organized around the main phenomena in a domain	1a. Knowledge structures of experts represent phenomena in the domain in relation to higher-order principles b. Knowledge is organized in the form of problem schema that include procedures for solving relevant problems
2. Inefficient use of short-term and long-term memory because knowledge often is stored in unrelated items	2a. Efficient use of short-term and long-term memory because recall occurs in chunks of related information b. Automatization of sequences of steps within problem strategies
3. Little or no time spent constructing representations of problems; represent problems at surface or superficial levels	3. Considerable time spent constructing representations of problems; represent problems at deep structural levels
4. Reliance on working backward strategies and, sometimes, trial and error	4. Reliance on working forward from information given in the problem
5. Frequent lack of awareness of errors and the need to check solutions	5. Use of strong self-monitoring skills that include testing and fine-tuning solutions

Note: Summarized from "Expertise in Problem Solving" by M. T. H. Chi, R. Glaser, and E. Rees, 1982. In R. J. Sternberg (Ed.), *Advances in the Psychology of Human Intelligence* (Vol. 1, pp. 7–75). Hillsdale, NJ: Erlbaum; Greeno (1980); Larkin (1980).

Metacognitive Skills.   Experts and novices also differ in their metacognitive skills. First, experts spend more time in planning, and they routinely self-monitor their decisions. As already stated, experts in diagnosing X-rays, for example, test and fine-tune their tentative diagnoses until all the characteristics of a particular film are accounted for (Lesgold et al., 1988). Novices, however, test and self-monitor their conclusions less often and are often unaware of their errors.

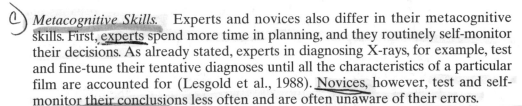

Particularly interesting in the study of radiologists is that third- and fourth-year radiology residents, in general, perform worse than either the experts or the first- and second-year residents. One explanation is that the schemata of the "true" novices are bound tightly to the perceptual data, while the expert rigorously tests possible schemata. The third- and fourth-year residents, in contrast, are beginning to replace perceptual decision making with cognitive reasoning, and rigorous testing is not possible in early stages of this process. In other words, the development of certain complex problem-solving skills is not linear.

Summary.   Research on the differences between experts and novices in problem solving indicates the role of knowledge and metacognition skills in thinking. The extensive knowledge base of experts also makes possible the efficient use of short-term and long-term memory.

In addition to a greater store of knowledge, experts in science and mathematics encode problems and procedures/solutions in schema organized around higher-order principles in the domain. They also spend time in constructing a representation of the problem, apply well-developed schema, and test and monitor their strategies through the process. In the humanities, experts construct explanations of situations or events that reflect the search for and identification of patterns of knowledge, and they also check and crosscheck their emerging deductions.

PRINCIPLES OF INSTRUCTION

Metacognition and problem solving are the complex higher-order capabilities described by cognitive theorists. However, a set of definitive learning principles related to these constructs has yet to be developed. Therefore, instructional principles may only be inferred from current developments.

Metacognition

Research on metacognition suggests areas that may be addressed by metacognitive instruction in the classroom. Among them are essential instructional conditions for any metacognitive instruction; knowledge of strategy applications, conditions, and cues; and self-monitoring and evaluation.

General Instructional Conditions

Four general conditions are essential for successful instruction for metacognition. First, any instruction on cognitive strategies should be "cognitive training with awareness" or "informed training" as opposed to "blind training" (Brown, Armbruster, & Baker, 1986; Rohrer & Thomas, 1989). For example, transfer of comprehension strategists to new tasks is far from automatic. Extensive teaching about when and where to use them is essential (Pressley, El-Dinary, Wharten-McDonald, & Brown, 1998).

Second, the performance criteria used to evaluate student achievement (higher-level) should require the kinds of metacognitive activities addressed in the instruction. If testing only includes low-level performances, students will have little incentive to engage in evaluating task demands, allocating resources carefully, evaluating performance, and monitoring progress. For example, students are unlikely to relinquish a summarization strategy that emphasizes rote recall if tests require only factual information. Instead, test items should be included that require the integration of disparate information to answer a novel question or solve a novel problem (Rohrer & Thomas, 1989, p. 113).

Third, instruction should provide supports for engaging in metacognitive activities. That is, instruction should present tasks that require cognitive strategies while providing training in the monitoring and evaluation of strategy use (Rohrer & Thomas, 1989, p. 113).

Of major importance is that instruction should avoid providing compensations, which are the conditions that decrease the demand for cognitive and metacognitive activities (Rohrer & Thomas, 1989). For example, a problem occurs when test items appear to require integrative processing, but students have received review materials that contain the integrated propositions needed for the test (p. 113). In other words, handouts and other aids should not provide the end product of metacognitive activities. Instead, they should facilitate students' constructions of such products.

Fourth, instruction should provide extensive practice in a variety of contexts with reinforcement. Teaching comprehension strategies with the accompanying metacognitive skills is a long-term process and, ideally, should continue across school years (Pressley et al., 1998). Also of importance, in addition to teacher reinforcement for student improvement, is that the teacher should demonstrate the use of self-reinforcement as he or she works through a strategy (e.g., "Great, this is a good reason") (Graham, Harris, & Troia, 1998, p. 28).

Knowledge of Strategy Applications. A key component of metacognitive knowledge is knowledge about the learning task and when and where to use particular learning strategies. For example, the initial steps in one program to teach writing skills are (1) develop background knowledge about the criteria for good writing and (2) introduce the strategy to be learned, the purpose, and when to use it (Graham et al., 1998). In addition to providing explanations, teachers introducing reading comprehension strategies should model them in a variety of naturally occurring contexts (Pressley et al., 1998). In addition, practice and adaptation of the strategies by the students is essential in helping students construct knowledge about when and where to use them. Then, as implementation of the strategy continues, learner-driven discussions about the ways students are adapting the strategies they know to new contexts and situations help develop reflective knowledge about strategy use (p. 53).

Three typical problems related to the execution of strategies for students have been identified by Butler and Winne (1995). One is the failure to recognize task conditions that should cue strategy use, referred to as the lack of conditional knowledge. The second problem is the misperception of task conditions (cues), which leads to selection of the wrong strategies and the selection of inappropriate criteria for judging performance. The third is the failure to recognize the relationships between task conditions and performance.

A fourth problem is the failure to make strategic use of new knowledge. One reason is that new concepts and strategies compete with old and, very likely, deeply ingrained procedures (Pressley, 1995). In addition, applying newly learned information requires more effort than relying on prior concepts. Finally, many more connections exist in knowledge between old strategies and misconceptions than to newly learned concepts (p. 209). Therefore, a few experiences with new concepts or new knowledge about tasks, conditions, and strategies are insufficient to develop use of the information. Instead, the self-monitoring use of newly learned strategies requires many experiences, and sophisticated use typically requires years (Pressley, 1995, p. 209).

One tool that can be helpful with adolescents is the Metacognitive Awareness of Reading Strategies Inventory (MARSI) (Mokhtari & Richard, 2002). The 30-item instrument addresses global reading strategies (e.g., previewing text for content), problem-solving strategies (e.g., adjusting reading rate), and support strategies (e.g., taking notes while reading). It may be used to assist students in developing awareness of strategy use in reading.

3. *Self-Monitoring and Evaluation.*   Students often do not realize the importance of monitoring and evaluating their learning. Research on computer-based instruction indicates that when students are given control over their involvement in instruction, they often exit prematurely (Steinberg, 1989). These findings indicate that the students were not adequately monitoring their understanding.

Further, one student in a program to teach strategies believed that admitting he did not know something meant that he was admitting he was dumb (Gaskins, 1994, p. 151). To illustrate the importance of explicitly noting lack of understanding, the teacher modeled monitoring as she solved a problem or wrote an essay. Self-talk demonstrated by the teacher included comments such as, "There's a lot of information in that last paragraph and I'm not sure I understand it. I'd better see if I can say it in my own words" (p. 151).

Because monitoring and evaluation activities require effort, instruction should include (1) teacher modeling and remodeling when necessary, (2) opportunities to practice strategies in pairs and in groups, and (3) teacher reinforcement. These steps are particularly important until the skills become less effortful for students and they begin to see the benefits of using them (Pressley et al., 1998).

Summary.   Explicit principles of instruction cannot yet be derived from the early work on metacognition. However, instructional guidelines may be suggested in three broad areas. They are essential conditions for metacognitive instruction, analyzing task purposes and conditions, and self-monitoring and evaluation.

The three general conditions that are essential for successful instruction in metacognition are (1) cognitive training should be implemented with awareness of applications, (2) performance criteria and test situations require metacognitive activities, and (3) instructional support should be provided for metacognitive activities. Of importance is that classroom handouts and other learning aids should not substitute or compensate for metacognitive strategies.

During instruction, brief class discussions can explore the purposes of key activities, such as reading and seatwork. Classroom activities can also be developed that make use of the learning from reading, seatwork, and other instructional activities. Discussions also can explore the relationships between task conditions, strategies, and the products from different tasks.

Self-monitoring and evaluation, according to some researchers, requires goal setting by students. Thus, instruction on setting subgoals may be helpful. Particularly important is teaching students to ask themselves questions during an activity, such as Do I understand this information? and evaluating the products of their efforts. However, learning appropriate metacognitive strategies involves the unlearning of inappropriate management behaviors.

Problem Solving

The terms *problem* and *problem solving* in the school curriculum have had multiple and contradictory meanings over the years (Schoenfeld, 1992). Stanic and Kilpatrick (1988) note that problem solving has become a catchall term for different views of education and schooling in general and mathematics in particular. In the late 1980s, however, the nature and role of problem solving in the curriculum began to undergo examination and revision.

Traditional Curriculum Approaches

College courses described as problem solving range across several perspectives. Among them are teaching students to think creatively and preparing students for competitions (e.g., the international Olympiads); providing instruction to potential teachers on some heuristic strategies; and providing a new approach in remedial mathematics (Schoenfeld, 1992, p. 237). Of interest is that thinking skills programs aimed at general improvement in intellectual ability have not presented convincing evidence of general transfer (Mayer & Wittrock, 1996, p. 51).

In elementary and secondary education, problems traditionally have been viewed as routine exercises. In mathematics, they serve to provide practice on a particular mathematical technique that has been demonstrated to the students (Schoenfeld, 1992, p. 337). Given the stated goal and needed numbers, the only task for students is to pick a suitable computation to apply to the situation. Often the problems or tasks are devised to introduce a technique, which is illustrated by the teacher and/or the text, and more problems or tasks are completed by the students for practice. This conventional mathematics, however, undermines reflective thinking (Pressley & McCormick, 1995, p. 415).

Lampert (1990) noted that the cultural assumption in mathematics is that doing math means following the teacher's rules. Further, mathematical truth is determined when the right answer is verified by the teacher. Similarly, typical student beliefs about mathematics identified by Schoenfeld (1985, p. 43) include "Problems are always solved in 10 minutes if they are solved at all," and "Only geniuses are capable of discovering mathematics."

In science, problems are often in the form of laboratory exercises. An analysis by Mergandoller, Mitman, Marchman, & Packer (1987) revealed three types. Explicit exercises pose the questions, prescribe the procedures, and specify the solution to be obtained. Implicit exercises pose the questions and prescribe the methods. Integrative exercises pose only the problem. An analysis of the laboratory exercises in seventh-grade science, however, revealed no integrative exercises. Instead, 45% of the assigned exercises were explicit and 55% were implicit (Mergandoller et al., 1987). In addition, 84% of the worksheet questions and 82% of the test questions required only verbatim recall.

In other words, instruction has traditionally focused on the content in the domain. Students are expected to master, in a preordained sequence, sets of facts and procedures that represent the content domain. Thus, the emphasis is on getting the right answer for problems and experiments.

Current Approaches

Explication of the subprocesses involved in problem solving and the associated metacognitive skills lead one to expect programs and classroom-based curricula targeted to these strategies. At present, however, some curricula continue to be text-based accompanied by specific routine problems. That is, these materials do not include problems that can challenge student thinking.

Some curricula that focus on developing dispositions to use mathematics in the real world and mathematical understanding address children's strategies in the context of "doing mathematics" (Lester, Garafolo, & Kroll, 1989). Required are exploring various ways to address problems, showing and discussing solutions, and discussing alternative solutions. Also required are developing rich knowledge structures and integrated understandings by all students. Thus, a key focus in such curricula is the various strategies that children engage in to solve problems. Lester et al. (1989) suggest using whole-class discussions to elicit ideas for possible ways to solve the problem. During team or small-group problem solving, early finishers can be challenged to generalize their strategies. As a concluding activity, children can present and discuss their different strategies, and the approaches can be extended or generalized to other situations. The teacher's role is to serve as a facilitator to provide hints when students experience difficulties.

One curriculum approach derives the content of problems from other activities that the children are involved in. For example, when discussing a book or an author, the children determine how old the author's book would be this year, how much older the book is than the child, and so on (Fennema et al., 1993, p. 565). Children also construct their own problems that they then solve, work in small groups, and discuss their strategies with each other, the class, and the teacher. Results indicate that all of the children solved problems that are more difficult than those typically found in first-grade textbooks (Fennema et al., 1993). Strategies ranged from representing the problem concretely (with manipulables) and counting to standard algorithms and complex invented algorithms (used by children in the middle and high performance ranges).

Implementing curricula that emphasize developing rich knowledge structures and integrated understandings by all students requires a reorganization of teacher beliefs and practices. The teacher must have an extensive knowledge structure of both mathematics and the ways that children think and learn. He or she also must be willing to permit children to work through their difficulties with hints or assistance from peers. That is, when the child becomes confused, the teacher's role is not to persuade the child about the "right" procedure.

Summary. The terms *problem* and *problem solving* have been interpreted in various ways in the curriculum. In the elementary and secondary school curriculum, problems traditionally have been viewed as routine exercises. They represent the organization of the content in the domain in terms of facts and procedures. Problems are introduced because they reflect a particular mathematical technique, and students then practice on additional problems so that they become proficient in the procedure. Thus, the cultural assumption of mathematics, for example, is that one must follow the teacher's rules and that the goal is the right answer. In science, the focus is on explicit exercises that pose the questions, prescribe the procedures, and specify the solution to be obtained.

Currently, the emphasis is on "doing mathematics" and mathematical understanding. This focus involves developing rich, integrated knowledge structures that result from an emphasis on the various strategies that may be used to solve basic representational problems. Implementing such curricula, however, requires a reorganization of teacher beliefs and practices and requires teachers with both mathematics knowledge and knowledge about how children think.

EDUCATIONAL APPLICATIONS

Classroom Issues

The basic issues related to cognitive perspectives of learning are discussed in chapter 8. Issues addressed by the research on complex cognitive processes are learning "how-to-learn" skills, recognizing learner differences, and teaching problem solving.

Learning "How-to-Learn" Skills

The term *metacognition* refers to the capabilities required to direct one's learning, remembering, and thinking. Included are knowledge about and awareness of one's own thinking and awareness of difficulties as they arise during learning so that remedial action may be taken.

Learner Differences

Differences in metacognitive capabilities between younger and older children have been identified. They include the extent of awareness of the purposes of instruction and different task demands, skills in monitoring one's understanding and applying new strategies, and awareness of strategy flexibility. In problem solving, differences in both knowledge base and strategy use have been identified between novice and expert problem solvers.

Teaching Problem Solving

Current perspectives on problem solving are addressing a new priority. Specifically, it is that students should acquire the same habits and dispositions to interpretations as experts in the domain. Therefore, problem solving in mathematics means "doing mathematics" and in viewing real-world situations as opportunities to model and quantify variables and/or types of data.

Relationships to Other Perspectives

Metacognition includes (1) knowledge about and awareness of one's thinking, (2) knowledge about the application of strategies to monitor, evaluate, and adjust one's learning activities, and (3) the execution of these strategies. The capabilities that control the management of learning, remembering, and thinking are described by Gagné as cognitive strategies. The goal setting, monitoring, and evaluation of one's learning also are components of models of self-regulation (see chapter 12). A key difference is that these models also address the motivational characteristics that influence the implementation of metacognitive strategies. Also of interest is that Vygotsky's cultural-historical theory addressed the self-regulation of attention and the conscious awareness and mastery of one's thinking processes in the school years (see chapter 11).

Prior theories and research typically conceptualized problem solving in terms of moves or changes in given conditions required to research a solution. Gagné's conditions of learning described problem solving as the search for and application of relevant rules. Current developments in cognitive theory describe the learner's internal subprocesses during the problem-solving process. This focus, particularly the emphasis on the individual's conceptualization of the problem, addresses the issues of problem organization and understanding raised by the Gestalt psychologists.

Developing a Classroom Strategy

Step 1: Select or develop meaningful problems.

1.1 What real-world situations can serve as the basis for problems to be solved?

1.2 Do the problems reflect broad operations or principles in the domain?

1.3 Are there situations for which the students can construct problems?

Step 2: Focus classroom discussion on alternative strategies.

2.1 Which problems are to be solved by teams and which ones by small groups?

2.2 What manipulations or other materials are needed to assist students in developing their strategies?

2.3 Will training be needed to refocus students on providing rationales for their work and listening to the rationales of others?

Classroom Example

Subject: Addition and subtraction in first-grade mathematics.

Organization of subject matter: Problems are organized by the following problem types: join, separate, part-part-whole, and compare.

Example of a "join" problem: Connie has 5 marbles. How many more marbles does she need to make 13 marbles altogether?

Example of a "compare" problem: Jim has 5 marbles. Connie has 8 more than Jim. How many marbles does Connie have?

The curriculum is an example of children learning to "do" mathematics. Beginning the first few days of school, children are asked to solve word problems that the teacher constructed. Later, children also construct and solve their own problems.

Content of the problems is derived from other activities that the children are involved in. For example, when discussing a book or an author, the children determine how old the author or book would be this year, how much older the book is than the child, and so on.

A key focus in the curriculum is the various strategies that children use to solve problems. Children are expected to be engaged in mathematics—solving problems they, their peers, or the teacher has written. They also are expected to persist in their work, and to report how they solved the problem. In addition, they are expected to reflect on their own thinking by comparing it with someone else's approach or on the difficulty of a particular problem for them (Fennema et al., 1993, p. 565). Finally, they are expected to listen to the solutions of others and to respect other solutions. The teacher encourages the use of multiple solution strategies and emphasizes the importance of children using a strategy that is most appropriate for them (p. 578).

Children often work in small groups, and they also present and discuss their work individually with the teacher and participate in whole-class sessions. In class discussions, the teacher often calls on children with less mature strategies first, challenging those with more mature strategies to think of alternative ways to solve the problem. For example, in response to the question, How many ways can you make 3?, strategies ranged from *6 − 3* and *1 + 1 + 1* to *3 + 3 + 3 − 3 − 3*.

CHAPTER QUESTIONS

1. What are some likely reasons for children's lack of implementation of metacognitive strategies following instruction on such strategies?
2. What are the major differences between the Gestalt view of problem solving and the information-processing perspective?
3. What are some of the potential advantages and disadvantages of having children construct their own problems?
4. Children often approach writing tasks as simply writing down somewhat appropriate information with each new sentence stimulating the next idea. What type of metacognitive deficiency do they have?

REFERENCES

Alexander, P. A., Schallert, D. L., & Hare, V. C. (1991). Coming to terms: How researchers in learning and literacy talk about knowledge. *Review of Educational Research, 61*(3), 315–344.

Ames, C. (1992). Achievement goals and the motivational climate. In D. Schunk & J. Meece (Eds.), *Student perceptions in the classroom* (pp. 327–348). Hillsdale, NJ: Erlbaum.

Anderson, J. R. (1985). *Cognitive psychology and its implications* (2nd ed.), New York: W. H. Freeman.

Anzai, Y. (1991). Learning and use of representations for physics expertise. In K. A. Anders & J. Smith (Eds.), *Toward a general theory of expertise* (pp. 64–92). New York: Cambridge University Press.

Bandura, A. (Ed.) (1995). *Self-efficacy in changing societies*. New York: Cambridge University Press.

Beal, C. (1989). Children's communication skills: Implications for the development of writing strategies. In C. McCormick, G. Miller, & M. Pressley (Eds.), *Cognitive strategy research: From basic research to educational applications* (pp. 191–214). New York: Springer-Verlag.

Bereiter, C. (1991). Implications of connectionism for thinking about rules. *Educational Researcher, 20*(3), 10–16.

Bjorklund, D. F., Muir-Broaddus, J. E., & Schneider, W. (1990). Knowledge and strategy development. In D. J. Bjorklund (Ed.), *Children's strategies: Contemporary views of cognitive development*. Hillsdale, NJ: Erlbaum.

Briars, D. J., & Larkin, J. M. (1984). An integrated model of skills in solving elementary school problems. *Cognition and Instruction, 1*, 245–296.

Brown, A. L., Armbruster, B. B., & Baker, L. (1986). The role of metacognition in reading and studying. In J. Orsanu (Ed.), *Teaching comprehension: From research to practice* (pp. 49–75). Hillsdale, NJ: Erlbaum.

Brown, A. L. (1987). Metacognition, executive control, self-regulation, and other more mysterious mechanisms. In F. Weinert & R. Kluwe (Eds.), *Metacognition, motivation, and understanding* (pp. 65–115). Hillsdale, NJ: Erlbaum.

Bruning, R. H., Schraw, G. J., & Ronning, R. R. (1995). *Cognitive psychology and instruction*. Upper Saddle River, NJ: Merrill/Prentice Hall.

Butler, D. L., & Winne, P. H. (1995). Feedback and self-regulated learning. *Review of Educational Research, 65*(3), 245–281.

Chase, W. G., & Simon, H. A. (1973). The mind's eye in chess. In W. G. Chase & H. A. Simon (Eds.), *Visual information processing* (pp. 215–218). New York: Academic Press.

Chi, M. T. H., Glaser, R., & Farr, M. (1991). *The nature of expertise*. Hillsdale, NJ: Erlbaum.

Chi, M. T. H., Glaser, R., & Rees, E. (1982). Expertise in problem solving. In R. J. Sternberg (Ed.), *Advances in the psychology of human intelligence* (Vol. 1: pp. 7–75). Hillsdale, NJ: Erlbaum.

Davidson, J., & Sternberg, R. (1998). Smart problem solving: How metacognition helps. In D. J. Hacker, J. Dunlosky, & A. C. Graesser (Eds.), *Metacognition in educational theory and practice* (pp. 47–68). Mahwah, NJ: Erlbaum.

Declos, V. R. & Harrington, C. (1991). Effects of strategy monitoring and proactive instruction on children's problem-solving performance. *Journal of Educational Psychology, 83*, 35–42.

Dole, J. A., Duffy, G. G., Roehler, L. R., & Pearson, P. D. (1991). Moving from the old to the new: Research on reading comprehension instruction. *Review of Educational Research, 61*(2), 239–264.

Duncker, K. (1945). On problem solving. *Psychological Monographs 68*(5), Whole no. 270.

Elliott, E. E., & Dweck, C. S. (1988). Goals: An approach to motivation and achievement. *Journal of Personality and Social Psychology, 54*(1), 5–12.

Fang, Z., & Cox, B. E. (1999). Emergent metacognition: A study of preschoolers' literate behavior. *Journal of Research in Childhood Education, 13*(2), 175–185.

Fennema, E., Franke, M. L., Carpenter, T. P., & Carey, D. A. (1993). Using children's mathematical knowledge in instruction. *American Educational Research Journal, 30*(3), 555–563.

Flavell, J. H. (1971). First discussant's comments: What is memory development the development of? *Human Development, 14*, 272–278.

Flavell, J. H. (1979). Metacognition and cognitive monitoring: A new area of cognitive development inquiry. *American Psychologist, 34*, 906–911.

Flavell, J. H., & Wellman, H. M. (1977). Metamemory. In R. V. Kalil, Jr., & J. W. Hagen (Eds.), *Perspectives on the development of memory and cognition* (pp. 3–33). Hillsdale, NJ: Erlbaum.

Garner, R. (1987). *Metacognition and reading comprehension*. Norwood, NJ: Ablex.

Garner, R. (1990). Children's use of strategies in reading. In D. Bjorklund (Ed.), *Children's strategies: Contemporary views of cognitive development* (pp. 245–268). Hillsdale, NJ: Erlbaum.

Gaskins, I. W. (1994). Classroom applications of cognitive science: Teaching poor readers how to learn, think, and problem solve. In K. McGilly (Ed.), *Classroom lessons: Integrating cognitive theory and classroom practice* (pp. 129–154). Cambridge, MA: MIT Press.

Gick, M. L., & Holyoak, K. J. (1980). Analogical problem solving. *Cognitive Psychology, 12*, 306–355.

Gick, M., & Holyoak, K. J. (1983). Schema induction and analogical transfer. *Cognitive Psychology, 15*, 1–38.

Glaser, R., & Chi, M. T. (1988). Overview. In M. Chi, R. Glaser, & M. Farr (Eds.), *The nature of expertise* (pp. xv–xxviii). Hillsdale, NJ: Erlbaum.

Graham, S., & Harris, K. (1994). The role and development of self-regulation in the writing process. In D. Schunk & B. Zimmerman (Eds.), *Self-regulation of learning and performance* (pp. 203–228). Hillsdale, NJ: Erlbaum.

Graham, S., Harris, K. R., & Troia, G. A. (1998). Writing and self-regulation: Cases from the self-regulated strategy development model. In D. J. Schunk & B. J. Zimmerman (Eds.), *Self-regulated learning: From teaching to self-reflective practice* (pp. 20–41). New York: Guilford Press.

Hacker, D. J. (1998). Self-regulated comprehension during normal reading. In D. J. Hacker, J. Dunlosky, & A. C. Gaesser (Eds.), *Metacognition in educational theory and practice* (pp. 165–191). Mahwah, NJ: Erlbaum.

Harnishfeger, K. K., & Bjorklund, D. F. (1990). Children's strategies: A brief history. In D. Bjorklund (Ed.), *Children's strategies* (pp. 1–22). Hillsdale, NJ: Erlbaum.

Hayes, J. R. (1988). *The complete problem solver* (2nd ed.). Hillsdale, NJ: Erlbaum.

Holyoak, K. J. (1995). Problem solving. In E. E. Smith & D. N. Osherman (Eds.), *Thinking*. Cambridge, MA: MIT Press.

Howe, M. J. A. (1988). Context, memory, and education. In G. M. Davies & D. M. Thomson (Eds.), *Memory in context: Context in memory* (pp. 267–280), New York: John Wiley.

Jacobs, J. E., & Paris, S. G. (1987). Children's metacognition about reading: Issues in definition, measurement, and instruction. *Educational Psychologist 22*(2 & 4), 255–278.

Karmiloff-Smith, A. (1979). Problem solving construction and representations of closed railway circuits. *Archives of Psychology, 47*, 37–59.

Katona, G. (1940). *Organizing and memorizing*. New York: Columbia University Press.

Köhler, W. (1969). *The Task of Gestalt psychology*. Princeton, NJ: Princeton University Press.

Kuhn, D. (1999). A developmental model of critical thinking. *Educational Researcher, 28*(2), 16–25.

Lampert, R. M. (1990). When the problem is not the question and the solution is not the answer: Mathematical knowing and teaching.

American Educational Research Journal, 27(1), 29–63.

Lesgold, A., Robinson, H., Feltovich, P., Glaser, R., Klopfer, D., & Wang, Y. (1988). Expertise in a complex skill: Diagnosing X-ray pictures. In M. Chi, R. Glaser, & M. Farr (Eds.), *The nature of expertise* (pp. 311–342). Hillsdale, NJ: Erlbaum.

Lester, F., Garofolo, J., & Kroll, D. (1989). *The role of metacognition in mathematical problem solving: A study of two grade seven classes*. Final report to the National Science Foundation of NSF project MDR 85-50346.

Maier, N. R. F. (1930). Reasoning in humans I. On direction. *Journal of Comparative Psychology, 10*, 115–143.

Mayer, R. E. (1992). *Thinking, problem solving, cognition* (2nd ed.). New York: Freeman.

Mayer, R. E., & Wittrock, M. (1996). Problem-solving transfer. In D. C. Berliner & R. C. Calfee (Eds.), *Handbook of educational psychology* (pp. 47–62). New York: Macmillan Library References.

Mergandoller, J., Mitman, A. J., Marchman, V. A., & Packer, M. J. (1987). Task demands and accountability in middle-grade science classes. *The Elementary School Journal, 3,* 251–265.

Midgley, C., Kaplan, A., Middleton, M., & Maeke, M. (1998). The development and validation of scales assessing students' goal orientation. *Contemporary Educational Psychology, 23*, 113–131.

Mokhtari, K., & Richard, C. A. (2002). Assessing students' metacognitive awareness of reading strategies. *Journal of Educational Psychology, 94*(2), 249–259.

Newell, A., & Simon, H. A. (1972). *Human problem solving*. Upper Saddle River, NJ: Prentice Hall.

Paris, S. G., Lipson, M. Y., & Wilson, K. K. (1983). Becoming a strategic reader. *Contemporary Educational Psychology, 8,* 293–316.

Polya, G. (1973). *How to solve it* (2nd ed.). Garden City, NJ: Doubleday.

Pressley, M. (1995). More about the development of self-regulation: Complex, long-term, and thoroughly social. *Educational Psychologist, 30*(4), 207–212.

Pressley, M., & Afflerback, P. (1995). *Verbal protocols of reading: The nature of constructively responsive reading*. Hillsdale, NJ: Erlbaum.

Pressley, M., & McCormick, C. B. (1995). *Advanced educational psychology for educators, researchers, and policy makers*. New York: Harper Collins.

Pressley, M., Borkowski, J. G., & Schmeider, W. (1987). Cognitive strategies: Good strategy users coordinate metacognition and knowledge. In R. Vasta & G. Whitehurst (Eds.), *Annals of child development* (Vol. 5, pp. 89–129). Greenwich, CT: JAI.

Pressley, M., El-Dinary, P. B., Wharton-McDonald, R., & Brown, R. (1998). Transactional instruction of comprehension strategies in the elementary grades. In D. Schunk & B. J. Zimmerman (Eds.), *Self-regulated learning: From teaching to self-reflective practice* (pp. 42–56). New York: Guilford Press.

Resnick, L. (1988). Teaching mathematics as an ill-structured discipline. In R. Charles & E. Silver (Eds.), *The teaching and assessing of mathematical problem solving* (pp. 32–60). Reston, VA: National Council of Teachers of Mathematics.

Resnick, L. B. (1988). Developing mathematical knowledge. *American Psychologist, 44*, 162–169.

Rohrer, W. D., & Thomas, J. W. (1989). Domain-specific knowledge, metacognition, and the promise of instructional reform. In C. B. McCormick, G. Miller, & M. Pressley (Eds.), *Cognitive strategy research* (pp. 104–132). New York: Springer-Verlag.

Schoenfeld, A. (1992). Learning to think mathematically. Problem solving, cognition, and sense making in mathematics. In D. A. Grouws (Ed.), *Handbook of research on mathematics teaching and learning* (pp. 334–370). New York: Macmillan.

Schunk, D., & Zimmerman, B. J. (Eds.) (1998). *Self-regulated learning: From teaching to self-reflective practice*. New York: Guilford Press.

Simon, H. A. (1980). Problem solving and education. In D. T. Tuma & F. Reif (Eds.), *Problem solving and education: Issues in teaching and research* (2nd ed., pp. 81–96). Hillsdale, NJ: Erlbaum.

Son, L. K., & Schwartz, B. L. (2003). The relation between metacognitive monitoring and control. In T. J. Perfect & B. L. Schwartz (eds.), *Applied metacognition* (pp. 15–38). New York: Cambridge University Press.

Spoehr, K. T. (1994). Enhancing the acquisition of conceptual structures through hypermedia. In K. McGilly (Ed.), *Classroom lessons: Integrating cognitive theory and classroom practice* (pp. 75–101). Cambridge, MA: MIT Press.

Stanic, G., & Kilpatrick, J. (1988). Historical perspectives on problem solving in the mathematics curriculum. In R. Charles & E. Silver (Eds.), *The teaching and assessing of mathematical problem solving* (pp. 1–22). Reston, VA: National Council of Teachers of Mathematics.

Steinberg, E. R. (1989). Cognition and learning control: A literature review, 1977–1988. *Journal of Computer-Based Instruction, 16*, 117–121.

Sternberg, R. (1998). Abilities are forms of developing expertise. *Educational Researcher 27*(3), 11–20.

Tuckman, B. W. (1996). The relative effectiveness of incentive motivation and prescribed learning strategy in improving college students' course performance. *Journal of Experimental Education, 64*, 197–210.

Van Haneghan, J. P. (1986). *Children's detection of errors in word problems: Evidence for comprehension monitoring in math* (Doctoral dissertation, University of Maryland, Baltimore County 1986). *Dissertation Abstracts International*, 47B: 2650.

Van Haneghan, J. P., & Baker, L. (1989). Cognitive monitoring in mathematics. In C. B. McCormick, G. Miller, & M. Pressley (Eds.), *Cognitive strategy research* (pp. 215–238). New York: Springer-Verlag.

Vosniadou, S., Pearson, P. D., & Rogers, T. (1988). What causes children's failures to detect inconsistencies in text? Representation vs. comparison difficulties. *Journal of Educational Psychology, 80*, 27–39.

Voss, J. A. (1989). Problem solving and the educational process. In A. Lesgold & R. Glaser (Eds.), *Foundations for a psychology of education* (pp. 251–294). Hillsdale, NJ: Erlbaum.

Vye, N. J., Goldman, S. R., Voss, J. F., Hmelo, C., Williams, S., and The Cognition and Technology Group at Vanderbilt (1997). Complex mathematical problem solving by individuals and dyads. *Cognition and Instruction, 15*(4), 435–484.

Wellman, H. M. (1985). The child's theory of mind: The development of conceptions of cognition. In S. R. Yussen (Ed.), *The growth of reflection in children* (pp. 169–206). Orlando, FL: Academic Press.

Wertheimer, M. (1959). *Productive thinking.* New York: Harper (original published 1945).

Wineburg, S. (1991). Historical problem solving: A study of the cognitive processes used in the evaluation of documentary and pictorial evidence. *Journal of Educational Psychology, 81*(1), 73–87.

Winne, P. H., & Hadwin, A. F. (1998). Studying as self-regulated learning. In D. J. Hacker, J. Dunlosky, & A. C. Graesser (Eds.) *Metacognition in educational theory and practice* (pp. 277–305). Mahwah, NJ: Erlbaum.

Wyatt, D., Pressley, M., El-Dinary, R. B., Stein, S., Evans, P., & Brown, R. (1993). Comprehension strategies, worth and credibility monitoring, and evaluations: Cold and hot cognition when experts read professional articles that are important to them. *Learning and Individual Differences, 5,* 49–72.

Zimmerman, B. J. (1995). Self-regulation involves more than metacognition: A social cognitive perspective. *Educational Psychologist, 30*(4), 217–221.

PART IV
Cognitive-Development Theories

Theories of learning address the particular events and conditions essential in the acquisition of knowledge and specific skills. In contrast, cognitive-development theories first identify the capabilities that represent the highest levels of human thought. Then they describe the events and conditions necessary to attain these levels of thinking. Although schooling, properly designed, may facilitate such development, the implication is that higher levels of human thinking cannot be taught directly.

The two cognitive-development theorists, Jean Piaget and Lev S. Vygotsky, described thinking in different ways. Jean Piaget, a Swiss psychologist, described logical thinking and reasoning about complex situations as the highest form of cognitive development. He grounded his investigations in the individual child's manipulation of and interaction with objects in his or her particular environment.

Lev Vygotsky, in contrast, viewed cognitive development as culturally based in that the signs and symbols essential for cognitive development are products of one's culture. Vygotsky identified logical memory, voluntary attention, categorical perception, and the self-organization of behavior as the highest forms of psychological functioning. He grounded his analyses in the cultural history of the human race and the child's interactions with knowledgeable adults in his or her particular culture.

CHAPTER 10
Jean Piaget's Cognitive-Development Theory

To present an adequate notion of learning one must first explain how the individual manages to construct and invent, not merely how he repeats and copies. (Piaget, 1970b)

The work of Jean Piaget is a major contribution to developmental psychology in several ways. First, prior to his research, young children were viewed simply as miniature adults. However, Piaget's theory and research clearly demonstrated the novel message that young children's thinking and ways of organizing experience differ qualitatively from adult thinking (Chandler & Chapman, 1991).

Second, the aim of Piaget's work was not to investigate changes in problem solving or cognitive skills. Instead, his purpose was to discover the characteristics of natural logic—the logic of the acting, speaking, reasoning individual in all of its various forms (Inhelder & deCaprona, 1990, p. 39). For example, at a certain point in development, the child knows, *without looking at a concrete set of examples,* that *A* is greater than *C* if he knows that *A* is greater than *B* and *B* is greater than *C*. He also knows that this conclusion must be true. Similarly, the child also knows that there are more *B*s than *A*s when *A* is included in *B,* and she does not waiver in her belief. This is the essence of Piaget's natural logic (Borel, 1987, p. 68). Discovering the characteristics of natural logic involved discovering the origins of knowledge and reasoning and the transitions from one form of reasoning to another. This goal requires the investigation of the roots of logical thinking in infancy, the kinds of reasoning that young children engage in, and the reasoning processes used by adolescents and adults.

Third, Piaget's approach to studying the development of natural logic was itself an innovation. He formed the framework for his research and theory from the disciplines of philosophy, biology, and psychology. From philosophy came the initial questions to be answered: What is the nature of knowledge? and What is the relationship between the knower and reality? For Piaget, the term *knowledge* refers to natural logic. Thus, the study of knowledge is the study of intelligence.

Biology, the second component in the framework of Piaget's work, is the source of his basic assumptions about the nature of intelligence. In Piaget's view, the adaptation and growth of organisms explain the problems and processes involved in the adaptation of intelligence to the environment (Piaget, 1980) (see section titled "A Constructivist View of Intelligence"). The role of psychology in Piaget's framework was to provide the method of study. Questions about the ways that intelligence grows and adapts to the environment can only be answered through psychological research (Piaget, 1972b, p. 9).

The fourth contribution of Piaget's work is that it consists of richly detailed analyses of thinking and reasoning, which Beilin (1992a) maintained is unrivaled in developmental psychology in both scope and depth. The areas addressed by Piaget include children's language and thought, children's understanding of causality and the world, moral development, arithmetic reasoning, stages in infant cognitive development, a theory of adaptation, the components of logical thinking, and analyses of prelogical thinking. Works published after Piaget's death address the role of possibility and necessity in logical thinking, analyses of the forms of knowledge in each of the sciences, and a theory of meaning. In addition, the group who collaborated with Piaget in Geneva at the Center for Genetic (developmental) Epistemology conducted hundreds of experiments on various aspects of children's reasoning and thinking.

Unfortunately, misinterpretations were made of Piaget's action-oriented model when it was assimilated in to the English and American empiricist tradition (Beilin, 1992b; Bickhard, 1997; Chandler & Chapman, 1991; Chapman, 1988; Dean & Youniss, 1991; Lorenço & Machado, 1996; Smith, 1991). First, his descriptions of the stages of reasoning were used to develop curricula in mathematics, science, and early childhood. In Piaget's view, however, the stages are not explanatory. Their purpose simply is to distinguish the various kinds of reasoning that were to be explained (Chapman, 1988, p. 338). Second, some researchers incorporated Piaget's concepts into their framework of questions while excluding issues the theory was intended to address. The result was a distorted version of the theory (Chapman, 1988; Chandler & Chapman, 1991; Dean & Youniss, 1991; Lorenço & Machado, 1996). Others, in efforts to remove extraneous factors from experiments on children's reasoning, developed tasks that required different and less complex forms of thinking than the Piagetian tasks (Chapman, 1988; Chandler & Chapman, 1991; Montangero, 1991). Thus, conclusions that some complex forms of reasoning were developed at earlier ages were in error. Further, some interpretations of Piaget's theory were so distorted that he was criticized for positions he had never taken (Bickhard, 1997; Chapman, 1988; Lorenço & Machado, 1996).

In addition, some researchers have developed psychometric measures of Piagetian concepts. First, this approach risks eliminating key constructs such as sequence, equilibration, universality, and generalization from the research agenda (Edelstein & Schroeder, 2000). Second, understanding individual differences in the context of Piaget's theory means a focus on interindividual variability as both input into and the outcome of development. Required are experiental interactions between the organism and the environment that deeply affect development across the lifespan (p. 842).

Understanding Piaget's work is hindered by at least three factors. One is that only some of his writings and the Genevan research are available in English. Second, Piaget, in his later writings, often did not restate the purpose and broad aims of his work, thus making it easier to misapply the theory to inappropriate questions (Chapman, 1988). Third, Piaget continued to revise and rework the theory based on continuing experimentation; he once described himself as its chief revisionist (Piaget, 1970b). For example, Piaget originally used the term *logico-mathematical* to refer to the child's construction of classes and relations involving number and quantity (Piaget, 1952). He later (1971) expanded the category to include all the organism's intercoordinations of its activities.

One of Piaget's last writings revisited the issues of the construction of the structures of logical thinking, specifically the role of possibility and necessity (Piaget, 1987a, 1987b). His last work on the logic of meaning (Piaget & Garcia, 1991) identified implications among actions as the basis for the later development of logical thinking.

PRINCIPLES OF COGNITIVE DEVELOPMENT

The focus of Jean Piaget's theory is the development of natural logic from birth to adulthood. Understanding the theory depends on understanding the biological assumptions from which it is derived and the implications for defining knowledge (Piaget, 1970b, p. 703).

Basic Assumptions

The basic assumptions of the theory are Piaget's conception of the nature of intelligence and the essential factors in cognitive development.

A Constructivist View of Intelligence

The introduction of Piaget's theory to the English-speaking community after World War II created a near-sensation with its bold theoretical claims and counterintuitive experimental data (Beilin, 1992a, p. 191). One of his counterintuitive claims was that intelligence and knowledge are not static quantities or things. Instead, intelligence and knowledge are ever-changing processes, and the role of the psychologist is to study the nature of the changes.

The Nature of Intelligence.   The basic assumption of Piaget's theory is that human intelligence and biological organisms function in similar ways. Both are organized systems that constantly interact with the environment. They also construct the structures they need in order to adapt to the environment (Piaget, in Bringuier, 1980, p. 3).

Piaget's view that the organism is not a passive agent in genetic development is supported by his research on mollusks. He found that certain mollusks, transported from their calm-water habitat to turbulent wind-driven waters, grew an extra "foot" to maintain a hold on the rocks in the fast current. Furthermore, these biological changes, constructed in response to an environmental change, were inherited by some descendants of the mollusks. For some of the organisms, this change persisted even when they were transported back to calmer waters (Piaget, 1980).

Piaget (1980) concluded that intelligence constructs the cognitive structures that it needs in the process of adaptation to the environment. Cognitive structures, like biological structures, "are not given in advance, neither in the human mind nor in the external world as we perceive and organize it" (Piaget, in Bringuier, 1980, p. 37). An example is the infant's coordination of her actions into the reaching-grasping-pulling scheme. This new structure enables her to pull a string to reach the object at the end of it (Piaget, 1967), to pull a blanket to get an out-of-reach toy, and so on. Other examples throughout childhood involve the gradual construction of logical ways of interacting with objects and events, instead of acting on the basis of perceptual cues. Therefore, intelligence is not a static trait that can be quantitatively assessed. Instead, intelligence is active, dynamic, and changing, for it seeks explanations and understandings both to construct itself and to function effectively.

The Relationship Between Knowledge and Intelligence.   The traditional view that learning involves acquiring static objective knowledge about a "real" world is based on two erroneous assumptions (Piaget, 1970b). One is that objective knowledge is some entity "out there" in objects and events that can be identified. The second erroneous belief is that the external environment and the individual can be separated into two entities in any definition of knowledge.

For Piaget, knowledge is knowing, and it is a process that is created by the activity of the learner. Knowing derives from the experience of transforming reality by interacting with it (Chapman, 1999, p. 32). In other words, "in the absence of action, the question of knowledge becomes mute within Piaget's system" (Pufall, 1988, p. 16). Moreover, in the creation of knowledge, the individual and the object are fused and cannot be separated. Knowledge also contains many subjective components; therefore, it is a relationship and not some a priori given.

More important, the relationship between the learner and the object is always undergoing transformation. "The relationship between subject (knower) and objects is in no way determined beforehand, and what is more important, it is not stable" (Piaget, 1970b, p. 704). The infant, for example, first learns about the environment by putting all objects into its mouth and later by shaking, dropping, pushing, or pulling them. At the most sophisticated level of intelligence, however, scientists and scholars build theories using abstract symbols that may have no concrete counterparts in the environment. Between the activities of the infant and the theoretical scientist lies a continuum of ever-changing development.

In summary, genetic epistemology "above all sees knowledge as a continuous construction" (Piaget, 1972b, p. 17). Since knowledge is constructed through the individual's interactions with the environment and intelligence also is so constructed, the issues in understanding knowledge and intelligence are reduced to the same question. In other words, to answer the question about how the individual progresses from a state of less sufficient to more sufficient knowledge is to determine the ways in which intelligence is interacting with the environment.

Essential Factors in Cognitive Development

Four factors are necessary for the developmental transitions from one form of reasoning to another. They are the physical environment, maturation, social influences, and the processes referred to as equilibration (Piaget, 1977).

Contact with the physical environment is indispensable because the interaction between the individual and the world is the source of new knowledge. However, such contact is insufficient for developing knowledge unless the individual's intelligence can make use of the experience. Maturation of the nervous system is, therefore, important because it permits the child to realize maximum benefit from physical experience. In other words, maturation opens up possibilities for development, whereas the lack of it establishes broad limits on cognitive achievement. The emergence of hand-eye coordination in the infant, for example, is essential for the construction of the infant's action schemes, such as reaching-grasping-pulling.

Although maturation is an important condition for cognitive development, the particular events are not predetermined. Development proceeds at different rates, depending on the nature of the contact with the environment and the learner's own activity.

The third factor, the social environment, includes the role of language and education and, particularly, contact with others. In the absence of social interactions, the child, subjectively certain in his or her beliefs, would be unlikely to initiate the actions required to change inaccurate ideas. Piaget (1926) stated, "Never without the shock of contact with the thought of others and the effort of reflection which this shock entails would thought as such come to consciousness" (p. 144). Also, differences in social experiences, like physical experience, can accelerate or retard the development of cognitive structures (Inhelder, Sinclair, & Bovet, 1974).

The foregoing three factors are the classical factors described by other theorists that influence development. Piaget maintained, however, that these three factors (either singly or in combination) were insufficient to explain the emergence of new forms of thinking (Chapman, 1988, p. 388). Also essential is the fourth factor, equilibration. This factor consists of the set of processes that maintain a steady state in intellectual functioning in the midst of transformation and change. Equilibration (described in the following section) regulates the individual's interactions with the environment and permits cognitive development to proceed in a coherent and organized fashion.

Summary

The purpose of Piaget's work was to discover the characteristics of natural logic, that is, the reasoning processes used at various phases during development.

The framework for Piaget's research and theory was formed from the disciplines of philosophy, psychology, and biology. The basic issues, the nature of knowledge and the relationship between the knower and reality, came from philosophy. The methodology for answering the questions came from psychology, and biology was the source of Piaget's assumptions about the nature of intelligence. Specifically, intelligence, like biological organisms, is an organized system that constantly interacts with the environment and constructs the structures essential for adaptation to the environment. Therefore, intelligence is an ongoing and changing process, and knowing is created by the activity of the learner. The key question for psychology thus becomes the ways that the learner progresses from one stage of knowledge construction to another.

The transition from one form of reasoning to another depends on four essential factors. They are the physical environment, maturation, social influences, and the processes referred to as equilibration. The role of equilibration is to maintain the functioning of intelligence while it undergoes major transformations.

The Components of Cognitive Development

The focal point of the theory is the processes that account for progress from one level of reasoning and thinking to a higher level. Two major topics in Piaget's theory illustrate these processes. They are the psychological nature of logical thinking and the fundamental processes involved in interactions with the environment.

The Psychological Nature of Logical Thinking

Three key concepts are important in understanding the nature of logical thinking in Piaget's theory. They are the psychological structure of operations, the role of possibility and necessity, and the logic of meaning.

Psychological Structure.   The basic units of logical thinking are particular kinds of cognitive activity that Piaget (1928, 1970b) referred to as *operations*. They are the cognitive structures that govern logical reasoning in the broad sense (Piaget, 1970a, 1970b). However, operations are not static structures of information. Instead, operations are transformations performed on data or objects that form a particular psychological structure. They are actions that are internalizable, reversible, and coordinated into systems. In other words, cognitive structures are not the conscious content of thinking. Instead, cognitive structures impose one particular way of thinking instead of another (Piaget, 1970/1976a, p. 64; 1976b).

Essential Characteristics.   Three key characteristics differentiate operations from other kinds of actions. First, the data or object transformation is one in which a change in one feature of the situation is exactly compensated by a change in another characteristic. For example, if a pile of 40 pennies is subdivided into four equal piles (transformation), the number of piles *increases* (from one to four) while the number per pile *decreases* (from 40 to 10). Second, as a result of these balancing compensations, the essential nature of the object(s) or the data remains invariant or constant. In the prior example, the total number of pennies (40) does not change. Recognition of the unchanging feature of the situation by the child is referred to as *conservation*. When a ball of clay is flattened into the shape of a pancake, for example, the amount of clay remains invariant; the quantity is conserved.

The third important characteristic of operations is that the transformation in the data or the object can be restored to the original by an inverse operation. The four piles of pennies, for example, can be recombined into the whole of 40 pennies.

The capability of a child to simultaneously coordinate an operation and its inverse is referred to as **reversibility**. When a child develops the understanding that a transformation *simultaneously* and necessarily implies its inverse, he or she can manipulate the situation and analyze it correctly without becoming confused. At that point, the child has constructed an operational structure (see the example in the following section).

In other words, both the data transformation and its inverse are essential elements of an operational structure. The inverse of adding $2 + 3 = 5$, for example, is subtraction (i.e., $5 - 3 = 2$). However, simply demonstrating the capability of adding numbers does not imply that operational thinking has been attained. The child must view addition as the inverse of subtraction and vice versa; that is, the existence of one requires the presence of the other (Murray, 1990, p. 199).

Example of a Psychological Structure.   Experiments on the conservation of quantity illustrate the phases involved in the child's invention of an operational structure. Children were shown little balls of clay that were then rolled into sausage shapes. When asked if the amount of clay was the same, three levels of development were found prior to operational thinking. Children focused only on the lengths of the sausage shape (Level I), began to notice that rolling out the clay makes it thinner (Level II), and then understood that rolling out the clay makes it simultaneously longer and thinner (Level III). Children at Level III also may understand that the sausage shape can be returned to the ball. However, they do not yet comprehend reversibility in terms of the compensatory relations between transformations of length and width (Chapman, 1988, p. 299).

Construction of the operational structure of conservation of quantity (Level IV) means that children can predict in advance the compensatory changes in length and thickness that result from rolling out the clay. In addition, they are able to identify the constant or invariant in the process.

Figure 10.1 illustrates the set of affirmations and compensatory negations that compose the structure referred to as conservation of quantity. The diagram illustrates the totalities of an operational structure that is identified by its own transformational rules about relations (Inhelder & deCaprona, 1990, p. 53).

To create an operational structure, the child must invent the opposite of factors x and y. Further, the child must determine exactly what non-x and non-y are, such that existence of one (x, y) requires the existence of the other (non-x, non-y) (Murray, 1990, p. 199). For example, when the child sequentially orders a dozen sticks of different lengths, she must realize simultaneously that "big" means "not little" and vice versa. Also, "bigger" means "less little," and a stick can be bigger or smaller than another depending on the comparison that is being made (Piaget, 1985, p. 104). Another is the late development of the concepts of possibility and necessity.

Operational structures develop slowly, over months and years, and their development requires reorganizations of prior thinking. One factor in this lengthy process is that only positive observables are registered perceptually. In contrast, negations are neglected or constructed slowly and laboriously after the development of positive observable characteristics (Piaget, 1985, p. 13). Another is the late development of the concepts of possibility and necessity.

The Role of Possibility and Necessity.   The interdependence of the factors and their inverses in Figure 10.1 illustrates a key concept in the construction of operational structures: necessity. That is, the child realizes that certain things he or she knows are true also *must* be true. Young children, and even adults, often are slow to appreciate the necessity that is inherent in situations (Murray, 1990, p. 192). For example, in two studies, children were able to accurately add numbers from one to three. However, from 30% to 70% of the children thought the answer also could be a different number (Cauley, Murray, & Smith, 1983; Murray, 1990).

The importance of distinguishing between necessary knowledge and "simply true" knowledge is that they differ in key characteristics. "Simply true" knowledge may be developed through induction, noting observable facts, probability, and contingent relations among events. In contrast, necessary knowledge (for example, conservation of number) depends on deduction, universality (can be acquired by any individual), certainty, and causal relations between states and affairs. That is, necessity is inherent in causal explanations, in the relationship between identified "causes" and the effects or outcomes they are said to produce (Ferreiro, 2001, p. 216).

Research by Piaget in his later years revealed the lengthy development by the child of possibility and necessity (Piaget, 1987a, 1987b). The child's understanding of these concepts in problem-solving situations emerges late in the

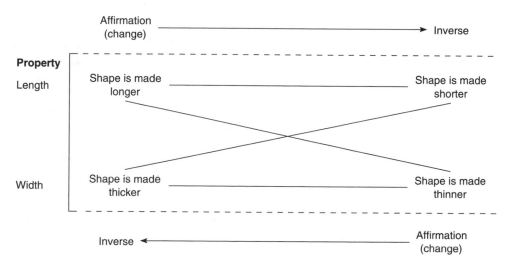

FIGURE 10.1
Illustration of the psychological structure of conservation of quantity

concrete operational period (Acredolo, 1997; Piaget, 1987a, 1987b). Beilin (1992a) views this work as one of the most important redirections of the theory.

At the preoperational level of thinking, children cannot differentiate between reality, possibility, and necessity. Shown a partially hidden box, young children stated that the hidden sides must be the same color as the visible portion (Chapman, 1988). This phase, in which only one possibility is viewed as valid, is referred to by Piaget (1987a) as "pseudonecessity."

At Level IIA, children think of a few concrete co-possibilities, such as the hidden sides could be "green, blue, violet, yellow, white—and that's all" (Piaget, 1987a, p. 44). At Level IIB, when concrete operations are firmly established, each possibility is treated as one among many others that are conceivable (Beilin, 1989, p. 115) (see Table 10.1).

Children at Level II also make some effort to rule out false possibilities on the basis of the data. In one experiment, the task was to arrange three animals in the same sequence as three animals hidden behind a screen. The six possible sequences of the sheep (S), the rabbit (R), and the chicken (C) are SRC, SCR, RSC, RCS, CSR, and CRS. The children were told the number of their correct positions after each attempt. This information can lead to the systematic elimination of certain possibilities until only one remains (the "necessarily" correct solution) (Chapman, 1988, p. 320). However, Level II children were able to eliminate only a few possibilities after feedback; none recognized that getting only two of the three animals correctly positioned is impossible.

TABLE 10.1
Levels of Reasoning About Possibility and Necessity

Level of Thinking	Possibility	Necessity
Level I (preoperations)	(a) Recognition of only a single possibility (b) Later recognition of at least one other possibility	(a) Reality as perceived or manipulated appears to be necessarily so (Piaget, 1986a, p. 148) (b) Lack of cumulative accounting of possibilities eliminated on successive trials of a problem (5–7 years)
Level IIA (onset of concrete operations)	Formation of concrete co-possibilities; limited to those the child can imagine	Some systematic exclusion of possibilities that proved to be false in previous trials; however, children sometimes forget the possibilities already excluded over an extended series of trials
Level IIB	Each possibility is one among many that are conceivable	
Level III (hypothetico-deductive operations)	Indeterminate unlimited possibilities are completely deducible	Systematic exclusion of possibilities; recognition that more than one series of trials is possible and leads inevitably to the correct solution

Level III children recognize unlimited possibilities and also systematically exclude possibilities until they arrive at the one that is necessary. In the animal sequence problem, for example, children at Level III systematically solved both the three-animal and four-animal sequences.

These transitions indicate that testing the development of operational thinking involves more than obtaining a correct answer to particular tasks. Genuine tests of operational thinking also must certify that the child's response is a necessary conclusion (Murray, 1990). Children may be asked, for example, if the outcome can be different, or if this outcome occurs only sometimes (p. 188). Equally important is eliciting the child's reasons for his or her conclusions.

The Logic of Meaning.   The logic of operational thinking is referred to as extensional logic. It involves the truth or falsity of a term or a statement based on its extensions or links to other terms or statements. Examples are part/whole and inclusion relations. For example, given a collection of both brown and white wooden beads, the statement, "There are more white beads than wooden beads" is false. The relative quantity of the white beads is determined by the other types of beads in the total collection.

Piaget's last work, *The Logic of Meanings* (Piaget & Garcia, 1991), laid the foundation for his theory of intensional logic, or a logic of shared meaning. In Piaget's view, the shared meanings in actions are the roots of operational or extensional logic. The major principles are as follows:

1. Knowledge always involves inference. That is, a relation between actions is a logical implication. For example, some infants at 9 to 10 months, when given empty cubes, sticks, and small plasticine balls, will insert an object into a cube. However, the infants first put the object into their mouths. According to Piaget and Garcia (1991, p. 5), they have constructed the content-container action scheme from the "insert into the mouth" scheme, and these schemes have, as a result, shared meaning. The infants then extend the content-container scheme to new schemes or subschemes, such as to insert and take out, to fill and to empty, and so on.
2. The meaning of an object includes what can be done with the object as well as descriptions of it (Piaget & Garcia, 1991, p. 119). Therefore, meaning is an assimilation to an action scheme (whether overt or mental). For example, the meanings of objects for an infant include pushing, opening, pulling, closing, and so on.
3. Logic begins at the moment a child is able to anticipate a relation between actions, referred to as *meaning implications* or *implications between actions* (Piaget & Garcia, 1991, p. 155). When the infant's action, such as inserting, is followed by the reverse action, emptying, the infant has begun to construct an implication between actions. In this example, the implication is that "action implies the possibility of the reverse action" (Piaget & Garcia, 1991, p. 6).

With the appearance of language, children can express action implications as statements and begin to construct logical links that represent "and" and "or."

In one problem, two tunnels *(A1* and *A2)* each branch into two *B* tunnels, which in turn each branch into two *C* tunnels. The task is to open as few windows as possible on the tunnels to determine the path taken by the car, which is indicated by a ribbon. (The problem consists of 12 branched tunnels, but is solved by opening three windows in the correct sequences). One 6-year-old first opened a window on an *A* tunnel, correctly inferring that the ribbon must be in either *A1* or *A2* and that the absence of the ribbon implies the car's path was through the other tunnel.

Although children can form logical connections that reflect "and" and "or" as well as negations of the combinations, their constructions do not yet represent operational thinking. Their constructions are context-bound fragments that later will become operational structures. Unlike the extensive research on concrete operations by Piaget and his colleagues, only a few experiments have been conducted on meaning implications (see Piaget & Garcia, 1991). Thus, this aspect of the theory remains incomplete. However, one analysis of this work by Ricco (1990) maintained that it provides a foundation for explaining necessity in operational settings.

Summary.   Three essential characteristics differentiate operational (logical) thinking from other kinds of actions. First, a transformation is exactly compensated by a change in another characteristic. Second, the essential nature of the object(s) or data remains invariant. Recognition of the unchanging feature of the situation and being able to explain why it does not change is referred to as conservation. Third, the transformation or change can be restored to the original by an inverse operation. When a child understands that a transformation simultaneously and necessarily implies its inverse, the child has developed the concept of reversibility. The child has constructed an internal operational structure and can analyze the situation accurately without becoming confused.

Essential to operational thinking is the child's construction of the concept of necessity. Young children cannot differentiate between reality, possibility, and necessity. At the onset of concrete operations, the child forms limited concrete co-possibilities but is only able to limit some of them in a systematic way. Eventually, the child is able to conceive of unlimited possibilities and to systematically exclude them.

Piaget's last work sketched the roots of operational thinking, which are found in the early actions of the infant and then the child. The basic principles are that knowledge always involves inference, the meaning of an object includes actions that can be carried out with it, and logic begins when a child is able to anticipate a relation between actions. Children's early logical connections, however, are context-bound fragments that later will become operational thinking.

The Fundamental Processes

Like biological systems, intelligence interacts with the environment, adapts to it, develops new structures as needed, and maintains a steady state while change and growth are occurring. Piaget, therefore, used terms derived from biological concepts to describe the essential nature of the interactions between intelligence and the environment. They are the processes referred to as *assimilation, accommodation*, and *equilibration*.

Assimilation and Accommodation.   The integration of external elements into the organism's structures is referred to as **assimilation**. Examples include the digestion of food and the incorporation of chlorophyll in a plant's growth (Piaget, 1970b, p. 307). In intellectual life, assimilation is "the incorporation of an external element, for example, an object or event, into a sensorimotor or conceptual scheme of the subject" (Piaget, 1985, p. 5). An infant grasping a toy, a child weighing an object in his hand, and a scientist reviewing experiments in light of a particular theory are examples.

Assimilation is not the process of passively registering a copy of reality, nor is it an association between some environmental stimulus and a response (S→R). Instead, it is the filtering of the stimulus through an action structure so that the structures are themselves enriched (i.e., S ⇄ R) (Piaget & Inhelder, 1969, p. 6).

An important requirement for assimilation is an internal structure that can make use of the information. Young children, for example, base many of their decisions about the environment on perceptual cues alone. Often they do not integrate new information because they lack an appropriate assimilatory structure. For example, when asked to draw a picture of a half-full bottle that is tipped to one side, young children typically draw the water line as always parallel to the bottom of the bottle (Figure 10.2).

When confronted with the physical situation, young children fail to see the discrepancy between their drawings and reality (Piaget, 1977, p. 4). They have not developed a coordinate spatial system that enables them to place the water in a frame of reference outside the bottle.

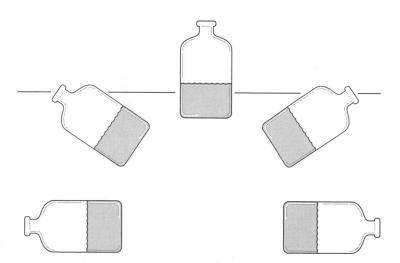

FIGURE 10.2
Young child's conception of the water line in containers placed at different angles

Accommodation is manifested in Piaget's theory in two ways. One is the adjustment of internal structures to the particular characteristics of specific situations. For example, biological structures accommodate to the type and quantity of food at the same time that the food is being assimilated.

Similarly, in cognitive functioning, internal structures adjust to the particular characteristics of new objects and events. The child assimilates the familiar characteristics of a green felt triangle (closed, three-sided) while accommodating to its particular features (in this case, color and material).

Assimilation and accommodation function together in encounters with the environment at all levels of cognitive functioning. When the infant has discovered that he or she can grasp everything he or she sees, everything becomes an object to grasp (i.e., assimilation) (Piaget, in Bringuier, 1980, p. 43). For a large object, however, both hands may be needed, and for a small object, the fingers may need to be tightened (accommodation). Similarly, the theories of the scientist and the scholar are assimilatory schemes that are then adapted to diverse situations (Piaget, in Bringuier, 1980, p. 43).

In cognitive development, accommodation also refers to the modification of the individual's internal cognitive structures. When the learner realizes that his or her ways of thinking are contradicted by events in the environment, the prior ways of thinking are reorganized. This reorganization, which results in a higher level of thinking, is also a form of accommodation.

Equilibration.   The processes involved in maintaining a steady state while undergoing continuous change is referred to as **equilibration**. However, equilibration is not a balance of forces (which would be an immobile state). Instead, it is the complex and dynamic processes that continuously regulate behavior (Piaget, in Bringuier, 1980, p. 41).

The three general forms of equilibrium identified by Piaget (1985) are (1) between assimilation and accommodation, (2) between schemes or subsystems, and (3) between the whole and its parts. Equilibrium between assimilation and accommodation is essential for the child's comparisons about the properties of objects. Equilibration balances assimilation and accommodation almost equally in most situations. However, the brief dominance of one or the other is sometimes necessary. Examples include symbolic play (the dominance of assimilation) and imitation (the dominance of accommodation). Equilibration, however, regulates these two types of childhood activities so that each occurs when appropriate (Piaget & Inhelder, 1969, p. 58).

Equilibration and the Construction of Operational Structures.   One of the sources of progress in the construction of both the action schemes of the infant and later logical operations is found in disequilibria (contradictions). Such events can force the individual to go beyond his or her current state and strike out in new directions (Piaget, 1985, p. 10). However, disequilibria do not always lead to progress. The various reactions to disequilibria described by Piaget (1985) are alpha, beta, and gamma reactions. Another important aspect of equilibration is the processes by which thinking is reorganized on a higher level. These processes are referred to as reflective abstraction.

Alpha, Beta, and Gamma Reactions.   The two types of alpha reactions are (1) ignoring or removing the disturbance, and (2) incorporating the conflict into one's beliefs without changing them. Examples of ignoring conflict involve failing to recognize (1) the true water line in a tilted bottle and (2) the changes in width when a ball of clay is lengthened into a cylinder (Level I thinking in the example discussed earlier in this chapter). An example of fitting a disturbance into core beliefs is the child who believes the Earth is flat and, when told the Earth is round, concludes that it is shaped like a disc (Vosniadou & Brewer, 1992).

In contrast, beta reactions involve a modification of thinking in order to accommodate the disturbance. For example, the child incorporates the thinning of the ball as it becomes longer into his or her thinking (Level III thinking). However, the child has not constructed a new cognitive structure that permits him or her to predict all the transformations in advance. Such a reorganization of thinking is a gamma reaction (Level IV thinking). That is, the child can predict *in advance* that rolling out balls of clay into sausage shapes involves changes in both length and thickness and that the changes are compensatory. That is, the thinning of the ball as it is lengthened becomes logically necessary (Piaget, 1985, p. 100).

Reflective Abstraction.   The equilibration process that accounts for the transition between relatively impoverished to richer cognitive structures is **reflective abstraction** (Piaget, 1986b, p. 142). This process consists of (1) projecting (reflecting) something borrowed from a lower level to a higher level and (2) cognitively reconstructing ("reflexion") what is transferred (Piaget, 1985, p. 29). An example is raising the step-by-step set of sensorimotor actions used to rotate an object, such as a cube, to the representational level (Piaget, 1980, p. 98). This process, although developed slowly over time, makes possible the visualization of the reverse side of the cube when only one aspect can be seen. Reflective abstraction is important because it is essential for the construction of concrete operations.

The subject matter in reflective abstraction is the individual's thought process. (In contrast, **empirical abstraction** refers to focusing on the observable characteristics of objects.) At the level of formal operations, thought processes are independent of any reference to physical manipulation (unlike concrete operations). This pure form of developing rich cognitive structures is referred to as reflected abstraction (Piaget, 1980).

Summary

The components of cognitive development consist of (1) the psychological structure of logical thinking and (2) the fundamental processes involved in interactions with the environment. Logical thinking in a particular domain has been achieved when the learner can simultaneously coordinate an operation and its inverse, can predict in advance the types of changes that will occur, and can support his/her decision on the basis of necessity.

The fundamental processes in the development of logical thinking are assimilation, accommodation, and equilibration. Assimilation is the integration of external elements into the learner's internal structures. Accommodation, in contrast, includes both adjustments in the learner's internal structures and qualitative transformations in thinking. Equilibration is the set of processes that maintains cognitive organization during the learner's changes in thinking. A major role for equilibration is that of maintaining intellectual functioning when disequilibria or cognitive conflicts occur. The alpha reaction involves either disregarding the disturbance or distorting the new information to maintain one's core beliefs. The beta reaction involves a modification of thinking in order to accommodate the disturbance. In contrast, a gamma reaction is the anticipation in advance of possible disturbances and the treatment of them as potential transformations. A gamma reaction indicates that the individual has constructed a new cognitive structure.

The processes responsible for the reorganization of thinking are referred to as reflective abstraction. The key characteristic is that the subject matter is the individual's thought processes. At the level of formal operations, the reorganization is referred to as reflected abstraction.

The Levels of Complex Reasoning

The early research conducted by Piaget (1967, 1970a) established the framework for his analyses of thinking processes. The framework consists of four broad periods or stages of cognitive development: sensorimotor, preoperational, concrete operational, and formal operational stages (see Table 10.2).

TABLE 10.2
Summary of the Qualitative Changes in Reasoning Processes

Stage	Reasoning Processes
Sensorimotor period (birth–1 year)	Presymbolic and preverbal intelligence involves the development of action schemes. Inference begins when the infant develops relations among actions. An example is constructing the container-content scheme from the "insert-in-the-mouth" scheme.
Preoperational period (2–3 to 7–8 years)	Partially logical thought begins; e.g., water poured into another container is the same water: a = a. However, the child reasons from one particular to another and decisions are made on the basis of perceptual cues. Young child does not differentiate between reality, possibility, and necessity in problem-solving situations.
Concrete operational period (7–8 to 12–14)	Logical ways of thinking linked to concrete objects are developed. Child comes to understand that a given operation simultaneously and necessarily implies its inverse. Child begins to develop co-possibilities in problem-solving situations and ways to systematically exclude them.
Formal operational period (older than 14)	The capability of dealing logically with multifactor situations begins. Individuals can deduce multiple possibilities and systematically exclude them. Reasoning proceeds from the hypothetical situation to the concrete.

Each one "extends the preceding period, reconstructs it on a new level, and later surpasses it to an even greater degree" (Piaget & Inhelder, 1969, p. 152). Contrary to early beliefs about Piaget's theory, the stages were not the goal of his work. Instead, they represent the kinds of logical issues the child can deal with at a particular phase in his or her development.

In addition to qualitative changes in reasoning processes, the stages also reflect changes in the child's awareness of his or her own thought processes. Piaget identified three levels (Pons & Harris, 2001). The first, practical consciousness, emerges in the sensorimotor period. It refers to the young child's awareness of his or her activities (p. 221).

The second level, conceptual consciousness, is associated with concrete operational thinking. Specifically, the construction of new concrete operations, as in the example in Figure 10.1, is accompanied by a conscious process of conceptualization (p. 221). The third level is reflective consciousness and is essential for the development of formal operational thinking. Here, the individual reflects on his or her own functioning. That is, the focus of reflective consciousness is the individual's thought processes rather than the content of the problem. Of importance in Piaget's conception of consciousness is that it is not an entity that is to be filled by a particular content (Ferreiro, 2001, p. 215). Like his other major concepts, it is a process—the developing awareness of one's thinking (*prise de conscience*).

Of the four major stages of reasoning, concrete and formal operational thinking represent complex reasoning. Both are logical forms of thinking, but they differ in qualitative ways.

Concrete Operations

Concrete operations are linked to the direct manipulation of objects. The common characteristic of concrete operational structures is that they consist of an equilibrium between "affirmations" (direct operations) and their inverses (opposites) (Piaget, 1985). The child has invented a "closed" concrete operational structure when he or she has constructed both the set of affirmations and their corresponding inverses.

Concrete operational structures are constructs in the domains of (1) numerical operations; (2) conservation (number, length, weight, area, mass, and volume); (3) classification and categorization (the addition and multiplication of classes); and (4) ordering relations (seriation). However, each is acquired independently of the others. For example, conservation associated with discontinuous quantities is acquired prior to the conservation of continuous quantities (e.g., weight and mass).

Unlike concrete operational thinkers, young children (preoperational thinkers) combine a sense of quantity, weight, and volume into a fuzzy concept of size (Smith, 1991, p. 85). They also use circular reasoning and the inconsistent application of criteria to justify their answers.

An earlier section in this chapter (Psychological Structure) describes an example of concrete operational thinking in relation to number and one on conservation of matter. Two other types of concrete operational thinking involve class inclusion operations and seriation. Class inclusion operations involve the separation of a collection into subclasses, such as subdividing a group of flowers into roses and tulips. The concrete operational child also can "double classify;" that is, she can divide the flowers into red roses, red tulips, white roses, and white tulips. Preoperational children, in contrast, can only focus on one feature at a time. When asked to identify the red roses, they will choose either all the red roses or all the red flowers.

Seriation is characterized by transitivity or the "transfer" of relations. If A = B and B = C, then A = C and C = B = A (the inverse). Seriation also includes asymmetric relations ("greater than" [>] and "less than" [<]), such as A > B > C. Concrete operational children understand that some element B is both longer and shorter than some other elements. Unlike preoperational thinkers who proceed haphazardly to form a series, concrete operational children systematically search for the longest (or shortest) stick, then the next one in length, and so on. They also can demonstrate that the reverse of A > B > C is C < B < A.

Of interest are the differences between the original Piagetian transitivity task and the task used by subsequent researchers who maintained that younger children also were proficient at seriation. In the original task, the child sees and compares two sticks at a time (A and B; B and C). The third stick is out of sight (Lorenço & Machado, 1996, p. 145). With this procedure, the inference that A is smaller than C is not based on any perceptual cues.

In contrast, other researchers began with all three sticks on the table in the order of increasing size. The sticks were separated so that length differences could not be perceived directly. The experimenter first placed A and B in front of the child, returned them to their original places, and then used the same procedure with A and C. The child then was asked to compare A with C. The problem with this procedure is that the child need only know the direction (right or left) in which the sticks increased in size (Lorenço and Machado, 1996). Chapman and McBride (1992) implemented both the standard and altered versions of the task with 6- to 9-year-old children. Performance was better on the altered version, but the children's justifications were that the bigger stick was on the right.

Formal Operations

The concrete operational thinker can only reason from empirical data in developing an explanation (Inhelder & Piaget, 1958, p. 251) and is limited to pairing characteristics two by two. This approach, however, does not take into account the possibilities that the variables are mixed. That is, one effect may be caused by several factors, or a single causal factor may be accompanied or masked by several varying factors that are not causes (Inhelder & Piaget, 1958, p. 282). Efforts in such a situation to classify or order events on the basis of covariation are inadequate.

Formal operational thinkers, in contrast, can solve multifactor situations (as opposed to only two-factor situations) because they have developed new ways of thinking. The formal operational thinker is able to conceptualize all combinations of the factors in a particular situation. For example, given four characteristics, such as red and white and tulips and roses, the formal operational thinker can generate the 16 possible combinations of these characteristics. Among the possibilities are white tulips and red roses, red roses and red tulips, and so on. The concrete operational thinker, however, can only generate the four subclasses (red roses, red tulips, white roses, white tulips). This example illustrates two of the essential characteristics for formal operational thinking. One is that reality is subordinated to possibility in that the individual can generate all the likely possibilities. Second, each hypothesis is a statement that combines several possible cases (observations) (Müller, 1999, p. 27). Therefore, they are interpropositional operations that each correspond to a logical operation.

The third characteristic of formal operations is that the hypotheses are related to each other in a combinatorial system. Specifically, Piaget (1970a) referred to the capability of generating the 16 possibilities as combinatorial operations. According to Piaget (Inhelder & Piaget, 1958, p. 313), this capability is essential for formal operational thinking because it makes possible the analysis of relationships in multifactor situations.

However, the individual, when faced with a complex situation, does not actually construct the table of combinations. Instead, he or she begins by conceptualizing some of the possible combinations and systematically testing hypotheses in order to isolate the correct explanation. The important characteristic that distinguishes formal operations from concrete operations is that the individual begins with a theoretical synthesis that implies certain relationships and then proceeds to test the hypothesized relationships (Karmiloff-Smith & Inhelder, 1975).

An example is the colorless liquids experiment (Inhelder & Piaget, 1958). The experimenter adds a substance g to each of two beakers of colorless liquid(s). In one case, the new substance produces no change; however, in the other, the color yellow appears. The task for the student is to identify which of four colorless liquids, singly or in combination, produces the yellow color (Figure 10.3).

Formal operational thinkers will figure out the possible combinations, often jotting them down, and then proceed to test them. Individuals who are at the concrete level of thinking will proceed to test combinations, two by two. However, this approach results in omissions and errors.

Piaget (1972a, p. 10) noted that his research into formal operations had utilized situations likely to be understood by children in an academic setting. However, the applicability of such situations to professional environments is questionable. In other words, carpenters, locksmiths, or mechanics may well reason hypothetically in their specialty. Their unfamiliarity with structured school subjects, however, would hinder them from reasoning in a formal way with the experimental situations used in the research.

Similarly, research conducted by DeLisi and Stewart (1980) indicated that college students reason hypothetically in the area of their college majors. However, formal operational reasoning was not observed in other areas. Some reviews of the research on formal operations concluded that the empirical evidence supporting the construct is equivocal. However, Bond (1998) concluded that studies attentive

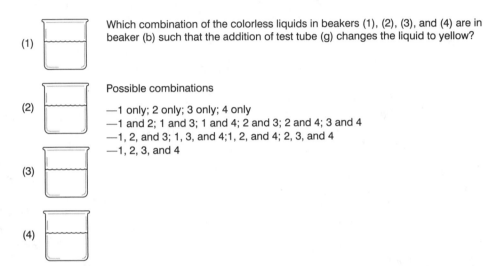

Beaker (a) + (g) = no color
(colorless)

Beaker (b) + (g) = yellow color
(colorless)

Which combination of the colorless liquids in beakers (1), (2), (3), and (4) are in beaker (b) such that the addition of test tube (g) changes the liquid to yellow?

Possible combinations

—1 only; 2 only; 3 only; 4 only
—1 and 2; 1 and 3; 1 and 4; 2 and 3; 2 and 4; 3 and 4
—1, 2, and 3; 1, 3, and 4;1, 2, and 4; 2, 3, and 4
—1, 2, 3, and 4

FIGURE 10.3
The colorless liquids experiment

to the definition of formal operations support inferences about formal operational thinking.

Of importance is to not confuse Piaget's use of propositional logic with the standard interpretation. In the standard use, p and q are combined in various ways, using logical connectives. The task is to determine whether a particular statement such as "if p then q" is true or false, given initial information about p and q. Piaget's application of prepositional logic, however, does not address truth or falsity in terms of the congruence of statements to given information. Instead, Piaget applied propositional logic as a description of the subject's experimental behavior (Müller, 1999, p. 28). That is, the subject is testing hypotheses based on causal models (p. 28).

Other Interpretations
Research summarized by Berk (1989) indicated that infants attain some accomplishments in the sensorimotor stage, such as object permanence, earlier than Piaget indicated. However, some researchers have used the reaction of surprise on the disappearance of an object (rather than a search for the hidden object) as evidence of the concept of object permanence (Lorenço & Machado, 1996). The

difficulty is that infants often display surprise at a change in a perceptual array of objects. Thus, the reaction is not a reliable indicator of object permanence. Further, as Piaget indicated, mental representations of hidden objects are rarely error-free until 18 months of age.

One line of theoretical development undertaken by Case (1985, 1992, 1993) has retained the broad perspective of Piaget's theory and introduced new concepts. This perspective, referred to as neo-Piagetian, has, according to Case (1992, p. 61), altered the Piagetian framework substantially. Further, the work is not a simple extension of Piaget's concepts nor a revision that he would have sanctioned (p. 62).

The broad concepts retained from classic Piagetian theory are that children create their own cognitive structures, assimilate experience to existing cognitive structures, pass through a universal sequence of structures, and incorporate earlier structures in later ones. Elements developed by Case (1985, 1992, 1993) are that (1) the general factor in children's development is their attentional or information-processing capacity (Case, 1992, p. 72), and (2) analysis of task performance should include children's goals and strategies and the information load required for the strategies.

Analyses of children's actions in different tasks led Case (1993) to conclude that children younger than 5 years approach computational tasks, such as telling time and making change with money, in a global fashion. In contrast, 5- to 7-year-olds have an integrated structure for such problems that includes counting and comparison. This integrated structure becomes automatic as children apply it in various situations and as functional working memory increases (p. 225).

Summary

The theory developed by Piaget traces the development of natural logic and reasoning from birth to adulthood. The transition from one form of reasoning to another depends on the physical environment, maturation, social influences, and the processes referred to as equilibration.

Two major concepts in Piaget's theory are the psychological nature of logical thinking and the fundamental processes in the functioning of intelligence. Three essential characteristics differentiate operational or logical thinking from other kinds of actions. They are that (1) each transformation in the data or object is exactly compensated by a change in another characteristic, (2) the essential nature of the data or object remains invariant, and (3) the transformation can be restored to the original by an inverse operation. A key concept in the construction of operational structures is that of necessity. That is, the individual is able to conceive of unlimited possibilities coupled with ways to exclude them and arrive at the necessary solution.

The three fundamental processes in intellectual functioning are assimilation, accommodation, and equilibration. Assimilation and accommodation are the basic processes in interactions with the environment, whereas equilibration maintains a steady state during growth and change. The three types of reactions to disturbances or cognitive conflicts are alpha, beta, and gamma reactions. When a gamma reaction occurs, the individual has reorganized his or her thinking into a more logical structure, a process referred to as reflective abstraction.

The qualitative differences in children's thinking form four broad periods or stages of development. They are the sensorimotor, preoperational, concrete operational, and formal operational periods. Presymbolic intelligence in the form of action schemes develops in the sensorimotor period while partially logical or transductive thought develops in the preoperational period.

At the level of concrete operations, the child develops logical structures in four domains. In addition to numerical operations, they are the conservation of number, length, weight, area, mass, and volume; classification and categorization; and ordering relations, or seriation. Concrete operations are linked to the manipulation of physical objects. Formal operational thinkers, in contrast, can solve multifactor situations because they are able to begin with a theoretical synthesis, and they then can test the hypothesized relationships in systematic ways.

PRINCIPLES OF INSTRUCTION

The derivation of instructional principles from Piaget's developmental theory requires careful and thoughtful analysis and interpretation. The primary reason is that the theory describes the qualitative changes in thought processes that lead to logical thinking. It does not address the learning of specific facts, such as state capitals. Early efforts to fit Piaget's developmental theory to curricula organized around specific objectives and goal-based evaluation resulted in misinterpretations. In recent years, some curricula based on the principle that children construct cognitive structures have been developed.

Basic Assumptions

One's perspective of the nature of the child's thinking has important implications for education (Piaget, 1970c). If childhood is believed to be simply a period that the child goes through to become an adult, then the relationship between the educational system and the child will be unilateral. The child will receive already finished products of adult knowledge and morality. Educational experiences will be organized and directed by the teacher and transmitted to the child. In such an educational climate, even individual tasks such as writing an essay will be directed toward obedience rather than autonomy (Piaget, 1970c).

However, if childhood is accepted as a necessary and important phase in the development of logical thinking, education will be viewed differently. The child's thought patterns undergo qualitative changes essential to the development of logical hypothetical thought. Therefore, the relationship between the educational system and the child must be a reciprocal one (Piaget, 1970c).

Piaget recommended the use of active methods that require the student to rediscover or reconstruct the truths to be learned. However, a highly industrialized and technological society presents problems in that it is not an ideal setting for exploration and spontaneous activity (Furth, 1980). How can a child apply his spontaneous curiosity to a television set, when only an expert knows how it works? Or to vegetables in a can when he has never seen them growing? The problem is that these children enter school with an intelligence that has not been well nourished. Thus, a "high-tech" society faces particular problems in developing individuals who are capable of constructing new knowledge.

The Components of Instruction

Instead of the verbal transmission of knowledge, education should be characterized by the use of methods that support the spontaneous research of the child or adolescent (Piaget, 1973). Such an approach is particularly important in the teaching of mathematics and science. Mathematics, for example, is composed of actions and operations, and therefore understanding mathematics should begin with action (Piaget, 1973). Such instruction should begin in nursery school with concrete exercises related to lengths, surfaces, numbers, and so on, progressing to physical and mechanical experiments in secondary school (Piaget, 1973, p. 104).

The basic need for education, according to Piaget (1973), is "to introduce both liberal arts and science students to experimental procedures and the free activity such training implies" (Piaget, 1973, p. 35). The solution he recommended is to provide mixed curricula—science classes that focus on self-directed experimentation and courses that use experimentation where possible. Some psychology classes, for example, could be devoted to individual experimentation in psycholinguistics.

Of course, subjects such as history or Latin cannot be "reinvented" by the students. That is, individuals cannot verify explanatory hypotheses with regard to Greek civilization (Piaget, 1973, p. 47). However, when research reveals some understanding of the ways in which students acquire spontaneous operational thought in historical understanding, methods may change.

A requirement that must accompany experimentation is that of collaboration and interchange among the students themselves (Piaget, 1973, p. 108). The traditional school often excludes this interchange, recognizing only the social exchange between teacher and student. However, both independent and collaborative student activity should be included. Using one's intelligence, according to Piaget (1973), assumes the exercise of a critical spirit. Such objectivity, however, can be developed only in the group situation in which give-and-take with one's peers occurs. Therefore, spontaneous activity, with small groups of students brought together by means of their mutual interest in a particular activity, should be a major feature of classroom learning. The classroom should be "a center of real (and experimental) activities carried out in common, so that logical intelligence may be elaborated through action and social exchange" (Piaget, 1973, p. 47).

Facilitating the Young Child's Construction of Knowledge

Organizing education around the child's spontaneous research implies an educational goal to develop the child's intelligence as an organized whole (Kamii, 1975). Important issues in preschool curricula are the problems with direct teaching, the role of make-believe play, the use of activities, sensorimotor activities, and the teacher's role.

Problems with "Direct Teaching."   Children do not learn by internalizing knowledge in ready-made form (Kamii & Kamii, 1990). Therefore, abstract ideas or principles should not be taught through verbal transmission (Kamii & DeVries, 1978). First, a logical rule contradicts the child's spontaneous beliefs and therefore confuses the child. The preoperational child does not notice the contradictions in his or her own explanations. One child, for example, stated that a wooden blade floats because it is thick, and copper wire sinks because it is long (Kamii & DeVries, 1978, p. 32). The fact that the wooden blade also was long was irrelevant to the child. Therefore, because the child is unaware of the contradictions, a logical rule to fit all contingencies at this point is only a verbalization that introduces confusion.

In addition, direct teaching of ideas stifles children's initiative in the construction of knowledge (Kamii & DeVries, 1978). Children may lose confidence in their ability to figure things out and focus instead on picking up cues from the teacher that indicate the desired right answer.

Make-Believe Play.   A key characteristic of preschool children, according to Piaget (1951), is that they manage to live in a world where the adult distinction between fiction and reality does not apply. This feat is accomplished in part through make-believe or symbolic play.

The importance of make-believe play is that it provides the child a temporary escape from the strange outside world. The child is free to accept from the environment what appeals to her or him and to ignore what is beyond immediate interest or understanding. For example, the child can "bake a cake" without having to be careful about breaking or burning. Also, the anger of an adult about some misbehavior can be reenacted using rules that the child understands. In other words, make-believe play provides a world of actions, symbols, and images where the child can feel free because it is under his or her own intellectual control (Furth, 1980, p. 67).

One of the current concerns about the use of VCRs and television as babysitters is the lost opportunities for creative play. The child is passive, instead of creating roles, actions, and thoughts through symbolic play. An important element in developing new ideas and ways of thinking is lost through reliance on these passive activities (Berk, 1989). Thus, an important activity to include in the preschool curriculum is some time in which children are free to engage in make-believe actions.

Use of Activities.   Many activities customarily included in preschool curricula can provide opportunities for cognitive development (Kamii & DeVries, 1978). Block painting, finger painting, musical games, cooking, dramatic play, and others are easily adaptable to a Piagetian curriculum. The first step is to evaluate the activities during preplanning for their potential to engage the children in the processes of empirical and logico-mathematical abstraction. That is, the activities should include problems that cannot be solved on the basis of perceptual cues only. Any activity, of course, can be inappropriate if used in the wrong way. Cuisinaire rods, for example, are inappropriate if the teacher demonstrates their uses and the outcomes that may be achieved (Piaget, 1973).

Some early curriculum developments advocated the diagnosis of the child's level of cognitive functioning and the provision of particular activities appropriate for the different levels in the classroom. In any one class of 30 children, however, various levels of development and breadth of understanding will be represented. Tailoring narrow exercises for individual children, though, is both impractical and unnecessary (Duckworth, 1979). First, the time required to test the children's level of cognitive development for different subsystems (number, space, length, etc.) is prohibitive. Second, logistical problems are generated by efforts to continuously provide a variety of activities and experiences for several different levels.

Third, activities or exercises that isolate and present one form of reasoning should not be used. They lack the element essential for progress, which is the dynamics of the conflict among modes of thinking (Inhelder et al., 1974, p. 265). Therefore, classroom activities should maximize the child's opportunities to construct and coordinate many relationships that he or she is capable of exercising (DeVries, 1978, p. 85).

Planning activities for classroom use should include consideration of two important factors: (1) the nature of the sensorimotor activities and (2) the use of teacher questions (i.e., the teacher's role).

Sensorimotor Activities.   For preschool children, Kamii and DeVries (1978, p. 49) identified four criteria for physical activities. Objects should be included that can be acted on directly by the child and for which different actions by the child will produce different effects. In addition, the effects of the child's actions on the object should be both immediate and observable.

Activities that meet these criteria can provide opportunities for the enrichment and clarification of the child's awareness of object characteristics, actions, and reactions (i.e., assimilation). Many such activities can also facilitate the process of accommodation that occurs when a cognitive structure adjusts to particular object characteristics and to the development of inferences about one's actions (meanings) (Piaget & Garcia, 1991).

Table 10.3 summarizes an activity for 4- and 5-year-olds that is appropriate for different developmental levels. The nature of the activity is such that it provides numerous opportunities for children to determine the physical properties of objects in the water. The interaction between blowing and speed of the objects contributes to the development of implications between actions.

The Teacher's Role.   Piaget (1973) indicated that no more difficult task exists for the teacher than that of becoming attuned to the spontaneous mental activity of the child or adolescent. Yet intellectual development depends on that constructive activity with all its errors and all the extra time that it seems to consume (p. 107).

TABLE 10.3
Summary of Classroom Activity for Young Children

Activity	Blowing objects with a straw across the water surface in a water table
Objects	A drinking straw for each child; assorted objects, including ping-pong balls, cotton balls, crayons, Ivory soap, paper cups, styrofoam bits, a round Tinker toy, and others
Follow-up activity	Suggest a race with some objects or a hockey game with the ping-pong balls
Potential logico-mathematical knowledge	"Lighter than," "heavier than," "faster than"; relationship between angle of straw, blowing effort, and speed
Sample follow-up questions	"What happened when you used two straws?" and "What would you like to try next time?" (Kamii & DeVries, 1978, p. 60)

Note: Summarized from *Physical Knowledge in Preschool Education* by C. Kamii and R. DeVries, 1978, Upper Saddle River, NJ: Prentice Hall.

The use of active methods does not mean that students are left to their own devices. Instead, the teacher's role is first to create and organize classroom experiences. Second, the teacher's responsibility is to provide examples that cause students to rethink hastily developed ideas.

Furthermore, children's "errors" that result from their experimentation must not be eliminated by coercion. The information that children use in reaching their conclusions may be inadequate for a correct solution of a specific problem. However, the choice is representative of a certain developmental stage that cannot be bypassed (Inhelder et al., 1974, p. 25). Therefore, games and activities should be reevaluated after implementation since children often take unexpected directions in pursuing their own questions.

In the implementation of activities, teacher questions can play an important role, but they must be carefully planned. Any questions that are used should be simply stated and should be real questions designed to provoke thinking; they should not be rhetorical statements in question form (Copple, Sigel, & Saunders, 1979, p. 213). Children's ideas, however, may be elicited through indirect questions, such as "Can you tell me about this?" or "What else feels (tastes, looks) like this?" (Copple et al., 1979, pp. 231–232). Examples of questions that keep children engaged are, "Can you find any more like that?" and "What did you do that was different from what she did?" (Duckworth, 1990, p. 46).

Prediction questions such as "What would happen if . . ." also may be used (Kamii & DeVries, 1978). These types of questions facilitate assimilation and accommodation and encourage children to go beyond physical reality in the construction of new knowledge. Questions such as "How did you know that the pudding was hot?" focus the child's attention on his or her strategy for reaching a conclusion.

However, with regard to direct actions on physical objects, young children often are unaware of which of their own actions produced a particular effect. For example, 4-year-olds can twirl an object on a string and time its release to land it in a box several feet away. Until the age of 9 or 10, their descriptions of the ways to accomplish this goal differ from their actions (Piaget, 1976b). Thus explanations of such effects by 4- and 5-year-olds, and their accompanying understanding of such causes, will be inaccurate.

In summary, rich opportunities to act on objects and to observe the resulting reactions develop the foundation for logical thinking. The major requirements for the curriculum, therefore, are opportunities for children to interact with the physical world in a variety of ways, to make their own mistakes, and to develop answers to their questions in interaction with their peers.

Facilitating Operational Thinking

True logical thinking, in the Piagetian view, is constructed by the learner in self-directed or peer-collaborative research on topics of interest to the students (Duckworth, 1978, 1990). As Piaget (1973) indicated, self-directed experimentation is particularly important in science and mathematics.

Applications in Science.   In elementary school science, the material world should be the starting point (Duckworth, 1990). The material world is both accessible and contains complexities children have never dreamed of (p. 25). For example, in one second-grade classroom, some children were interested in crystals. The children made a "crystal" museum of examples they collected, grew crystals, examined them under a microscope, and read books about them. One snowflake picture led to their building a 12-sided polygon with their pattern blocks. Some children were fascinated to discover that, within such a shape, patterns were found 1, 2, 3, 6, or 12 times. Their explorations to determine the basis for these numbers led to the factors of 12. Other children appreciated most the beauty of the patterns (Duckworth, 1990, p. 22).

Research in science education indicates that both children and older students hold a variety of intuitive beliefs about scientific concepts (Champagne, Gunstone, & Klopfer, 1985; Gilbert, Watts, & Osborne, 1985). Furthermore, these views are not merely isolated ideas. Instead, they are incorporated in conceptual structures that provide a coherent understanding of the world from the child's perspective. Judgments often are based on appearances, such as, "It has evaporated, but it has not gone into the steam form, because you can't see it" (Gilbert, Osborne, & Fresham, 1982). In one study, students as old as 19 held contradictory beliefs without being aware of their contradictions (Osborne & Gilbert, 1980). One student, for example, when asked if any force was acting on a man standing on the moon, replied, "There is no air up there, so there is no gravity" (p. 379). Later, in the same interview, the student indicated that there was some gravity, but no air.

The first step in altering the curriculum, suggested by Osborne and Gilbert (1980), is to determine the student's current level of thinking. They developed pictures of different events (e.g., a boy riding a bicycle, a man hitting a golf ball, and others) to use in determining students' concepts of force. Using interviews to determine the students' rationales for their answers provides the information for an assessment of students' thinking. Once the intuitive beliefs are identified, experimental activities may be implemented that produce cognitive conflict between the intuitive ideas and scientific thinking. For example, confronting student misconceptions about Newtonian mechanics is the goal of several process simulations in physical science (Flick, 1990; White, 1984). In one set of exercises, students perform several actions on a "spaceship" in a frictionless environment (space). In this way, they confront their misconceptions about force, velocity, and speed.

Constructivism in Mathematics.   As indicated in chapter 4, some developers have incorporated some of Piaget's concepts in curricula that also make use of classroom discourse. One perspective, referred to as radical constructivism, is derived directly from Piagetian principles. That is, essential learning processes are assimilation and accommodation following cognitive conflict and reflective abstraction. Another perspective, referred to as emergent (Cobb, 1995), advocates the Piagetian views that (1) knowledge is actively created by learners, (2) learners create new knowledge by reflecting on their physical and mental actions, (3) substantive learning occurs in periods of conflict and confusion, surprise, and over long periods of time, and (4) opportunities for learning occur during social interaction (Wood, Cobb, & Yaeckel, 1991, p. 591).

In one second-grade classroom, an example of this perspective, pairs of children first solve problems that may be resolved in more than one way. In the subsequent whole-class discussion, children are expected to justify and explain their answers and also to listen to other children's explanations (Wood et al., 1991). Important in this and similar implementations is the reconstruction of classroom social norms so that the children feel "psychologically safe" to explain their solutions to each other and the class (Wood et al., 1991, p. 598). Also important is that the teacher must be able to accept the students' incorrect answers unconditionally. In this second-grade classroom, the teacher learned, however, that letting children struggle to resolve conflicts in their thinking provided occasions for the children to learn. That is, the children's responses were not aimless, and her role was to create circumstances in which conflicts and confusions could be resolved through students' procedures (p. 699).

Role of the Computer.   Used appropriately, the computer can provide opportunities for children to exercise logic in action, a key concept in Piagetian theory. In the nonverbal computer program Symbol-Picture-Logic (SPL), for example, children discover the rules represented by symbols, complete symbol-logic statements, and, thereby, develop insights into logical necessity (Furth, 1986a, 1986b). The computer also can assist students to manipulate and construct objects that are impossible or impractical to use in the classroom. One computer environment is the Turtle Geometry and LOGO created by Seymour Papert (1980). The "turtle" in LOGO is a computer-controlled triangular symbol (Δ). Simple commands direct the turtle to move forward and backward as well as to change direction at any angle from 1 to 359 degrees. The turtle's movement leaves a trace (line) as though the student is drawing with pen or pencil. Any number of geometric figures may be designed, restricted only by the creativity and imagination of the student.

In creating a geometric figure, the student decides the kind of task that the turtle is to complete and sets about giving the turtle the computer commands (i.e., developing a computer program). When the turtle goes in an unexpected direction after receiving a particular command, the student must readjust his or her thinking and correct the command.

In this way, the student experiments with designing rectangles, triangles, squares, and circles, altering his or her strategy according to the performance of the turtle. Thus, students learn strategies for designing geometric figures without being directly taught (Clements & Gullo, 1984; Gallini & Gredler, 1989).

Such an environment is referred to as a microworld (Pufall, 1988, p. 27). It is an environment that does not prescribe what the child should know. Instead, a microworld is a context within which the child can construct knowledge. The developer of computer software, however, must not confuse *interactive* with *constructive*. This message is important because creating interactive environments is educationally appealing (Pufall, 1988). Interacting with the computer, however, is a necessary but not sufficient condition for the child's construction of knowledge.

Facilitating Formal Operational Thinking

The problems associated with placing students in multivariate problems before they have developed the conceptual structures to address such complex situations is illustrated in a study by Lavoie and Good (1988). Students were presented with a simulation in which some combination of five variables (temperature, waste type, dumping rate, type of treatment, and type of body of water) affected oxygen and waste concentration of the water. Problem-solving ability on prediction problems was related to high or moderate initial knowledge and performance at the Piagetian stage of formal operational thinking. Unsuccessful students tended to have both low initial knowledge and to be at the stage of concrete operational thinking. Kuhn, Black, Keselman, & Kaplan (2000) noted that students often have an incorrect mental model that impedes the multivariable analysis required in science inquiry. They lack the concept of additive effects of variables on the outcome. In Piagetian terms, they lack the combinatorial propositional logic of formal operational thinking.

Obviously, formal operational thinking cannot be acquired through "prepackaged experiments" or by solving end-of-chapter problems for a predetermined answer. Any experiment that is not carried out by the individual with complete freedom is not an exercise; it is simply drill with no educational worth (Piaget, 1973, p. 20).

Changes in thinking have been achieved in science and physics through situations that require the students to confront their inaccurate ideas through exploration (Champagne et al., 1985; Kuhn & Phelps, 1979). An essential characteristic of one intervention was described as "ideational confrontation." It is, of course, the disequilibrium described by Piaget.

In one study, students who showed no evidence of formal reasoning strategies were provided with a rich problem environment with opportunities to explore the causes of different events (Kuhn & Phelps, 1979). After three months of weekly problem-solving sessions, both fifth graders and adolescents showed changes in their reasoning strategies. However, the process was slow and uneven with setbacks along the way. "Conflicts and contradictions are encountered and resolved, not once, but many times over" (Kuhn & Phelps, 1979, p. 54). Similar to another study conducted by Kuhn (1979), the most common difficulty seemed to be not the mastery of new strategies but the inability to relinquish inadequate strategies.

Some students began by conducting experiments in such a way that their hypotheses could not be disproved (Champagne, Klopfer, & Anderson, 1980; Kuhn & Phelps, 1979). Other students, faced with findings that contradicted their hypotheses, simply ignored the conflicting data. Thus, open-ended exploration by itself is not sufficient to develop hypothetical reasoning. Probing questions and challenges to the student's thinking are essential.

Progress also requires that the instructor push students to formulate explanatory hypotheses and to test them repeatedly. Even so, "reconceptualization will be a slow tortuous process. It will come only after many alternative ideas and explanations have been tried and failed" (Champagne et al., 1980, p. 1078).

Summary
The focus of Piaget's theory is the development of logical thinking; therefore, it does not include specific guidelines for instruction. However, general guidelines for instruction to facilitate student thinking may be derived from the theory. First, knowledge, particularly in mathematics and science, should not be taught as though it were a set of truths that can be relayed through abstract language. Knowledge is constructed by the learner through self-directed and peer-collaborative research. The teacher's role is that of organizing and creating situations that present meaningful problems. Collaboration and interchange among the students also should accompany experimentation.

Many activities in the preschool curriculum can provide opportunities for cognitive development. Examples include block painting, finger painting, and musical games. Objects should be provided in the classroom that can be acted on directly by the child, and the child's actions should produce different effects that are immediate and observable. The teacher's role is that of asking thoughtful questions that provoke children's thinking.

At the elementary school level, a variety of materials for measurement and experimentation can provide children with opportunities to use their developing subsystems. Experimentation in science also is important to help children confront their intuitive beliefs about scientific concepts. In addition, used appropriately, computer environments can provide opportunities for students to construct and manipulate objects and thereby confront their intuitive beliefs.

Formal operational thinking also requires self-directed exploration. Students should be encouraged to formulate explanatory hypotheses, to test them, and to address conflicting data. However, reconceptualization will be a slow process.

EDUCATIONAL APPLICATIONS

The concepts developed by Piaget can be implemented in preschool and elementary school classrooms by providing rich activities for children's exploration. In mathematics and science, Piaget's concepts, combined with other concerns, such as developing a community of learners, have been implemented to develop curricula. Students are encouraged to solve problems in ways that make sense to them, to be able to justify and explain their answers, and to participate in class discussions to resolve conflicts and confusion.

Some of the curriculum misapplications resulted from the failure to coordinate a developmental curriculum with the academic curriculum. Kamii (1981) suggests three general objectives compatible with the school curriculum. Briefly summarized, they are (1) the development of children's autonomy through interactive situations; (2) the decentering and coordination of various points of view by children; and (3) the development of alertness, curiosity, initiative, and confidence in learning (Kamii, 1981, p. 24). These objectives may be integrated into the school curriculum without displacing it. Further, policies of the National Council of Teachers of Mathematics (NCTM) (1989) that advocate questioning others' thinking and supporting one's views are consistent with Piaget's theory.

Classroom Issues

Piaget's theory is neither a theory of academic learning nor a teaching theory. Nevertheless, it does address several educational issues.

Learner Characteristics

Jean Piaget's theory addresses the broad issues involved in cognitive development. Individual differences, readiness, and motivation are therefore viewed in terms of their relationship to long-term cognitive development.

Individual Differences.   The theory has been criticized by some educators for omitting specific references to individual differences. Piaget's standard response to such criticisms was that his focus was the identification of the most general and universal in all people (Furth & Youniss, 2000, p. 123). Thus, individual differences are outside the realm of the theory; the goal was to identify and to study the universal laws of cognitive development.

Nevertheless, cultural differences in the rate of attainment of cognitive structures have been observed. Children in some rural settings are slower than urban children in the attainment of concrete operations. Furthermore, formal operations are not attained by all individuals, nor are they acquired in all areas of expertise (e.g., physics, law, and engineering) (Piaget, 1972a).

Readiness.   Readiness has two meanings in the interpretation of Piaget's theory. One is that of the individual's capacity to assimilate new information; a requirement is a cognitive framework that can make use of the new information.

The second way in which readiness is manifested is in relation to the construction of logical cognitive structures, or operations. Specifically, logical constructions do not result until the subject experiences cognitive conflict and seeks to resolve it on a higher plane. Readiness, therefore, is the acknowledgment of conflicting statements coupled with the felt need to resolve two subsystems—for example, number and space.

Piaget has mistakenly been viewed at times as a maturationist because he identified four sequential stages of development. However, only the ordering of the stages is invariant; attainment requires learner experience with the environment, learner activity, and interaction with the social environment.

Motivation.   Two sources of motivation are identified by Piaget (1973). One is a general motivating factor that functions at all levels of development—that of need. As in other theories, needs may be physiological, affective, or intellectual. Since intelligence seeks both to understand and to explain, an intellectual need often appears in the form of a question or a problem (Piaget, 1967, p. 5). In Piaget's view, all action, whether movement, thought, or emotion, is in response to a need. In the theory, need is described as a manifestation of disequilibrium (Piaget, 1967). When the need is satisfied, equilibrium is restored.

Disequilibrium represents the general factor of need at all levels of development. The second source of motivation is the specifics or content of need at a particular age or period of development. These specific needs depend on the system of ideas that a child has developed plus his or her affective inclinations. For example, a young child may engage in behavior to gain the approval of a parent, but a teenager is more likely to seek the approval of peers.

Cognitive Processes and Instruction
Three important classroom issues are developing "how-to-learn skills," providing transfer of learning, and teaching problem solving. In the context of Piaget's theory, these issues take on a different meaning.

Developing "How-to-Learn" Skills.   The individual's ability to organize his or her own behavior efficiently in order to extract meaning from a situation or to initiate steps to solve some predetermined problem are typically defined as how-to-learn skills. In the context of genetic epistemology, however, manipulating and experiencing concrete objects in the environment is the foundation for knowledge construction. Children learn how to learn by generating problems, investigating questions, and examining their answers.

Transfer of Learning.   The facilitation of new learning that results from similarities to prior learning is an important classroom issue. Transfer of learning implies some sequencing of learning tasks in order to take advantage of their common properties.

Cognitive development, however, differs from specific learning. The attainment of particular cognitive structures do not "transfer" to the development of the next stage in the sense of isomorphic elements. The cognitive structures attained in any period of development do, however, prepare the learner to undertake the next stage.

Teaching Problem Solving.   According to Piaget (1973), the skill of problem solving cannot be directly taught. Instead, the rules of experimentation and, therefore, the rules for problem solution must be discovered or reinvented by each student. This experimentation and reinvention is essential to the development of problem-solving skills. In addition, Piaget maintained that the rules or theories that operate in any particular subject area must be reinvented by the individual; they cannot be conveyed verbally.

The Social Context for Learning

Unlike educational approaches that focus on teacher-student interaction, Piaget (1973) emphasized the importance of peer interactions in the context of self-directed experimentation. Only through this type of interaction does the student acquire the capability of viewing issues from other perspectives. Furthermore, in exchanges with others, students examine their own thinking, explore other alternatives, and reorganize their views and conclusions. The teacher, however, must create situations that promote exploration.

Relationships to Other Perspectives

Unlike operant conditioning, the conditions of learning, and the information-processing perspective, Piaget's theory does not address the factual and conceptual information that constitutes subject domains. Instead, his principles address the characteristics involved in thinking and reasoning about events, i.e., natural logic, and the various changes across the lifespan. Like Vygotsky, he was concerned with the individual's development of the awareness of his or her own thinking. However, he conceptualized the process differently.

The activities and strategies recommended by Piaget for the classroom, therefore, target children's spontaneous research in the development of reasoning and thinking skills. Although Piaget identified questioning and interaction among peers in the classroom as important, the teacher must create classroom situations conducive to a variety of student actions. Thus, in his view, the goal is not to become a community of learners, as is recommended by social constructivism. Further, the individual student, not the group, is the locus of learning.

Piaget's view of the role of make-believe play, children's egocentric speech, and the role of society also differed from that of Lev Vygotsky. These differences are discussed in chapter 11.

Developing a Classroom Strategy

The implementation of Piaget's concepts at any level of the curriculum can be accomplished using the following four general steps and the subquestions for each step:

Step 1: Determine which principles in a course or curriculum typically taught by verbal means may be replaced by student-directed research.

    1.1 Which aspects of the curriculum are conducive to experimentation?

    1.2 Which principles are conducive to problem-solving activity in a group situation?

1.3 Which topics (or concepts) can be introduced at a manipulable level using physical objects prior to verbal treatment?

Step 2: Select or develop classroom activities for the identified topics. Evaluate the selected activities using the following list of questions:

2.1 Does the activity provide opportunities for a variety of methods of experimentation?

2.2 Can the activity lead to a variety of questions by the students?

2.3 Can the student compare various modes of reasoning in working through the activity?

2.4 Is the problem one that *cannot* be solved on the basis of perceptual cues alone?

2.5 Is the activity one that generates both physical activity and opportunities for cognitive activity? (Inappropriate activities include constructing a picture or diagram or building objects prespecified by the teacher.)

2.6 Can the activity enrich an already learned construct?

Step 3: Identify opportunities for teacher questions that support the problem-solving process.

3.1 What probing follow-up questions may be used (e.g., predictions, "what if" questions)?

3.2 What potential comparisons can be identified within the material that are conducive to spontaneous questions?

Step 4: Evaluate the implementation of each activity, noting successes and needed revisions.

4.1 What aspect of the activity generated the most intense interest and involvement? Are there ways that this may be capitalized on in the future?

4.2 What aspect of the activity, if any, "fell flat"? Did the activity fail to engage the efforts of one or more learners? What are some alternatives to try next time?

4.3 Did the activity provide opportunities to develop new strategies of investigation or to enhance already learned strategies?

In summary, maximize the opportunities for students to construct knowledge for themselves through student-directed research. Discussions about research findings in which answers were developed through group interaction and that require consideration of a number of variables will enhance the student's construction of knowledge. Finally, whenever possible, provide direct student experience with constructs, rules, and theories prior to any verbalization. Otherwise, the information remains only verbalization and does not become knowledge.

Classroom Example

The following classroom lesson emerged as part of a research and development project in teaching conducted by Magdalene Lampert (1990). The goal was to determine in what ways the practice of knowing mathematics in the classroom could be brought closer to what it means to know mathematics within the discipline. The primary mechanism in this process is to alter the roles and responsibilities of both students and teacher during classroom discourse (Lampert, 1990, p. 29).

The goal was not to create a Piagetian curriculum. However, the construction of knowledge undertaken by the fifth-grade students, the role of the teacher, and the nature of the peer interaction reflect classroom characteristics described by Piaget as essential for cognitive development.

- *Basic premise:* "Doing" mathematics is not a matter of finding a right answer that is ratified by the teacher. Instead, mathematics develops as a process of "conscious guessing" about relationships that are examined and then tested through the use of counterexamples (Lakatos, 1976; Lampert, 1990).
- *Content:* Exponents, fifth-grade class
- *Purpose:* One can determine aspects of the characteristics of unknown quantities by studying patterns in numbers one can observe (Lampert, 1990; Polya, 1954). Also, students can acquire the attitudes and skills to participate in a disciplinary discourse that is knowledge *about* mathematics (Lampert, 1990; Schoenfeld, 1985).
- *Prior activities:* The use of mathematical discourse, and the rules for interchange, were already in use in the classroom (Lampert, 1990). When a problem was posed to the class, student conjectures and their names were written on the board. When students wanted to change a conjecture, they had learned to say, "I want to revise my thinking." When proposing a possible answer (conjecture), they were expected to provide a rationale. All the students had prepared their own tables of squares from 1^2 to 100^2 using calculators.
- *Constructing knowledge:* The teacher challenged the students to find patterns in their tables of numbers by examining the last digits of the numbers. They actively participated in this investigation for three 45-minute class periods. The key to the lesson was that "the mathematical content embedded in inventing the strategies that can be used to assert the answers without doing the calculations is mathematically significant and engages students in arguing about the key ideas behind how exponents work" (Lampert, 1990, p. 46).

The first assertion made by the students was that the last digits of the squares alternated between odd and even just as the base numbers did. Other assertions were that multiples of 10 would always end in 0, and the square of a number ending in 5 always ends in 5. They then began to explore further the hypothesis that "if the last digit is always n when you raise n to some power, the last two digits will always be n^2" (Lampert, 1990, p. 49). Two students asserted that the powers of 6 should end in 36, but other students quickly identified a counterexample.

Students also determined that the strings of last digits always will be symmetrical around both 0 and 5. A chart was used to work out the symmetrical pattern of last digits. The students also proved that the pattern would go on forever because numbers ending in 9 or 1 have squares that end in 1, numbers ending in 2 or 8 have squares that end in 4, and so on.

The final segment of the lesson shifted to strategies for figuring out the last digit in a number raised to the 5th power. In the discussion of 7^5, several digits were proposed along with the accompanying rationale. One student thought the pattern of last digits would be $1, 7, 9, 1, 7, 9$, and so on. However, after several assertions and discussions of each, the students determined that the pattern of last digits would be $7, 9, 3, 1, 7$; therefore, 7^5 ends in 7.

During the discussion, one of the students stated that 7^5 should end in 1. The teacher's role was to ask him to explain, to assert what some of the student's assumptions might have been, and, later, to ask him to articulate the revision in thinking he had made. The purpose is not simply for the student to rethink his assumptions, but to help the other students to see why those assumptions had led him to the conclusion that the last digit was 1. In other words, in this type of lesson, both students and teacher have a different relation to the subject matter than they would in a "knowledge telling exchange" (Lampert, 1990, p. 53).

Review of the Theory

Jean Piaget's theory of cognitive development redefines intelligence, knowledge, and the relationship of the learner to the environment. Intelligence, like a biological system, is a continuing process that creates the structures it needs in continuing interactions with the environment.

The essential characteristic of logical thinking is the construction of a psychological structure with particular characteristics. Specifically, the learner (1) clearly recognizes the changing (transformation) and unchanging (conservation) features of a situation, (2) understands the inverse operation for each transformation (reversibility), and (3) identifies the problem solution as logically necessary.

The development of the individual's different ways of thinking from infancy to adulthood include the action schemes of the infant, preoperations, concrete operations, and formal operations. The process by which each of these more complex structures is constructed are assimilation and accommodation, regulated by equilibration (Table 10.4).

The role of education, in Piaget's view, is to support the spontaneous research of the child. Experimentation with real objects and interaction with peers, supported by the teacher's insightful questions, permit the child to construct both physical and logico-mathematical knowledge. The major requirements for the curriculum are rich opportunities for children to interact with the physical world in a variety of ways, to make their own mistakes, and to develop answers through interaction with their peers.

Disadvantages

A major problem in the implementation of Piaget's ideas arises from the different perspective he casts on intelligence, knowledge, and learning. Considerable effort is required to alter one's perspective from intelligence and knowledge as products to treating these concepts totally as process.

The development of curriculum, according to Piagetian concepts, requires, as Piaget himself indicated, considerable work and effort. Implementation of a Piagetian curriculum is also complicated by the fact that his theory excludes the relationships between logical thinking and curriculum basics, such as reading and writing.

TABLE 10.4
Summary of Jean Piaget's Cognitive-Development Theory

Basic Element	Definition
Assumptions	Intelligence, like a biological system, constructs the structures it needs to function.
	Knowledge is the interaction between the individual and the environment.
	The growth of intelligence is influenced by four factors (physical and social environment, maturation, and equilibration).
Cognitive development	The growth of logical thinking from infancy to adulthood
Outcomes of cognitive development	The construction of new structures from prior structures (i.e., action schemes, concrete and formal operations)
Components of cognitive development	Assimilation and accommodation, regulated by equilibration
	Physical experience and logicomathematical experience
Facilitating logical thinking	Providing rich opportunities for experimentation with physical objects supported by peer interaction and teacher questions
Major issues in designing instruction	Maintenance of reciprocal relationship between child and education: avoidance of direct teaching and correction of children's "errors"
ANALYSIS OF THE THEORY	
Disadvantages	Understanding of basic terms and definitions is difficult.
	Piagetian curriculum is difficult to implement and maintain.
	Perspective excludes the relationship between logical thinking and basic learning, such as reading.
Contributions to classroom practice	Provides a rich description of the world through the child's eye.
	Identifies problems in curricula, particularly the teaching of mathematics and science as "socialized knowledge."
	Operationalizes the often-cited concept, "discovery learning."

Contributions to Educational Practice

A major contribution of Piaget's work is that he changed the view of a child from that of a little adult to one with distinctive and changing patterns of thinking. Another is that he identified the shortcomings of directly taught curricula. He clearly delineated the problems and effects of teaching mathematics and science, for example, as "socialized knowledge." In addition to providing us a rich description of the world from the child's eye, he has operationalized the often-cited concept "discovery learning." Table 10.4 summarizes Piaget's cognitive-development theory.

CHAPTER QUESTIONS

1. A student is using a computer software program to write an essay. She is required to use certain symbol keys to direct the computer to double-space, number the pages, and so on. In Piaget's view, what is this process?

2. A child feels the rush of air on his face made by fanning a paper. Later, on a windy day, he feels the wind and decides it is caused by the swaying trees (Wolfgang & Sanders, 1981, p. 117). Which stage of thinking does this notion of causality represent? Why?

3. A group of middle school students is asked to predict which of two objects, dropped at the same time, will fall faster. Most of the students predict that the heavier object will reach the floor first. When given several objects to experiment with, they are puzzled that they cannot determine any difference in the rate of descent. Some of the students conclude, in error, that the heavier object falls faster but that the difference is too small for them to observe. According to Piaget, what has happened in this situation?

4. How would the Gestalt psychologists describe the child's drawings of the water in Figure 10.2?

REFERENCES

Acredolo, C. (1997). Understanding Piaget's new theory requires assimilation and accommodation. *Human Development, 40,* 235–237.

Beilin, H. (1989). Piagetian theory. In *Six theories of child development: Annals of child development 6* (pp. 85–131). Greenwich, CT: JAI Press.

Beilin, H. (1992a). Piaget's enduring contribution to developmental psychology. *Developmental Psychology, 20*(2), 191–204.

Beilin, H. (1992b). Piaget's new theory. In H. Beilin & P. Pufall (Eds.), *Piaget's theory: Prospects and possibilities* (pp. 1–20). Hillsdale, NJ: Erlbaum.

Berk, L. E. (1989). *Child development.* Boston: Allyn & Bacon.

Bickhard, M. H. (1997). Piaget and active cognition. *Human Development, 40,* 238–243.

Bond, T. G. (1998). Fifty years of formal operational research: The empirical research. *Archives de Psychologie, 66,* 221–238.

Borel, M. (1987). Piaget's natural logic. In B. Inhelder, D. deCaprona, & A. Cornu-Wells (Eds.), *Piaget today* (pp. 65–75). Hillsdale, NJ: Erlbaum.

Bringuier, J. C. (1980). *Conversations with Jean Piaget* (B. M. Gulati, Trans.). Chicago: University of Chicago Press.

Case, R. (1985). *Intellectual development: Birth to adulthood.* New York: Academic.

Case, R. (1992). Neo-Piagetian theories of cognitive development. In H. Beilin & P. Pufall (Eds.), *Piaget's theory: Prospects and possibilities* (pp. 61–104). Hillsdale, NJ: Erlbaum.

Case, R. (1993). Theories of learning and theories of development. *Educational Psychologist, 28*(3), 219–233.

Cauley, K., Murray, F., & Smith, D. (1983). Necessity in children's reasoning: Criteria for conservation and operativity. Paper presented at the Eastern Educational Research Association, Baltimore, MD.

Champagne, A. B., Gunstone, R. F., & Klopfer, L. E. (1985). Effecting changes in cognitive structures among physics students. In L. H. J. West & A. L. Pines (Eds.), *Cognitive structure and conceptual change* (pp. 163–188). Orlando, FL: Academic.

Champagne, A. B., Klopfer, L. E., & Anderson, J. H. (1980). Factors influencing the learning of classical mechanics. *American Journal of Physics, 48*(2), 1074–1079.

Chandler, M., & Chapman, M. (1991). *Criteria for competence.* Hillsdale, NJ: Erlbaum.

Chapman, M. (1988). *Constructive evolution.* New York: Cambridge University Press.

Chapman, M. (1999). Constructivism and the problem of reality. *Journal of Applied Developmental Psychology, 22*(1), 31–43.

Chapman, M., & McBride, M. (1992). Beyond competence and performance: Children's class inclusion strategies, superordinate class cues, and verbal justifications. *Developmental Psychology, 28,* 319–327.

Clements, D. H., & Gullo, D. F. (1984). Effects of computer programming in young children's cognition. *Journal of Educational Psychology, 76,* 1054–1058.

Cobb, P. (1995). Continuing the conversation: A response to Smith. *Educational Researcher, 24*(6), 25–27.

Copple, C., Sigel, E., & Saunders, R. (1979). *Educating the young thinker: Classroom strategies for cognitive growth.* New York: Van Nostrand.

Dean, A. L., & Youniss, J. (1991). The transformation of Piagetian theory by American psychology: The early competence issue. In M. Chandler & M. Chapman (Eds.), *Criteria for competence* (pp. 92–100). Hillsdale, NJ: Erlbaum.

DeLisi, R., & Stewart, J. (1980). Individual differences in college students' performance on formal operational tasks. *Journal of Applied Developmental Psychology, 1*, 201–208.

DeVries, R. (1978). Early education and Piagetian theory. In J. M. Gallagher & J. A. Easley, Jr. (Eds.), *Knowledge and development: Vol. 2. Piaget and education* (pp. 75–91). New York: Plenum.

Duckworth, E. (1978). The having of wonderful ideas. *Harvard Educational Review, 42*, 217–231.

Duckworth, E. (1979). Either we're too early and they can't learn it or we're too late and they know it already: The dilemma of "applying Piaget." *Harvard Educational Review, 49*, 297–312.

Duckworth, E. (1990). Opening the world. In E. Duckworth, J. Easley, D. Hawkins, & A. Henriques (Eds.), *Science education: A minds-on approach for the elementary years* (pp. 21–59). Hillsdale, NJ: Erlbaum.

Edelstein, W., & Schroeder, E. (2000). Full house or Pandora's box? The treatment of variability in post-Piagetian research. *Child Development, 71*(4), 840–842.

Ferreiro, E. (2001). On the links between equilibration, causality, and 'prise de conscience' in Piaget's theory. *Human Development, 44*, 214–219.

Flick, L. B. (1990). Interaction of intuitive physics with computer simulated physics. *Journal of Research in Science Teaching, 27*(3), 219–231.

Furth, H. (1980). *The world of grownups: Children's conceptions of society.* New York: Elsevier North Holland.

Furth, H. (1986a). Piaget's logic of assimilation and logic for the classroom. In G. Forman & P. Pufall (Eds.), *Constructivism in the computer age* (pp. 37–46). Hillsdale, NJ: Erlbaum.

Furth, H. (1986b). *Symbol-picture logic (SPL)* (Vol. 2). Washington, DC: Computer Age Education.

Furth, H. G., & Youniss, J. (2000). Reflections on Piaget's sociological studies. *New Ideas in Psychology, 18*, 121–133.

Gallini, J., & Gredler, M. (1989). *Instructional design for computers: Cognitive applications in BASIC and LOGO.* Glenview, IL: Scott, Foresman.

Gilbert, J. K., Osborne, R. J., & Fresham, P. J. (1982). Children's science and its consequences for teaching. *Science Education, 6*, 623–633.

Gilbert, J. K., Watts, D. M., & Osborne, R. J. (1985). Eliciting student views using an interview technique. In L. H. T. West & A. L. Pines (Eds.), *Cognitive structure and conceptual change* (pp. 11–27). Orlando, FL: Academic.

Inhelder, B., & deCaprona, E. (1990). The role and meaning of structures in genetic epistemology. In W. F. Overton (Ed.), *Reasoning, necessity, and logic: Developmental perspectives* (pp. 333–344). Hillsdale, NJ: Erlbaum.

Inhelder, B., & Piaget, J. (1958). *The growth of logical thinking from childhood to adolescence* (A. Parsons & S. Milgram, Trans.). New York: Basic.

Inhelder, B., Sinclair, H., & Bovet, M. (1974). *Learning and the process of cognition.* Cambridge, MA: Harvard University Press.

Kamii, C. (1975). One intelligence indivisible. *Young Children, 30*(4), 228–238.

Kamii, C. (1981). Application of Piaget's theory to education: The pre-operational level. In I. Sigel, D. A. Brodzinsky, & R. M. Golinkoff (Eds.), *New directions in Piagetian theory and practice* (pp. 231–265). Hillsdale, NJ: Erlbaum.

Kamii, C., & DeVries, R. (1978). *Physical knowledge in preschool education.* Upper Saddle River, NJ: Prentice Hall.

Kamii, C., & Kamii, M. (1990). Why achievement testing should stop. In C. Kamii (Ed.), *Achievement testing in the early grades* (pp. 15–38). Washington, DC: National Association for the Education of Young Children.

Karmiloff-Smith, A., & Inhelder, B. (1975). If you want to get ahead, get a theory. *Cognition, 3*, 195–212.

Kuhn, D. (1979). The application of Piaget's theory of cognitive development to education. *Harvard Educational Review, 49*, 340–360.

Kuhn D., Black J., Keselman, A., & Kaplan, D. (2000). The development of cognitive skills to support inquiry learning. *Cognition and Instruction, 18*(4), 495–523.

Kuhn, D., & Phelps, E. (1979). A methodology for observing development of a formal reasoning strategy. *New Directions for Child Development, 5*, 45–57.

Lakatos, I. (1976). *Proofs and refutations: The logic of mathematical discovery*. New York: Cambridge University Press.

Lampert, M. (1990). When the problem is not the question and the solution is not the answer: Mathematical knowing and teaching. *American Educational Research Journal, 27*(1), 29–63.

Lavoie, D. R., & Good, R. (1988). The nature and use of prediction skills in a biological computer simulation. *Journal of Research in Science Teaching, 25*(5), 335–360.

Lorenço, O., and Machado, A. (1996). In defense of Piaget's theory; A reply to 10 common criticisms, *Psychology Review, 103* (1), 143–164.

Montangero, J. (1991). A constructivist framework for understanding early and late-developing psychological competencies. In M. Chandler and M. Chapman (Eds.), *Criteria for competence: Controversies in the conceptualization and assessment of children's abilities* (pp. 111–129). Hillsdale, NJ: Erlbaum.

Müller, U. (1999). Structure and content of formal operational thought: An interpretation in context. *Archives de Psychologie, 67*(260), 21–35.

Murray, F. B. (1990). The conversion of truth into necessity. In W. F. Overton (Ed.), *Reasoning, necessity, and logic: Developmental perspectives* (pp. 183–204). Hillsdale, NJ: Erlbaum.

National Council of Teachers of Mathematics (NCTM) (1989). *Curriculum and evaluation standards for school mathematics*, Reston, VA: Author.

Osborne, R. J., & Gilbert, J. J. (1980). A technique for exploring students' views of the world. *Physics Education, 15*, 376–379.

Papert, S. (1980). *Mindstorms*. New York: Basic.

Piaget, J. (1926). *Judgment and reasoning in the child*. New York: Harcourt.

Piaget, J. (1928). *Judgment and reasoning in the child*. London: Routledge & Kegan Paul.

Piaget, J. (1951). *Play, dreams and imitation in children*. New York: Norton.

Piaget, J. (1952). *The child's conception of number*. London: Routledge & Kegan Paul.

Piaget, J. (1965). *The moral judgment of the child*. New York: Free Press.

Piaget, J. (1967). *Six psychological studies* (A. Tenzer, Trans.). New York: Random House.

Piaget, J. (1970a). *Genetic epistemology* (E. Duckworth, Trans.). New York: Columbia University Press.

Piaget, J. (1970b). Piaget's theory. In P. H. Mussen (Ed.), *Carmichael's manual of psychology* (Chap. 9, pp. 703–732). New York: Wiley.

Piaget, J. (1970c). *Science of education and the psychology of the child*. New York: Orion.

Piaget, J. (1971). *The construction of reality in the child*. New York: Ballantine.

Piaget, J. (1972a). Intellectual evolution from adolescence to adulthood. *Human Development, 15*, 1–12.

Piaget, J. (1972b). *The principles of genetic epistemology* (W. Mays, Trans.). New York: Basic.

Piaget, J. (1973). *To understand is to invent: The future of education*. New York: Grossman.

Piaget, J. (1976a). The affective and the cognitive unconscious. In B. Inhelder & H. H. Chipman (Eds.), *Piaget and his school* (pp. 63–71). (Original published 1970)

Piaget, J. (1976b). *The grasp of consciousness: Action and concept in the young child*. Cambridge, MA: Harvard University Press.

Piaget, J. (1977). Problems in equilibration. In M. Appel & S. Goldberg (Eds.), *Topics in cognitive development: Vol. I. Equilibration: Theory, research, and application* (pp. 3–13). New York: Plenum.

Piaget, J. (1980). *Adaptation and intelligence: Organic selection and phenocopy* (S. Eames, Trans.). Chicago: University of Chicago Press.

Piaget, J. (1985). *The equilibration of cognitive structures*. Chicago: University of Chicago Press.

Piaget, J. (1987a). *Possibility and necessity* (Vol. 1). Minneapolis, MN: University of Minnesota Press.

Piaget, J. (1987b). *Possibility and necessity* (Vol. 2). Minneapolis, MN: University of Minnesota Press.

Piaget, J., & Garcia, R. (1991). *The logic of meanings.* Hillsdale, NJ: Erlbaum.

Piaget, J., & Inhelder, B. (1969). *The psychology of the child* (H. Weaver, Trans.). New York: Basic Books.

Polya, G. (1954). *Induction and analogy in mathematics.* Princeton, NJ: Princeton University Press.

Pons, F., & Harris, P. (2001). Piaget's conception of the development of consciousness. *Human Development, 44,* 221–227.

Pufall, P. B. (1988). *Function in Piaget's system: Some notes for constructors of microworlds.* In G. Forman & P. B. Pufall (Eds.), *Constructivism in the computer age* (pp. 15–35). Hillsdale, NJ: Erlbaum.

Ricco, R. B. (1990). Necessity and the logic of entailment. In W. F. Overton (Ed.), *Reasoning, necessity, and logic: Developmental perspectives* (pp. 45–66). Hillsdale, NJ: Erlbaum.

Schoenfeld, A. H. (1985). Metacognitive and epistemological issues in mathematical understanding. In E. A. Silver (Ed.), *Teaching and learning mathematical problem solving: Multiple research perspectives* (pp. 361–379), Hillsdale, NJ: Erlbaum.

Smith, L. (1991). Age, ability, and intellectual development. In M. Chandler & M. Chapman (Eds.), *Criteria for competence* (pp. 69–91). Hillsdale, NJ: Erlbaum.

Vosniadou, S., & Brewer, W. F. (1992). Mental models of the Earth: A study of conceptual change in childhood. *Cognitive Psychology, 24,* 535–585.

Wertheimer, M. (1959). Productive thinking: New York: Harper. (Original published 1945)

White, B. Y. (1984). Designing computer games to help physics students understand Newton's laws of motion. *Cognition and Instruction, 1*(1), 69–108.

Wolfgang, C. H., & Sanders, T. S. (1981). Defending young children's play as the ladder to literacy. *Theory into practice, 20*(2), 116–120.

Wood, T., Cobb, P., & Yaeckel, E. (1991). Change in teaching mathematics: A case study. *American Educational Research Journal, 28*(3), 587–616.

CHAPTER 11

Lev S. Vygotsky's Socio – Cultural-(Historical) Theory of Psychological Development

Culture creates special forms of behavior. . . . In the process of historical development social man changes the ways and means of his behavior, transforms the natural instincts and functions, [and] elaborates and creates new forms of behavior. (Vygotsky, 1931/1966, p. 19)

The work of Lev Vygotsky, which spanned the brief period from 1924 to 1934, has steadily grown in influence in the United States since the early 1980s. Unfortunately, however, misconceptions about his work have entered the mainstream of Western discourse, complicating the analysis of his contributions to educational psychology. Some scholars note that Vygotsky is credited with being 50 years ahead of his time for ideas that he himself credited to others (Cole, 1996; Valsiner, 1988; van der Veer & Valsiner, 1991). For example, some Westerners, unfamiliar with history, sometimes credit Vygotsky with the view that culture is a major influence on human cognitive development. However, the concept was introduced by two German academics, Moritz Lazarus and Hijam Steinthal, 60 years prior to Vygotsky's work, and it became the cornerstone of Wundt's "second psychology" (discussed in chapter 1). At the time Vygotsky entered psychology, anthropologists were debating various issues about the relationship between culture and individual development. Among them were the nature of the cultural influence on the individual, the relationship of different cultures to different forms of thinking (van der Veer & Valsiner, 1991), and whether different cultures form a continuum from "primitive" to "advanced" (Cole, 1996).

Initial misconceptions about Vygotsky's work are the result of several factors. One is the rapid acceptance and popularity of the theory, which Valsiner (1988) suggests is inversely related to the depth of understanding. Others are translation difficulties of some Russian words that do not have an English equivalent, lack of accessibility to many of his writings, and initial reliance on limited translations. Vygotsky's writings were banned in the USSR from 1936 until the 1950s (Valsiner, 1988). Then, in the 1970s and early 1980s, as U.S. interest in the theory emerged, 82.2% of the citations in English-language journals

(1969 to 1985) were to only two abridged translations of a few of his ideas (Valsiner, 1988).

Among the misconceptions about Vygotsky are (1) the often-repeated story about his entry into psychology, (2) the belief that the zone of proximal development is a major concept in the theory, and (3) omissions of the role of the teacher and formal schooling, particularly concept learning, in the development of higher cognitive functions. Clarification of these issues is facilitated by the detailed 10-year research and translation of many of Vygotsky's unpublished works, archival documents, and family correspondence by René van der Veer and Jean Valsiner (1991), and careful reading of the English editions of Vygotsky's collected works.

Vygotsky was born in Orsha, a town in western Russia near Minsk, in 1896, the same year that Piaget was born. Precocious as a child, Vygotsky was known for excelling in multiple intellectual pursuits. As an adolescent, with a circle of friends, he debated ideas such as Hegel's philosophy of history and the role of the individual in society (van der Veer & Valsiner, 1991).

On graduating from the gymnasium, he earned a gold medal, signifying the highest grade in all his subjects (Valsiner & van der Veer, 2000). He then engaged in studies at two universities in Moscow simultaneously, graduating from both in 1917, according to his daughter Gita (p. 330). Returning to his native province, Vygotsky taught at several institutes, set up a psychological laboratory at Gomel Teacher College, organized "literary Mondays" in the community for the presentation and discussion of literary works, wrote weekly theater reviews, co-founded a short-lived library journal, co-founded a publishing house, and headed the theater section of the Gomel Department of People's Education (Valsiner & van der Veer, 2000; van der Veer & Valsiner, 1991, p. 10).

Vygotsky's entry into psychology in 1924 was, in many ways, an accident of history. A humanist scholar with no formal training in psychology, Vygotsky came to the attention of the Director of the Moscow Institute of Experimental Psychology through one of the papers he presented at the second Psychoneurological Congress in Petrograd in January 1924. The presentation on the research methods of reflexology and psychology (Vygotsky, 1926/1971) discussed (1) the importance of psychology becoming a unified science that studies mind as well as behavior, (2) the inability of introspection to yield reliable, objective data, and (3) the need to go beyond the current methods of reflexology, which had "reached a dead end" (p. 47).

The often-repeated account of the paper is that it was such an electrifying presentation critical of Pavlov's reflexology that Vygotsky was invited to join the Institute. However, audience reaction seems to have been moderately enthusiastic (Joravsky, 1989). Nevertheless, the talk held appeal for the Institute director, Konstantin Kornilov, because (1) it raised questions about the rival discipline to Kornilov's reactology, and (2) Kornilov also subscribed to the view of a unified and objective study of the conscious mind (van der Veer & Valsiner, 1991, p. 43). In addition, both Kornilov and Vygotsky were interested in Hegelian synthesis as essential to understanding complex processes (p. 123). Further, after the dismissal of the prior Institute director and many of his staff for "idealism" (subjective psychology), Kornilov was hiring new personnel and offered Vygotsky a position (van der Veer & Valsiner, 1991).

Of interest is that, under ordinary circumstances, Vygotsky would not have obtained an academic position in psychology. However, in the reorganization of society under the Bolsheviks, old professional hierarchies had broken down, and educated individuals who did not oppose the Bolsheviks were in short supply in the largely illiterate country (Fitzpatrick, 1992). Valsiner (1988) noted that, 10 years earlier, psychology would not have been interested in Vygotsky, and, 10 years later, psychology would not have interested him.

Vygotsky's primary goal was to reformulate psychology as part of a unified social science (Joravsky, 1989; van der Veer & Valsiner, 1991). In his view, given the unique characteristics of humans (described in chapter 1), psychology should address the ways that human abilities develop, and it would fail in its major task if it could not explain the formation of human behaviors (Vygotsky, 1924/1979a; 1926/1997l).

Vygotsky further defined the broad focus of his theory as explaining the qualitative changes that account for the emergence of higher psychological (cognitive) functions at the levels of both the human species (phylogeny) and the individual (ontogeny). He began this quest by examining the writings of Western psychologists and sociologists that he and his colleagues translated into Russian. However, he found the psychological explanations of human cognition described by existing learning theories to be inadequate (Vygotsky, 1931/1997a, pp. 65–69; Vygotsky, 1926/1997h, pp. 149–151; Vygotsky, 1931/1997l, pp. 28–39; Vygotsky, 1926/1997l; Vygotsky, 1934/1997g). For example, although the Gestalt principle of structure is found in the intelligence of both the chimpanzee and the child, it is insufficient to explain the "central core" of human cognitive development (Vygotsky, 1934/1997g, p. 212).

Vygotsky also analyzed the writings of Western anthropologists and ethnopsychologists (van der Veer, 1991; Vygotsky, 1930/1997f; Vygotsky & Luria, 1930/1993, pp. 79–137), drawing on many of their concepts. Some he modified and supplemented with additional work, and he integrated this broad range of ideas into a theory that went beyond the disciplinary boundaries of the social sciences, humanities, and historical sciences (Wertsch, 1985a).

In addition to developing his theory, Vygotsky, like other psychologists in the war-ravaged country, fulfilled multiple roles. He addressed the problems of mentally retarded, blind, and deaf-mute children, became a skilled clinician, and participated in the founding of the Institute of Defectology, for which he was appointed "scientific leader" (van der Veer & Valsiner, 1991, p. 45). He was also involved in organizing child study in the Soviet Union (van der Veer & Valsiner, 1991). He also organized medico-pedagogical conferences in which doctors, psychologists, special education teachers, and others observed his examinations of special needs children with their parents (Vygodskaia, 1998).

This schedule of activities led to periodic life-threatening bouts of tuberculosis, a disease he had contracted as a young man while caring for his ill brother (van der Veer & Valsiner, 1991). Vygotsky was unable to defend his dissertation in the summer of 1925, and in October 1925, the dissertation, *The Psychology of Art*, was accepted for the Ph.D. degree without a public defense.

Although ill with tuberculosis, Vygotsky mustered a Herculean effort to accomplish his goals. Living in one room in a crowded apartment with his wife and two daughters, he often wrote after 2 A.M., the only time when he had a few quiet hours to himself (Wertsch, 1985a). Some of his writings were begun in the crowded, noisy barracks atmosphere of the sanatoriums where he was periodically hospitalized (see excerpts from Vygotsky's correspondence translated in van der Veer & Valsiner, 1991).

In the last three years of his life, Vygotsky completed manuscripts, articles, and books at an almost frenetic pace. Needless to say, his tuberculosis worsened and, in June 1934, he died at the age of 37.

A few of Vygotsky's writings were published after his death. However, his theory was receiving criticism for "bourgeois thinking" and in 1936 the intellectual climate changed. The Central Committee of the Communist Party banned all psychological testing in the USSR. At the same time the leading psychological journals ceased publication for nearly 20 years. Later some of Vygotsky's views were found to conflict with Stalin's 1950 essay on linguistics and thus were not published until 1956 (Wertsch, 1985a).

Vygotsky's major theoretical writings included the role of cultural signs and symbols in the development of attention, abstraction, language, memory, numeric operations, and reasoning (Vygotsky, 1929; 1931/1997a; 1930/1999b; 1931/1997j; Vygotsky & Luria, 1930/1993); his identification and discussion of the outcomes of cognitive development labeled the higher psychological or mental functions (Vygotsky, 1931/1997j; 1931/1966; 1930–1931/1998a); the key role of scientific (subject-matter) concepts in developing thinking (Vygotsky, 1934/1987a; 1934/1987b; 1930–1931/1998b); and the relationship of thinking and speech (Vygotsky, 1934/1987c; 1934/1987d).

However, Vygotsky's concept of the cultural and historical development of cognitive functions remained incomplete at his death. Among the issues he had begun to address at that time were the possible hierarchical relationships among mental functions and the development of affect and its role in intellectual processes (Bozhovitch, 1977, p. 15; Vygotsky, 1999c).

PRINCIPLES OF PSYCHOLOGICAL DEVELOPMENT

Vygotsky's goal was to create a psychology that was theoretically and methodologically equal to the task of investigating uniquely human characteristics.

Basic Assumptions

The framework for the analysis of human cognitive functions constructed by Vygotsky rests on three assumptions. They are (1) the nature of human intelligence, (2) the delineation of two different lines of psychological development, referred to as biological and cultural-historical, and (3) the design of an experimental method for the investigation of dynamic psychological processes.

The Nature of Human Intelligence

Vygotsky's description of the nature of human intelligence includes four related topics. They are (1) the differences between animals and humans, (2) the philosophical foundations that formed the basis of his theory, (3) the designation referred to as psychological tools, and (4) the influence of culture on human cognitive development.

Animal/Human Differences in Mental Activities.   Vygotsky took issue with the views of behaviorism and Gestalt psychology, because they based their views of cognition on research with animals. The stimulus–response paradigm, for example, reflects associations that are united only on the basis of a "purely external coincidence in time" (Vygotsky, 1931/1997i, p. 31).

Furthermore, the Gestalt structural principle, which maintains that the subject reorganizes her understanding of a situation by mentally restructuring the role of a tool available for solving problems, is not the same for chimpanzees and children (Vygotsky, 1934/1997g). First, a structured action is not necessarily an intellectual act (p. 205). The ape's goal-directed action is meaningful within the experimental situation, *but is meaningless beyond those boundaries* (p. 209). In contrast, the child's capability for speech liberates her activity and leads to the concept of the "objective nature of the tool," which is not dependent on any particular situation (p. 214).

Second, the universality claimed by the Gestaltists for the structural principle means that "the perception of a chicken [animal used in some Gestalt experiments] and the actions of a mathematician, which represents the most perfect model of human thinking, are equally structured" (Vygotsky, 1934/1997g, p. 225). If this is so, then the structural principle "is insufficiently dynamic to bring out the novel phenomena that arise in the course of development itself" (p. 225).

Philosophical Foundations.   Vygotsky drew on three philosophical perspectives for the foundation of his theory. One was a belief in rational man and the control of one's passions through the human mind, expressed by Benedict Spinoza, Vygotsky's favorite philosopher (Yaroshevsky, 1989; van der Veer & Valsiner, 1991, p. 15). Vygotsky's theory describes the ever-increasing mastery of one's behavior through the development of complex and powerful intellectual functions.

The second philosophical influence was the description of change as dialectical synthesis, described by G. W. F. Hegel. Briefly, dialectical synthesis involves (1) the negation of a thesis by its oppositive, antithesis, followed by (2) a resolution of that interaction in the form of a qualitatively new formation, a synthesis. For example, matter, which is the foundation of existence, is not viewed as absolute and unchanging. Instead, the world of matter is "a combination of processes, externally changing or developing" (Kornilov, 1930, p. 250). Light, heat, electricity, magnetic currents, chemical transformations, life, and psychological processes are examples; Vygotsky (1930/1997e) described the processes of cognitive development as both uninterrupted, "accompanied by leaps or the development of new qualities" (p. 112), and "a complex dialectical process" (Vygotsky, 1931/1997c, p. 99). The characteristics include a disproportionate development of separate intellectual functions, qualitative transformations of some forms of thinking into others, merging of the processes of involution and evolution in complex ways, and complex interactions of external and internal factors.

The third philosophical influence consisted of some general concepts from Karl Marx and Frederic Engels. They built on Hegel's concept that humans create diverse worlds (cultures) in which work provides the means through which humans perceive the world as independent objects and acting subjects. Marx and Engels maintained that humans affect the environment by changing it, and, through these efforts, change their own nature as well (Marx & Engels, *Collected Works*, Vol. 23, in Vygotsky, 1931/1997i, p. 55). The essential factor in changing human nature is the tools of work. Further, tool invention by pre-humans led to (1) the emergence of humans because it led to labor, the need for cooperation, and speech (Engels, 1925/1978); (2) through tool use, humans transform both nature and themselves; and (3) the particular social organizations that result from tool use determine human mental life (Engels, 1940). Thus, human labor transforms both nature and human experience. The discovery of fire, the invention of simple agricultural tools, and the discovery of electricity are examples.

The Role of "Psychological Tools."   Two difficult questions for psychology were left unanswered by the designation of tools as instruments of change. First, how does a relatively simple activity, tool use, account for such sweeping developments as the emergence of the human species and advanced cognitive development? Second, what are the relationships among tool use, social organizations, and differences in cognitive development?

Essential to bridging the gap between tool use and cognitive development was Vygotsky's designation of cultural signs and symbols as *psychological tools*. Likely sources for this concept were (1) Wolfgang Köhler's references to "the priceless tool of speech," and (2) Emile Durkheim's discussions of the collective representations of a society as "clever instruments of thought" (van der Veer & Valsiner, 1991, pp. 302, 206).

According to Vygotsky, the importance of these psychological tools (signs and symbols) is that they, rather than the tools of work, bring about the transformation of human consciousness and are the instruments essential to the development of higher cognitive functions. In other words, the essential difference between technical tools and psychological tools is that technical tools change an external situation but psychological tools direct the mind and change the process of thinking (Vygotsky, 1931/1997i, p. 62). Moreover, these psychological tools differ throughout human history and across cultures. The theory developed from this foundation was referred to by Vygotsky as the *cultural-historical theory of the psyche* (Leont'ev & Luria, 1968).

The Influence of Culture on Human Development.   Relationships among the use of signs and symbols (psychological tools), social organizations, and cognitive development at the species level discussed by contemporary anthropologists are found in Vygotsky's untranslated work (van der Veer & Valsiner, 1991). Among them are (1) thought and language are more well developed in contemporary cultures (Lévy-Bruhl, 1910/1922, 1922/1976), and (2) different cultures imply different kinds of cognitive growth through their various developments in law, music, art, language, religion, writing, and counting systems (Thurnwald, 1922). However, Vygotsky (1931/1966) retained only symbol systems from Thurnwald's list because they can serve as psychological tools to self-regulate cognitive processes and therefore transform behavior (van der Veer & Valsiner, 1991).

An early example is the so-called "messenger's wands" found in Australia (Leont'ev, 1959). They are large sticks or rectangular wooden slabs marked by a series of cuts. The sticks or slabs were given to messengers as they were sent out to deliver communications to distant tribes.

The notches were not arbitrary symbols of syllables or words, however. Instead, they were memory aids designed for the messengers. The notches designated certain persons and objects and their number and localities to the extent that they occurred in the given message. With the aid of this simple device, the messenger reconstructed the message at the time of delivery.

The uniquely human events associated with the use of these wands is that (1) new connections are established in the brain through the act of perceiving the external reminder and returning to the ideas they represent, and (2) the construction of the process of memorizing is accomplished by externally forcing an external object to remind the individual of something (Vygotsky, 1929/1977b, p. 69).

Further, agreeing with Thurnwald (1922), Vygotsky (1929; Vygotsky & Luria, 1930/1993) maintained that cultural diversity in symbols leads to differences in the level of mental functions. For example, in one village in Papua New Guinea, counting is accomplished by using body parts (Saxe, 1981). Counting begins with the right thumb, progresses around the hand, arm, shoulder, right ear, eyes, and then down the left side to the left forearm and fingers. Because the maximum number that may be counted using this method is 29, villagers have great difficulty with even simple addition and subtraction problems. Furthermore, the counting system limits the quantities that can be added and subtracted.

In contrast, cultures with advanced mathematical systems can produce individuals who think about differential equations in calculus. Therefore, the complexity of symbol use in a culture sets broad parameters for individual development.

Biological and Cultural-Historical Lines of Development
Analysis of the differences between animal and human behavior led to the identification of two qualitatively different lines of psychological development (Figure 11.1). One line is that of the biological factors that were a part of the evolutionary process. Included are the development of the central nervous system and physical growth and maturation. In the human species, biological factors dominate the early months of life, accounting for the development of perception, simple memory, and involuntary attention. The emergence of these elementary mental functions is also referred to as natural or primitive development (Vygotsky, 1929/1977b).

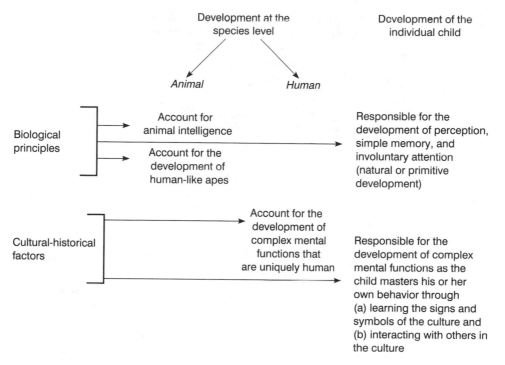

FIGURE 11.1
The influence of biological and cultural-historical lines of development

Part of the biological heritage of both animals and humans is the process referred to as **signalization**, which is the recognition of co-occurring stimuli in the environment (Vygotsky, 1929/1977b; 1931/1997i, p. 55). For example, the young gazelle learns to recognize the appearance of a lion as an indicator of danger. Similarly, a young child puts his hand on a hot stove and feels pain. On approaching the stove again, the child recalls the pain and exercises caution.

The essential difference between animal and human behavior is that humans progressed beyond their biological heritage. Early humans began to create and use culturally based signs and symbols, such as the knot-tying systems (quipu) used in ancient Peru for keeping count of those slain in battle and other events (Vygotsky & Luria, 1930/1993, p. 103). This and other creations of signs and their use is referred to as **signification** (Vygotsky, 1929/1977b; 1931/1997i, p. 55). This process differentiates human behavior from that of other animals; the signs created by early humans initiated cultural-historical development.

This second line of development also plays a key role in the cognitive growth of the individual child. The child inherits the symbol systems of his or her culture, and, depending on their complexity, these systems may lead to the development of rudimentary thinking skills (e.g., counting, simple addition and subtraction) or complex thinking skills (e.g., operating with differential functions and advanced probability systems). In other words, psychological development involves the transformation of primitive (or natural) mental functions to higher mental forms.

Although cultural-historical factors influence both the development of the species and of the child, three important differences may be identified. First, childhood does not repeat the stages that occurred in the development of civilization. (One early psychologist, G. Stanley Hall, maintained that childhood included the same stages as civilization, i.e., ontogeny recapitulates phylogeny. The theory, however, was found to be scientifically unsound.)

Second, in the development of the culture, humans are the creators and elaborators of sign systems. In contrast, the child is involved in the activity of mastering and internalizing the available sign systems and the associated reasoning processes. Third, when cultural development began for the human species, biological factors, in terms of influencing species development, were displaced. However, in the cognitive development of the individual child, biological factors become subordinated to cultural development in a complex transformative process.

In summary, the behavior of a modern cultured adult is the result of two different processes of mental development. One is the biological evolution of the animal species that gave rise to the species *Homo sapiens*. The second is the process of historical development that transformed primitive humans into humans who use signs and symbols to change their mental functioning (Vygotsky, 1931/1966).

The Experimental-Genetic (Developmental) Method

Vygotsky described the processes of cognitive development as complex and everchanging. However, the problem with experimental research is that these processes have not been studied (Vygotsky, 1931/1966, p. 21). Instead, psychological research has made use of only one model, that of stimulus–response. Regardless of the process under study, the psychologist exerts some action on the individual or exposes him or her to particular stimuli and analyzes the individual's reaction. Different constellations of stimuli and various reactions have been studied. However, not one fundamental step has been made beyond this basic model (Vygotsky, 1931/1966, p. 21). Until psychology bases its studies on the premise that psychological functions change under the influence of sociocultural experience, it will not discover the laws of human behavior (Leont'ev, 1977, p. 61).

To discover the dynamics of the development of human mental functions, Vygotsky (1929/1979b) and his co-workers devised experiments referred to as the **experimental-genetic method**. The researchers modeled their experiments on those that Köhler conducted with anthropoid apes (Vygotsky, 1929). The apes were placed in problem-solving situations with a means to the solution nearby. Similarly, Vygotsky and his colleagues presented children with tasks that were above their natural capacities, such as remembering a list of words. Objects were available nearby that could assist the child, such as a set of pictures. The researchers observed whether the additional stimuli ceased being neutral stimuli and became part of the problem-solving process, thereby changing the nature of the process. By implementing the tasks with children of different ages, the researchers identified differences in cognitive functioning (see Vygotsky & Luria, 1930/1993, pp. 175–192).

This experimental model is referred to as the functional method of double stimulation (Vygotsky, 1929, p. 430; 1984/1999a, p. 59). That is, the child's behavior is organized by two sets of stimuli, each of which has a function in behavior. One is the object of the task (such as remembering a set of words) and the other can serve as an auxiliary means to complete the psychological operation (e.g., a set of pictures). In the "forbidden colors" game, for example, the child forfeited points for "forbidden" answers, such as naming the color red and naming any color more than once. Examples of the 18 questions (the first stimulus set) included "Do you go to school? What color are the desks in school? Do you like to play? What color is grass?" (Vygotsky, 1929/1979b; Vygotsky & Luria, 1930/1993, p. 191). The child also received a set of cards, each a different color (the second stimulus set).

Observations indicated that preschoolers did not use the cards effectively, often looking at them at inappropriate times. However, older children (1) set aside the cards with the forbidden colors, and (2) added cards to the stack as they named other colors.

The importance of implementing this model with children of different ages was to explain the origins and causal-dynamic connections of a cognitive process to other processes that influence its development (Vygotsky, 1930/1977a, p. 76). In this way, research avoids addressing a complex reaction in its "finished and dead form . . . in its automatized form" (p. 75). At that point, processes have become a sort of fossil (p. 71).

Summary of Basic Assumptions

First, Vygotsky maintained that psychology should study humans, rather than animals, to discover the unique aspects of human cognition. Second, three philosophical views that formed the foundation of his work are (1) the Spinozan perspective that humans are rational and gradually gain control of their own thinking, (2) cognitive change can be characterized as the dialectical synthesis described by G. W. F. Hegel, and (3) the tools developed by humans changed their nature as well as the environment.

Third, Vygotsky identified psychological tools, which are the signs and symbols that serve as instruments of thought, as essential in the development of higher cognitive functions. These psychological tools, which are the products of one's culture, set broad limits on the level of higher cognitive thinking that the child can attain. That is, biological principles account for the development of natural (or primitive) functions whereas the signs and symbols of one's culture contribute to the development of complex ways of thinking.

Fourth, because cognitive processes are dynamic and ever-changing, they must be studied using research methods that reveal their dynamic nature. The aim of psychological research is (1) process analysis rather than object analysis, (2) an accounting that reveals real, causal, or dynamic relations, and (3) an explanation of the origins of cognitive processes (Vygotsky, 1931/1997a).

The Components of Cognitive Development

Key principles describe the transformation of primitive mental functions, such as involuntary attention and simple memory, into complex functions such as logical memory. Two principles are the two branches of cultural cognitive development and the general law of genetic development. The other major concepts are the role of imitation and the natural history of the sign.

The Two Branches of Cognitive Development

Vygotsky (1931/1966, 1931/1997m, p. 14) maintained that the development of higher mental functions encompassed two sets of processes that, initially, may seem to be unrelated. Instead, the development of higher cognitive functions consists of

> ... two inseparably connected but never confluent streams of development of the higher forms of behavior. These are, first, the processes of mastering the external means of cultural development and thinking—language, writing, counting and drawing, and secondly, the processes of development of the special higher mental functions. (Vygotsky, 1931/1966, p. 16)

Stated another way, "in the process of development, the child not only masters the items of cultural experience, but the cultural forms of reasoning" (Vygotsky, 1929, p. 415). That is, complex cognitive functions are developed in the process of subordinating symbol systems to human control to carry out cognitive tasks (Vygotsky, 1929/1979b). Using colored cards to monitor the color names that one has used in a game is an example. Constructing a hierarchy of related concepts in a subject area is another.

The inference that may be made from these statements is that learning to communicate with language is a necessary but not sufficient condition for the development of higher cognitive functions. This inference is supported by Vygotsky's description of signs and symbols as only potential psychological tools. Specifically, "a stimulus becomes a psychological tool not by virtue of its physical qualities ... (but) by virtue of its use as a means of influencing the mind and behavior" (Vygotsky, unpubl. manu./1997k, p. 85). Examples of psychological tools and their complex systems include "language, different forms of numeration and counting, mnemotechnical techniques, algebraic symbolism, works of art, writing, schemes, diagrams, maps, blueprints, all sorts of conventional signs, etc." (p. 85).

The General Law of Genetic Development

Central issues to understanding a basic principle of Vygotsky's theory are the components of the law of genetic development and the role of peers, teachers, and the learner (discussed in the section "Principles of Instruction").

The basis for Vygotsky's law of genetic development is the social-behavioral relationship described by the French psychologist Pierre Janet (van der Veer & Valsiner, 1988). Specifically, all higher psychological processes develop through the application of aspects of social relationships to oneself, and words are the most powerful social stimuli because they originated as commands (Janet, 1926, 1929, cited in van der Veer & Valsiner, 1988; Vygotsky, 1931/1966).

Vygotsky (1931/1997c) stated the general law of genetic development as

> every function in the cultural development of the child appears on the stage twice, in two planes, first, the social, then the psychological, first between people as an intermental category, then within the child as an intramental category. (p. 106)

In other words, every higher mental function was external or social before it became an internal mental function (p. 105). Included in the higher functions are categorical perception, conceptual thinking (verbal and mathematical), logical memory, and voluntary (self-organized) attention (see the section "The Nature of Complex Thought").

The law of genetic development also applies to learning the meanings of words, signs, and symbols. An example is a child learning the pointing gesture (Vygotsky, 1931/1966, 1931/1997c, p. 104). First, when the child tries to grasp an out-of-reach object, her hands are stretched toward the object and are left hanging in the air. The movement is objectively indicating an object. When the mother comes to help, the situation changes. That is, the response to the unsuccessful grasping movement of the child is a reaction by the mother, not by the object (pp. 104–105).

Later, the child is able to link her grasping movement to the total situation, and the child understands her actions as a pointing gesture. Here the function of the movement changes. Instead of a movement directed toward an object, it becomes a form of communication, a movement directed toward another person. The child then uses the gesture as a signal or indicator to others. In other words, the conscious use of the gesture is late in its development. The child also is the last one to realize its meaning. At this point, the gesture becomes a direction for the child herself.

The Role of Imitation

The process of the internal acquisition of the role of signs or symbols is not automatic. Instead, the transition from the external social plane to the internal psychological plane is one in which the child begins to practice with respect to himself the same forms of behavior that others formerly practiced with respect to him (Vygotsky, 1931/1997n, p. 88).

Particularly important is that such actions are the key to the individual's mastery of his or her behavior (p. 88). In other words, a basic path in the cultural development of the child is imitation (p. 95). However, in Vygotsky's (1931/1997n) view, imitation is not a simple mechanical transfer from one to another. Instead, the process of imitation requires "a certain understanding of the significance of the action of another" (p. 95). For example, if the individual knows nothing of chess, she cannot play a game even if a chess master shows her how (Vygotsky, 1934/1987b, p. 209). In other words, Vygotsky restricts the meaning of imitation to refer to "operations that are more or less directly connected with the mental activity of the child" (Vygotsky, 1930–1931/1998c, p. 202).

The Natural History of the Sign

The primitive mental functions—simple perceptions, natural memory, and involuntary (passive) attention—are linked to concrete experience. These functions are represented by the S–R model. More complex tasks, however, such as the operation of remembering, illustrate the role of auxiliary stimuli in thinking. However, learning to direct one's thinking is a complex, lengthy process that Vygotsky (1931/1997n) referred to as the natural history of the sign.

As indicated in Table 11.1, the first attempts to use signs, such as pictures to remember a set of words, is based on a lack of understanding of their role. That is, the child does not establish a clear semantic link from the pictures to the word. In stage 3, however, the child systematically establishes clear connections between the signs and the stimuli in the experiment. The fourth stage is that of internal sign use, the highest level of development. At this stage, individuals internalize the process of directing memory and attention through the use of self-generated stimuli. In one experiment, for example, one subject remembered the words *beach*, *hail*, and *dress* by creating the sentence, "A lady walked on the beach; it began to hail and ruined her dress" (Leont'ev, 1959, p. 94).

In a series of experiments on word recall, Leont'ev (1959) found qualitative differences among different age groups in the ability to make use of an auxiliary stimulus. A series of 15 words was read to each subject, one at a time, and the subjects were permitted to select a picture from a group for each word to assist them in later recall.

The preschool children either selected pictures randomly and were unable to use them, or they made associations between the pictures and words that did not facilitate word recall. In other words, the mere presence of an association is

TABLE 11.1
Natural History of the Sign

Stage of Sign Use	Characteristics	Arithmetic Example
1. Natural or primitive	Child tries to solve a problem by direct means, such as remembering different selection reactions (striking a particular key) through memorization	Young child can differentiate a group of 3 apples from a group of 7 apples by sight; cannot differentiate between groups of 16 and 19 apples
2. Recognition of the importance of signs	Attempts to use signs without realizing the method of their action; many errors	Beginning of counting on one's fingers, but makes errors and is unaware of the implications
3. External sign use	Systematically matches external signs to stimuli and establishes his/her own connection between them	Counts accurately using fingers, can subtract 2 from 7 in this way
4. Internal sign use	Child relies on internal or self-generated stimuli	The child is able to count in his/her head

Summarized from Vygotsky (1931/1997c, pp. 117–119; 1929, pp. 424–428)

insufficient to guide the child's memory. This level of functioning is analogous to the performance of a man who is able to press on a lever but who is unable to use the skill to move a heavy rock (Leont'ev, 1959, p. 141).

A qualitative change was found in the behavior of the school children. They formed word-picture links that indicated "an adaptation to the future conceived of *as a future*" (Leont'ev, 1959, p. 147). In this action, word and picture are combined into a complex integrated structure. This operation indicates that primitive or natural memory has been converted into an intellectual operation (i.e., a new form of memory).

In contrast, the adults formed complex verbal links between word and picture and often did not use the pictures during recall. Memory had become self-directed in that the created verbal association served as the cue. These phases in the development of mediated memorization indicate that intermediate forms of thinking appear between primitive mental processes and higher mental processes (Kozulin, 1990).

A similar developmental sequence was found in the experiments (described earlier) in which children were given colored cards to help them answer a series of questions. The young children often looked at the cards at inappropriate times or, when setting aside the forbidden colors, named that very color (Vygotsky, 1929/1979b). Older children, however, used the cards successfully to direct their attention and to assist their recall of acceptable colors. Also, the quality of their answers changed. For example, when the forbidden color was "green," grass was described as "In the fall, it is yellow" (Vygotsky, 1929/1979b).

The Development of Speech

In Vygotsky's (1934/1987d) view, the analysis of thinking and speech was a major task for psychology, and the central problem was "*the relationship of thought to word*" (p. 43). He noted that prior efforts to address this issue had oscillated between two extreme poles: the complete fusion of thought and word and the complete separation of thought and word, and neither was correct (p. 44). Instead, speech begins to develop independent of thought, and this stage is referred to as "preintellectual" (Vygotsky, 1934/1987c) (see Table 11.2).

Then, "at a certain point, the two lines cross: thinking becomes verbal and speech becomes intellectual" (Vygotsky, 1934/1987c, p. 112). This process begins when the child discovers the "instructional function" of a word; that is, everything has a name (Vygotsky, 1929, p. 429; Vygotsky, 1934/1987c). However, initially, the child treats the name as simply another characteristic of the object (Vygotsky, 1934/1987c, p. 118). That is, "the child masters the external structure earlier than the internal structure" (p. 118). Therefore, this stage is referred to as "naively psychological."

In the third stage, social speech differentiates into two types: communicative and egocentric (Vygotsky, 1934/1987e, p. 74). Egocentric speech first simply accompanies the child's practical activity. Then it takes on a planning function or the function of resolving problems (Vygotsky 1934/1987c). It is speech for oneself, although it is external physiologically (p. 114). Thus, egocentric speech is a "transitional form in the movement from external to internal speech" (Vygotsky, 1934/1987e, p. 76). When a child, using speech, begins to make a plan, his practical

TABLE 11.2
Stages in the Child's Development of Speech

Stage	Characteristics
1. Preintellectual	A means of social contact in the first year of life; includes laughter, babbling, pointing, and gesture
2. "Naively" psychological	Speech and thinking begin to coincide in second year of life when child discovers things have names; many words are used without grasping the true meaning (e.g., "because, but, when")
3. Dominance of external speech	
Communicative	Speech fulfills a social function
Egocentric	Speech first accompanies child's actions in planning and problem-solving, then becomes essential in planning; the "middle link" between external and internal speech
4. Intellectual	External operation moves to the internal plane and undergoes profound change; speech becomes soundless

Summarized from Vygotsky (1934/1987c)

thinking rises to a new level. Behavior is no longer determined by the structure of the visual field, "but by a new form of activity—verbal thinking" (Vygotsky, 1930–1931/1998a, p. 115).

Naturalistic observations of low-income Appalachian children conducted by Berk and Garvin (1984) supported Vygotsky's views. The researchers found that the major function of private speech is self-guidance and that it is greater during cognitively demanding academic tasks. Research also indicated that children who use private speech in conjunction with challenging tasks are more attentive and show greater improvement than their peers (Berk, 2000; Berk & Stuhl, 1995). Also, the rates of private speech are higher over a longer development period for children with learning problems (Berk, 2000).

The final stage of intellectual development is the internalization of egocentric speech. Egocentric speech becomes inner speech as well as the basic structure of the child's thinking. Inner speech, however, is speech carried out almost without words because it is speech for oneself, not for communication (Vygotsky, 1934/1987f, p. 277).

In summary, the child's intellectual growth requires that the child master the social means of thought, which is language. In other words, verbal thought is not an innate or natural form of behavior. Instead, it is determined by a cultural-historical process with characteristics that differ from natural (primitive) forms of thought.

Both Piaget and Vygotsky considered the acquisition of speech to be a major activity in cognitive development. They differed in their view of the child's egocentric speech. For Piaget, egocentric speech is a characteristic of pre-operational thinking, and this form of speech disappears as the child moves into concrete operations.

In contrast, Vygotsky viewed egocentric speech as an important transitional stage between external and inner speech. It is a significant phase in the child's learning to solve problems and to manage his or her own cognitive activity. Thus, egocentric speech is a transitional stage between social speech and inner speech for thinking.

Of importance is that the development of inner speech is determined by the nature of egocentric speech. Specifically, the structure of speech mastered by the child becomes the basic structure of the child's thinking (Vygotsky, 1934/1987c, p. 120). The implication is that children with impoverished vocabulary and a limited sense of word meaning will have difficulties in planning and problem solving. In other words, developing inner speech is not a guarantee that individuals reach the levels of advanced thinking (the higher psychological functions). For example, in the cross-cultural studies of Vygotsky and Luria (Luria, 1976), illiterate peasants were able to use speech in thinking that simply echoed practical and situational activity. In contrast, people with some education used abstract categories that restructured situational experience (Kozulin, 1984, p. 110).

Development in Children with Disabilities

The basic principles in Vygotsky's cultural-historical theory apply to children with disabilities as well. That is, cognitive development occurs in the context of the social activities of children with adults. The prevailing view at the time Vygotsky was writing was that a sensory defect or a mental weakness was regarded as a biological problem. The then-current belief was that a defect could be compensated for by a heightened sensitivity in another sensory function. Kozulin (1990) noted that examples are the senses of hearing and touch in the blind and vision in the deaf.

In contrast, Vygotsky viewed the problem of the disabling condition as primarily social (Gindis, 1995). That is, society's response to those with disabilities leads to social deprivation that results in defective development (Vygotsky, 1983/1993). The disability, in other words, alters the child's relationship with the world and affects his or her interactions with people. Thus, "the blindness of an American farmer's daughter, of a Ukrainian landowner's son, of a German duchess, of a Russian peasant—are all psychologically different facts" (Vygotsky, 1983, p. 50), in Gindis (1995).

Physical disabilities, such as blindness or deafness, alter the child's relationship with the world and affect his or her interactions with people. Vygotsky noted that self-reports from individuals with these disabilities indicated that the defects are not perceived as "abnormalities" until they are brought into the social context (Gindis, 1995, p. 78).

The disabilities prevent the children from mastering social skills and acquiring knowledge in the same ways and at the same rate as other children. Also, deafness is a more serious disability than blindness because it prevents the mastery of speech, blocks verbal communication, and limits entry to the world of culture (p. 78).

Vygotsky described disabilities in terms of primary and secondary defects. A primary defect is an impairment of biological origin. Secondary defects are the distortion of higher psychological functions that result from social factors. For example, many symptoms of disabling conditions, such as immature behavior and primitive emotional reactions, are secondary defects that are acquired in the process of social interaction.

Therefore, instead of training other sensory functions, such as acuteness of hearing, Vygotsky maintained that physical or mental defects can be compensated for through alternative, yet equivalent, means of cultural development (Gindis, 1995). Where necessary, symbolic systems should be changed, while preserving the basic meaning of social communication. Examples are the Braille system, sign language, lip-reading, and finger spelling. Further, societies should continue developing special psychological tools that can provide the social and cultural interactions essential for development. Many of today's computer developments, such as activating a keyboard through a breathing apparatus for paralyzed individuals, are examples.

Summary

Three general principles that are the components of cognitive development may be identified. First, Vygotsky (1931/1966) described two branches of cognitive development. One involves mastering the symbol systems of the culture and the other involves developing the cultural forms of reasoning.

Second, the law of genetic development states that all complex functions begin as social interactions between individuals and gradually acquire meaning and are internalized by the learner. However, also required is practice by the learner of the behaviors that adults used with him or her.

The third principle describes the process whereby speech and other artificial symbols are first mastered as a form of communication and then become instrumental in structuring and managing the child's thinking. The young child, for example, is unable to use pictures as cues to recall a set of words. However, adults often construct complex verbal relationships as memory aids. The lengthy process of learning to use artificial symbols to structure one's thinking begins with learning to use auxiliary stimuli to mediate one's memory. Gradually, over an extended period of time, the individual acquires the capability to construct symbols to aid in thinking. This process is referred to as the natural history (law) of the sign.

The use of speech also changes throughout childhood and follows the same four stages as the use of symbols in thinking. These stages are (1) preintellectual, (2) "naively" psychological, (3) dominance of external sign use, and (4) internalization.

The Nature of Complex Thought

Two conceptualizations developed by Vygotsky reflect his views on the nature of complex thinking. They are the higher mental functions and his concept of development.

The Higher Mental Processes

Like Piaget, Vygotsky (1930–1931/1998a, 1930–1931/1998b) believed that individuals did not attain the higher forms of thinking prior to adolescence. However, Vygotsky described the outcomes of cognitive development as including categorical perception, conceptual thinking (verbal and mathematical), logical memory (memory based on connections and relations among concepts), and voluntary (self-organized) attention. Of importance is that the higher mental functions are not merely a continuation of the elementary functions; instead, they are qualitatively new mental formations.

Table 11.3 illustrates the major differences between the primitive or elementary functions and the higher mental functions. Elementary functions are the natural inborn psychological structures conditioned primarily by biological characteristics (Vygotsky, 1931/1966, p. 31). They are represented by the S–R model and are characterized by immediacy, a reliance on concrete experience, and thought linked to action.

The transformations that lead from elementary to higher mental functions are the result of a lengthy period of development in which the control of one's

TABLE 11.3
A Comparison of Primitive and Higher Mental Functions

	Primitive Functions	Higher Mental Functions
1. Processes	Simple perception, natural memory, involuntary attention	Categorical perception, logical memory, conceptual thinking, self-regulated attention
2. Source of control	Stimulation from the environment	The use of both "object stimuli" and "means stimuli" by the individual to master and control his or her own behavior
3. Dynamics	Co-occurrence of two stimuli	Creation of new links through the individual's artificial combination of stimuli
4. Defining characteristics	Immediacy; bounded by concrete experience	Characterized by conscious awareness (of the processes), abstraction, and control
5. Thinking and reasoning	Determined by natural memory; limited to reproducing established practical situations	Abstract, conceptual; makes use of logical relations and generalizations
6. Origin	Biological factors	Cultural-historical development

mental processes shifts from the environment to the individual. A prerequisite to developing the higher mental functions is awareness of one's thought processes and some control of them. However, the young child is not consciously aware of her thought processes, and even the "school-age child realizes his own thinking operations inadequately still, and for this reason he cannot fully master them" (Vygotsky, 1930–1931/1998b, p. 65). In other words, perceiving one's own thought processes is a prerequisite to mastery and developing logical thinking.

Table 11.4 compares the specific characteristics of each of the elementary and higher cognitive functions. As indicated, the child's memory relies on visual images and concrete experience, whereas the memory of the adolescent (who has mastered the higher functions) relies on concepts with all the connections and relations with other concepts. Similarly, categorical perception is governed by conceptual thinking, and voluntary attention is organized through symbols. In other words, unlike the elementary functions, in which natural memory dominates throughout, the relationship is reversed in the higher mental functions. For the young child, "intellect is a function of memory, then, in the adolescent, memory is a function of intellect" (Vygotsky, 1930–1931/1998a, p. 96).

The Concept of Development

Referring to the work of Ernest Meumann, Vygotsky (1963) described two levels of development. One is actual or completed development. This level is determined by mental tests in which the child attempts to solve problems of increasing difficulty that are standardized for the child's chronological age level (Vygotsky, 1930–1931/1998c, p. 201). The problems that the child solves independently represent the actual level of development.

TABLE 11.4

A Comparison of Elementary and Higher Mental Functions

Simple memory	*Logical memory*
Relies on visual images and concrete experience	Recall is in the form of concepts "directly connected with comprehension, analysis, and systematization of material" (Vygotsky, 1930–1931/1998a, p. 98)
Simple perceptions	*Categorical perception*
Based on concrete experience	A synthesis of visual perception and abstract and conceptual thinking
Involuntary attention	*Voluntary attention*
Controlled from the outside; repelled by or attracted to different objects	Controlled internally; directed through symbols
Syncretic thinking	*Conceptual thinking*
Pre-conceptual; thinking proceeds from particular to particular	Involves recognizing a thing in all its connections and relations that are synthesized in the concept (Vygotsky, 1930–1931/1998b, p. 53)

Summarized from Vygotsky (1930–1931/1998a, 1930–1931/1998b, 1933/1997d).

However, equally important are the problems that the child can solve with assistance. This level is referred to as the zone of potential or proximal development and it represents the area of "immature, but maturing processes" (Vygotsky, 1930–1931/1998c, p. 202). Vygotsky suggested that the school psychologist should implement any of four strategies to determine this level of development. They are (1) demonstrate solving the problem and observe whether the child can imitate the demonstration, (2) begin solving the problem and ask the child to complete the solution, (3) ask the child to cooperate with another more developed child in solving the problem, or (4) explain the process of solving the problem to the child, ask leading questions, analyze the problem for the child, and so on (p. 202). In other words, these approaches can determine "precisely the mental maturation that must be realized in the proximal and subsequent periods of his stage of development" (p. 203). (Vygotsky [1930–1931/1998c] referred to determining the actual level of development and the zone of proximal development as comprising *normative age-level diagnostics* [p. 204].)

In summary, the higher cognitive functions are the uniquely human capabilities that are the products of cultural-historical development. Unlike the primitive or elementary functions, the higher cognitive functions are characterized by conscious awareness (of one's thinking), abstraction, and control. They also involve the use of logical relations and generalizations. Important for cognitive development is to assess both the child's level of actual development and the level or zone of proximal development. Such an assessment can identify the cognitive functions that are in a stage of maturation, but are not yet fully developed.

PRINCIPLES OF INSTRUCTION

Like Piaget, Vygotsky analyzed particular developmental processes responsible for complex cognitive functioning. Piaget emphasized the growth of logical thinking as the goal of cognitive development. Vygotsky, in contrast, described the transformation of simple perception, involuntary attention, and simple memory into categorical perception, conceptual thinking, logical memory, and self-organized attention.

Neither Piaget nor Vygotsky developed explicit principles of instruction. Although both theorists commented on certain aspects of the teaching process, instructional principles may be inferred only indirectly from their writings.

Basic Assumptions

The role of the culture in learning and the relationship between instruction and development provide the foundation for inferring basic assumptions about instruction.

Role of the Culture

According to Vygotsky, the culture does more than provide the setting in which learning occurs. Instead, the very structure of social functioning determines the structure of individual psychological functioning. That is, major concepts and ideas as well as the means of communication and ways of viewing the world are created by the culture. Thus, the child learns to think in ways that are directly fostered and developed by his or her particular culture.

Therefore, the basic structures of perception, representation, and self-awareness are likely to differ across different historical conditions. Vygotsky and Luria developed a research plan to analyze the cultural-historical shaping of mental processes. The research was conducted in the early 1930s in remote parts of the Soviet Union that had been faced with a radical restructuring of their economic system and culture (Luria, 1976). The research was conducted in the villages and mountain pasture lands of Uzbekistan and Kirghizia. The groups compared on various tasks were (1) Ichkari women in remote villages whose lives were controlled by strict Islamic codes; (2) peasants in remote villages who were not involved in socialized labor; (3) collective farm workers who had experience in planning, distributing labor, and monitoring work output; and (4) women students in a teacher's school.

The tasks, which were accompanied by in-depth interviews, involved perceptual and memory strategies, classification, and problem solving. In one task, the subjects were shown 27 different hues of skeins of wool. When asked to name the colors, the collective farm workers and women students used categorical names (red, blue, yellow) with occasional designations (light yellow, dark blue) (Luria, 1976). In contrast, the Ichkari women used graphic names, such as fruit-drop iris and spoiled cotton (p. 26).

When asked to group the different skeins, the collective farm workers and students usually arranged all the colors in seven or eight groups. In contrast, some of the Ichkari women maintained that the task could not be done while others arranged the skeins of yarn into series of colors according to increasing brightness. One series, for example, included pale pink, pale yellow, and pale blue. In other words, attempts by the experimenter to obtain a color grouping with only one primary color in a group led to failure to perform the task (Luria, 1976, p. 30). The study concluded that comparing objects according to logical attributes and generalizing them to well-known logical categories are not universal operations (Luria, 1971, p. 269).

Relationship Between Instruction and Development

According to Vygotsky (1934/1962; 1934/1987b), instruction influences development in two ways. One is that good learning precedes and leads development. That is, the tasks that the child can accomplish in collaboration with the teacher today, she can accomplish alone tomorrow (Vygotsky, 1934/1962, p. 104). Thus, both instruction and imitation play a major role in the child's development. "They bring out the specifically human qualities of the mind and lead the child to new developmental levels" (Vygotsky, 1934/1962, p. 104).

Planning instruction, therefore, includes determining the lowest threshold at which instruction may begin, since only a certain minimal development of cognitive functioning is required (Vygotsky, 1934/1962, p. 104). Like Montessori, Vygotsky believed that each subject of instruction is most influential at a certain period because the child is most receptive at that time. Therefore, important qualities for teachers include a sensitivity to the actions and words of the child and the ability to structure tasks so that the child may exercise his or her emerging capabilities.

The second way that instruction influences development is in the learning of school subjects, such as reading and mathematics. These subjects include operations that require awareness and deliberate control. Learning to master and consciously control operations (such as addition and multiplication) and to think in subject matter concepts furthers the development of complex mental functions (Vygotsky, 1934/1987b).

In summary, two basic assumptions related to instruction may be inferred from Vygotsky's theory. The first is that the structure of social relations in the cultural setting determines the individual's psychological structure. The second is that instruction should precede and thereby maximally influence development.

Components of Instruction

Important components of instruction are (1) determining the appropriate level of instruction, (2) implementing the genetic law of cognitive development, and (3) developing students' verbal thinking.

Determining the Appropriate Level of Instruction

Vygotsky (1934/1987b) maintained that school instruction plays an essential role in the child's cognitive development. To be useful, instruction must move ahead of development and lead it. Specifically, *"instruction impells (sic) or wakens a whole series of functions that are in a stage of maturation lying in the zone of proximal development"* (p. 212). To succeed in this role, instruction should focus on problems that the student can solve "in collaboration with or under the guidance of a teacher" (p. 211).

That is, instruction should occur between the lower threshold of development (the problems the child can complete independently, such as the problems on an I.Q. test) and an upper threshold represented by the problems the child can complete with assistance (Vygotsky, 1934/1987b, p. 211). The implication is that, if psychological testing does not include an assessment of the upper threshold of the child's cognitive functioning, then the teacher should schedule time to determine informally the level of the child's joint problem solving. This exercise can provide information to the teacher as to the appropriate level of instruction for the child.

Vygotsky (1934/1987b) cautioned that a particular lesson in a subject such as arithmetic will not correspond to a particular stage of development (p. 207). However, for example, arithmetic instruction can have an important influence on moving attention from the domain of lower mental functions to that of the higher mental functions (p. 207). Voluntary attention, a higher mental function, begins when "one controls one's own behavior with the help of symbolic stimuli" (Vygotsky, 1930/1999b, p. 36). Also "the first, second, third, and fourth components of arithmetic instruction may be inconsequential for the development of arithmetic thinking, but some fifth component may be decisive" (Vygotsky, 1934/1987b, p. 207). That is, the child, at that point, has learned a general principle.

An additional point is that the zone of proximal development is not always manifested in social interaction. For example, the school-age child operates in the zone of proximal development as he or she solves problems at home "on the basis of a model he has been shown in class," i.e., imitates the teacher through a process of re-creating previous classroom collaboration with the teacher. The "help," Vygotsky (1934/1987b) noted, is "invisibly present" (p. 216). Another example is a six-year-old who, growing up in a home with many books, newspapers, and magazines where the parents are avid readers, imitates them and learns to read without explicit instruction (Valsiner, 1988, p. 148).

Implementing the Law of Genetic Development

According to Vygotsky, internal psychological functions begin as interactions between the child and a knowledgeable member of the culture. However, the assumption should not be made that a sudden clean shift occurs from social to individual functioning. That is, a child does not simply work with someone on a task and then begin to carry it out independently (Wertsch, 1985b, p. 158). Instead, contemporary research indicates that several changes take place on the interpersonal level, and each is accompanied by a change on the intrapersonal level. Wertsch (1985b) identified five important factors in the transition from inter- to intrapsychological functioning. They are (1) the cognitive readiness of the child, (2) a willingness by the adult to transfer responsibility to the child, (3) the adult's use of "reflective assessments" as feedback to the child on the significance of particular behaviors, (4) the explicitness of the adult's directives, and (5) the construction of a joint definition of the task that gradually moves toward a culturally appropriate definition (Wertsch, 1985b, p. 166).

Establishing a joint definition of the task initially is particularly important because the adult and the child likely bring different concepts to a task setting. Therefore, the challenge to the adult is to find a way to communicate with the child so that he or she can participate in the task with the adult. This communication is the foundation for the transition to interpsychological functioning (Wertsch, 1985b, p. 161).

Vygotsky (1983/1997b) noted that in implementing lessons, it would be foolish not to consider the concrete and graphic nature of pupils' memory (p. 224). However, he also cautioned that "it would also be folly to cultivate this type of memory. This would be to keep the child at a lower step of development and to fail to see that the concrete type of memory is only a transitional step to a higher type, that concrete memory must be overcome in the process of teaching" (p. 224).

Also important is that social interaction is only the first step. The learner's subsequent activities are also essential. The student must imitate, invent, and practice with respect to himself the same forms of behavior that others formerly practiced with respect to him (Vygotsky, 1931/1966, p. 157).

An example is the teaching of composition to older Brazilian women in the College of the Bahamas (Fiore & Elsasser, 1982). Teaching began with the use of "generative themes," which are themes drawn from the students' daily lives. These themes were important because they allowed the students to explore the larger cultural and historical implications of personal experience. One generative theme, for example, was marriage. The students gradually moved from personal anecdotes to more sophisticated forms of expression, such as cause and effect, definition, and comparison and contrast. The increasing sophistication of the women's writing was accompanied by a more analytical approach to the issues.

Developing Students' Verbal Thinking

A major premise to Vygotsky's theory is that the signs and symbols used for communication in a culture are also the mechanisms for cognitive development. When the child enters school, word meaning and speech are two mechanisms that can facilitate the development of verbal thinking. First, the inner aspect of the word (word meaning) is key to freeing the child from perception and sensation (Vygotsky, 1934/1987d, p. 47). The reason is that "the word does not relate to a single object, but to an *entire group or class of objects*" (p. 47). In other words, from a psychological perspective, word meaning is primarily a generalization and is, therefore, *a verbal act of thought* (p. 47).

Therefore, following Vygotsky, a goal of school instruction should be developing word meanings. However, if the expectation is that the student is to internalize existing knowledge, thought processes are not required to grow, change, and develop. That is, teaching subjects that involve symbol systems, such as writing and mathematics, will not bring about the development of complex mental functions if the goal is the transmission of knowledge (Elsasser & John-Steiner, 1977, p. 363).

Second, "thinking depends on speech, on the means of thinking, and on the child's socio-cultural experience" (Vygotsky, 1934/1987c, p. 120). In other words, the structure of speech mastered by the child becomes the basic structure of the child's thinking (p. 120). Thus, the development of inner speech, an important mechanism of thinking, is dependent on the child's basic speech. In the classroom, this relationship has implications for children with poor vocabularies and those whose primary language is a dialect of English (non-standard English) or a language other than English.

Also important is that the child's internal speech at school age is a weak, unstable form that is not yet fully functional (Vygotsky, 1930–1931/1998b, p. 70). Therefore, "in order to think, the school child must think aloud" (p. 70). When a child's who has solved a problem on her own obtains an absurd answer, the teacher asks her to solve it aloud. Also important is to teach her to be conscious of her own operations, following each step, and to control the course of her thinking (p. 71).

The research conducted by Vygotsky and his colleagues indicated that children gradually move from external sign use to inner speech. School tasks should focus on developing word meanings (generalizations) and assist children to develop their speed as a means of thinking.

In summary, the appropriate level of instruction for a student is the problem that a child can solve with assistance. Such an assessment indicates the cognitive processes that are in the period of maturation, referred to as the zone of proximal development. Also important in the classroom is to implement the law of genetic development in which the teacher or other knowledgeable adult works with the student in school tasks. The student must then imitate, invent, and practice the forms of behavior that were the focus of the interaction with the teacher. Finally, teachers also should work with children to assist them in learning word meanings and in learning to use speech as a tool of thinking.

Designing Instruction to Develop Complex Cognitive Functions

Important issues in developing complex cognitive functions are (1) the "foundational" psychological functions, (2) teaching writing, (3) the role of scientific (subject-matter) concepts, and (4) the role of peers, the teacher, and the learner.

The Foundational Psychological Functions.   Vygotsky (1934/1987b) identified two broad psychological functions that form the foundation of the higher cognitive functions. These two functions are conscious awareness of and mastery (volitional control) of one's mental activities (p. 208).

The importance of the foundational functions is that they begin to emerge at school age and school instruction is essential in their development. That is, consciousness of and self-regulatory control of one's thinking are in the child's zone of proximal development. For example, the preschool child can use the correct case and verb form in oral speech but is unaware that such forms exist, and he or she cannot conjugate a verb fully (p. 206). An important effect of school learning is developing conscious awareness and control of such activities. For example, the child becomes aware of different verb forms and tenses and can choose the correct form when writing.

Teaching Writing.   Vygotsky (1934/1987b) identified reasons for the child's difficulty in learning writing that also explain its contribution to developing thinking. First, it does not reproduce oral speech but is a unique speech function (p. 202). It requires a high degree of abstraction that "uses representations of words rather than the words themselves" (p. 202). In other words, "written speech is the algebra of speech" (p. 203).

Second, it is a conversation with a sheet of paper rather than another individual. Therefore, the child must conceptualize the receiver of the message. Third, the motivations for oral speech are present prior to conversing with another, for example. However, the motivations for writing are less accessible to the child when he begins to learn to write (p. 203). In written speech, the writer must create the situation (p. 203). Finally, in choosing words and phrases, unlike most oral speech, the process is intentional and must reflect expected syntactic sequence.

Therefore, instruction in writing is one of the most important subjects in the child's early school years because it requires deliberateness and analysis. Learning to write assists the child to develop the foundational cognitive functions of conscious awareness and control of one's thinking processes (p. 211).

Some writing curricula in the early grades address the motivational and deliberateness of the process. Provided are uninterrupted reading and writing time; access to books, picture books, and magazines; opportunities; for other students to serve as an audience of early drafts; and publication of the children's favorite pieces (see Harste, Short, & Burke, 1988).

The Role of Subject-Matter Concepts.   The process of the development of subject-matter concepts (referred to as scientific concepts by Vygotsky) in students "contains the key to the whole history of the child's mental development" (Vygotsky, 1934/1987b, p. 167). One reason is that, even at the simplest level of development, the concept is "an act of generalization" (p. 169). It is "a complex and true act of thinking that cannot be mastered through simple memorization" (p. 169).

Another reason is, at the highest level of development, "thinking in concepts leads to discovery of the deep connections that lie at the base of reality, to recognizing patterns that control reality, to ordering the perceived world with the help of the network of logical relations cast upon it" (Vygotsky, 1930–1931/1998b, p. 48). That is, subject-matter concepts in a domain can be represented in terms of other concepts, and they form an interrelated system. Mastery of subject-matter concepts means that the student can define them easily, implement them in various logical operations, and identify the relationships among them (Vygotsky, 1934/1987b, p. 218).

In contrast, spontaneous or everyday concepts do not have these advantages. They are learned through the child's experience, and their weakness is in the incapacity for abstraction (Vygotsky, 1934/1987b, p. 169). An example is the child's concept of "brother," which is "saturated with the child's own rich personal experience" (p. 178).

Vygotsky (1930–1931/1998b) emphasized that the form of thinking (thinking in concepts that involves the higher cognitive functions) cannot be separated from the content of thinking (pp. 34–39). That is, mastery of a complex system such as algebra does not mean simply filling the forms of thinking present in a three-year-old with new content. New content requires new forms of thinking (p. 35). Particularly important is that "cognition, in the true sense of that word, science, art, various spheres of cultural life may be adequately assimilated only in concepts" (p. 42).

Implications for teaching subjects in middle and high school are (1) to focus on the system of interrelationships among the concepts in the domain, (2) to require students to explain the connections among them, and (3) to implement them logically in different problems and other situations.

The Role of Peers, the Teachers, and the Learner.   Many writings on instruction describe the primacy of large- and small-group discussions as an instructional approach, often citing Vygotsky as the source. O'Connor (1996) noted "These beliefs about classroom discussions are generally buttressed by reference to Vygtoskyan theory, in that collaboration or joint reasoning, the 'intermental' plane of cognition, is viewed as the genesis of a child's individual 'intermental' functioning" (p. 495). However, the term *collaboration*, when used by Vygotsky in reference to the school setting, refers to collaboration between teacher and student (Gredler & Shields, 2004). An example is "the teacher, working with the school child on a given question, explains, informs, inquires, corrects, and forces the child himself to explain; [and] when the child solves a problem, although the teacher is not present, he or she must make independent use of the earlier collaboration" (Vygotsky, 1934/1987b, p. 216). Also, some educators state that, as a part of instruction, the teacher should initially control task elements that are beyond the learner's capability to allow the learner to concentrate on the elements she can complete. This directive reflects Vygotsky's recommendations for *assessment* of the child's cognitive functions that are in the zone of proximal development, not Vygotsky's suggestions for instruction.

Further, on occasion, the general law of genetic development is described in some secondary sources as referring to the relations *among* people instead of the relations *between* people. This subtle change confuses the concept of adult-child collaboration described in the school setting by Vygotsky.

Vygotsky does name one situation in which a particular type of peer interaction can contribute to cognitive development. The situation is that of children contesting the statements of other children, the argumentation described by Piaget (Vygotsky, 1931/1966, p. 40). Specifically, argumentation among children becomes the process of reflection for the individual child. That is, these interactions provide the basis for the child's subsequent development and weighing of alternative perspectives on an issue.

Vygotsky's (1934/1987b) references to learning in the subject areas, in contrast, describe the teacher modeling, explaining, and asking the student for explanations. The importance of the verbalizations by the teacher is that they are the basis for the student's self-questioning and explaining of concepts when studying and reviewing materials.

In summary, designing instruction for complex cognitive functions includes attention to developing the child's conscious awareness and control of his or her own mental activities. These capabilities are the foundation for the higher cognitive functions, and they are beginning to emerge at school age.

Important in the development of the two foundational capabilities is the teaching of writing. The relationship of writing to these capabilities is that it is abstract. That is, sound images must be replaced by symbols, the message often is not addressed to a particular audience, and abbreviated inner speech must be expanded into intelligible form. Of importance is that both reading and writing should be organized for goals important to the child.

Subject-matter ("scientific") concepts also play an important role in the development of higher cognitive functions. Unlike everyday (spontaneous) concepts, subject-matter concepts are removed from the object or event they represent, and they also form a system. That is, concepts may be expressed in terms of other concepts. Thus, subject-matter concepts foster development of the processes of abstraction and generalization.

Essential in classroom instruction to develop higher cognitive functions is the collaboration between teacher and student. Although some individuals cite Vygotsky as the source for relying on small- and large-group discussions in the classroom, Vygotsky identified the specific activities that teacher-student collaboration should include.

EDUCATIONAL APPLICATIONS

Vygotsky's cultural-historical theory has received considerable attention in the United States in recent years. Two programs to teach reading to poor readers reflect Vygotsky's concepts of teacher-student collaboration, teacher modeling and imitation, and the abstraction of meaning from symbols. One is Reading Recovery designed by Marie Clay (1985) for first-grade children who have been unable to master the reading process in regular classrooms (the lowest 10%). The shared collaboration between teacher and child helps children monitor and integrate information from many sources. That is, they learn to use four types of cues (semantic, syntactic, visual, and phonological [oral language sounds]) and also develop meaning from reading (Clay & Cazden, 1990). The other is reciprocal teaching developed by Palinscar and Brown to teach comprehension strategies to older children with reading problems. Reciprocal teaching in reading helps the children develop the subjective judgment essential in monitoring whether they have understood the text (Brown, 1994, p. 6).

Vygotsky's principles have at least two other important implications. First, the meaning of signs and symbols used in the culture cannot be left to chance. Second, the theory also speaks to society in general as cultures attempt to understand the implications of a media-based society. Historically, thinking and new discoveries produced by civilizations increased as their symbol systems became more advanced. The implications of Vygotsky's theory, however, are profound for a civilization in which the major symbol system is one that makes use of co-occurring stimuli (images) and thus requires of the individual only primitive mental functions. Thinking, in other words, can regress in society as well as show progress from one generation to another.

Classroom Issues

The theory establishes the sociocultural setting as the genesis for cognitive development and learning. Therefore, learner characteristics, cognitive processes, and the context for learning are all viewed from that perspective.

Learner Characteristics
Individual differences and readiness are two issues that are specifically addressed by Vygotsky's theory.

Individual Differences.   One of the incomplete concepts in Vygotsky's theory is that of individual differences. However, Vygotsky (1930/1977a) noted that differences in the quality of memory are not the major differences between individuals. Instead, the power of attention and the force of one's drives are the critical differences. In other words, the way that the individual makes use of his or her own capacities, that is, their role in the personality, is the important factor in determining individual differences.

Readiness.   The zone of proximal development, in which cognitive functions are beginning to emerge, represents readiness. Because readiness refers to potential development, it cannot be determined by a standardized test.

Motivation.   One of Vygotsky's major interests that remained uncompleted at his death was the issue of affect. He believed that primitive emotions developed in the same general cycle and became moral, ethical feelings in the way that primitive mental functions are transformed into complex mental functions (Vygotsky, 1930/1977a). Also, he believed that subjective feelings regulated behavior, but the mechanisms of this regulation remain to be developed.

Cognitive Processes and Instruction

Transfer of learning, developing "how-to-learn" skills, and teaching problem solving are addressed by the theory in terms of the social nature of learning.

Transfer of Learning.   All higher mental functions first appear as interactions between a knowledgeable member of society and the child. "Transfer," then, in Vygotsky's view, involves the qualitative shift between interindividual actions and the internalization of these actions as complex intellectual functions. This process, however, is a lengthy one that first involves three major stages. They are (1) the use of the symbol system as communication, (2) the use of the symbol system to guide developing mental abilities, and (3) the development of internal cues and signs to monitor and regulate one's remembering and thinking.

Developing "How-to-Learn" Skills.   This issue is not addressed in the terminology familiar to American psychologists. However, Vygotsky does describe the highest level of symbol use—that of creating internal cues to monitor and regulate one's behavior. This activity involves the control of logical memory and thinking through symbol use and is one aspect of learning how to learn.

Teaching Problem Solving.   Like the learning of signs and symbols, learning to solve problems occurs in a social context. The teacher models the appropriate behaviors and then provides guidance as the learner works through the task.

The Social Context for Learning

Two aspects of the social setting determine the nature and extent of the child's learning. One is the historical developments inherited by the child as a member of a particular culture. That is, the culture may employ a primitive counting system, as in Papua New Guinea, or it may rely extensively on complex symbol systems, such as algebra, calculus, and complex probability systems. The nature of the symbol system inherited by the child sets broad parameters on the higher cognitive functions the child can develop.

The second crucial element is the nature of the child's social interaction with knowledgeable members of the society. Only through this interaction does the child acquire both meaning and utilization of important symbols and thereby develop his or her thinking abilities.

The implication in Vygotsky's theory is that the culture that teaches its children symbols as communication only is omitting the most important function of artificial signs, that of mastering and developing one's thought processes.

Relationships to Other Perspectives

Like Piaget, Vygotsky focused on the mechanisms by which individuals develop higher cognitive processes. However, cultural-historical theory defines them as self-regulated attention, categorical perception, logical memory, and conceptual thinking (instead of as logical reasoning processes). Other differences with Piagetian theory are the role of culture in cognitive development, the role of egocentric speech, and the pivotal role of school subjects. Egocentric speech does not disappear, but becomes inner speech. Vygotsky also placed greater emphasis on the role of make-believe play in that it provides opportunities for the child to extend his or her behavior beyond that of his or her average age.

Also of interest is that Vygotsky discussed the importance of developing the cognitive processes of abstraction and generalization through learning concepts some 40 years prior to their discussion in Gagné's conditions of learning and the instructional design literature. Further, particularly relevant, given the current interest in self-organized learning, is Vygotsky's identification of (1) the importance of self-regulated attention, (2) the role of signs and symbols in directing and managing one's learning, and (3) the identification of two key foundational processes in self-regulated learning. They are the learner's conscious awareness of the cognitive process to be developed and voluntary control (mastery) of one's actions. Further, he emphasized the importance of imitation prior to the introduction of modeling in American psychology. Finally, his focus on signification and learner development of meaning identifies Vygotsky (along with Piaget) as an early constructivist.

Developing a Classroom Strategy

Implementing Vygotsky's theory in the classroom changes the roles of both teacher and students. Ideally, one teacher would be working with one or two students; at most, the group should be limited to five or six. The steps for planning instruction inferred from Vygotsky's broad outline are as follows:

Elementary grades:

Step 1: Determine the appropriate instructional level for each child.

> **1.1** Which tasks/problems reflect important cognitive capabilities?
>
> **1.2** Which of the problems can the child solve with teacher assistance?

Step 2: Identify situations that can develop the children's verbal thinking.

 2.1 What are the key word meanings to be learned?

 2.2 In what ways can the learner demonstrate that key words are generalizations?

All grades:

Step 3: Structure the learning task as a collaborative teacher-student activity.

 3.1 What aspects of the task are to be modeled by the teacher?

 3.2 What self-regulatory skills are to be modeled by the teacher?

 3.3 In what ways is the student to use signs and symbols to regulate his or her own behavior?

 3.4 What teacher suggestions and feedback to students are needed to assist learning?

Step 4: Implement instruction and evaluate the results.

 4.1 Did the teacher gradually add other concepts as the students acquired mastery?

 4.2 Were the students able to function independently at the conclusion of instruction?

 4.3 Do the students' skills generalize to other settings and situations?

Classroom Example

The following lessons are taken from day one and day four of a Reciprocal Teaching Lesson (Palinscar & Brown, 1984, p. 138) with a student who met the minimal decoding standards but failed on comprehension. The lessons illustrate the gradual ceding of responsibility to the student.

> *Day 1:* The teacher and student have read one paragraph silently together, and the teacher has modeled the self-review questions one would ask to check comprehension. The second paragraph, also read silently, mentions several poisonous snakes called pit vipers. The paragraph explains the reason for the name and describes some characteristics of one pit viper known as the water moccasin, or "cottonmouth."

Teacher: This paragraph talks about several different kinds of poisonous snakes called pit vipers. What would be a good question to ask about pit vipers that begins with the word *why*?

Student: (no response)

Teacher: How about "Why are the snakes called pit vipers?"

Student: Why do they, uh, put vipers in a pit?

Teacher: Try it again. "Why are the snakes called . . . ?"

Student: Why are the snakes called pit vipers?

Teacher: Good for you. Now what would be a good question to ask about the water moccasin?

Student: The name?

Teacher: What about the name?

Student: Why is it called a moccasin?

Teacher: That's close; try again. What about the name "cottonmouth"?

Student: Why is it called a cottonmouth?
Teacher: Good. But we need to know which snake is called a cottonmouth.
Student: How about "Why is the moccasin called a cottonmouth?"
Teacher: Good. Now let's answer the questions to be sure we understand the paragraph. (Teacher and student review the questions and the answers in the same manner.)

Day 4: The brief paragraph is about a spinner's mate and his characteristics.

Student: (no question)
Teacher: What is this paragraph about?
Student: Spinner's mate. How do spinner's mate . . .
Teacher: Good. Keep going.
Student: How do spinner's mate is smaller than. . . . How am I going to say that?
Teacher: Take your time. You want to ask about spinner's mate and what he does, using the word *how*.
Student: How do they spend most of their time sitting?
Teacher: That's almost it. Sitting is the answer to the question. Can you ask the question without using *sitting*?
Student: How do they spend most of their time?
Teacher: Good, but we should name spinner's mate in the question. "How does a spinner's. . . ." Now you finish it.
Student: How does a spinner's mate spend most of his time?
Teacher: Good job.

Review of the Theory

Lev Vygotsky, like Jean Piaget, analyzed particular aspects of human cognitive development. Their approach to this task shares four major characteristics. They are (1) the establishment of a theoretical framework for the study of psychological processes, (2) the identification of different psychological structures constructed during development, (3) the analysis of the psychological processes required to attain the highest levels of cognitive development, and (4) an assertion that cognitive development does not proceed through small incremental changes. Instead, it undergoes qualitative transformations.

Vygotsky emphasized the complex mental functions of categorical perception, logical memory, conceptual thinking, and self-regulated attention. The potential for development of these capabilities is determined by the cultural-historical heritage of the child's culture and the child's social experience.

The key to the development of complex mental functions is mastering the signs and symbols of the culture and learning to use them to direct and regulate one's own behavior. The creation and use of arbitrary signs change the psychological nature of processes such as perception, memory, and attention into more complex forms.

Basic principles in cognitive development identified by Vygotsky include the two branches of cultural cognitive development and the general law of genetic development. Essential in the development of higher cognitive functions are interactions with knowledgeable adults to develop both the meanings of cultural symbols and the ways of thinking of the culture. Also important in this process are the imitation and intervention of the learner in applying actions modeled during adult-teacher interactions. (See Table 11.5.)

The major disadvantage of the theory is that Vygotsky was unable to complete his ideas before his death. Thus, educators are left with a broad outline but with few details on implementation.

Major contributions of the theory include the role of culture in learning and development, recognition of the psychological contributions of signs and symbols in psychological functions, and the importance of social interaction during learning.

TABLE 11.5
Summary of Vygotsky's Cultural-Historical Theory

Basic Elements	Definitions
Assumptions	(1) Human cognition cannot be explained by animal behavior. (2) Humans are rational and gradually gain control of their thinking. (3) Cognitive development can be described by dialectical synthesis. (4) The psychological tools developed by humans change their thinking. (5) Cognitive processes should be studied in ways that reveal their dynamic and changing nature.
Cognitive development	The development of complex mental functions that make use of both given stimuli and created stimuli
Components of development	The internalization of actions that first appear on an interpsychological plane; the mastery of the signs and symbols of the culture and learning to use them to master one's own behavior
Outcomes of cognitive development	Complex mental functions, including self-organized attention, categorical perception, conceptual thinking, and logical memory
Designing instruction for complex skills	Developing conscious awareness of and mastery of one's thinking through teaching concepts, and the use of writing for thinking
ANALYSIS OF THE THEORY	
Disadvantages	The incompleteness of the system and the lack of specific guidelines for implementation
Contributions	Recognition of the psychological contribution of created stimuli in cognitive development; the importance of social interaction and the social nature of learning

CHAPTER QUESTIONS

1. Low SES children typically are viewed as having a disadvantage in school because their homes lack magazines and other reading material and reading is not a regular activity for the parents. How would Vygotsky explain the children's disadvantage?

2. Why would Vygotsky not advocate the use of mechanized devices such as computers to provide remedial instruction?

3. What do you think Vygotsky meant when he said that written language is the algebra of language?

4. Schoenfeld (1985) and others express concern that individuals approach mathematical problems as mechanical exercises and seem to possess little awareness of what they are doing (see discussion in chapter 9). How would Vygotsky explain the problem, and what should instruction include to correct the problem?

5. How might writing be used to develop one's thinking?

REFERENCES

Berk, L. E. (2000). *Child development* (5th ed.). Boston: Allyn & Bacon.

Berk, L. E., & Garvin, R. A. (1984). Development of private speech among low-income Appalachian children. *Developmental Psychology, 20*, 271–286.

Berk, L. E., & Stuhl, S. T. (1995). Maternal interactions, private speech, and task performance in preschool children. *Early Childhood Research Quarterly, 10*, 145–169.

Bozhovitch, L. I. (1977). The cultural-historical development of the mind. *Soviet Psychology, 16*(1), 5–22.

Brown, A. L. (1994). The advancement of learning. *Educational Researcher 23*(8), 4–12.

Clay, M. (1985). *The early detection of reading difficulties* (3rd ed.). Portsmouth, NH: Heinemann.

Clay, M. C., & Cazden, C. B. (1990). A Vygotskian interpretation of Reading Recovery. In L. C. Moll (Ed.), *Vygotsky and education* (pp. 206–222). New York: Cambridge University Press.

Cole, M. (1996). *Cultural psychology*. Cambridge, MA: The Belknap Press of Harvard University Press.

Elsasser, N., & John-Steiner, V. P. (1977). An interactionist approach to advancing literacy. *Harvard Educational Review, 47*(3), 355–369.

Engels, F. (1940). *Dialectics of nature.* New York: International.

Engels, F. (1925/1978). *Dialectic on culture.* Berlin: Dietz Verlag.

Fiore, K., & Elsasser, N. (1982). Strangers no more: A laboratory literacy curriculum. *College English, 44*, 115–128.

Fitzpatrick, S. (1992). *The cultural front: Power and culture in revolutionary Russia.* Ithaca, NY: Cornell University Press.

Gindis, B. (1995). The social/cultural implications of disability: Vygotsky's paradigm for special education. *Educational Psychologist, 30*(2), 77–81.

Gredler, M., & Shields, C. (2004). Does no one read Vygotsky's words? Commentary on Glassman. *Educational Researcher, 33*(2), 21–25.

Harste, J., Short, K. G., & Burke, C. (1988). *Creating classrooms for authors.* Portsmouth, NH: Heinemann.

Janet, P. (1926). De l'angoisse a l'extrase. Vol. I. Paris: Alcan.

Janet, P. (1929). De l'angoisse a l'extrase. Vol. II. Paris: Alcan.

Joravsky, D. (1989). *Russian psychology: A critical history.* Cambridge, MA: Basil Blackwell.

Kornilov, K. N. (1930). Psychology in the light of dialectical materialism. In C. Murchison

(Ed.), *Psychologies of 1930* (pp. 243–278). Worcester, MA: Clark University Press.

Kozulin, A. (1984). *Psychology in Utopia*. Cambridge, MA: MIT Press.

Kozulin, A. (1990). *Vygotsky's psychology: A biography of ideas.* Cambridge, MA: Harvard University Press.

Leont'ev, A. N. (1959). *Problems of mental development.* Moscow: Publishing House of the Academy of Pedagogical Sciences RSFSR.

Leont'ev, A. N. (1977). The dialectical method in the psychology of memory. *Soviet Psychology, 16*(1), 53–69.

Leont'ev, A. N., & Luria, A. R. (1968). The psychological ideas of L. S. Vygotsky. In B. B. Wolman (Ed.), *Historical roots of contemporary psychology* (pp. 338–367). New York: Harper & Row.

Lévy-Bruhl, L. (1910/1922). *Les onctions mentales dans les societes inferieures.* Paris: Alcan.

Lévy-Bruhl, L. (1922/1976). *La mentalite primitive.* Paris: Retz.

Luria, A. R. (1971). Towards the problem of the historical nature of psychological processes. *International Journal of Psychology, 6*(4), 259–272.

Luria, A. R. (1976). *Cognitive development: Its cultural and social foundations.* Cambridge, MA: Harvard University Press.

Luria, A. R. (1979). *The making of mind: A personal account of Soviet psychology.* Cambridge, MA: Harvard University Press. (Edited by M. Cole & S. Cole)

O'Connor, M. C. (1996). Managing the intermental: Classroom group discussion and the social context of learning. In D. I. Slobin, J. Gerhardt, A. Kyratzis, & J. Guo (Eds.). *Social interaction, social context, and language.* Mahwah, NJ: Erlbaum.

Palinscar, A. S., & Brown, A. L. (1984). Reciprocal teaching of comprehension-fostering and comprehension-monitoring activities. *Cognition and Instruction, 1*(2), 117–175.

Saxe, G. B. (1981). Body parts as numerals: A developmental analysis of numeration among the Oksapmin in Papua New Guinea. *Child Development, 52,* 306–316.

Schoenfeld, A. H. (1985). Metacognitive and epistemological issues in mathematical understanding. In E. A. Silver (Ed.), *Teaching and learning mathematical problem solving: Multiple research perspectives* (pp. 361–379). Hillsdale, NJ: Erlbaum.

Thurnwald, R. (1922). Psychologie des primitiven Menschen. In G. Kafka (Ed.), *Handbuch der vergleichenden Psychologie Band 1.* (pp. 147–320). Munchen: Verlag von Ernst Reinhardt.

Valsiner, J. (1988). *Developmental psychology in the Soviet Union.* Bloomington, IN: Indiana University Press.

Valsiner, J., & van der Veer, R. (2000). *The social mind: Construction of the idea.* New York: Cambridge University Press.

van der Veer, R. (1991). The anthropological underpinnings of Vygotsky's thinking. *Studies in Soviet Thought, 42,* 73–91.

van der Veer, R., & Valsiner, J. (1988). Lev Vygotsky and Pierre Janet. *Developmental Review, 8,* 52–65.

van der Veer, R., & Valsiner, J. (1991). *Undertanding Vygotsky: A quest for synthesis.* Cambridge, MA: Blackwell.

Vygodskaia, G. (1995). Remembering father. *Educational Psychologist, 30*(2), 57–59.

Vygodskaia, G. (1998). Afterword. In K. Topping & S. Ehly (Eds.), *Peer-assisted learning* (pp. 329–332). Mahwah, NJ: Erlbaum.

Vygotsky, L. S. (1929). The problem of the cultural development of the child. *Journal of Genetic Psychology, 36,* 415–434.

Vygotsky, L. S. (1962). *Thought and language.* Cambridge, MA: Massachusetts Institute of Technology. (Original work published 1934)

Vygotsky, L. S. (1963). The problem of learning and mental development at school age. In B. Simon & J. Simon (Eds.), *Educational psychology in the U.S.S.R.* (pp. 21–34). London: Routledge & Kegan Paul.

Vygotsky, L.S. (1966). Development of the higher mental functions. In A. N. Leont'ev, A. R. Luria, & A. Smirnol (Eds.), *Psychological research in the U.S.S.R. Vol. I* (pp. 11–45). Moscow: Progress. (Original work published 1931)

Vygotsky, L. S. (1977a). *Talks on psychological systems, notes.* Cited in L. I. Bozhovitch, The cultural-historical development of the mind.

Soviet Psychology, 16(1), 5–22. (Original work published 1930)

Vygotsky, L. S. (1977b). The development of higher psychological functions. *Soviet Psychology, 16,* 60–73. (Original work published 1929)

Vygotsky, L. S. (1979a). Consciousness as a problem in the psychology of behavior. *Soviet Psychology 17*(4), 3–35. (Original work published 1924).

Vygotsky, L. S. (1979b). The development of higher forms of attention in childhood. *Soviet Psychology, 18*(1), 67–115. (Original work published 1929)

Vygotsky, L. S. (1983). *Sobraniye sochinenii* [Collected works] (Vol. 5). Moscow: Pedagogika.

Vygotsky, L. S. (1987a). An experimental study of concept development. In R. W. Rieber & A. S. Carton (Eds.), *Problems of general psychology, Vol. 1. Collected works* (pp. 121–166). New York: Plenum. (Original work published 1934)

Vygotsky, L. S. (1987b). The development of scientific concepts in childhood. In R. W. Reiber & A. S. Carton (Eds.), *Problems of general psychology, Vol. 1. Collected works* (pp. 167–241). New York: Plenum. (Original work published 1934)

Vygotsky, L. S. (1987c). The genetic roots of thinking and speech. In R. W. Rieber & A. S. Carton (Eds.), *Problems of general psychology, Vol. 1. Collected works* (pp. 101–120). New York: Plenum. (Original work published 1934)

Vygotsky, L. S. (1987d). The problem and the method of investigation. In R. W. Rieber & Carton (Eds.), *Problems of general psychology, Vol. 1. Collected works* (pp. 43–52). New York: Plenum. (Original work published 1934)

Vygotsky, L. S. (1987e). The problem of speech and thinking in Piaget's theory. In R. W. Rieber & Carton (Eds.), *Problems of general psychology, Vol. 1. Collected works* (pp. 53–91). New York: Plenum. (Original work published 1934)

Vygotsky, L. S. (1987f). Thought and word. In R. W. Rieber & A. S. Carton (Eds.), *Problems*

of general psychology, Vol. 1. Collected works (pp. 243–285). New York: Plenum. (Original work published 1934)

Vygotsky, L. S. (1993). *The fundamentals of defectology. Vol. 2, Collected works.* New York: Plenum. (Original work published 1982)

Vygotsky, L. S. (1997a). Analysis of higher mental functions. In R. W. Rieber (Ed.), *The history of the development of higher mental functions, Vol. 4. Collected works* (pp. 65–82). New York: Plenum. (Original work published 1931)

Vygotsky, L. S. (1997b). Cultivation of higher forms of behavior. In R. W. Rieber (Ed.), *The history of the development of higher mental functions, Vol. 4. Collected works* (pp. 221–229). New York: Plenum. (Original work published 1983)

Vygotsky, L. S. (1997c). Genesis of higher mental functions. In R. W. Rieber (Ed.), *The history of the development of the higher mental functions, Vol. 4. Collected works* (pp. 97–119). New York: Plenum. (Original work published 1931)

Vygotsky, L. S. (1997d). Mastering attention. In R. W. Rieber (Ed.), *The history of the development of the higher mental functions, Vol. 4. Collected works* (pp. 153–177). New York: Plenum. (Original work published 1983)

Vygotsky, L. S. (1997e). Mind, consciousness, the unconscious. In R. W. Rieber & J. Wollock (Eds.), *Problems of the theory and history of psychology, Vol. 3. Collected works* (pp. 109–121). New York: Plenum. (Original work published 1930)

Vygotsky, L. S. (1997f). Preface to Buhler. In R. W. Rieber & J. Wollock (Eds.), *Problems of the theory and history of psychology, Vol. 3. Collected works* (pp. 163–173). New York: Plenum. (Original work published 1930)

Vygotsky, L. S. (1997g). Preface to Koffka. The problem of development in structural psychology: A critical investigation. In R. W. Rieber & J. Wollock (Eds.), *Problems of the theory and history of psychology, Vol. 3. Collected works* (pp. 195–232). New York: Plenum. (Original work published 1934)

Vygotsky, L. S. (1997h). Preface to Thorndike. In R. W. Rieber & J. Wollock (Eds.), *Problems of the theory and history of psychology, Vol. 3. Collected works* (pp. 147–161). New York: Plenum. (Original work published 1926)

Vygotsky, L. S. (1997i). Research method. In R. W. Rieber (Ed.), *History of the development of the higher mental functions, Vol. 4. Collected works* (pp. 27–63). New York: Plenum. (Original work published 1931)

Vygotsky, L. S. (1997j). *The history of the development of the higher mental functions, Vol. 4. Collected works.* New York: Plenum. (Original work published 1931)

Vygotsky, L. S. (1997k). The instrumental method in psychology. In R. W. Rieber & J. Wollock (Eds.), *Problems of the theory and history of psychology, Vol. 3. Collected works* (pp. 85–89). New York: Plenum. (Archival manuscript)

Vygotsky, L. S. (1997l). The methods of reflexological and psychological investigation. In R. W. Rieber & J. Wollock (Eds.), *Problems of the theory and history of psychology, Vol. 3. Collected works* (pp. 35–49). New York: Plenum. (Original work published 1926)

Vygotsky, L. S. (1997m). The problem of the development of higher mental functions. In R. W. Rieber (Ed.), *The history of the development of higher mental functions, Vol. 4. Collected works* (pp. 1–26). New York: Plenum. (Original work published 1931)

Vygotsky, L. S. (1997n). The structure of higher mental functions. In R. W. Rieber (Ed.), *History of the development of higher mental functions, Vol. 4. Collected works* (pp. 83–96). New York: Plenum. (Original work published 1931)

Vygotsky, L. S. (1998a). Development of higher mental functions during the transitional age. In R. W. Rieber (Ed.), *Child psychology, Vol. 5. Collected works* (pp. 83–149) (M. J. Hall, Trans.). New York: Plenum. (Original work published 1930–1931)

Vygotsky, L. S. (1998b). Development of thinking and formation of concepts in the adolescent. In R. W. Rieber (Ed.), *Child psychology, Vol. 5. Collected works* (pp. 29–81) (M. J. Hall, Trans.). New York: Plenum. (Original work published 1930–1931)

Vygotsky, L. S. (1998c). The problem of age. In R. W. Rieber (Ed.), *Child psychology, Vol. 5. Collected works* (pp. 187–205). New York: Plenum. (Original work published 1930–1931)

Vygotsky, L. S. (1999a). Methods of studying higher mental functions. In R. W. Rieber (Ed.), *Scientific legacy, Vol. 6. Collected works* (pp. 57–60). New York: Plenum. (Original work published 1984)

Vygotsky, L. S. (1999b). The function of signs in the development of higher mental processes. In R. W. Rieber (Ed.), *Scientific legacy, Vol. 6. Collected works* (pp. 27–38). New York: Plenum. (Original work published 1930)

Vygotsky, L. S. (1999c). The teaching about emotions. In R. W. Rieber (Ed.), *Scientific legacy, Vol. 6. Collected works* (pp. 71–235). New York: Plenum. (Original work written 1930)

Vygotsky, L. S., & Luria, A. R. (1993). *Studies in the history of behavior: Ape, primitive, and child.* Hillsdale, NJ: Erlbaum. (Original work published 1930)

Wertsch, J. V. (Ed.) (1985a). *Culture, communication and cognition: Vygotskian perspective.* Cambridge, U.K.: Cambridge University Press.

Wertsch, J. V. (1985b). Introduction. In J. V. Wertsch (Ed.), *Culture, communication and cognition: Vygotskian perspective* (pp. 1–18). Cambridge, U.K.: Cambridge University Press.

Yaroshevsky, M. (1989). *Lev Vygotsky.* Moscow: Progress Publishers.

PART V
Social-Context Theories

As indicated by Vygotsky's cultural-historical theory, the social setting is a powerful influence on cognitive development. Other aspects of social influences on the individual are addressed by Albert Bandura's social-cognitive theory and models and theories of academic motivation.

The primary mechanism in social-cognitive theory is that individuals learn from observing the behaviors of others and the social consequences of those actions. Both live models and the symbolic models portrayed in the mass media are sources for learning. Factors that influence learning are the characteristics of the model and the learner's ability to process the observed events. The acquisition of skilled or accomplished performance, however, depends also on the learner's belief that he or she can execute the complex skill, referred to as perceived self-efficacy.

In contrast, the expectancy-value model, the goal orientation model, and attribution theory address particular characteristics of the individual and the learning setting that influence motivation. The expectancy-value model emphasizes students' expectations of success and the value they place on success, and the beliefs that support these motivations. Goal orientation models focus on students' intentions that determine the ways they approach and engage in learning activities and the effects of those intentions. Attribution theory addresses individuals' perceived causes of achievement-related outcomes and the links to subsequent behavior.

CHAPTER 12

Albert Bandura's
Social-Cognitive Learning Theory

A major function of thought is to enable people to predict events and to develop ways to control those [events] that affect their lives. (Bandura, 1995, p. 6)

Social-cognitive theory currently addresses the social, cognitive, and personal agency factors that influence learning and motivation. It began with Albert Bandura's clinical work with snake-phobic patients. Their observations of former patients handling snakes was a more effective therapy technique than persuasion and observations of others.

Early works identified the role of behavioral models in the learning of both prosocial and antisocial behaviors (Bandura, 1969, 1971a; Bandura & Walters, 1963) and the role of models in the modification of behavior (Bandura, 1965, 1971b). The theory then identified several social and cognitive factors that influence learning. Included are the capabilities of using symbols and engaging in intentional and purposive actions. Also included in the theory are the influences of the media on the values, attitudes, and behavior styles of the observers (Bandura, 1986).

Since the 1980s, the concepts of perceived self-efficacy and self-regulated learning have become a major focus of the theory. Self-efficacy refers to personal beliefs about one's capabilities to be successful in tasks with novel or ambiguous elements and includes teacher efficacy (Bandura, 1977a, 1997). Self-regulated learning refers to (1) students' proactive efforts to mobilize emotional, cognitive, and environmental resources during learning and (2) self-observation, judgment, and reaction to one's progress (Bandura, 1986; Schunk & Zimmerman, 1998; Zimmerman, 2001).

PRINCIPLES OF LEARNING

Albert Bandura's social-cognitive theory seeks to explain learning in the naturalistic setting. Unlike the laboratory setting, the social milieu provides numerous opportunities for individuals to acquire complex skills and abilities through the observation of modeled behaviors and the behavioral consequences.

Basic Assumptions

The assumptions of social-cognitive theory address the nature of the learning process and the outcomes of learning.

The Nature of the Learning Process

The definition of observational learning in social-cognitive theory is based on identified weaknesses in prior views of imitative learning.

Other Views of Imitative Learning.   Some theories maintained that the learner imitates a modeled behavior and is reinforced for the imitation, and later repeats the behavior. Other theories maintained that behavior imitation was the result of a particular relationship between the child and the adult. Examples include the child's identification with the same-sex parent, nurturance, power, envy, and others.

However, Bandura (1969) noted that these mechanisms are insufficient to explain much of the child's imitative behavior. For example, the learning of sex-role behaviors is facilitated by a variety of events. Included are the pink or blue treatment of the nursery, parental selection of particular clothing and toys, and parental reinforcement for sex-appropriate activities (Bandura, 1969, p. 215).

Early studies of observational learning also indicated that a nurturant relationship is not a prerequisite for imitation. Furthermore, fear of an aggressor is not a sufficient condition for imitation of aggressive behaviors. Instead, the appeal for imitating an aggressor is that dominance through physical and verbal force leads to possession of material resources and control over others.

Like prosocial behaviors, theories have proposed a variety of mechanisms to account for antisocial behavior. One belief is that frustration activates a frustration drive that then produces aggression. However, the term *frustration* is not a unidimensional state. Instead, it includes a variety of aversive conditions such as physical assault, insult, deprivation, harassment, goal blocking, and defeat (Bandura, 1979, p. 329).

More important, the aversive stimulation from these conditions leads to a variety of responses. Examples include withdrawal and resignation, achievement, self-anesthetization with drugs and alcohol, and aggression. Further, millions of people live in a state of deprivation. Yet comparatively few of those deprived engage in civil disturbances. The important question for social scientists, therefore, is not why aggression occurs in such conditions but why a majority of the ghetto population is resigned to dismal living conditions in the midst of affluence (Bandura, 1979, p. 333).

Other views of learning also assumed a unidimensional relationship between the individual and the environment. That is, either the environment or the individual is a controlling factor in learning. However, Bandura maintained that this simple relationship did not account for the development of complex behaviors.

Assumptions about Learning.   Prior theories have proposed a variety of mechanisms to account for the learning of prosocial and antisocial behaviors. Excluded from these explanations, however, is that the learner can (1) abstract a range of information from observing the behavior of others, and (2) make decisions about which behaviors to adopt and enact. A basic assumption of social-cognitive theory is that this observational and decision-making process is a key mechanism in the acquisition of both prosocial and antisocial behaviors.

Further, the acquisition of complex behaviors is not explained by a simple bidirectional relationship between the environment and the individual. Instead, most environmental influences on behavior are mediated by a variety of internal personal factors. Therefore, Bandura (1978) included in his explanation of learning the three factors first proposed by Kurt Lewin. They are behavior (B), the environment (E), and the internal events that influence perceptions and actions (P). In Bandura's view, a three-way interlocking relationship, referred to as **reciprocal determinism**, exists among these three factors. For example, after assertiveness training, an individual's behavior activates new environmental reactions (Bandura, 1977b). These reactions, in turn, generate self-confidence in the individual, which then mediates future behavior.

The relationships between the environment, internal events, and behaviors are often complex and subtle. Certain personal attributes, such as sex or race, often activate differential social treatment. The individual's self-conception, in turn, is influenced by the treatment such that biases are either altered or maintained. Also, the relative influence exerted by each of the factors will vary across individuals and situations. For example, behavior and its intrinsic feedback is a major influence for people who play the piano for their own enjoyment. In contrast, when deciding which book to check out of the library, cognitive factors are dominant (Bandura, 1986, p. 24).

The Outcomes of Learning

Most theories equate learning and performance or accept performance as an indicator that learning has in fact occurred. In contrast, Bandura believes that individuals acquire internal codes of behavior that may or may not be performed later. Therefore, learning and performance are regarded as two separate events. Learning is defined as the acquisition of symbolic representations in the form of verbal or visual codes that serve as guidelines for future behavior. An example is a child who sees an older boy in a fight with the class bully. Admiration from classmates may lead the observer to conclude that fighting in certain circumstances is both acceptable and rewarding. The younger child acquires both a set of behaviors and a tendency to enact the behaviors at a later point in time.

Visual codes consist of abstractions of the distinctive features of events instead of merely mental copies (Bandura, 1986). Included are activities, places, and objects. Examples are tennis, New Orleans, and the Eiffel Tower. Verbal codes include language symbols, numbers, musical notations, Morse code, and others (Bandura, 1971b). The importance of symbolic codes, both visual and verbal, is that they include a great deal of information in an easily stored form (Bandura, 1977b, p. 26).

In summary, three assumptions support social learning theory. First, the learning process requires both the cognitive processing and decision-making skills of the learner. Second, learning is a three-way interlocking relationship between the environment, personal factors, and behavior. Third, learning results in the acquisition of verbal and visual codes of behavior that may or may not later be performed.

The Components of Learning

In the naturalistic setting, individuals learn new behaviors through the observation of models and through the effects of their own actions. The components of learning are (1) the behavioral model, (2) the consequences of the modeled behavior, (3) the learner's internal processes, and (4) perceived self-efficacy.

Behavior, however, is demonstrated and observed in a variety of settings and under different conditions. For learning to occur, the modeled behavior, the reinforcement, and the learner's cognitive processing must meet certain requirements.

The Behavioral Model

Key issues in the role of the behavioral model are the effects of models, the types of modeling stimuli, the model characteristics, and the characteristics of observers.

The Effects of Models.   The primary function of the modeled behavior is to transmit information to the observer. This function may occur in any one of three different ways. One is that modeled behavior serves as a social prompt to initiate similar behavior in others. For example, a guest at an elaborate dinner party may observe the hostess in order to select the piece of silver appropriate for each course.

On the darker side, sensational crimes also serve as cues for copycat acts that erupt after the publicized event. For example, after the first airplane hijacking to Cuba in 1961, subsequent hijackings eventually involved 71 different countries over the next 14 years (Bandura, 1979, p. 325). A more recent concern about the extensive media coverage of school shootings is that repetitions of video reports of the incidents accompanied by national attention are powerful cues to individuals who may feel disenfranchised by society.

The second effect of modeling is to strengthen or weaken the learner's existing restraints against the performance of particular behaviors. Individuals' restraints typically are strengthened if the model receives punishment or other aversive consequences for the behavior. However, long-term exposure to reprehensible acts can influence the behavior of some observers. For example, the extensive research on exposure to media violence indicates it is a causal factor in the aggressive behavior of some individuals. The more than 1,000 studies led to a July 2000 joint statement by six professional organizations on the hazards of exposing children to media violence (Bushman & Anderson, 2001, p. 480).

The weakening of the learner's restraints toward the performance of particular behaviors can occur in two ways. One is the lack of punishment for reprehensible behavior (discussed in detail later in this chapter). The other is the modeling of defensible violence, which adds legitimacy to the use of violence as a solution to problems (Bandura, 1973, p. 33). Verbal and physical abuse by authority figures to restrain rioters is an example. Repeated exposure to such models results in a weakening of the individual's restraints on the use of aggressive solutions.

The third influence of modeling is to demonstrate new patterns of behavior. Models are particularly important in the socialization process of both children and adults. Language, mores, and familial customs as well as educational, social, and political practices are modeled in countless situations.

Types of Modeling Stimuli.   Defined functionally, a model consists of an organized stimulus array such that an observer can extract and act on the main information. The two principal types of modeling stimuli are live and symbolic models. Live models include family members, friends, work associates, and others with whom the individual has direct contact.

Symbolic models, in contrast, are pictorial representations of behavior. In contemporary American society, the greatest range of exposure to models is through the mass media. Symbolic models have supplanted the role of direct experience in learning about different aspects of the world (Bandura, 1982a, 1986). For example, the individual's only knowledge of an operating room, a criminal courtroom, a jail, and other settings may be from the mass media. Further, one report indicates that, by school age, a child will have spent more time watching television than would be spent in a college classroom (Gerbner & Gross, 1976, p. 176). Other reports indicate that children engage in more television viewing than in any other activity except sleeping (Berk, 1989; Carpenter, Huston, & Spear, 1989; Huston, Watkins, & Kunkel, 1989). Also, by the end of elementary school, the average child will have seen more than 8,000 murders and more than 100,000 other violent acts on television (Huston et al., 1992). Another report stated that a typical adult spends three hours each day watching television (Robinson & Godbey, 1997).

Television, however, is not real life. For example, the FBI reports that only 0.2% of crimes are murders, whereas about 50% of the crimes in reality-based TV are murders (Oliver, 1994; in Bushman & Anderson, 2001). Also, the cultural view often fostered by the mass media is one in which family problems are resolved in less than an hour, the criminal is always brought to justice, and the criminal's victims experience little pain or suffering. These "facts of life" are the hidden curriculum that no one teaches but that everyone learns (Gerbner, 1974). Thus, the viewer's knowledge about many settings is based on a symbolic fictional reality and may be distorted.

Characteristics of Models.   An important factor in the learning process is the degree to which the model is attended to by the learner. Some models, such as regular associates and peers, are more effective than others in attracting the learner's attention. For young children, both peer and adult models play an important role in the socialization process.

Responsiveness to models is influenced by three situational characteristics (Bandura, 1986, p. 207). One is the particular attributes or characteristics of the model. Important model characteristics are relevance and credibility for the observers. Models who have an impact on observers may be prestigious, appear to deserve trust, portray consensus in a group, offer believable standards to guide observers' aspirations, or provide realistic reference figures for observer comparison (Rosenthal & Bandura, 1978, p. 636).

In the classroom, observing success on school tasks achieved by those who are similar in age and competence should enhance the likelihood of observational learning (Schunk, 1987). In one study, children deficient in subtraction skills improved their performance after observing both the teacher and peer models solve problems (Schunk & Hanson, 1985).

The second factor that influences responsiveness to a model is uncertainty about a particular course of action. In such situations, the observer is likely to attend to the behavior of a prestigious model. Cues such as general appearance, speech, style, age, and signs of expertise are interpreted as indicators of past successes (Bandura, 1986, p. 208). Of importance, however, is that these characteristics exert the greatest influence when the consequences of the modeled action are unknown (Bandura, 1986).

The third stimulus characteristic that influences learning is the degree of intrinsic reward already present in the situation. Watching television is an example. The activity itself is satisfying to the observer (Bandura, 1971c).

Observer Characteristics. In addition to situational characteristics, the nature of the observer also affects responsiveness to modeling influences (Bandura, 1986). Some research indicates that those who lack self-confidence and have low self-esteem are especially prone to adopt the behavior of successful models. Such characteristics may in part explain tendencies of teenagers to emulate the dress and hairstyles of rock stars, for example.

However, when modeling is used explicitly to develop competencies, those who are more talented and venturesome are likely to derive the greatest benefit from observing proficient models (Bandura, 1986, p. 208). In other words, individuals with clear goals select models that are examples of valued skills. These observers differ greatly from insecure observers who turn to others because they lack confidence in their own abilities (Bandura, 1986, p. 208).

Summary. Behaviors performed by models are an essential component of learning in the naturalistic setting. The primary function of the modeled behavior is to transmit information to the observer in any of three different ways. They are (1) to serve as a cue for similar behavior in others, (2) to strengthen or weaken the learner's existing restraints against the performance of particular behaviors, and (3) to demonstrate new patterns of behavior.

The two principal types of models are live and symbolic. Live models are family members, teachers, friends, work associates, and others in the immediate social setting. Symbolic models are pictorial examples of behavior, such as the mass media. However, media often present fictional views of the world. Thus, the observer may obtain distorted views of various settings.

Three situational characteristics influence observer reactions to models. They are the attributes of the model, the extent of uncertainty about a particular course of action, and the degree of intrinsic reward present in the situation.

Responsiveness to models is also influenced by observer characteristics. Some research indicates that observers who lack self-confidence are likely to adopt the behaviors of successful models. However, when modeling is used to develop particular competencies, the talented and adventuresome observers are most likely to derive the greatest benefit from the modeling.

The Consequences of Behavior

Operant conditioning includes only consequences that impinge directly on the learner for behavior that he or she has executed. In contrast, social-cognitive theory also includes two other types. They are vicarious consequences and self-imposed consequences. Vicarious consequences are associated with the observed behaviors of others. That is, a model receives reinforcement or punishment for a particular behavior, and the consequence to the model generates emotional effects in the observer. The two types of such consequences are vicarious reinforcement and vicarious punishment. Also important in learning are the interactions of vicarious and self-imposed consequences with the direct consequences that the environment delivers for performance.

Vicarious Reinforcement.   For vicarious reinforcement to occur, (1) a model must be reinforced for the execution of particular behavior, and (2) positive emotional reactions must be aroused in the observer. This effect is used extensively by television commercials. For example, a well-known actress eats a particular low-calorie food and demonstrates her weight loss. A handsome actor dressed in a tuxedo demonstrates the features of a luxury car and then joins other expensively dressed people going to a party. In these situations, the vicarious reinforcement for a particular group of viewers is the positive feelings associated with being slim or acquiring social status.

Similarly, when playing a slot machine, for example, one sees and hears the other players win (Kazdin, 1989, p. 197). The loud noises and flashing lights announce the winners to others. Similarly, advertisements of contests often include reports of happy previous winners that may elicit positive emotional reactions in certain readers.

In addition to emotional reactions, vicarious reinforcement also conveys information about which behaviors are appropriate in which settings. A third effect occurs when the modeled behavior is repeatedly reinforced. When outcomes are viewed as personally attainable, seeing others reinforced for successful behaviors arouses expectations of similar results in observers. The observer anticipates the same reinforcement consequences for enactment of the same or similar behaviors. In other words, the model's continued reinforcement for a behavior predicts success for the observer. Such behaviors are described as having acquired **functional value** (Bandura, 1971b). (See Table 12.1 for a summary of the three effects.)

TABLE 12.1
Primary Effects of Vicarious Consequences

Vicarious Reinforcement	Vicarious Punishment
Conveys information about which behaviors are appropriate in which settings	Conveys information about which behaviors are inappropriate in which settings
Arousal of the emotional responses of pleasure and satisfaction in the observer	Tends to exert a restraining influence on imitation of modeled behavior (inhibitory effect)
After repeated reinforcements, incentive-motivational effects are generated; behavior acquires functional value.	Tends to devalue the model's status since a functional behavior was not transmitted

In one semester-long observational study of a third-grade classroom (Goetz, 1976), the children indicated that finishing on time, getting the right answers, and mastering the subject were important. These behaviors earned time for fun activities and had acquired functional value for the children.

Vicarious Punishment.   Like vicarious reinforcement, punishment received by a model tends to convey three primary effects. First, information is conveyed about behaviors that are likely to be punished and are therefore inappropriate. Second, a restraining influence on imitative aggressive actions is also likely to occur (inhibitory effect).

Finally, because the behavior transmitted to the observers was unsuccessful, the model's status is likely to be devalued. If the model enacts a behavior highly prized by a peer group, such as challenging unfair treatment, punishment may enhance the model's status.[1] Usually, however, the model's status is devalued.

Other outcomes may occur as the result of the presence or absence of punishment. One outcome is that of altering the observer's valuation of reinforcing agents (Bandura, 1977b, p. 51). The misuse of power generates resentment in observers and undermines the legitimacy of the agent's power. The observation of inequitable punishment may release angry observers from self-censure of their own behavior. The result is increased transgression rather than compliance. An example is that of excessive police reaction to crimes committed in certain urban neighborhoods or by members of particular subgroups in society. Outbreaks of vandalism and riots by other members of the subgroup often follow (Figure 12.1).

The Absence of Punishment.   The anticipation of punishment usually restrains the imitation of forbidden actions. However, when individuals are not punished for transgressions, the information conveyed is that of implicit acceptance. An example is a classroom in which the teacher is careless about

---

[1]Status is most likely to be enhanced by punishment for principled conduct. Personal communication from Albert Bandura, July 27, 1983.

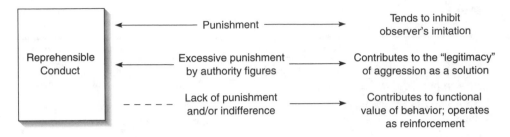

FIGURE 12.1
Some effects of consequences for reprehensible conduct

monitoring examinations and cheating occurs. If the cheating goes unpunished, others are more inclined to cheat on the next examination. The behavior has acquired functional value through the omission of punishment.

Similarly, when aggressive actions go unpunished or when people respond approvingly or indifferently, aggression is viewed as both acceptable and expected in similar circumstances (Bandura, 1973, p. 129). Aggression acquires functional value for the observer.

The lack of punishment for forbidden actions has important implications for the classroom. In one group of junior high classrooms, for example, some of the new teachers ignored students' initial disruptive actions and continued to teach or to wait until the situation was out of hand before trying to get order (Moskowitz-Hayman, 1976, p. 288). By the end of the school year, in one class, students were throwing chairs, pencils, and books; walking around the room; slapping each other; and humming, singing, and talking out loud. The importance of addressing disruptive actions early and consistently also is supported by a number of other classroom studies (see Doyle, 1986; Good & Brophy, 1987).

The absence of adverse consequences to the model fulfills a useful purpose in situations such as the treatment of phobic patients. Snake-phobic patients, for example, experienced reduced fear and anxiety after observing models handle snakes without incurring adverse consequences.

The influence of vicarious consequences, however, is relative rather than absolute. The extent of the influence varies with the observer's valuation of the type of outcome and the type of behavior (Bandura, 1977b, p. 119). In addition, observed consequences are of minimal influence if observers believe that the model's contingencies do not apply to them. For example, the physical aggression of a soldier is unlikely to enhance imitative aggression in the average citizen (Bandura, 1971b). Moreover, both vicarious and direct reinforcement are operating together in most situations. Therefore, the separate effects of either type are difficult to determine.

Self-Reinforcement.   Both direct and vicarious reinforcement involve consequences delivered by the environment. Gold stars awarded for attendance, prizes won on television quiz shows, and minimal prison terms imposed for heinous crimes are dispensed to individuals by some member or agent of society, and they may influence the behavior of others. Self-reinforcement, on the other hand, is independent of the consequences delivered by society. Furthermore, it must be consciously cultivated by the individual. Young children respond to immediate physical consequences (food and physical contact) and other material rewards. Then, symbolic consequences, including social reactions of approval and disapproval, followed by social contracting arrangements, become reinforcing or punishing. Finally, individuals become capable of establishing self-evaluative and self-produced consequences (Bandura, 1978, p. 103).

Self-reinforcement involves three subsidiary elements. They are (1) a self-prescribed standard of behavior, (2) reinforcing events under the control of the individual, and (3) the individual as his or her own reinforcing agent.

In general, individuals establish performance standards for themselves and tend to respond to their behavior in self-rewarding ways if their performance matches or exceeds the standard. Similarly, they respond in self-criticizing ways if their performance fails to meet the standard. Thus, although humans—like rats and chimpanzees—respond to reinforcement, the human capacity for thought and self-direction sets the species apart. Unlike human beings, "rats and chimpanzees are disinclined to pat themselves on the back for commendable performances, or to berate themselves for getting lost in the cul-de-sacs" (Bandura, 1971b, p. 249).

Interactions with External Consequences.   An important characteristic of self-imposed consequences is that they often operate together with external consequences (Bandura, 1974). These two sources of reinforcement either conflict with or supplement each other. When external rewards are outweighed by self-condemnation, external rewards are relatively ineffective. An example is the student who seeks to earn an *A* grade in every course. Earning a *B* in a particular course in which others earn *C*s and *D*s does not meet the individual's standards. Earning the highest grade is small consolation.

A second type of conflict that can occur is that of external punishment delivered by the environment for behaviors that the individual values highly (and therefore believes are worthy of reward). Nonconformists, dissenters, and, at the extreme, martyrs are in this category. For the latter group, their sense of self-worth is so strongly linked to particular beliefs that they suffer pain and even death rather than relinquish their values.

Summary.   Like operant conditioning, the consequences of behavior are essential to learning in social-cognitive theory. However, unlike operant conditioning, the theory incorporates other consequences in addition to reinforcement for behaviors that the learner executes. They are vicarious and self-imposed consequences. In vicarious reinforcement, the model is reinforced for a particular behavior, and positive emotional reactions are aroused in the observer. Vicarious reinforcement also conveys information about appropriate behaviors. Further, repeated reinforcements to the model for behaviors that the observer views as personally attainable raise expectations of similar results for the observer. Such behaviors have functional value for the observer.

Similarly, vicarious punishment delivered to a model also conveys three primary effects. First, information is conveyed about behaviors that are inappropriate. Second, punishment to the model exerts an inhibitory effect on imitation for the observer. Third, the model's status is devalued. Excessive punishment, however, can release observers from the self-censure of their own behavior.

In contrast to punishment for inappropriate behaviors, the absence of punishment implies implicit acceptance for those behaviors. For example, when aggression goes unpunished or is responded to indifferently, observers view it as acceptable and expected in similar circumstances. The implication for the classroom is that disruptive actions should be addressed early and consistently.

Although important, the influences of vicarious consequences on observers are relative rather than absolute. The extent of influence varies with the observer's valuation of the outcome and the behavior and the importance of the model.

Unlike direct and vicarious reinforcement, self-reinforcement is delivered by the individual for his or her own behavior. In general, individuals establish performance standards for themselves and tend to respond to their behavior in self-rewarding ways if their performance matches or exceeds the standard. They also tend to respond in self-critical ways if the performance fails to meet the standard. Self-imposed consequences also often operate in conjunction with external consequences. When external rewards are outweighed by self-censure, external rewards are relatively ineffective. Also, when external punishment is delivered for behaviors the individual values highly, it has little effect.

The Learner's Internal Processes

In social-cognitive theory, cognitive processes play a central role in learning. The learner's ability to code and store transitory experiences in symbolic form and to represent future consequences in thought are essential to the acquisition and modification of human behavior.

The cognitive processing of events and potential consequences guide the learner's behavior. For example, homeowners do not wait until their houses are burning to buy insurance. Instead, knowledge of the potential loss that can be the consequence of no insurance is the stimulus that prompts individuals to invest in homeowner's protection (Bandura, 1971b).

Four component processes are responsible for learning and performance. They are attention, retention, motor production, and motivational processes (Bandura, 1971a, 1977b). The relationships between the behavioral model, the learner's cognitive processes, and learning and performance are illustrated in Figure 12.2.

Attentional Processes.   New behaviors cannot be acquired unless they are attended to and accurately perceived (Bandura, 1977b). The learner's attentional processes, however, are influenced by a variety of factors. Included are the model's characteristics, characteristics and functional value of the behavior, and observer characteristics. Behavior that is successful for the model tends to be attended to and coded by the observer.

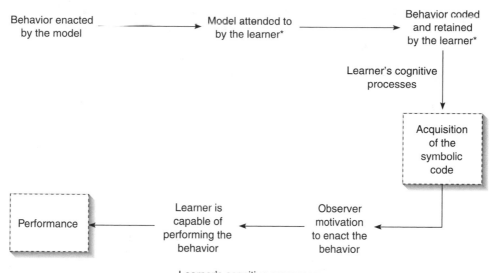

FIGURE 12.2
Sequence of steps in observational learning according to social-cognitive theory

Characteristics of the behaviors that influence attention include complexity and relevance. For example, long verbal sequences are too complex for young children to process. However, they are able to process visually presented models that are accompanied by a high degree of verbal repetition. The animal characters and dialogue in "Sesame Street" are an example.

Relevance, in general, refers to the importance of the behavior to the observer. Learning to drive a car, for example, is relevant for a teenager but not for a 2-year-old child.

Among the observer characteristics that influence attentional processes are perceptual set, observational skills, arousal level, past performance, and sensory capacities (Bandura, 1977b, p. 23). The learner's arousal level and perceptual set influence the selection of activities to be observed, whereas observational skills influence the accuracy of processing.

Learning from models also depends on the observer's skill in monitoring and interpreting ongoing events. Preschool children, for example, typically believe that an instant replay on television is a new example of the same event (Rice, Huston, & Wright, 1986). Also, Huston et al. (1989, p. 426) noted that preschool children typically do not differentiate between program content and commercials. Thus, developmental differences in abstracting information from symbolic models influence the interpretation of events.

Retention Processes.   These processes are responsible for the symbolic coding of the behavior and the storage of the visual or verbal codes in memory. These processes are important because the learner cannot benefit from the observed behaviors in the model's absence unless they are coded and retained for later use (Bandura, 1977b).

An important retention process is rehearsal. Both mental rehearsal, in which individuals imagine themselves enacting the behavior, and motor rehearsal (overt action) serve as important memory aids. Mental rehearsal requires that the learner internally represent the absent events. These representations can then guide the motor rehearsal.

Retention processes are, of course, influenced by the learner's development. The ability to represent behaviors in the form of labels and to generate verbal and visual cues enhances retention.

Motor Reproduction Processes.   After the observer has acquired a symbolic code, performance of the acquired behaviors depends on the learner's motor reproduction and motivational processes. Motor reproduction includes the selection and organization of responses at the cognitive level, followed by their execution (Bandura, 1977b). Like the processes of retention, motor reproduction is influenced by the developmental level of the individual.

Motivational Processes.   The three processes that function in observational learning as motivators are direct (external) reinforcement, vicarious reinforcement, and self-reinforcement. During the modeling of behavior, reinforcement to the model (vicarious reinforcement for the observer) is important in motivating the learner to attend to and code the observed behavior.

The Role of Self-Efficacy
The construct labeled self-efficacy refers to beliefs about one's capabilities, and these beliefs also motivate learners in particular ways. Important issues in self-efficacy are the essential characteristics, the sources of efficacy beliefs, and the effects on psychological processes.

Definition.   Perceived self-efficacy refers to a belief in one's capabilities to organize and execute the actions necessary to manage particular situations (Bandura, 1995, p. 2). Such judgments typically apply to situations that may include novel, unpredictable, or often stressful elements (Bandura, 1986; Bandura & Schunk, 1981).

Self-efficacy differs from self-concept in that self-concept is a general assessment. It is a global construct that includes several self-reactions (such as one's perceptions of popularity) (see Bong & Clark, 1999, for a discussion of the differences). Self-efficacy, in contrast, is a content-related judgment and, in the academic sphere, it refers to the belief that one can perform particularly academic tasks successfully (Zimmerman, 1995a, p. 218).

Efficacy expectations should not be confused with response–outcome expectations. A response–outcome expectancy is the belief that a particular behavior will lead to certain outcomes. However, an efficacy expectation is the belief in one's capability to execute the required behavior successfully

(Bandura, 1977b, p. 193). For example, the anticipated social recognition, applause, trophies, and self-satisfaction for the highest broad jump are outcome expectations. The belief that one can successfully high jump 6 feet is an efficacy judgment (Bandura, 1986, p. 391).

Perceived self-efficacy involves self-appraisal; it is not a fixed act, and it involves more than simply knowing what to do (Bandura, 1982b). Included in the self-appraisal are both personal and situational factors. For example, students who are capable of mastering a situation often make judgments that indicate they consider themselves to be inadequate (Zimmerman, 1986). University students often find their career options limited because they fear taking courses that involve quantitative methods (Henderson, 1986).

Faulty self-appraisal can, on occasion, lead to high self-efficacy that may be inaccurate. For example, in mathematics, children sometimes rely on "buggy algorithms." They are the systematic but inaccurate strategies that children often use in solving arithmetic problems. Knowledge of such strategies and being able to apply them well (they sometimes lead to correct answers) lead to a false sense of self-efficacy (Schunk, 1995, p. 214).

Sources of Efficacy Beliefs.   Four types of influence contribute to individuals' beliefs about their personal efficacy (Bandura, 1986; 1995). They are mastery experiences, vicarious experiences, social persuasion, and physiological and emotional states.

Mastery experiences provide the most authentic evidence about the individual's capabilities of mustering the resources required for success (Bandura, 1982a; 1995). Success tends to raise the judgment of efficacy, whereas repeated failures lower the judgment. For the individual who has a strong sense of efficacy, occasional failure will affect judgment very little. In contrast, failure is influential for individuals who are unsure of their abilities.

Mastery experiences designed to enhance students' self-efficacy should not consist of easy successes. Individuals who experience only easy successes are easily discouraged by failure because they tend to expect quick results (Bandura, 1995). Also, developing a sense of efficacy through mastery experiences must involve acquiring the cognitive and behavioral capabilities for executing appropriate courses of action (p. 3). Then, after individuals are convinced that they have the capabilities required to succeed, they are able to persevere in the face of setbacks.

Vicarious experiences provided by social models also contribute to self-efficacy. Observing similar individuals perform successfully can raise one's appraisals of efficacy. Vicarious experiences are particularly influential when people have had little or no direct experience in a situation. The models also demonstrate effective strategies for managing environmental demands and positive attitudes (Bandura, 1995, p. 4).

The third source of efficacy beliefs, verbal persuasion, can help counter an individual's mild self-doubts. Persuasion can assist individuals to avoid a focus on their personal deficiencies and to measure success in terms of improvement rather than outperforming others. However, persuasion cannot, in the absence of other influences, develop high beliefs of personal efficacy.

Physiological and emotional states also provide information about efficacy. Individuals tend to interpret stress reactions and tension as indicators of vulnerability to poor performance (Bandura, 1995, p. 4). Therefore, one way to alter personal efficacy is to reduce stress and negative emotional tendencies. In addition, individuals should learn to interpret the first signs of tension as an indicator that more focused effort is needed. Individuals with high self-efficacy tend to perceive heightened tension as a signal to energize one's efforts.

Effects on Psychological Processes.   Self-efficacy beliefs influence human functioning indirectly through four major processes. They are cognitive, motivational, affective, and selection processes (Bandura, 1995). Those with high self-efficacy construct success scenarios, whereas individuals with low self-efficacy do not. In specific, demanding situations, high self-efficacy contributes to continued analytical thinking, whereas low self-efficacy is accompanied by erratic strategies and thought processes (Wood & Bandura, 1989).

Efficacy beliefs enhance or limit motivation by influencing the types of goals that individuals set for themselves, the extent of effort they expend, and their persistence in the face of difficulties. A low sense of efficacy contributes to a slackening of effort and the tendency to give up easily.

Affective processes that are influenced by personal efficacy include anxiety, frustration, and depression (Bandura, 1993; 1995). A sense of efficacy assists in controlling disturbing thoughts and by supporting coping behaviors in difficult situations. For smokers, for example, research indicates that perceived self-efficacy in resisting smoking in stressful situations is related to relapses and the reinstitution of self-control after a relapse. Those with low self-efficacy relapse completely (Bandura, 1982b, p. 131). In other words, high self-efficacy contributes to the creation of a positive psychological environment for individuals that enables them to manage difficult situations.

Finally, efficacy beliefs influence the types of activities and environments that individuals choose (Bandura, 1995). Specifically, people avoid activities and environments that they believe are beyond their coping capabilities (p. 10). In contrast, individuals with a strong sense of efficacy approach difficult tasks as challenges to be mastered. Such an outlook, in turn, fosters personal accomplishment (Bandura, 1986).

Table 12.2 summarizes the task-related and long-term effects of high and low self-efficacy. As indicated, individuals with low self-efficacy focus attention on their deficiencies, set lower aspirations, and avoid the particular enriching environments that can enhance their competencies. Also of interest is that self-efficacy beliefs contribute to predictions of mathematics performance (Pajares, 1996; Pajares & Graham, 1999) and writing achievement (Pajares, Miller, & Johnson, 1997; Zimmerman & Bandura, 1994), and differentiate between high and low achievers in high school (Zimmerman & Martinez-Pons, 1986).

Summary.   Perceived self-efficacy is the learner's belief in his or her capabilities to successfully manage situations that may include novel or unpredictable

TABLE 12.2
Comparison of the Effects of Perceived High and Low Efficacy

	High Self-Efficacy	Low Self-Efficacy
Task-related behavior	1. Effort is strengthened in the face of difficulties.	1. Efforts slacken.
	2. Already-acquired skills are intensified and strengthened in the face of difficulties.	2. Task may be given up altogether in the face of difficulties.
	3. Effort and attention are focused on the demands of the situation.	3. Attention is focused on personal deficiencies and difficulties; these problems are magnified.
Long-term effects	4. Aids self-development through precipitating involvement in a variety of activities and experiences	4. Hinders development by facilitating the avoidance of enriching environments and activities
	5. Individual experiences little stress in taxing situations.	5. Individual suffers anxiety and stress in a variety of performance situations
	6. Typically leads to lack of effort rather than lack of ability as the cause for failure	6. Undermines the effective use of one's skills by directing attention to personal shortcomings
	7. Leads to goals that are challenging, that sustain interest and involvement	7. Leads to lowered aspirations as a mechanism for avoiding stress

Note: Summarized from *Social Foundations of Thought and Action: A Social-Cognitive Theory* by A. Bandura, 1986, Upper Saddle River, NJ: Prentice Hall.

elements. Perceived self-efficacy involves self-appraisal and it is not a fixed act. Students with similar academic abilities may differ in their sense of efficacy for particular subjects.

The four types of influence that contribute to efficacy beliefs are mastery experiences, vicarious experiences, social persuasion, and physiological and emotional states. Mastery experiences in which individuals acquire essential cognitive and behavioral skills for the situation and experience success are the most authentic evidence about capabilities. Vicarious experiences can be helpful when the observer can identify with the model, and verbal persuasion can help counter mild self-doubts. Physiological and emotional states that signal vulnerability to poor performance to the individual should be reduced or interpreted as a signal for increased effort.

Self-efficacy beliefs affect human functioning indirectly by influencing individuals' cognitive, motivational, affective, and selection processes. Individuals with high self-efficacy construct success scenarios, set challenging goals, persist in the face of difficulties, and control disturbing thoughts. Also, choices of activities, tasks, and even career choices are influenced by self-efficacy. Individuals avoid situations that they believe are beyond their coping abilities.

The Nature of Complex Learning

Unlike other theories, social-cognitive theory does not describe the forms of thinking and/or behavior that represent complex learning. Instead, the theory describes the factors essential to the attainment of superior performance in any domain or discipline. According to Bandura (1986), the essential factor in achieving complex capabilities is the individual's self-regulatory system. Important topics are the components of the system and the ways in which the self-regulatory system develops.

Personal, Behavioral, and Environmental Influences

A major goal of the self-regulatory system is to regulate the sources of personal, behavioral, and environmental influences that affect learning and performance. In addition to strategy knowledge and metacognitive knowledge, personal influences include perceived self-efficacy, learner goals, learner values and interests, perceptions of others (parents, teachers, and peers), and perceptions of learning environments (classrooms, libraries, and homes) (Zimmerman & Martinez-Pons, 1992; Schunk, 1995). Self-regulated learners view learning as a proactive enterprise. They set goals for themselves, are accurate self-monitors, and are resourceful in selecting learning strategies (Zimmerman, 1998).

Self-efficacy is important in self-regulation because it influences both the level at which goals are set and one's responses to failure to meet the preset goals. Goal setting and self-evaluation are critical for superior accomplishments in any area and particularly in the development of innovations. Self-generated standards and reinforcements sustain developments that often are resisted initially by society. In the absence of public recognition, self-reinforcement for meeting one's own standards maintains the artist's or innovator's creative efforts. Highly stringent standards, however, lead to self-created distress (Bandura, 1986). For example, the violinist in the second chair likely began as a prodigy with every expectation of dazzling the world. At 45 and balding, he is the most disappointed man on Earth (Bandura, 1986, p. 357).

The three major behavioral influences are self-observation, self-judgment, and self-reaction. Self-observation requires deliberate attention to one's behavior, whereas self-judgment refers to comparisons of one's present performance with pre-established goals (Schunk, 1995, p. 77). Graham and Harris (1994) described an anecdote about Ernest Hemingway in terms of these three processes. The author recorded his daily production of words (self-observation) on a mounted chart. If the amount was less than originally planned (self-judgment), Hemingway curtailed his time spent fishing (self-reaction) (p. 206).

Self-observation can be aided by recording key aspects of learning-related behavior. One course designed to help college students required that the students keep an activity log with 30-minute intervals for one week. Students often expressed surprise at the data, which indicated the amount of procrastination and non-productive time (Zimmerman, Greenberg, & Weinstein, 1994).

A key environmental influence on self-regulation processes is achievement outcomes. Individuals receive information about achievement, determine whether it meets their goals, and alter their behavior accordingly. If the achievement does not meet the preset goal, the individual may alter his or her strategies, increase effort, or lower the goals.

Measurement Issues.   The measurement of any unobservable construct, such as motivation, self-efficacy, or self-regulation, poses problems. Such constructs are not directly observable, and their presence must be inferred from behaviors that have been identified to occur only if individuals possess the particular construct. Measurement typically consists of observations of behavior in experimental or naturalistic settings (using checklists or other instruments) or self-reports of one's thoughts and typical behaviors.

The measurement of self-efficacy and self-regulation faces particular problems. They are: (1) data on self-efficacy, described as a dynamic construct, is in the form of cross-sectional snapshots (Henson, 2002, p. 142); (2) initial research on students' reports of their self-regulatory skills indicates a varying number of scale factors, depending on the instrument (Gredler & Garavalia, 2000a; Gredler & Schwartz, 1997; Pintrich & DeGroot, 1990); (3) some self-report instruments address primarily cognitive and metacognitive skills (e.g., how well do you remember information?); and (4) some assessments tend to focus on basic competencies rather than individual beliefs that they can manage and master situations with novel and ambiguous elements. Examples of items on writing competence are "When I have written a long or complex paper, I can find and correct all my grammatical errors," and "I can rewrite my wordy or confusing sentence clearly."

Some students tend to overestimate their self-regulatory skills (Pajares, 1996). In one study, eight entering graduate students with the highest scores on a measure of perceived self-regulatory skills had the lowest Graduate Record Examination and Miller Analogy Test scores (Schwartz & Gredler, 1998). Also, of 225 entering freshmen, provisionally admitted students (with insufficient SAT scores or high school grades) did not differ in their beliefs about their self-regulatory capabilities from fully admitted (qualified) freshmen (Gredler & Garavalia, 2000b).

Development of the Self-Regulatory System
The three-way interaction between personal factors, behavior, and the environment described by Bandura (1977a, 1978, 1986) contributes to the development of the self-regulatory system. A variety of models—teachers, parents, work associates, peers, and others—function as sources of information for standard setting and self-management of behavior. However, people do not passively incorporate everything they hear or see (Bandura, 1986). Instead, personal factors influence the development of generic standards from the behaviors of models in a variety of settings. In early childhood, for example, the approvals and punishments handed out by children to each other and to dolls or stuffed animals indicate the standards acquired by the children through modeling and direct experience (Bandura, 1986, p. 372).

The individual's self-regulated behavior influences the environment. In turn, however, environmental influences contribute to the development of self-monitoring and evaluative skills. They also provide support for the maintenance of internal standards (Bandura, 1986) (Figure 12.3). Self-regulation is cyclical because feedback on prior performance provides information for current adjustments in one's efforts (Zimmerman, 2001, p. 4).

Included in external reinforcements are rewards for excellence and negative sanctions for individuals who provide themselves with undeserved self-reward (Bandura, 1977b, 1978; Bandura, Mahoney, & Dirks, 1976). Examples include scholarships and other awards for outstanding academic achievements. Prizes, public acclaim, and monetary rewards reinforce winners of arduous sports events (e.g., the Indianapolis 500, the Wimbledon tennis tournament, and the Olympic Games). Negative sanctions also include public dishonor for cheating performances, such as that of Rosie Roiz, the marathon runner who faked a victory.

The behavioral standards used by the individual and the delivery of self-reinforcement depend on the relationship between the particular task and the individual's expertise. A mathematician, for example, would not consider that solving elementary arithmetic problems is deserving of self-reward. On the other hand, a humanities scholar would not devalue his or her poor performance on a test of engineering skills (Bandura, 1971b). Particularly important are the self-reinforcements for engaging in difficult tasks or aversive activities, such as completing homework or speaking up in social situations. Arranged self-reward bridges the gap between initiation of the new behavior and the environmental contingencies that will be activated by competent performance.

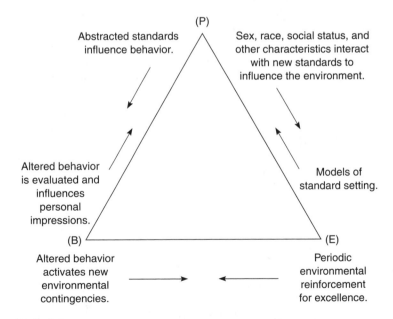

FIGURE 12.3
Reciprocal determinism in the development of self-regulatory systems

The three-way interaction between personal factors, environmental factors, and behavior, given different sets of circumstances, also can lead to the disengagement of self-evaluative capabilities. The result is the development and maintenance of reprehensible conduct and inhumane activities (Bandura, 1977a, 1979, 1986). Prior theories have proposed different internal "watchdogs" that are responsible for moral behavior, such as a conscience, a superego, or an internalized moral code. Such theories, however, encounter difficulties when they attempt to explain inhumane conduct by otherwise humane moral persons (Bandura, 1982a, p. 351).

In the social-cognitive analysis, such acts are performed through processes that disengage the behavior from a self-evaluative reaction. Among the dissociative practices that are responsible for this disengagement are moral justification (the end justifies the means), displacement of responsibility (I was only following orders), dehumanization of the victim (use of terms such as "gooks" and "wetbacks"), and euphemistic labeling. The role of euphemisms is to "sanitize" reprehensible or pernicious behavior by using benign expressions. Euphemisms also are used in everyday affairs to disguise negative situations or behaviors. Examples include "fourth quarter equity retreat" (decline in stock dividends) (Evans, 1989, p. 43), corporate "downsizing" (firing employees), and mercenaries "fulfilling a contract" (killing others).

The practices of dehumanizing victims, blaming victims to justify persecution, and other practices do not quickly transform a law-abiding citizen into an aggressor (Bandura, 1982a). Rather, the process is gradual, beginning with acts that do not generate excessive self-censure. Discomfort and self-approach then gradually diminish through repeated performance until brutal acts are committed with little distress (Bandura, 1982a, p. 354).

The importance of these analyses is twofold. First, the self-system is a critical factor in the development of accomplished skills and capabilities in any field of endeavor. Second, neither the development of self-evaluative reactions nor their disengagement is an automatic process. Rather, a series of particular types of reciprocal interactions between the individual and the environment is required.

Summary.   The self-regulatory system consists of informational cognitive structures on goals, outcomes, and behavior, and cognitive processes that perceive, evaluate, and regulate behavior. The self-system includes standards for one's behavior, self-observation, self-judgment, and self-reaction. The goal of self-regulated learning is to regulate sources of personal, behavioral, and social-environmental sources of influence. Individuals set goals for themselves, pay deliberate attention to their behavior (self-observation), and compare their performance with preset goals (self-judgment). Depending on the comparison, they may reward themselves and set higher goals, exert further effort to meet the goals, or lower the goals.

Achieving accomplished performance in any field requires goal setting and self-evaluation. Familiar examples are concert pianists and other artists. Self-generated standards and reinforcements are particularly important in the development of innovations that often are initially resisted by society. Self-efficacy is important in self-regulation because it influences the individual's choice of activities, effort and persistence, and toleration of failure.

Measurement issues related to self-efficacy and self-regulation include the need for a clear specification of the constructs to be measured and instruments that differentiate between the self-assessment of one's competencies and self-efficacy.

The development of the self-regulatory system depends on the reciprocal three-way interaction between the environment, personal influences, and behavior. Individuals abstract information from the behavior of others, and personal factors influence the development of generic standards from those behaviors. The individual's behavior influences both the environment and one's personal reactions. The consequences in the environment, in turn, influence both personal perceptions and subsequent behavior. In some situations, the three-way interaction can lead to the disengagement of self-evaluative capabilities and the development of reprehensible conduct that is sanctioned by some in the environment.

PRINCIPLES OF INSTRUCTION

A theory of instruction has yet to be derived from social-cognitive theory. However, the principles of the theory have major implications for the classroom. The theory has been implemented successfully in the acquisition of both motor and cognitive skills. Early applications to cognitive skills included linguistic rules, concept formation, and problem solving (see Rosenthal & Zimmerman, 1973, 1976, 1978). In recent years, modeling has been used to teach learning strategies. Examples include finding the main idea in paragraphs, setting up word problems, and monitoring one's own learning. Recall the references to teacher modeling in chapters 8 and 9.

Basic Assumptions

The three major assumptions that support the principles of social-cognitive theory also are applicable to classroom instruction. They are (1) the learner's cognitive processes and decision making are important factors in learning; (2) the three-way interaction between the environment, personal factors, and behavior are responsible for learning; and (3) the outcomes of learning are visual and verbal codes of behavior.

The Components of Instruction

In social-cognitive theory, the essential components of learning are a behavioral model, reinforcement to the model, and the learner's cognitive processing of the modeled behaviors. The components of instruction, therefore, are (1) identifying appropriate models in the classroom, (2) establishing the functional value of behaviors, and (3) guiding the learner's internal processing, which includes facilitating the learner's sense of self-efficacy.

Identifying Appropriate Models

In the classroom, both teachers and students can serve as live models for a variety of academic and social behaviors. For adolescents, the influence of peer models often is emphasized. However, the teacher is responsible for the classroom and is important as a model of responsibility, integrity, sincerity, and concern for both the individual and the collective welfare of the students (Brophy & Putnam, 1979, p. 196). At any level of education, the teacher or faculty member should model emotional maturity, rationality, "common sense," and consistent follow-through on commitments (Brophy & Putnam, 1979).

Community members, such as firefighters, police, doctors, nurses, and other models who are interesting to young children, can be invited to spend some time in the classroom. To be maximally effective, however, a planned program of community involvement is needed. Visits or talks that appear to fill up time or give everyone a break on Friday will be ineffective. They also may convey the message that being a responsible adult is not important and does not contribute to self-worth.

Symbolic models also are effective influences in the development of prosocial behaviors. Research on *Sesame Street* and *Mister Rogers' Neighborhood*, for example, indicated that the modeled prosocial behaviors enhance children's cooperativeness and friendliness (see Leifer, 1976).

Both live and symbolic models can teach abstract cognitive rules, problem-solving strategies, and sequences of integrated motor behaviors (see Carroll & Bandura, 1982; Rosenthal & Bandura, 1978; Rosenthal & Zimmerman, 1978).

The selection of a live or symbolic model often depends on practical considerations. For cognitive and motor skills, the advantages of the live model are (1) the physical demonstration of the behavior in front of the students and (2) the opportunities for student questions. The chemistry class in which the use of laboratory equipment often is demonstrated by the teacher is an example.

The major advantage of symbolic modeling is that the models may be viewed more than once by students. In one study, for example, a videotape was used to teach toothbrushing skills to children in Head Start classrooms (Murray & Epstein, 1981). In a project supervised by this author, videotapes of classroom teachers with their classes were made available to undergraduates about to undertake their own student teaching. The undergraduates returned to the tapes several times, reporting that they found something informative and interesting on each viewing.

In addition to the selection of the model, another important consideration is the selection of the behaviors to be modeled. They should be interesting to the observer and portrayed at a level of complexity to be understood by the learner. Also significant are the type and status of the model. Some research indicated that children are more likely to remember the actions of a friendly, powerful person than those of a cold, neutral person (Baldwin, 1973).

Nurturance of the model, however, must be implemented with care in powerful models. Because the young child seeks feedback from nurturant authority figures, expressive features can detract the child's attention away from modeled behaviors. This potential problem can be counteracted by the use of verbal directives focused on the relevant behavior as well as the display of minimal expressive reactions during modeling.

Establishing the Functional Value of the Behavior

According to social-cognitive theory, individuals pay attention to events in the environment that predict reinforcement (Bandura, 1977b, p. 85). They tend to ignore events that do not include reinforcement predictions. Therefore, Bandura (1977b) recommended that instruction should attempt to establish an expectancy for positive outcomes. Such an expectancy increases task attention.

Events that predict reinforcement have acquired functional value for the student and will be attended to. In the classroom, establishing the usefulness of new learning for the students is important. First-grade children, for example, frequently view the purpose of assignments as content coverage rather than content mastery (Anderson, 1981).

Also, in teaching learning strategies, students must learn when to use them and why they are used (the metacognitive knowledge described in chapter 9). For example, skimming is a strategy for previewing the information in a text passage. (It is dysfunctional if used merely to skip difficult words or sentences.) For a student to sense the need to use skimming and to spend effort in executing it, skimming must have utility (Paris, Lipscom, & Wilson, 1985, p. 304). Otherwise, it will be used only to comply with a teacher's request.

Establishing the functional value of social behaviors is also important in the classroom. Reinforcement to peer models for working quietly, proceeding in an orderly manner to recess, and so on can influence the adoption of those behaviors by classmates.

Two cautions, however, must be observed in the use of reinforcement. First, vicarious reinforcement differs from **implicit reinforcement**. Exemplary behavior that is praised in one individual and disregarded in others may to the teacher imply reinforcement to all the students who behaved well. To the slighted individuals, the direct consequences of their behavior (i.e., no reinforcement) may be perceived as punishment.

The second caution is that reinforcement, like beauty, is in the eye of the beholder. The same compliment, when given to two different individuals, can have different effects. Similarly, the omission of expected punishment conveys the impression of permissiveness. Behavioral restraints are reduced, and the formerly forbidden behaviors are performed with greater freedom (Bandura, 1971a). Therefore, clearly stated rules in the classroom must be maintained when transgressions occur.

Guiding the Learner's Internal Processes

The recommended instructional activities vary somewhat, depending on the type of skill to be learned. Different emphases are required for cognitive and motor skills. However, for both types of skills, instruction should provide opportunities (1) to code the observed behavior into visual images or word symbols and (2) to mentally rehearse the modeled behaviors. Unless imitative performances are symbolized in memory codes and then stabilized through rehearsal, neither the memory codes nor the behaviors can be retrieved later (Bandura & Jeffrey, 1973). Also important is facilitating the learners' sense of personal efficacy.

Motor Skills.   Successful performance of complex motor skills such as golf, skiing, and tennis depends on the individual's internal monitoring of kinesthetic feedback. A recommended strategy consists of (1) the presentation of a videotaped model, (2) the opportunity to develop a conceptual representation, and finally, (3) practice with concurrent visual feedback via a monitor (Carroll & Bandura, 1982). The strategy can be successful in teaching a new motor skill that is outside the learner's visual field, such as executing the backstroke.

Of primary importance is that mental rehearsal by the learner should precede physical execution of the skill (Jeffrey, 1976). Mental rehearsal fulfills an organizational function for the subsequent performance. Also, too early an emphasis on motor performance can jeopardize retention at a time when memory codes are unstable.

Delayed self-observation following modeling is also very useful for social and communication skills. Students in speech and debate, for example, can acquire essential information about needed changes in posture, voice level, gestures, and presentation and response styles.

Conceptual Behavior.   Initial studies indicated that children can infer judgmental rules from models when instructed to find consistencies across presented situations (Rosenthal & Zimmerman, 1978; Zimmerman & Rosenthal, 1974). However, in the classroom, the use of modeling alone appears to be less effective than when combined with some form of verbal instruction (Schunk, 1986). Verbalization during modeling should be carefully selected, however, so that it conveys important information. In addition, overt responding by the learner should not be required. Organizing and producing verbal responses appears to interfere with the observation of the behavioral sequence (Zimmerman & Rosenthal, 1974).

Facilitating Learner Efficacy.   Important for impulsive children is to exercise self-control when faced with new or ambiguous tasks. A plan developed by Meichenbaum and Goodman (1971) to teach impulsive children to manage their own behavior uses modeling combined with verbalized self-instruction. The method has been used for the self-regulatory training of underachieving children (see Fox & Kendall, 1983; Loper & Murphy, 1985).

An adult first models self-talk in three aspects of monitoring one's own learning. They are (1) problem definition ("What is it that I have to do?"), (2) self-instructions that focus on the task ("Now stop and repeat the instruction"), and (3) self-reinforcement and self-evaluation ("Good, I'm doing fine"; "That's OK, I can take my time until I get it right") (Meichenbaum & Goodman, 1971).

After observing the model, the students undertake four practice phases. The phases are (1) imitation of the model with guidance, (2) performance of the task while verbalizing aloud, (3) practice while whispering, and (4) practice using silent speech.

Student self-efficacy in the classroom also may be enhanced by observing the success of peers who are perceived to be similar in competence. Children with difficulties in subtraction who observed both the teacher and a peer model scored higher on self-efficacy, persistence, and achievement than those who observed only the teacher or no model (Schunk & Hanson, 1985).

The Role of Teacher Efficacy.   Teacher efficacy refers to the extent that the teacher believes he or she has the capabilities to affect student performance (McLaughlin & Marsh, 1978, p. 84). Specifically, it is a "teacher judgment of his or her capabilities to bring about desired outcomes of student engagement and learning, even among those students who may be difficult or unmotivated" (Tschannen-Moran & Woolfolk Hoy, 2001, p. 783). Several studies reported that teacher efficacy is related to student gains and that teachers in effective schools have a strong sense of efficacy (see Guskey, 1987, and Tschannen-Moran, Woolfolk Hoy, & Hoy, 1998, for a discussion).

One model of teacher efficacy maintains that it consists of two joint simultaneous decisions. One is analyzing the teaching task, which includes the various factors that contribute to the difficulty of the task weighed against available resources to facilitate learning; the other is the teacher's self-perceptions of his or her personal teaching competence (Tschannen-Moran et al., 1998, p. 228). In other words, like student efficacy, teacher efficacy refers to a particular context, such as teaching probability to middle school students.

Efficacy influences a variety of teachers' actions. Included are the goals they set, their level of aspiration, and effort invested in teaching. Teachers with a strong sense of efficacy are more open to new ideas, are more willing to experiment with different methods that may help their students, and exhibit greater enthusiasm for teaching (Allinder, 1994; Ashton & Webb, 1986; Tschannen-Moran & Woolfolk Hoy, 2001, pp. 783, 784). They also are nonauthoritarian, persist with struggling students, providing them with the help they need to be successful, and praise students for their accomplishments (Gibson & Dembo, 1994). In addition, they support the development of students' academic self-direction (Woolfolk & Hoy, 1990).

In contrast, teachers with a low sense of instructional efficacy tend to use a custodial orientation that relies primarily on external inducements and negative sanctions to promote academic work. Such teachers also spend more time in nonacademic activities and quickly give up on students if they do not get results (Gibson & Dembo, 1984; Woolfolk & Hoy, 1990). They also tend to identify low ability as the reason some students cannot be taught (Bandura, 2000, p. 4).

Teacher efficacy, however, does not function in isolation. Bandura (2000) noted that self-efficacy plays a key role in cognitive development and accomplishment through three pathways. They are (1) "students' beliefs in their efficacy to regulate their learning activities and master academic subjects, (2) teachers' beliefs in their personal efficacy to motivate and promote learning in their students; and (3) the faculty's collective sense of efficacy that their schools can accomplish significant academic progress" (p. 4). Collective teacher efficacy is the perception of teachers that the school faculty will have a positive effect on student achievement (Goddard, Hoy, & Woolfolk Hoy 2000, p. 486). However, it is not simply a summation of individual perceptions of themselves. Instead, collective teacher efficacy refers to "individual perceptions of the capabilities of the entire faculty in a school organization" (Henson, 2002, p. 142). It is an example of the collective efficacy concept described by Bandura (1997), which consists of the shared perceptions of group members about "the performance capability of a social system as a whole" (p. 469). Early research suggests that goal consensus among faculty is an indicator of collective teacher agency. However, people's shared beliefs in their collective capability to produce desired outcomes is the key component of collective agency (Bandura, 2000, p. 4).

Designing Instruction for Complex Skills

Social-cognitive theory addresses the learning of complex skills in three ways. One is that of modeling and teaching effective strategies for success in complex tasks. Examples in reading include analyzing word parts and using context to determine word meaning. The second application is that of modeling strategies for directing and monitoring one's own learning. The third application is that of developing the learner's self-regulatory system. Also essential in the classroom is a knowledgeable teacher with high self-efficacy.

Learning strategies are systematic plans that assist the comprehension of information and task performance (Schunk, 1989). Important in the learning of these strategies is the modeling that includes talking through unobservable processes. In this way, the cognitive and metacognitive processes are made explicit for students. Recall the example in chapter 9 in which the teacher verbalized her uncertainty in understanding a paragraph and noted she would reread it and summarize it in her own words.

Research indicates that such instruction is essential for low-achieving students. Unlike other students, low achievers do not develop these skills spontaneously (Brophy, 1988; Corno, 1986). Even if motivated to learn, low-achieving students tend to depend on rote memorization and other inefficient learning skills. Recall from chapter 11 the method referred to as reciprocal teaching, which teaches four strategies to enhance students' comprehension of text (Palinscar & Brown, 1984). Initially, the teacher models these strategies. Then, as students become more proficient, they become peer models for other students.

In two first-grade classrooms identified as supportive of self-regulation, classroom observations of reading and writing indicated that the teachers gave students choices, provided opportunities to control challenges, provided support, and gave feedback that was nonthreatening (Perry, VandeKamp, Mercer, Nordby, 2002, p. 9). In the area of writing, Graham and Harris (1994) derived suggestions for developing self-regulation based on prior research. The suggestions are to (1) make writing an enjoyable and interesting activity, (2) provide opportunities for students to initiate and direct their own efforts, (3) use writing tasks that require self-regulation (narrating a personal experience is not one), and (4) model self-regulation and provide strategy assistance to students as they write (p. 223).

EDUCATIONAL APPLICATIONS

Social-cognitive theory has two major implications for education. First, modeling is a primary source of information for learners. The theory identifies situations in which children acquire information from the models in the mass media as well as from family models and others. Second is the importance of a sense of personal efficacy and self-regulatory skills in becoming a successful learner.

Classroom Issues

Social-cognitive theory addresses some of the issues of concern in the classroom setting. It also addresses some learner characteristics and aspects of the social setting for learning.

Learner Characteristics
Individual differences, readiness, and motivation for learning are the student characteristics that interact with instruction. Both individual differences and readiness are discussed in social-cognitive theory in terms of their relationship to learning through observation.

Individual Differences.   Learners differ in their ability to abstract, code, remember, and enact the behaviors that they see. They also differ in their receptivity to models. Behaviors watched intently by nature lovers, for example, will be considered dull and boring by others. Receptivity to a particular model varies along the dimensions of (1) the valuation of the behavior for the observer and (2) the degree of similarity between the observed model/context of the behavior and the observer's status and situation.

In the classroom, after the early school years, students also will differ on the functional value of the learning outcomes established by the school or the teacher. Some students will enthusiastically engage in learning activities, many will be more or less passively compliant, and others who perceive no social value in the outcomes may engage in antisocial behavior.

Readiness.   The developmental level of the learner and receptivity to particular models are the two major factors that determine the individual's capability for observational learning. The learner's perceptual set and the degree of anticipated reinforcement influence the decision to attend to or to ignore the model. The ability to abstract the important features of the modeled behaviors and to recall them later without error also influences the extent and accuracy of the learning. Young children, for example, cannot process complex sequences of behaviors. Instead, they require short explicit visual sequences with repetition.

Motivation.   Although some activities are initiated for direct reinforcement (e.g., activities prompted by thirst, hunger, pain, and so on), the primary source of motivation is cognitively based (Bandura, 1977b, p. 161). Two types of cognitive motivators are included. One is the cognitive representation of future consequences for particular behaviors. "Past experiences create expectations that certain actions will bring valued benefits, that others will have no appreciable effects, and that still others will avert future trouble" (Bandura, 1977b, p. 18).

The second type of cognitive motivator may be referred to as self-motivation because it involves the standard setting and self-evaluative mechanisms of the learner. This type of motivation develops as part of the individual's self-regulatory system, discussed earlier.

Cognitive Processes and Instruction

Transfer of learning, developing the individual's learning-how-to-learn skills, and teaching problem solving are cognitive issues of importance to education. Of the three, social-cognitive theory discusses the first issue.

Transfer of Learning.   The concept of transfer has been researched in the social-cognitive context in two ways. One is the investigation of different treatments for phobic patients. Self-directed mastery experiences were found to be more effective in providing transfer to generalized threat situations than participant modeling alone (Bandura, 1976; Bandura, Adams, & Beyer, 1977).

Modeling of cognitive behaviors has provided both immediate and delayed transfer to similar tasks. Concept attainment, linguistic rule learning, and problem solution strategies were generalized to similar situations (Schunk, 1981; Zimmerman & Rosenthal, 1974).

The Social Context for Learning

Social-cognitive theory addresses the issue of learning in the naturalistic setting. Thus it describes specifically the mechanisms by which individuals learn from each other as they go about their daily lives. The observation of a variety of models (family members, regular associates, films, television) and the reinforcements delivered to peers and others are all important influences on learning. In particular, social-cognitive theory reminds the educational system that learning in a media-oriented society extends beyond the classroom in subtle and pervasive ways.

Relationships to Other Perspectives

Bandura's social-cognitive theory describes learning in the naturalistic setting. Observing peers and others (models), learners abstract behaviors relevant for them and later execute these actions. Bandura's concept of modeling plus reinforcement to the model is a key feature of Gagné's attitudinal domain. Further, cognitive theorists recommend teacher modeling and verbalization of learning and metacognitive strategies. Although the theory refers to the learners' attentional and retention processes, these processes are not prescribed in detail (unlike Gagné's internal conditions or the phases of information processing).

Like operant conditioning, social-cognitive theory incorporates both direct and self-reinforcement. A key difference is the inclusion of vicarious reinforcement, the physiological effects of observing reinforcement accorded the model.

The self-regulatory system, essential for complex learning, includes the metacognitive skills of monitoring and evaluation. However, descriptions of the self-regulatory system also include goal setting, learner values and interests, perceptions of the learning environment, and learner self-efficacy.

In the classroom setting, social-cognitive theory assumes that instruction is teacher managed and directed and the individual student is the locus of learning. Thus, it differs from social constructivist perspectives in which a community of learners is primary.

Developing a Classroom Strategy

The design of instruction for observational learning includes a careful analysis of the behaviors to be modeled and the processing requirements for learning.

Step 1: Analyze the behaviors to be modeled.

    1.1 What is the nature of the behavior? Is it primarily conceptual, motor, or affective, or is it a learning strategy (such as rereading difficult paragraphs and making notes)?

    1.2 What are the sequential steps in the behavior?

    1.3 What are the critical points in the sequence, such as the steps that may be difficult to observe and those for which alternative incorrect actions are likely?

Step 2: Establish the functional value of the behavior and select the behavioral model.

    2.1 Does the behavior or strategy carry a "success prediction," such as learning to operate equipment essential for a job promotion?

    2.2 If the behavior is a weak success predictor, which potential model is most likely to predict success? Examples include peers, the teacher, and status models that appeal to the target group.

    2.3 Should the model be live or symbolic? Consider cost, the need to repeat the experience for more than one group, and the opportunity for portraying the functional value of the behavior.

    2.4 What reinforcement(s) is the model to receive for the behavior?

Step 3: Develop the instructional sequence.

    3.1 For motor skills, what are the "do this" but "not this" verbal codes to be used?

    3.2 Which steps in the sequence are to be presented slowly? What are the verbal codes that supplement but do not supplant these steps?

    3.3 For a learning strategy, what unobservable processes and self-talk are to be modeled?

Step 4: Implement the instruction to guide the learner's cognitive and motor reproduction processes.

Motor skills:

4.1 Present the model.

4.2 Provide students the opportunity for symbolic rehearsal.

4.3 Provide student practice with visual feedback.

Conceptual behavior:

4.1 Present the model with supporting verbalization.

4.2 If a concept or a rule, provide students with opportunities to summarize the modeled behaviors.

4.3 If the learning is a problem-solving or strategy application, provide opportunities for participant modeling.

4.4 Provide opportunities to generalize to other situations.

4.5 Assist the students in analyzing their applications and setting goals.

Classroom Example

The behaviors modeled in the following example are note-taking skills. The identified population is middle school students (ages 10 to 14, grades 6 to 8).[2]

The teacher first models the strategy of note taking from written text. Important in this exercise is that the teacher model the process in which a particular recall cue is chosen over another. The teacher should "talk aloud" the cues that come to mind and the reasons for rejection of poor cues. After the teacher's demonstration, the students suggest the notes to be taken in the next two exercises. This activity provides for corrective feedback early in the learning. The students then complete a note-taking exercise on their own. This activity provides the symbolic coding and mental rehearsal necessary for conceptual behavior.

The follow-up exercise that demonstrates note taking from audiotaped material should be initiated only after the students have applied their skills for written materials in a variety of situations. Taking notes from an ongoing oral presentation is a difficult skill to learn. It is dependent on good listening skills and practice in the use of temporary auditory memory. In teaching this skill, exercises in listening and recall of oral material may be required prior to the note-taking exercise.

The teacher explains the importance of note taking in helping the students to remember material that they have heard or read. Also, good note-taking strategies should help them remember important information for tests.

Before beginning the actual classroom exercise, the teacher and students determine an initial goal for the skills to be learned. For example, they may decide that the goal should be to develop good recall cues for three important points in a short reading passage.

The teacher then distributes a four-paragraph reading selection and asks the students to read the first paragraph silently while the teacher reads it aloud.

---

[2]Example designed by Sharon Cohn, University of South Carolina.

A transparency that illustrates the note-taking format is placed on the overhead projector. It is divided into two columns, headed "recall cues" and "notes."[3] The teacher talks through the first paragraph in terms of its important points. Then under the "notes" column, two summary sentences for the paragraph and associated cues in the "recall cues" column are entered. The teacher verbalizes the ways in which these sentences and the recall words will help students to remember the paragraph.

The teacher then carries out the same procedure with the other two paragraphs. After reading each one aloud, the teacher talks though several alternatives for notes, selects one or two, and enters them in the appropriate column with associated cues. The importance of the exercise is that the students observe the ways in which the teacher analyzes the paragraph and selects summary sentences.

The students and the teacher then work through two or three exercises together, with the students suggesting the study notes. This activity is followed by independent note taking by the students on short passages that they have selected from other sources.

The teacher reviews the notes developed independently by the students on short passages they have selected and gives each student feedback on progress toward the initial goal. Suggested changes are made to students who are having difficulty with the assignment.

Reading Passage for Note-Taking Exercise[4]

A land grant of 10 million acres was given to George Calvert, a prominent nobleman from England known as Lord Baltimore. The land given by the king, Charles I, was located near Chesapeake Bay, and this gift enabled George Calvert to exert tremendous power. He was capable of establishing manors that resembled those of the feudal era, and of treating the inhabitants as serfs. He also functioned as a prosecutor and a judge of inhabitants charged with law breaking. George Calvert was called a proprietor, or an owner of landholdings, and his colony was known as a proprietary colony.

Prior to the king's seal being affixed to the charter describing the land grant, George Calvert died, and his son served as the first proprietor. The colony was known as Maryland, named after the wife of Charles I, Queen Henrietta Maria. Since the Calvert family was Catholic, they intended to establish a Catholic colony in Maryland.

In 1634 the first settlers arrived and established the town of St. Mary's. The settlers could obtain food and other provisions from the adjacent and prosperous colony of Virginia. They did not have to wait for ships from England. They did not waste time looking for gold; instead, they immediately began to grow tobacco.

---

[3]Suggested by W. Pauk, *How to Study in College* (New York: Houghton Mifflin, 1962).
[4]Paraphrased from J. A. Garraty ct al., *American History* (New York: Harcourt, 1982).

Recall Cues	Notes
Calvert	George Calvert, Lord Baltimore, was the proprietor of a large land area near the Chesapeake Bay.
Proprietary colony	He had a great deal of power, and his land was a proprietary colony.
Maryland	Calvert's son was the first proprietor of the colony called Maryland. Because Calvert's family was Catholic, they wanted Maryland to be a Catholic colony.
Tobacco	Early settlers in Maryland began to grow tobacco.

Note-Taking Exercise II

In this exercise, the teacher has previously recorded a script on audiotape. The speech is recorded with short pauses, much as one might give a talk to a group. In the modeling, the teacher plays each paragraph of the recorded tape and demonstrates how to take notes while the tape is playing. She writes recall cues and sentence fragments on the transparency during the brief pauses in the tape. The tape is stopped at the end of each paragraph, and the teacher completes the sentence fragments.

After the demonstration, the students and the teacher complete several short paragraphs together. This exercise is usually quite difficult for students because it involves listening and jotting down notes at the same time. Therefore, only very short paragraphs should be used until the students' skills are acquired; this may require several exercises over a period of time.

Taped Paragraph[5]

In the 17th century a cluster of religious reformers resided in England. These reformers were critical of the Church of England. However, they did not want to separate from the church. They wished to reform and to purify the church from the inside. These reformers were called Puritans.

Recall Cues	Sentence Fragments	Completed Sentence
Reform	the Church of England	The Puritans wanted to reform and purify the Church of England.
Purify		

Review of the Theory

Albert Bandura's social-cognitive theory began with his analyses of prior approaches to the learning of imitative behavior. Prior theories proposed a variety of mechanisms to account for the adoption of prosocial and antisocial behaviors. Included were reinforcement for imitation, nurturance, power, envy, and frustration.

[5]Paraphrased from J. A. Garraty et al., American History (New York: Harcourt, 1982).

In contrast, Bandura proposed a single paradigm to account for the acquisition of both prosocial and antisocial behaviors. The components are (1) the modeled behaviors, (2) the consequences of the model, and (3) the learner's cognitive processes (Table 12.3). The consequences received by the model that contribute to the observer's learning the behavior include vicarious reinforcement, vicarious punishment, and the absence of anticipated punishment. These consequences signal behaviors that have functional value and therefore may be useful to the observer. Later successful performance by the observer depends in part on the learner's cognitive processes (attention, retention, motor reproduction, and motivation).

Learning, according to Bandura, is represented by a three-way interaction among the environment, the individual's internal events, and the individual's behavior (reciprocal determinism). Also included in the theory is the development of the self-regulatory system, a necessary component in the development of outstanding performance in any area. Included in the system are a sense of personal efficacy, goal setting, self-evaluation, and self-directed rewards or punishments.

Disadvantages

Bandura identifies the importance of the learner's self-direction and sense of efficacy in interacting with the environment. However, in the limited classroom setting, developing the learner's self-regulatory system and sense of efficacy is a difficult task.

TABLE 12.3
Summary of Bandura's Social-Cognitive Theory

Basic Elements	Definition
Assumptions	Learning is a three-way interaction between the environment, personal factors, and behavior that also involves the learner's cognitive processes
Components of learning	Modeled behaviors, consequences to the model, and the learner's cognitive processes
Learning outcomes	Verbal and visual codes that may or may not later be performed
Designing instruction for complex skills	In addition to component skills, develop the learner's sense of efficacy and self-regulation
Major issues in designing instruction	Provide for mental rehearsal prior to practice; avoid omission of reinforcement or punishment when needed; avoid excessive use of punishment
ANALYSIS OF THE THEORY	
Disadvantages	Difficult to implement the requirements for self-efficacy and self-regulation along with other classroom priorities
Contributions	Description of the variety of attitudes and behaviors acquired from the mass media
	Provides a detailed description of the mechanisms of reinforcement and punishment in the group setting
	Identifies the importance of self-efficacy in learning

Contributions to Educational Practice

An important contribution is the detailed descriptions of the role of models and reinforcement and punishment in the classroom setting. That is, punishment or lack of it delivered to others as well as vicarious reinforcement are both operating in the classroom setting. Another contribution is the identification of the role of personal efficacy in learning.

CHAPTER QUESTIONS

1. In chapter 3, one technique for unconditioning children's fears made use of other children's acceptance of the feared object. According to social-cognitive theory, why was this technique successful?
2. Which types of reinforcement or punishment are likely to be operating in the following situations?
    _____a. Three classmates are allowed to go to the library early for completing assignments quietly.
    _____b. A student studying for a difficult final exam promises herself a day at the beach if she does well on the test.

    _____c. Kazdin (1989) indicated that when brief time-outs are given to disruptive students the number of similar incidents in the classroom tends to decrease.
3. Describe a television commercial in which an action or belief demonstrated by a model earns positive consequences for the model.
4. What are the meanings of the euphemisms "termination with extreme prejudice" and "uncontained engine failure"? What other euphemisms have you read and/or heard via the media?

REFERENCES

Allinder, R. M. (1994). The relationship between efficacy and the instructional practices of special education teachers and consultants. *Teacher Education and Special Education, 17*, 86–95.

Anderson, L. M. (1981). *Student responses to seatwork: Implications for the study of students' cognitive processing* (Research Series No. 102). East Lansing, MI: The Institute for Research on Teaching, Michigan State University.

Ashton, P. T., & Webb, R. B. (1986). *Making a difference: Teachers' sense of efficacy and student achievement.* New York: Longman.

Baldwin, A. L. (1973). Social learning. In F. Kerlinger (Ed.), *Review of research in education* (Vol. 1, pp. 34–57). Itasca, IL: Peacock.

Bandura, A. (1965). Behavioral modification through modeling practices. In L. Krasner & L. Ullman (Eds.), *Research in behavior*

modification (pp. 310–340). New York: Holt, Rinehart & Winston.

Bandura, A. (1969). Social-learning theory of identificatory processes. In D. A. Goslin (Ed.), *Handbook of socialization theory and research* (pp. 213–262). Chicago: Rand McNally.

Bandura, A. (1971a). *Psychological modeling: Conflicting theories.* Chicago: Aldine–Atherton.

Bandura, A. (1971b). *Social learning theory.* Upper Saddle River, NJ: Prentice Hall.

Bandura, A. (1971c). Vicarious and self-reinforcement processes. In R. Glaser (Ed.), *The nature of reinforcement* (pp. 228–278). New York: Academic.

Bandura, A. (1973). *Aggression: A social learning analysis.* Upper Saddle River, NJ: Prentice Hall.

Bandura, A. (1974). Behavior theory and the models of man. *American Psychologist, 29,* 859–869.

Bandura, A. (1976). Social learning perspective on behavior change. In A. Burton (Ed.), *What makes behavior change possible?* (pp. 34–57). New York: Brunner/Mazel.

Bandura, A. (1977a). Self-efficacy: Toward a unifying theory of behavioral change. *Psychological Review, 84*(2), 191–215.

Bandura, A. (1977b). *Social learning theory.* Upper Saddle River, NJ: Prentice Hall.

Bandura, A. (1978). The self-system in reciprocal determinism. *American Psychologist, 33,* 344–358.

Bandura, A. (1979). Psychological mechanisms of aggression. In M. von Cranach, K. Foppa, W. Lepenies, & D. Ploog (Eds.), *Human ethology: Claims and limits of a new discipline* (pp. 316–379). New York: Cambridge University Press.

Bandura, A. (1982a). The self and mechanisms of agency. In J. Suls (Ed.), *Psychological perspectives on the self* (Vol. 1). Hillsdale, NJ: Erlbaum.

Bandura, A. (1982b). Self-efficacy mechanism in human agency. *American Psychologist, 37,* 122–147.

Bandura, A. (1986). *Social foundations of thought and action: A social-cognitive theory.* Upper Saddle River, NJ: Prentice Hall.

Bandura A. (1993). Perceived self-efficacy in cognitive development and functioning. *Educational Psychologist, 28*(2), 117–148.

Bandura, A. (1995). Exercise of personal and collective self-efficacy in changing societies. In A. Bandura (Ed.), *Self-efficacy in changing societies* (pp. 1–45). New York: Cambridge University Press.

Bandura, A. (1997). *Self-efficacy: The exercise of control.* New York: W. H. Freeman.

Bandura, A. (2000). A sociocognitive perspective on intellectual development and functioning. Extended abstract of the E. L. Thorndike Award address. *Newsletter for Educational Psychology, 23*(2), 1–4.

Bandura, A., Adams, N., & Beyer, J. (1977). Cognitive processes mediating behavioral change. *Journal of Personality and Social Psychology, 35,* 125–138.

Bandura, A., & Jeffrey, R. W. (1973). Role of symbolic coding and rehearsal processes in observational learning. *Journal of Personality and Social Psychology, 26,* 122–130.

Bandura, A., Mahoney, M. J., & Dirks, S. J. (1976). Discriminative activities and maintenance of contingent self-reinforcement. *Behavior Research and Therapy, 14,* 1–6.

Bandura, A., & Schunk, D. H. (1981). Cultivating competence, self-efficacy, and intrinsic interest through proximal self-motivation. *Journal of Personality and Social Psychology, 41,* 586–598.

Bandura, A., & Walters, R. H. (1963). *Social learning theory and personality development.* New York: Holt, Rinehart & Winston.

Berk, L. E. (1989). *Child development.* Boston: Allyn & Bacon.

Bong, M., & Clark, R. E. (1999). Comparison between self-concept and self-efficacy in academic motivation research. *Educational Psychologist, 34*(3), 139–154.

Brophy, J. (1988). Research linking teacher behavior to student achievement: Potential implications for instruction of Chapter 1 students. *Educational Psychologist, 23*(3), 235–286.

Brophy, J., & Putnam, J. (1979). Classroom management in the elementary grades. *Classroom management. The eightieth yearbook of the National Society for the Study of Education* (pp. 182–216). Chicago: University of Chicago Press.

Bushman, B. J., & Anderson, C. A. (2001). Media violence and the American public. *American Psychologist, 56*(6/7), 477–489.

Carpenter, C., Huston, A., & Spear, L. (1989). Children's use of time in their everyday activities during middle childhood. In M. Block & A. Pellegrini (Eds.), *The ecological content of children's play.* Norwood, NJ: Ablex.

Carroll, W., & Bandura, A. (1982). The role of visual monitoring in observation learning of action patterns: Making the unobservable observable. *Journal of Motor Behavior, 14,* 153–167.

Corno, L. (1986). The metacognitive control components of self-regulated learning. *Contemporary Educational Psychology, 11,* 333–346.

Doyle, W. (1986). Classroom organization and management. In M. C. Wittrock (Ed.), *Handbook of research on teaching* (3rd ed., pp. 392–431). New York: Macmillan.

Evans, R. I. (1989). *Albert Bandura, the man and his ideas—a dialogue.* New York: Praeger.

Fox, D., & Kendall, P. (1983). Thinking through academic problems: Applications of cognitive-behavior therapy to learning. In T. Kratochwill (Ed.), *Advances in school psychology* (Vol. 3, pp. 269–301). Hillsdale, NJ: Erlbaum.

Gerbner, G. (1974). Teacher image in mass culture: Symbolic functions of the "hidden curriculum." In D. R. Olson (Ed.), *The form of expression: Communication and education. The seventy-third yearbook of the National Society for the Study of Education* (pp. 470–497). Chicago: University of Chicago Press.

Gerbner, G., & Gross, L. (1976). Living with television: The violence profile. *Journal of Communication, 26*(2), 173–199.

Gibson, S., & Dembo, M. H. (1984). Teacher efficacy: A construct validation. *Journal of Educational Psychology 76,* 569–582.

Goetz, J. (1976). Behavioral configurations in the classroom: A case study. *Journal of Research and Development in Education, 9*(4), 36–49.

Good, T. L., & Brophy, J. E. (1987). *Looking in classrooms* (4th ed.). New York: Harper & Row.

Goddard, R., Hoy, W. L., & Woolfolk Hoy, A. (2000). Collective teacher efficacy: Its meaning, measure, and impact on the student achievement. *American Educational Research Journal, 37*(2), 479–507.

Graham, S., & Harris, K. (1994). The role and development of self-regulation in the writing process. In D. Schunk & B. Zimmerman (Eds.), *Self-regulation of learning and performance: Issues and educational applications.* Hillsdale, NJ: Erlbaum.

Gredler, M., & Garavalia, L. (2000a). Students' perceptions of their self-regulatory and other-directed study strategies: A factor analysis. *Psychological Reports, 86,* 102–108.

Gredler, M., & Garavalia, L. (2000b, April). *The role of components of student regulation of learning, aptitude, and prior grades in explaining achievement.* Paper presented at American Educational Research Association, New Orleans.

Gredler, M., & Schwartz, D. (1997). Factorial structure of the self-efficacy for self-regulated learning scales. *Psychological Reports, 81,* 51–57.

Greenfield, P. (1984). *Mind and media: The effects of television, video games, and computers.* Cambridge, MA: Harvard University Press.

Guskey, T. R. (1987). Context variables that affect measures of teacher efficacy. *Journal of Educational Research, 81,* 41–47.

Henderson, R. (1986). Self-regulated learning: Implications for the design of instructional media. *Contemporary Educational Psychology, 11,* 405–407.

Henson, R. K. (2002). From adolescent angst to adulthood: Substantive implications and measurement dilemmas in the development of teacher efficacy research. *Educational Psychologist, 37*(3), 137–150.

Huston, A. C., Donnerstein, E., Fairchild, H., Feshbach, N. D., Katz, P. A., Murray, J. P., Rubenstein, E. A., Wilcox, B. L., & Zuckerman, D. (1992). *Big world, small screen: The role of television in American society.* Lincoln: University of Nebraska Press.

Huston, A., Watkins, B., & Kunkel, D. (1989). Public policy and children's television. *American Psychologist,* 424–433.

Jeffrey, R. S. (1976). The influence of symbolic and motor rehearsal in observational learning. *Journal of Research in Personality, 10,* 117–126.

Kazdin, A. (1989). *Behavior modification in applied settings* (4th ed.). Pacific Grove, CA: Brooks/Cole.

Leifer, A. D. (1976). Teaching with television and film. In N. L. Gagné (Ed.), *The seventy-fifth yearbook of the National Society for the Study of Education* (pp. 302–334). Chicago: University of Chicago Press.

Loper, A. B., & Murphy, D. M. (1985). Cognitive self-regulatory training for underachieving children. In D. L. Forrest-Pressley, G. E. MacKinnon, & T. G. Waller (Eds.), *Metacognition, cognition, and human performance* (pp. 223–265). Orlando, FL: Academic Press.

McLaughlin, M. W., & Marsh, D. D. (1978). Staff development and school change. *Teachers College Record, 80*, 70–94.

Meichenbaum, D. H., & Goodman, J. (1971). Training impulsive children to talk to themselves: A means of developing self-control. *Journal of Abnormal Psychology, 77*, 115–126.

Moskowitz-Hayman, G. (1976). Success strategies of inner-city teachers: A year-long study. *Journal of Educational Research, 69*, 683–689.

Murray, J., & Epstein, L. (1981). Improving oral hygiene with videotape modeling. *Behavior Modification, 5*(3), 360–371.

Oliver, M. B. (1994). Portrayals of crime, race, and aggression in "reality-based" police shows: A content analysis. *Journal of Broadcasting and Electronic Media, 38*, 179–192.

Pajares, F. (1996). Self-efficacy beliefs in academic settings. *Review of Educational Research, 66*(4), 543–578.

Pajares, F., & Graham, D. (1999). Self-efficacy motivation constructs and mathematics performance of entering middle school students. *Contemporary Educational Psychology, 24*(2), 124–139.

Pajares, F., Miller, M. D., & Johnson, M. J. (1997). Gender differences in writing, self-beliefs of elementary school subjects. *Journal of Educational Psychology, 91*(1), 30–61.

Palinscar, A. S., & Brown, A. L. (1984). Reciprocal teaching of comprehension-fostering and comprehension-monitoring activities. *Cognition and Instruction, 1*(2), 117–175.

Paris, S., Lipscom, M., & Wilson, K. (1985). Becoming a strategic reader. *Contemporary Educational Psychology, 8*, 293–316.

Perry, N. E., VandeKamp, K. O., Mercer, L. K., & Nordby, C. J. (2002). Investigating teacher-student interactions that foster self-regulated learning. *Educational Psychologist, 37*(1), 5–15.

Pintrich, P., & DeGroot, E. (1990). Motivational and self-regulated learning components of classroom academic performance. *Journal of Educational Psychology, 82*(1), 33–40.

Rice, M. C., Huston, A. C., & Wright, J. C. (1986). Replays as repetitions: Young children's misinterpretations of television forms. *Journal of Applied Developmental Psychology, 7*, 61–76.

Robinson, J. P., & Godbey, G. (1997). *Time for life: The surprising ways Americans use their time.* University Park, PA: The Pennsylvania State University Press.

Rosenthal, T. L., & Bandura, A. (1978). Psychological modeling: Theory and practice. In S. L. Garfield & A. E. Begia (Eds.), *Handbook of psychotherapy and behavior change: An empirical analysis* (2nd ed., pp. 621–658). New York: Wiley.

Rosenthal, T. L., & Zimmerman, B. J. (1973). Organization, observation, and guided practice in concept attainment and generalization. *Child Development, 44*, 606–613.

Rosenthal, T. L., & Zimmerman, B. J. (1976). Organization and stability of transfer in vicarious concept attainment. *Child Development, 47*, 110–117.

Rosenthal, T. L., & Zimmerman, B. J. (1978). *Social learning theory and cognition.* New York: Academic.

Schunk, D. H. (1981). Modeling and attributional effects on children's achievement: A self-efficacy analysis. *Journal of Educational Psychology, 73*, 93–105.

Schunk, D. H. (1986). Verbalization and children's self-regulated learning. *Contemporary Educational Psychology, 11*, 347–369.

Schunk, D. H. (1987). Peer models and children's behavioral change. *Review of Educational Research, 57*(2), 149–174.

Schunk, D. (1989). Self-efficacy and achievement behaviors. *Educational Psychology Review, 1*(3), 173–208.

Schunk, D. (1995). Inherent details of self-regulated learning include student perceptions. *Educational Psychologist, 30*(4), 213–216.

Schunk, D. H., & Hanson, A. (1985). Peer models: Influence on children's self-efficacy and achievement. *Journal of Educational Psychology, 77*(3), 313–322.

Schunk, D., & Zimmerman, B. (Eds.). (1998). *Self-regulated learning: From teaching to self-reflective practice.* New York: Guilford Press.

Schwartz, L., & Gredler, M. (1998). The effects of self-instructional materials on goal setting. *Journal of Research and Development in Education, 31*(2), 83–89.

Tschannen-Moran, M., & Woolfolk Hoy, A. (2001). Teacher efficacy: capturing an elusive construct. *Teaching and Teacher Education, 17,* 783–805.

Tschannen-Moran, M., Woolfolk Hoy, A., & Hoy, W. K. (1998). Teacher efficacy: Its meaning and measure. *Review of Educational Research, 68*(2), 202–248.

Wood, R. E., & Bandura, A. (1989). Impact of conceptions of ability on self-regulatory mechanism and complex decision making. *Journal of Personality and Social Psychology, 56,* 407–415.

Woolfolk, A., & Hoy, W. (1990). Prospective teachers' sense of efficacy and beliefs about control. *Journal of Educational Psychology, 82,* 81–91.

Zimmerman, B. (1986). Becoming a self-regulated learner: What are the key subprocesses? *Contemporary Educational Psychology, 11,* 370–404.

Zimmerman, B. (1995a). Self-efficacy and educational development. In A. Bandura (Ed.), *Self-efficacy in changing societies* (pp. 202–231). Hillsdale, NJ: Erlbaum.

Zimmerman, B. J. (1998). Developing self-fulfilling cycles of academic regulation: An analysis of exemplary instructional models. In D. H. Schunk & B. J. Zimmerman (Eds.) *Self-regulated learning: From teaching to self-reflective practice* (pp. 1–19). New York: Guilford Press.

Zimmerman, B. J. (2000). Attaining self-regulation: A cognitive perspective. In M. Boekarts, P. R. Pintrich, & M. Zeidner (Eds.), *Handbook of self-regulation* (pp. 13–39). San Diego: Academic.

Zimmerman, B. J. (2001). Theories of self-regulated learning and academic achievement: An overview and analysis. In B. J. Zimmerman & D. Schunk (Eds.), *Self-regulated learning and academic achievement* (2nd ed.) (pp. 1–37). Mahwah, NJ: Erlbaum.

Zimmerman, B. J., Greenberg, D., & Weinstein, C. E. (1994). Self-regulating academic study time: A strategy approach. In D. H. Schunk & B. J Zimmerman (Eds.), *Self-regulation of learning and performance: Issues and educational applications* (pp. 181–199). Hillsdale, NJ: Erlbaum.

Zimmerman, B. J., & Martinez-Pons, M. (1986). Development of a structured interview for assessing student use of self-regulated learning strategies. *American Educational Research Journal, 23,* 614–628.

Zimmerman, B. J., & Martinez-Pons, M. (1992). Perceptions of efficacy and strategy use in the self-regulation of learning. In D. Schunk & J. Meece (Eds.), *Student perceptions in the classroom* (pp. 185–207). Hillsdale, NJ: Erlbaum.

Zimmerman, B. J., & Rosenthal, T. L. (1974). Observational learning and rule-governed behavior by children. *Psychological Bulletin, 81,* 29–42.

CHAPTER 13

Cognitive Models and Theories of Academic Motivation

> *. . . Motivational psychologists and educators . . . are interested . . . in how [children's] thinking affects their actions—their important choices in school, their engagement with academic tasks, their ability to persist effectively in the face of setbacks (Dweck, 2002, pp. 80–81).*

Motivation is a construct of major interest to both psychological theory and educational practice. Although specific definitions vary, motivation, in general, is the process that plays a major role in an individual's choice of and continued engagement in particular activities. Early theories proposed inner forces, such as instincts, traits, and will, as the motivational factors that account for students' engagement in learning activities.

Since the mid-twentieth century, psychological models and theories of motivation began to focus on achievement motivation rather than a general focus on engagement in learning. That is, situations that can be judged as success or failure became the focus, and learner beliefs about one's competence became an issue (Nicholls, 1984).

Subsequent perspectives began to address students' cognitions and affects about aspects of the learning or achievement process as important factors in motivation. For example, John W. Atkinson's (1958, 1964) model of achievement motivation identified the individual's disposition to strive for success or avoid failure as key motivating factors. If the motive for success is high, individuals would be likely to engage in achievement tasks. However, if the disposition to avoid failure is high, individuals would avoid achievement tasks. Moreover, students would procrastinate and handicap themselves in other ways (Covington, 1992). Also important in Atkinson's model are the student's expectancy for success and the incentive value of success, identified as pride in accomplishment.

A different approach to motivation is the view that understanding the causes of past events influences an individual's future actions. This perspective began with the work of Fritz Heider (1958). He focused on the causes of events developed by "the man in the street" (p. 79). The two sets of conditions responsible for the outcomes of human action are factors within the person and factors within the environment. A subsequent development, referred to as locus of control (Rotter, 1966), specified that the perceived causes of behavior lie on a continuum between the two extremes of internal and external locus of control. Individuals who believe that reinforcements (positive consequences) are the result of hard work and planning also believe that they control their own destiny. They are, therefore, inner-directed and take responsibility for events in their lives. Arriving late to class is likely to be acknowledged as the result of leaving home too late to find a parking place, rather than some vague external condition.

In contrast, individuals who are outer-directed perceive no relationship between their behavior and reinforcements. Instead, luck, fate, or powerful others are in control. Therefore, the student may believe that a D on a test is the result of lack of ability (internal locus) or the result of teacher bias (external locus). A variation of this conceptual framework is described in the origin/pawn analysis by deCharms (1968). Origins initiate behavior intended to produce a change in the environment. Pawns, in contrast, perceive that they are pushed around by the environment.

Since the development of these initial models of motivation, society has become more complex and the importance of schooling also has increased. Careers typically require more than a high school diploma, and access to higher education often depends on meeting particular requirements. Therefore, research on motivation has moved beyond the laboratory to the classroom and incorporates various factors related to real-world settings. Currently, the major approaches to conceptualizing achievement-related motivation include the expectancy-value model, goal-orientation models, and attribution theory.

PRINCIPLES OF MOTIVATION

The prior chapters in this text discuss theories of learning or cognitive development that either describe the factors necessary for the achievement of particular skills and capabilities or the conditions essential to cognitive growth in thinking. Motivational models and theories, in contrast, focus on factors that influence students' engagement in achievement-related activities.

Basic Assumptions

The major approaches to the analysis of motivation share three major assumptions. First, an individual's motivation develops from a complex interaction of factors in the environment and factors within the particular child (Wigfield & Eccles, 2002a). Among them are social norms, the performance records of others (Weiner, 1974a), the affective reactions of teachers to students' successes and failures (Weiner, Graham, Taylor, & Meyer, 1983), types of classroom goal structures (Ames, 1992b), students' prior achievement history (Weiner, 1985b; Wigfield & Eccles, 2002b), and their beliefs about the nature of ability (Dweck, 2002).

Second, the student is an active processor of information. That is, self-assessment of one's capabilities and the interpretation of information from the environment are involved in achievement-related motivation. Third, and related to the prior assumption, is that a student's motives, needs, or goals are explicit knowledge. That is, the student can reflect on these beliefs and can communicate them to others (Murphy & Alexander, 2000, p. 38).

This assumption is important because many studies of the components of motivation rely on student self-reports. On occasion, these reports may be interviews. Typically, however, researchers use questionnaires with specific items to which students respond. Examples are I want to learn as much as possible in this class; Getting a good grade in class is important to me; and I work hard to get a good grade. Response options typically range on a 5- or 7-point scale with associated descriptors; for example, 1 = not true of me, 5 = very true of me. Wigfield (1994) noted that the questionnaire format only indirectly assesses children's beliefs. The reason is that the children respond to the constructs as defined by the researcher rather than generating their own definitions (p. 61).

In addition to the general assumptions, each particular view of motivation also includes assumptions specifically relevant to that perspective. For example, attribution theory focuses on individuals' perceptions of the causes of positive and negative achievement outcomes. Key assumptions of attribution theory are that the search for understanding is a major source of motivation (Weiner, 1979), people's belief systems and cognitive analyses of the causes of outcomes influence their future behavior, and causal inferences about outcomes are complex sources of information. Therefore, causal inferences are not unidimensional. For example, lack of ability and lack of effort are internal attributions for failure. However, they lead to different outcomes. A poor grade attributed to lack of ability will be expected to occur again. However, a poor grade attributed to lack of effort may not be expected in the future because effort expenditure can change (Eswara, 1972; Rosenbaum, 1972; Weiner, Neurenberg, & Goldstein, 1976). Also, lack of effort is punished more than lack of ability (Rest, Neirenberg, Weiner, & Heckhausen, 1973; Weiner & Kukla, 1970; Weiner & Peter, 1973). In other words, the one-dimensional descriptions of causal inferences, such as Rotter's (1966) locus of control perspective, are inadequate.

In contrast, goal orientation models focus on the motivational role of students' achievement-related goals. An assumption of one view of goal orientation is that the orientation of classroom goals influences students' personal goal orientations (Ames, 1992b).

In summary, common assumptions of current motivational perspectives are (1) an individual's motivation develops from a complex interaction of factors in the environment and factors within the child, (2) the individual is an active processor of information, and (3) students can reflect on and communicate their beliefs to others. In addition, particular motivational perspectives specify assumptions related to the aspect of motivation they emphasize.

Components of the Motivational Process

Three types of analyses of motivational processes in achievement-related settings may be identified. They differ in their emphasis on particular factors believed to influence motivation and the dynamics of the process. The three types of models or theories are (1) the expectancy-value model, (2) goal orientation models, and (3) attribution theory.

The Expectancy-Value Model

The current expectancy-value model is an expansion of Atkinson's (1958) model. However, unlike Atkinson's model, the current model focuses on the social-psychological reasons for students' choices of subject areas or courses (referred to as "tasks" in the model). Thus, the direct influences on achievement-related behaviors, identified as expectancy and value, are defined as cognitive rather than totally motivational constructs (Wigfield & Eccles, 1992, pp. 278–279).

The basic premise of the model is that students' expectations of success and the value they place on success are important determinants of their motivation to engage in achievement-related behaviors (Wigfield & Eccles, 2002b, p. 91). Of importance in the model is that "task" typically is measured at the domain level. That is, task refers to a subject area or a particular course, such as mathematics, biology, or social studies, not a specific activity (Wigfield & Eccles, 2000, p. 72; Wigfield & Eccles, 2002b, p. 94).

The model identifies five achievement-related behaviors that are influenced by motivational processes. They are choice, persistence, extent of effort, cognitive engagement, and actual performance. That is, motivational beliefs may influence students' choosing to enroll in biology, their persistence when faced with difficulties, the expenditures of considerable effort, and/or their final grade.

The two key motivational beliefs, task value and expectancy of success, are most directly determined by other achievement-related beliefs. (See Figure 13.1.) These related beliefs are summarized as the child's affective memories and the goals and general self-schemata of the child.

Task (Domain) Value and Expectancy Value.

Task value is an important component in the model because competence is an insufficient explanation of choosing to enroll in a subject or course. That is, a student may be competent in an area, but choose not to engage in it because it is not of sufficient value to the student (Wigfield & Eccles, 2002b, p. 94).

Task value in the model includes four components. They are attainment value, intrinsic value, utility value, and cost (Eccles et al., 1983; Wigfield & Eccles, 1992). Attainment value refers to the importance of doing well in a particular domain or course, and intrinsic value refers to the enjoyment for the student of doing well or the students' subjective interest. In assessing motivational beliefs in mathematics, the child indicates (1) the importance of being good in math on a range from not at all important to very important, and (2) the importance of being good in math compared to other activities.

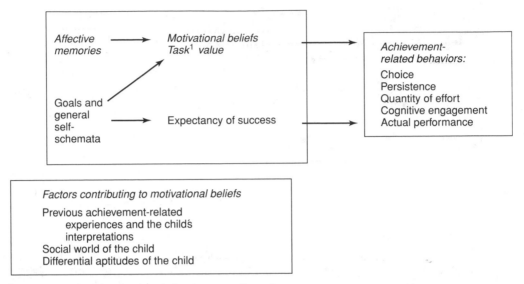

[1]Typically measured at the domain level, e.g., mathematics

FIGURE 13.1
A summary of the key components of the expectancy-value model

Intrinsic value is assessed by asking the child how much he or she likes doing math and the extent to which working on math assignments ranges from boring to very interesting (Wigfield & Eccles, 2000, p. 70). In this assessment, level of interest is documented as an index of enjoyment.

Utility value refers to the usefulness of the course or domain for the child. One assessment of utility states that some things in school can help in learning to do things better out of class. The example is that learning about plants might help to grow a garden (Wigfield & Eccles, 2000, p. 70). Then the student identifies the usefulness of the material he or she is learning in math. Thus, student responses may vary according to the topic currently under study.

Cost refers to the extent that choosing to engage in an activity, such as school work, limits the opportunity to participate in other activities (p. 70). However, data collection on aspects of the model has primarily focused on the other three subtypes of value (importance, intrinsic value, and usefulness).

In the model, expectancy value refers to children's beliefs about the extent to which they will do well. Children are asked how well they expect to do in math this year and how well they will be able to learn something new in math (Wigfield & Eccles, 2000, p. 70). Expectancy value, in other words, is, in part, an estimation by the child of his or her capacity of succeeding in the subject area or course. It is a prediction and, therefore, is future oriented.

Direct Determinants of Task (Domain) Value and Expectancy. The two sets of beliefs that directly determine task value and expectancy are the student's affective memories and his or her goals and general self-schemata (Wigfield &

Eccles, 2002b). Affective memories are activated by anticipation of engaging in the domain or course and involve the positive or negative emotions associated with prior similar experiences (Pintrich & Schunk, 2002, p. 62). For example, a student's motivation for enrolling in an advanced math class such as calculus is related to his or her affective reactions to prior math courses such as algebra.

The other set of supporting motivational beliefs, goals and self-schema, consists of the student's long- and short-term goals, perceptions of his or her "ideal self," perceptions of task (domain) difficulty, and the student's beliefs about his or her competence or ability. Ideal self refers to the kind of person the student seeks to become and is related to the student's perception of personal identity. For example, a student may view herself as someone who helps others. Her short-term goals may include volunteering at the local hospital during the summer break, and her long-term goal may be to become a social worker (Pintrich & Schunk, 2002, p. 62).

The model defines ability beliefs as the student's perceptions of his or her current competence in a particular area (Wigfield & Eccles, 2000). They differ from success expectancies, which focus on the future, whereas ability beliefs focus on the present (p. 70). Items that assess ability beliefs include: How good in math are you? and Compared to your other subjects, how good in math are you? and Compared to the other students in your class, where do you put yourself? (p. 70). In other words, students' affective memories of similar prior experiences, their goals, personal identity, perceptions of ability, and perceptions of the difficulty of the subject directly determine their expectancies for success and the value of the course or subject for them.

Factors Contributing to Motivational Beliefs.   The factors that contribute to students' motivational beliefs are the social world in which the student functions, his or her perceptions of the social experiences, environment, and prior achievement-related factors, and the student's aptitudes. Important elements in the child's social world, according to the model, include gender role stereotypes, cultural stereotypes of subject matter, and previous achievement-related experiences (Wigfield & Eccles, 2002b). For example, a cultural stereotype in the child's world may be that Hispanics cannot be engineers because they are not good at math. Important perceptions that contribute to motivational beliefs are the student's perceptions of stereotypes and his or her interpretations of previous achievement-related experiences.

Summary.   The current expectancy-value model expands Atkinson's (1958) model, but differs from it in two ways. The current model focuses on social-psychological reasons for students' choices, and tasks in the model refer to domains or courses of study. The two key motivational beliefs are task value (attainment, intrinsic, and utility values and cost) and expectancy value, the extent to which the child believes he or she will do well. These beliefs directly influence choice, persistence, extent of effort, and actual performance.

Task value and expectancy are directly determined by the child's affective memories and the goals and self-schemata of the child. Affective memories consist of the positive or negative emotional reactions associated with prior similar experiences. Goals may be both short- and long-term, and self-schemata includes perceptions of the "ideal self," perceptions of task (domain) difficulty, and beliefs about one's ability. Contributing to these beliefs are the child's social world, his perceptions of it and prior social experiences, and aptitudes.

Goal Orientation Models

In contrast to expectancy-value models, goal orientation models address students' reasons for engagement in academic tasks (Anderman, Austin, & Johnson, 2002; Pintrich & Schunk, 2002). For example, a student's goal in biology class may be to get an "A," but this statement does not indicate his or her reason for enrolling in the course. Goal orientation models, however, pursue whether the reason was to learn new concepts, demonstrate one's competence to others, or some other reason.

Formally stated, goal orientation refers to "a set of behavioral intentions that determine how students approach and engage in learning activities" (Meece, Blumenfeld, & Hoyle, 1988, p. 514). The importance of goal orientations is that they influence students' cognitive strategies, task selection, and perceptions of competence (Ames, 1992a; Ames & Archer, 1988; Anderman et al., 2002; Dweck, 1989; Elliott & Dweck, 1988; Jagacinski & Nicholls, 1987; Pintrich & Zusho, 2002). They also are related to the extent to which information is stored in long-term memory (Anderman et al., 2002). In addition, goal orientation influences the types of information students access to monitor their achievement-related activities. For example, students whose goal orientation is to outperform others will monitor the work and grades of others and will attempt to adjust their effort and cognition to demonstrate superiority (Pintrich, 2000, p. 473).

The original conceptualizations of students' goal structures contrasted two general orientations that reflect different purposes for engaging in achievement tasks. Examples are learning and performance goals (Dweck, 1986; Elliott & Dweck, 1988) and mastery and performance goals (Ames & Archer, 1988; Ames, 1992b). A similar conceptualization is task-involved and ego-involved orientations (Jagacinski & Nicholls, 1987; Jagacinski, 1992; Nicholls, 1984, 1989) in which the focus is the type of engagement in which students feel most successful.

Since the development of those models, some suggest that goal orientations are more multidimensional and nuanced. These views are reflected in the following discussion of learning or effort orientations, performance goal orientations, and work or failure avoidance.

Learning-Related Goal Orientations.   The three types of learning or effort orientations are summarized in Table 13.1. These orientations reflect a focus on mastering tasks, enhancing one's learning, and becoming more than superficially involved in achievement-related tasks.

The definition of success for students with learning-related goal orientations is that they master new tasks, make progress in learning new skills, or feel pleased when they have engaged in challenging tasks. A core belief associated

TABLE 13.1
Learning-Related Goal Orientations

Orientation	Definition
Learning goals (Dweck, 1986, 1989, 2002; Dweck & Leggett, 1988)	Increase one's competence; orientation related to an incremental theory of intelligence
Mastery goals (Ames & Archer, 1988; Ames, 1992b)	Develop new skills, try to understand one's work or achieve a sense of mastery based on self-referenced standards (Ames, 1992b, p. 262)
Task-focused goals (Anderman & Midgley, 1997; Kaplan & Midgley, 1997; Maehr & Midgley, 1991; Midgley et al., 1998)	Increase one's competence, attempt to master the task
Task orientation (Nicholls, 1984, 1989)	The extent to which students report feeling successful or pleased when they engage in certain tasks

with mastery goals is that effort and outcomes covary, and this belief maintains achievement-oriented behavior over time. Dweck (1989) also found that children with a learning goal orientation view intelligence as a dynamic, growing set of abilities. That is, intelligence is not a fixed entity.

Performance Goal Orientations.   The original conceptualizations of goal orientations identified performance and ego-involved goal orientations as counterproductive for learning. As illustrated in Table 13.2, performance goals involve a focus on demonstrating superior performance. This objective is accomplished by either outperforming others or doing well with little effort. This type of goal focuses on one's ability, and self-worth is based on perceptions of one's ability to perform. Social comparison information (how well others are doing or how much effort they are expending) is the standard for self-judgments about ability. Dweck (1989) also noted that children with performance goal orientations tend to view intelligence as a fixed trait, an "entity" view of intelligence.

The original conceptualizations of goal structure, according to Elliot (1997, 1999; Elliot & Church, 1997), are insufficient to explain the data on achievement-related behaviors and achievement outcomes. Specifically, neither a performance nor a mastery orientation can account for negative processes such as disorganized studying, low absorption during task engagement, procrastination, and unwillingness to seek help. Therefore, he proposed a distinction between performance-approach and performance-avoidance orientations. Performance avoidance involves fearing being thought stupid, avoidance of asking the teacher a "dumb" question, and often worrying about doing badly in school (p. 180).

Some studies (e.g., Harackiewicz, Barron, Tauer, & Elliot [2002]) have found that both mastery and performance-approach goals were linked to components of academic success for college students. Also, other studies have

TABLE 13.2
Performance Goal Orientations

Orientation	Definition
Performance goals (Ames & Archer, 1988; Ames, 1992b; Anderman & Midgley, 1997; Dweck, 1986, 1989, 2002; Elliott & Dweck, 1988; Kaplan & Midgley, 1997; Maehr & Midgley, 1991)	Determining one's ability by surpassing others; demonstrating ability to teachers and peers, and receiving public recognition for superior performance
Ego-involved orientation (Jagacinski & Nicholls, 1987; Jagacinski, 1992; Nicholls, 1984, 1989)	Feeling successful when one knows more than others
(a) Performance-approach component	Attainment of favorable judgments of competence by outperforming other students
(b) Performance-avoidance component	Avoiding unfavorable judgments of competence
(Elliot, 1997; Elliot & Church, 1997; Harackiewicz et al., 2002; Middleton & Midgley, 1997)	

linked performance-approach goals to such variables as task value (e.g., Bong, 2001), effort expenditure (e.g., Elliot, McGregor, & Gable, 1999), and performance (e.g., Lopez, 1999). Such findings have led to calls to revise goal theory to include performance-approach and performance-avoid orientations (e.g., Harackiewicz, Barron, Pintrich, Elliot, & Thrash, 2002). However, Kaplan and Middleton (2002) disagree. They note that the desirability of mastery goals, performance goals, or various combinations of them is dependent on the purposes expressed in the achievement setting (p. 648). In other words, one should question the nature of the educational setting where mastering and understanding the material does not contribute to higher grades (p. 648).

The problem with performance goals, in general, is that such an orientation leads to primarily superficial engagement in achievement-related tasks. A performance-avoidance orientation is further maladaptive in that even superficial engagement in learning activities is minimal.

Other Goal Orientations.   Two other goal orientations measured by researchers are work avoidance and failure avoidance. Work avoidance seems to represent the absence of an achievement goal, and the endorsement of just "getting through" task requirements (Archer, 1994; Elliot, 1999, p. 184). Briefly, examples are feeling successful when all the work is easy and not having any tough tests (Thorkildsen & Nicholls, 1998).

Failure avoidance involves avoiding looking stupid in one's classes through self-protecting strategies, such as not responding to teacher questions (Middleton & Midgley, 1997). Brophy (1999) suggested that students who attribute failure to uncontrollable causes seek to defend against perceptions of incompetence or to hide their incompetence from others (p. 76).

Summary.   Goal orientation models address students' reasons for engagement in academic tasks. The importance of goal orientations is that they influence students' cognitive strategies, task selection, perceptions of competence, and the extent to which information is stored in long-term memory. Original conceptualizations of goal orientations defined dichotomous contrasts, e.g., learning-oriented versus performance-oriented. Students with learning or effort orientations seek to master new tasks, make progress in learning new skills, or feel pleased when they have engaged in challenging tasks. One researcher also found that students with a mastery orientation viewed intelligence as a dynamic, growing set of abilities.

In contrast, students with performance or ego-involved orientations focus on demonstrating superior performance. This purpose is accomplished by either outperforming others or doing well with little effort. Social comparison information is the standard for self-judgments about ability. These students also tend to view intelligence as a fixed entity.

Some researchers have suggested that the performance goal orientation should be considered as two separate emphases: performance approach and performance avoidance. Performance avoidance involves fearing that one may appear "stupid," and worrying about how one is doing in school. However, the problem with performance goals, in general, is that they lead to superficial engagement in academic tasks. Two other goal orientations measured by researchers are work avoidance (endorsing just "getting through" work) and failure avoidance (avoiding looking stupid in class through self-protecting strategies).

Attribution Theory

The expectancy-value model and the goal orientation models describe particular anticipations, values, or rationales for approaching and engaging in achievement-related tasks. Further, goal orientation models identify positive and negative learning strategies associated with different goal orientations.

In contrast, attribution theory addresses individuals' thoughts, emotions, and expectancies following an achievement-related outcome (Weiner, 1980b). The theory also has been applied to the role of attributions in help-giving behavior (Weiner, 1979, 1980a, 1980c, 1982, 1983, 1995), in explaining children's reactions to unusual characteristics or behavior (Juronen, 1991, 1992), and in analyzing children's reactions to negative events precipitated by other children (Graham & Hudley; Graham, Hudley, & Williams, 1993; Hudley & Graham, 1993).

In achievement-related situations, the theory rests on three assumptions. They are (1) the search for understanding is a prime motivator of action, (2) attributions for achievement-related outcomes are complex sources of information, and (3) future behavior is determined, in part, by the perceived causes of prior outcomes.

The attributional process begins with an achievement-related outcome. The individual first appraises his or her performance and assigns it a subjective rating on a continuum from success to failure. Then the individual either identifies a cause or reflectively begins to look for the probable cause. A search is most often undertaken for unexpected outcomes, such as failure when success is expected.

The identification of the outcome as success or failure generates emotional reactions of satisfaction, or perhaps happiness, for success, and frustration or upset for a failure outcome. For example, in athletic competitions, one tends to experience happiness for a victory whether the win resulted from additional training, a poor competitor, or luck (Weiner, 1985a).

Sources of information that the individual draws on to identify a cause or attribution for the outcome include the individual's past success history, social norms, and the performance records of others (Weiner, 1974a, 1977). The importance of causal inferences or attributions for achievement-related outcomes is that they generate particular emotions. These feelings and the characteristics of some attributions influence the individual's expectancies for future outcomes.

Attributions and their Dimensions.   In the achievement domain, multiple causes of outcomes may be identified (Weiner, 1985b). Failure, for example, may be attributed to lack of effort, the absence of ability, poor strategies, bad luck, teacher bias, the hindrance of peers, and so on. However, the typical attributions for success and failure outcomes are ability, effort, task difficulty, and luck (Weiner, 1972). Sometimes other attributions are cited, such as mood, illness, or help from others. However, the most dominant attributions for success and failure, according to Weiner (1985a), are ability and effort. That is, success is attributed to high ability and/or hard work, and failure is attributed to lack of ability and/or lack of effort.

Particularly important in the attributional process are the characteristics or dimensions of the attributions. The important dimensions are stability, locus of causality, and controllability. The key questions are as follows: Is a particular attribution stable or unstable, internal or external, and under the individual's control or controlled by other individuals or events? For example, ability is internal, stable, and is not controlled by the individual; effort is internal, unstable, and controllable; and luck is external, unstable, and uncontrollable.

The dimensions of attributions may influence motivation in one of two ways. One is the expectancy for future goal attainment and the other is that particular dimensions generate a specific set of emotional reactions. Included are pride and self-esteem, confidence, anger, guilt, shame, gratitude, and hopelessness.

Currently, stability appears to be the only dimension that influences future goal expectancy. For example, success in mathematics that is attributed to ability, a stable cause, will be expected again. Also, the student who attributes a low test grade to low ability is likely to expect future failure and to believe he or she has no behavioral response that can alter subsequent events (Weiner, 1979). Therefore, little or no effort will be expended on achievement-related tasks.

Emotional Reactions.   Emotions are important in the attributional perspective because they are motivators of subsequent behavior. "Attributions tell us what to feel, and feelings tell us what to do" (Weiner, 1983b, p. 69). An individual who has experienced apathy, resignation, and feelings of incompetence will cease trying in achievement-related situations. On the other hand, one who feels gratitude and relief is motivated to express thankfulness. The individual who experiences feelings of competence, however, will approach achievement-related situations with confidence.

Following a positive outcome, the individual may experience feelings of pride and self-worth, confidence, or gratitude. The individual's identification of a personal characteristic as an attribution for a positive outcome generates feelings of pride and self-worth because it is internal (see Table 13.3). Kant described the locus of causality-pride linkage when he noted that everyone at a meal may enjoy the good food, but only the cook could experience pride (Weiner, 1985a, p. 561). In contrast, success ascribed to external causes, such as luck or help from others, does not influence self-esteem or future task engagement (Weiner, 1982). An example is receiving an A from a teacher who awards only good grades (external cause); pride is not experienced for the success. Instead, success attributed to external causes typically generates feelings of gratitude.

Success attributed to internal causes influences one's self-image. Similarly, failure attributed to internal causes contributes to negative self-image. Some studies (Brown & Weiner, 1984; Covington & Omelich, 1984; Jagacinski & Nicholls, 1984) have reported that shame-related affects (disgrace, embarrassment, humiliation, and/or shame) are associated with low ability, and guilt-related reactions are associated with lack of effort. The occurrence of shame, a more negative emotion than guilt, may be related to the stability and uncontrollability of ability (aptitude). In contrast, lack of effort, which is controllable, may tend to generate guilt but not the stronger emotion, shame. Graham and Weiner (1996) noted that "guilt tends to promote goal-directed activity, whereas shame gives rise to task withdrawal and is a motivational inhibitor" (p. 72).

Also important is that shame-related emotions often are followed by withdrawal and motivational inhibition. In contrast, guilt-related emotions

TABLE 13.3
Emotions Generated by the Dimensions of Causal Inferences for Achievement

Outcome/Dimensions Linkage	Emotional Reactions
Positive outcomes	
Internal cause	Feelings of pride and self-esteem
Controllable cause	Feelings of confidence
Stable cause	Maximizes feelings of pride, self-worth, and confidence (for internal causes)
Uncontrollable/external cause	Feelings of gratitude
Negative outcomes	
Internal cause	Feelings of embarrassment, guilt, and shame
Controllable cause	Feelings of guilt
Stable cause	Maximizes emotions of shame, apathy, and resignation associated with internal, controllable causes
Uncontrollable/external cause	Feelings of anger

often lead to reproach behavior and retribution (Hoffman, 1982; Weiner, 1985a). Thus, failure attributed to stable and uncontrollable factors generates strong negative emotions and exerts a debilitating influence on future achievement-related behavior as well.

Similar to success outcomes, the stability dimension maximizes the emotions generated by the internal cause of failure, lack of ability. Feelings of apathy, resignation, and hopelessness for the future typically occur. However, emotions resulting from unstable causes, such as lack of effort, are unlikely to be extended to future events.

An example of the attributional process is the Little League baseball player who performs poorly during a game. The boy has played poorly in the past, and the other children are playing well. The boy also has tried to improve by practicing many hours. On the basis of history, social comparison, and expenditures of effort, the boy is likely to conclude that he has failed because he is not good at baseball (lack of ability) (Weiner, 1985b, p. 566).

Antecedents of Causal Inferences.   As already stated, the individual makes use of several sources of information in the search for a causal attribution. They are specific information clues, which include success history, social norms, and performance patterns (Weiner, 1977, p. 181); the individual's general beliefs about success and failure, referred to as the individual's causal schema; and individual predispositions.

The individual's success history is the primary determinant for the selection of ability or lack of it as an attribution (Weiner, 1974a). A consistent record of prior achievements leads to attributions of ability for success, whereas a moderate success record is likely to generate effort as a cause of success. However, success for an individual with a consistently poor achievement record is likely to be attributed to luck, and failure will be attributed to lack of ability.

Social norms and the performance records of others also provide information. Succeeding at a task failed by others likely leads to the perception that one is able (Weiner, 1974a, p. 53). Similarly, failing a task that others accomplished successfully may lead to an attribution of lack of ability.

The individual's causal schema and individual characteristics also influence attributions. A sufficient causal schema is the belief that either ability or effort may account for success (Weiner, 1974a). In contrast, a necessary causal schema is the belief that ability *and* effort are essential for success, and is often the selected explanation for success on a difficult task. High-ability students tend to attribute their successes to both ability and hard work (Dai, Moon, & Feldhusen, 1998). An important individual characteristic that is related to the causal attributions made by children is self-concept. Elementary school students who are high in self-concept credit skill and ability for success. They also engage in more self-reward following success than low self-concept children (Ames, 1978; Ames, Ames, & Felker, 1977).

Developmental level also influences attribution selection. Most children in kindergarten and first grade hold high perceptions of their ability and high expectancies of success. They also are more likely to attribute success and failure to luck than are older children (Wigfield & Harold, 1992, p. 102).

Summary. The basic building blocks of the attributional model are the individual's attributions for success and failure outcomes and the dimensions of those attributions. The typical attributions are ability, effort, task difficulty, and luck. Others are mood, illness, fatigue, and help from others. Information that contributes to the identification of a particular attribution includes specific information cues, the individual's causal schema, and individual predispositions.

The causal meaning of attributions is determined largely by their underlying bipolar dimensions, which are stability, locus of causality, and controllability. The stability dimension influences future goal expectancy, and each dimension also generates particular emotions (see Table 13.4). The locus of causality is linked primarily to the individual's self-esteem. Causes attributed to the self either enhance feelings of self-worth (positive achievement outcome) or contribute to a negative self-image (negative achievement outcome). The affective relationship for stability is the intensification of emotions generated by other dimensions.

TABLE 13.4
Summary of the Properties of Major Achievement-Related Attributions

Attribution	Dimension	Consequence
Ability	Internal	Generates feelings of competence or incompetence and feelings of pride or shame
	Stable	Same outcome expected again; emotions of pride and shame magnified; for failure, resignation and apathy magnified
	Uncontrollable	For failure, magnifies feelings of resignation and apathy
Effort	Internal	Generates feelings of pride for success
	Unstable	Does not decrease success expectancy
	Controllable	Magnifies feelings of pride or guilt
Luck	External	Self-image not altered
	Unstable	No decrease in success expectancy
	Uncontrollable	Generates surprise for both success and failure
Others	External	Self-image not altered
	Unstable	No decrease in success expectancy
	Uncontrollable (by outcome recipient)	Generates gratitude for help and anger for hindrance
Task difficulty	External	No enhancement of self-esteem for success outcome
	Stable	Same outcome expected again
	Uncontrollable	Depression and frustration for failure outcomes

Summary

Three types of analyses of motivational processes in achievement-related settings may be identified. They are the expectancy-value model, goal orientation models, and attribution theory. Basic assumptions shared by these analyses are (1) an individual's motivation develops from a complex interaction of environmental factors and factors within the child, (2) the student is an active processor of information, and (3) a student's motives, goals, or attributions are explicit knowledge that can be communicated to others.

Each of the three analyses describes a different constellation of factors that account for the achievement-related behaviors of persistence, choice of tasks, cognitive engagement, and performance. The expectancy-value model identifies the value of the task and the expectancy of success as key motivational processes. The term *task* in the model refers to domain or course, such as mathematics or social studies. Direct determinants of these processes are the student's affective memories and self-schemata and goals. Contributing to these factors are the student's social world, his or her interpretation of that world, prior achievement-related experiences, and aptitude.

In contrast, goal orientation models address students' reasons for engagement in academic tasks. Personal goal orientations are important because they influence students' cognitive strategies, task selection, and perceptions of competence. The two general orientations are learning, effort, or mastery-oriented and performance or ego-oriented. Students with a mastery or learning orientation seek to develop new skills and increase their competence. They also tend to hold an incremental view of intelligence.

Currently, the performance-goal orientation includes two subcategories, performance approach and performance avoidance. The performance-approach orientation is accompanied by efforts to demonstrate superior performance by outperforming others or doing well with little effort. Performance avoidance, in contrast, is accompanied by avoiding unfavorable judgments of competence. Students with performance goal orientations tend to hold an entity view of intelligence.

The third motivational analysis, attribution theory, addresses an individual's determination of an outcome as success or failure and the reasons for that outcome (attributions). Sources of information in identifying attributions are the individual's success history, social norms, and the performance records of others. Typical attributions for success and failure outcomes are ability, effort, task difficulty, and luck. However, the properties or dimensions of the attribution are the key factors that generate emotional reactions and expectancy for the future. These dimensions are stability, locus of causality, and controllability by the student. For example, success attributed to help from others, which is unstable, external, and uncontrollable, may generate gratitude but not pride. Therefore, help from others does not influence self-esteem or future task engagement.

Of particular importance are the attributions of ability and effort. A negative outcome attributed to lack of ability generates feelings of shame, which may be followed by withdrawal. Also, because lack of ability is stable, internal, and not controlled by the individual, the same negative outcome is expected in the future.

The Cumulative Effects of Different Experiences on Motivational Beliefs

Two different motivational patterns that require intervention may be identified. One is the changes in children's motivations as they progress through school. The other is the extremely maladaptive pattern referred to as "learned helplessness."

Changes Throughout Schooling.   Children's motivational beliefs are not static; evidence indicates that they develop and change over time (Anderman et al., 2002, p. 203). Children's competence beliefs and expectancies for success for different tasks typically decline across the elementary school years into middle school (Wigfield & Eccles, 2002b). These declines, especially in mathematics, often continue into high school. Also, children's ratings of the importance and utility of school subjects, as well as their interest, are lower than the averages of the ratings of young children (Eccles & Midgley, 1989; Wigfield, 1994; Wigfield & Eccles, 1992).

Identification of likely attributions for achievement outcomes also changes throughout childhood. The subtle cues that indicate ability inferences often are not differentiated clearly by young children. Also, they typically do not differentiate between ability and effort. That is, young children tend to believe that success is related to working hard.

By the age of 11 or 12, children have begun to make normative evaluations of their ability. By that age, children use concepts such as effort, ability, task difficulty, and luck in an adultlike way, even if they cannot explain their reasons (Thorkildsen & Nicholls, 1998). Their ratings are more consistent with their report cards, their confidence is likely to decline under failure, and success expectancies decrease (Dweck, 1989; Nicholls, 1978; Ruble & Rhales, 1981). For example, if students attribute poor performance in math to ability, which is stable, they are likely to devalue math to protect their overall self-worth (Pintrich & Schunk, 2002; Steele, 1988; Wigfield & Eccles, 1992).

One rationale for the changes in motivation is that children become more proficient at understanding and interpreting the feedback they receive, and some self-assessments become more negative. Also, the nature of the school environment changes. Evaluation becomes more important and the likelihood of competition among the children increases (Wigfield & Eccles, 2002b, p. 97). In addition, the classroom tasks become more abstract as opposed to the more concrete tasks in elementary school (Dweck, 1989). Furthermore, in the early school years, more than half of the feedback addresses adherence to classroom procedures and conduct and not academic performance (Pintrick & Blumenfeld, 1985).

In addition to the decline in children's competency beliefs and expectancies for success, research indicates a decline in the endorsement of mastery goals by adolescents and an increase in the endorsement of performance goals (Anderman & Anderman, 1999; Anderman et al., 2002, p. 209). Several studies indicate that the student's increased endorsement of performance goals, which is often accompanied by self-handicapping strategies such as procrastination, is related to the implementation of performance goals at the classroom level (Ames & Archer, 1988; Anderman & Anderman, 1999; Anderman & Midgley, 1997; Midgley, Anderman, & Hicks, 1995; Urdan, Midgley, & Anderman, 1998).

As already stated, one rationale for the changes in children's motivations is the interaction between their information-processing skills and some alterations in the school setting. However, another rationale places a greater responsibility on the school setting. First, the instructional methods of middle-school teachers differ from those of elementary school teachers (e.g., Anderman & Maehr, 1994; Eccles & Midgley, 1989), relationships between teachers and students often are poor, opportunities are lacking for students to be involved in decision making, and grading practices are strict (Eccles et al., 1993; Anderman et al., 2002). That is, some schools function as "mini high schools" with a focus on grade and performance (Anderman et al., 2002, p. 211). In other words, students are developing strong needs for autonomy and control that conflict with the organization of the school.

"Learned Helplessness" Versus a Mastery Orientation.   Individuals low in self-concept who have experienced few successes are likely (1) to attribute failure to lack of ability and (2) to see no relationship between their success and their own actions. The belief that outcomes are independent of one's actions was researched originally as the construct known as "learned helplessness" (Seligman, 1975). In the initial experimental studies, dogs subjected to inescapable electric shock learned that no response, such as tail wagging, barking, or jumping, influenced the shocks. Then when placed in a situation in which knocking down a barrier terminated the shock, the animals first ran around frantically for a few seconds and then lay down, passively submitting to the shock. In other words, after the experience of uncontrollable trauma, the animals lost the motivation to respond, and depression and anxiety resulted. Further, even if a response was successful, the animal had difficulty in learning that the response was effective (Seligman, 1975, p. 22).

A major characteristic of helplessness in humans is whether individuals believe that outcomes are more or less likely to happen only to themselves or to relevant others as well. For example, a student may spend long hours studying, enroll in remedial courses, and still fail. The person eventually arrives at the conclusion that he or she is incompetent. In this case, important outcomes are available to others (they pass), but the student does not possess the behaviors to acquire them. The cause of the event is internal; this phenomenon is referred to as personal helplessness (Abramson et al., 1980, p. 11). The problem with personal helplessness, as in attributions for a single failure outcome, is that the internal nature of the attribution generates low self-esteem.

Research indicates that children of equal ability often react to failure in very different ways (Diener & Dweck, 1978; Dweck, 1975). Learned-helpless children attribute failure to stable factors, such as lack of ability. They also react to failure with solution-irrelevant statements, stereotypic responses, and derogatory comments. Examples include "I am stupid" and "I never did have a good memory" (Diener & Dweck, 1978). In addition, a marked and rapid decline typically occurs in the sophistication and appropriateness of the children's problem-solving strategies. In one study, by the fourth problem in a discrimination-testing situation, over two-thirds of the children made ineffectual responses.

In contrast, mastery-oriented children tend to acknowledge their errors but do not regard them as failures (Dweck & Licht, 1980, p. 199). They attribute the mistakes to unstable factors, such as bad luck, lack of effort, and unfairness of the experimenter. They also engage in self-instructional statements such as "I should slow down and try to figure this out" (Diener & Dweck, 1978, p. 459). Mastery-oriented children also maintain mature strategies in the face of failure. The unflagging optimism of these children, however, is perhaps the most striking difference between them and the learned-helpless group (Dweck & Licht, 1980, p. 201).

The two groups also differ in their reactions to success. In one study, learned-helpless children were less likely to attribute success to ability, and they underestimated their number of successes. They also tended to state that other children outperformed them, and they predicted poor future performance for themselves (Diener & Dweck, 1980). Mastery-oriented children, however, attributed performance to ability, correctly estimated their number of successes, thought they were doing better than other children, and expected continued success.

The underlying problem for "helpless" children is that they do not view themselves as instrumental in the determination of outcomes. They are therefore likely to consider adverse circumstances as insurmountable. Thus, the important factor is not the occurrence of aversive events but, rather, the perceived relationship between the individual's behavior and the event (Dweck, 1975, p. 75).

Classroom conditions can place children at risk for developing learned helplessness. When normative performance evaluations prevail in the classroom, low-confidence children react with ineffective strategies and attributions of lack of ability. However, when tasks are presented in terms of learning, such as to sharpen one's mind, maladaptive responses tend to decrease (Elliott & Dweck, 1988).

Summary. The two different motivational patterns that require intervention are the changes in children's motivational beliefs during the middle school years and the maladaptive pattern referred to as "learned helplessness." The declines in children's motivational beliefs, especially in mathematics, often continue into high school, and children often rate school subjects lower on utility and importance. Research also indicates a decline in their endorsement of mastery goals and an increase in the endorsement of performance goals.

One rationale for motivational declines is that by the age of 11 or 12, children differentiate between ability and effort. That is, they become more proficient at interpreting classroom feedback. Also, the school environment changes in the middle school years. Competition often increases, classroom tasks become more abstract, and evaluation becomes more important.

The concept of learned helplessness refers to individuals with low self-concept who have experienced few successes. They are likely to see no relationship between any success they have and their own actions. Learned-helpless children also attribute failure to stable factors, such as lack of ability. They differ from mastery-oriented children, who do not give up in the face of failure and who try various strategies.

The underlying problem for "helpless" children is that they do not see themselves as instrumental in the determination of outcomes. Thus, they view difficulties as insurmountable. Normative evaluations in the classroom also contribute to the development of this perspective.

PRINCIPLES OF INSTRUCTION

In the formal educational setting, children soon learn that doing well in school is an implicit goal, but an important one. Throughout the school years, in both formal and informal situations, students are faced with a continuing succession of achievement-related situations. These situations, and the inferences that students make about them, are important in the development of students' motivational beliefs. Unlike learning and cognitive-development theories, motivational models and theories have not developed explicit principles of instruction. However, they have identified characteristics of classroom instruction that influence students' motivations.

Basic Assumptions

The shared assumptions of the expectancy-value model, goal orientation models, and attribution theory also apply to classroom instruction. They are (1) academic motivation develops, in part, from a complex interaction of classroom factors and factors within the student, (2) the student is an active processor and interpreter of the classroom setting, and (3) students can reflect on and report their perceptions to others. A fourth assumption is that motivation is subject-specific; that is, students' values and goals may differ for mathematics, biology, history, literature, and other courses.

Classroom Influences on Student Motivation

The classroom setting is one in which hundreds of interactions occur between teachers and students. These interactions are sources of information for both teacher and student beliefs about students' abilities and students' motivational beliefs. Discussed in this section are classroom goal structures, teacher reactions to student performance, and implementing a learning goal orientation.

Classroom Goal Structures

A major focus on the identification of mastery and performance goal orientations by Ames (1992b; Ames & Archer, 1988) is that classroom goal orientations influence students' goal orientations. The activities and emphases in the classroom may be categorized as mastery/learning-oriented or performance-oriented, and the associated classroom environments influence students. Mastery-oriented classrooms emphasize effort, improvement, and challenge and establish an environment in which students can experience improvement and feelings of mastery.

In contrast, teachers who focus on ability perceptions, make evaluations public, and show only the best students' work are performance-oriented. Examples include announcements of the highest and lowest scores; posted charts of students' projects, scores, and progress; and public displays of selected projects and achievements (Ames, 1992b, p. 264). Frequent use of written assignments that are graded, the display of only A or mostly correct papers, and the use of both positive and negative feedback in a public context also reflect a performance orientation in the classroom (Stipek & Daniels, 1988). Such practices provide many opportunities for students to question their ability and to judge themselves inadequate (Ames, 1984, 1992a; Mac Iver, 1987; Stipek, 1981).

Other studies also support the linkage between classroom practices and students' goal orientations (e.g., Anderman & Young, 1994; Meece, 1991; Meece, Blumenfeld, & Hoyle, 1988). In addition, some studies have identified links between the type of classroom goal structure and students' motivations and/or strategy use. One study of 570 students in third through sixth grades from twelve schools found that performance-oriented classroom goals were associated with a decline in students' valuations of mathematics and reading (Anderman et al., 2001). Other studies of middle school students have found that performance goals in the classroom were linked to both performance-approach and performance-avoidance goals in students. Further, students' performance-avoidance goals were predictors of students' self-handicapping strategies (Middleton & Midgley, 1997; Midgley & Urdan, 2001). Included in handicapping strategies are putting off studying until the last minute and avoiding seeking help in the classroom.

One difficulty in implementing a learning-goal orientation in middle and junior high schools is the shift in grading practices from elementary school. The focus in elementary school classrooms is on task mastery, improvement, and intellectual development. However, middle and junior high schools are perceived by teachers, students, and observers to be performance-focused with the emphasis on competition and social comparison (Anderman & Midgley, 1997; Covington, 1999; Wigfield, Eccles, & Pintrich, 1996). Grading practices tend to be stricter at those levels, and grades often are determined relative to the performance of others. Covington (1999; Covington & Teel, 1996) refers to this structure as the "ability game." In such a competitive, zero-sum situation, an inadequate supply of rewards (good grades) is available to only a few students. When one player "wins" (receives a high grade), then other students must lose (receive lower grades). Classrooms in which only a few high grades are available tend to foster the perception that self-worth is related to success (Covington, 1999) and contributes to student goal orientations of performance-approach, performance-avoidance, and failure avoidance. Anderman and Maehr (1994) maintain that the motivational problems of adolescents are largely the result of a performance-goal orientation in the classroom.

Teacher Reactions to Student Performance

Research indicates that the teacher's classroom goal orientation is related to students' personal goal orientations and related strategy use in the classroom. In addition, teacher reactions to student success or failure in the classroom, for formal or informal assessments, can influence students' attributions for the assessment outcome.

Specifically, the teacher evaluates the performance as success or failure, makes an attribution for the outcome, and communicates the outcome to the student. Both the verbal feedback and the teacher's nonverbal reactions (e.g., facial expression, hesitation) send messages to the student. The basis for this conclusion is the research on reactions to success and failure. In one series of studies, research participants responded to hypothetical situations as "teachers." In the success conditions, they rewarded high effort more than ability, and, for failure, punished lack of effort more than lack of ability.

In other studies, both children and adults, when presented failure situations and "teacher" reactions of anger, inferred lack of effort as the cause. For teacher reactions of pity, they inferred the cause of failure to be lack of ability (Graham & Weiner, 1983; Weiner, Graham, Stern, & Lawson, 1982). In other words, sympathy expressed to certain students following failure is one of the cues for low-ability inferences by others (Graham, 1984, 1988, 1990). More important, the sympathy may (1) prevent the teacher from providing challenging tasks to the student and/or (2) lead to too much teacher help to the student, thereby removing student responsibility for learning (Weiner, 1980d, p. 10). Unsolicited aid may lead the student to conclude that the teacher perceives his or her ability to be low. Such behaviors also may lead to devaluation of the subject by the student by contributing to negative affective memories and may contribute to a work avoidance goal orientation.

Other teacher behaviors may contribute to negative motivational beliefs of students. That is, teachers who expect certain students to perform poorly will treat them differently, thereby reducing their opportunities to learn and contributing to poor achievement. Good (1980) listed 11 ways that students designated as low achievers are rated differently in some classrooms. Included are seating low achievers farther from the teacher and/or in a group, asking for less work and effort from them, and paying less attention to them. Less attention includes less eye contact, fewer opportunities to respond to teacher questions, less time to answer questions, and less detailed feedback on errors (p. 88). In one study, fifth-grade students were asked to evaluate teacher expectations for a hypothetical smart student (G) and a low-ability student (E). The children indicated that the teacher would not expect the low-ability student to remain task involved (Thorkildsen & Nicholls, 1998).

Good (1980) suggested that teachers should be proactive by building classroom structures in which the needs of low achievers can be met without ignoring the needs of other students. Also important is to avoid feedback to students that sends negative messages. Rohrkemper and Brophy (1983) found that the teacher's affective reaction typically influences his or her subsequent actions, which also convey messages about ability. Pintrich and Blumenfeld (1985) found that teacher feedback about work was a better predictor for children's ability and effort perceptions of themselves than other interactions with teachers or peers.

Implementing a Learning Goal Orientation

Characteristics of learning-oriented classrooms include flexible instructional groups, variations in assignments according to students' skill levels, discouragement of normative comparison, frequent group projects, encouragement of peer assistance, and substantive comments on student work (Stipek & Daniels, 1988). Also, one study indicated that implementing grading policies based on specific, clearly defined criteria was effective in discouraging negative achievement goals in at-risk middle school students (Teel, DeBruin-Parecki, & Covington, 1998). Furthermore, initial discussions of classroom goal orientations identified procedural and cognitive priorities that are important in learning-oriented classrooms (Ames, 1992b). Examples are permitting students to participate in decision making and designing tasks that provide reasonable challenges to students (see Figure 13.2).

Another mechanism that can contribute to a positive learning environment is some form of cooperative learning. Examples include small-group teaching; the Jigsaw method; Teams, Games, and Tournaments (TGT); and Student Teams and Achievement Divisions (STAD). In small-group teaching, students typically select subtopics within a general area and then organize themselves in groups of two to six to prepare for presentation to the total class. In the Jigsaw method, groups of students who are working on the same portion of the material help each other learn and prepare the material for presentation to their original group (Aronson, Stephan, Sikes, Blaney, & Snapp, 1978). Teams, Games, and Tournaments and Student Teams and Achievement Divisions are group study approaches that each conclude with a formal method of evaluating student learning on a weekly basis. Use of the Jigsaw method with one class in a science museum resulted in several minutes at the designated exhibits rather than the typical time spent by students of less than one minute (Hidi, Weiss, Berndorff, & Nolan, 1998).

Perhaps most important, recent research indicates that motivational statements of teachers, their respect and support for students, and their expressions of the nature of learning also are important in implementing a mastery or learning goal orientation (Patrick, Anderman, Ryan, Edelin, & Midgley, 2001). Practices observed in two fifth-grade mastery-oriented classrooms are summarized in the following paragraphs.

Student Participation.   In one classroom, the teacher engaged the students in generating the rules for the class. When discussing math problems, both teachers called on all students in the class, not only the ones who volunteered. Also, because the emphasis was on the strategies used by students in working through problems, students were encouraged to share their approaches.

Autonomy.   Students were given considerable freedom in the classroom to talk with others, go to the pencil sharpener, and so on, provided they were

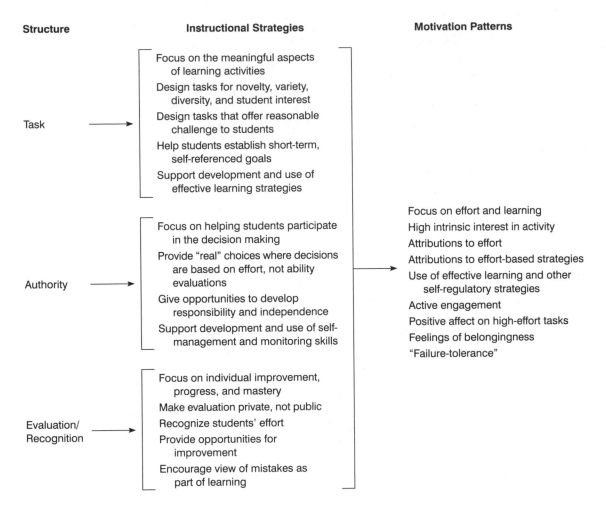

Structure	Instructional Strategies	Motivation Patterns

Task →
- Focus on the meaningful aspects of learning activities
- Design tasks for novelty, variety, diversity, and student interest
- Design tasks that offer reasonable challenge to students
- Help students establish short-term, self-referenced goals
- Support development and use of effective learning strategies

Authority →
- Focus on helping students participate in the decision making
- Provide "real" choices where decisions are based on effort, not ability evaluations
- Give opportunities to develop responsibility and independence
- Support development and use of self-management and monitoring skills

Evaluation/ Recognition →
- Focus on individual improvement, progress, and mastery
- Make evaluation private, not public
- Recognize students' effort
- Provide opportunities for improvement
- Encourage view of mistakes as part of learning

→
- Focus on effort and learning
- High intrinsic interest in activity
- Attributions to effort
- Attributions to effort-based strategies
- Use of effective learning and other self-regulatory strategies
- Active engagement
- Positive affect on high-effort tasks
- Feelings of belongingness
- "Failure-tolerance"

FIGURE 13.2
Classroom structure and instructional strategies essential for mastery goal orientation
Note: From "Classrooms: Goals, Structures, and Student Motivation" by C. Ames, 1992, *Journal of Educational Psychology, 84*(3), p. 267. Copyright 1992 by the American Psychological Association. Reprinted with permission of the author.

not distracted from learning and did not distract others (Patrick et al., 2001, p. 46). They also were permitted to decide whether they worked individually or with others, and the order in which to complete tasks during seatwork.

Recognition and Support. Teachers recognized student efforts in learning with "warm praise that was also task-related, clear, contingent and credible," and was not limited to only a few students (p. 47). For example, when one student was reading aloud, he struggled with one word and finally read it correctly. The teacher commended him for not giving up and referred to him as a good reader (p. 47). Also, when several students raised their hands to answer a question, the teacher commented on what a bright class they were, with so many hands raised.

The teachers also voiced positive expectations for the students. They stated often that the students could do the work, even if they were having difficulties (p. 47). In addition, feedback focused consistently on the particular academic activity and provided specific suggestions for improvement. Students also were encouraged to help each other.

The Nature of Learning.   Both mastery-oriented teachers emphasized that learning is a process. One teacher said that seeing, hearing, and doing were ways of learning and the class would do all three. Both teachers also stressed the importance of understanding and improvement, which were more important than getting the right answer (p. 45). Also, mistakes were viewed as indicators that a shift in strategy was needed.

The importance of teacher structuring of the social environment for learning in these ways is indicated by a survey of 233 seventh and eighth graders from three ethnically diverse schools. Results indicated that teacher caring and support, opportunities to interact with classmates about academic work, and teacher encouragement of mutual respect led to more adaptive patterns of learning and engagement in learning (Ryan & Patrick, 2001).

Summary

The shared assumptions of the expectancy-value model, goal orientation models, and attribution theory in the classroom are those that are also general assumptions of these perspectives. A fourth assumption is that motivation is subject-specific.

Two classroom influences on the development of students' motivational beliefs are the nature of classroom goal structures and different teacher reactions to students who differ in ability. Mastery-oriented classrooms facilitate the development of positive student motivations because such classrooms emphasize effort, improvement, and challenge, and establish an environment in which students can experience improvement and mastery. In contrast, a focus on perceptions of ability, public evaluation, and showcasing only the best students' work are performance-oriented.

Also, teacher feedback, both verbal and nonverbal, sends messages to students about the teacher's attributions for a failure outcome. That is, teacher reactions of anger typically are interpreted as lack of effort as the cause for failure. Expressions of pity and unsolicited help are interpreted as sympathy, which indicates lack of ability. Other teacher behaviors that send messages of low-ability are seating low achievers farther from the teacher, less eye contact, and fewer opportunities to respond to teacher questions.

Implementing a learning or mastery goal orientation includes flexible instructional groups, variations in assignments due to skill levels, encouragement of peer assistance, and substantive comments on student work. Observed characteristics of two mastery-oriented classrooms included student participation in generating class rules, considerable student autonomy, recognition and support of students' efforts, and a view of learning as a process that focuses on understanding and improvement.

Developing Programs for Motivational Change

Two types of maladaptive motivational patterns may be identified. One is the decline in positive motivational beliefs in some children during the middle school years. Included are competence beliefs and success expectancies, the importance and utility of school subjects, decline in the endorsement of mastery goals and an increase in performance goals, and a change in attributions for failure from effort-related to ability-related (Anderman & Anderman, 1999; Anderman et al., 2002; Eccles & Midgley, 1989; Wigfield, 1994; Wigfield & Eccles, 1992, 2002b).

Students who have developed these beliefs are likely to have implemented self-handicapping and other avoidance strategies at least part of the time. As a result, they are likely to be lacking some important knowledge and skills in one or more school subjects. Therefore, skill-building in one-on-one or small-group situations is essential. Also of importance in these sessions is to promote autonomy by giving students choices in which tasks to address first, providing recognition and support for students' efforts, and providing feedback on student mistakes that demonstrates the information value of errors in learning.

Particularly important, if at all possible, is to ensure that the students' regular classrooms value learning, understanding, and improving knowledge and skills. Some research indicates a relationship between disruptive behavior and classroom goals (Kaplan & Maehr, 1999; Kaplan, Gheen, & Midgley, 2002; Roeser, Midgley, & Urdan, 1996). Disruptive behavior is likely to be high in classrooms in which students perceive that the classroom values demonstration of ability and performing better than others (Kaplan et al., 2002, p. 203). In contrast, classrooms perceived to value understanding and learning are likely to be low in disruptive behavior. In other words, classrooms that are mastery-oriented provide fewer reasons and fewer opportunities for students to develop avoidance goals and strategies.

The second type of maladaptive motivational belief is referred to as "learned helplessness." Typically, most attribution retraining programs are designed to change undesirable or maladaptive attributions for failure from lack of ability to lack of effort. However, according to the attributional model, both success and failure outcomes should be addressed. In other words, instead of being viewed as a random event, success becomes predictable when related to ability *and* effort. Both are internal factors, and extent of effort is controlled by the individual. On the other hand, failure is changed from an expected (highly predictable) event to one that is under some individual control through the control of effort.

However, building the high, stable, and resilient expectancies that accompany challenge seeking and persistence requires attention to several variables. Among them are an environment that supports risk taking and tasks that include challenge, and even failure, within a learning-orientation setting (Dweck, 1989, p. 118).

Planning an attributional change program should include at least three steps. The first step is to develop an analysis of the attributional cues that currently signal failure in the child's experience. The second step is to identify and implement alternative teacher behaviors that can serve as attributional cues to the student. Examples are legitimate, positive comments for both effort and partial activities completed correctly. The third is to identify group activities that foster beliefs in the importance of developing alternative strategies to reach a goal and that emphasize realistic goal setting.

EDUCATIONAL APPLICATIONS

A major contribution of motivational perspectives to education is the analyses of classroom interactions. In the classroom setting, researchers have applied these frameworks to analyze both student and teacher behaviors and to suggest remedies (Ames, 1992b; Ames & Archer, 1988; Anderman et al., 2002; Covington, 1999; Dweck, 1989; Eccles et al., 1983; Elliot, 1999; Elliott & Dweck, 1988; Jagacinski & Nicholls, 1987; Stipek & Daniels, 1988). On a broader scale, attribution theory has implications for the ways that our culture defines success. Frieze, Francis, & Hanusa (1983) described several analyses of the American definition of success. It is viewed as attainable by the individual who outperforms others in competitive situations. Such a societal value, by its very nature, relegates some people to failure status. In contrast, other cultures define success in terms of group accomplishment and cooperation. At the very least, attribution theory suggests success definitions that emphasize accomplishment through effort and the exercise of learned skills (Frieze et al., 1983).

Classroom Issues

The issues of student characteristics, cognitive processes and instruction, and the social context for learning are viewed from the perspective of motivational perspectives.

Learner Characteristics
The characteristics of major concern to education include individual differences, readiness for learning, and motivation. Motivational perspectives do not directly address individual differences or readiness for learning.

Individual Differences. Motivational models and theories identify various factors, such as achievement history and the learner's social context, that influence the individual's motivational beliefs. However, they do not identify particular constellations of these factors that differentiate individuals.

Readiness for Learning. Although readiness is yet to be researched by the motivational perspectives, the implications are clear. Low expectancy for success, low task value, the adoption of performance-avoidance, work or fail-ure-avoidance goal orientation, and attributions of lack of ability for failure influence students' receptivity to instruction.

Motivation.   Theories of learning typically treat motivation as a concept that is an adjunct to the principles for generating learning in the student. For the most part, these theories focus on some environmental manipulation that may lead to student motivations, such as arousing the student's attention, examin-ing the role of incentives, or making the material relevant, meaningful, or interesting (Weiner, 1974b).

In contrast, motivational perspectives view certain classroom processes and student characteristics as important sources of motivation. Classroom processes, for example, include supporting a mastery goal orientation, the teacher's affec-tive reactions to students' successes and mistakes, support for autonomy, and recognition and support of effort.

Cognitive Processes and Instruction
The three cognitive issues of importance to education are transfer of learning, teaching problem solving, and learning how-to-learn skills. Motivational per-spectives indicate that self-handicapping and avoidance strategies are likely to be transferred to subsequent achievement tasks as are maladaptive problem-solving approaches. Acquiring how-to-learn skills is most likely to occur in classrooms with mastery goal orientation in which errors are treated as clues to remedy one's learning.

The Social Context for Learning
Goal orientation models and attribution theory address aspects of the class-room that influence students' motivations. Classrooms with a mastery goal ori-entation establish a climate that facilitates learning. The classroom supports student development and the use of self-management skills, avoids competition, and provides reasonable challenges. Attribution theory identifies the teacher as an important source of information for students' beliefs about their capabilities.

Relationships to Other Perspectives
Unlike the learning-process and cognitive-development theories, motivational perspectives identify the learner as a major factor in developing motivation for school learning. Through the interpretation of information in the social setting and past experiences, the learner develops a set of beliefs that encour-age or discourage engagement in achievement-related tasks.

Some concepts in attribution theory and social-cognitive theory are com-plementary. Learners who attribute success to effort or ability and effort also hold positive self-efficacy beliefs and are self-regulated learners.

Developing a Classroom Strategy

The application of motivational perspectives in the classroom implies a need for proactive strategies rather than a reliance on reactive responses to students' achievement-related activities. It also implies a classroom climate that fosters an emphasis on the process of learning rather than on competitive achievement. Such a classroom climate minimizes the number of success–failure judgments with their accompanying self-worth assessments and expectancy consequences. Instead, classroom goals emphasize improved learning strategies, class time is structured to minimize interpersonal competition, and feedback to students minimizes ability or lack of ability as an attribution for classroom outcomes. In other words, the classroom is structured to reinforce the belief that learning is acquired through constructive effort. The following strategy is suggested for the development of a positive proactive environment.

Step 1: Restructure classroom objectives in terms of learning processes or strategies.

1.1 Which objectives can be rewritten to emphasize a learning strategy?

1.2 Which classroom tasks currently in use can be varied to provide novelty and diversity and enhance student interest?

Step 2: Identify appropriate evaluation methods.

2.1 Where can formative evaluations or tests be implemented that focus on identifying mistakes to improve learning?

2.2 Does the classroom contain wall charts, progress reports, or grades that can be replaced with rotating displays of all students' work?

2.3 Are classroom rewards consistently distributed for effort, not ability?

2.4 Are students given a variety of opportunities to demonstrate what they have learned?

Step 3: Identify classroom activities that (1) deemphasize interpersonal competitiveness and (2) facilitate the development of effective task-approach strategies and effort.

3.1 Is the percentage of time devoted to class activities as compared with small-group and individual seatwork activities too high, for example, 80% as compared with 20%?

3.2 What changes can be made in tasks to increase student decision making?

3.3 Which small-group activities may be used to increase the cooperative nature of learning?

3.4 What individual or group games are available that can enhance student effort and/or improve learning strategies?

Step 4: Develop verbal feedback statements that convey appropriate attributional messages.

4.1 Is praise appropriately used (i.e., avoided for success at easy tasks, provided for persistence and appropriate strategies as well as success at difficult tasks)?

4.2 What constructive teacher strategies may be used instead of sympathy for unsuccessful performance? Are external factors, such as luck, avoided as explanations for success and failure?

4.3 What strategies may be used to encourage students to take responsibility for their own learning?

Classroom Examples

Two classroom strategies are discussed. The first is an academic learning game known as STRATAGEM (Bell, 1982), and the second is a group learning arrangement.

STRATAGEM

STRATAGEM was developed to ease the pressure of studying for examinations and to increase student effort in thinking through issues in the subject area. The game has been used successfully by the author with high school and college students. Other teachers have reported success with middle school students.

The game is a cooperative learning activity in which teams of two to four students take turns in answering questions typed on 3×5 cards placed face down in front of the players. Each game requires a banker and two teams of players. Thus, a classroom may have as many as five games operating simultaneously to accommodate the entire class.

Each team is given $1,000 in artificial money at the beginning of the game. The team decides, before seeing the question to be answered, the amount of money to be staked on the team's ability to answer the unseen question. Amounts from $10 to $50 may be selected. The information used by the team in this decision is the coding information provided about the question. This information is on the reverse side of the question card and, thus, is face up to the team. Questions are coded as one of three levels: 1 = recall; 2 = application; and 3 = inference. The topic of the question is also listed. An example is "Asking children to draw pictures about a story that they have just read is an example of _____," which is coded "Level 2—Application; Topic: Information-Processing Theory."

After the wager, one member turns the question card over and reads the question aloud. The team then has 3 to 4 minutes to discuss possible answers. Typically, the members of the other team in the game also are trying to determine the answer. If the team answers a level 1 question correctly, the bank matches the amount wagered. For a level 2 question, the bank pays double the wager, and it triples the amount for level 3 questions. Thus, the team, for a $10 wager, may receive an additional $10, $20, or $30. Similarly, for a $50 wager, the bank would pay $50, $100, or $150, depending on the level of the question.

To emphasize the learning process and to ensure that no team runs out of money, the teams lose only the amount of the wager for incorrect or incomplete answers. That is, the level of the question enters only into the reward for correct answers.

When the team announces the selected answer, it is either compared with a list of answers provided to the banker or evaluated by the teacher, who is circulating among the players. In practice, after learning the correct answer, both teams typically discuss the answer for a few minutes before the next team takes a turn on the next question. These brief discussions are permitted because (1) they do not lessen the enthusiasm for the game and (2) they contribute to the learning.

The teacher's role is to circulate among the games, clarifying questions or keeping the discussions from inhibiting the play. In a 45-minute class period, from 25 to 30 questions can be completed. Of the 50 questions developed for each use of the game, approximately two-thirds are application and inference questions. The nature of the questions precipitates discussions that enhance learning.

The ideal time to implement the game is a week or two before a major examination, that is, before the students have begun their detailed study. This practice equalizes performance on the game questions and emphasizes learning.

Teaching Students to Identify the Main Idea

In this classroom strategy, the following instructional events are presented by the teacher (see chapter 7):

1. Gain attention.
2. Inform learner of the objective.
3. Stimulate recall.
4. Present distinctive stimulus features (topic + something special about the topic = main idea) plus two or three examples.
5. Provide learning guidance. This event is carried out with small groups. Each group is given the task of selecting four favorite movies or television programs, identifying the main idea of each and describing why the statement is the main idea. As each group progresses in the activity, the teacher provides feedback about needed changes in the choices. Differences between story details, sweeping statements, and the main idea are pointed out where needed. At the conclusion of the activity, each group presents its program choices and main idea identifications to the class.
6. Elicit performance.
7. Provide feedback.

Events 6 and 7 are completed in the form of a written diagnostic exercise. Children are given a set of eight story lines with four choices of the main idea for each. Feedback is given in the form of changes needed to realign the child's conception of *main idea* with the concept characteristics.

8. Assess performance.
9. Provide retention and transfer.

Events 8 and 9 make use of the academic game "Natural Topics," described in chapter 7.

Review of Perspectives on Motivation

Three perspectives, the expectancy-value model, goal orientation models, and attribution theory, focus on factors that influence students' engagement in achievement-related activities (see Table 13.5). They maintain that motivation develops from a complex interaction of environmental and internal factors, the individual is an active processor of information, and achievement-related beliefs are explicit information. The expectancy-value model also maintains that student's expectations of success are key determinants of task (course) choice, persistence, extent of effort, cognitive engagement, and actual performance.

TABLE 13.5
Summary of Motivational Perspectives

Basic Elements	Definitions
Assumptions	Motivation develops from a complex interaction of internal and external factors; the individual actively processes information; and achievement-related beliefs are explicit information.
Motivational processes	Key determiners of achievement-related behaviors are students' (1) success expectancies and task (domain) values, (2) achievement-goal orientations, or (3) attributions for success/failure outcomes.
Components of motivation	(1) students' affective memories, goals, and self-schemata, which directly influence expectancies and values, (2) mastery, performance-approach, and performance-avoidance orientations, or (3) major attributions (ability, effort, task difficulty, mood or illness, luck) and the dimensions (locus of causality, stability, and controllability)
	Analysis
Disadvantages	Specific classroom procedures are yet to be developed
Contributions to classroom practice	Identification of classroom activities that contribute to maladaptive student behaviors and the problems inherent in competitive classrooms
	Provide a framework for the research and analysis of affective events operating in the classroom

Direct influences on these values are the student's affective memories and goals and self-schemata. Contributing beliefs are the student's social world and perceptions of it, and prior achievement-related experiences.

In contrast, goal orientation models address students' reasons for engaging in academic tasks because they influence students' cognitive strategies, task selection, and competence perceptions. Major types are mastery or learning-oriented, which lead to positive task strategies, performance-approach, and performance-avoidance orientations. The latter two orientations focus on obtaining favorable judgments of one's competence and avoiding unfavorable judgments, respectively. Both orientations lead to superficial engagement with the subject matter.

The third perspective, attribution theory, maintains that the search for understanding is a prime motivator of action, attributions are complex sources of information, and future behavior, in part, is determined by one's attributions for success and failure outcomes. Typical attributions are ability, effort, task difficulty, luck, others, and mood or illness. They differ on the dimensions of locus of causality, stability, and controllability, which can generate different expectancies for future outcomes and different emotions.

In the classroom, many children's expectancies for success, competence beliefs, and beliefs in the effectiveness of effort typically decline as they enter middle school. This decline may lead to self-handicapping and other avoidance strategies. However, classrooms that focus on mastery-oriented goals, provide student choice on tasks, and provide recognition and support for effort can facilitate the valuing of knowledge and learning by students.

Disadvantages

Specific classroom procedures are yet to be developed for the implementation of the motivational perspectives in the classroom.

Contributions to Educational Practice

The motivational perspectives have identified a major problem in the American classroom. It is the competitive nature of learning and the effects that such an atmosphere can have on many children. Competitiveness, by its very nature, relegates someone to last place, often in a race that has limited long-term value. These perspectives provide a framework for the research and analysis of many affective events operating in the classroom.

CHAPTER QUESTIONS

1. According to the expectancy-value model, what is the difference between attainment value and intrinsic value?
2. How does the portrayal of goals in the expectancy-value model and the goal orientation models differ?
3. What is the rationale for subdividing performance goals into performance-approach and performance-avoid goals?
4. What is the relationship between attributions for success and Bandura's concept of self-efficacy?
5. How might a learner's theory of intelligence interact with classroom events to influence attributions for achievement outcomes?

REFERENCES

Abramson, L. Y., Garber, J., & Seligman, M. E. P. (1980). Learned helplessness in humans: An attributional analysis. In J. Garber & M. E. P. Seligman (Eds.), *Human helplessness: Theory and applications* (pp. 3–33). New York: Academic.

Ames, C. (1978). Children's achievement attributions and self-reinforcement: Effects of self-concept and competitive reward structure. *Journal of Educational Psychology, 70,* 345–355.

Ames, C. (1984). Competitive, cooperative, and individualistic goal structures: A motivational analysis. In R. Ames & C. Ames (Eds.), *Research on motivation in education* (Vol. 1, pp. 177–207). New York: Academic.

Ames, C. (1992a). Achievement goals and the motivational climate. In D. Schunk & J. Meece (Eds.), *Student perceptions in the classroom* (pp. 327–348). Hillsdale, NJ: Erlbaum.

Ames, C. (1992b). Classrooms: Goals, structures, and student motivation. *Journal of Educational Psychology, 84*(3), 261–271.

Ames, C., & Archer, J. (1988). Achievement goals in the classroom: Students' learning strategies and motivational processes. *Journal of Educational Psychology, 80*(3), 260–267.

Ames, C., Ames, R., & Felker, D. W. (1977). Effects of a competitive reward structure and valence of outcome on children's achievement attributions. *Journal of Educational Psychology, 60,* 1–8.

Anderman, L. H., & Anderman, E. M. (1999). Social predictors of changes in students' achievement goal orientation. *Contemporary Educational Psychology, 25*, 21–37.

Anderman, E. M., & Maehr, M. L. (1994). Motivation and schooling in the middle grades. *Review of Educational Research, 64*, 287–309.

Anderman, E. M., & Midgley, C. (1997). Changes in goal orientation, perceived academic competence, and grades across the middle-school levels. *Contemporary Educational Psychology, 22*, 260–298.

Anderman, E.M., Austin, G. G., & Johnson, D. M. (2002). The development of goal orientation. In A. Wigfield & J. S. Eccles (Eds.), *Development of achievement motivation* (pp. 197–222). San Diego: Academic.

Anderman, E. M., & Young, A. J. (1994). Motivation and strategy use in science: Individual differences and classroom effects. *Journal of Research in Science Teaching, 31*(8), 811–831.

Anderman, E. M., Eccles, J. S., Yoon, K. S., Roeser, R., Wigfield, A., & Blumenfeld, P. (2001). Learning to value mathematics and reading: Relations to mastery and performance-oriented instructional practices. *Contemporary Educational Psychology, 26*, 76–95.

Archer, J. (1994). Achievement goals as a measure of motivation in university students. *Contemporary Educational Psychology, 19*, 430–446.

Aronson, E., Stephan, C., Sikes, J., Blaney, N., & Snapp, P. (1978). *The Jigsaw classroom.* Beverly Hills, CA: Sage.

Atkinson, J. W. (1958). Towards experimental analysis of human motivation in terms of motives, expectancies, and incentives. In J. W. Atkinson (Ed.), *Motives in fantasy, action, and society* (pp. 288–305). Princeton, NJ: Van Nostrand.

Atkinson, J. W. (1964). *An introduction to motivation.* Princeton, NJ: Van Nostrand.

Bell, M. E. (1982). STRATAGEM: A problem-solving game for use in revision. *Simulation/Games for Learning, 12*(4), 157–164.

Bong, M. (2001). Between- and within-domain relations of academic motivation among middle and high school students: Self-efficacy, task value, and achievement goals. *Journal of Educational Psychology, 93*, 23–34.

Brophy, J. (1999). Toward a model of the value aspects of motivation in education: Developing appreciation for particular learning domains and activities. *Educational Psychologist, 34*(2), 75–86.

Brown, J., & Weiner, B. (1984). Affective consequences of ability versus effort ascriptions: Controversies, resolutions, and quandaries. *Journal of Educational Psychology, 76*, 146–158.

Covington, M.V. (1992). *Making the grade: A self-worth perspective on motivation and school reform.* New York: Cambridge University Press.

Covington, M. V. (1999). Caring about learning: The nature and nurturing of subject-matter appreciation. *Educational Psychologist, 34*(2), 127–136.

Covington, M. V., & Teel, K. M. (1996). *Overcoming student failure: Changing motives and incentives for learning.* Washington, DC: American Psychological Association.

Covington, M. V., & Omelich, C. L. (1984). Task-oriented versus competitive learning structures: Motivational and performance consequences. *Journal of Educational Psychology, 76*, 1038–1050.

Dai, Y. D., Moon, S. M., & Feldhusen, J. F. (1998). Achievement motivation and gifted students: A social cognitive perspective. *Educational Psychologist, 33*(2/3), 45–64.

deCharms, R. (1968). *Personal causation.* New York: Academic.

Diener, C. I., & Dweck, C. S. (1978). An analysis of learned helplessness: Continuous changes in performance, strategy and achievement cognitions following failure. *Journal of Personality and Social Psychology, 36*, 451–462.

Diener, C. I., & Dweck, C. S. (1980). Analysis of learned helplessness II: The processing of success. *Journal of Personality and Social Psychology, 39*, 940–952.

Dweck, C. S. (1975). The role of expectations and attributions in the alleviation of learned helplessness. *Journal of Personality and Social Psychology, 31*, 674–685.

Dweck, C. S. (1986). Motivational processes affecting learning. *American Psychologist, 41*, 1040–1048.

Dweck, C. S. (1989). Motivation. In R. Glaser & A. Lesgold (Eds.), *The handbook of psychology and education* (Vol. 1, pp. 187–239). Hillsdale, NJ: Erlbaum.

Dweck, C.S. (2002). The development of ability comparisons. In A. Wigfield & J. S. Eccles (Eds.), *Development of achievement motivation* (pp. 57–88). San Diego: Academic.

Dweck, C., & Leggett, E. (1988). A social-cognitive approach to motivation and personality. *Psychological Review, 95*, 256–273.

Dweck, C. S., & Licht, B. G. (1980). Learned helplessness and academic achievement. In J. Garber & M. Seligman (Eds.), *Human helplessness: Theory and application* (pp. 197–221). New York: Academic.

Eccles, J. S., & Midgley, C. (1989). Stage-environment fit: Developmentally appropriate classrooms for young adolescents. In C. Ames & R. Ames (Eds.), *Research on motivation in education* (Vol. 3, pp. 139–186). San Diego: Academic.

Eccles (Parsons), J., Adler, T. F., Futterman, R., Goff, S. B., Kaczala, C. M., Meece, J. L., & Midgley, C. (1983). Expectancies, values, and academic behaviors. In J. T. Spence (Ed.), *Achievement and achievement motivation* (pp. 75–146). San Francisco: W. H. Freeman.

Eccles, J. S., Midgley, C., Wigfield, A., Miller-Buchanan, C., Reuman, D., Flanagan, C., & MacIver, D. (1993). Development during adolescence: The impact of stage-environment fit on young adolescents' experiences in schools and families. *American Psychologist, 48*, 90–101.

Eliot, A. J. (1999). Approach and avoidance motivation and achievement goals. *Educational Psychologist, 35*(3), 169–189.

Elliot, A. J., McGregor, H. A., & Gable, S. (1999). Achievement goals, study strategies, and exam performance: A mediational analysis. *Journal of Educational Psychology, 91*(3), 549–563.

Elliot, A. J. (1997). Integrating the "classic" and "contemporary" approaches to achievement motivation: A hierarchical model of approach and avoidance motivation. In M. Maehr & P. Pintrich (Eds.), *Advances in motivation and achievement* (Vol. 10, pp. 243–279). Greenwich, CT: JAI Press.

Elliot, A. J., & Church, M. A. (1997). A hierarchical model of approach and avoidance achievement motivation. *Journal of Personality and Social Psychology, 72*, 218–232.

Elliott, E. E., & Dweck, C. S. (1988). Goals: An approach to motivation and achievement. *Journal of Personality and Social Psychology, 54*(1), 5–12.

Eswara, H. A. (1972). Administration of reward and punishment in relation to ability, effort, and performance. *Journal of Social Psychology, 87*, 139–140.

Frieze, I., Francis, W., & Hanusa, B. (1983). Defining success in classroom learning. In J. Levine & M. Wang (Eds.), *Teacher and student perceptions* (pp. 3–28). Hillsdale, NJ: Erlbaum.

Good, T. (1980). Classroom expectations: Teacher–pupil interactions. In J. H. McMillan (Ed.), *The social psychology of school learning* (pp. 70–122). New York: Academic.

Graham, S. (1984). Communicating sympathy and anger to black and white children: The cognitive attributional consequences of affective cues. *Journal of Personality and Social Psychology, 47*(1), 40–54.

Graham, S. (1988). Can attribution theory tell us something about blacks? *Educational Psychologist, 23*(1), 3–21.

Graham, S. (1990). Communicating low ability in the classroom: Bad things good teachers sometimes do. In S. Graham & V. S. Folkes (Eds.), *Attribution theory: Applications to achievement, mental health, and interpersonal conflict* (pp. 17–36). Hillsdale, NJ: Erlbaum.

Graham, S., & Hudley, C. (1992). An attributional approach to aggression in African-American children. In D. Schunk & J. Meece (Eds.), *Student perceptions in the classroom* (pp. 75–93). Hillsdale, NJ: Erlbaum.

Graham, S., Hudley, C., & Williams, E. (1992). Attributional and emotional determinants of aggression among African-American and Latino young adolescents. *Developmental Psychology, 28*, 731–740.

Graham, S., & Weiner, B. (1983). Some educational implications of sympathy and anger from an attributional perspective. In R. Snow & M. Farr (Eds.), *Aptitude learning, and instruction: Vol. 3. Conative and affective policy analysis* (pp. 199–221). Hillsdale, NJ: Erlbaum.

Graham, S., & Weiner, B. (1996). Theories and principles of motivation. In D. C. Berliner & R. C. Calfee (Eds.), *Handbook of educational psychology* (pp. 63–84). New York: Macmillan.

Harackiewicz, J. M., Barron, K. M., Tauer, J. M., & Elliot, A. J. (2002). Predicting success in college: A longitudinal study of achievement goals and ability measures as predictors of interest and performance from freshman year through graduation. *Journal of Educational Psychology, 94*(3), 562–575.

Harackiewicz, J. M., Barron, K. M., Pintrich, P. R., Eliot, A., & Thrash, F. (2002). Revisions of achievement goal theory: Necessary and illuminating. *Journal of Educational Psychology, 94*(3), 638–645.

Heider, F. (1958). *The psychology of interpersonal relations*. New York: Wiley.

Hidi, S., Weiss, J., Berndorff, D., & Nolan, J. (1998). The role of gender, instruction, and a cooperative learning technique in science education across formal and informal settings. In L. Hoffman, A. Krapp, K. Renninger, & J. Baumert (Eds.), *Interest and learning: Proceedings of the Sceon Conference on interest and gender* (pp. 301–316). Kiel, Germany: IPN.

Hoffman, M. L. (1982). Development of prosocial motivation: Empathy and guilt. In N. Eisenberg-Borg (Ed.), *Development of prosocial behavior* (pp. 281–313). New York: Academic.

Hudley, C., & Graham, S. (1993). An attributional intervention to reduce peer directed aggression among African-American boys. *Child Development, 64*, 124–138.

Jagacinski, C. M. (1992). The effects of task involvement and ego involvement on achievement-related cognitions and behaviors. In D. H. Schunk & J. Meece (Eds.), *Student perceptions in the classroom* (pp. 287–306). Hillsdale, NJ: Erlbaum.

Jagacinski, C. M., & Nicholls, J. G. (1984). Conceptions of ability and related affects in task involvement and ego involvement. *Journal of Educational Psychology, 76*, 909–919.

Jagacinski, C. M., & Nicholls, J. G. (1987). Competence and affect in task involvement and ego involvement: The impact of social comparison information. *Journal of Educational Psychology, 79*, 107–114.

Juvonen, J. (1991). Deviance, perceived responsibility, and negative peer reactions. *Developmental Psychology, 27*, 672–681.

Juvonen, J. (1992). Negative peer reactions from the perspective of the reactors. *Journal of Educational Psychology, 84*, 314–321.

Kaplan, A., & Maehr, M. L. (1999). Achievement goals and student well-being. *Contemporary Educational Psychology, 24*, 330–358.

Kaplan, A., & Midgley, C. (1997). The effect of achievement goals: Does level of perceived academic competence make a difference? *Contemporary Educational Psychology, 22*, 415–485.

Kaplan, A., Gheen, M., & Midgley, C. (2002). Classroom goal structure and student disruptive behavior. *British Journal of Educational Psychology, 72*, 191–211.

Kaplan, A., & Middleton, M. J. (2002). Should childhood be a journey or a race? *Journal of Educational Psychology, 94*(3), 646–648.

Lopez, D. F. (1999). Social cognitive influences on self-regulated learning: The impact of action-control beliefs and academic goals on achievement-related outcomes. *Learning and Individual Differences, 11*, 301–319.

Mac Iver, D. (1987). Classroom factors and student characteristics predicting students' use of achievement standards during self-assessment. *Child Development, 58*, 1258–1271.

Maehr, M. L., & C. Midgley (1991). Enhancing student motivation: A school-wide approach. *Educational Psychology, 26*, 399–427.

Meece, J. L. (1991). Students' motivational goals and the classroom context. In M. Maehr & P. Pintrich (Eds.), *Advances in motivation and achievement: Goals and self-regulatory processes* (Vol. 7) (pp. 261–285). Greenwich, CT: JAI.

Meece, J. L., Blumenfeld, P. C., & Hoyle, R. (1988). Students' goal orientations and cognitive engagement in classroom activities. *Journal of Educational Psychology, 80*, 514–525.

Middleton, M., & Midgley, C. (1997). Avoiding the demonstration of lack of ability: An underexplored aspect of goal theory. *Journal of Educational Psychology, 89*, 710–718.

Midgley, C., & Urdan, T. (2001). Academic self-handicapping and achievement goals: A further examination. *Contemporary Educational Psychology, 26*, 61–75.

Midgley, C., Anderman, E. M., & Hicks, L. (1995). Differences between elementary and middle school teachers and students: A goal theory approach. *Journal of Early Adolescence, 15,* 90–113.

Midgley, C., Kaplan, A., Middleton, M., Maehr, M. L., Urdan, T., Anderman, L., Anderman, E., & Roeser, R. (1998). The development and validation of scales assessing students' achievement goal orientation. *Contemporary Educational Psychology, 23,* 113–131.

Murphy, P. K., & Alexander, P. (2000). A motivated exploration of motivation terminology. *Contemporary Educational Psychology, 25,* 3–53.

Nicholls, J. G. (1978). The development of the concepts of effort and ability, perception of academic attainment, and the understanding that difficult tasks require more ability. *Child Development, 49,* 800–814.

Nicholls, J. G. (1984). Achievement motivation: Conceptions of ability, subjective experience, task choice, and performance. *Psychological Review, 91,* 328–346.

Nicholls, J. G. (1989). *The competitive ethos and democratic education.* Cambridge, MA: Harvard University Press.

Patrick, H., Anderman, L. H., Ryan, A. M., Edelin, K. C., & Midgley, C. (2001). Teachers' communication of goal orientation in four fifth-grade classrooms. *Elementary School Journal, 102*(1), 35–58.

Pintrich, P. R. (2000). The role of goal orientation in self-regulated learning. In M. Boekarts, P. R. Pintrich, & M. Zeidner (Eds.), *Handbook of self regulation* (pp. 451–502). San Diego: Academic.

Pintrich, P.R., & Schunk, D. H. (2002). *Motivation in education: Theory, research, and applications* (2nd ed.). Upper Saddle River, NJ: Merrill/Prentice Hall.

Pintrich, P. R., & Blumenfeld, P. C. (1985). Classroom experiences and children's self-perceptions of ability, effort, and conduct. *Journal of Educational Psychology, 77,* 646–657.

Pintrich, P.R., & Zusho, A. (2002). The development of academic self-regulation: The role of cognitive and motivational factors. In A. Wigfield & J. S. Eccles (Eds.), *Development of achievement motivation* (pp. 249–284). San Diego: Academic.

Rest, S., Neirenberg, R., Weiner, B., & Heckhausen, H. (1973). Further evidence concerning the effects of perceptions of effort and ability on achievement evaluation. *Journal of Personality and Social Psychology, 28,* 187–191.

Roeser, R.W., Midgley, C., & Urdan, T. C. (1996). Perceptions of the school psychological environment and early adolescents' behavioral functioning in school: The mediating role of goals and belonging. *Journal of Educational Psychology, 88,* 408–422.

Rohrkemper, M., & Brophy, J. (1983). Teachers' thinking about problem students. In J. Levine & M. Wang (Eds.), *Teacher and student perceptions* (pp. 75–103). Hillsdale, NJ: Erlbaum.

Rosenbaum, R. M. (1972). *A dimensional analysis of the perceived causes of success and failure.* Unpublished doctoral dissertation, University of California, Los Angeles.

Rotter, J. B. (1966). Generalized expectancies for internal versus external control of reinforcement. *Psychological Monographs, 80* (1, Whole No. 609).

Ruble, D. N., & Rhales, W. S. (1981). The development of children's perceptions and attributions about their social world. In J. Harvey, W. Ickes, & R. Kidd (Eds.), *New directions in attribution research* (Vol. 3, pp. 3–26). Hillsdale, NJ: Erlbaum.

Ryan, A.M., & Patrick, H. (2001). The classroom social environment and changes in adolescents' motivation and engagement during middle school. *American Educational Research Journal, 38*(2), 437–460.

Seligman, M. E. P. (1975). *Helplessness.* San Francisco: Freeman.

Steele, C. (1988). The psychology of self-affirmation: Sustaining the integrity of the self. In L. Berkowitz (Ed.), *Advances in experimental social psychology* (Vol. 21, pp. 261–302). New York: Academic.

Stipek, D. J. (1981). Children's perceptions of their own and their classmates' ability. *Journal of Educational Psychology, 73,* 404–410.

Stipek, D. J., & Daniels, D. H. (1988). Declining perceptions of competence: A consequence of changes in the child or in the educational environment? *Journal of Educational Psychology, 80*(3), 352–356.

Teel, K. M., DeBruin-Parecki, A., & Covington, M. V. (1998). Teaching strategies that honor and motivate inner-city African American students: A school university collaboration. *Teaching and Teacher Education*, *14*, 479–495.

Thorkildsen, T. A., & Nicholls, J. G. (1998). Fifth-graders' achievement orientation and beliefs: Individual and classroom differences. *Journal of Educational Psychology*, *90*(2), 179–201.

Urdan, T., Midgley, C., & Anderman, E. M. (1998). Classroom influences on self-handicapping strategies. *American Educational Research Journal*, *35*, 101–122.

Weiner, B. (1972). *Theories of motivation from mechanism to cognition.* Chicago: Markham.

Weiner, B. (1974a). An attributional interpretation of expectancy-value theory. In B. Weiner (Ed.), *Cognitive views of human motivation* (pp. 51–69). New York: Academic.

Weiner, B. (1974b). Motivational psychology and educational research. *Educational Psychologist*, *11*, 96–101.

Weiner, B. (1977). An attributional approach for educational psychology. In L. Shulman (Ed.), *Review of research in education* (Vol. 4, pp. 179–209). Itasca, IL: Peacock.

Weiner, B. (1979). A theory of motivation for some classroom experiences. *Journal of Educational Psychology*, *71*, 3–25.

Weiner, B. (1980a). A cognitive (attribution)-emotion-action model of motivated behavior: An analysis of judgments of help-giving. *Journal of Personality and Social Psychology*, *39*, 186–200.

Weiner, B. (1980b). *Human motivation.* New York: Holt, Rinehart & Winston.

Weiner, B. (1980c). "May I borrow your class notes?" An attributional analysis of judgments of help-giving in an achievement-related context. *Journal of Educational Psychology*, *72*, 676–681.

Weiner, B. (1980d). The role of affect in rational (attributional) approaches to human motivation. *Educational Research*, *9*, 4–11.

Weiner, B. (1982). The emotional consequences of causal ascriptions. In M. S. Clark & S. T. Fiske (Eds.), *Affect and cognition: The 17th annual Carnegie symposium on cognition* (pp. 185–208). Hillsdale, NJ: Erlbaum.

Weiner, B. (1983b). Speculations regarding the role of affect in achievement-change programs guided by attributional principles. In J. Levine & M. Wang (Eds.), *Teacher and student perceptions* (pp. 57–73). Hillsdale, NJ: Erlbaum.

Weiner, B. (1985a). An attributional theory of achievement motivation and emotion. *Psychological Review*, *92*(4), 548–573.

Weiner, B. (1985b). *Human motivation.* New York: Springer-Verlag.

Weiner, B. (1993). On sin versus sickness: A theory of perceived responsibility and social motivation. *American Psychologist*, *48*(9), 957–965.

Weiner, B. (1995). *Judgments of responsibility: A foundation for a theory of social conduct.* New York: Guilford.

Weiner, B., & Kukla, A. (1970). An attributional analysis of achievement motivation. *Journal of Personality and Social Psychology*, *15*, 1–20.

Weiner, B., & Peter, N. (1973). A cognitive-developmental analysis of achievement and moral judgments. *Developmental Psychology*, *9*, 290–309.

Weiner, B., Graham, S., Stern, P., & Lawson, M. (1982). Using affective cues to infer causal thoughts. *Developmental Psychology*, *18*, 278–286.

Weiner, B., Graham, S., Taylor, S., & Meyer, W. (1983). Social cognition in the classroom. *Educational Psychologist*, *18*, 109–124.

Weiner, B., Neirenberg, R., & Goldstein, M. (1976). Social learning (locus of control) versus attributional (causal stability) interpretations of expectancy of success. *Journal of Personality*, *44*, 52–68.

Wigfield, A. (1994). Expectancy-value theory of achievement motivation: A developmental perspective. *Educational Psychology Review*, *6*, 49–78.

Wigfield, A., & Eccles, J. S. (1992). The development of achievement task values: A theoretical analysis. *Developmental Review*, *12*, 265–310.

Wigfield, A., & Eccles, J. S. (2000). Expectancy-value theory of achievement motivation. *Contemporary Educational Psychology*, *25*(1), 68–81.

Wigfield, A., & Eccles, J. S. (2002a). Introduction. In A. Wigfield & J. S. Eccles (Eds.),

Development of achievement motivation (pp. 1–11). San Diego: Academic.

Wigfield, A., & Eccles, J. S. (2002b). The development of competence beliefs, expectancies for success, and achievement values from childhood through adolescence. In A. Wigfield & J. S. Eccles (Eds.), *Development of achievement motivation* (pp. 91–120). San Diego: Academic.

Wigfield, A., & Harold, R. D. (1992). Teacher beliefs and children's achievement self-perceptions: A developmental perspective.

In D. Schunk & J. Meece (Eds.), *Student perceptions in the classroom* (pp. 95–121). Hillsdale, NJ: Erlbaum.

Wigfield, A., Eccles, J., & Pintrich, P. (1996). Development between the ages of 11 and 25. In R. C. Calfee & D. C. Berliner (Eds.), *Handbook of educational psychology* (pp. 148–187). New York: Macmillan.

Zucker, G. S., & Weiner, B. (1993). Conservatism and perceptions of poverty: An attributional analysis. *Journal of Applied Social Psychology, 23,* 925–943.

Epilogue

Competing perspectives progress and degenerate, or coexist indefinitely, depending on their capability to generate new hypotheses that lead to empirical discoveries (Lakatos, 1970).

Early in human history philosophers and educators sought to understand the events that explain the process of learning. Philosophers approached the task by first defining the nature of knowledge consistent with a particular belief about the nature of reality. If knowledge is defined as the innate ideas present in the mind at birth, then learning must be the process by which those ideas acquire form and substance. In contrast, if knowledge is defined as sensory experience, then learning is the process whereby the information derived through the senses becomes organized in a systematic way.

In the early centuries of civilization, knowledge was a commodity reserved for an elite group—priests, kings, and philosophers. Society was not required to educate large numbers of citizens in a variety of complex skills in order to survive. Therefore, explanations of learning were not viewed as prescriptions for educational practice.

Since that time, however, societies and cultures have evolved and changed. Included in these changes were continued expansion of the available knowledge base of the culture and the ways that knowledge is to be transmitted to future generations.

Progress in the sciences in explaining physical phenomena in the 18th and 19th centuries led to interest in the derivation of learning principles from empirical data. Also, education, however rudimentary, had become a process whereby individuals received some instruction in at least the basic skills of reading, writing, and arithmetic (ciphering). Thus, the acquisition of organized knowledge, however simplified, was no longer the province of a few.

In the climate of expanded scientific investigations of physical phenomena, researchers interested in mental events pressed for experimental investigations of the human mind. The result was the emergence of psychology as the discipline that applied the experimental method to analyses of learning.

CONTRIBUTIONS OF LEARNING THEORY

The early theories of learning were charting new, unexplored territory and in many ways seem quite primitive from the perspective of the early 21st century. Nevertheless, they provided experimental paradigms for research and introduced basic constructs that could be studied systematically in the laboratory or in the school setting. Moreover, they were appropriate for the learning needs of society at the beginning of the 20th century. For the most part, individuals were expected to acquire rudimentary skills in ciphering (arithmetic) and reading. Only a few became scholars or thinkers. Pavlov's classical conditioning and Thorndike's instrumental conditioning addressed these basic learning situations, which involve the linking of a stimulus and a response. Classical conditioning demonstrated the association of a response to a stimulus through stimulus pairing, and instrumental conditioning demonstrated the linking of stimuli and responses through the use of consequences. Although Gestalt theory addressed the role of perception in problem solving, the problems were either of the puzzle type or relatively rote school problems. Functional fixedness and problem set, two Gestalt concepts, refer to difficulties that can arise in these situations.

Classical conditioning failed to fulfill Watson's bold promise that it would explain all behavior. Nevertheless, the paradigm addresses the attachment of emotional responses to otherwise neutral stimuli, such as calendar dates and particular locations.

Unable to explain the acquisition of complex skills, behaviorism was foundering in the late 1930s when B. F. Skinner introduced operant conditioning. Focusing on response consequences as the key to behavioral change, operant conditioning led to programs in behavior modification, the teaching machine, and programmed learning materials in reading and other areas. The widespread popularity of Skinner's principles led to many misapplications; nevertheless, reinforcement is a powerful principle that plays a key role in efforts to develop new behaviors.

The training needs of World War II and the later perceived threat from the USSR raised new questions about learning. Efforts to teach individuals to operate and repair complex equipment revealed that teaching the component skills of a complex task is essential. The role of component skills, a variable previously unaddressed, became the nucleus of Robert Gagné's conditions of learning.

The 1960s curriculum reform, precipitated by the launch of *Sputnik*, raised the issue that U.S. schools had failed to produce sufficient numbers of scholars and scientists. Gagné's domain of intellectual skills, which differentiated problem solving from less complex interactions with symbols, addressed this priority.

The communications research emerging after World War II and the advent of the computer raised another issue in human learning. If computers process information for a specific task, are humans engaged in a process no less complex? These developments validated the concerns of theorists and researchers interested in the long-neglected issue of mental processes. What followed is referred to as the cognitive revolution because the focus on the internal cognitive operations in information processing and problem solving was a major paradigm shift.

A different dimension of cognitive processing was introduced by the discovery of Piaget's theory and research in the 1960s. Piaget described the richness and complexity of the development of natural logic and the broad qualitative transformations from the preverbal logic of the infant to the cognitively complex thinking of the scientist. Piaget's research demonstrated that the thinking of children was not simply that of little adults, but, instead, was a very different set of processes.

Of interest is that the cognitive revolution of the 1960s and 1970s was a major discontinuity for psychology, and especially educational psychology (Pintrich, 1994). The interest in cognitive development generated by Piagetian theory and the attention to cognitive processes initiated by information-processing theory had a profound effect on both theory development and recommendations for educational practice. That is, the cognitive revolution changed the basic constructs addressed by psychology and educational psychology. Instead of observable events in the form of stimuli and responses, the basic constructs became the mental structures, activities, skills, and processes that represent the inward life of the mind (p. 138). Currently, perspectives on learning disagree on the best ways to represent the inner workings of the mind. Nevertheless, this focus addresses an issue raised by William James and other early psychologists.

The prevalence of electronic media in the decades following the 1960s has introduced another dimension into both society at large and educational institutions. Specifically, the images, ideas, settings, beliefs, and actions transmitted by television have changed the larger social reality with which individuals have contact. Albert Bandura's social-cognitive theory addressed this new reality in his analyses of the effects of models on observers. According to Bandura, much of learning is an indirect process in which the reinforcements and punishments accorded to others are influential in the observer's acquisition of particular behaviors.

Western society has become more complex in other ways as well. As computers become mainstays of business and industry, individuals in the work force are expected to become much more proficient at processing information and solving problems. Thus, cognitive psychology has a major role to play in addressing learning essential for such tasks.

In addition, the prevalence of the computer for both communication and work has extended both learning and work beyond the confines of a particular setting. Some businesses presently are implementing the use of computers by employees in their homes to generate communication with others and to carry out their basic activities.

The use of computers in the home setting to carry out one's work depends on individuals who are highly skilled, motivated, and self-directed. However, until the late 20th century, motivation was not a pivotal issue in theory development. Currently, both Bandura's social-cognitive theory and other motivational perspectives address motivation as integral components of learning and achievement. Bandura describes the role of personal efficacy and the development of the individual's self-regulatory system as major components in acquiring both expertise and self-direction. Other views address academic motivation or attributions for achievement-related outcomes.

As the 21st century unfolds, the number of individuals from diverse cultures who are becoming part of the mainstream are raising new questions for both education and the workplace. Vygotsky's cultural-historical theory describes the role of the signs and symbols of one's culture in determining the substance and form of one's learning. It places new emphasis on the ways that signs and symbols are learned and the ways that they are used to direct one's own learning. The implication is that individuals from different cultural backgrounds can come together to solve community problems, but developing mutually understandable forms of communication within educational and work settings is essential.

Each of the seven theories has addressed particular issues relevant both to learning and to education. Each has developed principles based on particular assumptions about the nature of learning or cognitive development. Further, each theory has provided insight into different issues in the classroom, and each has made a major contribution to an understanding of human learning (see Table 1).

CURRENT ISSUES

In recent years, theory and research have begun to address the many complexities inherent in the learning process. However, theory development and research face conceptual, theoretical, and social issues in their efforts to contribute to our understanding of learning and instruction.

They are (1) the gap between theory development and understanding (conceptual), (2) the importance of affect and motivation (theoretical), (3) the role of technology in learning (theoretical), (4) the gap between the reality of many classroom settings and the theory (social), (5) the disparity among children entering school (social), and (6) the tension between universalistic and particularistic theories.

The Gap Between Theory Development and Understanding.   The rapid popularity of a theory often leads to misconceptions and misapplications. Valsiner (1998) noted that the depth of understanding of a theory is inversely related to its popularity. If the misconceptions are not corrected, the theory often is questioned or discredited. An early example in the 1960s was the rush to publish so-called programmed learning materials. On the surface, they resembled Skinner's mode of programming instruction. However, the developers simply left blanks in sentences from textbooks instead of carefully designing the instructional sequence. The problems generated by the poorly designed materials led to criticisms of operant conditioning as a basis for developing individualized instruction.

More recently, the attempted application of the Piagetian stages of cognitive development to the design of curriculum and the stated mandate that Vygotsky

TABLE E.1
Brief Summary of Seven Contemporary Theories

Theory	Summary of Assumptions	Basic Components	Major Issues in Designing Instruction	Major Contributions
B. F. Skinner's operant conditioning	Learning is behavior; behavioral change, represented by response frequency, is a function of environmental events and conditions.	(S^D)–(Response)–$(S^{reinf.})$	Transfer of stimulus control, timing of reinforcement, avoidance of punishment	Analysis of states, such as readiness; analysis of aversive classroom practices; individualized learning materials
Robert Gagné's conditions of learning	Human learning in all its variety is the focus of study. Learning is more than a single process, and these distinct processes cannot be reduced one to the other.	The five varieties of learning, each with its own set of internal and external conditions	Identification of capabilities to be learned; selection of appropriate instructional events; task analysis for cumulative learning	Identification of the psychological processes in cumulative learning; accounts for the diversity of human learning; linked instruction to phases in information processing
Information-processing theories	Human memory is a complex and active processor and organizer of information that transforms learning into new cognitive structures.	The processes of perception, encoding and storage in long-term memory, metacognitive knowledge and processes, and problem-solving processes	Linking new learning to schema; providing processing aids in comprehension, developing metacognitive skills, and problem solving	Identification of the active processes in the learning of new information, developing learner-directed skills, and development of models of problem solving
Jean Piaget's cognitive-development theory	Intelligence constructs the cognitive structures that it needs to function. Knowledge is an interactive process between the learner and the environment.	Assimilation and accommodation, regulated by equilibration; physical experience and logico-mathematical experience	Provide rich opportunities for experimentation with physical objects with peer interaction and support from teacher questions	A rich description of the world through the child's eyes; identifies current curriculum problems; operationalizes discovery learning

Theory	Basic Assumptions	Key Concepts	Educational Applications	Contributions
Lev Vygotsky's cultural-historical theory of psychological development	The processes of human cognitive development are part of the process of historical development.	The processes of mastering the signs and symbols of the culture; also, learning to use symbols to direct and master one's own behavior	The role of subject matter concepts in developing higher cognitive skills; the creation of zones of proximal development during teaching	Recognition of the psychological contributions of created stimuli in cognitive development; the importance of social interaction and social collaboration in learning
Albert Bandura's social-cognitive theory	Learning is a three-way interaction among the environment, personal factors, and behavior.	Modeled behaviors; direct, vicarious, and self-reinforcement; and the learner's cognitive processes	Provide models, reinforcement, and rehearsal; develop efficacy and learner's self-regulation	Description of learning from models in the social-setting and influence of mass media; development of the self-regulatory system
Cognitive models and theories of academic motivation	Academic motivation arises from a complex interaction of factors in the environment and within the child; the student is an active processor of information; and the student's motives and goals are explicit information	Key motivational factors: expectancy of success, goal orientation, and self-attributions about success and failure outcomes	Implement mastery-oriented classroom goals, student decision making, autonomy, and recognition and support	Identification of the psychological linkages between beliefs and action and the linkages between classroom activities and children's beliefs about themselves

advocated group-directed school instruction are examples. The result is curriculum or instruction that fails to meet the potential suggested by the theory.

This issue is difficult to address in an era of prolific publications and rapid information dissemination through the Internet. Methods of addressing this issue include verifying the source of the theoretical interpretation, e.g., an established Vygotskian or Piagetian scholar, checking original sources (or translations by established scholars), and comparing suggested implementations with verified sources about the theory.

The Importance of Affect and Motivation.   Self-regulatory constructs are likely to become even more important as educators and others attempt to address the almost overwhelming problems in school and society today (Pintrich, 1994, p. 140) (see the following sections). Further, the rapid increase in knowledge and information as well as rapid transformations in the workplace place a premium on self-directed learners who value learning for its own sake and who can make use of new information. Brophy (1999) noted that a challenge for theory is to address ways to develop learners who value the subject matter and learning. His suggestion of the need for models who exemplify enthusiasm for the subject as well as the structuring of reinforcements for student development of insights about the subject area are useful. Nevertheless, theory and research also must explore other individual and social factors that influence the development of positive dispositions toward learning.

The Role of Technology in Learning.   Bandura's social-cognitive theory refers to models in the electronic media; however, most theories address the learning of the individual student in interacting with objects or events in the environment. Yet to be developed are learning principles that address teacher–student interactions, student-to-student communication, and student-to-subject-matter interactions for various uses of computer technology. The structuring of information, the nature of questioning, the nature of informative feedback, and the scheduling of reinforcements are among the many issues to be addressed in relation to technology. Complicating these issues is the potential of telecommunication exchange projects among classrooms in different cultures to promote simplistic and sanitized views of others (Fabos & Young, 1999). For example, in one project, computer exchanges among students in the United States and New Zealand revealed that the students watched the same television shows and listened to the same music. Such exchanges may indicate the dominance of U.S. media in the world, but they do not foster in-depth understandings of students' backgrounds and cultural contexts.

The Gap Between the Reality of Many Classrooms and Theory.   Typically, learning-process theories identify specific components of learning in isolation and the processes required to learn complex skills and capabilities. They are, in one sense, the "ideal" components of learning.

In many classrooms, however, the pressure of standardized testing and suggestions to base teacher remuneration on student performance have introduced other variables into the learning process. Content coverage and test achievement are pervasive, if unstated, priorities. Principles of instruction are often a secondary, not a primary, goal for theories of learning and cognitive development. Nevertheless, in addition to identifying differences between novices and experts, developments are needed that can address optimum ways for teachers (1) to identify key concepts and (2) integrate "learning-how-to-learn" strategies into subject matter learning.

The Disparity Among Children Entering School. Programs that teach basic concepts about the nature of print and books and the nature of numbers to children were described in prior chapters. The need for these programs indicates the disparity in basic pre-instructional concepts among children entering school. Prerequisite capabilities are discussed in Gagné's conditions of learning, and readiness is referred to in other theories. Further, Vygotsky identified the differential use of signs and symbols in different cultural settings as setting broad parameters on cognitive development.

Nevertheless, specific constructs that address the nature of learner readiness in terms of world knowledge, observational strategies for noting and recording data about events and objects in the environment, and other related issues are needed.

The Tension Between Universalist and Particularistic Theories. The learning-process theories, Piagetian theory, social-cognitive theory, and academic motivation models and theories are universalist perspectives. That is, the goal is to define principles of learning, cognitive development, or motivation that universally apply across settings, contexts, and learners. Vygotsky's theory, in contrast, identifies setting, in the form of a cultural context, as a major variable in cognitive development. That is, the extent of sophistication of the symbol system of the culture and the ways of thinking used in the culture establish broad limitations on learning. Further, social interaction with capable adults is an essential component of learning. Thus, his theory breaks down the barrier between the individual learner and the context.

Vygotsky provided a new perspective in the form of the role of one's culture in learning. However, theorists and researchers must guard against further development that becomes so particularistic that generalizability is not possible. Bronfenbrenner (1993) noted that both universalist and particularistic theories are needed. Universal theories can provide information about the processes, activities, and skills that are to be found across learning settings. Particularistic theories then flesh out the details and fill in the gaps for various applications of the universal theories. In other words, each needs the other, and work should not proceed on one without the other.

Finally, the world at the beginning of the 21st century is experiencing rapid and major shifts in political relationships and world economies. The centuries-old shift from an agricultural/industrial basis of production to an industrial/cybernetic basis is dominated by electronically mediated political economies

(Gordon, 1991, p. 99). One result is that education is likely to become critical to society's survival and to be appreciated as an increasingly complex process. In addition to the prior issues, some of the new realities that theory development is facing are as follows:

1. A redefinition of culture to address the electronic dimensions of interpersonal interactions
2. The complexities involved in learning to harness a changing technology to master one's thinking and learning
3. The role of human support in rapidly changing work and learning environments

In other words, the increasingly complex needs of society in the area of learning will require theory development that addresses ever-more-complex issues. This effort, however, has just begun, and, we hope, the best is yet to come.

REFERENCES

Bronfenbrenner, U. (1993). The ecology of cognitive development: Research models and fugitive findings. In R. H. Wozniak and K. W. Fischer (Eds.), *Development in cognition* (pp. 3–44). Mahwah, NJ: Erlbaum.

Brophy, J. (1999). Toward a model of the value aspects of motivation in education: Developing appreciation for particular learning domains and activities. *Educational Psychologist, 34*(2), 75–86.

Fabos, B., & Young, M. D. (1999). Telecommunication in the classroom: Rhetoric versus reality. *Review of Educational Research, 69*(3), 217–259.

Gordon, E. W. (1991). Human diversity and pluralism. *Educational Psychologist, 26*(2), 145–155.

Lakatos, I. (1970). Falsification and the methodology of scientific research programmes. In I. Lakatos & A. Musgrave (Eds.), *Criticism and the growth of knowledge* (pp. 59–89). Cambridge, U.K.: Cambridge University Press.

Pintrich, P. R. (1994). Continuities and discontinuities: Future directions for research in educational psychology. *Educational Psychologist, 29*(3), 137–148.

Valsiner, J. (1988). *Developmental psychology in the Soviet Union.* Brighton: Harvester Press.

Glossary

Abstraction, empirical. The process of constructing internally the physical characteristics of objects.

Abstraction, reflective. The process of reorganizing or coordinating one's actions on a higher level.

Accommodation. (1) The adjustment of internal cognitive structures to particular characteristics of specific situations; (2) the modification of internal cognitive structures that takes place when thinking is reorganized.

Adaptation, active. The adaptation to the environment undertaken by the human species in which nature is controlled and mastered. The two results of this process are (1) the creation of new natural conditions of existence and (2) altered internal psychological structures.

Adaptation, passive. The adaptation to the environment undertaken by animals in which tasks are mechanically executed according to inherited experience and materials available in the environment.

Advance organizer. An "umbrella" statement that provides a conceptual link between the learner's existing knowledge and the new learning.

Affect. The general and specific emotions that result from a particular outcome. General emotions include happiness and frustration. Specific emotions include gratitude, pride, incompetence, and guilt.

Antecedent information. The sources of information available to the individual prior to the causal attribution about success or failure. They include success history, the individual's beliefs about events and associated causes, and individual predispositions, such as need for achievement.

Applied behavioral analysis. The application of Skinner's experimental analysis of behavior to real-world settings such as classrooms and hospitals (also referred to as *contingency management*).

Assimilation. The process by which information from the environment is integrated with the subject's internal structure; not a matter of passive registration of characteristics, however.

Attention. The processes of dealing with incoming stimuli; may be automatic, such as attending to usual household sounds, or deliberate, such as attending to unusual noises, a question, a problem, a television program, and so on.

Attitudes. The internal capabilities that govern the individual's disposition toward or away from events, objects, and individuals.

Attribution. An inference made by an individual about the causes of a particular outcome.

Autonomy. The capability of existing independently; a process or activity carried on without outside control.

Aversive stimuli. Those stimuli from which an individual seeks avoidance or escape.

Axon. The "tail" of a neuron that carries the signals to be transmitted to other neurons.

Behaviorism. The term applied to the study of the relationships among environmental conditions and events and behavior.

Capabilities. The changes in states of memory that make possible the prediction of many instances of performances by the learner; the outcomes of learning.

Causality dimensions. The characteristics of attributions that lead to different consequences. The three causality dimensions are *locus* (source of the cause), *stability* (temporary or permanent cause), and *control* (internal to the individual or external). Attributions that are internal and stable, for example, strongly influence the individual's feelings of self-worth in contrast to external or unstable causes.

Class inclusion. The ability to deal simultaneously with a general class defined by a general property (e.g., flowers) and with subclasses of the general class that are defined by a restrictive property (e.g., roses). Included are combining classes (A + A' = B) and the reverse operation (B − A' = A).

Classical (reflex) conditioning. The procedure by which physiological reactions to particular stimuli (e.g., salivation, finger retraction) are trained to respond to new stimuli.

Cognitive behavior. An outward sign of the assimilatory and accommodative capacities of a living organism.

Cognitive strategy. An activity undertaken to facilitate understanding, such as comparing, describing, or summarizing.

Cognitive structures. Internal structures that govern the individual's interactions with the environment; internalized actions.

Concept learning. The skill of classifying objects or events into categories.

Concrete operations. The first forms of logical thought that begin at age 7 or 8 and continue until age 11 or 12.

Conditional procedure. A set of steps (procedure) that requires decisions about alternative steps at certain points in the sequence.

Conditioned response (CR). A reflex reaction that has been trained to respond to a new stimulus.

Conditioned stimulus (CS). After training, the new stimulus that elicits the reflex reaction.

Connectionism. A synonym for Thorndike's theory of learning, implying that connections are established between stimuli and voluntary behaviors. Also, a view of learning that approximates the neural networks in the brain. Memory is described as consisting of interacting connection nets composed of elements (units) and links referred to as connection weights. Processing occurs in the elements, and knowledge is stored in the connection weights.

Constructivism. Several related perspectives that view knowledge as a human construction. Radical constructivism, derived from Piaget's perspective of learning, views the learner's knowledge as adaptive. The teacher's role is to challenge the child's way of thinking. Social constructivist views, in contrast, view knowledge as a social product.

Contingency-governed behavior. The changing consequences of behavior that bring about behavioral change.

Culture.

   In operant conditioning—a set of social practices defined as the contingencies maintained by a group. Such contingencies shape the behavior of each member of the group and also transmit social practices and rituals to new or younger members.

   In Vygotskian theory—the society that (1) transmits the verbal and other codes essential for self-directed thinking and (2) serves, through the interactions inherent between individuals, as the agent of cognitive development.

   In Vygotsky's cultural-historical theory—the particular social setting in which the child grows up. It includes both past historical achievements and contemporary customs and rituals.

Dendrites. Branching fibers on a neuron that receive signals from other neurons.

Developmental (genetic) epistemology. The study of the growth of logical thinking from infancy to mature thought.

Differential reinforcement. The reinforcement of particular responses to the exclusion of others.

Discriminative stimulus (S^D). The stimulus that gains control over a subject's behavior by its continued presence when responses are reinforced. Examples include red and green traffic lights and verbal stimuli such as "Please pass the salt."

Disequilibrium. A state of nonbalance in the individual's cognitive development that leads to equilibrium on a higher level; for example, the child's recognition that his or her judgments about a situation are in conflict.

Drive reduction. The satisfaction of a biological need that strengthens the link between the drive (hunger, thirst, etc.) and the response.

Dual-code model. The position that maintains that the information stored in long-term memory may be in either visual or verbal form.

Einstellung. See Problem set.

Elaboration. One of the mechanisms by which stimuli are transformed for storage in long-term memory and later retrieval. Included are stimulus substitution, association, and other stimulus modifications (also referred to as *secondary* or *constructive rehearsal*).

Elicited responses. Responses that are triggered by a particular stimulus. Included are reflexes and conditioned emotional reactions.

Emitted responses. Behaviors for which no known correlative stimulus can be identified; operants.

Encoding. The process of transforming stimuli so that the information may be stored in long-term memory and retrieved for later use.

Environment. The situation in which behavior occurs. It includes both *potential environment* and *actual environment*. The potential environment includes the range of possible consequences that can occur following an individual's response. Actual environment includes all the changes in the situation that occur as a result of the actions of the individual. The learner's behavior transforms the potential environment into the actual environment.

Equilibration. The set of processes that coordinate cognitive development in the individual's search for "true" equilibrium. Included are alpha, beta, and gamma reactions and reflective abstraction.

Equilibrium. A temporary level of understanding to be surpassed by later constructions; for example, concrete operational thought is the equilibrium toward which preoperational thinking is striving.

Events of instruction. The set of stimuli in the environment that supports the internal processes of learning; each learning event has a parallel stimulus situation. The set of instructional events comprises the external conditions of learning.

Expectancy. The anticipation that some performance will lead to a particular consequence.

Experimental analysis. The methodology used to identify the variables of which behavior is a function; accounts for behavior in terms of physical conditions that are both observable and manipulable.

Experimental-genetic (developmental) method. The experimental method that permits psychologists to study the causal-dynamic roots of a process. Included are (1) placing subjects in tasks somewhat too difficult for them and introducing other factors into the process, such as auxiliary stimuli or possible disruptions, and (2) comparing the behavior of young children with that of older subjects.

External conditions of learning. The set of events deliberately planned to support the phases of learning; also referred to as *instructional events*.

Extinction. The weakening and eventual disappearance of emitted responses through nonreinforcement.

Formal operational period. Mature hypothetical reasoning.

Fossilized behavior. An action or behavior that has had a very long history in human development and therefore is executed in a mechanized or automatic fashion. The problem for research is that of discovering the internal features of such behaviors and the causal-dynamic roots.

Functional fixedness. The inability of the problem solver to perceive elements of a situation in a new relationship or a new way.

Functional method of double stimulation. The experimental method that provides both a typical stimulus and a neutral stimulus for the subject and then tabulates uses and applications of the neutral stimulus.

Functional value. The utility of a particular behavior. The utility of a behavior is established when the observed behavior leads to positive consequences.

General law of genetic development. Every function in the child's cultural development appears first on the social level between people (interpsychological) and then inside the child (intrapsychological).

Goal orientation. A student's purpose or reason for participation in achievement-related tasks.

Higher psychological (mental) functions. The psychological processes that are uniquely human. Included are logical memory, voluntary attention, and the activities of generating artificial or self-generated stimuli and mastering and regulating one's own behavior.

Implicit reinforcement. Behavior that is praised in one individual and disregarded in others may be regarded by the teacher as implicit reinforcement. However, it may be perceived by the students as punishment.

Inhibition. The reduction in a response caused by the introduction of new stimuli.

Insight. A particular reorganization of the perceptual field such that it is seen in a new way.

Instantaneous matching. Imitative learning in which the learner copies the behavior immediately after the presentation.

Instructional event. See External conditions of learning.

Instructional systems design. The development of instruction for specified goals and objectives in which (1) the organized sequential selection of components is made on the basis of information, data, and theoretical principles at every stage and (2) the product is tested in real-world situations both during development and at the end of the development process.

Instrumental conditioning. The term applied by Thorndike to his theory to indicate that it addressed the association of voluntary behaviors to new stimuli.

Intellectual skills. The organized set of human capabilities that involves the use of symbols in interacting with the environment. Included are discrimination, concepts (concrete and defined), rules, and higher-order rules (problem solving).

Intelligence. The individual's adaptation to the physical and social environment; a growing, developing, changing process that is represented moment by moment in the ways that the individual deals with the world.

Internal conditions of learning. The learner's internal states, such as motivation, and the processing steps that facilitate learning.

Keyword method. A mnemonic method for learning new vocabulary, particularly foreign languages. The word to be learned is encoded in a visual image that combines its meaning and its pronunciation (or some other distinguishing feature).

Knowledge. In Piagetian theory, the constructive interaction between the individual and the object. Knowledge is neither some predefined entity in the environment, nor is it a preformed innate cognitive structure.

Explicit knowledge. *In information-processing theory*—knowledge that is easily available to consciousness and is the object of thought.

Tacit knowledge. *In information-processing theory*—knowledge that typically operates below the level of conscious awareness.

Latency. The length of time between a stimulus and a response.

Latent learning. The acquisition of skills that may or may not be performed.

Law of contiguity. The principle that a combination of stimuli accompanied by a movement will tend to be followed by the same movement on its recurrence.

Law of equivalence. Any concept may be expressed in any of a variety of ways using other concepts at the same level of generality. For example, "1" may be expressed as "3 – 2," "4 – 3," "5 – 4," "2/2," "4/4," and so on.

Learning. The process(es) by which humans acquire the range and variety of skills, knowledge, and attitudes that set the species apart from others.

> *In operant conditioning*—a change in the likelihood or probability of a response.
>
> *In Gagné's conditions of learning*—the process by which humans acquire unique capabilities.
>
> *In information-processing theories*—the set of cognitive processes that transforms a state of the individual's memory from one state to another, resulting in one or more capabilities.

Learning hierarchy. An organized set of intellectual skills from simple to complex that indicates the set of prerequisites for each capability to be learned.

Learning task analysis. The process by which the true (i.e., essential) prerequisites of an intellectual skill are determined.

Measure of generality. Position of a concept within the total system of concepts in terms of its coordinate, superordinate, and subordinate relationships. It determines both the equivalence of concepts and the intellectual operations possible within a given concept.

Memory, episodic. Personal or autobiographical information characterized by the vividness of the memories.

Memory, long-term. Information in an inactive state that, unless forgotten, may be recalled for future use.

Memory, procedural. Information that enables the individual to respond adaptively to the environment.

Memory, semantic. General information that is part of the common store of knowledge (e.g., historical facts, technical information, addresses, phone numbers, and other bodies of knowledge).

Memory, short-term. Sometimes referred to as *working memory;* refers to information that is in the active state.

Metacognition. Knowledge about and awareness of one's own thinking and learning and the use of strategies to guide, monitor, and redirect one's thinking and learning.

Method of loci. An associative mechanism for aiding the encoding and storage of stimuli in memory. It involves the construction of bizarre visual images that link the stimuli with familiar, related locations, such as rooms in a house or landmarks on a familiar walk.

Microworld. A context or environment in which the learner can construct knowledge; usually refers to computer software.

Model. Any stimulus organized so that an observer can extract the principal information conveyed by environmental events without first performing overtly.

Modeling. A process in which a demonstrated behavior is the stimulus for learning. The primary function of the model is to transmit information.

Motor skills. The capabilities that govern the individual's execution and performance of particular physical acts.

Natural history (law) of the sign. The series of transformations that sign-using activity in directing one's own behavior undergoes. Included are the transitional stages between elementary mental functions and the development of higher mental functions.

Natural or primitive development. The domination in the early months of the child's life of biological principles of development. Included are the development of perception, simple or natural memory, and involuntary attention.

Natural selection. The process whereby certain behaviors are reinforced by survival of the species.

Negation. A form of reversibility; for example, in class inclusion, negation is expressed by $B - A' = A$. The action negates the combining of classes. Also, the characteristic of an object that must be constructed by the child; for example, the positive characteristic of lengthening a ball of clay is accompanied by increasing thinness (negation). The construction of operational structures depends on the child's development of both affirmations (positive characteristics) and negations.

Negative utility. A variable-ratio schedule of reinforcement in which the ultimate outcome is the long-term detriment of the subject. Compulsive gambling and drug addiction are examples.

Neurotransmitter. A chemical messenger that transports signals across the synapse from one neuron to another.

Operant. Any response that acts or operates on the environment to produce some consequence or change.

Operant conditioning. The process of modifying a subject's behavior through the reinforcement of appropriate responses in the presence of the appropriate stimuli.

Operations. Cognitive structures described by Piaget that govern logical reasoning in the broad sense.

Perceived self-efficacy. The belief that one can perform successfully the behaviors that lead to positive outcomes.

Personal helplessness. Identified by Seligman, this state is the perception that outcomes inaccessible to the individual are nonetheless accessible to others.

Phases of learning. The nine internal phases of information processing that transform stimulation from the environment into a new capability. The set of events constitutes the internal conditions of learning and is executed in different ways for different capabilities.

Phi phenomenon. The projection of two brief illuminations of light such that they are perceived as light in motion.

Philosophy. An organized belief system that provides a consistent and unified view of the external world and the inner world of the individual. A philosophy is developed by defining the nature of reality first. Then questions such as "What is truth?" and "What is knowledge?" are answered consistent with the definition.

Prägnanz. The Gestalt law that states that a psychological organization can be only as "good" as prevailing conditions permit.

Precurrent responses. Activities often referred to by others as "thinking"; behaviors that make other behaviors more probable (e.g., reviewing a problem).

Premack principle. The rule that describes the relative power of certain reinforcers. Specifically, preferred activities may be used to reinforce less preferred activities.

Preoperational thinking. Prelogical thought processes that are governed by perceptions. This type of thinking takes place from about the age of 2 to 7 or 8. During these years, the child also develops representational thought and social relations with peers.

Primitive psychological (mental) functions. The basic psychological processes that are continuations of the basic process in animals. Included are perception, simple memory, involuntary attention, and practical tool-using intelligence, such as pulling a string to reach the object at the end of it.

Problem set. A view of a problem or situation that immediately predisposes one to a particular conscious act.

Problem solving. In general, problem solving involves dealing with new and unfamiliar tasks or situations that present some obstacle, and relevant solution methods are not known. In Gagné's conditions of learning, problem solving is the skill of recalling and applying a set of rules in the proper sequence to solve a problem. Also referred to as *higher-order rule learning.*

Procedures. The organization of discrete motor skills into complex activities; usually requires the learning of related concepts and rules. Examples include administering an injection and dissecting a frog.

Program. A series of changing contingencies that shapes behavior until the identified terminal behavior is generated.

Propositional network theories. The position that information is stored in long-term memory only in verbal form. This perspective describes networks of verbal information composed of nodes and the pathways that link the nodes.

Punishment. The withdrawal of a positive reinforcer or the addition of a negative reinforcer to a behavioral situation.

Reciprocal determinism. The mutual influence of the individual and the environment on each other.

Reciprocity. The reversibility of an ordered series; for example, if $A > B > C$, then $C < B < A$.

Rehearsal, elaborative. Also referred to as *constructive rehearsal* or *elaboration;* the process of modifying stimuli for storage and later retrieval.

Rehearsal, primary. Also referred to as *maintenance rehearsal;* the process of repetition in order to preserve information in memory.

Reinforcement. Any consequence of a response that increases the probability of the behavior's recurrence.

> Negative reinforcement—the withdrawal or termination of a stimulus that strengthens behavior; also known as *escape conditioning.*
>
> Positive reinforcement—the situation in which an organism's behavior "produces" a new stimulus that increases the frequency of the behavior.
>
> Vicarious reinforcement—according to Bandura, observation of positive consequences received by the model.
>
> Conditioned or secondary reinforcers—stimuli that acquire reinforcing power through repeated association with primary reinforcers. Examples include rocking and cuddling an infant while feeding it.
>
> Contrived reinforcers—artificial reinforcers that are not normally provided by the environment.
>
> Generalized reinforcers—reinforcers that function in a variety of situations.
>
> Natural reinforcers—nonaversive feedback provided by the environment.

Representational systems. The symbolic codes that are stored in the learner's memory. *Visual codes* are vivid images. *Verbal codes* include language symbols, numbers, and musical notation.

Resistance to extinction. The tendency of a response to persist after the supporting conditions are withdrawn.

Reversibility. An essential characteristic of operational structures; the capability of returning an operation to its starting point. For example, addition is reversed through subtraction.

Rule-governed behavior. Verbal stimuli, such as advice, maxims, rules, and laws, that can alter behavior. Unlike reinforcement contingencies, the probability of behavioral changes remains undetermined.

Rule learning. The skill of recalling and applying a rule to make a prediction, determine an effort, or deduce a consequence.

Scaffolding. A term introduced in recent years to describe the process of controlling task elements that are initially beyond the learner's capacity.

Schedules of reinforcement. The delivery of reinforcement according to different specifications.

> Interval schedule—delivery of reinforcers based on elapsed time; may be fixed (e.g., every 5th second) or variable (e.g., every 5th, 8th, and 12th second).
> Variable-ratio schedule—delivery of reinforcers based on emitted responses; may be fixed (e.g., every 5th response) or variable (e.g., every 5th, 10th, and 13th response).

Schema. A term with no fixed definition that is used to refer to knowledge structures; typically used as a synonym for prior knowledge.

Scientific concepts. The domain-specific concepts that are learned in subject areas in formal schooling, according to Vygotsky.

Scientific empiricism. The accumulation of facts through carefully designed experiments or "controlled experience."

Self-efficacy. The sense that one can execute successfully a behavior required to produce a particular outcome.

Self-perception. An individual's ability to respond differently to his or her own behavior.

Self-reinforcement. Anticipated and evaluative consequences that are generated by the individual for his or her behavior.

Sensorimotor thinking. The action schemes developed by infants to solve problems in their environment. An example is grasping the edge of a blanket and pulling it toward oneself to get the object lying on it (i.e., reaching-grasping-pulling).

Seriation (serial ordering). The operational structure by which individuals are able to place objects in a linear sequence from shortest to longest, smallest to largest, and so on. Included is the ordering of both a series A < B < C and its reciprocal C > B > A.

Shaping. The process of developing complex repertoires of behavior through (1) specifying the terminal skill to be learned and (2) reinforcing successive approximations to the terminal behavior.

Signalization. The system of connections that is a copy or the reflection of the natural ties among all kinds of natural events that indicate the appearance of immediately beneficial or destructive events.

Signification. The creation and use of signs, that is, artificial signals.

Signs. Artificial or self-generated stimuli that become the immediate causes of higher mental functions.

Social behavior. The tendency for an individual to match the behaviors, attitudes, or emotional reactions that are observed in actual or symbolic models.

Spontaneous concepts. The concepts—such as "dog," "cat," "hungry," and countless others—that are learned naturally in a child's daily interactions with family members and others.

Stimulus generalization.

> *In classical conditioning*—the tendency of similar stimuli to elicit the same reflex.
> *In operant conditioning*—the tendency of two or more stimuli that share a common feature to acquire control over an operant response (e.g., a child's verbal identification of "p" and "P").

Stimulus–response (S–R) theories. Behaviorist theories that define learning as an associative link between a particular stimulus and a particular response.

Strategy. A set of actions over and above the processes involved in a task.

Symbolic codes. The representations of information in long-term memory. Theorists disagree as to their forms (i.e., verbal only or visual and verbal [see Propositional network theories and Dual-code model]).

Symbolic model. A visual image of the live model, such as a film or televised presentation.

Synapse. The minute space between neurons across which messages are transmitted from one neuron to another.

Teacher efficacy. The extent to which the teacher believes he or she has the capacity to affect student performance.

Terminal contingency. The complex set of behaviors expected as the outcome of a series of differential reinforcements for related subskills and/or approximations of the complex behavior. Such behaviors have an almost zero probability of occurring naturally in the environment. Instead, behavior must be shaped through a carefully planned sequence of behaviors and reinforcements. Examples include a pigeon bowling and a student writing a term paper.

Transfer of learning. The increased ease of a particular learning task that results from the prior learning of a similar task.

Transitivity. The property that represents the relationships among objects in a series; that is, if $A > B > C$, then $A > C$. Similarly, if $A = B$ and $B = C$, then $A = C$.

Unconditioned response (UCR). The reflex reaction that naturally occurs following a particular stimulus.

Unconditioned stimulus (UCS). The stimulus that naturally is followed by a particular reflex reaction.

Varieties of learning. The five categories of human learning that (1) are differentiated by at least one unique requirement for learning, (2) result in different classes of performance, and (3) are generalizable across subject areas, grade levels, and learners. The five varieties of learning are verbal information, intellectual skills, cognitive strategies, motor skills, and attitudes.

Verbal information. The variety of skills that includes the acquisition of (1) labels and facts, (2) meaningfully connected selections of prose or poetry, and (3) organized bodies of knowledge.

Name Index

Miyakc, A., 201
Mokhtari, K., 252
Montessori, M., 324
Moon, S. M., 392
Moreno, R., 135
Morgan, J. J. B., 32
Morris, E. K., 28
Morris, P. E., 205, 209
Moskowitz-Hayman, G., 350
Mozart, W., 102, 103
Müller, U., 281, 282
Muir-Broaddus, J. E., 235
Muris, P., 34
Murphy, D. M., 365
Murphy, G., 29, 31, 49,
    52–53, 58
Murphy, P. K., 382
Murray, F., 270–271, 273
Murray, J., 363

Neath, I., 198–199, 204–205
Neirenberg, R., 382
Neisser, U., 78, 80, 204
Nelson, C. A., 93, 96, 106
Newell, A., 78, 80, 202, 244
Newman, F., 102
Nicholls, J. G., 380, 386–388,
    391, 395, 400, 405
Nolan, J., 401
Nordby, C. J., 10, 367
Norton, T. L., 151
Nowakowski, R. S., 95
Nyberg, L., 108

O'Connor, M. C., 330
O'Connor, M. G., 84
O'Connor, T. G., 103
Ohlsson, S., 56
Oliver, M. B., 346
Omelich, C. L., 391
Ormerod, T. C., 56–57
Osborne, R. J., 289
Oyama, S., 96

Packer, M. J., 87, 254
Paivio, A., 200–201
Pajares, F., 356
Palinscar, A., 89, 334, 367
Papert, S., 290
Paris, S. G., 234, 238–240, 364

Patalano, A. L., 57, 68
Patrick, H., 401–403
Pauk, W., 372
Pavlov, I., 17, 28–31, 36, 118, 152,
    159, 420
Pearson, P. D., 203, 235, 239
Perfetto, G., 215
Perkins, D., 89
Perlmutter, M., 202
Perry, N. E., 10, 367
Peter, N., 382
Peterson, S., 208
Phelps, E., 291–292
Phelps, M. E., 96
Phillips, D. C., 10, 81–83
Piaget, J., 7, 14, 16, 18–23, 75,
    80–81, 85, 107, 146,
    263–300, 319, 321, 323, 330,
    333, 335, 421, 423
Pierce, W. D., 78, 142
Pintrich, P. R., 359, 385–386, 388,
    395, 399, 400, 421, 425
Pizlo, F. J., 49
Pizlo, Z., 49
Plato, 6, 7, 13
Plaud, J. J., 31
Poincar, H., 57–58
Polya, G., 244, 297
Pons, F., 279
Poplin, M. M., 88
Popper, K., 74
Prawat, R. S., 202
Premack, D., 135
Pressley, M., 217–222, 234, 241,
    251, 252–254
Price, B. H., 107
Pufall, P. B., 267, 291
Putnam, J., 363
Pylyshyn, Z., 201

Quillian, M. R., 201

Rafshoon, E., 95
Raichle, M. E., 104, 106, 107
Rayner, R., 32
Reed, E. S., 8
Rees, E., 248
Reiser, R. A., 181
Resnick, L., 148, 232, 242
Rest, S., 382
Rhales, W. S., 395

Ricco, R. B., 274
Rice, M. C., 353
Richard, C. A., 252
Riego, W. H., 96
Rilling, M., 32–33
Ritchie, B. F., 65
Robins, R. W., 78
Robinson, J. P., 346
Roediger, H. L., 210, 212
Roehler, L. R., 203, 235
Roeser, R. W., 404
Rogers, T., 239
Rohrer, W. D., 222, 241, 249, 251
Rohrkemper, M., 400
Rohwer, W., 75
Ronning, R. R., 209, 238, 248
Roper, R. M., 34
Rorty, R., 82
Rosenbaum, R. M., 382
Rosenthal, T. L., 347,
    362–363, 365, 369
Rosenzweig, M. R., 96
Rothkopf, E. Z., 166
Rothman, D. L., 104, 106–107
Rotter, J. B., 381–382
Ruble, D. N., 395
Rumelhart, D. E., 199
Rutherford, A., 77
Rutter, M., 103
Ryan, A. M., 401, 403
Ryan, R. M., 142

Sadoski, M., 207
Sargeant, M., 135
Sarter, M., 104, 106
Saunders, R., 288
Sawyer, K., 58
Saxe, G. B., 310
Scarff-Seatter, C., 89
Scatton, B., 107
Schall, M., 96
Schallert, D. A., 202, 234, 246
Schank, R. E., 202
Schatscheider, C., 88
Scheibel, A. R., 96
Scheu, J., 88
Schneider, W., 199, 219, 234, 236
Schoenfeld, A. H., 102, 222, 233,
    242, 246, 249, 253–254, 297
Schooler, J. W., 56
Schraw, G., 207, 209, 238, 248

Subject Index

450   Subject Index

Social-cognitive theory of
Bandura, *(Continued)*
assumptions of, 343–345, 362
attentional processes in,
352–353
background of, 342–343
behavioral model in, 345–348
classroom example of, 371–373
classroom issues in, 368–369
classroom strategy based on,
370–371
complex learning in, 358–364
components of learning in,
345–347
consequences of behavior in,
348–351
disadvantages of, 374
educational applications of,
368–370
influence of, 421
instructional principles based
on, 362–368
on media, 346, 348, 425
motivational processes in, 354
motor reproduction processes
in, 354
retention processes in,
353–354
self-efficacy and, 354–358
summary of, 373–374, 424
Society, learning and, 3–4, 79–81,
186, 223, 332–333, 369, 406
Somatosensory cortex, 99
Spacing effect, 211
Speech, in Vygotskian theory
egocentric, 317–319
stages in development of,
317–319
State concept, of memory, 198
Stimuli
aversive, 125, 137–138
selection of, 134–135
types of, 118–119
in Vygotskian theory, 312–313
Strategic knowledge, 166, 180
Strategies
for constructive meaning,
219–221

teaching of, 218–219, 221–222,
367
Subject-matter (scientific)
concepts, 325, 329, 330–331
Summarizing, 219, 221, 223, 234
Synapses, 94, 103
production of, 95–96
Syntactic knowledge, 203
Systems design model, 187–189

Tacit knowledge, 202, 207
Task value, 383–384
determinants of, 384–385
Task-focused goals, 387
Teachers
goal orientation of, 398–399
influence of, 400–401
recognition of student by,
402–403
role in classroom, 287–289,
330, 363
self-efficacy of, 366–367
Teaching machines, 77, 80,
140–141, 290–291
Technology
and cognitive psychology, 78
computers, 196, 215–216,
290–291, 421, 424
effects of, 426–427
media, 181–182, 424
and neuroscience, 103–104
teaching machines, 140–141,
290–291
Television, as behavioral model,
346, 421
Temporal cortex, 99
Text-structure knowledge, 203, 214
Thalamus, 97, 101–102
Theory
barriers of classroom
application of, 425–426
and cognitive-development
perspective, 75–76
and cognitive psychology,
78–79
compared to other knowledge
sources, 13–14
components of, 12

current developments in,
78–81
in instructional psychology,
74–75
Threshold method, of breaking
habits, 43
Time-out, 142
Token economies, 78
Traditional wisdom, 5
Transfer of learning, 39–40,
144–145, 169–170, 185, 223
instructional events for,
177–178, 294, 332, 369
Transfer of training, 60–61
Turtle Geometry, 290
Type S conditioning, 118

Unconditioned response, 30
Unconditioned stimulus, 30
Universalist perspectives, 426
Utility value, 384

Variable-ratio schedule, 130, 132
Varieties of learning, 162–167, 176
Verbal codes, 344
Verbal information, 163–164, 176,
180
Verbal thinking, 318, 327–328
Vicarious punishment, 349
Vicarious reinforcement, 348–349
Visual codes, 344
Völkerpsychologie, 9

Water jar problems, 62–64
Wernicke's area, 102
Work avoidance, 388
Working memory, 168, 199, 207,
209
Writing, teaching of, 328–329

X–ray problem, 61–63

Zone of proximal development,
305, 323, 325–326, 332